The Bank Analyst's Handbook

The Bank Analyst's Handbook

Money, risk and conjuring tricks

Stephen M Frost

John Wiley & Sons, Ltd

Other Wiley Editorial Offices

John Wiley & Sons, Inc., 111 River Street, Hoboken, NJ 07030, USA

Jossey-Bass, 989 Market Street, San Francisco, CA 94103-1741, USA

Wiley-VCH Verlag GmbH, Boschstr. 12, D-69469 Weinheim, Germany

John Wiley & Sons Australia Ltd, 33 Park Road, Milton, Queensland 4064, Australia

John Wiley & Sons (Asia) Pte Ltd, 2 Clementi Loop #02-01, Jin Xing Distripark,
Singapore 129809

John Wiley & Sons Canada Ltd, 22 Worcester Road, Etobicoke, Ontario, Canada M9W 1L1

Wiley also publishes its books in a variety of electronic formats. Some content that appears in print may
not be available in electronic books.

Library of Congress Cataloging-in-Publication Data

Frost, Stephen M.
The bank analyst's handbook : money, risk, and conjuring tricks / Stephen M. Frost.
    p.   cm.
  Includes bibliographical references and index.
  ISBN 0-470-09118-5 (alk. paper)
  1. Banks and banking. I. Title.
HG1601.F76 2004
332.1–dc22   2004002790

British Library Cataloguing in Publication Data

A catalogue record for this book is available from the British Library

ISBN 13: 978-0470-09118-0 (hb)

Typeset in 10/12pt Times by TechBooks, New Delhi, India
Printed and bound in Great Britain by MPG Limited, Bodmin, Cornwall
This book is printed on acid-free paper

For my children
Natasha, Thomas and Juliet

Contents

Contents

Foreword

BRIDGING A GAP

Financial institutions have few friends. However, despite their poor image, they provide a range of services without which it is difficult to envisage how a modern economy could operate. It is also true that banks attract some of the brightest and most highly qualified people of any industry. Money is one factor, banks pay well for top talent, but many are also attracted by the intellectual challenges of the business. Banks are difficult to analyze but they also provide fascinating and challenging problems to solve.

No single person could now write the definitive text on financial systems because the scope of the subject matter is too broad, the level of detail too deep and it is in a state of constant flux. One can, for example, go to any large bookshop and buy a 600+ page 'introductory text' to value at risk, techniques used in controlling trading risk. Books that focus on a particular, narrowly defined subject tend to be very detailed and are usually written for specialist practitioners or finance academics.

Books that aim to give a general introduction to banking, securities and financial markets are often rather superficial and most suited to a high-school audience. They tend to be full of rather boring tables showing such interesting things as international bank rankings by assets and charts illustrating the growth in the nominal value of interest rate swap agreements. This book represents an attempt to bridge the gap between the more superficial introductions and the specialist tomes. In writing this book I have tried to follow these guiding principles:

- **Scope and detail.** That all important functions and subjects related to the financial services industry be covered. That the key principles related to each subject are clearly identified and that the level of detail is sufficient for the reader to understand their nature, rationale and shortcomings.
- **Brevity.** That explanations and subjects are covered in a clear and concise manner. Many specialist finance texts weigh in at an impressive 1000+ pages. The longer a book on principles is, the less likely it is to be concerned with principles. Einstein's original paper on special relativity was a mere 80 pages long. Less is more.
- **Universality.** That the coverage is of universal applicability rather than country specific, and will date only slowly. This is achieved by focusing on principles and the underlying economic reality of transactions. Where there are important differences in practices between countries these are identified.
- **Motives.** That the motives of people and organizations are clearly identified and conflicts of interest highlighted. Power, greed, fear and corruption all play their parts in financial dealings.

TARGET READERSHIP

In a very real sense, this is the book that I wish I had had when, fresh out of business school, I started out as a bank analyst. An important objective is to demystify a vital industry that many find to be baffling and impenetrable. People who will benefit most from reading this book include the following:

- **Business school students and other graduates.** MBA and finance students will find that while the main courses are based on fundamental principles, they come with a pinch of worldly cynicism. The book also highlights issues such as the failure of financial statements to provide a true view of banks' condition and the arbitrary nature of regulatory capital requirements. Several important areas, such as credit risk management and banking crises, are also covered that are rarely addressed in general financial works. Anyone who is seriously considering a career in financial services should find that reading this book helps them in making their decision.
- **Finance professionals.** Many front-office finance professionals are specialists working in a narrowly defined field. This book will help them to gain a wider perspective on other parts of the industry with which they are less familiar. Many other professionals work in back-office, systems and other support functions. In some cases they have only a limited understanding of the businesses they are supporting and frequently feel too intimidated to admit their ignorance. This book will help them to gain a better understanding of the businesses they support and improve their communications with other people working in the industry.
- **Analysts and portfolio managers.** Financial analysts and portfolio managers are likely to find the chapters on bank valuation approaches of particular interest. Portfolio managers apply diversification techniques in the context of fund management but they will gain a new perspective from seeing how these techniques are also applied in trading, credit risk and in turn drive bank capital management and requirements.
- **Consultants, accountants, auditors and legal practitioners.** Many external professionals provide a wide range of services to financial institutions. This book will help them to understand better their clients' requirements. It will also help to break down the barriers to communication created by industry jargon.
- **Financial journalists.** Most financial journalists are journalists first and finance specialists second. This book will give them a solid grounding in theory and practices as they relate to the financial services industry and help them to understand and interpret bank results, new developments and regulatory changes better. As Warren Buffett put it "The smarter the journalists are, the better off society is. People read the press to inform themselves, and the better the teacher, the better the student body."
- **Corporate management.** "If you know the enemy and know yourself, you need not fear the result of a hundred battles. If you know yourself but not the enemy, for every victory gained you will suffer a defeat. If you know neither the enemy nor yourself, you will succumb in every battle" (from Sun Tzu's *The Art of War*). Corporate treasuries face many of the same risk management issues as banks.

I have assumed a basic understanding of accounting and level of numeracy. Some parts of this work are rather technical but I have tried to keep the level of mathematics in the body of the text itself relatively low and provided more formal derivations and proofs in stand-alone exhibits and primers.

BOOK STRUCTURE

The main body of this work is organized around seven relatively discrete parts:

- **Part I – Financial systems.** We start by painting a big picture showing the principal means whereby capital from investors is channeled to borrowers, and the roles played by commercial banks, investment banks and fund managers and securities markets in that process. We lay the foundations for the approaches and methods used to value financial assets. We conclude by looking at how money is created, the functions of central banks and the tools they have to influence the supply and price of money.
- **Part II – The spread business.** The main source of commercial banks' income comes from the spread they generate between the returns they earn from loans and the costs of attracting deposits to fund those loans. In the second part of this book we examine deposit taking and retail and corporate lending. We also cover the most common operational services they provide to their corporate clients.
- **Part III – Risk management.** Risk management lies at the heart of core bank competencies. In Part III we focus on interest rate, foreign exchange and credit risk management. We look at how risk can be measured in terms of volatility of returns and losses and the way in which portfolio diversification reduces risk. We also explore the fundamental basis for value-at-risk (VaR) methods for controlling market risk and how this can be used in the context of credit risk assessment. We conclude by looking at why bank capital should be considered as a buffer to absorb a level of losses determined by management and how VaR approaches can be used to define the level of capital that a bank should hold. The Basel Accord on regulatory capital requirements, in its old and proposed form, is introduced and we take a hard look at its main features and arbitrary nature.
- **Part IV – Capital markets.** In this part we look at the roles played by fund managers and investment banks as capital markets intermediaries. We look at the different types of fund managers and investment products offered and examine the methods used to assess portfolio performance. We look at investment banks' key capital markets' intermediation role in the primary and secondary markets and at their organization and other services offered. We also examine the nature of asset securitization and how asset backed securities are used to redistribute risk and returns.
- **Part V – Bank valuations and acquisitions.** The subject of equity valuations is both broad and complex. We restrict ourselves to the methods used to value commercial banks using the dividend discount model as the primary tool and show how to approach valuations of banks with excess capital and how to accommodate short-term explicit earnings forecasts using multiple-stage models. We look at the worldwide pressures for consolidation and the fundamental and management incentives for bank acquisitions. We look at the practical constraints on using cash to make acquisitions and the fundamental constraint imposed by minimum regulatory capital requirements.
- **Part VI – Problem loans and banking crises.** Under "normal" conditions credit losses can simply be treated as a cost-of-doing-business. When credit quality starts to deteriorate, either at individual banks or on a system-wide level, the focus of attention becomes problem loans. We look at why corporates fail and how banks manage the resultant problem loans. Banking crises are relatively uncommon but when they do occur their impact is severe. We examine the major causes of banking crises and the methods most commonly used in their resolution.

- **Part VII – Supervision and financial statements.** In the final part of this book we look at how the financial services industry is policed by regulators and supervisors and the functions of accounting authorities and audit bodies. We also look at the most important balance sheet items and income statement lines and their related ratios. We show how to go about forecasting the balance sheet and income statement looking at loan growth forecasts and net interest income in particular detail.

PRIMERS

There are also three self-contained primers at the back of this book. The first gives a relatively concise but formal introduction to the various statistical methods referred to in this book. The second a formal derivation of duration and convexity. The third provides thumbnail sketches of all of the various institutions that play a part in financial services.

There are very few formal sources in this book, these are well-travelled roads and the foundations of modern financial theory were laid more than a quarter of a century ago. I have included a list of finance books currently on my bookshelves.

Acknowledgments

The story behind this book differs from that of most financial texts and this is not the place to tell it in full. Nor do I have much time, however, for seemingly endless lists of people and platitudes. I met hundreds of people in my professional capacity, many of whom were very helpful. Two groups of commercial bankers do stand out, HSBC country managers and ex-Citibankers. So very different and yet so alike. I will concentrate on those people who actually made a real difference to me. I hope they all know how grateful I am to them.

This book might never have seen the light of day save for an element of serendipity. I first met Chris Matten when he was appointed CFO of a Singapore bank I covered. He is also the author of an excellent book "Managing Bank Capital" that I had already read. It had given me much food for thought, not least because it had been written by a practitioner rather than an academic. I don't know what he first thought when my rough first draft arrived on his desk with a hastily scribbled plea for any feedback or suggestions. It was 18 months since we had last spoken. The draft (or manuscript as I now know it is called) was posted the day I flew to the UK for a three-week holiday with my children. This was the first time anyone had had a look at any of it so I awaited his response with a degree of trepidation.

Chris was very generous with his comments. By e-mail he effectively gave me a crash-course in how publishers work. I hadn't done any of the things I was supposed to have done. No proposal. No defined target audience and so on. I'm glad I didn't know what I was supposed to do, the book has life because I breathed it into it. I am not sure I could have done that if I had followed some tightly structured plan.

He made the critical introduction to Rachael Wilkie, a senior editor with John Wiley in the UK. I was able to delay my return to Singapore and we met up for my first literary lunch. It was all going much faster than I'd planned. I hadn't intended approaching any publisher until the work was completed, still some months away. I flew back to Singapore if not with a firm commitment then with at least good reason to hope. Other reviews had to be sought and I had to put together all of those marketing related materials that I had avoided preparing.

Dr Alistair Milne of the Cass Business School in London reviewed the book for John Wiley at this relatively advanced stage and I took note of his insightful suggestions on book structure. Acting on them meant adding two new chapters and re-ordering the rest. It was well worth doing. He is not responsible for the rather pragmatic approach I've taken to the application of text-book financial theory.

Rachael had the courage of her convictions and put the proposal forward to Wiley's commissioning committee. I sent off the completed manuscript a few months later and the contract followed. I thank the team at John Wiley for their subsequent efforts.

Then there were my friends and family. Most of whom were in the UK and we kept in touch by phone and email. Alan Spence made a very important contribution. He got me to send him back-ups of the work as it progressed. As a result, when an incompetent computer repair shop wiped my hard disk it was painful but possible to recover. He held my hand as the labor progressed and the book began to emerge, albeit from the distance of 11,500 kilometers. He asks the right questions and that is often more important than having the right answers. Alan has always been there when it mattered.

Paul Hallas gamely agreed to be the lay guinea pig and made some useful suggestions. Anne Marie, Mike, Amanda and Suzi in the UK demonstrated that one's oldest friends are often also the best. My other great friend, Alan Stewart, died of a brain tumor around the time this book was started. He was so pleased when, just months before he died, he was awarded his PhD. It is a tribute to his own spirit that he was able to savor the moment even as he faced death. He does, however, appear in the book in the guise of one of three young men who bought a house on credit cards. I am sorry that I have not been in a position to give his widow Karen more support. We all miss him.

I was suffering from acute depression when I started this work. I had cut myself off from the world, stayed at home with my cat, tuned in to the BBC World Service and thought and wrote. I might never have written this book if it had been otherwise. My friends and family in the UK were very supportive and very far away. Ed Manser, Damaris, Gary, Nick, Hugh and Gemy in Singapore defied the cynic's definition of a friend. Katya Watmore showed great strength of character and compassion when she reached out her hand to help me pull myself out of the very deep, dark hole into which I had fallen. I am not sure why Katya, in particular, placed such faith in me but my family and I will be forever indebted.

This book is dedicated to my children, bound for New Zealand, who are far away but close to my heart. By the time this book is published I will have completed development of a course and workbook that are intended to complement this book. And after that, who knows. It is a big world out there.

I would welcome any feedback and can be contacted by e-mail at the address below. Please include the word "Handbook" in the subject line to avoid being filtered out as spam.

Stephen Frost
February 2004
s_m_frost@hotmail.com

Prologue

The love of money is the root of all evil.

The Bible, Timothy, Chapter 12

LANGUAGE, GENERAL RELATIVITY, TECHNOLOGY AND LIBERALIZATION

Language

It is not uncommon to meet professionals in financial services who have only a vague idea about what their colleagues actually do, even though they work on the same floor. The root cause is specialization and the subsequent development of languages, or *patois*, that makes communication between common specialists faster and more precise but are virtually impenetrable to everybody else.

Some of the terms in these languages can be quite evocative (butterfly spread, fallen angels, chastity bonds, baked-in-the-cake, sinking funds, double witching day, bottom fishing, concert party, dressing up, flip-flop notes, ever-greening, barefoot pilgrim) and sound quite fun. Other terms (collateralized debt obligation, contingent immunization, continuous net settlement, non-cumulative preference stocks, death-backed bonds, disintermediation, correlation coefficients, dynamic asset diversification, subordinated limited irredeemable preference shares) are quite intimidating and sound as though they should have come from a German-speaking lawyer.

Most lay people have no idea what most of these terms mean but assume quite reasonably that people who work in finance do. This is like assuming that all Europeans speak the same language. The terms that we meet in day-to-day life are usually the ones we would rather not have to think about such as bounced check, over credit limit, minimum payment, bank charges, commission rates and, at ATMs, service suspended.

General Relativity

It is not necessary to understand Einstein's theory of general relativity or be able to recall Newton's laws to know that if you drop a brick onto your foot it is going to hurt. We only have to know enough about the effects of gravity to avoid dropping a brick on our toes in the first place. One does not have to be able to derive the highly complex and very difficult Black–Scholes model for valuing financial options to be able to understand how they can be used, what factors determine their price and how changes in these factors will affect a traded option's price.

Richard Feynman (a jazz-playing, womanizing, fun-loving physicist who won the Nobel prize) believed that understanding what lies behind a natural phenomenon described by a set of equations was more important than the ability to write them. He also argued that if one can't explain a phenomenon without having to resort to equations, one doesn't really understand what is going on. This is how it should be with financial theory.

Much of financial theory tries to formalize what we instinctively believe to be true. We know that if we back a winning long-shot the payout will be far higher than if it had been the clear favorite. Risk and reward are inextricably linked. Many of us are experts in liquidity management and recognize credit and settlement risks when we see them.

Significant advances have been made in finance theory over the past 40 years, particularly in the areas of asset portfolio management and option valuation techniques. People still joke about weather forecasting but short-term forecasting is actually pretty good these days, made possible by very powerful number-crunching computers. I doubt, however, that any progress has been made in terms of predicting market behaviour reliably and profitably using mathematical computer models. This lack of progress would be consistent with the fundamental premise that security price movements are inherently random. An awful lot of people are paid a great deal of money in the belief that this premise is false.

We also need to maintain a healthy level of skepticism about theories that rely on unrealistic simplifying assumptions and those that cross the line between science and psychology. An attractive theory may be supported by historic data but fail the acid test of successfully forecasting future results.

Technology

Most of the academic papers on financial theory submitted to journals would lie gathering dust in various libraries around the world if it had not been for the huge advances in information technology and data processing that have been made over the past 30 years or so. In 1666 (the same year as the Great Fire of London) Isaac Newton was able to calculate the velocity required for a rocket to escape earth's gravity but it took nearly 300 years before the technology was developed to allow this to be achieved.

Computer hardware, databases, software applications and huge increases in cheap bandwidth and telecommunications capabilities have allowed financial institutions to apply these advances in financial theory. Academic financial journals are now full of articles seeking to support or disprove these theories by mining the rich vein of digital financial data now available.

Few really understand that the world's financial system has become entirely dependent on technology. It became fashionable, after the event, to dismiss the warnings of possible Y2K disasters as hysterical, self-serving hyperbole. If Captain Smith had reduced speed the *Titanic* might have escaped from its appointment with destiny. On arrival in New York some would have criticized him for being too cautious and for failing to meet the promised crossing time. Financial institutions make huge investments in technology where a successful outcome is one where nothing happens.

Liberalization

It is difficult to gain a historical perspective of the times through which we live. Each new paradigm gains its supporters and has its 15 minutes of fame before being casually discarded. In the 1980s there were scores of books extolling the Japanese way of doing things. American politicians inflamed fears that the Japanese would end up owning most of the USA. This hysteria reached a peak when Japanese investors bought the symbolic Rockefeller Center in New York. By the early 1990s most of these books had been remaindered and were being used for landfill. Many so-called new paradigms are simply the same old ideas packaged in a different form whose time has come again, and are used to sell consultancy services.

Liberalization, in all of its forms, has passed into and out of favor many times. The last 25 years of the twentieth century are likely to be viewed by posterity as a period when it was in ascendancy around the world (despite occasional set-backs). Most industries were affected and financial services were no exception. A major inflexion point was the collapse in the early 1970s of the fixed exchange rate system between major industrialized economies established at the end of the Second World War.

Commercial banking and financial brokerage were among the few industries where national price controls, in the form of regulated deposit and lending rates and commission rates for buying and selling stocks, still existed. The types of activities that financial institutions could undertake were also highly restricted. Deposit-taking banks in many countries were prohibited from stock exchange membership and from owning insurance companies or writing insurance policies. Significant regulatory barriers had been erected in countries around the world to prevent domestic financial systems falling into the hands of foreigners.

Banking cartels had become well entrenched in many countries. Banks and their regulators enjoyed a cozy co-existence with incumbents enjoying considerable shelter from the harsh light of competition. This was at the expense of their customers of course. Liberalization occurred for a number of reasons. Financial institutions started to shift their international business to those regimes with the most laissez-faire attitude and lowest taxes and costs. Facing a continuing loss of jobs and revenues the more highly regulated centers were under relentless pressure to act to "create a level playing field". Boundaries between different types of businesses became increasingly difficult to define. Companies could borrow from a commercial bank or raise funds from the capital markets. Insurance companies and brokerages sold investment products that competed head on with bank deposit products.

Progress on World Trade Organization (WTO) agreements on financial services has been slow and is likely to remain so. Competition and market forces do not stand still, however. Financial crises have also forced some governments to relax maximum limits on the level of foreign ownership and lower barriers to entry in order to attract foreign capital.

PUBLIC IMAGE LIMITED

Historic Perspective

The most basic financial services, such as money lending, date back to the earliest use of money as a store of value and a means of exchange. Banks, however, have never enjoyed universal popularity. In the Bible, we read about Jesus Christ throwing out the moneychangers from the temple two thousand years ago. The Quran prohibits the payment of interest on loans and deposits. Shakespeare mocked Shylock, a moneylender, in the play *The Merchant of Venice*.

Banks were blamed widely for the 1930s depression in the US when Gross Domestic Product (GDP) halved and millions lost their jobs. Thousands of banks failed and many retail depositors saw their life savings vanish. People who had taken out mortgages to buy their homes, but were unable to make the required monthly payments, found themselves homeless after banks acted to seize the property and evict the occupants.

Retail Banking Blues

In more recent years banks around the world have taken action to dissuade low-income retail customers from using their services. This has been a three-pronged attack. The first prong involved the introduction of automated teller machines (ATMs) to try to coax retail customers away from bank branches. The second prong was widespread closures of marginal branches. The third prong involved the introduction of account and transaction-based fees. In many cases these fees are waived for customers who maintain a specified minimum balance in their deposit account. Inevitably it has tended to be the people who can least afford these fees that have ended up paying them. This has left banks open to continuing political attack and in some countries legislators have acted to force banks to provide a free basic banking service.

Banks have also been attacked by consumer advocacy groups for offering easy credit and charging excessive rates of interest to consumers. Inevitably banks have been guilty of misleading advertising. Banks and finance companies may calculate, and highlight, the "interest rate" charged on installment loans by taking the total interest paid divided by the initial value of the loan. As this takes no account of the loan's reducing balance over its term this rate is well below the effective rate being charged. In many countries lawmakers have had to resort to legislation to prohibit such practices.

Many banks have also been guilty of selling investment products to ill-informed retail customers without explaining the nature of the underlying downside risks. On occasion when things have gone badly wrong banks refer complaining customers to the small print in the lengthy agreement that the customer signed. These "agreements" always seek to indemnify the bank against any claims or customer losses. As these agreements are usually written in an archaic form of financial legalese it is not surprising that few members of the general public understand their detail.

The Pig Trough

Best-selling books and box-office hits have shaped popular perception of investment banking. Michael Douglas, in his Oscar-winning portrayal of an investment banker in the 1984 movie *Wall Street*, caught the public eye with his battle cry that "Greed is good". There are many books, both fiction and non-fiction, that have chronicled the excesses of investment bankers, "Masters of the Universe". One of the best of these books is Burrough's *Barbarians at the Gate* which gave a riveting account of the takeover of RJR Nabisco, at the time the largest ever such deal, warts and all.

Any doubts about whether such accounts exaggerated the level of avarice in the 1980s were probably dispelled by the closure of Drexel Burnham, a US investment bank that pioneered the issue of (junk) bonds for companies with a low credit standing. The US District Attorney prosecuted Michael Milken, its high profile CEO, for criminal and racketeering charges. Milken pleaded guilty and was sentenced to two years in jail and "agreed" to pay a fine of $850m.

Most insurance companies seem to have been designed to avoid paying out on any claims and on the rare occasions when they do they never seem to meet the claims in full. Claims on damage from minor auto accidents always seem to be finely balanced between the costs of the claim and losing the no-claims bonus. Life insurance policies always seem to cost more than originally expected and to give worse returns than alternatives. The people selling such investment products rarely understand how these actually work but follow a script and are trained to give stock responses to frequently asked questions.

Retail brokers push speculative stocks in order to persuade clients to place buy and sell orders and hence generate brokerage commission. Many so-called "independent" financial advisors recommend those investment policies that generate the highest commission for the advisor rather than those that are in their clients' best interests. Investors who have bought mutual funds find that if they try to sell those funds that the amount they actually receive is well below the value of their investment due to high redemption charges. Nobody likes cold calling but in many countries such practices are legal and used with high-pressure sales techniques to persuade unsophisticated investors to buy investment funds that are totally inappropriate to their needs. Money and morality are words that both start and end with the same letters but have little else in common.

PART I

Financial Systems

Financial intermediation

* Money & risk as raw materials
* Problems with direct investments,
* Bank intermediation
  - Credit, liquidity, interest rate risk & maturity transformation
  - Credit & deposit products
* Securities market intermediation
  - Securities, legal rights, ownership, liquidity
  - Primary & secondary markets
  - Money markets, bond markets, asset backed securities, equity markets
  - Role of investment banks
* Other intermediary roles
  - Mutual fund managers, pension funds, life insurance companies, private banks

Central banks and the creation of money

* Money
  - Functions & roles, money with intrinsic value, move towards paper based
  - Creation of money, reserve requirements, money multiplier
* Discount rate & open market operations
  - Impact on yield curve
* Moral suasion
* Managed currency systems
  - Currency boards, pegged, managed devaluation, trade weighted baskets, capital controls
* Examples of central banks
* Supranational institutions
  - The IMF, World Bank, the Bank for International Settlements (BIS)

Introduction to securities valuation

* Fundamental concepts
  - Time value of money, present & net present value (NPV), internal rate of return
* Yield-to-maturity, annual, semi-annual, zero coupon bonds, compounding frequency

* The yield curve
  - Term spread, impact of yield curve shifts on bond value, credit spreads
* Option returns structures
* Callable, putable & convertible bonds
* Equities

1

Securities Markets and Financial Intermediation

There is no such thing as absolute value in this world. You can only estimate what a thing is worth to you.

Charles Dudley Warner, US Journalist

RAISON D'ÊTRE

Pure capitalist economies are market-based. The allocation and prices of capital, labor, goods and services are determined by market forces alone, based on supply and demand. This differs from that of command, or planned, economies where allocation is determined, and prices set, by a central authority. The former Soviet Union provides an example of a command economy.

Developed economies today can be viewed as "mixed" economies where private enterprise and market disciplines are the major determinants of capital allocation and the establishment of prices but the state also plays a role. Even in those countries where market forces are given most freedom to act the state usually intervenes to correct the most egregious forms of market failures and in particular to protect groups, such as individual depositors and investors, from abuses such as fraud.

Market-based economic systems need financial organizations and structures to facilitate pricing, market making and redistribution of money and financial risk in order to operate efficiently:

- **Money.** A fundamental requirement of efficient modern economies is that capital is transferred from those parties with a surplus and allocated to those individuals, companies and sectors that can generate the highest economic returns. The main mechanism used to determine this allocation is the action of financial markets.
- **Risk.** All human activities involve a degree of risk. There is, however, a wide range of the level of risk associated with specific activities. Some institutions and individuals exposed to a particular form of risk may wish to reduce that exposure and will be prepared to pay to do so. Others are prepared to accept those risks at a certain price. As a result there is a market for risk. Financial service organizations help these markets to function by taking such risks onto their own account, acting in an intermediary role and providing products to redistribute risks.

In this first chapter we set the scene by painting a big picture showing the principal flows of money from investors to borrowers. An impressionist work is created with thousands of brushstrokes but only makes sense when seen from a distance. Individual brushstrokes have little meaning in themselves. Readers may come across terms in this chapter with which they are unfamiliar or whose precise definition is unclear. My advice to readers is to gloss over any such terms. We will be looking at all of the areas covered here in more detail later.

The glossary at the end of this book contains definitions of many of the more important financial terms. The dictionary definition of a glossary, however, is "a detailed list of specific terms on a particular subject area that never contains the one you are looking for".

PRINCIPAL CHANNELS

One of the most important functions of a financial system is to facilitate the flow of capital from those with excess (the providers of capital) to those with a financing need (the users of capital). I will tend to use the term investors rather than the unwieldy providers of capital and borrowers rather than users of capital. Members of the former group are also referred to as savers and members of the latter group as security issuers.

It is convenient to identify four distinct groups: individuals, private corporations, public sector entities such as municipal authorities and governments. Members of each group may play either role and at times will play both. There are three principal channels for flows of money between investors and borrowers:

- **Direct investment.** These are direct flows of money from individual investors to individual borrowers. Most of these flows are in the form of equity investments and dividends and capital returns on these investments. Direct investments suffer from a number of fundamental and practical problems. These flows account for only a very small proportion of the total flows between investors and borrowers.
- **Bank intermediation.** Banks take deposits from savers and pass these funds on to borrowers. They pay interest on the deposits and charge interest on the loans. Their profits come from the spread between the rate they pay for funds and the rate they charge. The pooling of individual deposits and banks' ability to lend to many different borrowers eliminate many of the problems associated with direct investments.
- **Securities markets intermediation.** Using securities markets provides a way to avoid bank intermediation by bringing together many individual investors to invest in securities, such as equities and bonds, issued by many different borrowers. Securities market intermediation also eliminates many of the direct investment problems. By eliminating the banks' spread this may provide better returns to investors and lower cost funds to borrowers.

A third type of intermediary exists, not identified explicitly above, that offers investment products by packaging securities in a number of different ways and selling these to investors. The relative importance of bank versus securities market intermediation varies significantly from country to country but we can make these general observations:

- **Level of development.** Securities market intermediation becomes increasingly more important as the level of development of a country increases. In the most developed economies securities intermediation to meet corporate financing requirements has become much larger than bank intermediation. In emerging markets the low level of income is reflected in a limited demand for investment products and a lower level of domestic institutional investors. This is one factor in bank intermediation remaining more important than securities markets intermediation in these countries.

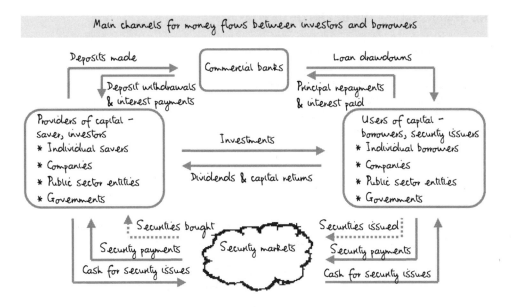

- **Corporate versus retail.** As the level of bank intermediation for corporate financing has fallen in relative importance retail lending has become far more important. In the most developed markets banks have increasingly looked to exploit their advantages in originating retail loans and sell such loans on rather than fund these loans themselves. They have done so by using the securities markets.

In this chapter we will look at the following:

- The demand side, and in particular the characteristics of the financing requirements of corporates, individuals and governments.
- The supply side in terms of the range of investors' requirements.
- The specific problems associated with direct investments.
- The nature of bank intermediation in terms of the way in which it eliminates the problems associated with direct investments and an outline of the range of credit products and deposits offered.
- The nature of securities and the features of, and difference between, primary and secondary securities markets.
- The four main securities markets (money market, bond markets, asset backed securities and equity) and the main forms and characteristics of the securities issued in each market.
- The role and importance of fund managers (mutual funds, pension fund and life insurers) and how their functions add value to the investment process.
- Finally we will pull these all together to get a complete picture of the flows of funds and legal rights between investors and borrowers.

THE DEMAND SIDE – THE USERS OF CAPITAL

Corporate Financing Requirements

The characteristics of financial undertakings vary across two primary axes. First the risks involved in the undertaking and second the timing and value of the associated cashflows. To a large extent these risk and timing characteristics dictate the nature of the financing required. Most corporate financing requirements fall into one of the following broad categories.

Corporate financing requirements – major categories

Fixed assets
* Productive capability
  - Plant, equipment, new products, distribution capability, computers
* Medium-term financing
* Used up - replacement cycle

Seasonal
* Christmas, summer
  - e.g. toy manufacturer, leisure industry
* Cashflow negative for parts of the year
* Peak period performance critical

Working capital
* Inventory - raw materials, work in progress, finished goods
* Accounts receivable less accounts payable
* Continually growing requirement

Short-term self-liquidating finance
* Trade finance prime example
* Short-term finance
* Paid back when buyer pays

Bridging finance
* Acquisition prime example
* Short-term financing required
* To be replaced with bonds or equity
  May be paid off from disposals

Project finance
* Specific project. e.g. toll road, power plant, oil refinery
* Long-term financing requirement
* Ability to service any debt
  - Dependent on project success versus
  - Borrower has other income & assets

Real estate development
* Commercial real estate
  - office, retail malls, leisure, hotels
* Residential
  - Apartment buildings, condominiums, large & small scale developments, landed property
* Medium-term financing requirement
* Project financing characteristics

Real estate investment
* No means to repay principal quickly save through disposals
* Long-term financing requirement
* Project financing characteristics

It is possible to meet a long-term financing requirement with short-term funds that are continually rolled over but this exposes the user of the funds to significant risks. If liquidity tightens, or investors become more risk averse, the borrower may find it difficult to raise short-term money and even if this is possible may have to pay through the nose to get it. The process of continually paying off old debt while raising new debt also incurs transaction costs that over the life of the financing requirement are likely to be significant.

There is a significant variation in the level of risk associated with different financial investments. Short-term self-liquidating finance for trade is very low risk while medium- to long-term project financing, where the project owner is completely dependent on the success of the project to service its financing, is usually very high risk.

In general, the financing term should match the economic term of the undertaking being financed, returns should reflect the risks associated with the undertaking and financing should be provided by parties willing to accept such risks for such returns.

Retail Financing Requirements

The range of retail financing requirements is much narrower than for corporations:

- **Homes.** Many people, for a number of reasons, aspire to own their own home whether it be a castle in the English countryside, a condo in New York or a semi-detached house in suburbia. Financing for such purchases is long term in nature and usually paid for from the income of the occupier or occupiers.
- **Automobiles.** Automobiles are usually second only to property in terms of retail big-ticket acquisitions. These are depreciating assets and most owners look to pay off any financing they obtain within three to five years.
- **Seasonal.** While an individual's behavior may be impossible to predict with any certainty people as a whole still tend to act as a herd. Spending on many goods rises in winter as people go out to buy carefully chosen gifts for their loved ones and socks and chocolates for their other relatives. Spending on vacations peaks in the summer months as the masses head for the beaches. During the rest of the year people either save for their next holiday or work to pay off their last.
- **Consumer goods.** White goods such as washing machines and refrigerators have now become so cheap that their cost relative to income has fallen sharply. Most men love toys, however, and there is always the next generation of mobile phone, personal digital assistant, plasma screen or home entertainment system to salivate over. Many women are fashion victims and this may help to explain why the smaller bikinis become the more they seem to cost. These types of purchases are often made on a whim and have to be paid for either from savings or by borrowing. Real consumers would need a dictionary to find out the meaning of the word savings. And such people are easy prey for predators such as unscrupulous finance companies and banks.
- **Occasional.** Certain events, weddings and medical emergencies are good examples, occur infrequently but may require significant outlays. The timing of such events cannot usually be predicted well in advance.
- **Education.** Most students have to pay for tertiary education. Financing is usually provided by a combination of parental contributions, income from part-time or summer jobs and long-term education loans.

Government Financing Requirements

The focus of this book is on financial markets and financial institutions. The subject of public sector finance is fortunately well outside our scope other than to the extent that it impacts on these markets and institutions. In brief, however:

- **Income.** Government income comes from taxes imposed on corporates and individuals. The receipt of these taxes is highly seasonal. The absolute level of taxes expected is based on government economists' forecasts for economic activity. The best economists are all born with two hands, thick skins and a good sense of humor. The actual level of tax receipts is often very different from that expected.
- **Expenditure.** Certain parts of government expenditure are fixed but larger parts depend on the level of economic activity and unemployment. Little, if any, provision is made for major unexpected events, such as a war. The actual level of expenditure is usually very different from that expected.
- **Political pressures.** Political pressures mean that forecasts for income have a bias towards being too high while forecasts for expenditure are biased towards being too low.

The difference between income and expenditure has to be financed through borrowing and this is usually achieved through the issue of bonds. The level of borrowing should also be affected by the economic cycle. Deficits tend to be largest during recessions and smallest (or even become surpluses) at the peak of the cycle. It is difficult, however, to differentiate between deficits that are due to cyclical factors and those that are structural in nature.

The overall result is that most governments are continually paying off debt from old bond issues while attracting new financing by issuing new bonds. These bonds are issued across a range of maturities varying anywhere between three months and 30 years. The level of government borrowing has a direct effect on the demand for, and hence price of, money. Excessive levels of government borrowing make it harder and more expensive for the private sector to borrow and this is the phenomenon referred to as "crowding out" by economists. Just what constitutes excessive requires a political as much as an economic judgement.

THE SUPPLY SIDE – INVESTORS, SAVERS, PROVIDERS OF CAPITAL

Individuals, corporations and even governments and state institutions may have savings or money that is surplus to their current requirements. For convenience sake we will refer to them all as investors. Investors seek the following:

- **Risks and returns.** To get the highest level of return available for a given level of risk taken, or the lowest level of risk possible for a given level of return. These are not at all the same thing. There is a wide range of tolerances to risk between investors.
- **Economic term.** To make investments whose economic term matches that of their liabilities. An individual seeking to invest in order to generate an ongoing income in their retirement will look for investments that meet that objective rather than investments offering a short-term return only, for example.
- **Liquidity.** To match the liquidity of their investments with their own liquidity requirements. Some investors need to keep most of their funds in investments that are close to being cash equivalents and can be easily and quickly liquidated. Other investors may be willing to accept a much lower level of liquidity in return for higher long-term returns.
- **Counterparty risk.** To minimize counterparty specific risk.

- **Costs.** To keep the costs associated with making the investments, and liquidating them if necessary, as low as possible within the primary constraints of meeting the overall objectives in terms of risks and returns.
- **Diversification.** To select a level of diversification that matches their risk tolerances. Diversification reduces specific risks and individual investors may be willing to pay for diversification benefits that they cannot readily achieve on their own.

Although these investment objectives appear relatively straightforward, when taken in combination they result in very many different specific objectives. Many financial intermediaries (fund managers) have developed whose only products are investment funds tailored to meet these varying, and conflicting, objectives. All investors would like to make the investments that have the highest returns and the lowest risks. The only place where such investments exist is in their dreams.

DIRECT INVESTMENT

Direct investments are largely restricted to private family-owned companies and start-up companies that have attracted specialist venture capital or private equity interest. Many small companies have to rely on direct investments for the bulk of their financing. In general, however, direct investments present a number of specific problems to both the providers and users of capital:

- **Matching.** It is difficult for individual investors to find suitable companies or projects to invest in. It is also difficult for these companies to identify individual potential investors. There is also a matching problem between the size of individual's savings and the financing needs of large companies.
- **Liquidity.** Direct investments are inherently illiquid, due to the absence of a secondary market, and this means that savers cannot readily turn their investment into cash. Parties needing to raise funds in a hurry from direct investments would also find it extremely difficult.
- **Counterparty risk.** It is difficult for individual investors to determine the credit-worthiness or viability of the company or project they are investing in. This makes such investments relatively high risk. This higher risk is reflected by the higher returns demanded by investors and hence higher financing costs for the users.
- **Costs.** Appraisal costs for investors in total will be high if each investor has to carry out their own analysis. The costs of attracting investments will also be high if each investor has to be persuaded of the merits of the case. It is much cheaper and more effective for a company to raise a relatively large amount in one go than raise relatively small amounts from many investors and have to service each investor individually.
- **Diversification.** It is difficult for individual savers to diversify their risks by finding lots of attractive companies or projects to invest in directly.

There is, however, one common form of direct financing that is easy to overlook. This is the credit that many suppliers provide their customers for services and products that have been delivered and on which payment has not yet been made. Most of this credit is very short term (30- to 60-day payment terms are common) but in a few specialized industries, the aviation business is a good example, vendor financing can be very long term.

COMMERCIAL BANK INTERMEDIATION

Credit Risk, Liquidity Risk, Interest Rate Risk and Maturity Transformation

The primary form of commercial bank intermediation involves, of course, taking deposits and making loans. Banks effect four key transformations:

- **Credit risk.** Lenders are exposed to the risk of losses arising from borrower default. Depositor credit (or counterparty) risk is with the bank itself rather than with the end-users of the funds. By making loans to a large number of diverse borrowers banks are able to spread out losses arising from default at individual borrowers across a wide base. They maintain a certain level of capital to be able to absorb unexpected losses and shield depositors from defaults by the end-users.
- **Liquidity risk.** Most depositors want to be able to withdraw their deposits with a minimum amount of notice. Most borrowers, on the other hand, would be unable to comply with bank demands for immediate repayments of their loans. At any moment in time while some depositors will be withdrawing their deposits others will be making new deposits. As a result of pooling together funding from many individual sources banks are able to provide funding for loans that are inherently illiquid from deposits that are highly liquid.
- **Interest rate risk.** Most borrowers with long-term financing requirements need stable funding costs to be able to assess project viability and to be able to service their debt from their income. They are therefore vulnerable to changing (higher) interest rates. There is usually a stronger demand for fixed rate loans than for floating rate loans. Given the short-term nature of bank deposits these are effectively priced as floating rate. Banks have a number of tools available that allow them to take floating rate deposits and make fixed rate loans using securitization, interest rate swaps and derivatives.
- **Maturity transformation.** A high proportion of borrower financing requirements is long term in nature. Short-term rates are relatively volatile but borrowers demand stable funding. Most deposits are very short term, at least in a legal sense. Few have a legal term above three months and many are effectively overnight. Their economic, or effective, term is much greater, however, as the bulk of these short-term deposits is continually rolled over. The deposit pooling process means that banks are able to provide long-term loans from short-term deposits. Banks "fund short and lend long".

Commercial banks are widely viewed as "spread managers" with most of their income coming from the difference or spread between the rate they pay for their funding and the rate at which these funds are lent out. The spread has to be sufficient to cover operating costs, credit losses, compensate for the risks they have taken onto their own account and generate a return on the capital tied up in their business. It's a little bit more complicated than that, of course, but then there wouldn't be a need for a book such as this if it wasn't. Bank intermediation reduces the specific problems identified with direct investments:

- **Matching.** Branch networks, branding and advertising are all methods banks use to attract customers. Corporates and individuals know that banks are in the business of selling loans and approach them directly. Savers know that banks offer interest bearing deposit accounts. A bank can "package" together deposits from many individual savings accounts and provide much larger individual loans to companies.

- **Liquidity.** Depositors can determine the level of liquidity they require for themselves. Some deposits can be withdrawn on demand or with minimal restrictions on the notice period required. They can also choose to put their funds into higher-yielding time deposits where early withdrawal is usually possible but will attract a penalty charge.
- **Counterparty risk.** Depositors' credit risk lies with the bank rather than the end-user. Banks conduct their own credit appraisals of borrowers, they also assume a certain level of expected credit losses as the cost of doing business. Banks hold capital that acts as a first line of defense to protect depositors from suffering losses as a result of unexpected credit losses from end-user defaults.
- **Economics of scale.** By combining funds from many depositors banks can make relatively large individual loans. Appraisal and other transaction costs are relatively independent of loan size and fall as a percentage of the proposed advance as loan size increases.
- **Diversification.** Banks make loans to large numbers of individuals and individual companies allowing them to diversify credit risk.

Credit Products

The most common forms of credit products (financing) that banks offer are as follows:

- **Term loans.** Most term, also known as installment, loans are made for periods of between six months and three years. Borrowers pay a certain amount each month, part interest and part principal, for the term of the loan until all interest has been paid and there is no outstanding principal. Very few corporate loans extend beyond five years (at least in a legal sense). Mortgages, however, typically have terms of between 20 and 30 years. Interest may be paid at a fixed or floating rate. The actual interest rate charged on a floating rate loan at a particular time is based on a specified benchmark or reference rate.
- **Interest only loans.** These are loans where the borrower services the loan by making payments of interest due only until the loan reaches term when the principal is due to be repaid.
- **Bullet loans.** These are loans where there are no payments until the loan reaches its term. At term the borrower is due to repay both principal and capitalized interest.
- **Revolving credit.** The most common form of revolving credit is that provided by credit cards. Revolving credit usually has no term as such but requires borrowers to keep the total outstanding balance below some pre-approved level.
- **Facilities.** Facilities, overdrafts and revolving credit are very similar. When a bank grants (and it charges for this favor) a customer a facility it allows them to draw down up to a specified limit without having to seek bank approval. Such facilities may be for a fixed period (committed) or may be withdrawn without notice by the bank (uncommitted).
- **Trade finance.** Banks provide short term finance to facilitate trade between companies.
- **Credit lines.** Banks grant credit lines to provide short-term credit to facilitate customer transactions and transactions with counterparties.

Some banks offer specialized financing of the following form:

- **Bridging loans.** Some banks provide short-term bridging loans to finance specific transactions. These loans are to be repaid once the company has found alternative sources of long-term funding (bonds and equity) or from the proceeds from asset disposals.

- **Asset financing.** Some banks provide financing for assets such as airplanes and equipment. These may be structured as leases but are best regarded as loans with the assets concerned pledged as collateral.
- **Project financing.** The term project financing in its strictest sense is financing provided to a company for the purposes of a specific project and where in the event of the project failing the borrower has no other means to repay its loan.

Most bank loans are made in a secured form whereby the borrower pledges specific collateral to shield the banks from any losses arising from the borrower either failing or defaulting on the loan. Syndicated loans are a particular form of loan made by a group of banks working together. This allows them to make a larger single loan to one counterparty than any one of them would be prepared to make individually.

Funding

The main source of bank funding is customer deposits. The names and terms (conditions) of bank deposit products vary from country to country but in substance they take two principal forms:

- **Demand.** These are accounts where depositors can withdraw their funds either immediately or with minimal notice. These accounts are used to support customer payment services (checkbooks, direct debits, and standing orders). They may or may not pay interest and if they do it is at a relatively low rate.
- **Time.** These are deposits made for a fixed term of requiring advance notice of withdrawal, varying anywhere between overnight to one year. Banks are not bound to meet any depositor withdrawal demands until the maturity date. In practice early withdrawal is permitted but is subject to a penalty fee. These deposits offer a higher return than demand deposits but still have lower rates than expected returns from most other investment products.

Banks also have a certain amount of long-term debt and equity. Equity is one of the most important sources of funding for non-bank institutions but banks do not hold capital for this purpose but rather as a buffer to protect the bank from failing as a result of unexpected losses. Equity and long-term debt do provide a source for funding but they make up only a small percentage of total commercial bank liabilities.

SECURITIES MARKET INTERMEDIATION

Securities markets provide another means of intermediation. The use of the term security is much abused and means different things in different contexts. In the context of securities markets a security may be characterized in broad terms by the following:

- **Legal rights.** A security is a legal title that confers various clearly defined rights to its owner. These rights are most commonly with regard to the ownership of other assets or claims on future cashflows from the issuer of the security.

- **Ownership.** Ownership may be established by physical possession (a bank note is a form of bearer security) or through records maintained in a central registry. Very few securities in developed markets are issued in a paper form.
- **Traded.** Security ownership, together with all associated rights, may be transferred or sold to another party. This transfer is usually made as a result of a trade whereby the holder of the security sells it in exchange for a cash consideration. (Just why the amount of cash paid for a security is always called the consideration is not immediately obvious, it just is.)

Financial securities are issued through the primary market and, once issued, trade in the secondary market:

- **Primary market.** When an institution wishes to raise funds through the issue of securities issuers and investors are brought together in what is called the primary market. Investment banks are normally used to facilitate this process. The primary market has no physical presence and is more of a concept than anything else. Successful subscribers pay the investment banks for the individual securities they have been allocated.

  The lead investment bank then pass on the proceeds from the issue to the issuer, less any fees payable for its services. Investment banks also provide an underwriting service whereby they guarantee to take and pay for any securities outstanding from issues that have not been fully subscribed. They charge an additional fee for this service.
- **Secondary market.** The secondary market is used for the trading of issued securities. This provides investors who subscribe to primary issues with a means to sell their securities at a time of their choosing and not have to hold them to term. The depth and liquidity of secondary market trading is an important factor in the pricing and success of primary issues. Trading may take place on an exchange, may be carried out through an intermediary (market makers) or may be between individual parties. One of the most important consequences of secondary markets is that they establish a market price for existing securities that can then be used to help determine the pricing of new primary market issues.

Securities market intermediation reduces the specific problems that we identified with direct investments:

- **Matching.** Investment banks maintain close relationships with the largest institutional investors and this allows them to identify those that are likely to be interested in subscribing to a particular new issue. They also maintain close relationships with likely key corporate and other issuers. Companies looking to raise finance may approach investment banks directly. A single primary market issue will usually comprise millions of individual securities. This allows issuers to raise a large amount in one go and for individual investors, both large and small, to determine the size of their own investments.
- **Liquidity.** The existence of an active secondary market is often a prerequisite for a successful primary issue. This can create the classic chicken-and-egg problem in developing markets. Liquid secondary markets give rise to market prices and, in theory at least, a means for investors to sell their holdings quickly.
- **Counterparty risk.** The holders of individual securities are exposed to counterparty risk. This is the risk that the issuer fails or defaults. Most securities markets are highly regulated

and new issues are subject to stringent disclosure requirements. Specialist agencies exist whose main functions are to determine the credit-worthiness of issuers and specific issues and to assign them credit ratings. This removes (or at least reduces) the need for individual investors to carry out their own credit appraisal.

- **Costs.** Appraisal and application costs for investors are low. The main costs to the issuers are the fees paid to the investment banks and other professionals for their services. In absolute terms these costs can be very large but for the largest issue are only a small fraction of the total issue size.
- **Diversification.** A typical security issue involves the actual issue of many hundreds of millions of individual securities. An individual investor can hold relatively small numbers of individual securities issued by many different issuers and hence diversify their risks.

SECURITIES MARKETS

There are four principal forms of securities markets. Money markets used for short-term financing requirements, bond markets for medium- to long-term financing, asset backed securities (segmented largely by risk and return characteristics rather than by time) and equity markets. When people in the industry talk about capital markets they are usually, but not always, referring to the bond and equity markets.

Money Markets

Money markets are used to deal in short-term "fixed income" securities. Few, if any, of these securities have terms beyond one year and most are six months or less:

- **Treasury bills.** Many governments issue short-dated debt instruments, in the US these are called Treasury bills. This form of security is issued at a discount to its redemption (also known as par) value. An investor might buy a six-month Treasury bill at $9667 which has a par value of $10 000. This gives the investor the equivalent of an annualized return of 7%. Treasury bills offer low yields, are usually highly liquid and can be regarded as risk free.
- **Commercial paper.** The most common form of corporate money market instrument is commercial paper. The issue of commercial paper may be facilitated by either commercial or investment banks. In practice a company establishes an informal commercial paper program giving an indication of likely size and number of future issues to a lead bank. This bank identifies specific institutional investors likely to have an interest in future issues. When the company wants to make an issue these investors are contacted and offered a part of the issue. They may choose to take some of it or they may decline. The bank may take some of the issue itself in which case this is best regarded as a short-term unsecured loan.

  Credit agencies give issuer ratings for short-term debt rather than issue-specific ratings. The short-term nature of commercial paper means that credit risks on issued paper are usually relatively low (or nobody would buy them in the first place). Their short term also means that their value is relatively insensitive to changes in the overall level of interest rates. Most companies use commercial paper to help manage their cash positions rather than as a form of long-term financing.

- **Bills of exchange and banker's acceptances.** Bills of exchange and banker's acceptances arise out of banks' services to facilitate trade. When a buyer (importer) has to make payment on goods from a seller (exporter) that have been shipped it may do so by instructing its bank to pay the seller (exporter) with a bill of exchange or time draft, payable a specified number of days after presentation.

  Once the exporter's bank is satisfied that all the conditions of the letter of credit have been met it "accepts" the draft and it then becomes a banker's acceptance. This provides a guarantee from the bank that it will pay the amount due on the due date. This is a negotiable instrument and the seller (exporter) can sell this at a discount to its face or redemption value in a secondary money market in order to get paid sooner.

- **Certificates of deposit (CDs).** Certificates of deposit are the equivalent of bank time deposits issued in the form of a security. They are actively traded, and usually issued with a longer term (up to two years) than time deposits advertised in branches. Returns from CDs are slightly lower than returns on equivalent time deposits offered by the issuing bank. This is because investors place a value for the liquidity afforded and are prepared to pay for this.

The interbank market is a form of wholesale money market that allows banks with a shortfall of funds at a particular maturity to borrow from banks with a surplus. The vast majority of these loans/deposits are very short term with few having a term beyond three months. Individual banks quote a bid rate and an offer rate for a given term and currency. The offer rate is the rate at which one bank is prepared to lend to another and the bid rate is what it is willing to pay for any deposits that another bank wants to make with it. The Federal Reserve rate is the rate at which US banks will lend US$ to one another.

In liquid markets (and this is the case for all major currencies) the bid–offer spread is very thin. Each bank gives their own bid and offer prices. Banks looking to place excess funds will look for the highest bid rate while banks looking for funds will look for the lowest offer rate. The prices offered by individual banks adjust on a continuous basis based on each bank's changing balance sheet position and requirements.

London is one of largest international banking centers in the world and the rates quoted between banks there are frequently used as reference points in other markets. These rates are referred to as LIBOR and LIBID and are quoted for each currency traded. These are calculated taking an average of the rates of a number of the largest, most active banks. For historic reasons the value for LIBOR used as a reference for the repricing of floating rate instruments is taken as of 11:00 am on the day in question, a convention followed in many other interbank markets.

Bond Markets

Bonds belong to the family of "fixed income" securities. The bond market is far more important than most individuals realize. Equity markets are more familiar because they receive far more media attention and many individuals have either invested directly in the stock market or know people who have. The reality is that in developed markets bond markets are a more important source of new financing for companies than equity markets and individuals' direct stock holdings are only a small fraction of those of institutions. The most important issuers of bonds are governments, local municipal bodies and private sector corporations:

- **Governments.** Governments use bond issues as part of their overall management of state finances. Domestic government bonds are regarded as risk free in the sense that it is assumed that there is no default risk. Old bonds are continually being redeemed and new bonds issued across a wide range of maturities. The government usually gives a schedule of planned issues. Certain types of issue, for example 10-year bonds, are issued on a regular basis with the only variable being the size of the issue (and the price determined at the time of issue). Prices and allocation of individual issues (i.e. how many bonds each subscriber will get) are determined using a form of auction.

  Potential investors make their bids in terms of price and quantity. Those investors making the highest bids receive the quantity they bid for. Although the bonds are issued at par (the redemption value) the actual price that investors pay may be higher (at a premium) or lower (at a discount) than this value. The pricing of new issues and the prices of issues traded in the secondary market allows a yield curve to be derived showing risk-free yields against term.
- **Municipal bonds.** Municipal authorities (cities, states etc.) may also issue bonds. Their risk is usually judged to lie somewhere between that of government bonds and high-quality corporate bonds, although it is possible to think of specific instances when this has not been the case. The combination of higher yields than government bonds and a favorable tax treatment of interest income afforded such bonds in some countries makes them of potential interest to particular groups of investors.
- **Corporate bonds.** Corporate bonds are issued in a greater variety of forms than government bonds but the most important difference is that they are not risk free. Primary issues have to be priced such that corporate bonds give higher yields than government bonds with equivalent terms. This difference between yields on risk-free bonds and those on "risky" bonds is referred to as the credit spread. Credit spreads vary depending on the perceived credit-worthiness of the issuer and also vary with the overall state of the economy.

Bonds may be issued in any of a number of forms, of which these are the most common:

- **Coupon bonds.** Coupon bonds pay interest to their holders on a regular basis and pay a notional principal at term when they mature. Most bonds issued pay a fixed interest rate (referred to as its coupon rate) on an annual or semi-annual basis. A government seeking to raise $1 bn might look to issue 100 000 bonds each with a principal (also known as par) value of $10 000, annual payments, coupon rate of 6% and five-year term. Each bondholder will receive $600 in interest payments at the end of each of the first four years and $10 600 at the end of the fifth year. Almost all government securities, other than short-dated instruments such as Treasury bills, are issued in this form.

  The actual issue price of bonds is likely to be higher or lower than the nominal par value (i.e. be issued at a premium or a discount) depending on the bond's terms and the overall balance between supply and demand.
- **Zero coupon bonds.** Zero coupon bonds do not make any interest payments as such but are issued at a discount to their principal value. In order for a five-year zero coupon bond with a par of $10 000 to give the same annualized returns as the above coupon bond issued at par the zero would have to be issued at a price of $7470.

- **Floating rate notes.** The term bond is usually restricted to fixed coupon and zero coupon bonds. Companies also issue debt securities where interest paid is pegged against a variable benchmark rate. These are more commonly referred to as floating rate notes (FRNs).
- **Index linked bonds.** Some governments issue bonds where the level of interest payments is tied to a retail price index. They are a particular form of an FRN and are usually marketed at retail investors.
- **Callable bonds.** These are coupon bonds in which the holder has the right (or option) to call, or redeem, them before the nominal term. Call terms for individual issues vary significantly but usually specify the price at which they will be redeemed (usually, but not always, par) and specific dates on which the call option may be exercised. The terms of some issues only allow for a certain proportion of the issue to be called on any given call date. Some terms lay out a schedule of call dates with differing call prices. Callable bonds trade at a discount to the equivalent vanilla bonds.
- **Putable bonds.** Putable bonds are similar to callable bonds with the difference being that the redemption option is at the discretion of the holder of the bond. Putable bonds trade at a premium to equivalent vanilla bonds. These are far less common than callable bonds.
- **Convertible bonds.** Convertible bonds are straight coupon bonds that also give the holder the right to exchange (convert) the bonds for a defined amount of the equity of the issuer. This may or may not also require an additional cash consideration. Convertible bonds trade at a premium to equivalent vanilla bonds.

Bonds may be issued in the domestic currency of the issuer or may be issued in a foreign currency. A Eurobond, for example, is simply a bond issued and traded outside the country of its denominating currency, e.g. a US$ bond issued in London.

It is worth repeating the point that the par value is the value on which coupon payments are based and is also the final value at redemption. It has little to do with either the issue price or traded price. The issue price and the price of bonds trading in the secondary market will only be equal to their par value by chance. The issue price and traded value will vary depending upon the level of interest rates at a particular time. As a bond approaches its redemption date its traded price will start to converge on its par value, however.

Asset Backed Securities (ABSs)

Securitization involves the issue of securities that give the holders of the securities the right to receive a stream of payments based on, or guaranteed by, the cashflows generated from a pool of underlying assets. Asset backed securities have become commonplace in most developed markets but are still relatively rare in developing markets. The main features that asset backed securities share in common are as follows:

- **Payment backing.** Payments to holders of asset backed securities are based on, or guaranteed by, income received from an underlying asset or pool of assets,
- **Title.** The rights to the cashflows generated from the securitized assets are transferred to the holders of the securities but there is no transfer of title of the individual assets.
- **Tranches.** Securities based on the securitized assets are usually issued in a number of tranches each with its own characteristics of risks and returns. This helps to attract a wide range of investors with varying degrees of tolerance to risk.

- **Default risk.** Securities may be issued with a form of credit enhancement to reduce default risk. This enhancement, or guarantee, may be provided by the issuer or by a third party guarantor.
- **Secondary market.** Asset backed securities can be traded in a secondary market.

The most common types of financial asset backed securities are mortgage backed securities, credit card receivables, auto loans, other loans and bonds. Corporates may securitize some of their operating assets such as properties they occupy, ships and airplanes. Such issues reduce the level of their assets and hence funding requirement.

The pricing of different tranches associated with a single issue varies considerably depending upon the level and nature of their underlying risks and expected returns. High-quality tranches (where the level of certainty of expected payments is high and default risks low) can be valued in much the same way as high quality corporate bonds. Valuing tranches that are susceptible to particular risk factors (resulting in a higher degree of uncertainly in the level of expected payments) requires the use of complex modeling techniques.

Equity Markets

Securities in the form of stocks or shares represent a claim on the common equity of a company and on the payments made to equity holders. Most shares also have voting rights that allow shareholders to vote on certain matters concerning the conduct of a company. In practice most decision-making powers are delegated to a board of directors and only in certain clearly defined cases is shareholder approval for their actions required.

Primary issues are usually referred to as Initial Public Offerings (IPOs). Investment banks advise issuers on pricing matter and facilitate the placement of shares. Publicly traded companies may raise additional capital from existing investors through rights issues, from new investors by private placements and through the exercise of various convertible instruments and stock options. Secondary market trading is normally carried out through a regulated stock exchange. Equities differ from bonds in a number of fundamental ways:

- **Term.** Equities are regarded as perpetual while bonds are issued with a finite term.
- **Certainty.** Equity holders are entitled to their share of any dividends paid by the company but these dividends are not certain. They may rise or fall from one year to the next and may be missed completely.
- **Seniority.** In the event of a company incurring losses equity holders are the first class of creditors to absorb those losses. All other creditors are senior to equity holders, in terms of claims, in the event of liquidation.
- **Required returns.** Return risks are higher for equity holders than for any other class of creditors. It should not be surprising that equity holders demand higher returns than bondholders to compensate for these higher risks.
- **Valuations.** It is much harder to value equities than it is to value bonds because of the uncertainty over expected returns and level of required returns to be used as a discount rate. So far we have avoided getting into any detail on security valuation methods. This is a complex subject but in the next chapter we will introduce the general approach, based on discounted cashflows, used to value securities.

The following graphic provides a summary of the key characteristics of the four most important financial securities.

Characteristics of main forms of financial securities

MONEY MARKETS
* Short dated debt instruments (e.g. treasury Bill, commercial paper, bankers' acceptances)
* Issuer specific ratings
* Issued at discount to par
* Governments, corporates & financial institutions
* Liquidity/cash flow management

BOND MARKETS
* Medium-to long-term debt instruments
* Range of forms (coupon, zeros, fixed rate, floating, callable, putable, local & foreign currency, convertible bonds)
* Governments & Corporates
* Issue-specific ratings
* Discount rate – term yield plus credit spread

ASSET BACKED SECURITIES
* Confer rights to payments based on cashflows from pool of assets
* Financial & physical assets
* Issued in series of tranches – risk & return
* Financial institutions major issuers
* Credit enhancement – tranche-specific ratings
* Complex valuation techniques

EQUITIES
* Confer equity ownership rights, perpetual
* Rights to dividends (may rise, fall or be missed)
* All other creditors have senior claims in event of liquidation
* Higher risk & highest required returns
* Discount rate – risk-free rate, equity risk premium, stock specific premium

Investment Banks

Investment banks specialize in securities market intermediation. They are wholesale businesses and their customers are corporates, municipal authorities, governments and other financial fund management intermediaries (mutual funds, pension funds, life insurance funds and private banks). Their four main areas of particular specialization are securities issuance, brokerage, securitization and proprietary trading:

* **Securities issuance.** When a company is looking to issue bonds or equities it appoints an investment bank to manage the issue. The investment bank will put together all of the information required by securities regulators in the form of a prospectus that sets out the terms of the proposed issue.

  In most cases the bank leading the issue will put together a syndicate of other investment banks. Between them they will give a guarantee to the issuer to buy any paper left outstanding in the event of the issue being undersubscribed.
* **Brokerage.** When investors need to trade securities in secondary markets they usually have to deal through brokerages. These take orders from customers and provide an execution service. Some brokerages are run as independent business but all investment banks have large brokerage operations.

- **Securitization.** Investment banks act as securitization packagers and distributors. Their customers include commercial banks. They structure the securitization issues and, using their sales force, sell them to their institutional fund management customer base.
- **Proprietary trading.** Investment banks have large proprietary trading operations. They trade in vanilla instruments such as bonds and equities but also trade in commodities and more esoteric instruments such as derivatives (options and futures).

We will be looking at the functions of investment banks in more detail in Chapter 16.

CORPORATE FINANCING – A PRACTICAL PERSPECTIVE

Companies have a large number of possible ways to finance their business. Given that there is also a wide range of their financing requirements it should not be surprising that there is no single "right" answer as to how a company should be financed. It is, however, worth spending a little time looking in broad terms at the specific factors that a company will need to take into account, and in particular its balance sheet structure and the nature of its cashflows. The major balance sheet items are as follows:

On the asset side:

- **Cash.** All companies must maintain a certain amount of assets in the form of cash or cash equivalents. Liquidity requirements vary depending on the volatility of expected future payments, both to and from the company concerned.
- **Accounts receivable.** The level of accounts receivable at a company such as a water utility is both relatively stable and predictable. The level of accounts receivables at most companies is determined by the actual level of sales and the speed at which customers pay their bills. Volatility may be due to seasonality, the size of individual unit sales, rising or falling sales and changes in customer payment behavior (financially stressed customers will delay settling invoices as long as possible). Most companies have limited control over the level of accounts receivable.
- **Finished goods.** Volatility in the level of finished goods also depends upon the level of sales. Its volatility varies with the length of the production process and between orders being placed and fulfilled. Some operations (steel mills are an example) have to continue producing finished goods even when sales have collapsed.
- **Raw materials.** The level of raw materials will vary with the expected production schedule. A key source of volatility is the price of raw materials and the extent to which the company has hedged its costs.
- **Fixed assets.** Equipment, computers and other means of production will have to be replaced over the medium term as they wear out or become obsolete. The level of volatility varies with the length of the replacement cycle.
- **Facilities.** Facilities such as head office, regional offices and factories are long-term investments. It may be possible to reduce the level of such assets through securitization but this cannot be done quickly.

On the liabilities side:

- **Equity.** Equity is perpetual. It takes time to raise and it is the most expensive form of financing. Its level is difficult to change quickly.
- **Longer-term bonds.** Longer-term bonds provide a stable source of financing. Where these are fixed rate the company reduces its exposure to rising interest rates. In practice it is difficult to issue corporate bonds with a term greater than five years and this is a relatively expensive form of financing.
- **Medium term.** Stable medium-term financing may be provided by issuing medium-term bonds or by taking out a term loan from a bank. The key determinant is likely to be price but bank loans usually afford more flexibility in terms of the borrower being able to negotiate revised terms.
- **Accounts payable.** The level of accounts payable is driven by raw material and component orders and this in turn is driven by sales expectations. Most companies have a reasonable level of control over the level of this account. Some companies, and supermarkets provide a good example, are able to meet all of their non-equity financing requirements from accounts payable. They turn their stock over quickly, receive cash from their customers and pay their suppliers on 30–60-day terms.
- **Short-term financing.** For short-term financing companies have two broad alternatives. They can establish a regular commercial paper program, although the success of actual issues is not assured, however. They can also request a committed facility or overdraft from a bank. This will allow it to draw down up to the specified limit at any time of its choosing. Banks are usually willing to consider commitments for up to one year. Some banks impose requirements that at some point during the year the balance of the overdraft must be brought down to zero. Such facilities are particularly useful for companies with volatile or seasonal cashflows.

The following graphic shows the main classes of a typical company's assets and liabilities. No significance should be attached to the relative sizes of each class in this graphic.

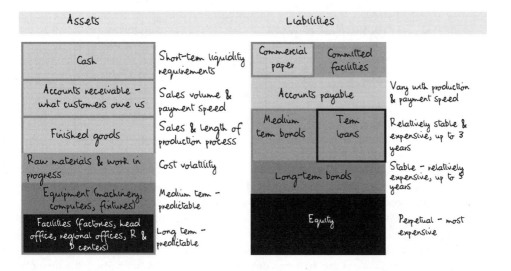

The company will have to decide what level of net debt to equity gearing it is targeting. Higher gearing usually results in higher returns on equity but this is at the expense of higher risk to equity holders. There are few free lunches. The level of financial risk is driven by gearing and volatility.

The actual means of financing used will be driven by the nature of those risks and the level of risk that management, on behalf of shareholders, and in effect other creditors, are willing to bear.

CORPORATE GEARING – MODIGLIANI AND MILLER

Companies are financed with a mixture of debt and equity and questions on corporate debt–equity gearing have long dogged academics. How should a firm determine the best level? Is there, in fact, an optimum mix? Does the mix matter? The "standard" textbook conceptual framework is due to Modigliani and Miller and dates back to the late 1950s. Their "famous" Proposition I proposed that how a project was financed had no impact on the value of the project itself. This appears to make intuitive sense but merits further investigation. In this context it is helpful to talk in terms of a project but this analysis extends to listed companies.

The total market value of all of the debt (including loans) and equity is often referred to as a firm's enterprise value (EV). For the enterprise value to equal the project's value the weighted returns on these securities must equal the project's expected returns:

$$W_{Debt} \times R_{Debt} + W_{Equity} \times R_{Equity} = ER_{Project} = \text{Weighted cost of capital} = WACC$$

This is also referred to as a project's weighted average cost of capital. The debt and equity weightings are given by:

$$W_{Debt} = D/(E + D) \text{ and } W_{Equity} = D/(E + D)$$

After rearranging the equation we get:

$$R_{Equity} = ER_{Project} + D/E \times (ER_{Project} - R_{Debt})$$

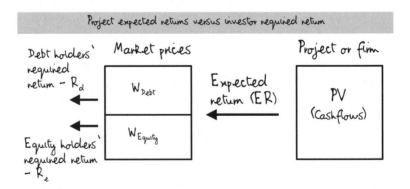

This is the form for their second proposition. The required (expected) return for the equity holders is proportional to the ratio of the market values of the project's debt to its equity.

This holds provided there is no relationship between the required return on the project's debt and its capital structure.

This provides a way to obtain higher equity returns through gearing. Let us take a case where the project's expected returns are 10% and debt holders' required returns 5%. If the project is entirely equity financed then equity expected returns will, of course, be 10%. At a 2 × debt equity level this rises to 20%.

$$R_{Equity} = 10\% + 2/1 \times (10\% - 5\%) = 20\%$$

The capital structure (mix of debt and equity) does have an impact on the required returns of debt holders. Debt holders have a senior claim over equity holders in the event of liquidation. Any reduction in the amount of equity financing and corresponding increase in debt increases the risks of losses to the debt holders. At low gearing levels this has a relatively modest effect but as the loss risk increases it starts to become material. Above a certain level further increases in debt–equity gearing do not result in a corresponding increase in expected returns for equity holders.

There are a couple of issues that are worth highlighting. The basic framework above ignores taxes and has to be adjusted to take these into account. It also assumes perfect markets such that the stock's market value is equal to its intrinsic value. Putting semantics to one side there is no *a priori* reason why this should be the case in the real, imperfect, world.

Free lunches are few and far between and the higher returns are accompanied by an increase in earnings risk (volatility). A firm's capital structure is a subject that we have not yet finished with but we will have to defer further study until we have taken a more detailed look at risk and returns when expressed in terms of volatility of returns. We will pick this up again in Chapter 14 "Fund management".

THE ROLE OF OTHER INTERMEDIARIES

So far we have talked about investors in a general sense of the term. Many people have an erroneous impression that investments in securities (and in stocks in particular) are driven by direct investments made by individuals. This is not the case. Retail holdings in most markets account for a very small proportion of securities market value. Institutional investment firms, working on behalf of individuals, provide the principal means of channeling capital from the providers of capital to the users in many countries.

Institutional investment firms make up the final form of financial intermediary and include mutual funds, pension funds, life insurance companies and private banks. We will be looking at these in more detail in Chapter 15 but the following outlines their major functions.

Mutual Fund Managers

Fund managers provide an investment service by pooling funds from investors and investing these funds in securities markets. Individual funds are offered with a range of investment objectives in terms of return and risk characteristics. They include mutual funds targeted largely at retail investors and hedge funds marketed at more sophisticated investors:

- **Mutual funds.** Examples of types of mutual funds include bond, equity, balanced, sector-based, country-based, value and growth. Most funds are open-ended with the number of shares varying with redemptions and new subscriptions. These funds do not trade on a secondary market and the fund manager in effect acts as a market maker with bid–offer prices based on appraised market value of holdings.

- **Hedge funds.** Hedge funds differ from mutual funds in a number of ways. They usually use leverage (borrowing) to increase returns. Most are higher risk than mutual funds and the range of instruments in which they trade is much wider.

Fund managers are private sector companies seeking to generate a return on their owners' capital. Most funds bear an initial subscription charge, a redemption charge and also charge an annual management fee based on the value of the assets being managed. Fund managers also profit from the bid–offer spread. The latter is often quite large.

Investors benefit in two ways. Investing in mutual funds allows them to diversify their investment portfolios more effectively, and at lower cost, than if they tried to do this on their own. Second, having selected a particular mutual fund based on its style and investment objectives individual investors do not need to get involved directly in the investment process itself.

Pension Funds

Pension fund managers exist to meet the demands of current workers to be able to generate an income in retirement from savings made while employed. Pensions take one of two forms:

- **Defined benefit.** Some employers provide defined benefit pensions plans to their employees. Pensioners receive a guaranteed income based on length of service and final salary. The companies bear the investment risk. Employees bear a counterparty risk arising from the risk that the employer fails or is unable to honor its legal commitments under the terms of the plan.
- **Defined contribution.** These are plans where members make regular contributions to a fund but are given no guarantee of future benefits. They therefore bear both investment and counterparty risk. These are best viewed as a form of mutual fund with a specific long-term investment objective.

Pensions are long-term liabilities and most pension funds hold a large proportion of their assets in the form of fixed income securities.

Insurance Companies

Life insurance companies offer products that combine a traditional investment approach with insurance to cover events such as unexpected death and for which policyholders pay regular premiums:

- **Life insurance.** Life insurance (assurance) policies are offered in two principal forms. The simplest are those where the policyholder pays a premium to the insurer in exchange for a guarantee that in the event of their death nominated beneficiaries will be paid a lump sum. These policies are intended to protect policyholder dependants from the financial effects of the holder's death. The second form offers a similar cover but adds an investment element to the product. Part of the premiums paid go to pay for the pure insurance cover and the balance to the equivalent of a mutual fund. Policyholders may opt to cash in the investment portion and allow the insurance cover to lapse.

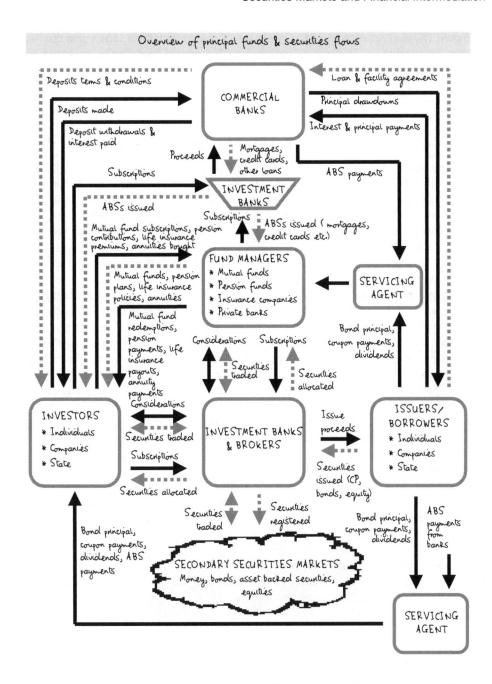

Overview of principal funds & securities flows

Life insurance companies are exposed to what is charmingly referred to as longevity risk. This arises as a result of any difference between when they expect their customers to die and when these people actually oblige.

- **Annuities.** Most annuities take the following form. An investor buys an annuity with a single payment. At some future date the annuity holder starts to be paid a specified fixed amount on a regular basis. These payments continue until the universe comes to an end or the holder's death. The life insurance company has to fund this long-term fixed liability and does so by investing primarily in fixed income instruments. The annuity holder bears the counterparty risk.

Others

Other similar intermediaries are private banks, independent financial planners and brokers:

- **Private banks.** Private banks cater to the financial (and sometimes other) needs of very rich individuals. The level of service provided ranges from advisory through to full discretionary fund management. Most private bankers advise on asset allocation. Within asset classes their focus is often more on particular mutual funds than individual securities.

  Some clients, however, have a high tolerance for risk and may even actively seek it. Part of the thrill of being very rich for some people involves being able to take big bets. Casinos around the world bear testament to this fact. These clients will trade in highly speculative investments and often on the most flimsy of pretexts.

- **Independent financial planners.** Most investment firms employ financial planners to "help" investors in their financial planning. The most suitable investments that they identify are usually those provided by their employer. Independent financial planners do not work for a company manufacturing investment products. The most suitable investments that they identify for their clients tend to be those that generate the largest commission income for themselves.

  No doubt most independent financial planners aspire to act in an ethical way and other professionals do face similar issues concerning moral hazard. This is an area where it is much easier to regulate and lay down standards than it is to police them. The risk of abuse will remain so long as compensation is commission driven and this risk will be higher when such commissions are not disclosed to the client.

- **Brokers.** Some brokers offer forms of cash management services to their clients. When clients maintain cash balances with the broker the broker will look to combine these individual balances and invest them in money market instruments. By doing so their clients receive wholesale, rather than retail, rates on their balances.

The diagram on page 25 shows the principal flows of capital from providers to users. Lines in black indicate the actual flow of funds while dotted lines indicate the transfer of securities or future commitments (e.g. a life insurance policy).

2

Introduction to Securities Valuations

Albert Einstein when asked what he considered to be the most powerful force in the universe answered: Compound interest! What you have become is the price you paid to get what you used to want.

Mignon Mclaughlin, US author

INTRODUCTION

In the first chapter we looked at financial systems from a top-down perspective and tried to paint a big picture of the nature of financial intermediation. This chapter is still very much about principles but is very much bottom-up. We will be looking at the fundamental drivers of financial investments' and securities' valuations, how options work and how various hybrid instruments can be viewed as a combination of a vanilla instrument plus an option. Finally we briefly introduce some of the issues raised concerning equity valuations.

The concepts covered in this chapter appear under a variety of guises throughout this book. Readers who are not familiar with these concepts face a relatively steep learning curve but should not feel intimidated. Financial options, for example, have a reputation for being hard to master but there is nothing inherently difficult about understanding how they work and the factors that drive their valuations. The biggest obstacle to understanding these concepts is probably the relatively large number of new terms with which it is necessary to become familiar.

THE TIME VALUE OF MONEY AND INTERNAL RATE OF RETURN

Three of the most fundamental concepts in financial analysis are the time value of money, internal rate of return (*IRR*) and the present value (*PV*) of a stream of future cash payments:

- **Time value of money.** $1000 in your pocket today is worth more than the $1000 you receive in one month's time. We can, for example, use the initial $1000 to make a one-month deposit with a bank that pays 1% interest each month. At the end of the month we withdraw the deposit and receive back $1010. The extra 10 bucks represents the time value of this money.

  It is worth noting that we will get back more than $1120 if the $1000 was invested under these conditions for a year. This is because the interest earned in the first month will in turn earn interest in subsequent months. This is the compounding effect of interest. The actual return is given by $(1.01)^{12}$ and a simple calculation shows that you should receive $1126.83c at the end of the year.

- **Internal rate of return.** Suppose we have a choice of two projects in which we could invest our $1000. The first project will generate cash returns of $600 at the end of the first year, $600 at the end of the second year and $200 at the end of the third year. The second project will generate cash returns of $600 in the first year, $300 in the second year and $500 in the third year. In nominal terms both projects generate $1400 in cash but they differ with respect to the timings of the cashflows.

One way to compare the investments is to calculate their "internal rate of return". This is a measure of a project's annualized returns over its life. More formally, the internal rate of return is the discount rate that takes the value of the future cash payments back to the value of the initial investment.

It is necessary to use an iterative approach to calculate the internal rate of return. With just a little effort this can be done by using a function provided within the spreadsheet application (in other words Excel's *IRR* function). The dumb, lazy way is to adjust the discount rate manually until arriving at a solution:

$$\text{First project: } \$1000 = \frac{\$600}{(1 + IRR)^1} + \frac{\$600}{(1 + IRR)^2} + \frac{\$200}{(1 + IRR)^3}$$

$$\text{Second project: } \$1000 = \frac{\$600}{(1 + IRR)^1} + \frac{\$300}{(1 + IRR)^2} + \frac{\$500}{(1 + IRR)^3}$$

The discount rates required to make the future cashflows equal to the initial $1000 are 22.38% for the first project and 16.80% for the second. The first project therefore has a higher internal rate of return.

We can express the above in a generalized form where Cf_n are the cashflows in the nth period, and $\sum$ means simply "add up the following":

$$\text{Initial investment} = \sum_{n=1}^{N} \frac{Cf_n}{(1 + IRR)^n}, \text{ equation to solve for IRR}$$

- **Present value.** The present value of a stream of future cashflows is simply the value of these cashflows discounted at a required rate of return (RR):

$$PV = \sum_{n=1}^{N} \frac{Cf_n}{(1 + RR)^n}$$

- **Net present value (*NPV*).** The net present value is simply the present value of the future cashflows less the cost of the initial investment:

$$NPV = PV - \text{Initial investment}$$

A project or investment with an *NPV* equal to zero is achieving its required returns. A positive *NPV* means that it has higher returns than required, and one with a negative *NPV* lower than required returns. We can use this to compare the relative attractiveness of two investments.

Let us assume that we require a 20% return on a proposed investment. To calculate the *NPV* of a proposed investment we need to take account of all of the cashflows, including the initial investment as shown in the following table.

The first project has a positive *NPV* of $32 and the second project a negative *NPV* of $56. The first project meets our investment criteria while the second project fails to meet the target required return, otherwise known as the hurdle rate. *NPV* and *IRR* are closely linked. A project that has an *IRR* equal to its required return will have an *NPV* of zero. One of the big advantages of using *NPV* for project appraisal purposes rather than *IRR* is that individual *NPVs* can be simply added together to arrive at a total *NPV*. It is impossible to get an overall *IRR* from individual project *IRRs*. The only way to do this is to take the cashflows for the individual projects and add them up in each time period and use these to calculate the overall *IRR*. Adding a new project means the whole process has to be done again. Looking at individual project *NPVs* also helps to put the projects into perspective in terms of their contribution to total *NPV*.

		Start	Year one	Year two	Year three	*NPV*
First project	Cashflows	($1000)	$600	$600	$200	
	Discount factor		1.2	1.2^2	1.2^3	
	Discounted cashflows	($1000)	$500	$417	$116	$32
Second	Cashflows	($1000)	$300	$500	$600	
	Discount factor		1.2	1.2^2	1.2^3	
	Discounted cashflows	($1000)	$250	$347	$347	($56)

Calculating the net present value (NPV) — table title

YIELD-TO-MATURITY

We will now take these fundamental concepts and apply them to bond valuations. We will start with two government coupon bonds. Each one has a par value of $10 000 and pays on an annual basis:

- The first bond has an annual coupon rate of 6% and remaining term of three years. It is currently trading at $10 412.
- The second bond has an annual coupon rate of 5% and remaining term of five years. It is currently trading at $9180.

It is important to note that either bond could have had a much greater term when issued. What is important is not the term at issue but the remaining term. The cashflows associated with the two bonds are as follows. The internal rate of return on the first bond is 4.5% and on the second bond 7.0% (calculated using a spreadsheet function).

	Remaining term	Coupon rate	Price	1	2	3	4	5	Internal rate of return
						Years			
First bond	3 years	6.0%	−10412	600	600	10600			4.50%
Second bond	5 years	5.0%	−9180	500	500		500	500	10500	7.00%

Bond cashflows — table title

We can confirm that these are the internal rates of return by calculating the discount factors to use for each year using the *IRR* as the discount rate. This shows that the present value of the first bond is equal to $10 412 and for the second bond $9180, the same as the current market prices.

The internal rate of return in the context of a bond is called its yield-to-maturity, often abbreviated to simply yield. By convention it is quoted as an annualized rate.

Semi-annual Payments

Most bonds pay their coupon on a semi-annual basis, twice a year, rather than an annual basis. Let us take the same two bonds in terms of coupon rate and market prices but assume that

Present value using *IRR* as discount rate							
	Coupon rate	Years					Total
		1	2	3	4	5	
First bond	6.0%	600	600	10 600			
Discount factor		(1.045)	$(1.045)^2$	$(1.045)^3$			
		1.045	1.092	1.141			
Present value		574	549	9289			10 412
Second bond	5.0%	500	500	500	500	10 500	
Discount factor		(1.070)	$(1.070)^2$	$(1.070)^3$	$(1.070)^4$	$(1.070)^5$	
		1.070	1.145	1.225	1.311	1.403	
Present value		467	434	408	381	7486	9180

they pay on a semi-annual basis. Their cashflows are as shown below. The annualized yield-to-maturity for the first bond is 4.57% (compared with a yield of 4.50% for the bond with annual payments) and 7.30% for the second bond (versus 7.00%).

Semi-annual coupon payments												
Year		1		2		3		4		5		YTM
First bond	−10 412	300	300	300	300	300	10 300					4.57%
Second bond	−9180	250	250	250	250	250	250	250	250	250	10 250	7.30%

Zero Coupon Bonds

Government Treasury bills are short-dated securities issued at a discount to par and that do not pay any interest. These are generally referred to as zero coupon bonds or simply zeroes. It is very easy to calculate the annualized yield to maturity for a zero coupon bond.

We will take two such bonds. The first bond matures in 90 days (three months) and the second in 180 days (six months). US$ interest rates are quoted on a 360-day basis. We will follow this convention and explain the difference between this convention and the 365-day convention when we look at the generalized treatment of increasing the frequency of payments.

The first bond is trading at $9970 and the second at $9900. The cashflows and internal rate of return are as follows. The first zero has an annualized yield-to-maturity of 1.204% and the second 2.020%.

Zero coupon bond (ZCB) examples						
		Price	Par	Discount factor	Discount factor	YTM
First ZCB	3-months	−9970	10 000	1.0030	(1 + Annualized YTM/4)	1.204%
Second ZCB	6-months	−9900	10 000	1.0101	(1 + Annualized YTM/2)	2.020%

This is actually a simplified example, just taking the annualized rate and dividing it by the number of periods is a first order approximation. A rigorous approach has to take full account of the compounding frequency and this is explained as follows.

Exhibit: Compounding frequency

The frequency at which interest is calculated affects the total interest paid. If we have a bond that has an annual rate of 12% but interest is paid semi-annually the effective annualized rate is given by $(1 + 0.12/2)^2$ – this is equal to 12.36%.

More generally the effective annualized yield is given by the following equation where n represents the number of compounding periods in one year, r the simple annual rate and r_{EAR} the effective annualized rate:

$$\left(1 + \frac{r}{n}\right)^n = 1 + r_{EAR}$$

By increasing the frequency at which the interest is compounded the effective annualized rate increases but starts to reach a limit as shown by the following chart:

Effective annualized rate versus compounding frequency

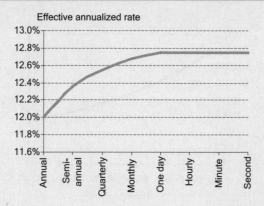

Mathematically as n gets increasingly large (tends to infinity) the effective annualized rate is given by the following equation where e is the natural number, approximately equal to 2.71828. This is known as continuous compounding. In our example the effective annualized rate using continuous compounding is close to 12.75%:

$$\left(1 + \frac{r}{n}\right)^n = e^r \quad as\ n \to \infty, = 1 + r_{EAR} \Rightarrow r_{EAR} = e^r - 1$$

This is actually a very useful result as it can be generalized to the following, where t is the number of years. With continuous compounding if we invest P dollars today we should receive V in t years' time where V is given as follows:

$$V = P \times e^{+rt}$$

This is useful because t can be fractions of a year, for example if V is to be received in one and a quarter years then $t = 1.25$. For example, we will receive $1172.4 in one and a quarter years for an initial investment of $1000 with an effective annualized rate of 12.75%:

$$V = \$1000 \times e^{+(0.1275 \times 1.25)} = \$1000 \times 1.1728 = \$1172.8$$

IMPACT OF CHANGING RATES ON BOND VALUES

Let us assume that we have a 15-year US Treasury bond with a coupon rate of 4.5% and yield-to-maturity of 7.36% and trading at $7453. The following chart shows the sensitivity of this bond's price to yield-to-maturity. Two immediate things to notice are:

- Its price rises with falling yields, this is due to the lower discount rate of course.
- The rate of increase of price increases as yields fall, and this is because of the inverse relationship between price and discount rate.

We will be looking in much more detail at the effect of changing yields on bond valuations in Chapter 10 "Managing interest rate and FX risk".

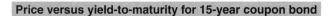

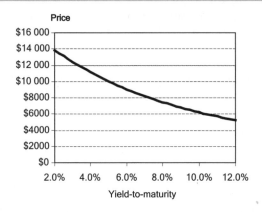

This chart is typical of what are referred to generically as "price charts" where the price of an instrument is plotted against a single factor, in this case the yield-to-maturity. An option price chart would have option price plotted against the price of its underlying instrument. Other factors also play a part in an option's price but the price of its underlying instrument is the primary factor in determining an option's value.

THE YIELD CURVE

The yield curve is one of the most widely watched of all economic and financial indicators. The yield curve has these characteristics:

- **Graphical representation.** The yield curve is a graphical representation of the yields-to-maturity that can be obtained from buying government securities across a range of maturities, plotted against term.
- **Construction.** Yields-to-maturity are taken from the prices of government issues trading in the secondary market and the prices of recent new issues. For issues trading in the secondary market it is the remaining term that is taken rather than the term at issue.

It is important to have a number of such issues across a range of maturities to construct a yield curve. Yield curves are normally constructed using a number of large, liquid benchmark issues. Yields-at-maturities where there are no benchmarks are inferred from yields on close bonds with maturities that are slightly longer and shorter. The yield at four and a half years might be inferred from yields on bonds with a remaining term of four and five years, for example.

- **Risk free.** Government bonds are generally regarded as risk free and the yield curve is therefore a representation of risk-free yields against maturity.
- **Liquidity.** In developed markets such as the US and the UK government debt markets are highly liquid. This is a necessary condition for quoted prices to be meaningful.
- **Slope.** In "normal" situations the yield curve is usually described as, and is, upward "sloping". Yields on long-term bonds being higher than those on short-term bonds. When this is reversed the yield curve is described as being inverted.

From the prices of these bonds a yield curve can be constructed. The following charts show textbook, stylized examples of an upward sloping and an inverted yield curve.

The real world, like many of our lives, is messier. We will look at some real examples of the yield curve in the next chapter when we look at central bank functions, and in particular how central banks respond to changes in the yield curve and also act to influence its shape and level. For the moment we will stick with these cozy idealized shapes and put on hold discussions about why they may shift in shape from one form to the other.

Term Spreads

One of the key transformations that banks make is that of maturity transformation. An upward sloping yield curve tends to favor banks because they fund short and lend long. Fortunately for banks, in most countries, for most of the time the yield curve is upward sloping. When yield curves do invert few commercial banks are able to escape the pain.

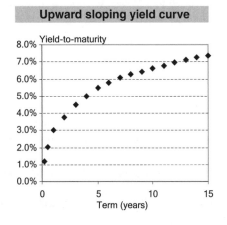

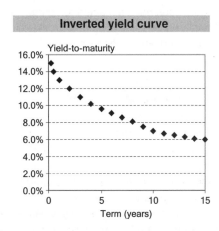

The yield curve is used to identify spreads that are due solely to differences in term. In the above example of an upward sloping yield curve yields-to-maturity for bonds with a term of one year are 1.20% while yields on 10-year bonds are 6.62%. The term spread between one year and 10 year yields is therefore 5.42 percentage points. It is common to talk about term spreads between yields at the short end and those at the long end but there is no hard definition as to which terms to use at either end. At the long end this may be constrained by the availability of long-term liquid benchmarks, common short-end yields used are the discount rate (the rate at which the central bank will lend to banks) and yields on three-month government securities.

Financial spreads of all kinds are measured in basis points. One hundred basis points is equal to one percentage point. The above term spread is hence 542 basis points. Basis point is usually abbreviated to either bpt or bp. Using, and talking in terms of, basis points soon becomes second nature to anyone who works in financial services. This is because they provide an appropriate scale for measuring financial spreads.

Impact of Shifts in Yield Curve on Bond Valuations

Changes in the supply of and demand for money occur for many different reasons causing the yield curve to shift. We will consider two possible cases:

- **Parallel shifts.** Demand for fixed income investments at all maturities falls. This will push down the price of money and hence result in lower bond prices and higher yields. Investors will demand higher yields on new issues and prices for bonds already issued will fall until they offer the same yields as equivalent new issues. We will assume that yields fall by 100 bpts at all maturities. This is referred to as a parallel shift in the yield curve.
- **Non-parallel shifts.** For our second case we will assume that supply of new money at the short end is restricted but that demand for bonds with longer maturities increases. This will push up returns demanded (reduce prices) for bonds at the short end and push up prices (lower yields) of bonds at the long end. This type of change in the shape of the yield curve is called a non-parallel shift. The following example is a tilted shift but non-parallel shifts can take many forms.

  This particular example is characteristic of changes in yield curves that take place when inflationary expectations have risen, pushing up yields on long-term instruments and the central bank has then acted to tighten liquidity and push up the level of short-end rates. As liquidity tightens the economy starts to slow, inflationary fears recede and long-term required returns and hence bond yields fall.

VANILLA CORPORATE BONDS

So far we have focused on risk-free government bonds. Corporate bonds, even from the most credit-worthy of companies, are not free of default risk. In this sense they are regarded as risky assets.

Take the case of a five-year corporate bond with a 5% annual coupon and currently trading at $8444. Its yield-to-maturity is 9%.

The yield-to-maturity for an equivalent risk-free bond is 6%. Yields on three-month government securities are 2%. The term spread is therefore 400 bpts.

Example of parallel shift in yield curve	Example of non-parallel yield curve shift

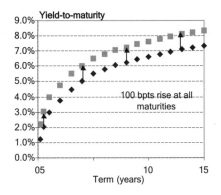

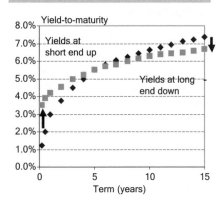

The credit spread is the difference between the yield on the corporate bond less the yield on the equivalent risk-free bond. In this case the credit spread is 300 bpts. We can break down the yield on a corporate bond into three components as follows:

Yield on corporate bond = Short-term risk-free returns + Term spread + Credit spread

Using the 90-day bill yield as the short-term yield we get the following for this corporate bond:

Yield on corporate bond = 200 bpts + 400 bpts + 300 bpts = 9.0%

The value of a corporate bond is therefore affected by three factors: changes in the overall level of interest rates (short-term risk-free rates), non-parallel shifts in the shape of the yield curve (term spreads) and changes in returns demanded for default risk (credit spreads).

Credit spreads, in general, are likely to widen in the face of an anticipated deterioration in the financial conditions of corporates in general and to narrow when the market starts to price in a recovery of corporate fortunes.

When there is a general widening of credit spreads they do not increase uniformly for all issuers. Credit spreads for weaker companies increase more than those on the strongest companies. In the face of an anticipated deterioration people usually talk in terms of a "flight to quality". There are a couple of ways to look at this. Investors shift out of corporate bonds regarded as high risk to those regarded as low risk and from low-risk corporate bonds into risk-free government bonds. Another way to look at this is that investors demand higher returns for holding risky bonds and the increase in returns demanded is greatest for those companies perceived as being highest risk.

The valuations of callable, putable and convertible bonds are complicated by the presence of embedded options. We need to look at the basic characteristics of financial options before we can look at their valuations.

FINANCIAL OPTIONS

Call and Put Options

There was a time when opening the mail was something that people looked forward to. That is no longer the case. So imagine your surprise if one morning you received a letter from your stockbroker enclosing a certificate, given in recognition of past business you have given them, that gave you the "opportunity" to buy a 15-year government bond at a price of $11 500. The offer is for one month only and can be taken up by presenting the certificate plus $11 500 in cash to the broker at any time till then. A quick look at a financial newspaper, however, shows that its current market price is just $11 015. At first glance this does not appear to be a very attractive offer. If you wanted to hold the bond then you could simply buy it in the market today at $11 015.

A little thought, however, shows that the certificate is worth holding onto. If the bond price rises above $11 500 at any time during the offer period then you can exercise this "option" and immediately sell the bond in the market. The difference between the then market price and the exercise price will be straight profit.

There are two types of options, call options and put options:

- **Call option.** The above free offer is an example of a call option. In formal terms a call option gives the holder the right, but not the obligation, to buy a specified asset at a specific price (the exercise or strike price) until a particular date (the expiry date). The party giving the option is called the option writer.
- **Put option.** The second type of option is a put option. This gives the holder the right, but not the obligation, to sell a specified asset at a specific price (the exercise or strike price) until a particular date (the expiry date). If the price of the bond is below the bond price then the holder can simply buy the bond in the market and exercise the option to immediately sell the bond at the exercise price. The holder's profit then is the difference between the bond's market price and the strike price.

The returns for this option for the holders and writers of a call option and a put option, plotted against bond price, are shown in the following charts. It is worth noting that trading options is a zero sum game, what one party gains another loses.

- **Call option.** The call option returns have the following characteristics:
    - If the price remains below the strike price the holder will not exercise the option and it will simply expire.
    - The returns to the holder and the writer are mirror images of one another.
    - The returns are asymmetric in form with regard to bond price.
    - If the price rises above the strike price profits to the holder and losses to the writer have no limit.
- **Put option.** The put option returns have the following characteristics:
    - If the price remains above the strike price the holder will not exercise the option and it will simply expire.
    - The returns to the holder and the writer are mirror images of one another.
    - The returns are asymmetric in form with regard to bond price.

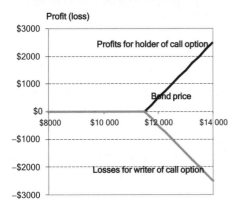

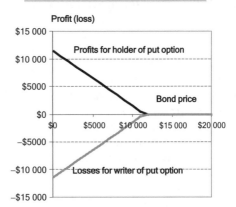

- The profits to the holder and losses to the writer in the event of the option being exercised are constrained. The maximum profit or loss is the option's strike price.

Options are talked about in terms of whether they are in-the-money, at-the-money or out-of-the-money:

- **In-the-money.** If the market price of the underlying instrument is higher than the call option's strike price the option can be exercised at a profit. The option is then described as being "in-the-money". When the underlying instrument's price is much greater than the call option's strike price it is described as being deep in-the-money. A put option is in-the-money when the price of the underlying instrument is less than the option's strike price.
- **At-the-money.** If the price of the underlying instrument is at the strike price it is described as being "at-the-money".
- **Out-of-the-money.** If the market price of the underlying instrument is less than the strike price a call option is described as being "out-of-the-money". In like manner if the market price of the bond is lower than the put option's strike price the option is in-the-money and, if higher, is out-of-the-money.

Given that the writer of the put and call options has no potential upside as a result of changes in the prices of the underlying instrument they will not give them away for free. Instead the writer requires compensation in the form of a premium paid when the option is written that they retain whether the option is exercised or expires.

Premiums and Values of Traded Options

The asymmetric nature of returns with regard to the price of the underlying instrument, and mirror image of returns to the holder and the writer, mean that options have a value to the holder even if the current stock price is below the call option's strike price or above the put option's strike price. The holder of such an option should be able to sell the option for a certain amount to a third party. This is referred to as the option's premium. The price of a traded option can be broken into two parts, its intrinsic value and its life or time value:

- **Intrinsic value.** The intrinsic value is simply the profit that would be realized if the option was in-the-money and exercised. The intrinsic value is zero when the option is either at-the-money or out-of-the-money.
- **Life or time value.** In addition to the price of the underlying instrument there are three factors that determine the value of an option's premium, the volatility of the price of the underlying instrument, time to expiration and the level of interest rates.
  - **Time.** The longer the exercise period the greater the value of the option's value. This is pretty obvious. If the option is out-of-the-money and expires next week there is less opportunity for the bond's price to rise above that of the strike price than if it expires in six months.
  - **Volatility.** The value of the bond will vary with changes in the yield curve. The more volatile that interest rates are the more volatile will be the bond's price. Higher volatility is good for option holders due to the asymmetric nature of returns relative to the bond's price. If the bond price falls below the strike price it doesn't matter if it falls a little or a lot as we won't exercise the option in any event. If the bond's price rises a lot our profit on exercise will be much greater than if it only rises a little.

The writer (or seller) of an option is paid a premium by the holder (buyer) of the option. This price may be lower or higher than the value implied from option valuation models.

The option's premium also varies with the level of interest rates but this is far less significant as a factor than either time or volatility. Its effect is also far more subtle and difficult to explain simply. For our purposes it is sufficient to note that the level of interest rates does affect an option's value and leave it at that for now.

The first of the following two charts shows the traded and intrinsic values of the above call option plotted against bond price. The following characteristics are worth noting:

- The value of the premium falls as the option moves deep into or out-of-the-money.
- When the option is either deep in-the-money or deep out-of-the-money its value varies with that of the bond's price.

The second chart shows the rate of change in percentage terms of the option's traded value against the bond's price. In the context of this chapter this has little significance but we will be picking up on this in Part III when we look at trading strategies and risk management. This has the following important characteristics:

- The rate of change of the option's value does not vary in a linear way with bond price.
- The rate of change is greatest when the option is close to being at-the-money and
- The rate of change reverses direction at a particular bond price.

Charts of the first form, which plot the price of one instrument against a single factor (in this case bond price), are sometimes referred to as delta charts. Risks resulting from changes in the price against this factor are referred to as delta risk.

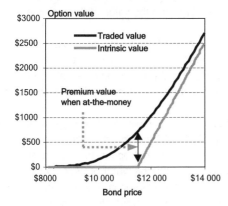

Call option's traded value versus intrinsic value against bond price

Rate of change of traded option value against bond value

Charts of the second form are known as gamma charts and the risks resulting from changes in the rate of change of the price as gamma risk. It is striking to note how the direction of the rate of change of the option's price reverses. I have deliberately omitted the actual percentage changes, it is the non-linear nature and this reversal characteristic that are important.

Wheels within Wheels

A few words of caution are in order. It is conventional to use stocks rather than bonds to illustrate the characteristics of options. In part this is because in reality exchange traded stock options are the norm and futures contracts the norm for bonds and other interest rate instruments (we will look at futures later in Chapter 10 when we consider the management of interest rate risk).

Whether we use stocks or bonds as the underlying instrument it is necessary to skirt around a number of real life complications. Readers should just bear in mind that although the above examples demonstrate the chief characteristics of financial options they do not tell the full story. The following gives an indication of some of the complexities that are usually glossed over but need to be taken into account in an in-depth analysis:

- Most textbook explanations are based on European-style options and it is sufficient to understand that equivalent American-style options will always be worth more because of their greater flexibility.
- Simplified explanations for stock option behavior ignore the complications created by dividend payments (whether known or not yet declared) and corporate actions such as rights issues.
- In using bonds as the underlying instrument I've ignored the complications arising from coupon payments and from the change in the value of the bond resulting from the passage of time. The volatility of a stock's price can be determined directly from stock prices but the volatility of the bond's price has to be inferred from the volatility of interest rates. These factors explain, in part at least, why exchange traded bond options are less common than futures contracts.

Profit and Loss Diagrams

The return diagrams we used earlier showed returns assuming no premium. These charts are, however, usually shown as profit and loss diagrams that include the value of the premium paid by the buyer of the option to the writer.

Let us assume a call option with a strike price of $11 500, which at a bond price of $11 000 has a premium of $1000. The buyer of the call option will only make a profit if the bond price trades above $12 500. If the option expires and the price remains below $11 500 the option writer will earn the full $1000 premium and the buyer incurs a loss of the same amount.

The second chart shows the profits and losses for a put option with the following terms. The strike price is $10 000, at a market price for the bond of $11 000 the option's premium is $1000. The price would have to fall below $9000 for the buyer of the put option to make a profit. If the option expires with the bond price remaining above $10 000 the writer of the put option will earn the full $1000 in premium and the holder takes an equivalent loss. The maximum profit theoretically possible for the holder is $9000 (bond price of zero versus strike price of $10 000 less $1000 premium).

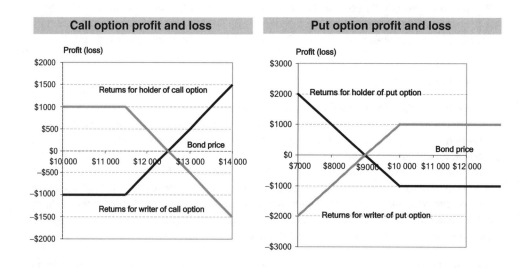

Gearing

Suppose the bond is trading at $11 000. The above call option should actually be trading at a premium of $468. Rather than buying the bond we could buy 23 call options and still have $246 in cash left over. This provides a much higher level of gearing to changes in the price of the bond itself. The first chart shows that if the bond's price rises to $11 500 the value of the option holding would rise to nearly $17 000. The higher gearing also, of course, results in greater downside risk.

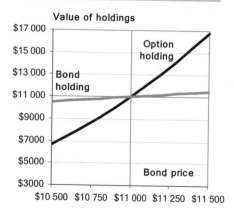

Bond versus option holdings value

Other Options

Financial options exist for many financial instruments. The most common form of exchange traded options are stock options. These are usually restricted to the largest stocks in a market. They have highly standardized terms. They usually have a common expiry date, in other words on a particular day each month a number of contracts will all expire. It is usually possible to trade options across a range of exercise dates.

Options can be issued in a number of different forms:

- **American versus European.** An option may be written that can be exercised on any date until the expiry of the option contract or can only be exercised on its expiry date. The former is referred to as American style and the latter as European style.
- **Asian.** Asian-style options are a relatively recent innovation and differ from traditional options in that they use an average price of the underlying instrument over a specified period rather than a single spot price.
- **Warrants.** Warrants are simply a form of long-dated call option contract. While exchange traded options are highly standardized, exist for a range of expiry dates and have a common expiry date warrants are issued in a particular form and for a specific expiry date. They may be issued in a "covered" form, where the issuer owns the underlying instrument, or uncovered where in the result of their exercise the issuer will have to buy the stock in the market.
- **Rights issues.** Companies may look to raise more capital from their shareholders by having a rights issue whereby shareholders are "invited" to subscribe for additional, new shares. These new shares are usually priced at a significant discount to the current market price. These rights are a form of European-style call option. Rights for larger companies may be listed and traded on an exchange.
- **Convertible bonds.** Convertible bonds comprise a straight bond plus a stock call option. When companies issue convertible bonds these options are usually implicit but investment

banks may buy these bonds and break them up into their constituent parts and sell on the straight bond equivalent and option separately.

- **Exchange traded versus over-the-counter.** Option contracts may be traded on an exchange or be "over-the-counter" (OTC), that is a private agreement reached between two parties. Exchange traded options are issued in a highly standardized form. OTC contracts may take many forms giving greater flexibility than exchange traded options. They are, however, inherently illiquid, and bid–offer spreads given by the (usually) single market-maker may be very wide.

- **Black–Scholes.** Various models have been developed to value traded options based on a framework derived by Fischer Black and Myron Scholes. These models require a relatively high level of mathematical skills to understand well. My first degree was in theoretical physics and I struggle with them. For all save option specialists it is probably sufficient to treat Black-Scholes as a fairly reliable black-box model. Give it these four inputs (price of underlying instrument, volatility of price of the underlying instrument, time and interest rate) and it will give a plausible value for an option's premium.

  Three of these four factors are well defined and can be measured with a high degree of certainty. The exception is the volatility of the price of the underlying instrument. The historic level of volatility varies over time and its measured value depends on the frequency (hourly, daily, weekly etc) and time period selected. Valuation models need the future (rather than past) volatility and there is no guarantee that the historic level of volatility will be maintained. The value these models put on an option is therefore an estimate and two traders are likely to arrive at different (but close) estimates for an option's premium.

  It is helpful to remember the following relationships. Both call and put options become more valuable as they move deeper into the money. Their value increases with the time to expiry and volatility of the price of the underlying instrument. Rising interest rates result in higher stock call option prices but lower stock put option prices.

- **Embedded options.** Many financial instruments, including loans and deposits, contain embedded options. These differ from traded and OTC options in that they are not defined in explicit terms. Someone who has taken out a 30-year mortgage has effectively bought a prepayment option allowing them to pay off the loan before it comes to term.

CALLABLE, PUTABLE AND CONVERTIBLE BONDS

Callable Bonds

Some corporate bonds are issued as callable bonds. These are bonds issued that contain an option exercisable at the discretion of the issuer to "call" or redeem the bond at a particular price. The exact call conditions are often more complicated than this but we will look at the case of a single call price where in the event of the issuer calling the bond it buys back all issued bonds.

This call option alters the way in which the bond's price changes. We will use a 15-year bond with a coupon rate of 4.5% trading at $8000. The call price is $10 000, the bond's par value. In effect while the issuer of the bond has sold a bond the buyers of the bond have also written a call option to the issuer.

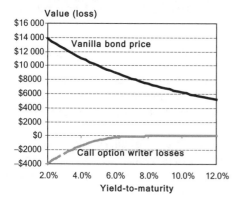

Vanilla bond price and call option losses versus yield-to-maturity

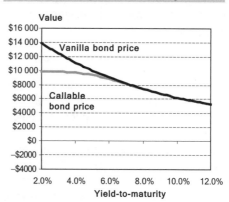

Vanilla and callable bond prices versus yield-to-maturity

(The reader should bear in mind that corporates cannot in practice issue bonds with such long terms but the longer term makes it easier to see the how the bond's value is affected by the presence of the option.)

As yields-to-maturity fall the value of the vanilla bond rises. The position for the writer of the call option is opposite. As the bond's price rises the writer's losses increase. These are shown in the first of the following two charts.

As the holder of the bond and the writer of the call option are the same party we can get the price of the callable bond by simply adding together the two positions, as shown in the second chart. The effect is a form of price truncation, as yields fall and the bond's price approaches that of the call price further price increases are truncated.

We can express this as follows:

Value of callable bond = Value of equivalent straight bond − Value of call option

The exact terms of the call option vary in terms of call price and call schedule. Some bonds are issued with a schedule of possible call dates, call price on each date and may specify a maximum percentage of the issue that can be called on each date. When comparing yields-to-maturity of callable bonds to other bonds one of two yields is used:

- **Yield-to-call.** The yield-to-call is the yield of the bond assuming it is called at the call price at the next call date.
- **Yield-to-worst.** The yield-to-worst is used for callable bonds with a schedule of call dates and call prices. The yield-to-worst is the yield-to-call for the call for the combination that is most disadvantageous to the holder of the bond.

Callable bonds have lower value than equivalent vanilla bonds. When issued pricing has to reflect the "premium" paid to the writer of the call option. Callable bonds always have lower yield-to-maturity than their vanilla equivalent.

Putable Bonds

Putable bonds are the opposite of callable bonds and entitle the holder of the bonds to sell them back to the issuer before the maturity date. This is equivalent to the issuer of the bond writing a put option:

Value of putable bond = Value of equivalent straight bond + Value of put option

The put option gives the holder of the putable bond some protection against the effects of higher yields (which may be due to upward shifts in the yield curve or may be due to a widening of credit spreads). If market prices fall below the put price the bondholder can exercise their option at the put price.

As the holder of the bond and the holder of the put option are the same party we can get the price of the putable bond by simply adding together the two positions, as shown in the second chart. The effect is a form of price compression, as yields rise and the bond's price approaches that of the put price further price falls are truncated. The put price is $7500.

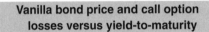

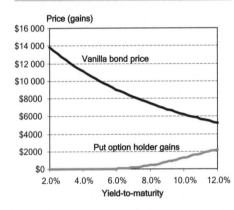

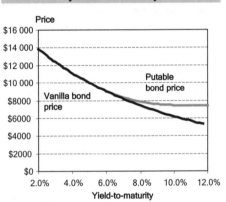

Putable bonds are worth more than their vanilla equivalent and trade at higher yields to maturity. Put options on long-term bonds are potentially dangerous to issuers because their exercise is out of the control of the issuer.

Bondholders may demand such an option because of concerns about a company's creditworthiness. The protection offered by put options is, however, limited. If credit spreads at a particular issuer widen this is likely to be because of specific problems or weaknesses at the issuer. In the event that bondholders seek to exercise their put option the company may not be able to honor its commitment.

Convertible Bonds

Convertible bonds are bonds issued by companies that have an embedded option that entitles the holder to exchange the bond for a predefined amount of equity in the company at a specified price. In some countries convertible bonds are referred to as debentures. The price of such a convertible bond is given by the following:

Convertible bond price = Straight bond price + Value of stock call option

The conversion terms for individual issues vary widely. There is nothing to stop a company issuing a bond that contains an embedded option that gives the issuer the right to force conversion. In this case the holder of the bond has effectively sold a put option on the bond:

Convertible bond price = Straight bond price − Value of bond put option

Most equity analysts dislike having to incorporate the effects of convertible instruments because they complicate calculations of future fully diluted earnings per share (EPS) and hence valuations. Institutional investors are likely to be able to take account of the potential dilution from the issue of new shares; this is not, however, true for most retail investors.

Asset Backed Securities

Asset backed securities are issued in a number of different tranches each with a particular mix of risk and returns. Some of these tranches are relatively easy to value but others are not. We will defer any discussion of approaches to their valuation until we look at securitization issues in Chapter 17.

Equity Valuations

Securities in the form of stocks or shares represent a claim on the common equity of a company and on the payments made to equity holders. The reader will recall that in its most generalized form a security's value is given by the sum of its discounted expected future cashflows, as shown below, this is also referred to as its present value:

$$\text{Intrinsic equity value} = \sum_{n=1}^{N} \frac{Cf_n}{(1 + RR)^n}$$

There is an extensive body of well-tested academic theory on how to value US Treasury bonds. We have already looked at these methods in some detail. They work well for two principal reasons:

- **Certainty of cashflows.** The cashflows associated with these bonds in terms of coupon and principal payments are clearly defined in advance. These bonds are generally treated as risk free and hence there are no default risks to take into account.
- **Discount rate.** The depth of the US Treasuries market means that the appropriate discount rate to use is provided by yield-to-maturities taken from a yield curve taken from the prices of traded benchmark issues and new issues.

It is harder to value corporate bonds. Term yields can by taken from the risk-free yield curve but a level of default risk exists and is reflected in higher yields (lower prices) than for an equivalent risk-free instrument and attributed to a credit spread. These default risks, and hence credit spreads and prices, are likely to change over time. In deep markets where most issues have an external credit rating the credit spreads for a particular issue can be estimated from credit spreads on other issues with similar terms and from issuers of the same credit rating.

There may also be some uncertainty in future cashflows due to the presence of embedded call or put options. Various methods have been developed to try to take these factors into account.

Valuing equities is much harder than valuing bonds, whether risk free or corporate, for the following reasons:

- **Uncertain future dividends.** The main source of cashflows generated from stocks is dividends paid. Future dividend payments may rise or fall and in some years may be missed completely.
- **Corporate actions.** Companies may also raise additional capital through rights issues to which existing shareholders will have to subscribe or face a dilution in their share of the ownership. Dilution may also occur from the exercise of convertible instruments or stock options. Companies may also decide to return excess capital via share buy-backs, special dividends or capital reduction programs.
- **Discount rate.** Equity holders are the first set of creditors to bear losses. All other creditors have a senior claim in the event of the corporate's liquidation. Investors therefore demand higher returns from equity than for other asset classes. The discount rate to the used, the company's cost-of-equity, can be viewed as being based on three factors as shown in the following equation:

$$\textit{Cost-of-equity} = \textit{Risk-free rate} + \textit{Stock beta} \times \textit{Equity risk premium} = \textit{COE}$$

- **Risk-free rate.** CAPM does not state which risk-free rate to use. Most analysts take the yield on the longest-dated government bonds available as the risk-free rate, and this seems like the most appropriate market-based rate to use given the perpetual nature of equities. In many developing markets there is a default risk, local markets lack depth and there is often a complete absence of government issues at the long end of the yield curve.
- **Equity risk premium.** The equity risk premium cannot be measured directly. It is possible to argue that stocks are cheap or expensive depending on the equity risk premium assumed. The equity risk premium does not have an absolute, unchanging value in the same way as real would constants such as the speed of light or Planck's constant appear to have.
- **Stock betas.** That leaves stock-specific risks to be taken into account. This is captured through a stock-specific factor, beta, and is based on the relationship between returns on an individual stock versus those of equities as an asset class.

This above approach is based on the widely used capital asset pricing model which we will look at in more depth in Chapter 15 on "Fund management" and when we look at methods to value commercial banks in Chapter 18.

3

Central Banks and the Creation of Money

Authority doesn't work without prestige, or prestige without distance.

General Charles de Gaulle, French President

MONEY

The most important feature of central banks is their egregious power to affect the supply and price of money and hence the level and shape of the yield curve. One of the most widely watched economic indicators is the US$ yield curve. Given the sensitivity of the valuations of financial assets to the level of interest rates it is important to understand the factors and forces that determine the shape of the yield curve and changes to that shape.

These shifts in the yield curve provide both opportunities and risks to individual banks. At any given moment in time the Treasury has to decide whether to position its balance sheet to try to take advantage of shifts in the yield curve. Taking such a position is speculative and to be successful requires the bank to be better at forecasting future interest rates than the market. Alternatively it can attempt to structure its balance sheet such that yield curve shifts are neutralized and have minimal impact on bank earnings and economic value.

In this chapter we also look at the way that central banks may exert moral suasion and explain the different managed currency systems that some central banks try to maintain.

It is useful to take a step back and first examine the way in which money is created. Most of us find the whole process a complete mystery even though in essence it is actually quite straightforward. With his usual acute eye the eminent economist J. K. Galbraith observed that "The process by which banks create money is so simple that the mind is repelled." Central and commercial banks both play key parts in this process. By understanding how money is created it is much easier to understand where central banks get their powers of leverage.

Functions and Roles of Money

Money is a commodity that we tend to take for granted. Most of us think of money as cash, but cash is just a small portion of broad money. Most financial transactions are conducted using checks, electronic transfer of funds or credit cards. Economists have a number of different definitions of money. We do not need to define these here particularly as definitions vary from country to country and this is very much moving into the realm of macroeconomics. It is, however, worth reviewing the three fundamental functions that money performs.

- **Accounting basis.** Money provides a means of accounting for the value of real goods. It allows, for example, one to compare the cost of a cup of coffee with the price of a telephone call.
- **Store of value.** Money represents a form of savings, whether it is in the form of a bank deposit or cash. It provides a means of making purchases of real goods and services in the future. It is not a good store of value in an inflationary environment, however.

- **Means of exchange.** Money provides a means of exchange for real goods and services. In the absence of money transactions between two parties would have to be done on a barter basis. Barter is a very inefficient means of effecting transactions. Money reduces transaction costs and makes the real economy more efficient.

The first subjects to examine are how money is created and the role of banks in that process. In most countries the central bank controls how much money is created. The creation of money has always reminded me of a magician's sleight of hand. While your intellect tells you one thing no matter how many times you see the trick it is still impossible to work out how it is done. The ancient street hustle of the "three cup" trick is a good example. In the case of money the con is contained in the word confidence.

Money with an Intrinsic Value

For most of human history societies have functioned without money. The development of tokens to represent value is a relatively modern development and for thousands of years those tokens were deemed to have an intrinsic value. It is only in the last 500 years or so that money has been represented by tokens with a legal status but no intrinsic value. At first such notes were issued backed by real physical assets (gold) but today that linkage has been completely broken.

The most commonly used mediums for money in historic times were gold and silver. Other more exotic currencies, to our way of thinking at least, have included salt and cowry seashells.

Gold in particular has always had a fascination because of its unique physical qualities. Gold does not tarnish as silver does or rust as iron does. It can be beaten into extremely thin leaf. It has attractive, decorative qualities and is used widely in jewelry. It is of a uniform standard – gold from Egypt cannot be distinguished from gold extracted from the New World. This is not the case with organic products such as coffee or saffron. At the time of writing the price of saffron was around $400 an ounce, in line with that of gold, but prices vary depending on quality and source. Gold also has a scarcity value. It is not a common element and is difficult to extract from the ground. It is a very dense element and requires little storage space.

When gold is used as a medium of exchange it provides a way in which different products and services can be given equivalent values in terms of a given weight of gold. To illustrate this point we use a highly stylized example taken from Dreamworld.

Dreamworld is a wonderful place where cream and chocolate are not fattening and airplanes leave on time. When necessary in Dreamworld we can assume no transaction costs, no taxes, no bid–offer spread, we can borrow or lend what we choose at the risk-free rate whenever we want, companies pay dividends only when required, there is no counterparty risk and we don't need to worry about capital allocation issues! Dreamworld has a very convenient location and is populated largely by finance academics. One group can use the power of its simplifying assumptions to formulate fundamental theories. The second group woks on how to modify these theories to take the chosen assumptions into account.

In this example we will ignore the costs of capital investments, taxes and transaction costs, the impact of skill levels on labor costs and so on. We will take only human labor into account. Suppose it takes 10 days of human labor to produce one ounce of gold, five days to make a table, 20 days to build a cart and one day to clean a house. For the markets to be in equilibrium the table should be sold at half an ounce of gold, the cart for two ounces and the cleaner should get one-tenth of an ounce for his daily efforts.

In periods of high inflation or uncertainty over the future value of paper money many people turn to gold as a way to preserve value. A paper currency may lose all of its value in the event of a regime change or a military defeat. Gold hidden in a hole in the garden provides a way to preserve value. It is a generally accepted axiom (although not always borne out by facts) that the price of gold rises in terms of political and economic uncertainty. There are, however, significant problems with using tokens that have an intrinsic value as money:

- **Transaction costs.** Gold is completely negotiable and there is no foolproof way to establish ownership. Gold ornaments or coins can be melted down and recast as standard bars. Its density makes it difficult to move large amounts easily and this also makes it vulnerable to loss. The physical delivery of gold involves risks arising from natural disasters such as a ship sinking in a storm or human intervention in the form of theft. Gold has to be kept in a secure location and shipments require tight security. Transport has been both slow and difficult for most of human history. All of these factors push up transaction costs.
- **Costs to the economy.** Gold's intrinsic value comes from demand for its use in jewelry, in specialist applications such as the decoration of churches and temples and, in modern times, in the electronic and space industries. Gold extraction requires significant capital investment and labor and is the source of damaging environmental pollution. Using gold as a medium for money ties up capital and human resources that could be used in a more productive manner. King Midas learnt the hard way that gold cannot satisfy human hungers.

  The world's central banks all have vaults where they store their gold reserves. Between them they hold thousands of tons of gold. The US gold reserve is held at Fort Knox, one of the world's most secure facilities, where it is jealously guarded. At least squirrels use their hoards to help them survive the winter. There is something delightfully ironic about a system where one group of people expend huge effort to extract a metal from one hole in the ground which is then sold to another group of people who, at huge expense, put it in their own hole in the ground.
- **Supply and demand.** Our simple example showing the equivalence of values in gold based on labor inputs looked only at the supply side. Suppose that demand for carts exceeded that which could be produced. In this situation cart builders might be able to sell each cart they made at $2\frac{1}{2}$ ounces of gold. This would attract people making tables or digging for gold to switch to making carts and would result in a reduction in the supply of gold and tables, pushing up the price of tables relative to carts and lowering the price of carts in terms of gold. This would continue until equilibrium between the markets was re-established.

  When the Spanish discovered huge quantities of gold in the New World, much of it already extracted and refined, they thought they had made their fortunes – and many of the early conquistadors did. But the huge influx of gold had a much wider impact. With the supply of gold (money) expanding rapidly the price of real goods and services in terms of gold rose. In modern times this would be seen as a period of high inflation. There was no change in the real output of the Spanish economy but a transfer of wealth took place from those who had held gold as a store of value and those on fixed incomes to people who had invested in real assets.
- **Debasement.** A gold or silver coinage can be debased in one of three ways. Very pure gold is very soft and is usually mixed with a base metal, such as silver, to make a harder alloy. A carat, or karat, is a measure of the proportion of precious metal in an alloy. Twenty-four-carat

gold is pure gold while 18-carat gold is 18/24 or three-quarter gold. The authority to mint coins in medieval times usually rested with the monarchy.

A king could make his gold go further by increasing the level of silver contained in newly minted coins. In some instances the coinage in circulation would be recalled, melted down and reissued in a debased form. For obvious reasons people preferred to hold onto older coins with the same nominal face value but a higher gold content. People tried to pay for goods and services with coins that had the lower gold content. This is the basis for what is known as Gresham's law, "Bad money drives out good money", after Sir Thomas Gresham the master of the royal mint in the reign of Elizabeth I. In modern times the US dollar has become the preferred currency in many developing and transitional economies. This reflects greater confidence in the US dollar retaining its value and being convertible than in the local currency.

A second method was to shave metal off the edges of the coins. To try to prevent such practices coins were produced with serrated edges. Most countries continue to produce coins milled in this manner but the serrated edges are now only useful in slot and vending machines. The last method was to take a lower value base metal, such as lead, and to produce counterfeit gold-plated coins.

In the Middle Ages alchemists sought to find a way to transmute a base metal into gold. This would have been as remarkable an achievement then as the discovery of cold fusion would be today. Alas, while such an alchemist might have found fame he was unlikely to have made his fortune in any case. Recognition of intellectual property rights and patent laws in medieval times were relatively undeveloped. The only way he could have made his fortune would have been to buy real goods with the gold he had made as quickly as possible before others found out about his discovery. Once everyone knew how to make gold its value would have plummeted.

The Move Towards Paper-based (Fiat) Money

What do gunpowder and pasta have in common? According to the Chinese both of these were invented in China long before they appeared in the West. It is generally accepted that the earliest use of paper money was in China more than 1000 years ago towards the end of the Tang dynasty. These were issued by private banks but backed by the state. The use of the paper currency reduced the need to transport silver to make payments. This paper was effectively a form of negotiable IOU or promissory note. The holder of the note could present it to the issuer and receive the stated weight of silver in return.

While Italians may dispute this version of history as it relates to pasta they can at least claim to have laid the foundations for the modern banking system in the sixteenth century. This was the perfect scam because while the perpetrators profited no-one was obviously hurt through their system provided it worked as intended. The perpetrators were respected (or at least rich) goldsmiths.

Goldsmiths had to keep quantities of gold on their premises in the form of raw material, work-in-progress and finished products. This gold had to be kept in a secure place and yet be readily accessible. This allowed them to provide a service to rich merchants and landowners to store their gold. They were able to offer one of the earliest safekeeping, or custody, services to their customers. Customers would deliver their gold, usually in the form of coins, to the goldsmith who would issue a receipt for the gold. The receipt represented a claim on this stored gold. The goldsmith would return the gold when this receipt was presented.

A merchant who had to pay a supplier would present his receipt to the goldsmith, take the gold and then make the payment. The supplier would then take the gold back to the goldsmith for safekeeping and receive a receipt in turn. Over time customers realized that it was safer and more convenient to make large payments using these receipts as the medium of exchange. Two issues had to be resolved. The first was that the receipts presented were genuine and represented real claims. The second was that the goldsmith would, and could, honor these claims. The first issue was resolved through the use of wax seals. The second issue depended largely on the reputation of the goldsmiths and perceptions of their integrity and solvency.

Over time the gold receipts increasingly displaced gold coins for the settlement of large payments. Coins continued to be used to settle smaller transactions and to make up any difference between the value of the receipts and the required payment. As an aside, these early forms of paper money can be viewed as an asset backed bearer security but by convention it is usually referred to as cash.

These developments led to the adoption of the equivalent of paper money but it did not involve either the creation of money or the establishment of a banking system. These required a leap of imagination. It is difficult to believe this innovation emerged from a committee but the name of the original visionary has been lost in the mists of time. As will become clear goldsmiths had every incentive to keep the workings of this system to themselves.

On any given day the amount of actual gold withdrawn by customers was normally only a very small proportion of the gold that had been deposited with the goldsmith. It became clear that some of this stored gold could be lent out without the knowledge of the depositors. The latter were not concerned whether the coins they received on presentation of their receipt were those initially deposited – only that their value (weight) was the same.

The borrowers rarely withdrew gold itself but instead were issued receipts that acted as a negotiable currency just as those issued to the actual depositors did. The goldsmiths agreed terms and conditions for these loans with the borrowers. The latter paid interest on these loans. The nominal value of receipts circulating in the economy exceeded the value of the gold held by the goldsmiths. In this way money was created.

The system had two potential weaknesses. The first was that the goldsmiths might get greedy and lend out too high proportion of the gold they held leading to a high level of receipts circulating in the system. This in turn could result in people starting to question whether the goldsmiths could meet their claims. If enough people with a claim on the goldsmith presented his or her receipts at the same time the goldsmith would be unable to meet all of the claims. The system only worked if depositors were confident that their claims would be met.

The second weakness arose from borrowers who took their loans in the form of gold and subsequently defaulted. This was a real risk when borrowers included kings using such loans to finance wars and merchants buying goods abroad to be shipped home for resale. Members of the first group were at risk from losing their war or being held for ransom, the second of their ship sinking or being attacked by pirates and losing their cargo.

The banking system created by the goldsmiths was unregulated, there were no legal reserve or capital adequacy requirements, for example. There was no form of depositor protection provided by the likes of the US Federal Deposit Insurance Corporation (FDIC). It also still relied on the backing of a commodity (gold) with an intrinsic value.

We now have the basis for the modern money system but we need to get rid of the convertibility into gold. We have already discussed some of the practical problems with using gold as a currency such as the tying up of resources to produce and store it that could be better used elsewhere. This is not the major problem, however, which lies in the realm of macroeconomics.

By linking the domestic currency to gold a country's money supply is effectively constrained by gold supply. Although there have been periods when gold supply has risen much faster than the real economy, such as happened in Spain, the supply of gold is relatively fixed. In an expanding economy an insufficient level of money supply growth will lead to disinflation, higher unemployment and a lower level of real output. This link can be broken by prohibiting gold withdrawals. This would effectively mean that no-one would know whether the gold was there or not! Policy makers could then determine money supply as deemed necessary by economic conditions.

These problems are, however, amplified by trade when countries have their own currencies linked to gold. This results in the adoption of what is known as the gold standard and results in a fixed exchange rate system. If holders of sterling were entitled to exchange a £100 note for one ounce of gold and the holders of US dollars could exchange $200 for one ounce this would force a fixed exchange rate of £1 for $2.

Under a gold standard countries with a trade deficit (where the value of their exports in terms of gold was less than the value of their imports) settle this difference by transferring gold to those countries with a trade surplus. The outflow of gold leads to a fall in money supply in those countries with a deficit and lower prices making exports more competitive as a result. Inflows of gold at creditor nations result in increased money supply, higher prices and less competitive exports. As a result of these two pressures the trade balance tends to equilibrium.

Higher trade levels result in higher overall output and trade has expanded much more rapidly than economic output since the time of the industrial revolution. The demand for exchange currency has hence grown much faster than the supply of gold. The only way for this demand to be satisfied is for prices to fall, and again leads to higher unemployment and a lower output level than would otherwise be the case.

A gold standard puts policy makers into a straitjacket with no effective means to determine or influence money supply other than through trade tariffs and other barriers that reduce the level of trade. The last attempt to operate using a global fixed exchange rate system failed in 1974 and today few seriously countenance the return to either a fixed exchange rate system or a gold standard.

RESERVE REQUIREMENTS AND THEIR ROLE IN THE CREATION OF MONEY

Reserve requirements play an important role in determining the level of money that can be created. To show how money can be created we will assume a Dreamworld financial system and then relax these assumptions until we get to a reasonable approximation of a modern financial system.

We will assume one commercial and one central bank, that all companies have opened checking accounts with the commercial bank, all payments have to be made by check and the central bank requires the commercial bank to maintain cash equivalent to 10% of all deposits (referred to as cash reserves). We will view the creation of money and credit as a series of discrete steps.

The first step involves the central bank printing $100m in cash and depositing it with the commercial bank. The commercial bank now has $90m that it can lend out after putting aside the required $10m in cash reserves. A company then borrows $90m and has it credited to its checking account. It then writes checks equal to this amount to pay its suppliers. The suppliers then have $90m in checks that they have to deposit with the commercial bank. The commercial bank has to set aside $9m in additional reserves but now has an additional $81m it can lend out.

Commercial bank balance sheet ($m) – end of round one			
Assets ($m)		**Liabilities ($m)**	
Cash reserves	19	Deposits from central bank	100
Cash on hand	81	Deposits from customers	90
Loans to customers	90		
Total assets	**190**	**Total liabilities**	**190**

The second round is very similar but the bank can now lend out only $81m. The borrower writes checks for this amount to suppliers who deposit the proceeds with the bank. The bank has to set aside $8.1m in additional reserves leaving it with $72.9m that it can lend out.

Commercial bank balance sheet ($m) – end of round two			
Assets ($m)		**Liabilities ($m)**	
Cash reserves	27.1	Deposits from central bank	100.0
Cash on hand	82.9	Deposits from customers	181.0
Loans to customers	171.0		
Total assets	**281.0**	**Total liabilities**	**281.0**

This process can continue until the bank has exhausted its cash on hand and it is all held in the form of cash reserves. The final bank balance sheet is as follows. The initial deposit of $100m has been transformed into total deposits of $1000m and created $900m in new credit. The multiplication factor m is given by the following equation where r is the proportion of deposits that must be held as cash reserves:

$$\text{Money multiplier } m = \frac{1}{r}$$

Commercial bank balance sheet ($m) – at completion			
Assets ($m)		**Liabilities ($m)**	
Cash reserves	100.0	Deposits from central bank	100.0
Cash on hand	0.0	Deposits from customers	900.0
Loans to customers	900.0		
Total assets	**1000.0**	**Total liabilities**	**1000.0**

Having the legal power to adjust bank reserve requirements gives the central bank a tool to influence the growth of money (and hence of credit). An increase in reserve requirements will lead to a lower money multiplier and a reduction in credit growth or even a contraction in credit. To return to our Dreamworld assumptions:

- It does not matter if there is one or are 10 commercial banks. In a closed system the checks written on one bank's accounts will be deposited with another. Changes in market share may take place but have no effect on the overall analysis.
- Some drawdowns will be in the form of cash and not all transactions will be settled by check. Companies will keep a buffer of cash and positive balances for short-term contingencies. The practical effect is to reduce the value of the money multiplier. It is not unreasonable to expect this buffer level to vary over time.
- Banks will need to keep cash for immediate withdrawals other than that required as cash reserves by the central bank. Failure to do so would result in it either failing to keep the required cash reserves in the event of a deposit withdrawal or forcing it to reduce its deposit and loan base. The latter is difficult to achieve quickly. This will further reduce the money multiplier.

In practice not all reserves are required to be held in the form of cash (although the central bank is likely to allow them to count towards meeting reserve requirements) and most are held as deposits held with the central bank known as reserve deposits.

It is widely accepted that over time broad money should grow in line with the level of economic activity. If it grows faster this is likely to lead to inflationary pressures and if slower to deflation. This is a huge simplification as it ignores the cyclicality of capitalist economies but will suffice for our purposes, this is not an economics book. The central bank has three tools to help it achieve this objective, reserve requirements, adjusting the discount rate and open market operations.

By increasing reserve requirement the central bank can reduce money supply and by adjusting it downwards increase money supply. In practice, few OECD central banks actively use reserve requirements to manage money supply because it is a fairly blunt instrument. This is not the case in some emerging markets (Malaysia and the Philippines are examples) where adjustments in reserve requirements have been extensively used as a policy tool. The two central bank tools used most often are the discount rate and open market operations.

It should also be noted that the central bank is printing money and charging interest to commercial banks that borrow this money. This is clearly a good business. These profits are referred to as seigniorage. There was a story in the national press in the early 2000s about an unfortunate UK company to which the Royal Mint had subcontracted work. It must have been the only company in the world that literally had a license to print money and that was operating at a loss.

Factors Affecting the Shape of the Yield Curve

Economists have time in their busy little lives to ponder on the factors that determine the shape of the yield curve. At its most fundamental its shape is, of course, determined by supply and demand for money at certain maturities. This just shifts the question to one of what determines supply and demand. Most theories have to contend with the irritating constraint imposed by the real world that yield curves rarely take the pure forms suggested in the previous chapter. Their precise form varies from day to day. They often have kinks and do not have a smooth shape, this will be apparent from the actual examples we look at later in this chapter.

The three basic theories that have been put forward by economists are those of unbiased expectations, liquidity preference and market segmentation:

- **Unbiased expectations.** At its most basic the unbiased expectations theory holds that forward rates reflect expectations of future spot rates. An inverted yield curve therefore implies that the market expects future spot rates to fall. This may be because the market expects either real rates or inflation to fall.

  Take an investor with $10m to invest for two years. The investor has the choice of buying two-year paper with an annual yield of 8% or buying one-year paper today with a yield of 6% and reinvesting it in one-year paper a year hence at the prevailing spot rate. Proponents of this theory argue that for the market to be in equilibrium the following should hold:

$$(1.08)^2 = (1.06) \times (1 + R_e) \Rightarrow R_e = 10.04\%$$

  where R_e is the expected future one-year spot interest rate. If this equality does not hold there is a potential (albeit not risk-free) arbitrage opportunity.
- **Liquidity preference.** This theory starts with the premise that investors prefer to hold short-dated securities to long-dated securities. Investors buying long-dated securities will therefore demand a premium. Issuers will be prepared to pay such a premium because it means they avoid the refinancing costs of, and risks associated with, redeeming, issuing and rolling over short-term debt.
- **Market segmentation**. The third theory asserts that there are different markets at different maturities. Supply and demand within specific market segments then establish clearing prices.

All three theories have their merits but simple and busy equity analysts usually assume the following:

- **Long-term yields.** That changes in long-term yields are a good reflection of changing inflationary expectations.
- **Short-term rates.** That short-term rates largely reflect central bank views on the economy's inflationary and growth prospects, and that market forces play a secondary role.
- **Medium-term rates.** That medium-term rates will fall somewhere between short-term and long-term rates, or may be higher than or lower than both short-term or long-term rates! Such humped shapes are usually short-lived.

DISCOUNT RATE AND OPEN MARKET OPERATIONS

The most commonly used central bank tools are those of adjusting the discount rate, to affect the price of money, and buying and selling government bonds, to affect the level of money supply. The discount rate is the rate at which banks can borrow from the central bank. In practice the transmission mechanism is often through the interbank market. The Federal Funds rate, for example, is the rate at which US banks with cash and deposits with Federal Reserve banks in excess of their reserve requirements will lend to banks that have a shortfall:

- **Discount window.** Banks that regularly borrow from the central bank will find themselves being charged punitive rates. The discount window provides a mechanism for the central bank to influence the level of short-term interest rates through its role as the lender of last resort. Their ability to influence rates at the long end of the yield curve is more limited. The use of the discount window is highly visible.

- **Open market operations**. The final way in which central banks can influence money supply is through open market operations. If the central bank wishes to increase money supply then it intervenes to buy government securities. It does this by "printing" cash. If it wants to reduce money supply then it sells government securities. The effectiveness of open market operations is due to the effect of the money multiplier. The central bank has a very long lever.

The central bank can choose the term of the securities it buys or sells and while its effectiveness is limited in can influence yields at a particular maturity. Its action in terms of money supply and its impact at the short end enjoy considerable leverage but as just one more participant in bonds at a particular term it has no such gearing.

EXAMPLES OF CENTRAL BANK ACTIONS

Fed Action and the Yield Curve, May 1994–February 1996

I'm going use two examples of Federal Reserve board action to illustrate how central banks can effect the yield curve. The first example dates back to 1994–1996. The yield curve charts tell us much pretty much what took place and how the yield curve influenced, and was affected by, Fed actions:

- **July 1992–January 1994.** The Fed left the discount rate unchanged through this period. The yield curve had a normal upward structure with long-term rates steady to drifting down. They reached a low in January 1994.
- **April–May 1994.** By April 1994 rates at the long end had increased by more than 100 bpts from their January lows signaling market expectations of higher inflation. In May 1994 the Fed increased the discount rate by 50 bpts.
- **June 1994–February 1995.** Yields at the long end continued to rise driven by fears of inflation and an overheating economy. The Fed continued to increase rates by a further 50 bpts in September, 25 bpts in November, a further 50 bpts in December and a further 50 bpts in February. The total increase was 225 bpts over less than a year, from a low of 3% to 5.25%.
- **March 1995–February 1996.** By March 1995 the tightening of liquidity was starting to have an effect, inflationary expectations were abating and long-term rates had fallen back to 7% around the level at which the Fed started tightening. The Fed left rates unchanged at 5.25% until February 1996 when long-term rates had fallen and were below 6%. In February 1996 it cut rates for the first time since July 1992.
- **Impact on term spreads.** Between January 1994 and February 1996 the term spread between discount rates and 10-year bond yields had narrowed from approximately 280 bpts to around 80 bpts. The yield curve did not invert but it came close to being flat.

People at the Fed had good reason to be satisfied with themselves. By taking early action they reduced the threat of inflation and cooled off an economy at risk of overheating but without pushing the economy into a recession or even a downturn.

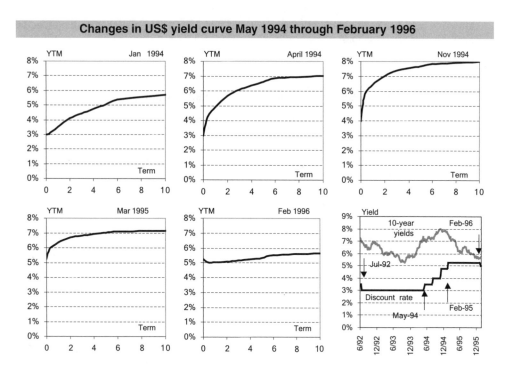

Changes in US$ yield curve May 1994 through February 1996

Fed Action and the Yield Curve, November 1998–July 2003

The previous example occurred in the middle of what became known as "goldilocks" economics, not too hot and not too cold. It shows an example of a central bank taking early action to choke off inflationary pressures. While inflation remained in check through the 1990s the economy enjoyed one of its longest ever periods of sustained growth. The previous example demonstrated the success of the Fed's monetary policy at that time. It had a much harder job in the period November 1998 through to July 2003 with the threat of a deflationary recession a real possibility:

- **November 1998–October 1999.** The Fed left the discount rate unchanged through this period. Rates at the long-end started to drift up and despite their low nominal level they were relatively high in real terms and suggested rising inflationary expectations.
- **November 1999–January 2001.** Over the course of a year the Fed increased the discount rate by approximately 150 bpts. These hikes continued through the first half of 2000 even though long-term rates had peaked in January and (with the benefit of hindsight) appeared to be heading down. By January 2001 long-term rates had fallen about 150 bpts from the peak and it appeared as though the Fed had overdone its tightening. The yield curve was inverted in January 2001. This coincided with the bursting of the technology and stock market bubble.
- **February 2001–December 2001.** Over the course of 2001 the Fed continued to cut rates aggressively and by the end of the year had cut nearly 500 bpts in total. At 1.25% the discount rate was at a historic low. Despite these cuts long-run rates continued to fall and by June 2002 had fallen a further 100 bpts. With very mixed signals of the economic outlook the Fed cut a further 50 bpts in November 2002 but these had little visible effect. The shape of the yield curve at the end of July 2003 remained largely unchanged from June 2002. The

outlook in July 2003 remained very mixed with risks of a deflationary recession balanced by hopes of a modest recovery.

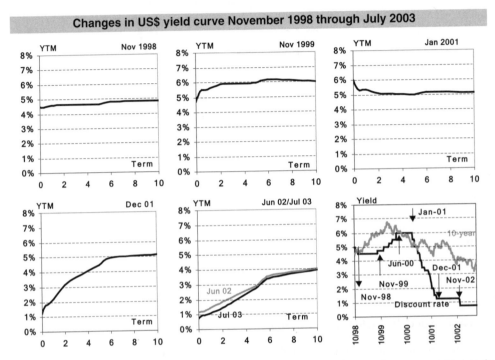

Changes in US$ yield curve November 1998 through July 2003

Managing an economy the size of the US is very much like trying to steer a supertanker. It takes time between turning the wheel and actually turning course. Once headed in a particular direction it is also difficult to stop.

Neither of these examples is intended to pass any judgment on the Fed's policies during these periods (I most certainly lack the credentials to do so in any case) but rather to illustrate the following:

- **Market expectations and central bank actions.** There is a complex interplay between market expectations and central bank actions, action takes time to have an effect, and the effectiveness of such actions varies.
- **Forecasting difficulty.** Forecasting interest rates is difficult because it is necessary not only to identify the fundamental drivers but to second-guess the central bank in terms of the actions it is likely to take in response to its perceptions of the underlying drivers.
- **Range of shifts.** Shifts in the yield curve may be parallel, with rates at all maturities going up or down by the same amount, but this occurs rarely. They may be non-parallel in which the levels of changes in rates at varying maturities differ. An extreme example of a non-parallel shift in the yield curve is the shift from an upward-sloping yield curve to an inverted one.
- **Variety of shapes.** Although we have talked about upward-sloping curves and inverted curves in the previous example we have one case where medium-term rates were higher than both short- and long-term rates and another where they were lower.

THE RISK-FREE FALLACY OF GOVERNMENT BONDS

Bonds issued by governments are generally regarded as risk free in the sense that it is assumed that there is zero default risk. The implicit assumption is that if a government could not redeem its bonds it always has the option of printing more money. This assumption has always been flawed as holders of bonds issued by Napoleonic France, pre-revolution Russia and China would have found. Many of these bonds still exist but are traded as collector items for aesthetic reasons.

In more recent years experience with Argentina, Brazil and Mexico in the mid-1980s has also showed that this is a fallacy when the bonds are issued in a foreign currency and bought by foreign investors. In most OECD countries today, however, these government's securities are generally regarded as providing a risk-free return. In the early part of this century Japanese governments ran significant deficits, funded by bond issues, to try to break out of their deflationary slump. Despite continuing current account surpluses and massive foreign currency reserves they had to suffer the indignity of being warned by rating agencies that the status of their debt was under review.

MORAL SUASION

Central banks are powerful organizations. In addition to being endowed with significant statutory powers most are usually able to leverage these powers by applying what is referred to as "moral suasion". This is politically correct talk for arm-twisting. Implicit threats or rewards may accompany the arm-twisting. Moral suasion is the art of getting banks to do things that the central bank wants but has no legal power to impose.

Their ability to influence domestic banks' actions in the "national interest" is one of the reasons why most central banks act to ensure that locally controlled banks remain dominant in the domestic market. They usually seek to achieve this end by two means:

- **Foreign limits on control and ownership.** They often impose limits on the proportion of shares in local banks (usually set at 40%, of issued shares) that can be held by foreign individuals or institutions. This usually results in two classes of shares and in many cases a "foreign premium" where shares on the "foreign board" trade at a premium to those on the local board. Individual holdings are also usually subject to a 5% limit. Central banks or regulators can also exercise their powers to approve senior management and board level appointments to ensure that management control remains in local hands whatever the ownership structure.
- **Restrictions on foreign banks' operations.** They also often try to restrict the market share of foreign banks. Measures include limits on the total number of banking licenses given to foreign banks. This often prevents the entry of new foreign banks. Other restrictions that are often imposed concern the sorts of businesses they are allowed to undertake, limits on the number of branches and ATMs and being prohibited from being a member of the domestic clearing system (forcing them to clear all such transactions through a local bank). This heavy level of protection and regulatory requirements has had a significant influence on industry structures in many developing countries.

Examples of moral suasion by central banks and bank regulators include the following:

- **Bailouts.** A healthy domestic bank may be asked to rescue a smaller failing bank. Privately owned banks are better able to resist this particular pressure than state-controlled banks but may be given little option. A foreign-owned bank is much better placed to resist such coercion.
- **Lending restraints.** The central bank may ask banks to restrain their lending to a particular sector, usually the real estate market. This may be done informally or through the imposition of a limit on the proportion of total loans that a bank can lend to a particular sector.

  In Hong Kong, for example, the Hong Kong Monetary Authority effectively imposed a 40% limit on the proportion of loans that a bank could extend to real estate developers and investors and for residential mortgages in the mid-1990s. Rapid asset inflation had pushed property prices to the point where they were among the highest in the world. The prudence of this policy was shown when property prices reversed in the late 1990s and approximately 40% of mortgagors found themselves with negative equity.
- **Directed lending.** The central bank may set loan growth targets for individual banks at an overall level, by economic sector or by group of customers. These targets are intended to support government policy whether economic or social. The following are just a few such examples
    - In Taiwan the ruling government has at times instructed banks to give preferential treatment to people and companies adversely affected by earthquakes. This may be worthy but could have been addressed in a more equitable way by the government making direct grants to the affected parties so that they could meet their financial obligations.
    - In the US banks have to meet legislative requirements to lend to particular groups of people to support national housing policies and to prevent discrimination based on location. A high proportion of deposits gathered in a particular area, such as an inner city ghetto, must be lent out in that locale, for example.
    - In South Korea in the 1990s successive governments encouraged banks to lend to particular industrial groups and sectors. Banks were expected to support governments' objectives to create and nurture national champions.
    - In some countries tax relief is given on part of the interest paid on home loans but is not given for rental expenses. This distorts the housing market by encouraging home ownership at the expense of those living in rented accommodation. In addition profits made from an individual selling their primary residence are exempt from capital gains taxation which is applied to profits made from trading other forms of assets.

MANAGED CURRENCY SYSTEMS

Another explicit objective of some central banks is to maintain a stable currency. Central banks have to decide between two distinct options, to allow the currency to float freely against other currencies or to attempt to manage the exchange rate. Most economists would agree that central banks can make a reasonable stab at maintaining a stable exchange rate or a stable inflationary environment but that it is not possible to achieve both at the same time.

Over the past 20 years central banks in most developed economies have chosen to target stable inflation and allow their currency to float freely. Floating systems may lead to more volatile exchange rates but those rates adjust gradually over time and reflect market perceptions of underlying economic fundamentals. Central banks in many developing countries have persisted with trying to achieve both objectives with a bias towards targeted stable exchange rates. There are a number of ways for a central bank to try to manage its country's exchange rate. These include currency boards, fixed currency pegs, currency bands, managed devaluation and the use of trade-weighted baskets of currencies:

- **Currency boards.** A currency board is a system where the local currency is based on that of another currency, usually the US dollar. It is for this reason that the adoption of managed currency systems is frequently referred to as "dollarization". The system requires the central bank to maintain a reserve of US$. A conversion rate between the US$ and the local currency is then fixed. The amount of local currency that the central bank can issue is then constrained by the amount of US$ reserves. In other words the local currency is fully backed by the foreign currency.

  If those foreign reserves fall, by people or institutions selling the local currency and buying US$, the amount of local currency in circulation is automatically reduced by a corresponding amount. This has the effect of pushing up local interest rates. Currency boards can result in a stable exchange rate even at times of crisis but only at the cost of local pain. A potential currency crisis can usually be avoided through disciplined adherence to the currency board. This can only be achieved by imposing very high interest rates and at the expense of a recession. The Hong Kong dollar peg is one of the best-known currency boards.

- **Fixed currency pegs.** Fixed currency pegs are another method of linking a local currency to the US$. The central bank attempts to fix the exchange rate at a particular level even though the local currency is not fully backed by US$ reserves. There are then two ways to try to maintain this level, open market operations by the central bank and capital controls.

  In open market operations the central bank intervenes directly in the foreign currency market. If holders of the local currency sell it and buy US$ the central bank steps in to supply the US$ at the specified rate. If on the other hand institutions sell US$ and buy the local currency the central bank issues the local currency. It then normally acts to sterilize these inflows by issuing bonds to mop up the additional local currency. The Thai baht and Argentine peso were both fixed currency peg systems maintained by open market operations, before their demise.

- **Currency bands.** Some countries have operated using currency bands. Before the adoption of European Monetary Union European currencies traded within specified bands against one another in a system called the European Rate Mechanism (ERM). When a currency came close to the top of its band European central banks would sell the currency and when it came close to the bottom they would buy it. The risks involved in such systems were highlighted when the British pound was forced out of the ERM by speculators who believed that sterling had entered the system at too high an exchange rate.

- **Managed devaluation.** Some countries have tried to adopt a policy of a managed devaluation. Indonesia in the mid-1990s gives us an example of a currency where the central bank made it clear that it was aiming for a managed devaluation of approximately 10% per year. When the currency collapsed in 1997, however, it fell from 2500 to the US dollar to reach a low of 17 000.

- **Trade-weighted basket.** This is a system that avoids some of the above problems. The objective is to manage the currency against a trade-weighted basket of currencies. No official target is given, which makes the currency less of a target. This system is intended to help maintain a country's competitiveness with trading partners and shield the economy from imported price inflation.

The basic problems that most of these systems share are that the central bank risks pitting itself against the market and that in the event of a crisis there is no mechanism for a flexible adjustment. The result has often been a sharp correction resulting in a significant dislocation to both the financial system and the real economy. Argentina provided a good example in 2001 of the effects of the collapse of a managed currency system and its devastating impact on Argentineans' life.

Capital controls are another way in which central banks may seek to manage their exchange rate and level of foreign reserves. These prevent a currency from being fully convertible. The degree of capital controls imposed may vary widely. The least onerous capital controls simply make foreign exchange more difficult by requiring central bank approval for all transactions above a specified level, with approval usually being granted after a certain period. Capital controls encourage companies to look for ways to circumvent such constraints and also usually result in some form of black market where rates offered differ significantly from official rates.

Organizations such as the IMF are usually opposed to the use of capital controls under any circumstances but, as we will argue in Chapter 21 "Banking crises", the combination of open capital accounts and an overreliance on short-term foreign funding is an important source of potential instability in developing countries.

EXAMPLES OF CENTRAL BANKS

The US Federal Reserve

The US Federal Reserve, usually referred to as the Fed, acts as both the central bank and one of the key regulators of the commercial banking system. The main board is based in Washington but there are also 12 regional reserve banks operating in what are referred to as Federal Reserve Districts.

The main board has seven members drawn from the reserve banks in the Federal Reserve Districts. The US President appoints these members with the appointments being ratified by the Senate. The members serve 14-year terms. This appointment system means that political interference is very limited and that the Fed has effective day-to-day political independence. Inevitably the board does work closely with whoever is the current incumbent of the position of Secretary of the Treasury even though they do not always see eye to eye.

The board is responsible for setting bank reserve requirements. It also shares responsibility with the regional reserve banks for establishing discount rate policy. Combined with open market operations these provide the principal tools for managing US monetary policy.

It should be obvious that as the US Federal Reserve is the world's most powerful national central bank its monetary policies can have wide reaching effects in other countries, particularly those with currencies linked to the US$.

The Federal Open-Market Committee (FOMC) meets on a regular basis, normally about once every six weeks, to establish a target Federal Funds rate and hence monetary policy necessary to achieve it. The Federal Funds rate is the rate that banks with surplus reserve deposits with a Federal Reserve Bank charge on overnight funds to banks with a shortfall.

The Fed is able to influence the actual Federal Funds rate through open market operations by buying or selling Treasury bills and notes in the market. Minutes of the meetings are published as are the voting records of the individual members in terms of their bias towards interest rate and monetary policy. In this context hawks favor tightening monetary policy and a bias towards higher rates and doves the opposite. The minutes and statement from the chairman are closely watched for signals on likely future Fed monetary and interest rate policies as they may have a significant impact on equity and bond markets not only in the US but around the world. The Fed is very careful of language and does not actually issue a formal bias statement but rather a "balance of risks" statement. Most people interpret the latter as a statement of bias in any case.

The chairman of the Fed is also authorized by the FOMC to act if necessary between meetings. Such occasions are relatively rare, it is difficult to see when an emergency tightening of money supply would be necessary. There have only been three instances in recent memory when the Fed has pumped short-term liquidity into the market. One of those was flagged well in advance in the case of the Y2K switchover. The other two followed the collapse of the Long Term Credit Management group, a highly leveraged US hedge fund, which failed in dramatic style in 1998 largely due to positions it took in Russian instruments, and the reopening of US financial markets after the events of September 11th 2001.

The European Central Bank

The European Central Bank (ECB) was established following the decision of a number of European countries, including Germany, France and Italy, to adopt a common European currency. Individual central banks had to relinquish their powers to manage money supply and set domestic interest rate levels. A few countries, such as the UK, opted out although in time that may well change.

There are clear advantages and disadvantages of having a common European currency. Cross-border transaction costs are reduced in part because there are no foreign exchange related charges for business conducted between members. Risks arising from companies having foreign exchange positions are also reduced. Business travelers and tourists in Europe no longer have to carry cash in a dozen different currencies.

The disadvantages stem from a lack of labor mobility and variations in national fiscal policies. In a unified economy such as the US workers will react to a downturn in one part of the country by moving to a part of the country with better economic prospects. This is much harder to accomplish in a continent with many different languages and where there is a limited tradition of cross-border labor movement.

National central banks' ability to use monetary policy to influence economic growth, the level of unemployment and inflation have been largely subjugated to the ECB. They cannot cut interest rates, for example, to give a boost to a local economy in recession or hike rates to choke off inflation. The extent to which this lack of flexibility will result in future problems remains to be seen.

The ECB has specific quantitative inflation targets to meet but also has the power to take action against countries that fail to keep their government's financing deficit as a percentage of GDP below a predetermined level.

The Bank of England

The Bank of England is worth a mention because it was the first modern central bank. It was established in 1694 but it is only in the nineteenth century that its operations started to differ greatly from central banks in continental Europe such as the Bank of France and the German Reichsbank. The latter both had branch networks and made loans directly to businesses. They accounted for a substantial proportion of the banking business in each country.

The Bank of England was different because it had no direct lending to companies. It influenced credit conditions indirectly through its actions in trying to control, or at least have an impact on, the behavior of commercial banks. It did this primarily by adjusting the rate at which it would lend to commercial banks.

The Bank of England was established to act on behalf of the government. In the post Second World War period this meant that politicians effectively made many of its decisions. By way of contrast the German Bundesbank and US Fed both enjoyed a high degree of independence from political interference.

Political control meant that the Bank of England was usually required to increase money supply in the run-up to a general election by the party in power. This was intended to give the economy a short-term boost and the electorate the "feel-good" factor. Such an increase in money supply, without a corresponding increase in the real productive capacity of the economy, usually fed through to higher inflation, a depreciation (or devaluation) of the currency and a subsequent tightening of money supply. This gave rise to a period characterized by what became known as "stop-go" economics.

Around the turn of the century the Bank of England was given effective operational independence, being free to set sterling base interest rates and manage supply as it saw fit to keep inflation within a target range defined by Parliament. It also lost its responsibilities as a bank supervisor to a newly established, unitary financial services regulator, the Financial Services Authority (FSA).

SUPRANATIONAL INSTITUTIONS

Bretton Woods

Two of the key supranational institutions, the International Monetary Fund (IMF) and the World Bank, were established following a conference of leading countries held at Bretton Woods in the USA in 1944 to establish a post-war framework to facilitate currency and economic stability. The IMF now has nearly 200 member countries. Both organizations are centered in Washington.

The objectives of the two organizations were always clearly delineated. The IMF was intended to provide relatively short-term financing to stabilize economies that had got into trouble with their foreign currency debts and reserves. The World Bank to provide long-term financing to support development.

Both organizations have their own agendas and this has led to significant controversy over their roles, objectives and policies. I will try to avoid being judgmental and simply describe what their principal objectives are and how they seek to achieve them. In this day and age it is usually safer to talk about sex than it is about politics. Most people are more interested in the former than the latter in any case.

The third key supranational financial institution is the Bank for International Settlements (BIS). This is based in Basel, Switzerland and its establishment predates that of the IMF and World Bank.

The International Monetary Fund (IMF)

The simplest way to view the IMF is that it is the world's lender of last resort. The principal stated objectives of the IMF are as follows:

> To promote international monetary cooperation, exchange stability, and orderly exchange arrangements; to foster economic growth and high levels of employment; and to provide temporary financial assistance to countries to help ease balance of payments adjustment

In practice the IMF's most high profile activity is to provide funding to countries experiencing balance of payment problems while imposing conditions on the governments of these countries to implement economic reforms in return for being given such loans:

- **Financing.** The IMF is financed by contributions from its member countries. Each member's contribution is based on its relative economic size and condition. These contributions are referred to as quotas and are denominated in a special currency unit, the Special Drawing Right (SDR), based on a weighted basket of four major currencies (at the time of writing this basket was made up of the US dollar, the euro, the Japanese yen and UK sterling).

  Quotas are reviewed periodically and may be adjusted to reflect changes in either an individual member's economic condition or changes in the IMF's financing requirements. The latter depends largely on the state of the global economy.

  The IMF pays interest on members' positive balances based on short-term money market rates of the currency basket.

  In addition to providing the IMF with its funding, quotas are used to define each member's maximum contribution, and, in principle at least, to determine their ability to borrow from the fund in times of financial distress.

- **Management.** The head of the IMF is, by tacit agreement, always a European. Quotas are used to determine each member's voting rights. As the world's largest economy the US has a significant influence on the IMF's management and policies and the heaviest voting weighting.

  In practice the IMF is run by an executive board. This 24-strong board is made up of permanent representatives from the USA, Japan, Germany, France, the UK, China, Russia and Saudi Arabia plus 16 other representatives from other countries elected for two-year terms. Few decisions are, however, made based on formal votes.

- **Borrowing rights.** Member countries can borrow the equivalent of their quota in any given year and up to three times their quotas in total. In exceptional circumstances these lending limits may be lifted.

  When trouble starts politics become an overriding consideration, both domestic and international. Domestic politics affect the ability of governments to make reforms while international politics has an important influence on the IMF's willingness to provide funds.

- **Conditionality.** Conditionality is the most controversial aspect of the IMF's operations. Before making a loan to a distressed country the IMF will seek to impose conditions for economic, and sometimes political, reform to ensure that the financing is genuinely short term and that the borrower will be able to repay the loan.

These conditions can be wide ranging and usually require the borrower to meet defined monetary and budgetary targets, the removal of subsidies on selected products, the opening up of markets, reduction in import tariffs and removal of foreign ownership restrictions. These conditions frequently lead to hardship and with the IMF also being widely seen as a tool of US foreign policy tend to lead to popular political opposition in affected developing markets.

It is easy to make the IMF the bogeyman and it does not have a perfect record in terms of corrective action proscribed. These attacks miss the point. In an open global economy the world needs an organization such as the IMF. Trade and capital flow imbalances in individual economies will occur from time to time. These may be the result of poor government or central bank policies. They may also be a consequence of supply side or demand side shocks, such as a sharp increase in energy prices or a fall in commodity prices.

It is also fair to add that many governments have taken advantage of the intervention of the IMF to impose unpopular policies that it can blame on the IMF but had actually wanted to pursue in any case. IMF conditions that a government reduces its fiscal deficit do not normally define in detail exactly how this is to be achieved. A government may choose to cut public employees' salaries, for example, but maintain its chosen level of military spending.

The World Bank

The World Bank was established as the International Bank for Reconstruction and Development (IBRD). The latter, somewhat cumbersome, title provides a more accurate description of the bank's role. The IMF has more of the functions and responsibilities one would expect from a world central bank.

The World Bank was set up to address long-term development issues and to reduce global poverty. It provides funding for basic infrastructure projects to developing countries. It is also mandated to facilitate reforms to reduce global poverty. This is clearly well intentioned but the evidence shows that it has had limited success. Its efforts in sub-Sahara Africa have had few positive results, for example.

The gap in terms of wealth between developed and many developing economies has widened. The blame for this should not be laid at the feet of the World Bank, however. Its resources are a small fraction of private investment flows and subsidies on agricultural products and other commodities by developed countries have taken their toll on incomes in developing countries.

The Bank for International Settlements (BIS)

The Bank for International Settlements (BIS) was established in Basel, Switzerland, in 1930 and hence its formation predates that of the IMF and the World Bank. The BIS is owned exclusively by the world's central banks. Its primary functions are to coordinate and facilitate banking and settlement services between the world's central banks. It is probably best known for helping to bring about the Basel Accord that established capital adequacy requirements for OECD banks.

These are rules that define how much capital a bank should maintain relative to its asset size and risks undertaken to comply with minimum international norms.

In common with the IMF and the World Bank the BIS conducts economic and monetary research, although it has a different focus. This diversity is probably positive as it results in a range of views. It also gives a lot of post-doctoral economists jobs. The BIS also undertakes research and provides advice and training on reducing risks in settlement systems, both domestic and cross-border.

PART II

The Spread Business

Deposit taking

* Retail & wholesale deposits
* Other forms of financing
* Distribution & delivery channels
* Account charges
* Deposit substitutes
* Impact of reserve requirements on funding costs
* Liquidity risk management
* Deposit insurance schemes

Mortgage lending

* Fixed versus floating rate
* Home equity & others
* Credit appraisal
  - Price-to-value
  - Ability-to-pay
* Negative equity - system level

Corporate lending

* Bank versus corporate credit ratings, disintermediation, regulatory capital
* Corporate financing requirements
* Substitutes (bonds, commercial paper)
* Bank flexibility & issue costs
* Small & medium enterprises
* Macro- & microlevel pricing factors
* Credit approval & loan agreement
  - Collateral, guarantees & covenants

Credit cards

* Basic functions
  - Payment means
  - Guarantee
  - Revolving credit
* Supplementary features
  - Competition & market segmentation
* Mass-market versus premium
* Issuers & merchant banks, network operators
* Standard transaction & merchant payment
* Credit approval, fraud prevention & detection
* Other consumer loans
  - auto loans, education, consumer

Operational services

* Cash management, trade finance, custody, remittances, factoring, trust

4

Deposit Taking and Other Funding

It's a wise man who lives with money in the bank. It is a fool who dies that way.

French proverb

INTRODUCTION

Banks are highly geared businesses that rely for the bulk of their financing requirements with non-equity funding. Shareholders' equity rarely accounts for more than 5–10% of total liabilities; this is equivalent to a debt–equity ratio of $10\times$ to $20\times$. A non-financial firm with such a high gearing would generally be regarded as a company close to failure.

A big difference between banks and corporates is that deposits and other liabilities are not a source of external funding for the business – they are an integral part of the business. The bulk of most commercial banks' funding comes from deposits from non-bank customers.

Most people see their deposits held with banks as a form of savings that earn interest, and they do fulfill this function to an extent, but they can also be seen as loans made to banks that allow them to remain in business. Wholesale customers are more aware of this distinction than retail depositors.

DEPOSIT TAKING

Retail and Wholesale Segments

The deposit market can be conveniently divided into retail and wholesale segments, although the boundary between these two segments has became somewhat blurred by the increase in the numbers of the "mass affluent". The retail and wholesale segments have very different characteristics. Retail deposits can be broadly characterized by the following:

- **Priced by banks.** Retail deposits are priced on the basis of rates published by individual banks. These rates can be changed at will and retail depositors' only choice is to accept those rates or take their deposits elsewhere.
  - Rates on retail deposits offered by banks in most countries have been highly regulated in the past and in many countries continue to be set centrally. In some countries regulators determine these rates, while in others they are set by individual banks acting as a cartel. The global trend over the past two decades has been towards de-regulation and liberalization.
- **Relatively sticky.** Retail customers do not switch banks very often. There is a high degree of inertia. This can be explained by the relatively high switching costs that are entailed with, for example, moving standing instructions to pay regular bills automatically from an account at one bank to an account at another bank.
  - These switching costs act as an impediment to competition and in some countries lawmakers have introduced legislation to require banks to transfer details of standing

instructions set up for a customer at one bank to another bank when instructed to do so by the customer.

- **Relatively price insensitive.** Most retail depositors do not move their deposits from one bank to another for the sake of an extra 50 basis points (bpts). The degree of price insensitivity depends partly on the size of the deposits and partly on the reason why the customer has made the deposit. A customer using an account primarily as a transaction account will be less price sensitive than a customer using the deposit account as a savings account or as a means to generate an ongoing income.
- **Location and convenience.** Attracted on the basis of location, convenience and branding. The number and geographic spread of branches, opening hours, and access to automated teller machines (ATMs) are of particular importance.
- **High administrative costs.** Can be relatively expensive in terms of operating costs per dollar of deposit, particularly if depositors make frequent, small deposits and withdrawals.

Wholesale deposits can be characterized by the following:

- **Prices set by supply and demand.** Wholesale deposit rates are largely set by supply and demand and are usually priced against a market rate such as the three-month interbank rate. Wholesale depositors may be able to negotiate for better rates by threatening to move their deposits to another bank.
- **Very mobile.** Wholesale deposits can be switched from one bank to another by means of electronic instruction.
- **Highly price sensitive.** An extra 10 bpts on a $100m deposit is worth $100 000 on a one-year deposit.
- **Highly counterparty credit quality sensitive.** Wholesale depositors are conscious of their counterparty risk and manage it actively. At the first sign of any real problems, or even perception of problems, at a bank wholesale depositors will switch their funds to other banks perceived as lower risk.
- **Low administrative costs.** They are very low cost per dollar to administer, and involve limited human intervention.

Most commercial banks take both retail and wholesale deposits. They do have to make a strategic decision on competitive positioning. The choice is between maintaining a (relatively) large, expensive distribution network and attracting cheaper retail deposits and operating with a smaller number of branches, at relatively low cost, and rely on more expensive, higher risk wholesale deposits.

There has been a global trend towards the liberalization of deposit products. In many countries restrictions on regulated accounts have included the following:

- **Demand deposit accounts.** An account on which US banks are not allowed to pay interest on any outstanding balance.
- **Savings accounts.** A retail account offering a fixed rate of return. Notice of withdrawal normally has to be given above a minimum prespecified limit.

- **Time deposits.** Deposits with a fixed rate and fixed term. Early withdrawal is usually subject to a penalty fee or may even be prohibited.
- **NOW deposits.** A US deposit account (negotiable order of withdrawal account). One of the first US bank deposit accounts on which interest rates were deregulated.

The original objective of regulating the rates that banks could pay on deposits was to eliminate what was perceived as potentially dangerous, destabilizing price competition.

The reasoning being that some banks would bid up deposit rates to attract funds but then have to make higher-risk, high-yield loans to generate an economic return. Other banks would then be forced to match those rates to keep their own deposit base intact leading to a spiraling crisis. Ignorant retail depositors would not understand the higher risks they were accepting in return for the higher rates and would go to the bank with the highest rates.

There is some evidence to support this. The Bank of Credit and Commerce International (BCCI), which collapsed in 1991, offered rates that were significantly higher than at other banks. BCCI was widely referred to, in the City of London, by financial professionals as the "Bank of Crooks and Criminals International", well before it failed. But, many of its predominantly Asian depositors were unaware of its reputation or the risks they were taking and they all lost almost all of their deposits in the aftermath of its failure.

OTHER FORMS OF FINANCING

In addition to deposits banks have a range of other short- and long-term financing alternatives.

Short-term Finance

From a bank's perspective there is little difference between a negotiable certificate of deposit (NCD) and a time deposit. The big difference to the holder of NCDs is that they can be traded in a secondary market. NCDs are also generally relatively longer term than time deposits but shorter term than bonds. They may be issued in the local currency or a foreign currency, usually the US$. In the latter case proceeds may be used to finance foreign currency assets or swapped back into the local currency.

Medium- and Long-term Finance

Banks have a similar range of medium- and long-term financing options as industrial and service companies. These include equity raised through private placements or rights issues, straight bonds, convertible bonds, preference shares and subordinated debt. These usually comprise only a relatively low proportion of a bank's funding and capital management factors are usually the main consideration in raising medium- to long-term finance and we will look at these in Chapter 14 "Capital management".

The Inverted Pyramid

Bank liability structures are sometimes represented as an inverted pyramid and the following diagram is approximately to scale for a typical commercial bank. The first thing to notice is just how small the equity base at the apex of the pyramid is. The bulk of their funding comes from customer deposits and these are relatively short term (the proportion of time deposits with a maturity beyond 90 days (three months) is usually very small). Long-term debt is usually only a small fraction of total liabilities.

Deposits from other banks are usually made to support a correspondent banking relationship where the bank provides a local service to another bank operating in a different region or country. Some deposits arise from bank's activities in the wholesale interbank markets where they lend to and borrow from one another, usually on relatively short terms.

The interbank market is an important source of funding for many foreign banks operating in emerging markets. Branching restrictions mean they frequently lack the local currency deposit base enjoyed by domestic banks. This does, however, tend to put them at a disadvantage in terms of funding costs relative to local banks. Interbank rates in developing markets are often rather volatile as a consequence of their lack of depth and liquidity.

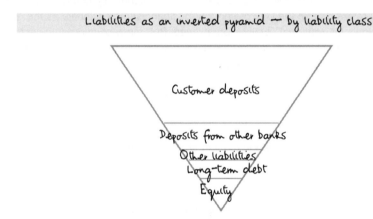

Liabilities as an inverted pyramid — by liability class

Customer deposits

Deposits from other banks

Other liabilities

Long-term debt

Equity

DISTRIBUTION AND DELIVERY CHANNELS

Branches have been the traditional means banks have used to provide services to their customers. In many countries local banks have been protected from foreign bank competition by restrictions imposed on the number of branches the latter can open. This is proving less effective as a barrier to entry as more delivery channels are now available.

The main issues concerned with providing basic banking services through branches are:

- **Costs.** Branches provide a relatively expensive delivery channel. The cost of a simple transaction, such as depositing a check or making a cash withdrawal, in a branch is many times higher than if the transaction was carried out through an ATM.

  In the early days of the introduction of ATMs many US banks made the mistake of trying to use ATM networks as a way to generate revenues and to differentiate their service. In many cases they actually discouraged usage by charging fees for transactions carried out using ATMs. This is understandable. The initial investments were high and banks sought to recoup their costs but this policy was also shortsighted and misguided. The initial competitive advantage from being able to offer a differentiated service was soon lost once other banks introduced their own ATMs.

Over time banks have realized that the key benefit of ATMs lies in cutting, or at least containing, costs. Now, many banks provide an incentive to customers to use ATMs by not charging for ATM transactions but imposing a charge for transactions done in a branch. Some banks have gone as far as to actually pay their customers for carrying out certain transactions made through ATMs!

- **Tying up capital.** Banks that own their own branches tie up capital. Capital is a scarce resource and its management is one of the key factors in adding value to the business.
- **Scalability.** The costs of transactions carried out in branches scale with the volume of transactions. This is not the case with most other delivery channels. The marginal cash cost of a transaction carried out at an ATM or through the Internet or other electronic means is close to zero.
- **Rental risk.** Banks that do not own their branches are exposed to the risks that rents will rise pushing up their operating costs.

Banks have made a huge effort to coax retail customers away from branch-based banking by providing a range of other delivery and distribution channels including the following:

- **ATMs.** From basic cash-dispenser functionality automated teller machines (ATMs) have evolved to provide many of the services available through a branch. These range from basic account management services such as transferring funds from one account to another, paying bills, setting up standing orders and so on, to more sophisticated functions such as buying mutual funds or subscribing to an Initial Public Offering (IPO).
- **Cash-back services.** In many countries banks and retailers have combined to provide cash-back services. A customer paying a bill at a retailer using a debit card can opt to pay for their goods and withdraw some cash from their bank account at the same time.

    This has benefits for customers, banks and retailers. For the customers it gives convenience. For the banks it provides an additional cash-dispensing channel relieving pressure on their ATMs. It also reduces the need to replenish their ATMs with cash. For the retailer it reduces the amount of cash they hold and have to bank. Most banks charge a fee to business customers for large cash deposits to cover the expense of counting it.
- **Phone banking.** In many countries, phone banking has become highly automated providing similar functionality as an ATM machine. Call centers have become increasingly sophisticated and automated. A few banks established stand-alone phone-based banks differentiated from their parent through branding and pricing. The loss of business due to cannibalization of customers in their traditional bank has to be balanced with the new business gained by attracting customers from other traditional competitors.

    The reduction in telecommunication costs has also enabled large, global banks to locate call centers in countries where labor costs are low. India, for example, has a relatively well-educated English-speaking workforce but labor costs are but a fraction of those in OECD countries.
- **Internet and other electronic banking.** During the period of the Internet boom a number of stand-alone Internet banks were established by non-bank companies. Their business model was based on rapidly attracting a large, retail deposit base by marketing aggressively and offering higher rates than traditional banks. They then planned to market mortgages, credit

cards and other retail products to that base. Other less ambitious operators chose to offer specialist services such as searching the Web to get the best terms for a mortgage loan, car loan or insurance policy. Only a few of the hopeful new entrants have survived the test of time.

Larger, established banks saw the Internet as less of a threat than an opportunity. They already had the customer relationships and multiple distribution channels that would make it difficult for new entrants to compete. Some did establish their own "Internet bank" with different branding from their parent (and these are among the few survivors) but most eventually decided that it was better to simply use the Internet as one more delivery channel.

Some estimates put the cost to a bank of a customer making a transaction through the Internet at less than 1% of the cost of having it done through a branch. The emergence of Internet banking has had three major effects on competition. The first is that it has raised customer expectations on pricing and availability of service. The second is that it is helping to force banks to strive for an optimal balance between providing services through branches, ATMs and other delivery channels. The third is that it has increased the level of potential scale economies and hence pressures for consolidation.

- **Service stations/Convenience stores.** Citibank, for example, has been able to circumvent regulatory restrictions on branch openings in a number of countries by making agreements with outlets such as convenience stores, service stations and taxi firms, to display application forms for Citibank credit cards and accounts.
- **Direct marketing.** Retail banks often claim that sophisticated "data mining" tools allow them to leverage their investments in Customer Relationship Management (CRM) systems to identity potential fee-paying customers. These people are then inundated with direct marketing materials and unsolicited phone calls and e-mails.

In the early stages of the development of credit cards some US banks did not wait for customers to apply for credit cards but simply mailed them credit cards with a pre-approved credit limit. This practice was subsequently made illegal by legislators concerned about the impact on consumer indebtedness.

ACCOUNT CHARGES

In most countries as deposit rate liberalization has progressed banks have moved to offset the cost of higher rates that competition has produced by introducing account charges for selected retail deposit accounts. The most common fee structure is for the bank to impose account charges if the balance in a low or non-interest-bearing account falls below some specified minimum amount.

Many companies prefer to pay charges than be required to leave non-interest-bearing compensating balances with a bank. The charges are tax deductible while foregone interest has no tax benefit.

The structure of these charges varies between banks and also between countries. Banks love fees and are always looking for ways to extract more of them from customers. Retail customers hate bank fees and in many countries have got used to the idea that basic banking services should be free. Some banks impose transaction-based fees based on factors such as the number of checks written, standing order instructions and bounced (or returned) checks.

In many businesses an approximate 80:20 rule applies, that is 80% of a company's profits come from 20% of its customers. At many retail banks in developing markets this is probably more like a 150:20 rule, with the other 80% of customers loss making. This can have important social and competitive implications. Banks play an important social role in any economy. Large domestic banks in developing markets cannot turn away mass-market customers simply because they are unprofitable. They also find it difficult to impose onerous account charges because of political considerations.

The more sophisticated foreign banks do not generally experience such constraints. They try to impose high minimum balance requirements in order to "cherry-pick" the most profitable customer segments while avoiding having to service those that are loss making.

BANK DEPOSIT SUBSTITUTES

There is a wide range of non-traditional financing products competing for savings. These include the following:

- **Direct investments in the stock market.** Investors maintaining equity portfolios by buying individual stocks through a brokerage firm. The proportion of the US population directly invested in the stock market rose steadily during the 1990s. The advent of Internet-based no-frills (discount) brokerages offering low, fixed cost transactions has made trading on the stock market accessible to a younger mass market.

  The collapse in prices of technology and telecommunication stock prices and general weakness of stock markets around the world in the early part of the twenty-first century led to large losses for many investors. This dampened the appetite of many to invest in stocks.
- **Mutual funds.** These are funds, marketed and managed by asset management companies such as Fidelity, Putnam and Merrill Lynch Asset Management, that invest in a mix of bonds and stocks. They allow individual investors to diversify their portfolio holdings.

  These asset managers spend large amounts on advertising. Many of the largest players have global brands.
- **Government and municipal bonds.** These may be attractive to sections of retail investors paying tax as such bonds are often tax exempt. They may also have a longer maturity than deposits offered by banks. They are, however, relatively difficult for the average retail depositor to buy and sell individually.
- **Corporate bonds.** Corporate bonds are held largely by institutional investors and may offer a higher return than bank deposits. Higher returns are usually earned in exchange for the acceptance of a higher degree of risk.
- **Insurance products.** Insurance companies offer a wide range of products that compete with bank deposits including annuities and minimum guaranteed return funds.
- **Money market funds.** These are funds, marketed by retail brokerages, that work by combining funds from many retail customers' funds, and then investing them in the wholesale market, in this way retail depositors can get higher rates than by acting alone.

RESERVE REQUIREMENTS

Many people, quite reasonably, get confused between reserve requirements, reserves for credit losses, asset revaluation reserves and other reserve accounts contained within shareholders' funds. There is also frequently confusion between deposit reserve requirements and capital adequacy requirements. The two have no direct connection. In order to dispel this potential confusion the most common reserve accounts that banks report are as follows:

- **Asset revaluation reserves.** These are reserves used to adjust the value of assets carried at cost to their market value. In some countries banks are allowed to include certain revaluation reserves within their shareholders' funds. In Japan, for example, banks include unrealized gains (if they have any) on their substantial equity holdings within shareholders' funds. In Hong Kong banks include revaluation reserves for their real estate holdings (primarily their branches and head office) within the shareholder's account. In both countries the regulatory body allows part of these reserves to count towards their regulatory capital requirements.
- **Reserves for credit losses.** Also known as "allowance for bad debt losses" and "loan loss provisions". In a sense they are equivalent to asset revaluation reserves in that they are used to adjust the value of loans on the books downwards to reflect expected future losses and hence lower market value. In most countries these are a contra asset account, in which case they appear as a negative number on the asset side of the balance sheet. In a few countries they are presented as a positive liability account. The presentation method used has no impact on a bank's economic value or the function of these reserves.
- **Other equity reserves.** Many banks report a number of other reserves within shareholders' funds, including reserves for foreign exchange translation differences. Banks in some countries also report "statutory reserves", these have no physical existence but represent a minimum level of equity that a bank must keep to maintain its license. They cannot be distributed to shareholders without the central bank's permission. These statutory reserves are a throwback to a time when there were no formal capital adequacy requirements and have no real significance today.
- **Reserve requirements.** Central banks impose reserve requirements on deposit-taking banks. This requires banks to maintain a specified percentage of their funding in the form of cash within the bank's vaults, in accounts held with the central bank or in Treasury securities. The formula used to calculate the level varies from country to country, as do the actual levels imposed. In some countries it is based solely on the level of non-bank deposits, in others the definition is broader encompassing other liabilities such as negotiable certificates of deposit (NCDs) and money market funds.

Banks are required to adjust their balances with the central bank to ensure that they comply with the regulatory requirements on a regular basis. This is usually once a month. They are usually also required to report their daily compliance over the course of the month. Banks with a shortfall of reserve deposits are able to borrow these funds on an overnight basis from those with an excess of funds at a rate set by the central bank.

In developing countries the lack of depth of financial markets means that on these specified dates interbank rates are frequently highly volatile as banks are forced to borrow from one another or from the central bank to be able to meet the reserve requirements.

Reserve requirements impose a form of tax on deposits. In some countries, such as the Philippines where reserve requirements have been as high as 16% of eligible liabilities, these can have a material impact on a bank's cost of funds. Most central banks do not pay interest on the balances that the commercial banks keep with them. In some countries the central bank does pay interest but at a rate well below that of the market.

A bank paying 5% for its deposits and which is subject to a 6% reserve requirement only has 94% of these deposits available for on-lending. In effect the cost of these funds has been pushed up by 32 bpts (5%/94% = 5.32%).

Impact of reserve requirements on effective funding costs									
Reserve requirement	0%	2%	3%	4%	5%	6%	7%	8%	9%	10%
Effective funding cost	5.00%	5.10%	5.15%	5.21%	5.26%	5.32%	5.38%	5.43%	5.49%	5.56%

Reserve requirements are one of the ways in which central banks can adjust money supply and we have already looked how they influence the creation of money in Chapter 3.

LIQUIDITY MANAGEMENT

Bank Runs

In the 2001–2002 Argentine banking crisis the world was treated to pictures of peoples in panic attempting to withdraw their deposits from banks. Better to have physical US dollars under the mattress than risk holding them with a bank where they earn interest but the entire principal may be lost, either as a result of bank failure or government expropriation.

During the US depression of the 1930s, many banks failed as a direct consequence of bank runs. A loss of confidence in the banking system led to a situation where rumors of possible bank failures led to panic withdrawals by depositors. Banks are highly vulnerable to deposit runs because while the bulk of their liabilities (deposits) are short term the bulk of their assets (loans) are both long term and inherently illiquid.

All companies have to manage their liquidity or cashflows carefully. Many companies fail due to cashflow problems and, on the surface at least, banks appear to be even more at risk given the structure of their balance sheets. Liabilities are predominantly short term. A relatively small proportion of their deposits has a term in excess of three months. A large proportion of retail deposits are either "on demand" or can be taken out with less than seven days' notice.

Long-term debt is issued largely to meet capital management objectives rather than for liquidity management purposes. Even when taken together with a bank's equity these long-term liabilities form only a small part of a bank's total liabilities.

Most of a bank's assets are inherently medium to long term. Some assets, such as overdrafts and revolving credit, have formal terms that may give the bank the legal right to call in the loans without notice. That is of limited comfort in terms of liquidity management given that most companies and individuals with such credit would be unable to comply with the bank's demands. Getting the principal back on such loans might require legal action and in any event would take some months.

Liquid Assets

Banks deal with short-term liquidity requirements by keeping a proportion of assets in the form of marketable government securities and a small level of vault cash (typically 1%–2% of deposits). The following diagrams represent a typical commercial bank's asset and liability breakdowns classified by liquidity. They are approximately to scale based on area.

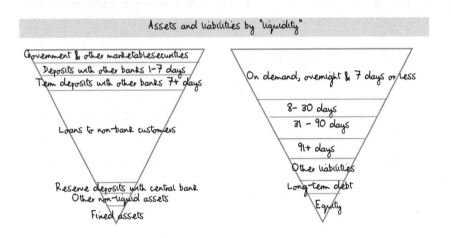

By making some simplifying assumptions it is relatively easy to make a back-of-the-envelope estimate of how long a bank could survive in the event of a bank run. Examples of these assumptions are: all demand deposits are withdrawn on the first day, 1/30th of all one-month time deposits and 1/90th of all three-month deposits each day until exhausted. Where a large proportion of a bank's depositor base is retail this will overstate the speed at which funds are withdrawn. This is because the effective term of many retail deposits is greater than their legal term.

On the asset side all securities can be assumed to be sold immediately, an estimate made for vault cash and similar calculations made on its deposits with other banks. Carrying out this exercise on Asian banks shows that many could not survive more than one day and the most conservative banks no more than 10 days. In the US and most developed countries banks with theoretical survival period greater than 5 days are uncommon. Holding more negotiable securities can lengthen the survival period but these have lower yields than loans and such a shift would reduce the bank's returns.

Banks depend on two factors for their survival, avoidance and the largesse of a central bank. The first line of defense then is to avoid getting into situations that create a real risk of a bank run. Wholesale creditors are far more aware of counterparty risk than retail customers and even in countries where there is a form of depositor protection insurance their deposits are usually outside the scope of coverage of such schemes.

Bank regulators are, of course, aware of this risk, and go to great pains to avoid making statements that imply solvency problems at individual banks and might precipitate a bank run. The central bank will usually step in to act as the lender of last resort to banks suffering from short-term liquidity problems. A bank can survive a protracted period of technical insolvency provided it receives such liquidity support. Few solvent banks, however, can survive a deposit run without such support.

DEPOSIT INSURANCE SCHEMES

Objectives

A partial solution to the problem of discouraging bank runs adopted in some countries is to provide a level of third-party deposit guarantee. In such schemes banks are usually required to pay for deposit insurance to a central agency. If a government guarantees to bail out any bank that fails there is no incentive for depositors to consider the credit-worthiness of banks. In turn this reduces the incentive for banks to lend and trade prudently, knowing that the government will meet these downside risks. The main criticism of deposit insurance schemes is that they subsidize banks taking above-average risks and penalize banks that are more conservative.

Deposit insurance schemes are likely to be most effective when two conditions are met. First that the maximum level of deposit protection is kept relatively low. The US Federal Deposit Insurance Corporation (FDIC), for example, only provides protection to depositors with deposits of $100 000 or less. Wholesale depositors are considered to be more sophisticated and better aware of counterparty risks. Second that the deposit insurance agency charges different insurance premiums to different institutions to reflect varying degrees of risk.

In other countries, and particularly in Asia, depositors have assumed an implicit government deposit guarantee. This guarantee has generally only extended to commercial banks. Other institutions such as finance companies, securities companies and merchant banks have generally not been included in the implicit guarantee that depositors will be protected in the event of failure.

On the positive side these schemes define exactly how much protection depositors will receive in the event of a bank failure. This increases confidence in the banking sector overall and reduces the risks created from bank deposit runs.

However, if the coverage of the protection is too broad, it will have a similar effect as a government guarantee. This problem is usually addressed by guaranteeing deposits only up a specified maximum level. This gives protection to retail depositors but forces wholesale depositors to consider credit risk.

The last criticism of these schemes is that they tend to favor riskier banks at the expense of sound banks. This can be addressed by varying the premiums that banks are charged for the insurance protection based on the risk profile of the bank. In addition the insurance company may impose restrictions on the activities that a bank can undertake such as a limit on the amount of listed equities that the bank may hold for trading on its own account.

5

Corporate Lending

I hate banks. They do nothing positive for anybody except take care of themselves. They're first in with their fees and first out when there's trouble.

US Judge Earl Warren

INTRODUCTION

The Herd Instinct

There can be few natural sights as impressive as that of the African wildebeest on its annual migration. Herds stretch across the Serengeti as far as the eye can see. They reach rivers that must be crossed where crocodiles wait in ambush. Individual wildebeest are taken but instinct is so strong that the rest press on regardless. In the swinging 1960s a British group (The Kinks) had a popular hit with their song "For he's a dedicated follower of fashion". Primates live in groups, lions in prides and whales and dolphins in pods. People lived in villages, then towns and increasingly in mega-cities with their ethnic ghettos and residential districts. There is an ancient Chinese saying that can be translated as "The nail that sticks out will be hammered in."

Bankers are often criticized for acting as a herd. If one bank determines that this is a good time to be expanding its mortgage/consumer finance/SME/corporate loan book then you can be reasonably confident that most other bankers have reached the same conclusion. In the 1980s most large international banks bought US$ bonds issued by South American governments. They were all confident that "countries can't fail" and few of these banks were spared from the huge losses that resulted when they did.

Unfortunately, when an economy moves into recession and companies are most in need of financial support all banks seek to restrict new loans and reduce their exposure to those segments perceived to be of highest risk. This can end up being a self-fulfilling prophecy as cutting off the life-blood of working capital at these companies can result in liquidation of viable companies simply because they lack the cash in the short term to pay their employees, utility bills and for raw materials.

These criticisms of bank herd behavior are both valid and unreasonable. It is irrational to expect people to act rationally and bankers are people. It takes a great deal of strength to swim against the tide and some that try drown. In any case being a part of a herd can make sense. The wildebeest most likely to be taken by the crocodiles are those that cross first and the stragglers. The safest time for an individual to cross is at the peak of the migration when the sheer weight of numbers affords most protection. It is not so very different in banking.

Banks normally classify companies as corporate customers based on sales or asset size criteria. The minimum size criteria vary from country to country and from bank to bank but a company with sales of less than $100m would be unlikely to be given corporate status at most banks in developed markets. Corporate bankers are usually organized along industry lines such as telecommunications, technology, real estate, oil and energy, transport, utilities etc.

This specialization is necessary because bankers need to understand the dynamics of the industries in which their customers are operating to assess the underlying credit risk and likelihood that the company will be able to meet its financial obligations.

The credit appraisal process for loans to corporates is normally done on a case-by-case basis. Large loans have to be approved at executive or even board level. Lending to corporates in most countries has been in relative decline, however, with the decline greatest in more developed markets. The three most important factors behind this shift are arguably the following:

- **Credit ratings.** Many large blue-chip corporates have better credit ratings than the banks themselves. There is little reason why such a corporate should pay more for loans from a bank than it receives on any deposits it makes with the bank.
- **Disintermediation.** Another major change has been the increased access for corporates to capital markets. Bond, equity and wholesale money markets provide a means for corporates to go directly to investors bypassing the commercial banks as a result. This has been helped by the better credit ratings that many corporates have relative to their aspiring lenders.

  This process has been given the accurate, albeit unwieldy, term of disintermediation. These trends have benefited the investment banks at the expense of the traditional commercial banks. The former are able to earn fees from the issuance process and from underwriting guarantees.
- **Regulatory capital.** No account is taken of counterparty risk in determining regulatory capital requirements under the terms of the original Basel Accord. A loan to a top-rated corporate is treated in exactly the same way as an exposure to a small, high-risk company. This state of affairs is due to change in 2006–2007 when a new Basel Accord is adopted but even then corporate loans are likely to attract a higher regulatory capital charge than retail loans.

Substitutes

Corporates have a wide range of financing alternatives, both short and long term to bank loans. The most important substitutes are the following:

- **Commercial paper.** Commercial paper issues are corporate IOUs. They are short term in nature, typically 90 days to one year. They do not pay interest, are issued at a discount to par and are unsecured. In most countries commercial paper can be traded in a secondary market. In effect commercial paper is a form of short-dated zero coupon bond. Commercial paper investors include banks, insurance companies and corporate and institutional treasuries.

  Commercial paper issues are most suitable for companies with a short-term or seasonal financing requirement. Some companies do, however, rely on them for long-term funding by continually rolling over their commercial paper. As one issue matures the company makes another.

  This funding approach runs the risk of liquidity tightening and the company being unable to roll their paper over or having to pay a steep premium to do so. This occurred in 2002 in the US, for example, after the collapse of a number of large, high profile companies raised widespread investor concern about further corporate failures.

- **Corporate bonds.** Bond markets have developed to meet the needs of companies to source stable medium- to long-term funds and investors seeking medium- to long-term investments with varying yields and risk levels. A company is likely to be able to raise a larger amount through a bond issue, bought by a larger number of investors, than by borrowing from a single bank. The latter may be unwilling to take on an exposure of such a size to one company and may be constrained by regulatory single borrower limits (the amount it can lend to any one group expressed as a percentage of its capital base).

  Bonds are normally issued with a number of restrictive covenants, as is the case with many bank loans. These are legally binding commitments, made by the issuer, and documented in the bond prospectus to adhere to conditions that protect debt holders from being adversely affected relative to equity holders. These conditions typically cover areas such as dividend policy, share buy-backs and the company taking on further debt.
- **Other straight debt.** Other forms of non-bank debt include subordinated debt and preference shares. These are forms of long-term debt that rank low in terms of seniority. Banks are rarely willing to offer commercial loans with terms greater than three to five years.
- **Convertible bonds.** Convertible bonds provide a form of debt financing with an option to convert the debt into equity at some future date.
- **Asset securitization.** Over the past 30 years an entire industry has developed, led by investment bankers, to develop and sell asset securitization products. These provide an alternative way for companies to finance their operating assets. We can illustrate this by using a simple example of a company that owns its head office. By entering into a sale and leaseback type of arrangement the company can reduce its assets and hence borrowing requirement.
- **Equity.** Equity is the money that the owners of the company have invested in the business. As equity is effectively perpetual it provides the longest-term financing option. It is also the most expensive form of financing.

Despite a range of financing options many corporates borrow from banks because of greater flexibility and lower transaction costs:

- **Flexibility.** Commercial banks are able to offer relatively flexible financing. It is difficult to change restrictions arising from bond issues at a later date because of the number of bond-holders. A bank will also seek such covenants but is likely to be relatively flexible in terms of renegotiating the conditions at a future date. The borrower may also be able to extend the term of the loan, increase its balance or repay the loan earlier than originally agreed depending on changed business conditions.

  An example of the sort of flexibility banks can offer is provided by the use of caps and collars. Take the following case as an example. A borrower with a floating rate loan is prepared to accept a level of interest rate risk but wishes to cap that risk at a certain level. This is shown in the first of the following charts where the interest rate paid is capped at 11%. If the borrower is prepared to forego some of the potential upside from lower interest rates a cheaper alternative is a collar and in this example the actual rate paid will vary only between 9% and 11%. Caps and collars provide further examples of the use of options.
- **Transaction costs.** There are significant transaction costs relating to the issue of paper into capital markets. Investment banks charge fees for managing and underwriting an issue. The lower upfront costs of borrowing from a bank may well outweigh any savings from a lower level of interest expense from issuing bonds.

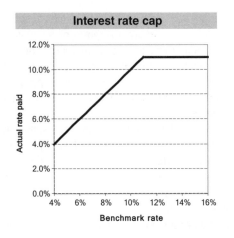

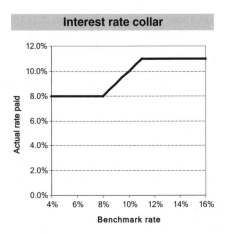

Syndicated loans remove one advantage that bond issues may have. A syndicated loan is a loan made by a group of banks to a large borrower (the group of banks is referred to as the syndicate). The advantages of syndicated loans to borrowers are that they can borrow more in one go than they would be able to obtain from one bank alone. In this sense the syndicated loan market is in direct competition with the bond market. Such loans are either very large or higher risk than single-bank loans. Most loans usually have an arrangement fee. They may be traded in a secondary market. The lead manager usually takes responsibility for collecting interest and principal payments from the company and passing it on to the members of the syndicate.

Corporate loans have tended to become more specialized, for example providing short-term funding for an acquisition until the corporate has put in place longer-term funding from the bond or equity markets.

Banks have had to increasingly look at the total relationship with the corporate to justify low margin lending by also looking at the profitability of other fee generating businesses that the bank has with the client. This has become generally referred to as "credit leverage" or "tying" where the bank will only make the loan if the corporate agrees to give it business in another area where the bank can generate a compensating return, such as in investment banking.

SMALL AND MEDIUM ENTERPRISES

Small and medium enterprises (SMEs) are other companies or partnerships that fall below the criteria defined for corporates. Individual banks have different definitions of what constitutes a corporate customer rather than an SME. A separate small and medium size enterprise division usually handles smaller companies, and the smaller companies may well be included within retail banking.

There is no hard and fast definition of an SME. Banks, however, generally regard loans to the SME segment as higher risk than loans to corporates. Large corporates are usually tracked by credit rating agencies such as Moody's and Standard and Poor's. Corporates usually have alternative ways to raise finance, such as equity and bond issues, other than borrowing from banks. This combination of perceived higher risk and lack of alternatives means that most SMEs are charged more for loans than larger corporates.

Small companies frequently find that larger suppliers demand shorter payment terms, and may even require cash on delivery, but that their larger customers insist on longer credit terms. This pushes up the need for working capital. Successful expanding companies usually find that working capital requirements grow rapidly, most SMEs have no option other than to turn to banks to meet these financing requirements.

Start-ups frequently find that trying to get a loan from a bank is like trying to get blood out of a stone. Most banks insist on a minimum of three years' audited accounts before they will consider making a loan. Many start-ups fail and banks find it difficult to price the risk of failure in the absence of any operating track record. This means that most start-ups have to rely on equity, and possibly venture capital, for all of their funding requirements.

MACRO-LEVEL FACTORS AFFECTING PRICING AND BANK POSITIONING

Individual banks are affected by macro-level factors such as the economic outlook, competition and the availability to bank customers of substitutes to bank products. These factors will affect not just loan pricing but how the bank tries to position itself.

Economic and Interest Rate Outlook

The macro-economic and interest rate outlook will affect the level of loan demand, the ability and willingness of banks to meet that demand and whether it is better to make fixed or floating rate loans. It will also have a significant impact on the level of delinquencies and resulting credit losses.

When an economy is experiencing strong growth this is likely to be accompanied by investment in new capacity and robust consumer demand. Demand for credit is likely to be strong and, in the absence of inflation, interest rates low. Economies are cyclical, however, and investment starts to turn into overinvestment. With signs of an overheating economy and concerns about inflation increasing the central bank is likely to start to increase the discount rate and take action to tighten money supply.

If this is accompanied by a demand side shock (whether domestic or export oriented) capacity utilization levels are likely to fall as will investment in new capacity. The strongest demand for loans is likely to come from companies that became overextended when the economy was expanding and to whom banks are reluctant to increase exposure. In many cases they will be trying to reduce it. Layoffs will start to have an impact on unemployment levels and hence consumer confidence and spending. The central bank is likely to change its bias for interest rates to neutral and then start to cut them in order to give the economy a boost. Supply and demand eventually come back into balance.

We have already noted how difficult economists find identifying turning points. The old wry comment is that "economists have forecast 10 of the last four recessions". Extrapolation represents the triumph of hope over experience, however. Management has to have a view, whether that view is contrarian or consensus.

The general rules of thumb for a bank anticipating a sharp slowdown are as follows. Cut back exposure to the industries and sectors that have enjoyed the strongest growth. Cut back exposure to companies with stretched balance sheets (high net debt to equity ratios) or where debt servicing depends on continued growth and to those that require a high level of capacity utilization to break even. Increase exposure to defensive sectors such as fast moving consumer goods and utilities. Reduce the term of new loans (if the ship is going to sink it is best to be one of the first to the lifeboats). Increase the level of collateral cover and quality. All of these actions are easiest to achieve with the benefit of hindsight, of course.

Competition

In the past lending rates in many markets were regulated and set by regulators or by banks operating in a cartel. The global trend has been towards liberalization and allowing market forces to set lending rates. In most OECD countries, and in increasing numbers of emerging markets, free competition determines lending rates. Competition has resulted in lower spreads (the difference between what banks pay for deposits and earn on loans) in most traditional lending segments including corporate.

Other banks may have different cost structures and strategic objectives. One bank may decide to attempt to gain market share by undercutting on price or be prepared to make unsecured loans. Decisions have to be made as to whether to accept a lower market share or respond by matching or undercutting the rates and terms offered by the bank initiating the price war. Price wars can be dangerous and what starts as an attempt by one bank to gain market share can result in unchanged market shares and lower yields on these loans than before for all banks.

The following diagram provides a summary of the major macro-level factors that have an influence on loan pricing and bank positioning.

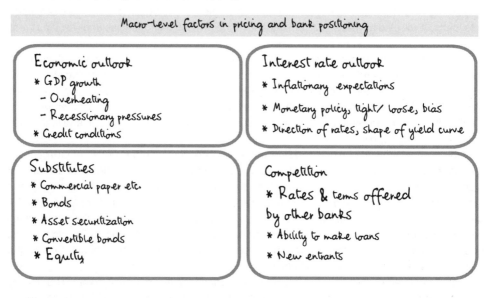

Macro-level factors in pricing and bank positioning

Economic outlook
* GDP growth
 - Overheating
 - Recessionary pressures
* Credit conditions

Interest rate outlook
* Inflationary expectations
* Monetary policy, tight/ loose, bias
* Direction of rates, shape of yield curve

Substitutes
* Commercial paper etc.
* Bonds
* Asset securitization
* Convertible bonds
* Equity

Competition
* Rates & terms offered by other banks
* Ability to make loans
* New entrants

MICRO-LEVEL FACTORS AFFECTING PRICING

In addition to external factors beyond the bank's control loan pricing will be affected by inputs from other groups within the bank and by specific factors concerning a particular loan. The funding costs will depend on the bank's deposit taking effectiveness and on the spread that treasury takes. From the lending department's perspective this is a given cost. Operating costs will depend on the productivity of back-office and cost allocation methods (for example, how head office overheads are treated). The lending department is also likely to have a target return on capital employed and to have capital allocated to it. This will usually be both at a business unit level and for specific loans. The level of likely credit losses must also be considered. Pricing has to take these factors into account.

Funding Costs

Loan departments at banks do not get their funding directly from external sources but instead request the required funding from the bank's treasury department. Treasury will quote a rate that it will charge for the funds provided. The term of the loan will also affect pricing. In general terms the longer the term of the loan the higher the rate that banks will require. Many loans are priced against yields from equivalent bonds on the yield curve. Banks are exposed to the risk that borrowers may repay their loans early. This prepayment risk may be priced in a number of ways.

Short-term loans are inherently lower risk. Banks with shorter-term exposure can reduce that exposure at an early stage of a company showing symptoms of financial distress.

Operating Costs

All loans incur an origination cost and ongoing processing costs. Origination and processing costs include direct costs related to the loan, such as any legal fees and costs relating to the credit appraisal process, and indirect costs such as management and administrative overhead, marketing expenditure and use of shared data-center facilities. The problem of how best to allocate overheads and indirect costs to specific transactions, or even business units, is not unique to banks. There are plenty of books on management accounting that address these issues at great length. For our purposes we will assume these costs are given.

Credit Risk

In addition to the spread that banks seek to take account of the term of the loan, banks seek an additional spread to compensate for credit, or default, risk. There are very few occasions when a bank will make a loan to a customer where it expects the borrower to be unable to meet the terms of the loan agreement. Nevertheless, experience has shown that there is a default risk for all loans.

In conceptual terms the level of expected credit losses, stated in terms of net present value (*NPV*) is given by the sum of the probability of default in a particular time interval, multiplied by the expected actual losses arising from the default, discounted at an appropriate discount rate.

The likelihood of defaults will be influenced by any covenants that the bank can obtain from the borrower. In the event of default the level of losses will be influenced by the level and quality of collateral that the borrower pledges. Loans can be either secured, whereby the borrower pledges a form of security to the bank as collateral against the loan, or unsecured. In general banks only make unsecured loans on relatively small ticket retail loans, on loans to the most credit-worthy corporates and loans that are very short term.

Banks gain a benefit in terms of lower volatility of expected credit losses when they have a well-diversified loan book. We will examine this more fully in Chapters 13 and 14 when we look at the subjects of credit risk and capital management. In principle a bank with a better diversified loan book should be able to offer lower prices than a bank with the same operating cost structure and funding costs but still achieve the same return on its equity as the less well-diversified bank.

Required Returns

In most cases the primary objective is to price the loans at a level that gives the bank a return on the capital employed above some target rate set by management, this is sometimes referred to as the hurdle rate. Provided that this hurdle rate is equal to, or greater than, the business unit's cost-of-equity then granting the loan or facility will create "economic value", more on this in Chapter 14 "Capital management".

There are exceptions, however. State controlled banks may be pressured by the government to make "soft loans" to selected parties. These are loans priced below market rates. Commercial banks that are part of a universal bank may be required to accept lower returns on loans to specific corporates to help the investment bank win business. Banks controlled by conglomerates may be required to extend cheap credit to parties related to the conglomerate or its owner.

The lending department will normally be informed how much capital has to be set aside by a central capital management group working within Treasury. A distinction has to be made between the capital that regulators require banks to maintain to support a particular business and capital that bank management deems necessary to protect the bank from unexpected economic losses. We will not consider the detailed issues involved in the allocation of capital at this point.

Micro-level factors in pricing

Required returns
* Bank cost of equity
* Target bank & business unit returns
* Capital allocated
* Tying / market share

Funding costs
* Maturity - term spread
* Distribution of repayments
* Fixed versus floating
* Pre-payment risk

Credit losses
* Credit spread
* Expected credit losses
  - Default probability, losses in event of default
* Guarantees, credit derivatives

Costs
* Costs of attracting funding
* Origination / termination
* Processing

CREDIT APPROVAL AND THE LOAN AGREEMENT

Credit Approval Process

The credit approval process at most banks is usually rigorous and follows established documented procedures. In simple terms, however, the key issues can be boiled down to the following:

- **Ability to repay.** The borrower must be able to demonstrate that they will be able to service and repay the loan and show when it will be repaid. The bank will require a complete set of accounts including an audited balance sheet, profit and loss statement and, most important of all, a cashflow statement and an analysis of future cashflow projections. These should be supported by a business plan that justifies the key assumptions in the financial projections.
- **Security.** Banks look for borrowers to pledge security against the loan. This is intended to protect the bank from credit losses in the event that the borrower is unable, or unwilling, to honor its loan repayment obligations.
- **Credit risk.** The bank must also determine the likelihood of default and level of losses as a result. Banks do not generally make loans where they expect the borrower to default but experience shows that a proportion will do so. These risks must be recognized and priced in. Specific loans can add to a bank's overall risks by increasing the concentration of loans to companies in particular industries or locations.
- **Returns.** Management must also ensure that the pricing structure is such that the bank is able to generate returns on the capital tied up with making the loans that are equal to, or greater than, its target return level.

The Loan Agreement

The loan agreement provides a legal contract between the borrower and the bank. It spells out in detail the terms of the loan. This normally specifies the amount(s) to be drawn down, the interest rate that will be charged and sets out a schedule of the dates when interest payments and principal repayments are due. It will also contain a detailed breakdown of any fees to be paid and penalties that the bank may charge for minor transgressions such as late or missed payments. For secured loans it will also include details of the collateral being pledged by the borrower. Most agreements also contain clauses indemnifying the bank against potential liabilities arising from specified events.

If the loan is a floating rate loan the loan agreement will specify the underlying benchmark rate, the margin over that benchmark, the conditions under which the rate charged to the customer will be changed and the notice to be given when such a change is made.

The bank will try to ensure that the loan agreement covers all possible eventualities. If the value of the collateral pledged falls below a certain level the agreement may require the borrower to provide additional collateral to restore the original value.

In countries such as the US where litigation is a constant potential threat it is important that the agreement states clearly any risks arising out of taking out the loan.

COLLATERAL, GUARANTEES AND COVENANTS

Collateral

Banks prefer to make secured loans rather than unsecured loans. In the event of the borrower failing secured creditors are in a much stronger position than unsecured creditors and are able to recover a much higher level of the debt due. Pledged security is called collateral and can take many forms. These include the following:

- **Real estate.** Real estate is the most common type of collateral provided. It has some clear advantages over many other sorts of collateral. It can't move for a start. Land registries exist in most developed countries that enable clear ownership to be established. The bank has to establish that no other party already has a claim to the title. The bank will need to lodge a claim at the land registry to establish its rights.

  This may be the actual asset being purchased, as in the case of a mortgage, or may be some unrelated property that the borrower has title to. The bank has to establish that no other party has a "lien" on the property and that the borrower has clean title. While the lien is lodged with the land registry the company will not be able to sell the underlying asset whether land or buildings.

  The main problems for banks with taking real estate as collateral are as follows:
  - **Subjectivity.** Appraised values are inherently subjective and may not reflect the actual market-clearing price.
  - **Liquidity.** Real estate is inherently illiquid and even in "normal" market conditions it may take many months before the bank is able to find a willing buyer at a price that covers the losses resulting from an actual default.
  - **Exposed to market corrections.** Banks are exposed to the risk of a property market correction reducing the value of pledged collateral and making it harder to sell in the event of foreclosure.
  - **Title.** Establishing title is an issue in many emerging markets where no central land registry exists. It is a very real problem in Japan, Eastern Europe, much of Asia and the countries that comprised the former Soviet Union.
- **The underlying asset being bought.** For retail borrowers this might be a car or a motor-cycle. In the corporate world this includes assets as diverse as airplanes, ships and machinery.

  The main issue here is that the borrower will carry the asset on its own balance sheet at cost, less any depreciation. This provides a realistic assessment of economic value when the accounting concept of "going concern" applies but in event of the liquidation of a firm, specialist machinery is likely to fetch far less than its book value.
- **Financial securities.** Banks are willing to accept some financial securities as collateral. These securities can include government paper, such as Treasury bills and bonds, and corporate paper, such as bonds and commercial paper. Many banks will also accept traded equity stocks.

  Where the loans are used by the borrower to purchase securities the loans are usually subject to margin requirements, where the borrower makes a cash deposit of a defined percentage of the market value of these securities. The minimum margin requirements are usually set by the central bank, bank regulator or securities regulator. Most agreements stipulate that the borrower must provide additional collateral to restore the original level of cover or face the risk that the bank will be entitled to call in the loan or sell part or all of the securities pledged to make good the shortfall.

- **A back-to-back deposit.** In addition to margin loans there are two occasions when a borrower may both draw down a loan and make an agreed deposit with the bank. Tax can provide an incentive where the interest expense on the loan is in a tax regime that allows it as a taxable expense while the interest income from the deposit is earned in a tax haven where it is not taxed.

  A company that has highly seasonal cashflows may find itself in a situation where for parts of the year it is cash rich but for other parts of the year it needs external funding. One solution to this financing problem would be for the bank to agree a facility under which the borrower has the right, but not the obligation, to draw down against it up to a specified limit without notice. Another solution is for the bank to make an equivalent loan for the whole cycle but require the customer to deposit its periodical surplus cash with the bank. The bank may be able to offer better pricing for the second solution.

- **Accounts receivables.** Accounts receivables represent the money due from customers for products or services delivered that have been invoiced but where payment has not yet been received. The composition of accounts receivables is the key factor in terms of its value as collateral. Accounts receivables at a utility company with hundreds of thousands of customers would be regarded as high quality. Historic default rates can be used to establish the likely level of future losses to a high level of confidence. Banks would also probably accept accounts receivables at companies that had only a handful of investment grade customers.

  Banks are generally reluctant to accept accounts receivables as collateral from many companies, however. We will look at factoring services that banks do provide to free cash locked up in company accounts receivables in Chapter 6 "Operational services".

- **Inventory.** For a small manufacturer of furniture the inventory will consist of raw material (wood, cloth, screws, glue etc.), semi-finished items (table tops, cupboard doors etc.) and a proportion of finished items that have not yet been dispatched.

  As a going concern the accounts reflect the historic costs of these materials, including labor expended, and not their market value. In the event of liquidation, however, the price that the bank would obtain from a sale of these assets is likely to be well below that of their actual cost and book value.

  When the inventory is technology based and there is a sudden build-up of inventory the value of the inventory is likely to fall rapidly as a result of obsolescence. Most manufacturers of Internet infrastructure equipment failed to forecast the sharp fall in demand that took place when the technology boom of the 1990s came to its abrupt halt. These companies were forced to write down the value of the subsequent inventory build-up and one major US company alone wrote off more than $3bn in one quarter.

In most cases the bank will seek to ensure that the value of the collateral is at least 20%–30% higher than the loan principal. This buffer is intended to meet four objectives:

- **Incentive for borrower.** The collateral buffer provides a strong incentive to the borrower to meet their agreed obligations. If a borrower fails to meet the terms of the loan agreements the bank has the right to seize and sell the underlying asset. This is frequently done at auction at fire sale prices.

The bank seeks to recover as much of its losses as possible and then has to return any remaining balance to the borrower. If the value of the collateral that could be obtained from a more orderly sale is greater than the value of the outstanding loan it is in the interests of the debtor either to keep the loan current or to repay the loan.

- **Fire sale prices.** The buffer provides a margin for valuation error and the likelihood that in the event of foreclosure the bank will not succeed in gaining the maximum price possible. The bank cares about recovering its losses but has little incentive to maximize any surplus to be returned to the debtor.
- **Offset foreclosure costs.** The buffer also provides a margin to cover professional fore-closure costs. Many legal systems, particularly in developing markets, are biased against creditors. Banks are often better placed than other creditors but there are still significant legal and professional costs associated with foreclosure.

In most countries, the bank will have to obtain a court ruling to establish that it has the right to foreclose and sell the asset concerned. It has to establish that the terms of the loan have been breached, that the bank has a legitimate claim on the asset, that no other creditor has a legitimate claim on the asset and that the bank has a right to sell the asset:

- **Litigation costs.** In complicated cases litigation costs can represent a significant proportion of the outstanding balance due. This is an area we will revisit when we look at "non-performing loans" (NPLs) in more detail in Chapter 13 "Managing credit risk" and Chapter 20 "Corporate failures and problem loans".
- **Protection against drop in market value of collateral.** Finally, having a buffer gives the bank some protection against a drop in the market value of the assets. It is common for loan agreements to require the borrower to provide additional collateral if the value of the pledged collateral falls below a specified level.

Collateral provides banks with a comfort factor but does not obviate the need to carry out a cashflow-based appraisal process. One of the factors that contributed to the Asian financial crisis of the late 1990s was that many banks lent on the basis of collateral cover alone rather than as a result of a cashflow analysis.

Guarantees

Guarantees can take many forms and banks generate fee income from providing a range of guarantees, such as a standby letter of credit, to its customers. A bank may also be offered a guarantee from a third party with respect to a loan the bank is making to a customer. In the event of default the guarantor is required to meet the borrower's outstanding obligations. Loan or credit guarantees can be considered as a form of collateral. They are treated as contingent liabilities by the guarantor unless it becomes likely that it will be forced to honor its guarantee. Guarantors may be private or public sector organizations:

- **Public sector.** These include state-sponsored organizations that specialize in guaranteeing loans for a particular type of borrower such as small companies or cooperatives. Some spe-cialist public sector banks (such as national import–export banks) also provide guarantees. These guarantees are useful in helping the guarantor achieve objectives of funneling credit to selected borrowers or facilitate exports without having to actually fund such loans itself.

- **Private sector.** Most corporate guarantees are made by parent companies on behalf of subsidiaries or associates. Occasionally a large company may provide such a guarantee for a company that has no direct affiliation, an example might be a small, independent but strategic supplier. If the guarantor is the company's major customer it is in an excellent position to assess the risks of making such a guarantee. Insurance companies issue surety bonds that can also act as loan guarantees.

Being given such a guarantee does not obviate the need for the usual credit appraisal of the borrower but in respect of the guarantee the bank also needs to take into account two factors in order to determine its value as collateral: enforceability and ability of the guarantor to honor its guarantee:

- **Enforceability.** For guarantees provided by an American parent for a US-based subsidiary it should be a trivial exercise to determine enforceability. Standard contracts exist and have been tested through the courts. This is more of an issue when guarantees are cross-border. A guarantee made by a US multinational corporation on behalf of a subsidiary incorporated in a developing country may pose problems. In the absence of precedents legal opinions may have to be obtained and eventually require a judgment call from the bank.
- **Ability to honor.** The guarantee effectively shifts the credit risk from the borrower to the guarantor. Where the guarantor is an institution such as an insurance company the value of its guarantees and ability to make them is highly dependent on its credit rating. A bank should never accept a guarantee where the credit rating of the guarantor is lower than that of the borrower.

These cross-border guarantees can also create internal credit problems for the lender where the guarantee is perfectly acceptable and well within the total credit lines authorized for use by the guarantor but the loan breaches head office limits on country exposure. It can be frustrating for bank officers in the international branches of a global bank to have a loan or credit line application from a subsidiary of an American triple-A corporate, and guaranteed by that company, turned down on credit grounds.

Covenants

There is an inherent conflict between the providers of debt and equity to companies. Most providers of debt financing require the borrower to agree to conditions on the way in which the borrower runs their business to protect the lenders from actions that would weaken their own positions. These conditions are called covenants. Examples of such conditions include the following:

- **Debt–equity level.** The bank may impose a limit on the company's net-debt-to-equity ratio. The objective of such a covenant is to prevent the company from taking on more debt by borrowing from another bank or issuing bonds or commercial paper. Any such action would result in a reduction in the company's ability to service its borrowings and increase the bank's risk.

- **Dividend policy.** A common covenant is to require the company to pay its debtors before making a dividend payment. In many cases such restrictions are extended to cover actions such as share buy-backs and capital reduction programs. There is an intrinsic conflict between shareholder interests and creditor interests and banks need to protect themselves from action that could result in a material deterioration in their own position.
- **Asset sales.** The lending bank may impose restrictions on the company's right to dispose of assets, even if these are not explicitly pledged as collateral. The objective of this covenant is to prevent the company from disposing of its highest quality assets at a discount to their underlying value.
- **Interest cover.** The bank may require the company to maintain a minimum specified level of operating cashflow to interest payments.

In the event of any of these covenants being broken the bank has the right to force the company to take corrective action or risk the bank calling in the loan. If the company cannot repay the loan promptly the bank may take legal action against the borrower and act to foreclose on the pledged collateral.

Most legal agreements between banks and counterparties also include a "force majeure" clause. This is a clause that the bank can invoke in the event of a change in the regulatory environment or a specified external event beyond their control. Legal and regulatory changes, the imposition of capital controls or the outbreak of war are examples of the sort of events that would allow a bank to invoke this clause. The clause absolves the bank of responsibility for any losses or other adverse effects experienced by the customer.

CREDIT DERIVATIVES

Credit derivatives are a relatively recent development and are only available in the more developed financial markets and then only for specific companies. They provide insurance policies that banks can buy to shield themselves from some losses arising from loan default. They are contracts between two parties where the seller of the credit derivative agrees to pay the buyer of the contract a pre-agreed amount when a specific condition or set of conditions is met. The sellers of these policies are usually insurance companies or SPVs (special purpose vehicles) set up by insurance companies. These conditions relate to the credit-worthiness of a corporate. Examples of trigger conditions include the following:

- **Default event.** An actual default on a payment on a loan on a bond. This could be defined as either interest or principal.
- **Credit spreads.** The spread on a corporate bond rising above a specific level against a specified benchmark such as a government Treasury note of similar maturity. If the credit spread widens the market is pricing in a higher default risk.
- **Rating downgrades.** A downgrade of a particular corporate by one of the leading credit-rating agencies. If a downgrade occurs, or is expected, the credit spread on bonds issued by the company is likely to widen and prices fall. The risk of default on any banks' loans will also rise and the bank's economic value will fall.

These products can best be viewed as 'insurance' policies but can also be used as a means to trade on credit quality. The writer of such a product would be betting that a default was in fact unlikely and that the option will expire valueless. Their profit will then be the premium paid by the buyers of the contract. Credit derivatives are usually represented by customized contracts that can be structured in a number of ways.

The form of the payment varies depending on the terms of agreed contract. The payment may be one of the following:

- **A spread-based payment.** The credit spread is measured by comparing a company's bond yields against those of Treasury notes with similar structure and term. If the bond's credit spread rises above a predetermined level the contract pays out on a notional principal outstanding based on the difference between the actual spread and that defined in the contract.

  This is best illustrated with an example. Suppose that the contract is for a notional principal of $100m and that the issuer will pay out if the credit spread reaches more than 500 bpts above the yield on a specified, comparable Treasury note. At 600 bpts the annual payment from the issuer of credit derivative would be $1m.

- **A principal-based payment.** The contract could be structured as a straight insurance policy that pays out a defined amount in the event of a trigger condition being met, such as a payment being missed, the company seeking bankruptcy protection or being liquidated.

  Credit derivatives are not traded on exchanges but are further examples of instruments that are traded OTC (over-the-counter). They provide a way for insurance companies to compete with banks. By issuing credit derivatives they can enhance the credit quality of a company's debt and make it easier to sell. In this way they are going head to head with banks in terms of pricing credit risk.

A bank may buy credit derivatives even if it has no direct exposure to the underlying company as proxy insurance. If a bank, for example, has exposure to a number of suppliers of a particular company buying a credit derivative against this company will reduce risk. Its suppliers will be adversely affected if the company cannot pay its bills. That in turn will impact on their ability to service their debt.

An insurance company may write a credit derivative on a company where in its view the market is mispricing default risk. If the writer of the policy is also a lender to that company it may have an inside track on the likelihood of a trigger condition being met. In this case the bank's incentive is to sell an option that the bank believes will expire worthless.

Credit derivatives are only likely to be successful in markets where there is perceived to be a high degree of transparency and high standard of corporate governance. In emerging markets this is rarely the case and as a result credit derivatives are largely confined to developed markets such as the US and UK. The word "perceived" used here was chosen carefully.

CONCLUSION

Given all of the factors involved in determining pricing and granting approval it is a wonder that a bank ever makes any loans. Adam Smith's "invisible hand" plays a major role in pricing. This is more apparent in the bond market where information and terms on issues are in the public domain. Bonds are also issued in a standardized form. Term spreads and credit spreads can both be inferred from market prices.

Banks hide behind secrecy laws and a desire to keep potentially price-sensitive information on the loans that they are making to themselves. The best sources of information on actual loan pricing (rather than published rates such as *Prime*) are the borrowers themselves and the syndicated loan market. Customers may tell one bank what another is offering to try to get the best terms available.

Over the past 50 years or so there has been a shift away from "relationship" banking to "transaction" banking with customers always taking the deal with the lowest price. Relationship banking was arguably helped by the presence of local monopolies in some countries and by regulated lending rates in others. Their breakdown has led to an increased level of price-based competition.

While this shift has certainly occurred relationship banking is not yet dead. Maintaining banking relationships with a relatively small number of banks has its advantages. Account managers at these banks build up a better understanding of the company's longer-term financing requirements, seasonality and cyclicality of cashflows. Credit decisions can be made relatively quickly.

These banks are likely to be able to approve requests for credit faster than banks that lack that experience. The acid-test, however, comes from the actions that the bank takes when a company is going through a difficult period, whether this is due to external factors such as a change in the macro-level environment or changes in industry structure or competition. A bank that cuts credit lines to a company at the first signs of trouble is likely to find itself frozen out in the future.

Management at most banks have to deal with the reality that corporate loans have very little product differentiation. Barriers to entry are low and there is a wide range of substitutes. Under such conditions banks in most countries are price-takers. The best they can do is to get their operating and appraisal costs down and to get the optimal balance between the costs of attracting cheaper funding and the costs of those funds.

6

Operational Services

It's the little things that make the big things possible. Only close attention to the fine details of any operation makes the operation first class.

J. Willard Marriott, US hotelier and businessman

INTRODUCTION

Commercial banks also provide a range of traditional operational services. These are not generally perceived as sexy but most are relatively low risk, have low capital requirements and their income is relatively high quality in the sense that while growth expectations are low it is less volatile than income from most other banking activities.

These include cash management, trade finance, custody, remittances, trust and clearing and payment services. In some of these businesses entry costs and the costs of maintaining investments in the technology necessary to remain competitive have become prohibitively high. In some services, such as global custody, the number of players has fallen drastically over the past two decades from more than a dozen banks to just three or four.

CASH MANAGEMENT

Most companies have multiple bank accounts. At any particular moment some of these may have positive balances and others be overdrawn. The problem of managing these account balances is exacerbated when the company operates in a number of countries and has accounts in a variety of currencies. Corporate treasurers have four prime objectives in terms of cash management:

- **Minimize funding costs.** Multinationals maintain bank accounts in many countries. At any given moment in time some accounts may have a positive balance and others be overdrawn. It is therefore important to minimize funding costs on those accounts that have a negative balance.
- **Maximize returns.** In like manner the treasurer seeks to maximize returns on accounts with positive balances.
- **Manage liquidity.** The company must also manage its cash positions in order to be able to pay its suppliers, employees and other creditors in a timely manner.
- **Remain within the law.** In many developing countries the laws concerning cross-border foreign exchange transactions are complex and may be open to interpretation. A multinational has to take care to remain within the legal restrictions that exist in each country in which it operates.

This is where banks come into play. Their cash management groups ensure that they remain current on all the legal constraints and provide the necessary systems infrastructure. There are two principal methods employed:

- **Sweeping.** Sweeping involves the physical transfer of funds (albeit by electronic means) between accounts in different countries. Care has to be taken for two reasons. Countries with foreign exchange controls do not permit sweeping. The second reason is that such transfers may be viewed as intercompany loans and this may have adverse tax implications.
  To further complicate matters differences in time zones between countries, and even within countries, must be taken into account.
- **Pooling.** Pooling involves a notional consolidation of a company's accounts. The bank then calculates interest to be paid or due after netting the returns on the balances.

This is a gross simplification of what is a highly complex business segment requiring sophisticated infrastructure, an international distribution capability and secure systems. Some banks use cash management as a loss leader because it gives a huge insight into its customers' cash positions and flows and because it is likely to give rise to related business in areas such as trade finance and foreign exchange.

TRADE FINANCE

The financing of cross-border trade is one of the earliest services that banks provided to corporates and merchants. The fundamental problem for an exporter or supplier is that there is a risk that the buyer or importer will not make the agreed payment on receipt of the goods. This may be the result of one of two specific factors:

- **Company-specific risk.** This is the risk that the importer is unable or unwilling to make the payment due. Pursuing a company through the courts in a foreign country is likely to prove an expensive and time-consuming undertaking and has no guarantee of success.
- **Country-specific risk.** This is the risk that the government of the importing country will introduce measures, such as the introduction of capital controls, to prevent money leaving the country and hence from allowing the buyer to pay the exporter.

An importer faces the risk of non-delivery if they make payment in advance. Banks step in to break this impasse by providing guarantees of payment to exporters when the goods are delivered to the buyer.

The most basic and common form of this guarantee is the "letter of credit", commonly referred to as an L/C. This is a highly standardized contract and is internationally recognized. It is treated as a contingent liability by the issuing bank as payment is conditional on a number of conditions being met. The following diagrams show the two main phases involved from the placement of an order by an importer to an exporter and the subsequent delivery of the goods and payment:

- **Initiation.** The importer and exporter agree that payment will be made using a letter of credit and agree the terms under which payment will be made. The importer places its order and then approaches its bank and asks it to issue an L/C to the exporter's bank. This gives the exporter's bank a guarantee that the importer's bank will make the required payment when the goods have been received at the buyer.

- **Delivery of goods and payment.** In the second phase the exporter provides its shipper with the documentation, in particular the bill of lading, necessary for the buyer to collect the goods from the port of entry. The importer's bank then makes the required payment to the exporter and debits its own customer's account. This is shown in the following chart but a common means of payment involves the use of bills of exchange and banker's acceptances.

Bills of exchange and banker's acceptances arise out of banks' service to facilitate trade. When a buyer (importer) has to make payment on goods from a seller (exporter) that have been shipped it may do so by instructing its bank to pay the seller (exporter) with a bill of exchange or time draft, payable a specified number of days after presentation.

Once the exporter's bank is satisfied that all the conditions of the L/C have been met it "accepts" the draft and it then becomes a banker's acceptance. This provides a guarantee from the bank that it will pay the amount due on the due date. This is a negotiable instrument and the seller (exporter) can sell this at a discount to its face or redemption value in a secondary money market in order to get paid sooner.

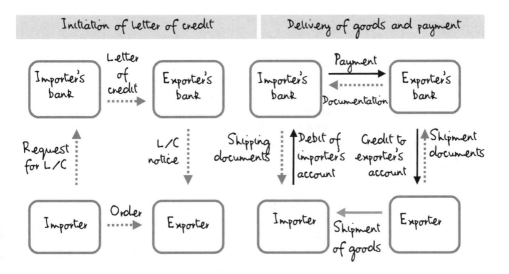

The entire process is documentation driven based on standardized international terms for documentary credits. The most important document is the bill of lading which the exporter passes to the shipper and is used to establish title to the shipped goods.

Banks do not perform these services for free. First, they are able to generate fees from the L/C issue. Second, they may provide short-term funding for the transaction. Third, they are able to obtain a spread on the actual FX transaction.

In the past this has been a highly paper-intensive activity requiring extensive clerical work and attention to detail. Advances in communications technology, the widespread expansion of the Internet and the adoption of Electronic Data Interchange (EDI) standards mean that the whole trade finance business is becoming increasingly automated and integrated with cash management services that banks provide to corporates.

Letters of credit protect exporters from importer default but leave them open to the risk of default at the guarantor bank and to country risk. Getting a second guarantee reduces these risks. This may be either from a bank in its own country or from a specific state bank or agency. The original letter of credit is then known as a confirmed letter of credit. The second level of guarantee creates what is known as a standby letter of credit that only pays in the event that the primary guarantor defaults.

The matter of guarantors is more important at times than it might seem. In the aftermath of the Asian financial crisis there were still some successful exporters in business in Indonesia. They had actually benefited from the devaluation of the Indonesian currency, the rupiah (it fell from a level of around 2500 rupiah to the US$ to reach a low of 17 000 at one point). They had one huge problem, however, they needed to import various components and raw materials from abroad to remain in business but had no means to pay for them.

All of the domestic banks were technically insolvent and it was impossible for them to open letters of credit. The only way around this was for one of the few foreign banks still operating in Indonesia to open the L/C on behalf of the domestic bank and they were only prepared to do so if they could obtain guarantees from foreign state controlled import–export banks.

CUSTODY

Most banks provide basic custody services to investors holding bonds and stocks. A small number of commercial banks also provide more sophisticated custody services to institutional clients such as fund managers. Specialist banks provide a service of collecting and remitting interest income from bonds and dividends from stocks. They are active in the stock lending business.

The whole business has changed dramatically with technology. In the past all securities were issued in paper form. Bonds, for example, had coupons attached to them that had to be clipped off and sent to the issuer's bank in order to get payment. There are still vaults full of such paper that were issued many years ago but have not yet matured and have to be processed in this way.

Now most securities are issued and traded in scrip-less form, eliminating much of the paper trail. Now what custodian banks provide are computer interfaces to large numbers of incompatible clearing and settlement systems, obviating the need for the client to do so themselves.

The custody business is split into two distinct segments. Local custody services provided by banks providing services in individual countries and global custodians coordinating client holdings with local custodians and pulling these holdings together for their clients.

The global custody business has become highly concentrated, largely as a result of the high costs of investing in technology necessary to compete in this business segment. There are now only three or four global custodian banks still competing with one another. At present this still appears to be an attractive business segment with high barriers to entry and customer switching costs. In the long term this may change as more exchanges and clearing systems adopt open standards but that is a long way away.

REMITTANCES

In many countries, such as the Philippines, India and Mexico, large numbers of workers support their families by working abroad. In some Middle East countries foreign workers outnumber local residents. In countries such as Singapore and the Hong Kong SAR (Special Administrative Region) there are hundreds of thousands of foreign domestic workers from the Philippines and Indonesia.

This has created a retail demand from foreign workers to send funds to their families back home. Banks are just one of a number of financial institutions that provide remittance services. Banks effect this by means of electronic transfer.

There is also a large informal, lightly regulated business for transferring money home. A mainland Chinese worker in Singapore wanting to remit funds to his family in Shanghai will go to a moneychanger and hand over the cash. The moneychanger will then call, or send a fax, to instruct their counterpart in Shanghai to make payment to the named recipient.

This practice creates a number of problems. It leaves workers open to fraud and distorts published statistics on cross-border fund flows. It also facilitates money laundering. It is difficult to see how these businesses can be either better regulated or eliminated, however.

FACTORING

We have already alluded to the fact that a large portion of working capital is tied up in accounts receivables at many companies. These are moneys due from customers for services or products that have been delivered and invoiced but for which payment has not yet been received. This is not unusual, typical payment terms are 30–60 days and may even be as long as 90 days. Companies wanting to receive their cash faster look to banks and specialist finance companies for factoring services by selling them the rights to the cashflows represented by accounts receivable. Factoring may be arranged such that the factor collects directly from the seller or the seller carries out this function and remits proceeds as they are received.

Factoring may be carried out in one of two principal ways, known as discount or maturity factoring:

- **Discount factoring.** Here the seller is paid by the factor in advance (before the average due date) and receives an amount based on the invoiced amount less an allowance for credit losses. In turn the factor is paid interest on average balances some way above that paid on loans made to companies of a similar credit standing.
- **Maturity factoring.** The buyer pays the seller for the outstanding receivables on their average due date. The factor carries out the entire credit and collection process. The factor is paid a fee for providing this service that takes into account estimated credit losses.

The receivables may be sold with or without recourse.

TRUST

The trust business covers a wide range of activities and the degree to which banks provide trust services varies significantly between countries. They both compete with and cooperate with legal firms in some of these areas. In many of these areas they have specific fiduciary responsibilities that may be laid out by law or established through the terms of their appointment:

- **Estate.** Banks frequently provide estate planning and act as the executor for the winding up of estates. This involves handling the legal matters, managing the estate's assets and arranging for their disposal and the subsequent disbursements.
- **Guardianship.** Banks may be appointed to act in a guardian capacity on behalf of a beneficiary and take overall responsibility for their financial dealings under the terms of the guardianship.
- **Trust management.** In some countries many education institutions and charities rely upon income from endowments and other bequests. Banks may act as the trustee itself or in an advisory role to the trustees. A few of these trusts are personal trusts usually set up to effect a transfer of wealth from one generation of a family to the next while minimizing future death duties.

In all of these areas banks usually act in a very conservative manner. They are high-volume, low-margin businesses. In some countries "trust" has taken on a different meaning and may be employed as part of an overall strategy to attract customer deposits by guaranteeing returns. These businesses are extremely difficult for external analysts to analyze due to the opacity of publicly available data.

CLEARING AND PAYMENT SYSTEMS

In a modern economy transactions between parties usually involve the exchange of items such as capital goods, labor, manufactured goods, services and legal claims for a "cash" consideration. The exchange may involve more than one currency and may involve a time difference between delivery of goods and actual payment. Such exchange transactions carry with them a number of risks including settlement failure and fraud. Financial organizations cooperate with one another to establish the infrastructure and procedures necessary to minimize these risks and transaction costs. These include formal markets such as stock exchanges, and automated systems to enable payments to be made both within individual countries and also cross-border.

The provision of clearing and payment systems is one of the most important operational services that banks provide. Payment systems may be either national or cross-border.

The most important international system is provided by the Society for Worldwide Interbank Financial Telecommunications (SWIFT). This is a cooperative owned by 7000 members operating in approximately 200 countries. SWIFT was established in 1973 and is based in Brussels, Belgium, but has operational centers around the world.

SWIFT provides two key services. First it provides a global telecommunications network to enable banks and other financial institutions to exchange electronic messages to instruct transfers of funds in a secure manner. Second it coordinates the standardization of the format of these messages. The latter is vital to allow banks to send, receive and interpret electronic payment instructions in an automated way.

SWIFT has three principal challenges. It must ensure it provides a secure service, maintains an extremely high level of reliability and has a well-managed implementation of changes in message formats or communications protocols.

Most countries have their own clearing systems for payments made between banks, and on behalf of customers with accounts at these banks. The vast majority of these systems concern electronic transfers of funds but other means have to be used for payments involving paper checks.

Many interbank clearing systems take the form of end-of-day clearing (as opposed to continuous). Payments due between each of the clearing house members are calculated on a gross basis but payments are done on a net basis. Netting reduces overall risks arising from the failure of one member. Examples of clearing systems in the US are Fedwire, for payments between US Federal Reserve bank members, and CHIPS, for payments between New York-based banks.

Check clearing poses some practical problems. In more developed countries check details are captured at the branch of the bank where they are deposited, using a combination of different methods. Some data is encoded in magnetic form of the checks and can be scanned. Some data can be captured using optical character recognition (OCR) systems and the rest has to be input manually. Checks are then only retained as part of the process of maintaining a paper audit trail. In less developed countries checks have to be delivered in physical form to a regional or national data entry center where the data is captured.

Some countries also have specialist payment systems used for salary payments, payments to suppliers, standing orders and so on. Members of these systems include non-financial organizations. These systems are a part of what is now more generally referred to as e-commerce and cover settlement of B2B (business-to-business) and B2C (business-to-consumer) transactions. Despite the introduction of the euro no single European clearing and payments systems exists and banks must rely on other means such as sending instructions via SWIFT or their own networks and using national payments systems.

In "continuous" systems net settlement is done on a much more frequent, intra-day basis. These systems are often associated with secondary capital market transactions (bond clearing, for example). Continuous net settlement is generally accepted as further reducing risk.

7

Mortgage Lending

Figure it out. Work a lifetime to pay off a house. You finally own it and there's no one to live in it.

Arthur Miller, Death of a Salesman

RETAIL CREDIT PRODUCTS

Many banks subdivide the retail segment further in terms of their own organization into personal banking (mortgages, credit cards, overdrafts and other services) and consumer finance (auto loans and other loans to finance consumer purchases). In recent years there has been a move to base the retail banking organization more on the delivery method used, for example branch-based banking and products delivered electronically. This trend is likely to persist as more people use the Internet to search for the best terms available and to apply for loans.

Most retail loans are highly commoditized. Credit approval procedures are highly automated and pricing and approval decisions result from bank policy decisions rather than being made individually. Key success factors in this segment include access to customers, ease of application, speed of credit approval and pricing. For specialist lending services, such as loans to individuals with a poor credit record, collateral requirements may be lowered in return for a higher price. The major types of retail loans are as follows:

- **Housing mortgage.** Typically a loan with a term of 15–30 years made for the purchase of a specific property. The borrower gives the bank a "lien" on the property. This is a legal term that entitles the bank to the title of the property in the event of the borrower failing to make payments as scheduled. Mortgages may be fixed rate, floating rate or some combination of the two forms, for example fixed for the first three years and then reverting to a floating rate based on some prespecified benchmark.
- **Credit card.** A form of unsecured revolving credit but also providing an electronic point of sale payment service. Credit cards provide a specified period of free credit after which the issuer charges a relatively high rate on any balances not paid off. These balances are referred to as "rollover" balances. Some cards also have some form of annual fee.
- **Consumer finance.** Car loans and loans for the purchase of other consumer items such as washing machines, motorbikes and televisions fall into the broad category of consumer finance. Banks compete with a number of non-bank institutions in this segment such as stores, auto manufacturers and specialist consumer finance firms.
- **Unsecured overdraft.** A short-term facility granted to meet some specific financing requirement such as the costs of a wedding.
- **Margin loans.** Loans made to support customer share trading. The loans are secured against the value of the stock. In the event of the stock falling the bank may issue a "margin call" requiring the customer to "top up" their account with a cash deposit or face a forced sale of their stock.

- **Education loans.** In many countries banks provide loans to students to help pay for college fees. In some cases these loans are subsidized by the state.

In the most developed countries, and in particular in the US, securitization has had a marked impact on the development of the mortgage lending business. Securitization involves selling the rights to the cashflows generated from a pool of assets, of which mortgages make up the largest class. In such markets commercial banks may find it more profitable to originate mortgage loans and then to sell those loans than to hold and fund them. We examine securitization issues in detail in Chapter 17.

THE MORTGAGE BUSINESS

Types of Loans Available

Housing loans are the largest and most important retail loan segment. For most individuals the mortgage is likely to be the largest single loan they ever take from a bank. Governments in many countries have encouraged the growth of mortgage lending in order to increase the level of private home ownership. In many instances governments provide tax incentives to borrowers.

Credit losses on mortgages are generally lower than on other retail or corporate loans and also more predictable. It is quite common to hear bankers and analysts argue that the Basel Accord requirements also provide an incentive for banks to make housing loans because they are only required to "set aside" 50% of the regulatory capital required for all other loans to support a mortgage. Such comments often reveal a lack of understanding of the nature of the difference between risk and regulatory capital. This is an issue that we will return to in Chapter 14 "Capital management".

Housing loans can be either fixed rate or floating rate. In the US the latter are commonly referred to as Adjustable Rate Mortgages (ARMs). These have different advantages to issuer and mortgagor:

- **Fixed rate mortgages.** Fixed rate mortgages are the dominant form in the US. The advantage to the mortgagor is that the monthly payments are not affected by rising interest rates and this also reduces the risk of default to the issuer. The two disadvantages to the issuer are:
  - Banks are funded largely with short-term deposits. If interest rates rise their cost of funds will increase but the return from their fixed rate mortgages remains unchanged. This exposes the lending organization to significant interest rate risk. Mismanagement of this risk was an important factor in the US S&L (saving and loans) crisis of the 1980s.
  - If on the other hand banks seek to avoid this risk by obtaining matching fixed rate funding they are left exposed to prepayment risk. That is the risk that interest rates fall and that mortgagors pay off their existing loans and take out a new mortgage at the prevailing lower rates. The lender has, in effect, sold a loan with an embedded put option.
- **Floating rate mortgages.** These are much more common in Asia, Latin America and Europe than in the US. The main advantage to the issuer is that making such loans leaves them less exposed to interest rate and prepayment risk. The main disadvantage is that default risk is likely to be higher in the event of a sharp rise in interest rates.

In those countries where floating rate mortgages are the norm banks will generally only offer fixed rate mortgages when they expect interest rates to fall, and in many cases the fixed rate offer normally applies only to the early years of the mortgage before reverting to floating

- **Endowment/investment linked mortgages.** Endowment or investment linked mortgages are a combination of a standard loan and an investment policy. Monthly payments go to pay interest on the loan as in a traditional mortgage loan but a part also goes to pay the premiums on an investment policy. The investment policy is normally invested in bonds and equities. The intention is that the endowment policy will generate sufficient returns that when the loan has to be repaid there will be sufficient investment profits to pay the principal and a bonus to the policyholder.

  Actual monthly payments are in line with those of a traditional mortgage in which a part of the principal is paid off each month. Banks liked these because they were able to extract upfront fees for the policy. Mortgagors liked it less when they found that returns on their investment policies were insufficient to repay the outstanding principal at term.

- **Home equity.** Home equity loans are second mortgages secured against a residential property. They are possible when either property prices have risen sufficiently to increase the homeowner's equity or the borrower has paid down a significant proportion of their original mortgage. Such loans may be used for home improvements, to repay higher cost debt, to make investments or for consumer spending.

- **Other housing loans.** Subject to regulatory restrictions there is no real limit on the different ways that housing loans can be structured. A loan could have a monthly payment that steadily increases over time. This might be attractive to young people who expect their earnings to rise relatively sharply. A loan could be structured with negative amortization, where the monthly payments are insufficient to pay interest and reduce outstanding principal. Unpaid interest is rolled into the outstanding principal and this grows over time. This could be advantageous if property prices are rising or the borrower expects a large capital inflow, possibly from a bequest, in the future.

  Retired people may find themselves where they own a valuable asset (their house) but have insufficient income to meet their needs. Where there is a demand financiers will look for ways to meet those demands and make a profit. Insurance companies and banks both offer competing products to such customers. A typical policy from an insurance company pays a perpetuity until death, allows the customer to continue to live in the house but eventually gets title to the house. A competing bank product would be for the bank to make a loan to the retiree with the property as collateral. The retiree would then redeposit this loan as a deposit with the bank and live off the interest earned. The interest due on the loan would be capitalized. The total outstanding balance is then paid off from the proceeds from the borrower's estate when he or she dies.

Credit Appraisal

Housing loans are subject to the same basic checks as are applied to loans for consumer finance but will be subject to additional scrutiny. A letter from the employer containing current salary, position and the length of service with the company is frequently required.

If all the basic checks are confirmed then attention switches to ability to pay and the impact of a potential default risk. For most consumer finance loans the major focus is whether borrowers will repay, based on their past credit record, rather than whether they can repay based on visible income. For housing loans the reverse is generally the case:

- **Ability to pay.** Many individual lenders and regulators impose limits on the amount that can be lent based on household income. A common restriction is that monthly mortgage payments cannot be more than 40% of disposable income after tax.

  This puts an effective cap on the value of the loan that can be made. Under the above condition a couple earning $10 000 per month after tax would be allowed to pay a maximum of $4000 per month in mortgage payments – $48 000 per year. At a 7% mortgage rate this equates to a maximum loan of approximately $600 000 for a 30-year loan.
- **Loan-to-value.** The second measure that many lenders and some regulators use to reduce the potential impact of default is to set an upper limit on the amount that can be lent against the appraised value, or market price, of the property. This is referred to as the loan-to-value ratio.

  A very common loan-to-value limit is 80% of the appraised value or purchase price. In the example above this would correspond to an appraised value of $750 000. This means that the couple would have to fund $150 000 of the total purchase from their own savings.

There have also been attempts to use indemnity insurance to provide the bank with the required buffer without the borrower having to make a down payment. This works by the mortgagor taking out an insurance policy that will pay out to the mortgage lender in the event of the borrower defaulting.

Bankers always maintain that their lending policies are prudent and conservative. I have never visited a bank where management said anything other than this. Several of these banks subsequently failed under the weight of credit losses.

Lenders are, however, prone to herd behavior. When the property market is strong there is a temptation to lower the loan-to-value multiple figuring that even if they lend at current valuations (i.e. 100% loan-to-value ratio) within a year rising property prices will have restored the bank's collateral buffer. Markets do not go up indefinitely, however; from time to time they correct. Sometimes this correction can be severe and last for many years.

EXAMPLE OF PAYMENT STRUCTURE FOR FIXED RATE MORTGAGE

Mortgages are among the longest-term loans that banks provide. In most countries the normal term at the onset is between 20 and 30 years. In the case of a fixed rate mortgage both the actual rate and the monthly payment are fixed. In each month a proportion of the payment goes towards repaying the principal and the remainder towards paying interest on the remaining outstanding balance.

We will base most of our analysis using a simplified example of a 20-year, fixed rate mortgage. We have simplified the payments to assume that they are done on an annual basis, rather than a monthly basis. We still need to input the basic variables in order to determine the pricing structure necessary to meet our 24% required rate of return. The following table gives a breakdown of the net cashflows associated with the loan together with the outstanding balance on the mortgage and the capital required at the end of each year.

Simplified structure of payments and outstanding balance for 20-year mortgage loan								
Lending rate	Funding costs	Processing costs	Origination costs	Capital required	Expected losses	Monthly payment	Required return	Actual return
7.23%	6.00%	120	2,000	2.50%	300	38,420	24%	23.4%
Year Balance	Interest payment	Funding costs	Net int. income	Capital charge	Capital repaid	Net cashflow	Principal payment	Capital required
0	400 000						− 12 300		10 000
1	390 480	28 900	−23 400	5500	−2400	238	3218	9520	9762
2	380 272	28 212	−22 843	5369	−2343	255	3161	10 208	9507
3	369 327	27 475	−22 246	5229	−2282	274	3101	10 945	9233
4	357 591	26 684	−21 606	5078	−2216	293	3036	11 736	8940
5	345 007	25 836	−20 919	4917	−2146	315	2966	12 584	8625
6	331 514	24 927	−20 183	4744	−2070	337	2891	13 493	8288
7	317 045	23 952	−19 394	4558	−1989	362	2811	14 468	7926
8	301 532	22 907	−18 547	4359	−1902	388	2725	15 513	7538
9	284 898	21 786	−17 640	4146	−1809	416	2633	16 634	7122
10	267 062	20 584	−16 667	3917	−1709	446	2534	17 836	6677
11	247 937	19 295	−15 623	3672	−1602	478	2428	19 125	6198
12	227 430	17 913	−14 504	3409	−1488	513	2314	20 507	5686
13	205 442	16 432	−13 305	3127	−1365	550	2192	21 988	5136
14	181 865	14 843	−12 018	2825	−1233	589	2 062	23 577	4547
15	156 585	13 140	−10 639	2501	−1091	632	1 921	25 280	3915
16	129 478	11 313	−9160	2153	−940	678	1 771	27 107	3237
17	100 413	9355	−7574	1780	−777	727	1 610	29 065	2510
18	69 248	7255	−5874	1381	−602	779	1 437	31 165	1731
19	35 831	5003	−4051	952	−415	835	1 252	33 417	896
20	0	2589	−2096	493	−215	896	1053	35 831	0

The result of this payment structure is that in early years the bulk of the monthly payment goes towards interest payments. In our example of a 20-year mortgage, in the early years less than 30% of the payments go towards principal repayment. A borrower who pays off the loan after five years will find that while they have made $192 100 in total payments the outstanding balance has only fallen by $54 993 from $400 000 to $345 007.

As the principal starts to reduce, however, the proportion that goes to principal repayment starts to rise. Principal repayments account for more than half of the monthly payments from the twelfth year onward in this example.

These characteristics mean that the shorter the average remaining term of a portfolio of mortgages the greater the level of capital repayments and the lower the level of outstanding mortgage loans and interest income. This has implications for both Treasury and the capital management division. As a portfolio of mortgages ages the outstanding principal falls and less capital is required to be set aside and more and more capital is released to the capital management group. It must find an alternative use for this capital to continue to generate the required 24% pre-tax return.

For a bank to simply maintain its mortgage portfolio at a particular absolute level it must continuously write more new mortgages. This takes no account of the new mortgages that have to be written to replace loans that have been repaid as a result of a mortgagor selling her

Breakdown of monthly payments	**Outstanding balance on 30-year loan**
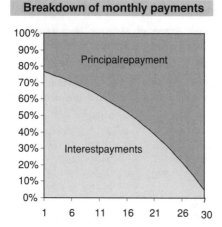	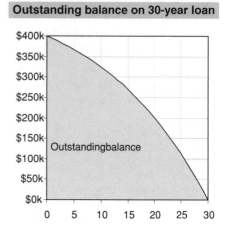

property or paying off the loan by getting refinancing at a lower rate from another lender. This brings us to the subject of mortgage prepayment risk.

Fixed rate mortgages are more attractive to borrowers than floating rate mortgages because borrowers hold an embedded call option, allowing them to repay their loan before the formal term. This can be represented as follows:

Value of mortgage loan = Value of equivalent straight loan – Value of embedded call option

If interest rates fall borrowers can repay their outstanding mortgage and take out a new mortgage at the then lower prevailing rates. This exposes the lending bank to prepayment risk. We will defer an examination of the impact of prepayments and consider these issues in Chapter 17 when we deal with the subject of asset securitization.

ESTIMATING SYSTEM-LEVEL NEGATIVE EQUITY

Real Estate Price Indices

In markets where the residential property market has been through a boom–bust cycle one of the most common requirements for analysts is to estimate the level of negative equity within the system.

Estimating system-level negative equity is only really possible if a representative property index exists. In many emerging markets that is rarely the case but it is usually possible to find some proxy or failing that actually goes to the land registry (if there is one) and check a select number of transaction prices on comparable properties.

The following example shows how to go about estimating the level of negative equity in a market. We will assume that all of the mortgages had an original term of 20 years and that banks lent on an 80% loan-to-price basis.

The starting point is to estimate how much prices have fallen over time. We will assume that the bubble took place in the late 1990s and that we are at the end of December 2000. The value of properties bought in 2Q96 is 50% lower now than when bought. All of the properties bought between 3Q95 and 3Q97 are worth less now than when bought, as shown in the following table.

Change in residential property prices												
	1Q95	2Q95	3Q95	4Q95	1Q96	2Q96	3Q96	4Q96	1Q97	2Q97	3Q97	4Q97 4Q00
Residential index	90	100	135	150	180	200	210	160	120	115	110	100 100
Change in prices	11%	0%	−26%	−33%	−44%	−50%	−52%	−38%	−17%	−13%	−9%	0% 0%

Historic Mortgage Drawdown

Next we need to estimate the level of new mortgages drawn down over time. If residential mortgages were rising very rapidly (and this is usually the case when real estate bubbles develop) a reasonable first approximation is to take the net increase in mortgage loans and assume that it is close to the gross increase. This may be done at the system level or for individual banks. Some countries actually publish gross drawdowns and these should be used when available.

Estimated mortgage drawdowns ($m)										
	2Q95	3Q95	4Q95	1Q96	2Q96	3Q96	4Q96	1Q97	2Q97	3Q97 4Q97
Housing loans	10 500	11 130	11 798	12 388	13 379	14 048	14 329	14 615	14 907	15 206 15 510
Gross drawdown	500	630	668	590	991	669	281	287	292	298 304
Purchase price	625	788	835	737	1239	836	351	358	365	373 380

Next we estimate how much of these loans have been repaid. Based on our example of a 20-year mortgage we know approximately how much capital is repaid in each year.

Mortgage principal repayment ($m)						
	Year 1	Year 2	Year 3	Year 4	Year 5	Year 6
Principal repayment	9520	10 208	10 945	11 736	12 584	13 493
As % of original loans	2.4%	2.6%	2.7%	2.9%	3.1%	3.4%
Cumulative	2.4%	5.0%	7.7%	10.6%	13.7%	17.0%

We are only interested in the loans made in 1995, 1996 and 1997. These are the only loans that are at risk of being "under water". A mortgage taken out in 1995 is approximately six years old and hence approximately 17% of the original principal has been repaid. This could be done on a quarter by quarter basis but besides from adding complexity and increasing the risk of computational error it does little to increase the accuracy of the estimates.

Mortgage principal re-paid			
Year in which mortgage drawn down	1995	1996	1997
Principal repaid	17.1%	14.7%	12.2%

We then calculate the estimated balance outstanding and subtract it from the current estimated value of the properties bought. This shows that the only properties at risk were those bought between 1Q96 and 4Q96.

Mortgage principal repaid ($m)											
	2Q95	3Q95	4Q95	1Q96	2Q96	3Q96	4Q96	1Q97	2Q97	3Q97	4Q97
Gross drawdown	500	630	668	590	991	669	281	287	292	298	304
Principal repaid	86	108	114	87	146	99	41	35	36	36	37
Balance outstanding	**414**	**522**	**553**	**503**	**845**	**570**	**240**	**252**	**257**	**262**	**267**
Purchase price	625	788	835	737	1239	836	351	358	365	373	380
Change in price		−204	−278	−328	−619	−438	−132	−60	−48	−34	
Current value	**625**	**583**	**557**	**410**	**619**	**398**	**219**	**299**	**318**	**339**	**380**
Collateral (shortfall)	**211**	**61**	**3**	**−93**	**−226**	**−172**	**−20**	**47**	**61**	**77**	**113**

Finally, we can make a reasonable first-cut estimate of the level of negative equity. Approximately 12% of mortgage loans, by value, have negative equity with the level of negative equity highest for people who bought in 3Q96 at approximately 30% of their outstanding balance.

Estimated mortgages with negative equity ($m)					
	1Q96	2Q96	3Q96	4Q96	Total	As% of total mortgages
Balance outstanding	503	845	570	240	2158	12.0%
Negative equity	−93	−226	−172	−20	−511	
As % of balance outstanding	19%	27%	30%	8%		

Part of the reason for including this example is to illustrate how in an imperfect world, where the data to arrive at a definitive answer either does not exist or is not reported, it is still possible with many problems to make some reasonable quantified conclusions using the data that is available, some clear approximations and a bit of creativity.

This method of estimating the level of mortgages with negative equity will not work in markets with significant levels of mortgage securitization.

MORTGAGE DEFAULT RATES

The historic default rates on mortgages have been generally much lower than on other consumer and corporate loans. They have also generally remained low even when borrowers have significant levels of negative equity. There are a number of reasons why this should be the case:

- **People have to live somewhere.** Negative equity represents an unrealized loss. There is no incentive to realize this loss provided the borrower can service the loan. The advantage of moving to cheaper rented accommodation has to be balanced against the disadvantages of defaulting.
- **Bankruptcy avoidance.** If a borrower defaults on a property with significant levels of negative equity they are likely to face bankruptcy proceedings. In addition to the stress and loss of assets that such proceedings bring they are also likely to make it impossible for the borrower to ever own their own property.

Exhibit: The residential property market trap

Property markets are at their most dangerous after they have enjoyed a strong run for many years. First time buyers start to panic as the prices of houses and apartments threaten to move out of reach. They become desperate to get a foot on the ladder. They are egged on by friends who have already done so and are sitting on large unrealized gain. The high level of gearing that mortgages provide accentuates this. Suppose someone buys an apartment for $750 000 with an initial down payment of $150 000, equivalent to 20% of the purchase price. If the market value of the apartment rises by 10% their equity increases by 50% to $225 000. If the market value goes up by 20% then their equity doubles.

Suddenly all the talk at dinner parties centers on how much prices have gone up for particular types of properties and locations. The market develops a momentum of its own with property prices rising well above the level implied by historic affordability measures such as average transaction prices versus average salaries.

All parties have to come to an end, however. The trigger is usually a change in the economic environment. Higher property prices increase the level of mortgage payments for people trading up and for first time buyers. Asset inflation also feeds through in the form of higher rents as landlords try to maintain yields. Employees then seek wage increases to maintain the real value of their earnings. These put upward pressure on inflation.

The usual response of central banks to rising inflationary pressures is to raise interest rates to slow the economy and choke off inflation. Interest rates for mortgages with floating rate loans follow and monthly payments start to rise. In countries where fixed rate mortgages are the norm the cost of new mortgages rises. This makes it harder for first time buyers to buy and for people looking to trade up to afford the payments on the next mortgage.

First, the volume of property transactions falls. Potential sellers are reluctant to cut asking prices. With the higher mortgage payments potential buyers cannot afford to meet the monthly mortgage payments implied by asking prices. The immediate result is that there is no market clearing price, that is a price at which sellers are prepared to sell and buyers to buy. At that time "appraised value", the value that realtors and surveyors assign to properties, becomes increasingly meaningless.

In time these appraised valuations adjust to reflect the new reality. Sellers are urged to cut asking prices to "realistic" levels. As these agents make their money from commissions based on actual transactions they have a strong incentive to ensure that a clearing level is reached. Their profitability is more dependent on the actual volume of transactions than the absolute prices being paid.

It is at this point that first time and highly geared borrowers begin to realize that they are in a serious predicament. The gearing that works so well when prices are rising now kicks in with a vengeance when prices are falling. The borrowers find themselves facing the "negative equity" trap. This means that the market value of their property is less than the principal outstanding on the mortgage.

- **Long dated option.** A mortgage can be viewed as a long dated option. Given long enough most property markets eventually recover, even though it may take years. Option holders do not simply throw away an option that is out-of-the-money for the simple reason that it also has a "time value". Given the typical term of mortgages the time value is significant, particularly as the "premium" they have paid (the down payment) represents a significant portion of their accumulated savings.

The level of defaults in the UK rose sharply after the residential property market crashed in 1986. A close examination of the problem showed that many defaulters had not actually made any down payment on their mortgage. Instead the lending bank had sold indemnity policies to them issued by an insurance company. These policies protected the banks from the first 20% of losses. Having paid very little for the option and being well out-of-the-money borrowers had little incentive to stay current and simply dropped off the keys after moving out.

The actual losses experienced by banks were relatively modest and the insurance companies simply responded by increasing the premiums charged for these policies. Few banks went through formal bankruptcy proceedings and, in the absence of a central register of defaulters, borrowers were able to go to another bank and took out a new mortgage on a different property. It's a wonderful world.

8

Credit Cards and Other Retail Loans

Dream as if you'll live forever, live as if you'll die tomorrow.

James Dean, US actor

CORE CREDIT CARD BUSINESS

Basic Functions

Although a number of stores had introduced charge cards for the use of customers in their own stores the first credit card proper was introduced by Bank of America in 1958. Approximately two billion cards are now in issue worldwide with the major brands being Visa and MasterCard.

Credit cards have been one of the most successful and profitable retail financial products. Their adoption worldwide has resulted in a huge complex industry. Many credit cards now offer supplementary features but at its most basic a credit card provides three functions:

- **A method of payment.** Credit cards provide a cashless form of payment. In early years this was done through the use of paper slips but today the vast majority of payments are made electronically.
- **A method of payment guarantee.** Most hotels require either a cash payment in advance or a credit card imprint to shield them against the risk of a customer checking out without paying.
- **A revolving credit facility.** This provides customers with a credit line with a preset limit that they can draw down against without having to seek specific approval. The cardholder is not required to pay off the entire balance at the end of the statement period but has to make a minimum payment generally defined as a percentage of the outstanding balance.

Many banks now offer debit cards. These cards provide the first two of the above functions. The major difference is that they are linked to the customer's bank account and this is debited at the time of payment. They are either issued under the Visa or MasterCard brand using their network services or under a country-specific brand. These are more common than credit cards in some countries, particularly those where there have been regulatory restrictions on the issue of credit cards to customers. In some countries, for example, credit cards can only be issued to customers meeting minimum income requirements specified by regulatory authorities.

SUPPLEMENTARY FEATURES

As the industry has developed the number of supplementary features available has increased sharply. This has been accelerated by two factors:

- **Competition.** Issuers are competing with each other for customers. Supplementary features provide them with a way to compete which is not simply based on the annual fee charged or interest rate applicable.
- **Market segmentation.** By providing a number of different branded cards with different pricing structures and features issuers can segment the market more effectively. A basic mass-market card may have a low, or no, annual fee and high interest rate. A premier card may have a high fee, low interest rate and offer many supplementary features.

Examples of supplementary features include the following:

- **Insurance.** A traveler paying for an airline ticket with a particular card automatically receives some form of travel insurance. These policies can provide cover for cancellation, medical expenses, loss of life, lost luggage, travel delays and so on.
- **Discounts.** Suppliers make agreements with issuers to offer discounts to customers paying with a particular card. In return the issuers give the supplier a rebate in the form of free advertising.
- **Loyalty schemes.** "Air Miles" are one of the earliest examples of loyalty schemes. These were originally devised as a means to lock frequent flyers into using a particular airline or group of airlines. Credit card issuers offer the equivalent by offering "points" based on the value of transactions charged on a card. These points may be exchanged for the waiver of any annual fee, a cash rebate, free gifts and other promotional items and in some cases can be transferred to airline frequent flyers programs.
- **A lower rate credit line.** American Express is better known as a charge card operator than as a credit card issuer. In addition to a number of other supplementary features some of these cards are linked to a bank account with a pre-approved overdraft limit and with an interest rate below that charged on most credit cards.

Market Segmentation

The basic rationale for this segmentation is based on issuers' knowledge that the demands of customers in the mass-market and mass-affluent (premium) segments are different:

- **Mass-market.** Mass-market customers are generally price sensitive in terms of annual fees but relatively ignorant about the real level of interest being charged on their rollover balances. Rollover rates on mass-market cards are usually high while transaction values, otherwise referred to as billings, are relatively low.
- **Mass-affluent.** Mass-affluent customers are less price sensitive to annual fees than mass-market customers and more concerned about the status attached to a particular card and the level of credit limit granted. The latter is important, as the costs associated with international travel in particular can be very substantial. Anyone who has experienced having their card rejected when presented as a payment means knows how embarrassing this is, and how dangerous this can be if this happens in a country that is thousands of miles from their home. Issuers require holder of various cards to have a certain minimum income level. Someone paying with a gold credit card is indirectly making a statement about her income level.

Billings on mass-affluent cards are generally high, particularly for people using cards to pay for business trips. Rollover rates are generally much lower than on mass-market cards, however, with many holders using them primarily as charge cards and paying off the full outstanding balance each month.

By segmenting the market credit card issuers seek to extract the maximum profit possible from each segment.

Key Participants

The key players in the business include the following:

- **Network/brand operators.** Visa and MasterCard operate the two largest international networks on behalf of their members. Both organizations have been subject to legal action and regulatory investigation concerning the extent to which they provide and charge for these services constitutes an anti-competitive practice. They do not issue credit cards as such nor do they manage or finance credit card receivables.
- **Issuers.** In the early days most issuers were banks but over time the number of non-bank institutions issuing credit cards has risen sharply. A small number of these issuers manage their own credit card business and finance the receivables. Many other cards, commonly called affinity cards, are issued in the name of a particular organization or association with a large membership base but the business is actually run by a bank. The association is able to negotiate better terms for its members in terms of pricing and supplementary features. The bank gains the benefit of a relatively cheap method of origination.
- **Merchants.** The term "merchant" is used for all of the organizations that accept payment by credit card. These include retail outlets, hotels, airlines, travel agents, and restaurants. The list goes on. Today most enterprises that sell products or services to retail customers accept credit cards. The explosive growth of the number of companies operating through the Internet has made the ability to pay by credit card even more important.

  In countries such as China, where the banking, clearing and payment systems are relatively undeveloped, many companies use credit cards to pay suppliers.
- **Merchant processing banks.** These are the banks that process the payments made to a merchant. They ensure that the funds are remitted to the merchant's bank account on the agreed date. In the early years when payment was made using paper slips the processing was highly manual but it is now highly automated.

  For this service the bank changes the merchant a fixed transaction fee. This fee is negotiated between the merchant and the bank. For small retailers it is often in the region of 3%–4% of the transaction value. For large retailers, such as Wal-Mart and Carrefour, with huge bargaining power, pricing is both much lower and negotiated.

The fee charged to the merchant is split three ways between the merchant processing bank, the network provider and the issuing bank.

Standard Credit Card Transaction

The following diagram shows the flows associated with a standard credit card transaction. When the entire transaction is carried out electronically the following takes place and the entire transaction normally takes between one and two seconds to complete.

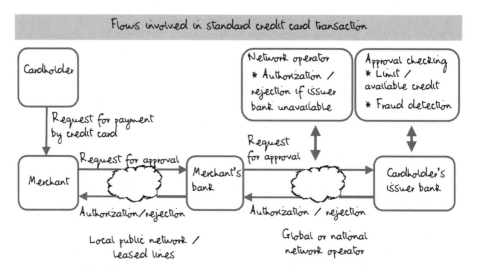

Flows involved in standard credit card transaction

- The cardholder requests to pay by credit card, presents their card which is read by the merchant's card reader and details of the card plus requested purchase amount are transmitted to the merchant's processing bank.
- The merchant's processing bank then sends a request, routed through the credit card operator's network, to the cardholder's issuer bank. This network may be a global network for cross-border transactions or one that is completely national. There will be occasions, particularly for the biggest banks in a country, when the merchant's bank and the cardholder's issuer bank are the same.
- Provided the issuer bank's systems are in operation and a network communication established, the card's details are verified and the issuer bank determines whether to authorize or reject the payment request. This involves checking the value of the transaction against the cardholder's available credit and carrying out a number of security checks intended to detect any fraud attempt. The request is then either approved or rejected. The response is then transmitted back to the merchant's bank, together with an authorization code if approval is granted.
- If for some reason the issuer bank's systems are inaccessible arrangements may have been made with the network operator to authorize approval of transactions up to some specified level. The network operator will then act on behalf of the issuer.
- The merchant then receives the authorization response or rejection. The cardholder signs and given a paper copy of the transaction details. The transaction is then completed.

If a merchant does not have a card reader or the equipment to send the request for authorization electronically they normally have to seek authorization by making a telephone call to their processing bank. The resulting sales drafts are the only record of the transaction having taken place and the merchant bank arranges for these to be collected, or they are delivered to the bank's processing center, at the end of each day.

Merchant Payment

At the end of the business day the merchant's processing bank takes all of the collected sales drafts and inputs them into its system. These are then combined with those advises collected electronically during the day to produce a file, in a format defined by the credit card network operator, and transmitted to the relevant network operator.

The network operator then combines together all of the sales advices from all of the merchant processing banks. These are then sorted by issuer bank. Each transaction in a foreign currency is converted into the issuing banks' base currency. Individual files are then transmitted to each of the issuer banks.

The issuer bank then carries out basic validation checks on this data, checking that authorization codes are correct, for example, and that transactions received are not simply duplicates of others already received and processed. The issuer posts each transaction to the relevant individual cardholder's account. It also generates payment instructions for each of the merchant banks that are owed payment. These are then settled though a clearing or payment system. The system used will depend on whether the issuer and merchant banks are in the same country or not.

When the transfer has cleared the merchant's processing bank credits each of its merchants' accounts with the requisite amount, less fees due. In this way the merchant is finally paid, usually within two to three working days of the actual purchase. This fast and guaranteed method of payment goes some way towards offsetting the fees charged. Responsibility for losses due to fraud lies with the issuer bank and cardholder, if the issuer bank authorized the payment, and with the merchant if no authorization was given. At the end of the billing period the issuer bank prepares and sends a statement of transaction activity to the cardholder.

Approval Process

Credit appraisal and approval processes are highly standardized and frequently highly automated. Banks must strike a balance between the losses avoided from rejecting applications of lower quality and the income foregone as a result. If the criteria are too conservative many potentially profitable applicants will be turned away and get a card from a less conservative issuer. In most cases the approval process consists of no more than three controls:

- **Basic checks that applicant details are correct.** A recent payslip and tax return are usually required to verify income claimed. A recent utility bill in the name of the applicant is frequently used to check the applicant's address.
- **A basic search of a credit bureau's database.** Credit bureaus capture financial data from many sources in order to create credit histories for individuals. They then sell the results from this collated information on the basis of specific requests from banks or other creditors. This will identify people with a poor credit history. Ironically people who have never borrowed or had a credit card may find it harder to get their applications approved than applicants who have borrowed often and frequently been late with their payments. At least the latter have a credit history.

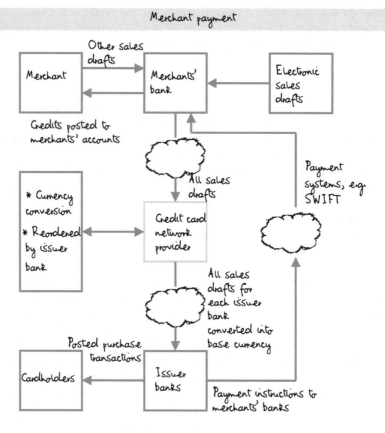

Merchant payment

There is always the risk that the data held against individuals is inaccurate, resulting in them being effectively blacklisted for new credit. Consumer advocacy groups have campaigned to give individuals the right to check the accuracy of data held on them. Legislation in most developed countries has been enacted to establish procedures to enable this to be done.

- **An in-house credit rating score.** Most banks have automated consumer credit scoring systems. These rely on the use of statistical data to determine likely risk of default. Non-quantitative factors that will be taken into amount include location, type of residence (house or apartment), rented or owned, children, and highest education qualification. An unmarried actor living in a rented apartment who dropped out of school may well be deemed a higher credit risk than a married lawyer with two children living in a townhouse she owns. This is likely to be the case even if the actor earns significantly more than the lawyer.

In the US there is a body of legislation intended to protect consumers from discrimination by prohibiting banks from making credit decisions on a number of grounds including race, gender and location. This is the exception rather than the rule. In most countries banks make such decisions with few legislative constraints.

CREDIT CARD FRAUD

Credit card fraud is a serious problem in many countries. The problems are most acute at smaller issuers operating in developing markets. The main types of fraud are:

- **Theft.** The simplest form of fraud involves simply stealing someone's card, impersonating the cardholder and faking his or her signature to make a purchase.
- **Interception.** Some fraud is carried out by interception of credit cards sent through the post to customers. This may involve an inside agent, a postal worker, for example, or may involve theft from a post box. The latter is most common in apartment blocks with communal post boxes.
- **Skimming.** Sophisticated criminal organizations operate that specialize in copying the electronic details of the credit card. When someone pays a restaurant bill it rarely occurs to him or her that while the restaurant is getting authorization a restaurant worker is copying the details of the card. Low paid service workers can find this a useful supplement to their wages, provided the risks are low. This can be done using an electronic reading device about the size of a cigarette packet.

  A more sophisticated development involves breaking into a point-of-sale device and placing a more advanced reader into the device. The reader is left in place for a period of time and then removed allowing details of all of the cards that have been used for purchases to be extracted. These details can be sent electronically anywhere in the world and then transferred to cloned cards. These cards can then be used until the skimmed cards are identified and blocked. Banks also have to cope with remote scanning devices placed in proximity to ATMs and used to attempt to obtain details of cards and related passwords used in these machines.
- **Identity theft.** Many purchases may be made over the phone or Internet and do not require the actual presentation of a physical card. Details required are simple, name as written on card, credit card number and expiry date. In its more sophisticated form this is a part of what has become known as "identity theft".
- **Merchant fraud.** The most common merchant fraud is probably carried out in shady bars in the small hours of the morning. The first indication that the cardholder has that they have been victim of fraud is when they see a $500 entry on their account statement for a bill that was actually $50.

The advent of the Internet has increased the potential for fraud. Credit card details can be stolen in bulk by stealing details from Internet retail operations with weak security. Banks have had to develop countermeasures to protect against fraud. Many issuers courier the credit card to the holder or send it by some form of registered post. Other issuers require the cardholder to come to a branch in person to collect a new card. These measures are aimed at prevention of fraud based on mail interception.

Some issuers, such as Citibank, have put photos of the holders onto the card itself. This appears to be more of a marketing gimmick than a protection against fraud. There is little evidence that this measure significantly reduces the level of losses and if it did it is reasonable to assume that other issuers would have followed suit. Retailers are supposed to verify that the signature on the card matches that made at payment time. In my experience few bother. The tipping system in the US creates a disincentive for service personnel to challenge a customer's identity before receiving their tip.

The most surprising thing is that there has been no widespread introduction of personal identification numbers (PIN) as a means to ensure that the person using the card is also the holder. Many banks have introduced this for their own cards used in ATMs. The only reasonable conclusion is that the banks collectively have decided that the costs of system and technology changes would be higher than the savings achieved from reducing fraud. At some stage there is likely to be a great leap forward in technology with the adoption of smart cards. The cost of smart cards has come down below a dollar a card and they could be used to provide many functions, such as a "wallet" of cash, that cannot be provided with the traditional swipe card. A few hundred million of these cards worldwide had been issued at the time of writing.

The very success of credit cards has made any changes in technology a major challenge and such a migration would be on a par with efforts expended by financial institutions to deal with Y2K. Simply replacing all issued cards with smart cards would cost about $2bn worldwide. This takes no account of the costs involved in either replacing or upgrading ATMs and card-reading equipment at the merchants.

Fraud Detection

Having done what they can to prevent fraud from happening in the first place, banks face the problem of detecting fraud either when it is attempted or after the event to prevent repetitions. In order to do this banks have implemented sophisticated computer systems to identify potentially suspect transactions. These rely on a combination of two factors:

- **Statistical sampling and analysis.** These systems search for unusual transaction behavior, for example a sudden increase in activity on a card that is only used infrequently, or a transaction well above usual levels.
- **Improbable events.** These systems look at multiple transactions and attempt to identify whether they are mutually incompatible. It is completely feasible that I could pay a hotel bill in London on Friday and buy an expensive camera in New York the following day. It is infeasible that someone could pay a hotel bill in Hong Kong and simultaneously buy a mobile phone in Italy. (This actually happened to me and the issuing bank caught the infeasible transactions.)

The gap between the large sophisticated issuers and those of small, inexperienced banks new to this business is illustrated with this example. I once visited a bank in Taiwan that was too small to be of interest to institutional investors but was a possible target for a bid. They had fairly recently entered the credit card business as an issuer and were very pleased with the growth in number of cards issued that they had been able to achieve. Their approach to fraud detection was breathtakingly simple. Once an hour they would print out a record of all the transactions over a certain minimum dollar value that had been automatically approved by their systems in the last hour. A handful of individuals then went through these printouts looking for any suspicious transactions. If they found one they then called the cardholder concerned to check whether the transaction was legitimate.

MANAGING REVOLVING CREDIT

Managing retail revolving credit exposures calls for different approaches than used for term or installment loans. The conditions under which a term loan is classified as non-performing can be defined quite clearly in terms of failure to meet the conditions specified in the loan agreement. The main reason why credit card bills have some form of minimum monthly payment is to provide a default type of trigger. If the outstanding balance rises above the approved limit (due largely to the effect of capitalizing unpaid interest) and the cardholder fails to make the payments necessary to take the balance back below that limit within a defined period of time this provides a second default trigger.

Credit card receivables are usually managed on a "pooled" basis from a default loss perspective. An issuer may have one or more pools based on issued card characteristics (e.g. mass-market and premium cards). Due to their large number and small individual exposures default losses can be relatively well modeled using statistical techniques. This is also true of repayment patterns and seasonality.

Many legal systems disallow personal bankruptcy proceedings on outstanding debts below a certain minimum level, well above that of most credit card holders' individual limits. Few banks actively pursue delinquent credit card accounts to the full extent allowed by the law in any case. They usually pass over delinquent accounts to specialist debt recovery agencies and write off the outstanding balance at that time. The delinquent account details would be submitted in the usual way to a credit bureau. Any subsequent recoveries would be netted against future write-offs and, again, at a pooled level, can be reasonably well anticipated.

Other Retail Loans

- **Consumer finance.** Consumer finance loans are made for a range of consumer products such as autos and white electrical products such as refrigerators. In addition to the basic checks made on applications for credit cards lenders look to get security for larger-ticket items. For auto loans, for example, the bank will seek to get physical custody of the car ownership documents. This may be more of a symbolic act than an effective control.

   The bank's possession of these documents means that the only way the borrower can sell the asset is by reporting the loss of the documents to the relevant authorities and obtaining replacement documentation. In the event of default the borrower would be liable not just to a civil action but also risk facing criminal charges for fraud. A high proportion of other consumer finance loans is unsecured.
- **Overdrafts and installment loans.** Many banks and finance companies offer overdrafts and personal installment loans that are unsecured and are not granted for a specific purpose or purchase. An overdraft is a form of revolving credit akin to that provided by a credit card. Most of these loans and facilities have lower interest rates than those charged on credit card rollover balances and many borrowers take such loans to consolidate and repay outstanding balances on their credit cards.

Exhibit: Buying a house on credit cards

Three friends of mine claim to have bought a house on credit cards. Their plan was quite simple and very deliberate. They never actually lied but they did exploit weaknesses in the system. They found their house by accident at a party where the hosts turned out to be looking to sell their house for a price of the current equivalent of $200 000. They agreed there and then to buy it provided they could raise the funds to finance the purchase.

None of them had any savings although all three had jobs. Banks would lend the equivalent of 80% of the price of a house but it was possible to get this increased to 90% by paying a premium on an insurance policy that paid out the 10% shortfall in the event of default. So they needed to raise about $30 000 between them to make the down payment required by the bank and cover legal and appraisal costs. All three of them applied for credit cards, their first applications as they had only recently left college. They could state truthfully on each application that they had no other credit cards as they applied for all of them simultaneously. Some of the applications were turned down but enough were approved to give each of them credit lines of about $10 000.

No bank would make such a housing loan to three young single men so two of them applied as a stable gay couple. The loan was immediately approved. They made the necessary cash withdrawals on their credit cards and after the usual legal process found themselves proud owners of one house. They had drawn up an agreement between themselves that basically committed all three to owning the house for a minimum of three years. After that any of the three could bring the association to an end and the house would be sold and proceeds divided three ways.

Even with three incomes they could only just make the mortgage payments. So they made no attempt to pay off the credit card debt and allowed it to build up. They made minimum payments on one card by taking a cash advance from another. From time to time they would request a higher limit on their cards. With unembellished credit records these requests were always granted. They sold the house three and a half years after they bought it. Their combined credit card debt had risen to approximately $60 000 but they sold the house for $400 000. They made $200 000 on trading the house and after paying off the credit cards that left around $140 000 in total. Each one of them walked away with more than $45 000.

Retail bankers who hear this story usually cringe. The outcome would have been very different if property prices had fallen. The three perpetrators were convinced that property prices were going to continue to rise or they would not have engineered the scheme in the first place but it also came down to the asymmetry of returns. It was close to being a one-way bet. They had little to lose. They had no assets of their own to lose. They acted in a completely rational and legal way.

- **Margin loans.** A margin loan is a loan made by both brokerages (securities companies) and banks to enable investors to buy stocks using borrowed money, or at margin. A simple example shows how this is usually structured. An investor wishes to buy $100 000 worth of stock. The lender agrees to lend the $100 000 but also requires the investor to make a $20 000 deposit with the bank. Interest is usually charged on the whole $100 000 but not earned on the deposit. If the value of the stock lent by the margin borrower falls to $90 000 the lender will make a "margin call", and require the investor to make an additional $10 000 deposit. If the investor is unable to do so, or for some reason cannot be contacted, the lender has the right to sell stock to the value of $10 000 in the market. When stock markets fall sharply many investors are likely to receive margin calls and forced selling by margin lenders adds further downward pressure on markets.

Borrowing at margin provides investors with gearing and in a rising market will enhance returns. It is a relatively-low risk business for the lenders unless markets fall sharply and liquidity dries up. The actual margin level required is frequently imposed by bank or securities' regulators.

- **Education loans.** Students (or their parents) have to meet their own day-to-day expenses while studying at college or business school. They may also have to pay tuition fees and other charges imposed by the college. Bursaries and scholarships are available for some students but many can only finance their education by taking out student loans. These loans are long term and may be made at relatively low interest rates. Governments may subsidize the costs of loans from banks or give borrowers a favorable tax treatment on interest paid on such loans.

PART III

Risk Management

The controls cycle

* Identification of requirements
* Development of controls
* The role of Treasury & capital management
* Enforcement of controls
* Review controls & requirements

Managing interest rate risk

* Duration & convexity
  - Impact of changing interest rates on asset & liability values
  - Effective duration
* Economic value
* Use of duration to manage interest rate risk - duration gap
* Interest rate derivatives
  - Forward rate agreements
  - Interest rate swaps
  - Interest rate future
* Practical issues with use of duration as tool
* Mark-to-market accounting issues
* Gap analysis
* Managing FX risk
  - Forward contracts
  - Currency swaps

Trading

* Reasons to trade
  - Spot forward, future markets
  - Current business requirements, hedging
* Arbitrage
  - Interest rate parity
  - Interest rate futures
  - Stock index future
  - Exchange
  - Options (call-put parity)
  - Holding company
* Speculation - outright positions
* Fundamental speculation
  - Equities, foreign exchange, interest & credit
* Short selling
* Reversion to mean
  - Trading volatility - advanced option strategies
* Technical analysis

Managing trading risk

* First order price risks
* Realization risks
* Model risks
* Value at risk (VaR)
* Statistical skeletons
  - Distributions, standard deviation, confidence levels, holding periods
* Portfolio diversification
  - Correlation, application to portfolio VARs
  - Portfolio examples
* Multiple variable dependency
  - Foreign currency bond, forwards
* Risk factor decomposition & aggregation
* Weaknesses of VaR approaches
* VAR conversion
  - Common holding period & confidence level

Managing credit risk

* Expected versus unexpected losses
* Default probabilities
  - Sources, cyclicality, time frame, changing conditions
* Losses in event of default
* Non-normal distributions
  - Chebyshev estimating system level losses
* Loss distributions by loan type
* Proprietary (internal) databases
  - Internal ratings, decomposition & aggregation
* Portfolio diversification
* Providing for credit losses
  - Incentives, methods, regulatory requirements
* Bad loan resolution
  - Foreclosure, liquidation, restructuring

Capital management

* Forms of capital
  - As funding source, risk, economic & regulatory capital
* Capital allocation & return measures
* Excess of regulatory capital
* Capital allocation & diversification

* The Original Basel Accord
  - Key features & exclusions
  - Unintended consequences
* The Market Risk amendment
* The New Accord – Basel II
  - External & internal ratings
* Who's afraid of the Basel Accord?

9

The Controls Cycle

There are things in your life you can control – and there are variables you can't. The more diligent you are at controlling what you can, the more influence you'll have over your destiny. You just have to figure out which are which.

Carlton Young

RISK TAKERS

Many people see banks and other financial services companies as conservative risk-averse organizations. Nothing could be further from the truth. Banks and insurance companies are in the business of managing and pricing risk. In essence they seek opportunities where the market price for accepting risk is higher than their own assessment of its likely cost. The risks that banks undertake can be looked at in many different ways:

- **Credit risk.** Credit risk is the risk that a counterparty that owes, or potentially owes, a bank money fails to meet its obligations. For most commercial banks this is the most important risk to manage and price. A triple-A US company, such as General Electric, has very different risk characteristics than a small manufacturing company in an emerging market. The challenge for banks is to determine a pricing structure for their products that is competitive but compensates for the underlying risks.
- **Interest rate risk.** Bank balance sheets are made up of a mix of fixed and floating rate assets and liabilities whose composition is continually changing over time. A bank that makes a lot of fixed rate loans, such as car loans, funded with floating rate deposits is exposed to the risk that interest rates rise. This will push up its cost of funds while the returns on its assets will remain largely unchanged.
- **Foreign currency risk.** A foreign bank that borrows US$ and lends it out in its local currency is exposed to exchange risk. The main risk here is that the US$ appreciates against the local currency leaving it with a liability that in local currency terms it is greater than the value of its matching asset.
- **Market risk.** This is the risk that the prices of financial instruments, such as equities, in which a bank has a position falls. This could result in the bank suffering unrealized losses on any open positions it has.
- **Liquidity risk.** Banks are usually funded with relatively liquid, short-term deposits which are lent out long term as loans. Loans are inherently illiquid. Companies and individuals rarely borrow unless they have a financing need. Banks face the risk that a large portion of their depositors will demand their funds back at the same time. Management has to determine the appropriate balance between holding low yield, but liquid, assets such as government securities that can be readily sold and higher yielding, but illiquid assets such as loans.
- **Settlement risk.** This is the risk that the settlement of a transaction with a counterparty fails. A bank that exchanges US$ with another bank for yen has a potential settlement risk due

to the time difference between the USA and Japan; it will deliver the US$ before it receives the equivalent in yen.

- **Model risk.** Banks use models to estimate the value of instruments such as options and to assess the level of risk that the bank is exposed to in its trading activities. These models are complex and errors in these models pose a risk to banks. They may overpay for financial instruments or underestimate the level of market or trading risk being taken.

- **Regulatory risk.** Banks are highly regulated organizations. They are at risk from regulatory and legislative changes that increase the costs of doing their business and may even prohibit them from undertaking it at all. They may breach regulatory requirements and be fined, face losing their license or suffer loss of reputation.

- **Country risk.** A US bank with operations in a foreign country is, for example, at risk from the imposition of capital controls preventing it from remitting any profits or other funds it has in that country. In extreme cases foreign banks may even have their assets appropriated.

- **Fraud.** Banks are at risk from fraud and other criminal behavior by their staff, customers and counterparties. In some cases these actions may involve actual theft but in other cases it may simply involve the concealment of losses that do not become apparent until a later date.

- **Judicial and legal risk.** Financial contracts are frequently complex and banks are exposed to the risk that their understanding of an agreement differs from that of a court. Legal disputes between American commercial banks and a number of insurance companies on credit derivative contracts written by the latter on failed energy trading companies around the turn of the century involved billions of dollars in disputed claims.

- **Actuarial risk.** Insurance companies sell policies that pay out in the event of death or disability. The premiums charged on these policies are based on actuarial assumptions about factors such as mortality rates. If those assumptions prove to be incorrect such policies may be loss making.

- **Operational risk.** Operational risk is a catchall category for other things that could go wrong. It includes potentially catastrophic events such as earthquakes, flooding and fire and other more mundane factors such as power, computer or telecommunications failures.

- **Pre-payment and reinvestment risk.** Reinvestment risk arises when a bank has fixed rate interest-earning assets, such as housing loans, where the borrower has the right to repay those loans early. If interest rates fall and borrowers repay their loans the bank will have to reinvest the proceeds received at the then prevailing lower rates.

- **Replacement risk.** Replacement risk arises when a bank has an obligation to one party where the discharge of that obligation is conditional on a third party meeting its obligation to the bank. For example, the bank may have sold stock to the first party. It intends to deliver this stock using stock it has bought but not yet received from a third party. If the third party fails to deliver its stock the bank will have to buy it from the market at a potentially higher price.

The most common primary cause of bank failures is insolvency arising from credit losses. This is followed by failure to manage interest rate risk and foreign exchange risk. Failures arising from fraud, market risk and liquidity risk tend to hit the headlines but are far less common than those due to these first two factors.

The Management of Risk

Risk management overlays all financial institution functions. Banks cannot generate the returns required by shareholders without accepting risk. The two key challenges for the management of banks and other financial service companies are how to manage and price that risk.

Buying the equivalent of an insurance policy can reduce many of these risks, but insurance bears a cost. Management has to balance the costs of those implicit or explicit insurance premiums against the level of protection afforded. A bank analyst has to understand enough about the techniques and tools available to make a judgment on whether management at a particular bank has the skills and infrastructure to make these decisions effectively. The starting point is to establish the organizational infrastructure for risk management. The controls cycle is made up of a number of specific steps that need to be taken:

- **Identify control requirements.** Specific control requirements may be the result of a need to correct weaknesses in existing controls or from the introduction of new products or transactions. Weaknesses in existing controls are usually identified through a review process. Well-managed banks establish procedures to break down and identify the specific risks associated with new transactions or products. Other requirements may arise from operational factors such as data center and network security and from changes in the legal or regulatory environment.

    The next step is to attempt to quantify the potential for losses from possible control failures. This step is necessary to assess how urgent the requirements are and the downside risk of delaying or not taking action. Controls do not come cheap and action has to be prioritized.

    It is possible to control losses to a bank arising from petty pilfering of the stationery cupboard but the direct costs of the controls necessary would likely be greater than the losses avoided. Horses for courses.

    For most risks this quantification requires establishing an acceptable maximum level of potential losses, a confidence level that those losses will not be exceeded and a time frame during which those potential losses could be incurred.

    This is easier to do with some risks than others. The likely credit losses arising from credit card operations can be determined relatively well given sufficient historic data. It is far harder to quantify the potential impact from operational risk that involves assessing the impact of possible, but unlikely, future events.

    Once the requirements have been identified specific actions to meet these requirements are initiated. Some of these actions are likely to be relatively minor while others may require wholesale changes to systems and procedures.

- **Develop and implement controls.** Having identified and quantified business risks, banks need to amend or put into place systems to control those risks. These systems will usually be a combination of automated and manual systems. Most control systems use a method of checks and balances and define a clear division of responsibilities. A trivial, but familiar, example is that individuals at most companies are not usually allowed to sign off their own expense claims.

    Credit risk, for example, can be managed by setting limits on exposures to companies, business sectors, geographical regions and countries. Positions and individuals within a bank will need to be identified and given the power to set limits up to a defined level. Those limits must be captured and incorporated into systems to ensure that lending officers and other individuals are prevented from taking action that results in these limits being breached.

The way in which banks are organized is also important. In trading operations there has to be a clear distinction between the people making the trades and those accounting for and reporting the results of those trades. Designing and building integrated global systems that incorporate these controls requires great skill but this is only generally acknowledged in the event of failure.

- **Enforce compliance.** Day-to-day compliance is the responsibility of line management supported by their control systems. Some systems will identify transactions that break no controls but meet certain criteria for manual investigation.
- **Review existing controls.** Risk management is an ongoing process with no real start or end. Existing systems and controls may be reviewed on an ad-hoc basis, on a scheduled regular basis (a full external audit is normally undertaken at least once a year and may be done on a semi-annual basis). Most financial institutions will also be subject to on-site examination by the relevant supervisory authorities.

One of the results of the review process is to identify control weaknesses in existing systems and these then feed through into control requirements. The following diagram provides a visual representation of the controls cycle.

Controls cycle

Identify control requirements
* Weaknesses in current controls
* Requirements from new products
* Infrastructure requirements - data centers, networks, physical security
* Legal and regulatory requirements and changes
* Initiation of projects to meet requirements

Develop & implement controls
* Automated & manual systems
* Checks and balances
* Clear division of responsibilities
* Documented authorization procedures
* Service level agreements
* Establishment of approval committees

Review compliance with existing controls
* Internal audit
* Compliance departments
* External audit process
* On-site supervisory examination
* Identify weaknesses in current controls

Enforce compliance
* In-built system features (e.g. input and authorization screen access controlled)
* Trigger alarm levels
* Clear separation between recommended action & authorization
* Line management responsibility

TREASURY

Treasury lies at the very heart of any bank. Asset liability management (ALM) is one of the most important functions of commercial banks given their extremely high gearing. All banks have an asset liability committee, frequently referred to as an ALCO, responsible for asset liability management. Its major responsibilities are to manage the following four risks:

- **Interest rate risk.** All banks are exposed to interest rate risk. Interest rates may rise or fall. The shift in rates may be parallel or non-parallel. These shifts will have a direct impact on the economic value of a bank's assets and liabilities. Treasury is responsible for managing this risk. A wide range of financial derivatives has evolved that help banks manage these risks.
- **Foreign exchange risk.** International banks take deposits and make loans in many different currencies. They also actively trade currencies on their own behalf and for their customers. This can create risks that the bank's position will be negatively affected by changes in foreign exchange (FX) rates between currencies.
- **Market risk.** Treasuries of major banks take positions in many different instruments in order to manage the preceding three risks and to try to profit from market movements. This leaves them exposed to market risk.
- **Liquidity risk.** Banks are also exposed to liquidity risk. This is the risk arising from depositors unexpectedly seeking to withdraw their funds from the bank. A bank can fail if it is unable to liquidate assets to meet these withdrawal demands.

We have already examined the issues associated with the management of liquidity risk in Chapter 4 "Deposit taking and other funding". We will look at the management of interest rate and foreign exchange risk in the next chapter. We will examine methods used to manage market risk in Chapter 12 "Managing market risk"

Commercial banks operate in the money markets, the bond and equity markets, the foreign currency markets and buy and sell derivatives for the underlying instruments in all of these markets. Treasurers also need to take into account expected and unanticipated new deposits and withdrawals, and drawdown and repayments on loans.

They are also constrained by regulatory requirements on capital adequacy and reserve deposits. Banks unable to meet reserve requirements may buy Repos, borrow from other commercial banks or borrow from the central bank through its discount window.

The following diagram provides an overview of a typical commercial bank's Treasury interactions with other markets, other divisions of the bank and the central bank. It illustrates the complexity involved in managing a bank's Treasury operations. The diagram does not include one-on-one interactions between Treasury and bank customers and other banks.

The role of equity at a bank differs from that of equity at a non-financial company. Capital is maintained to be able to absorb a certain level of losses without causing the bank to fail. The level required then comes out of the whole risk assessment and control process. The function of capital management may reside within Treasury or be carried out by a specialist capital management group. We will address these issues in Chapter 14 "Capital management".

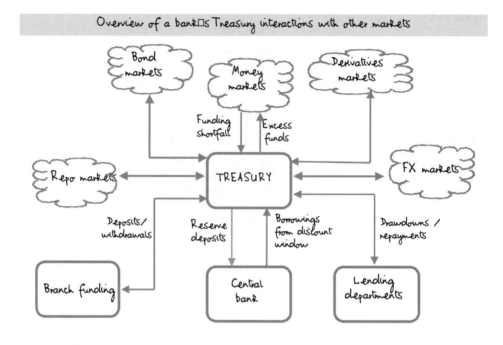

Overview of a bank's Treasury interactions with other markets

Treasury Professionals

The professionals who work in Treasury tend to fall into one of three broad groups:

- **Specialists with a very short time horizon.** These include spot FX and floor traders. Some of these trades are executed on behalf of customers. Banks generate income through a bid–offer spread or a standard transaction charge. Some of these traders are acting in a proprietary capacity, using the banks' capital to trade in large amounts on very small changes in prices between different rates. Others are, on a commission basis, responsible for the execution of customers' orders.

    Management imposes limits of the size of traders' open positions and many traders are required to have a flat or closed position by business close. We will look at this more closely in Chapter 12 "Managing market risk".
- **Specialists with a long time horizon.** Individuals whose job is not to spot potential short-term pricing arbitrages but to identify longer-term trends such as whether interest rates will go up or down over the next 12 months or whether the yen will strengthen against the US$.
- **Professional managers.** Individuals whose job it is to manage these specialists, put in place control systems to shield the bank from unexpected losses and take action to position the bank to either take advantage of forecast long-term trends or to minimize earnings volatility whatever the change in interest or exchange rates.

The economists and strategists are the people to talk with when you want a view on what is likely to happen in the world economy and to exchange rates over the next 12 months. These people are usually highly educated, with master's degrees and doctorates very much the norm. The traders rely on these people for their insight into wider developments that may have an impact on the prices of instruments that they trade. It is an odd mix of street traders and cerebral academic types.

10

Managing Interest Rate and FX Risk

In theory there is no difference between theory and practice. In practice there is.
Yogi Berra. US baseball player, coach and commentator

INTEREST RATE RISK

In this chapter we are concentrating on interest rate risk, arguably second only to credit risk in importance to most banks. The value of banks' assets and liabilities are highly sensitive to changes in the level of interest rates. Forecasting shifts in yield curves accurately and with a high degree of confidence is difficult. These shifts may be parallel, but rarely are, where yields change by an equal amount at all maturities or non-parallel. If bank asset liability management were a simple matter then people working in Treasury would get paid a lot less. There are three methods available and used for the assessment of interest rate risk:

- **Duration matching.** Duration matching involves analyzing the price sensitivity of assets and liabilities to changing interest rates. We will focus on the techniques associated with duration matching.
- **Gap analysis.** Gap analysis is essentially a method based on placing assets and liabilities into one of a number of different "time buckets" determined by when they are due to be repriced.
- **Sensitivity analysis.** This method involves subjecting a portfolio to a wide range of possible changes in interest rates and assessing the potential impact of each scenario. Management has to assign a probability to each scenario.

None of these methods is without its problems. One of the fundamental issues faced is that of balancing a perceived need to maintain stable reported earnings with maximizing economic value. In practice management at most commercial banks prioritize earnings stability.

We looked at the methods used to value bonds and other securities at a given discount rate in Chapter 2. In this chapter we focus on the change in instrument values due to changes in those discount rates or yields.

PRICE SENSITIVITY TO YIELD CHANGES

Duration

To assess how changing yields will affect the price (value) of a bond portfolio we need to be able to calculate the percentage price change of the portfolio for a given yield change, usually measured in basis or percentage points.

To a first approximation, the percentage change in price of a bond for a given change in yield, ΔY, is given by the following equation. D represents a factor referred to as duration (this is formally defined as modified duration but we will ignore this historical complication for the moment):

$$\frac{\Delta P}{P} = -D \times \Delta Y$$

Duration is simply a measure of the slope of the bond's price against yield and is measured in units of years. (For a formal derivation of duration refer to the relevant primer at the back of this book.) Duration is longer, all other factors remaining constant, when the following apply:

- **Lower the coupon rate.** The greater the weighting of cashflows further into the future the greater the impact of changing yields on price. For a coupon bond this means that the lower its coupon rate the greater the duration and hence price volatility relative to yields. A zero coupon bond will always have a greater duration than a coupon bond with the same maturity.
- **Longer the maturity.** It follows from the above that the longer the maturity the greater the duration. Pushing out the terminal value in time adds to volatility.
- **Lower the yield.** The rate of change of price for a zero coupon or coupon bond increases as yields fall.

Take a zero coupon bond with a face value of $10 000 that matures in 10 years and has a current market price of $5084 and yield-to-maturity of 7%. Its duration at this yield is 9.35 years. Using duration to estimate the change in price when yields rise to 8% we get the following:

Change in price if rates rise to 8% $= -9.3458 \times \$5084 \times 0.01 = -\$475.1$

This suggests that the price of the bond should fall to $4608.9. As already mentioned using duration gives only a first approximation of the price change and the bond should actually trade at $4631.9.

Repeating the exercise for the case where yields fall to 6% we get the following:

Change in price if rates fall to 6% $= -9.3458 \times \$5084 \times (-0.01) = +\$475.1$

Note the change in sign. Using duration alone suggests that the bond's price should rise to $5559.1. (It should in fact trade at $5583.9.)

The price derived by using duration alone will always be lower than the actual price. This is because simply taking the account of the rate of change of price at a single point only works for very small changes in yields. It takes no account of the curvature of the price-versus-yield graph. This results in an approximation error as shown in the following chart. Using duration alone to estimate the change in the value of our portfolio would give a value of P_1 while the actual value calculated using the present value formula is P_2.

The second chart shows the rate of change of duration with yield, this shows that the rate of change gets larger as yields fall.

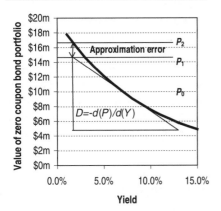

Bond portfolio price versus yield

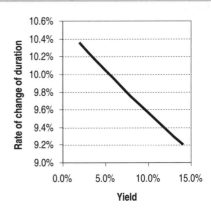

Rate of change of duration versus yield

Convexity

The effect of curvature is taken into account by adding a second term to our equation where *C* is a factor defined as convexity which measures the rate of change of duration against yield:

$$\frac{\Delta P}{P} = -D \times \Delta Y + \frac{1}{2} \times C \times (\Delta Y)^2$$

Taking our zero coupon bond example, its convexity is 96.1. Plugging this into our equation we can calculate that the impact of convexity on the change in bond price of a 100 basis point change in yields is $24.4:

$$\frac{1}{2} \times 96.1 \times \$5084 \times (0.01)^2 = \$24.4$$

Taking both duration and convexity into account gives a result that is very close to the bond's theoretical price.

	Duration	Convexity	Bond price given by duration alone	Bond price given by duration plus convexity	Actual bond price
At 6%			5559.1	5583.5	5583.9
At 7%	9.3458	96.1			5083.5
At 8%			4608.9	4633.3	4631.9

Bond price given by duration and convexity versus actual prices ($)

It should be clear from the above that given a choice between two bonds with the same duration it is preferable to own the bond with the higher convexity as its value will rise more when yields fall and drop less when yields increase.

In broad terms convexity is a "good" thing and bond portfolio managers are likely to be prepared to accept a lower yield in return for additional convexity, particularly when interest rate volatility is high. It is rare to find a financial attribute that gives greater upside potential but also provides greater downside protection.

To wrap up on convexity, this is greatest when the following apply:

- **Yields are low.** Convexity increases as yields fall. As rates increase convexity falls.
- **Lower the coupon rate.** Convexity will be greater for bonds with a given yield and maturity the lower the coupon rate. This implies that zero coupon bonds have greater convexity than coupon bonds of the same maturity. However, for bonds with a given yield and duration, the lower the coupon rate the lower the convexity.
- **Greater the dispersion of cashflows.** Bond portfolios may have identical duration but very different convexities. The following diagram shows the structure of the cashflows of three model portfolios. One contains a single bullet (zero coupon) bond, the second contains a combination of bonds with short duration and bonds with duration longer than that of the bullet (this is descriptively referred to as a barbell portfolio) and the third has a collection of bonds with evenly spaced duration.

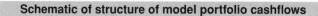

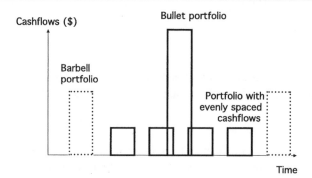

All three portfolios have the same duration but the bullet portfolio will have the least convexity and the barbell the greatest.

ECONOMIC VALUE

Market Value of Assets less Liabilities

There are four ways in which to specify the "value" of a bank, its reported book (accounting), its exchange traded value as a listed, going concern, its estimated intrinsic value based on the present value of its discounted future cashflows and its economic value. The economic value (EV) of a bank is given by the market value of its assets less the market value of its liabilities. It is hence a snapshot in time and takes no account of future earnings resulting from growth:

$$EV = PV_A - PV_L$$

The change in the economic value of a bank is given by the change in the market value of its assets less the change in the market value of its liabilities.

$$\Delta(EV) = \Delta(PV_A) - \Delta(PV_L)$$

Now if the change in market values is solely due to parallel shifts in interest rates we know that the change in the values of its assets and liabilities is given by their duration multiplied by their starting value, to a first approximation:

$$\Delta(EV) = D_A \times PV_A \times \Delta Y - D_L \times PV_L \times \Delta Y$$

Suppose we have a bank with a balance sheet where the present value of its assets is $100bn and the present value of its liabilities is $95bn. The economic value of the bank at current interest rate levels is therefore $5bn.

The duration of its assets is four years and their convexity 50. The duration of its liabilities is three years and their convexity 100. If interest rates rise by 100 bpts then the value of its assets and liabilities will both decline, as shown below:

Value of assets:

$$= +\$100bn + (-.01 \times 4 \times \$100bn) + (0.5 \times 50 \times (0.01)^2 \times \$100bn) = \$96.25bn$$

Value of liabilities:

$$= +\$95bn + (-.01 \times 3 \times \$95bn) + (0.5 \times 100 \times (0.01)^2 \times \$95bn) = \$92.625bn$$

The bank's economic value will fall to $3.625bn:

$$\$96.25bn - \$92.625bn = \$3.625bn$$

If interest rates fall by 100 bpts then the value of its assets and liabilities will both increase, as shown below:

Value of assets:

$$= +\$100bn + (.01 \times 4 \times \$100bn) + (0.5 \times 50 \times 0.01^2 \times \$100bn) = \$104.25bn$$

Value of liabilities:

$$= +\$95bn + (-.01 \times 3 \times \$95bn) + (0.5 \times 100 \times 0.01^2 \times \$95bn) = \$98.325bn$$

The bank's economic value will rise to $5.925bn. The increase in the value of the bank for a 100 bpt drop in interest rates is less than the fall in its value for a 100 bpt increase in rates and this is due to the lower duration and higher level of convexity of its liabilities compared with its assets:

$$\$104.25bn - \$98.325bn = \$5.925bn$$

USING DURATION TO MANAGE INTEREST RATE RISK

We have already examined how changes in yields will affect a bank's economic value:

$$\Delta(EV) = D_A \times PV_A \times \Delta Y - D_L \times PV_L \times \Delta Y$$

Dividing through by PV_A we get:

$$\frac{\Delta(EV)}{PV_A} = \left(D_A - \frac{PV_L}{PV_A} D_L \right) \Delta Y$$

This gives an approximate measure of the volatility of the economic value of the bank's balance sheet and is called the "duration gap". A bank can choose to shield itself from small parallel shifts in interest rates by using derivatives to adjust the duration of its assets and liabilities such that:

$$D_A \cong \frac{PV_L}{PV_A} \times D_L$$

The larger the duration gap the more exposed a bank is to interest rate risk. If a bank seeks to position itself for falling interest rates it will lengthen the duration of its assets or shorten the duration of its liabilities.

EMBEDDED OPTIONS – EFFECTIVE DURATION

Callable and Putable Bonds

We looked at callable and putable bonds in Chapter 2 "Introduction to securities valuations". A callable bond gives the issuer of a bond an option to call, or redeem, a bond before its formal term. A putable bond allows the holder of the bond to sell it back to the issuer before term. We can express the value of these two types of bond in the following way:

Value of callable bond = Value of equivalent straight bond − Value of call option
Value of putable bond = Value of equivalent straight bond + Value of put option

Callable bonds are affected by what is called negative convexity. In the example illustrated in the following diagram the bond has been issued with a call price of $10 000. As yields fall and the price starts to approach the call price the price–yield curve flattens. The reason for this is simple. If yields fall further the issuer is likely to call in the bond in which case holders will only receive $10 000.

This situation is reversed with putable bonds. If prices of an equivalent straight bond fall below the put price the price of the putable bond will remain at the put price as the holder has the right to sell the bond back to the issuer at this price.

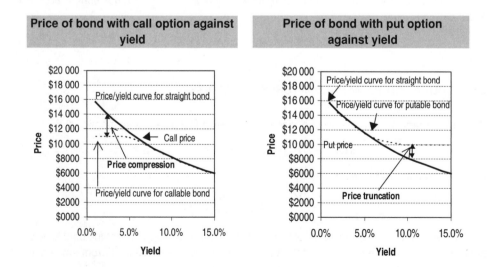

This truncation effect occurs with callable bonds because the bond's price–yield curve has negative convexity as the price approaches the call price. The holders of callable bonds are exposed to two interest rate related risks:

- **Reinvestment risk.** If the issuer calls the bond it is likely to be because interest rates have fallen. The owner of the bond is exposed to reinvestment risk because it will receive lower returns when it reinvests the cash paid out by the issuer to redeem the bonds.
- **Price compression.** The second factor is that, as interest rates fall, the market will increasingly price in the expectation that the issuer will call in the bond at the specified price. As a result the price of the bond will not increase as interest rates fall but will be truncated and tend towards the call price.

The value of the call option will rise when interest rates are falling (price of underlying instrument is rising) and when interest rate volatility increases (more volatile price of underlying instrument). The issuers of putable bonds are exposed to:

- **Refinancing risk.** If the owners of bonds decide to sell the bond back to the issuer it is likely to be because interest rates have increased. (Another reason why bondholders might choose to put the bonds back is because they doubt the ability of the issuer to repay the principal at maturity.) The issuer is exposed to the risk that they will have to refinance the debt at a higher financing cost. The issuer is also exposed to the risk that it can not refinance the debt and will be unable to meet its obligations.

  In this case the issuer of the bond has sold a put option to the buyer of the bond. The value of the underlying instrument will fall as interest rates rise increasing the value of the put option.

The duration to be used for assets and liabilities with embedded options has to be adjusted to take account of their presence. The duration then estimated is referred to as effective duration.

BANK EXPOSURES TO NEGATIVE CONVEXITY

Many bank assets and liabilities have embedded options and can usefully be looked at in terms of callable and putable bonds:

- **Callable bond equivalents.** When a bank makes a loan this is equivalent to the borrower issuing a bond. Many loans allow the borrower the option to repay its loan before term. This is equivalent to the borrower owning a call option. Many people complain when they decide to repay a loan early about the bank charging them a penalty fee. To them it seems grossly unfair. Penalty charges are completely understandable. The bank wishes to discourage early repayment and also has to be compensated for the value of the option it has written to the borrower.

  The most obvious example of prepayment risks is that of fixed rate mortgages. These loans are long term and hence have long duration. When interest rates fall borrowers have a potential incentive to pay off their current loan and refinance it with a loan at the then prevailing lower interest rates. They are *likely* to do so when the savings from lower financing costs are greater than the costs of refinancing. We will look in more detail at mortgage prepayment risks in Chapter 17 "Securitization".

- **Putable bond equivalents.** Banks have to differentiate between legal and economic duration. Most banks will allow early withdrawal of time deposits but impose a penalty charge. Many short-term deposits in the form of demand and savings deposits have legal terms that are much shorter than their economic term. Many savings type deposits offer a fixed rate of return (or only change the rate infrequently). In the event of a modest increase in interest rates most depositors will leave these funds in their savings accounts. As rates rise, however, there is a shift away from demand and savings type deposits into term deposits offering higher rates. This alters the economic duration of such liabilities.

PRACTICAL ISSUES OF USING EFFECTIVE DURATION TO MANAGE INTEREST RATE RISK

There are a number of practical issues with using effective duration to manage interest rate risk, however:

- **Calculation and modeling complexity.** Calculating the effective duration of all of a bank's assets and liabilities is not a trivial exercise. As we have seen many of these assets and liabilities contain embedded options.

  Bond markets can be reasonably certain that an issuer able to refinance its debt will exercise its call option if it is deep in-the-money. This is not the case for many bank assets and liabilities that contain embedded options, such as fixed rate mortgages and time deposits, where it is more a matter of probabilities and many of these options will not in fact be exercised even though they are in-the-money. Estimating effective economic duration requires the use of sophisticated modeling techniques.
- **Rebalancing.** A portfolio's duration will change over time. It is therefore necessary to continually rebalance the balance sheet to maintain a target duration gap.
- **Large shifts.** Using modified duration to assess the change in value of assets and liabilities for changing interest rates is only effective for relatively small changes in interest rates. In a volatile interest rate environment where there are extreme swings in interest rates, convexity and the impact of embedded options will play a greater role.
- **Non-parallel shifts.** This theoretical framework assumes parallel shifts in interest rates across the yield curve and, as we have seen, in the real world these are the exception rather than the rule.
- **Credit spreads.** The use of duration as a measure of interest rate risk implicitly assumes that there is no relationship between credit spreads and the level of risk-free rates. In fact it ignores credit spreads completely. In a stable interest rate environment, but where credit spreads are widening, the use of duration as a measure of changing economic value will tend to overstate the value of a bank's assets and hence its economic value.
- **Basis spreads.** Not all floating rate assets and liabilities are priced off risk-free rates and benchmark rates may not move in line with risk-free rates leading to changes in basis spreads.
- **Timing.** Not all floating rate bank assets and liabilities will reprice at the same time. This further complicates analysis of the impact of shifts in risk-free rates.

- **Management discretion.** The rates for many assets and liabilities are set by the bank itself taking into account a number of factors of which changing risk-free yields is just one. In general they will, for example, seek to cut deposit rates faster than lending rates when interest rates are falling.
- **Depth of derivative markets.** In many developing markets the range of derivative products available to hedge interest rate risks is limited. A bank treasurer may know what he or she should do to control interest rate risk but be unable to position the bank accordingly because of the immaturity and lack of depth of the domestic financial markets.

USE OF INTEREST RATE DERIVATIVES

There is now a wide range of interest rate derivatives available in most developed markets. These derivatives provide bank treasuries with tools to change their exposure to shifts in interest rates without having to act to change the composition of the banks' balance sheet directly. The latter is difficult to achieve quickly and efficiently in practice.

Derivatives are not recorded on the bank's balance sheet and are hence described as "off-balance sheet". Over the years most regulators have acted to force greater disclosure of these off-balance sheet items and their related exposures.

Banks have resisted this trend to greater transparency arguing that by providing more information they risk giving commercially sensitive information to competitors that will be able to exploit perceived weaknesses in balance sheet structure at an individual bank. There is little merit to this argument.

We now need to look at some of these derivatives in order to show how a bank can use them to adjust its exposure to shifts in the yield curve.

Forward Rate Agreements (FRAs)

A forward rate agreement is a contract, based on a notional principal, between two parties to exchange interest at some defined future date based on the difference between two different benchmark rates. These benchmark rates may be floating, such as an interbank rate, or fixed.

It is easiest to explain most of these derivatives using diagrams. The following example of a 90-day FRA assumes a notional principal of $100m. One part of the agreement is based on payment at a fixed 12% annual rate. The other part is based on LIBOR + 4% (LIBOR is the rate at which credit-worthy banks lend to one another and stands for the London Inter Bank Offer Rate). For our example we will assume LIBOR currently stands at 8%.

Let us assume that on the settlement date LIBOR has risen to 12%. On this day both parties calculate how much each owes the other. The floating rate payer owes the fixed rate payer $4m while the fixed rate payer owes the floating rate payer $3m. These are simply netted and the floating rate payer pays the resulting $1m to the fixed rate payer. If interest rates had fallen the payment would be in the opposite direction.

There is no exchange of principal, a FRA is simply a contractual agreement.

In this example we have used a fixed/floating FRA but the range of possible benchmarks is much wider. A floating/floating FRA could be based on yields at different maturities on the yield curve, 90-day LIBOR rates versus five-year government bond yields for example. FRAs are highly standardized contracts and have been successful for two principal reasons:

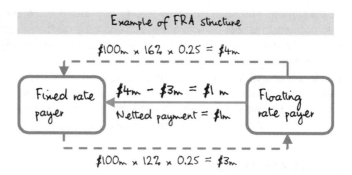

Example of FRA structure

- **Flexibility.** Because FRAs represent single netted payment transactions they provide huge flexibility to treasurers.
- **Comparative advantage.** One party may have a relative cost advantage at borrowing floating rate but require fixed rate funding. The other may have the opposite position.

Interest Rate Swaps

Interest rate swaps are simply a form of multiple period FRAs. The term of the agreements may be a matter of many months or even years. As is the case with FRAs there is no exchange of principal. The following diagram represents the cashflows over time for a 10-year floating–fixed swap, nominal principal of $100m with settlement every 30 days (the equivalent of 120 FRAs), where the fixed rate payer pays at an annual rate of 6% and the floating rate payer pays LIBOR plus 150 bpts.

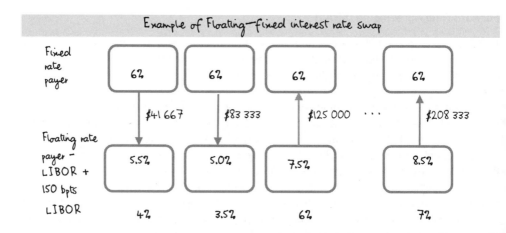

Example of Floating–fixed interest rate swap

The netting effect disguises the true nature of this transaction. The duration of an asset or liability that is repriced against market rates on a frequent basis is close to zero. That is not the case for a fixed rate asset or liability. In fact the fixed rate payer has effectively shortened duration while the floating rate receiver has lengthened it.

An international swaps dealers association is largely responsible for having established standardized international swap agreements. One of the early legal challenges was to come up

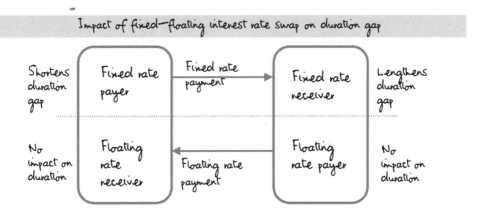

Impact of fixed—floating interest rate swap on duration gap

with a structure where in the event of one party breaching a swap agreement on which it is due to make payments the other party is under no obligation to continue to make payments on other swap contracts. This reduces the potential exposures of both participants in the event of either party becoming bankrupt. In entering into swap agreements banks are potentially exposed to credit risk. For swap contracts where the bank is a net payer there is clearly no credit risk. Credit risk only arises on contracts where the bank is a net receiver.

FINANCIAL FUTURES

Futures represent a contractual agreement to buy or sell a financial instrument or commodity at a fixed price on a fixed future date. Futures differ from forward contracts in that they are traded on an exchange while forwards are contracts between two parties. A crucial difference between an option and a future contract is that returns for the participants of futures contracts are symmetric.

These are contracts to buy or sell interest-earning assets, at a predefined level of interest rate at a future date. In most cases these assets take the form of government securities. There are two types of US$ futures contract, Treasury-bill (T-bill) futures and Eurodollar futures. T-bill futures provide a contract to buy short-term US government paper while Eurodollar futures are based on short-term time interbank deposit rates. When interest rates fall the value of interest rate futures contracts rises.

I shall use an example based on our 15-year government bond, currently trading at $7453 and a 90-day futures contract priced at $7500. If we buy the contract then in three months' time we are committed to buying the bond at that price.

If the bond's price is $7500 (including accrued coupon payment) then neither the seller nor the buyer of the contract will make any profit or loss. If, however, the price of the bond is above that of the futures price the buyer of the contract will make a profit and the seller a matching loss. If, on the other hand, the price of the bond falls then the situation is reversed. The seller will make a profit and the buyer a loss.

The second chart shows how the holder of such a bond can fully hedge their position against changes in yields by selling a futures contract on the bond. The gains (losses) on the bond are exactly compensated by the losses (gains) on the futures contract.

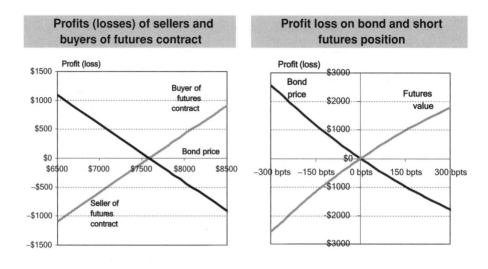

The symmetry of returns means that no premium is involved. Both parties are, however, potentially exposed to counterparty risk. At the end of each day each members' contracts are marked to market. Where a member's net position is at a loss they are required to make a matching deposit with the exchange to cover those potential losses. Exchange members are also required to contribute to an exchange fidelity, or insurance fund, to further reduce risk.

It is worth noting that no cash payments are involved even if interest rates rise and we have a loss on our futures contract. This is because the bond can be used to meet the margin requirement. Futures contracts do not exist for all issues or for all maturities. If this is the case a close equivalent has to be used. This will result in a partial hedge.

When interest rates fall the value of interest rate futures contracts rises. The buyers of interest rate futures contracts effectively lengthen net duration while the sellers shorten duration.

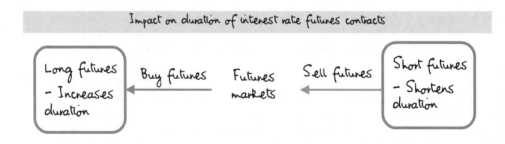

The actual mechanisms involved in futures trading are quite complex. Contracts are standardized and are often based on notional instruments and settle on common dates in much the same way as exchange-traded options. Members settle with the exchange rather than with each other. Other futures contracts include the following:

- **Index and stock futures.** These are contracts based on an index, such as the S&P 500, or individual stocks. An investor holding a portfolio of equities may sell index futures in order to hedge against a falling market. When equity prices fall the value of the short futures position rises and this can offset the losses on the individual holdings.
- **Commodity futures.** These are standardized contracts based on an underlying commodity. These include metals (gold, silver, copper, tin etc.), agricultural products (pork bellies, orange juice, flour, coffee etc.) and energy (oil, gas, coal, electricity etc.). Futures contracts are highly standardized specifying the grade or quality of the underlying commodity

Contracts may involve physical delivery of the underlying asset but in many cases do not. In the latter case the transaction is purely financial and members settle with the exchange rather than with each other.

Speculators play an important role in futures markets. Some of these are individuals trading on their own account while others work for banks or specialist trading houses. They are important because they provide liquidity and eliminate arbitrage opportunities and these help to create an efficient market.

Other More Exotic Interest Rate Instruments

This is a relatively simple introduction to the sort of interest rate-based instruments available to both banks and corporates to enable them to manage interest rate risk. Other more exotic instruments include the following but are really beyond the scope of an introductory book such as this, and we will restrict ourselves to a brief description of each instrument without getting into any real detail:

- **Swaptions.** Swaptions give the holder the right but not the obligation to enter into a future defined swap agreement.
- **Interest rate swap futures.** These are futures contracts in which the underlying instrument is the value of a specified interest rate swap contract.
- **Basis spread contracts.** It is possible to trade futures contracts based on basis spreads, for example on the spread between two benchmark rates such as those from an interbank market and those from government bonds.
- **Bond indices futures contracts.** A relatively few standardized bond indices exist on which it is possible to trade futures contracts.
- **Caps and collars**. We examined the structure of caps and collars in Chapter 5 "Corporate lending". It is possible to create a number of different positions based on combinations of call and put options.
- **Strips and synthetic zeroes.** Investment banks can create a variety of synthetic products based on actual or notional coupon bonds. A government coupon bond can be used to create two securities. The first security entitles the holder to the coupon payments only, these securities are referred to as strips. The second makes no coupon payments but has the structure of a zero coupon bond.

The number of possible instruments is virtually limitless. The existence of actual futures contracts is largely determined by supply and demand. Futures contracts come and go as these change, some start life as over-the-counter contracts while others die a quiet death as market conditions change rendering the contract redundant.

ACCOUNTING ISSUES

Economic Value versus Reported Book Value

Economic value represents the net market value of the assets and liabilities at a moment in time. It represents the value if the assets were sold and used to buy back its liabilities assuming that their sale and repurchase have no direct impact on market prices:

Economic value = Market value of assets − Market value of liabilities

Economic value is very different from the accounting-based definition of value, where reported shareholders' funds are given by:

Shareholder funds = Book value of assets − Book value of liabilities

Under the accounting version a bank's value remains unchanged whether rates rise or fall.

There are three methods that may be used to account for securities holdings. In some countries all three methods are used depending on the security's classification:

- **Carried at cost.** Under this method the value of the security on the books is left unchanged at the acquisition price. In a rising interest rate environment this will result in a reported book value that is greater than a bank's economic value.
- **Marked-to-market – income statement.** Under this method the security is revalued at the current market price. Any unrealized gain or loss is taken through the income statement.
- **Marked-to-market – balance sheet treatment.** The security is again revalued at current market price. The unrealized gain or loss is not, however, taken through the income statement but is reflected in an additional account within shareholders' fund. This account is usually called something like "Reserve for unrealized gains or losses on securities". The loss or gain is only taken through the income statement when realized.

Accountants employed by banks, regulatory bodies or working for standards bodies have an ongoing tussle over whether, and how, to make bank accounting policies provide a realistic picture of the underlying economic value. Banks have by and large resisted moves towards market-based valuations on the grounds that this would make their reported earnings increasingly volatile and that it is difficult to determine a market price for many of their loans.

The result has been, and is likely to continue to be, an uneasy compromise that accepts implicitly that published bank accounts do not provide an accurate measure of economic value. This compromise involves the acceptance of a number of internal inconsistencies.

An example of this inconsistency would be at a bank that has both fixed rate mortgages and fixed rate bonds. There will be a negative impact on the economic value of both the mortgage loans and the bonds if interest rates rise.

In most countries banks are required to recognize the fall in the value of the bonds but will not have to recognize the fall in the value of the fixed rate mortgages.

One of the problems associated with not "marking to market" all investments is that it can provide an incentive for banks to sell investments that have a market value above their book value while retaining other instruments on which the bank has a paper loss. This will result in a book value that is inflated relative to its economic value and artificially inflate reported earnings.

Accounting Treatments Based on Intent

The accounting method used affects reported earnings, book value and the value for Tier I capital as defined in the Basel Accord. Under US GAAP banks are permitted to use both the carried-at-cost and mark-to-market methods. From an economic value perspective this is clearly nonsense. The same security held in different accounts will be valued in different ways based on intent!

A bank could have holdings in an identical bond booked in three different accounts based on "intent". If the intention is to hold the bond to maturity it is included at cost. If booked as "available-for-sale" the asset is held on the balance sheet at current market prices with unrealized gains or losses included in a reserve account within the equity account. If the bond is counted as a "trading security" the bond is marked to market with any gains or losses taken through the earnings statements. Finally, if the bank had raised finance itself by issuing its own bond with identical economic characteristics as the bond held as an asset this will be carried at cost.

The rigorous application of accounting standards results in book value numbers that are precise but have limited real meaning (although they are of consequence). Numbers that reflect economic value, by their very nature, should be approximate and based on estimates but would at least have a real significance.

Most banks have argued against compulsory mark-to-market accounting on the basis that it will result in more volatile reported earnings, book value and level of reported regulatory capital. So what? External auditors usually sign off a company's accounts with a statement along the lines of "these financial statements give a true and fair view of the state of ABC Bank as of December 31 2006 and of the profit of ABC Bank for the year then ended". If the economic reality is volatile then this should be reflected in financial statements and management should be prevented from trying to hide this fact through accounting obfuscation and obstruction.

The main criticism of those efforts that have been taken to make reported book value reflect economic value better is that they did not go far enough. The main area where there has been some progress in this direction has been in the treatment of traded securities. It is difficult, however, to see the sense of taking just selected parts of the interest rate-sensitive portion of a bank's balance sheet and marking them to market, while ignoring the much larger proportion held in loans and also non-equity liabilities such as bonds that a bank has issued.

GAP ANALYSIS

In many countries banks are required to disclose their period-end interest rate gap positions in the form of the following report. These reports show balance sheet assets and liabilities broken down by when they are next due for repricing. The effects of off-balance sheet items such as swaps are also included within the summary.

A positive interest rate gap means that more assets than liabilities are due to be repriced in a particular time interval. The following bank has a negative yield gap over the next 12 months and as such net interest margins should benefit from falling interest rates.

This would suggest that we can quantify the impact of rate changes within a specific time interval. The impact of an increase in short-term rates for a specific interval is given in general by:

$$\textit{Impact on net interest income} = \textit{Balance sheet gap for time interval} \times \Delta r$$

For the three-month or less time interval for a 100 bpt increase in rates would imply:

$$\textit{Impact on net interest income} = -(\$7500m \times 0.01) = -\$75m$$

Bank interest gap sensitivity report ($m)							
	3M or less	3–6 M	6–12 M	1–3 Y	3–5 Y	5 + years	Equity
Assets	19 500	12 500	6000	9000	6000	25 500	
Liabilities	−25 000	-8000	−4500	−5000	−4000	−23 000	−9000
Off balance sheet	−2000	−1000	−3000	2000	3000	1000	
Gap	−7500	3500	−1500	6000	5000	3500	
Cumulative gap	−7500	−4000	−5500	500	5500	9000	−9000

Concentrating on managing short-term interest rate gaps can help banks report relatively stable spreads but this may have the effect of ignoring duration gaps for assets and liabilities with long duration. This will lead to increased risks of losses in economic value.

In practice analysts do not find gap reports of much use for a number of reasons:

- They represent a snapshot in time and by the time they are released are usually well out of date. They indicate how a bank was positioning itself for changing interest rates rather than what they are now expecting. The use of the off-balance sheet instruments allows banks to adjust their gap positions in the medium and long term relatively quickly.
- They do not take any account of embedded options whether explicit as with mortgage pre-payments, or implicit options that exist in many deposits. If interest rates rise some demand deposit holders will exercise their option to withdraw their funds and redeposit them in an interest-bearing account.
- The time intervals are generally very broad and banks do not report an average repricing period. An analyst usually makes simplifying assumptions, for example that all deposits in the three to six-month time frame are repriced after four and a half months.
- Interest rates can remain stable for a protracted period but at times may change on a regular basis over a period of many months. It becomes increasingly difficult to estimate the potential impact of multiple interest rate changes on repricing.
- Rates across the yield curve do not usually change in parallel.
- Banks are not passive observers. When interest rates are falling they will try to cut borrowing rates more than they cut lending rates. Lending rates are generally relatively sticky in a falling interest rate environment.

Accounting standards, the nature of the Basel Accord, reporting requirements and the way in which markets react to earnings releases all mitigate against using economic value as the principal driver for managing interest rate risk even though it has by far the best arguments in its favor. Treasuries have a range of tools that allow them to adjust their exposure to both parallel and non-parallel shifts in the yield curve using off-balance sheet instruments. Whether they use these tools wisely is a different matter. Banks in emerging markets lack widespread access to such tools and are generally more exposed to interest rate risk.

Analysts are frequently asked how rising or falling rates are likely to impact on a bank's net interest income. Sales people and investors do not want to hear answers from analysts that start with "it's very difficult to tell" or "that's not really the important question".

So analysts always do a back of the envelope calculation to come up with some quantified explanation together with some plausible sounding qualitative reasons to support the numbers. This is relatively easy when there is an obvious price war in a particular segment where there is little that an individual bank can do in the face of industry-wide price pressures. It's much harder when one doesn't know what positions they have been taking with off-balance sheet products.

MANAGING FOREIGN EXCHANGE RATE RISK

Banks are exposed to a number of potential foreign exchange risks. Foreign exchange risks may arise as a result of cash exposures or from exposures to instruments denominated in a foreign currency. Risks arise when there is a mismatch between the value of assets it owns denominated in a foreign currency and the value of what it owes in the same currency. A mismatch may also occur as a result of payments it expects to receive, or is committed to make, in a foreign currency at a future time. The former exposures are referred to as spot positions and the latter forward positions:

- **Long.** A bank may have a long spot foreign currency position if it has foreign currency in the form of cash or owns an asset denominated in a foreign currency. It may have a long forward position if it expects to receive a future payment in a foreign currency or expects to receive an asset at a future date that is denominated in a foreign currency.
- **Short.** A bank may have a short spot foreign currency position if it owes foreign currency in the form of cash (for example, in the form of a deposit taken by a bank in a foreign currency) or a financial instrument denominated in a foreign currency. It may have a short forward position if it is committed to making a future payment in a foreign currency or to deliver an asset at a future date that is denominated in a foreign currency.

The overall spot and forward position is calculated for each foreign currency by adding up the individual spot and forward positions in that currency. It has a flat position if its assets in one currency are equal to its liabilities in both the spot and forward markets.

A US bank that has a long spot position in euros worth $100m at current exchange rates but also owes yen to the value of $100m does not have a flat position. It has a long euro position and a short yen position. If the bank also owes the equivalent of $100m in euros at current exchange rates for delivery in one month's time the bank does have a flat euro position overall even though it is long in the spot market and short in the forward (we will look at this in more detail a little later in this chapter).

Short-term Positions

When a bank has, or owes, a foreign currency it has a potential foreign exchange risk. Short-term outright exposures may arise directly from holding a foreign currency, for example. Retail customers can usually obtain relatively small amounts in cash of a major foreign currency from larger branches in major cities or at international airports. For larger amounts it is always necessary to give some notice. In the overall scheme of things these exposures are not material. Most short-term positions are due either to banks' trading operations or arise out of services provided by the bank to customers to facilitate trade financing.

A bank with an outright spot position can hedge that position by entering into a forward contract. Let us take the following case. A US bank has a cash position of ¥100bn, the current ¥:$ exchange rate is 100, 90-day annualized ¥ interest rates are 2% and 90-day annualized US interest rates are 3%. The bank can hedge its position by entering into a forward contract to sell ¥1005bn into US$ in three months' time. The current 90-day forward rate is 99.7519.

This works as follows. Our ¥ cash position will earn ¥5bn in interest over the 90 days. We can fund this by borrowing $1000m on which we will pay interest of $7.5m. When we convert the ¥1005bn at 99.7519 we will receive $1007.5m allowing us to repay our US$ loan plus interest due on the loan.

The above assumes, of course, that we can enter into a forward contract at an exchange rate of 99.7519. It turns out that given the interest rates in the two currencies this is exactly the level that the forward rate will take. This is due to the effects of arbitrage and we will look at arbitrage in detail in the following two chapters on trading and the management of market risk. In brief, arbitrage ensures that spot and forward exchange rates adjust in response to changing interest rates in the currencies concerned to ensure that no risk-free profit can be made from the following combination of transactions:

- A bank borrows in one currency,
- lends in another for a fixed term
- and enters into a forward contract to convert the proceeds from the loan back into the currency borrowed.

The bank will make a profit if the proceeds from the exercise of the forward contract are greater than the amount we borrowed to finance the transaction.

This effect whereby such profit opportunities are eliminated through arbitrage is called interest rate parity and is explained for the general case in the next chapter.

Long-term Positions

Positions that are of longer term are more often hedged through swap markets than forward markets. The structure of a foreign currency swap is very similar to that of a floating rate interest rate swap. We will take the case of a floating rate ¥1000bn five-year loan with interest paid every three months. In order to hedge the annual interest payments we would enter into a yen–dollar swap agreement with terms as follows:

- Nominal values of the contracts are ¥1000bn and $1bn.
- The amount to be paid by the yen payer is set at the current spot yen 90-day interest rate for settlement 90 days after.
- The amount to be paid by the US$ payer is set at the current US$ 90 day interest rate for payment 90–days after.

Interest rate parity ensures that the US-based bank has fully hedged the interest payments due from the loan. (This is a simplified example and in practice we would have to look more fully at the pricing basis and payment terms of the loan and take these into account.)

The following, slightly more complex, worked example is of a three-year euro–yen swap. The conditions of the two parties are as follows:

- **Nominal value.** Nominal values of the contracts are ¥500bn and €600m.
- **Payment calculation.** Interest to be calculated on a quarterly basis. Payments by the yen payer are to be based on the spot yen 90-day London interbank rate plus 150 bpts and at the spot euro LIBOR for the euro payer. On the day that the agreement starts the two payments due are calculated based on 90-day yen rates of 0.75% and euro rates of 2.25%, giving payments due of ¥281.250m and €3.375m.
- **Settlement.** Settlement is to be made 90 days after the date of calculation on a netted basis in US$. The calculated payments are converted into US$ based on the then yen:US$ spot rate of 99.50 and a euro:US$ spot rate of 1.205. The yen payment due is US$2 826 633 while that of the euro payer is $2 800 830. The yen payer pays the difference of US$25 803 to the yen receiver.

These are shown in the following diagrams.

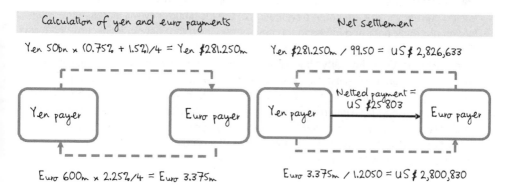

Calculation of yen and euro payments

Yen 50bn x (0.75% + 1.5%)/4 = Yen ¥281.250m

Euro 600m x 2.25%/4 = Euro 3.375m

Net settlement

Yen ¥281.250m / 99.50 = US$ 2,826,633

Netted payment = US $25 803

Euro 3.375m / 1.2050 = US $ 2,800,830

Future payments are calculated and paid in exactly the same way on a quarterly basis until the agreement ends.

The possible precise conditions of foreign currency swaps are limitless. One of many different bases may be used in the calculation. Net settlement may be in a third currency or in one of the two currencies involved in the swap. Standardized foreign currency swap agreements exist for all the major trading currencies but their volume in terms of notional principal is much lower than that of domestic currency interest rate swaps.

PRACTICAL LIMITS AND RISKS

There are practical limits on how far forward it is possible to hedge a foreign exchange exposure using forwards, futures or swaps. Banks do not usually try to hedge equity positions they hold in foreign subsidiaries where the position is effectively perpetual. This limit also depends on the depth and liquidity of the currency markets. For major currencies the practical limit is in the region of three to seven years. For exposures in minor currencies and in particular those of developing countries the ability to hedge may be very limited.

Banks in developing markets are exposed to particular risks associated with managed currency systems. When interest rates on foreign currency loans are lower than rates on local currency loans borrowers may be tempted to take out foreign currency loans. When exchange rates are floating this offers no real benefit as the borrower also takes the risk of exchange rate movements. If the borrower hedges this exposure interest rate parity ensures that there is then no benefit to the borrower of taking a foreign currency loan.

Under managed currency systems the central bank provides a form of guarantee of future rates. If the local currency is pegged against the foreign currency then banks may be tempted to borrow in the foreign currency and lend these on. Superficially at least it has a flat FX position and is not exposed to changes in exchange rates. This is a fallacy. It faces three specific risks. The first is the potential impact on its capital adequacy ratios, the second is the transformation of exchange risk into credit risk and the third its transformation into liquidity risk:

- **Impact on capital adequacy ratios.** If the foreign currency appreciates against the local currency and it is fully hedged the value of its assets and liabilities will both increase by the same amount. Its equity base, however, is in local currency terms. As the value of its foreign currency assets rises its capital adequacy ratio (in approximate terms equity divided by assets) will fall. If a bank has material levels of foreign loans and there is a sharp devaluation its capital adequacy ratio may fall below regulatory requirements.
- **Transformation into credit risk.** Although the bank is hedged its borrowers who have taken foreign currency loans are not. A devaluation of the local currency will increase the value of foreign currency debt and increase the cost of servicing that debt in local currency terms. These two effects result in a much higher risk of default.
- **Transformation into liquidity risk.** When a bank has funded foreign currency loans with short-term foreign funding it is exposed to the risk of a flight of funds. Foreign lenders to the banks may decide not roll to over their deposits to the bank when they reach term. Local borrowers with long-term foreign currency loans will not be able to repay their loans quickly. A bank may not be able to attract foreign currency deposits at all (because of credit concerns) and if it does so it may have to pay punitive rates. If it is able to pass those higher rates onto borrowers then this will further increase default risk.

11

Trading

REASONS FOR TRADING

The fundamental driver of trading is that one party has goods or services that they wish to sell and that another party wishes to buy. A trade can be made if they are brought together and can agree a price for the transaction. Markets have developed to facilitate this process. This is as true for financial products as it is for any other. The real drivers of the volume of trading in financial instruments are, however, fear and greed. Fear drives individuals, companies and financial institutions to take action to reduce or hedge risk. Greed drives the same parties to look for ways to profit from the trading activity itself.

We will start by looking at how spot markets operate and why hedging needs naturally result in the development of forward or future markets. Our main focus in this chapter will be on the nature of arbitrage transactions and their importance in influencing financial instrument prices, and how financial institutions seek to profit from trading activities. We will look at the methods used to manage the risks taken in such activities in the next chapter.

Spot, Forward and Future Markets

Companies needing to buy or sell assets immediately deal through spot markets. Spot market prices are determined by supply and demand at the time the trade is made and can be quite volatile and are generally difficult to forecast well. These transactions usually result in the exchange of an asset for a cash consideration. Settlement may take place immediately, as is usually the case in street markets, but in financial markets there is usually a short delay between the trade being agreed and its actual settlement of one or two working days.

Companies dealing through spot markets are exposed to a number of risks, in particular concerning price and the certainty of sale or purchase. The example of the farmer and the food processing company is almost always used to illustrate the nature of risks arising from relying on spot markets. At the time the farmer sows his seed he has no idea what spot prices will be at harvest time. Good weather conditions may result in a glut pushing down spot prices. The food processing company is exposed to the risk that crops fail and spot prices rise sharply. Commodity futures markets developed to allow both parties to hedge their risks without having to deal directly with the other.

Most texts stop at this stage and fail to point out that both parties are still exposed to other forms of risk. The farmer is committed to deliver at the agreed price even if his crop fails and prices rise sharply. The food company is committed to pay and take delivery even if it subsequently finds that it has no need for the raw materials.

The key difference between futures and forwards is that the former are contracts intermediated through an exchange while the latter are agreements made directly between individual parties. Futures contracts are always standardized. Futures exchange operations are designed to eliminate direct counterparty risk. They do so by requiring all exchange members to contribute to an "insurance" fund that pays out in the event of the failure of a member. In addition those holders of futures contracts that have a paper loss are required to make a cash or security deposit equal to the net sum of their losses on all contracts with the exchange on a regular basis, usually at the end of the business day. Most forward contracts are also highly standardized but usually allow for more flexibility than futures contracts. Parties are also exposed to counterparty default risk.

Many people fail to recognize that although most of their day-to-day transactions are carried out through spot markets their most important transactions are actually in the form of forwards. An itinerant Mexican farm-worker in California is far more aware of the difference between the spot and forward markets for labor than the average salaried white-collar professional. Mortgages are a form of multiple-period forward rate agreement where the borrower is either a fixed or floating rate payer.

TRADING PROFITS

A large proportion of trading activity is not performed for genuine business reasons but is down to traders and speculators whose objective is to generate short-term profits from buying low and selling high or even from selling high and buying low. Most large banks trade in a wide range of instruments. These include foreign currency (FX), bonds, stocks, interest rate instruments, commodities and derivatives. Banks provide an execution service to their customers and together with proprietary traders provide much of the liquidity and turnover necessary to allow these markets to operate efficiently.

As in most banking activities trading requires a managed balance between risk and returns. The reward system at most banks encourages risk taking because it is asymmetric in structure. A trader may be given a huge bonus on the back of huge trading gains but in the event of making large losses may face the prospect of losing their job but does not face the prospect of having to compensate the bank for the losses. Sophisticated control systems have to be put in place to ensure an appropriate division of responsibilities and control the level of potential losses that may result from ill-considered or negligent trading or from bad luck.

The most basic controls concern the booking of trades, position reporting and the related division of responsibilities. Traders should be separated from the people booking these transactions, marking positions to market and preparing management reports on current positions and any losses or gains.

The traders tend to be the people to join for a wild evening out. Collectively they are also among the most boring people in all professions to meet and this is particularly so when they are found in a group. This should not be surprising as many of them spend the entire working day focusing on the third and fourth decimal points of the prices of the instruments in which they specialize. Traditionally their skills owed more to street markets than to university education but this has changed, as complex instruments such as derivatives have become more important.

Trading strategies can be divided into those based on arbitrage, outright speculation, regression to mean and technical analysis.

ARBITRAGE

Arbitrage opportunities arise as a result of mispricing or pricing inefficiencies between markets or between financial instruments. It is worth starting with a simple practical example to illustrate the key principles behind attempts to profit from arbitrage opportunities and explain how those attempts result in the subsequent elimination of such opportunities.

Suppose we have a type of goods (Widgets) that is widely sold in two adjacent countries but where the price in one country (Costlia) is higher than in the other (Cheapa). There is a potential opportunity to make a profit by buying Widgets in Cheapa, transporting them to Costlia and selling them at the higher prices prevailing there.

There will, however, be direct costs associated with buying, transporting and selling the Widgets. There may also be some form of import duties or taxes. The aspiring entrepreneur will also have to finance the purchase until she receives the proceeds from their sale. There is also a risk that prices of Widgets in Costlia fall before the entrepreneur is able to sell the goods. If the purchase was financed with a loan taken in Costlia's currency and is to be repaid from the sale proceeds received in Cheapa's currency there are risks associated with an adverse exchange rate movement. These risks, however, can be eliminated through hedging actions taken at the time of the initial purchase. In general arbitrage profit is given by the following:

Arbitrage profit = Profit due to difference in prices between markets − Transaction costs
− Financing costs − Associated hedging costs

In Dreamworld we can ignore transaction costs and taxes and the actual transaction described above would be structured as follows:

- **Initiation.** Buy Widgets by borrowing the required amount in Cheapa's currency. At the same time enter into the following forward contracts. First, to sell the Widgets at a specified future date and fixed price. Second, a forward foreign exchange contract for the date when the proceeds from the sale are received to convert sufficient Costlia currency into that of Cheapa's to be able to repay the balance of the loan taken out in Cheapa plus the interest due.
- **Completion.** Deliver Widgets and receive guaranteed payment from the buyer in Costlia's currency. Honor forward FX contract and repay outstanding debt in Cheapa.

The successful entrepreneur should be left with a positive balance, which in the structure of the above transaction would be denominated in Costlia's currency. This amount is fixed at the time the transaction was initiated and is independent of changes in the price of Widgets or in the exchange rate between the two currencies.

If such an arbitrage profit exists then traders will buy more Widgets in Cheapa and sell them in Costlia. The increased demand in Cheapa will put upward pressure on the price of Widgets in that country. The increased supply in Costlia will put downward pressure on Widget prices in that country. These pressures will persist until the arbitrage profit possible is eliminated. At that time the markets are in equilibrium. We need to look now at some specific examples of financial arbitrage transactions.

(The above example glosses over some factors such as transportation costs and ability to find a buyer to agree to such a forward contract. In financial trades transaction costs are usually a very small fraction of a transaction's value and the ability to easily find counterparties depends on the depth and liquidity of a particular market. The transaction is "risk free" in the sense that the main risk factors have been hedged away but some secondary, or residual, risks remain such as those relating to counterparty exposures and from actions such as the imposition of capital controls preventing the remittance of the proceeds from Costlia to Cheapa.)

Interest Rate Arbitrage

The simplest, and most commonly referred to, type of financial arbitrage is that of interest rate arbitrage. Suppose we have two freely traded currencies, the zloty and the peno, currently trading at an exchange rate of 1 zloty for 2 peno and the following conditions exist:

- A one-year deposit in the zloty earns 15% and in the peno 10%.
- The one-year forward exchange rate is 0.55 zloty for 1 peno.

Suppose we have Z100 000 to invest over one year and are considering two alternative investments:

- In the first alternative we can make a Z100 000 deposit in zloty, this will earn a 15% return and at the end of the year we will have Z115 000.
- Or we can convert the zloty into peno at spot and deposit the P200 000 proceeds in a peno deposit while simultaneously entering into a forward contract to convert our penos back into zloty in one year's time.
- At a 10% deposit rate we will receive P220 000 in one year's time. Converted back into zloty at the forward rate of 0.55 zloty to the peno will leave us with Z121 000.

The second alternative is clearly a more attractive investment and we end up with Z6000 more at the end of the year than if we had gone for the first alternative. This forms the basis of the arbitrage.

If we assume that we can borrow at the same rate as deposits earn then we can create the arbitrage position by entering into the following transactions:

- Borrow Z100 000 today, we will have to repay Z115 000 in one year's time. Convert the Z100 000 at spot into P200 000 and make a matching one-year deposit. Take out a forward contract to convert the P220 000 proceeds back into zloty in one year at the forward rate of 0.55.
- After one year we receive the P220 000 from the matured time deposit. This is converted into Z121 000 from the original forward FX agreement. We can then repay the Z115 000 due on our zloty loan and end up with a clean profit of Z6000. This profit is locked in and does not depend in any way on how spot rates vary over the course of the year and is simple arbitrage profit.

Other arbitrageurs will also seek to earn these same profits and undertake similar transactions. As a result demand in the spot market for penos will rise while demand to sell penos in one year's time will fall. The zloty–peno spot rate will tend to rise while the peno–zloty forward rate will tend to fall. This will continue until no arbitrage opportunity exists. If we assume that all of the adjustment is due to the forward rate adjusting then the forward rate at which the arbitrage opportunity is eliminated is given by:

$$Forward_{Z-P}\ rate = Spot_{Z-P}\ rate \times \frac{(1 + R_Z)}{(1 + R_P)}$$

$$Forward_{(Z-P)}\ rate = 0.5 \times (1 + 0.15)/(1 + 0.10) = 0.5227$$

Exhibit: Interest rate parity

Interest rate parity is expressed in terms of the following equality. If this equality does not hold a profitable arbitrage opportunity exists, at least in theory:

$$F_{ab} = S_{ab} \times \frac{(1 + r_a)}{(1 + r_b)}$$

Where F_{ab} represents the forward rate between the two currencies, S_{ab} the spot rate, r_a the interest rate on currency a and r_b the interest rate on currency b.

The forward rate will adjust until any arbitrage opportunity is eliminated. The forward rate does not, however, tell us what the future spot rate will be. That will be determined by supply and demand at that time. The forward rate is simply an exchange rate that takes account of current interest rate differentials between currencies.

The forward rate adjusts because there are traders looking for such arbitrage opportunities and they help to ensure that foreign exchange markets are efficient.

This can be simplified to a first approximation. When r_b is small we can use the binomial expansion to restate the denominator in the interest rate parity equation and this can be expressed as follows:

$$\frac{1}{(1 + r_b)} = (1 + r_b)^{-1} \cong (1 - r_b)$$

Replacing this term in the original equation we get the following:

$$F_{ab} \cong S_{ab} \times (1 + r_a) \times (1 - r_b) = S_{ab} \times (1 + r_a - r_b - r_a r_b)$$

Under most normal conditions both r_a and r_b are relatively small percentages and their product can therefore by ignored. We therefore end with this approximation:

$$\frac{F_{ab}}{S_{ab}} \cong 1 + r_a - r_b$$

If the interest rates of the two currencies are the same then the forward rate should be the same as the spot rate.

Traders face a number of practical problems with trading emerging market currencies. The first is simply the limited size, depth and liquidity of these markets compared with those for OECD currencies. There is also a lack of derivatives and settlement systems are relatively inefficient. Credit departments at head offices of international banks also impose limits on total exposure to individual countries. This constrains the size of positions that traders can take. Finally, banks are wary of possible developments such as the imposition of capital controls or other restrictions on convertibility.

Stock Index Futures Arbitrage

Stock index futures also give rise to potential arbitrage opportunities. Index trading involves a form of program trading where an entire series of related trades is executed simultaneously.

Suppose it is June 2005. The Blue Chip 50 Index level is 1000 and a December Blue Chip 50 Futures contract is selling for 1100 and each futures contract is worth $1 per index point. The expected annualized dividend yield over the six-month period is 4% and yield of Treasury bills is 6%. We have $100 000 to invest and two alternative investments to consider:

- Buy $100 000 in the index weighted constituent stocks of the Blue Chip 100 Index, hold them for one year and sell them on the delivery date of the December Blue Chip 50 Index futures contract.
- Buy 100 Blue Chip 50 December futures contracts and invest $100 000 in Treasury bills maturing in December.

The proceeds from these two alternatives are as follows:

- The $100 000 invested in stocks will earn approximately $2000 in dividends and when we sell the basket of stocks we will receive $100 000 × (1 + g), where g is the growth in the Blue Chip Index in percentage terms over the six-month period:

$$\textbf{\textit{Proceeds in December}} = \$100\,000 \times (1 + g) + \$2000$$

$$= \textbf{\$102\,000} + \textbf{\$100\,000} \times \textbf{\textit{g}}$$

- Buy 100 Blue Chip 50 Index 1100 futures contract and invest $100 000 in Treasury bills. No cash outlay is required to buy the futures contracts because the Treasury bills can be used for the margin requirement. The futures contract will be determined by the growth in the index level over this period less the cost of the futures contract:

$$(100 \times 1000 \times (1 + g) \times \$1) - (100 \times 1100 \times \$1)$$

$$= \$100\,000 + \$100\,000 \times g - \$110\,000$$

$$= \$100\,000 \times g - \$10\,000$$

At the end of December our investment in Treasury bills will give us $103 000:

$$\textbf{\textit{Proceeds in December}} = \$103\,000 + \$100\,000 \times g - \$10\,000$$

$$= \textbf{\$93\,000} + \textbf{\$100\,000} \times \textbf{\textit{g}}$$

Neither outcome is certain but, irrespective of what happens to the index level, the first alternative produces returns that are $9000 higher than the second alternative. This forms the basis for the arbitrage trade. The investor follows this strategy:

- Buy the constituent stocks of the Blue Chip Index, hold them for one year and sell them on the delivery date of the December Blue Chip Index futures contract.
- Sell December Blue Chip Index December futures contracts. The margin is provided by the stocks bought in the first part.
- Sell (short) Treasury bills that mature in December.

This structure locks in a "guaranteed" $9000 profit. The profit is not in fact completely guaranteed, as the actual dividend yield from the index constituents may be less than expected. The opportunity cannot last, of course. Buying stocks in the market will tend to push up their prices while shorting the December Blue Chip Index futures contract will tend to push the price down from 1100. If we assume that all of the adjustment takes place in the futures market then the price would fall to 990 and at this level no arbitrage opportunity exists.

In general terms the following equality must hold for there to be no arbitrage opportunity:

$$P_f - P_c = (R_f - DY) \times P_c$$

P_f is the price of the futures contract, P_c the current level of the index, R_f the yield on Treasury bills and DY the dividend yield from the constituents of the index.

Exchange Arbitrage

Some financial instruments are traded on more than one exchange. India, for example, has several stock exchanges. A very simple arbitrage is to buy the stock on one exchange and to simultaneously sell it on a second exchange where the price is higher. This is only possible in countries where communications are relatively poor and even then such opportunities are infrequent.

Some stocks trade on two or three international exchanges and price differences on the stock persist over time. There are a number of reasons why this may be the case. Transaction costs in terms of brokerage commissions and stamp duties may be lower on one exchange than the other. Many funds are also constrained in terms of the markets and instruments in which they are allowed to invest. They may only be able to hold securities listed on a domestic exchange, for example.

Many major international stocks trade in the form of American Depository Receipts (ADRs) or Global Depository Receipts (GDRs). These are securities that represent a specified number of shares in a foreign company and are traded on US and certain other major international exchanges. These securities are issued by a depository institution (usually a major custodian bank) on behalf of the company, are priced in US$ and entitle the holder to all of the dividends from the foreign company. US and other international investors can therefore effectively trade in the underlying stock without having to deal through a foreign exchange. This cuts out a lot of risks and hassles for international investors.

The number of ADRs for a particular stock is fixed and, with supply constrained, ADRs normally trade at a premium to the market price of the underlying stock on its own exchange.

Options Arbitrage

Options arbitrage looks to exploit differences in values between the cash market and the options market. Consider the following conditions:

- A call option exists on a stock currently trading at $102 with an exercise price of $100, that has one year to maturity and a current price of $12.
- The equivalent (in terms of strike price and exercise date) put option has a price of $4.
- The continuously compounded annualized risk-free rate, at which it is assumed we can lend or borrow, is 5%.

This combination of factors provides an arbitrage opportunity. To exploit it we would enter into the following transactions:

- Sell a call option and buy a put option, this will give us $8 ($12 less $4).
- Borrow $94, being the difference between the stock's current price ($102) and the net proceeds from writing the call option and buying the put option. This will allow us to buy the stock at $102. We will need to pay back $98.82 ($94 × $e^{+0.05}$) in one year's time.

The net result is a profit of $1.18. Why should this be the case? Suppose the stock price at expiry rises to $120. The call option will be exercised, we will deliver the stock we hold and we will receive $100 in return. This is used to pay off the funds borrowed plus interest due leaving us with $1.18. The put option will simply expire worthless.

If on the other hand the stock price falls to $80 we would exercise the put option, deliver the stock we hold and receive $100, used to pay off the funds borrowed. The call option will simply expire. Again our net profit is $1.18.

The elimination of options arbitrage opportunities results in what is called call–put parity, as shown below:

$$\text{Call–put options parity: } C - P = S - Xe^{-rT}$$

The pioneering work on option valuation theory was carried out by Fischer Black and Myron Scholes, who published the first such framework in 1973. The actual equation is pretty intimidating and we do not need to delve into its workings here. The following provides a formal demonstration of call–put parity.

Exhibit: Call–put parity

Equilibrium Between Cash and Options Markets

Suppose we are considering an investment in a stock today that we intend to sell after six months. There are two ways we could do this. We could establish this position through the cash market by borrowing the funds to buy the stock or through the options market by buying a call option and selling a put option. These two alternatives must have the same present value or a profit could be made by buying in the undervalued market and selling in the overvalued market. Arbitrage forces the following equality and we will demonstrate how this works with an example:

$$PV_A = PV_B$$

- **Take out position through cash market.** We could do this by borrowing the funds to effect the stock purchase today and repay this loan with interest when we sell the stock in six months' time (t). The stock is currently trading at S_0 and the annualized continuously compounded risk-free rate is r. In six months' time we will receive S_1 and have this available to repay our loan. The value of our position today is the present value of the stock sale proceeds less the value of the loan taken out. Mathematically this is given as follows:

$$\text{Present value of alternative } A = S_1 e^{-rt} - S_0 = PV_A$$

We will make a profit only if the present value of the proceeds from selling the stock is greater than the value of the loan taken out to buy them in the first place.

- **Use options to create same position.** We can create the same returns using a combination of call and put options. Suppose we buy a call option and sell a put option today, each with an exercise price of X.

  If the stock price in six months, S_1, is greater than the exercise price, X, we will exercise our call option to buy the stock from the option writer and then sell it in the market at the higher price S_1. The put option will lapse unexercised. If the stock price is less than the exercise price the call option will lapse but the holder of the put option will sell us the stock at X which we can then sell in the market at S_1. The returns are the same whether the stock price is greater or less than the options' exercise price as shown below:

$$\text{Present value of alternative } B = +C - P + S_1 e^{-rt} - X_1 e^{-rt} = PV_B$$

Present value (today) on exercise date		
	$X > S_1$	$X > S_1$
PV from buying call option	$-Xe^{-rt} + S_1 e^{-rt}$	0
PV from selling put option	0	$-Xe^{-rt} + S_1 e^{-rt}$
Total	$-Xe^{-rt} + S_1 e^{-rt}$	$-Xe^{-rt} + S_1 e^{-rt}$

- We have already asserted that the cash and options market must offer identical returns because of arbitrage. We must also take into account C, the premium we pay for the call option, and P, the premium we are paid for writing the put option:

$$PV_A = PV_B \Rightarrow S_1 e^{-rt} - S_0 = -C + P + S_1 e^{-rt} - X_1 e^{-rt}$$

The terms $S_1 e^{-rt}$ cancel out (the equality does not depend on the future price of the stock). We are left with the following:

$$- S_0 = -C + P - X_1 \times e^{-rt}$$

and after rearranging we get the following equation which is the usual form in which call–put parity is expressed:

$$+ C - P = S_0 - X_1 \times e^{-rt}$$

Interest Rate Futures Arbitrage

Two broad strategies exist for interest rate futures arbitrage. Interest rate futures contracts on US Treasury bonds or bills allow for the delivery of the actual bond or a close equivalent (Eurodollar futures involve cash settlement).

Take a 20-year bond, with a 8% coupon rate trading at par ($10 000). Assume that this is the deliverable for a three-month futures contract currently trading at $10 200. The annualized risk-free rate is 6%.

- **Initiation.** Sell the futures contract at $10 200. Purchase the bond in the spot market at $10 000 by borrowing $10 000 for three months. The bond can be used for the margin requirement and hence there is no net cashflow.
- **Settlement.** Deliver the bond and receive $10 200 plus accrued interest of $200. Pay back the principal and accrued interest of $10 150 on the borrowings. Net profit is $350.

Take the same scenario but assume a futures contract price of $9700. The first strategy would result in a loss and the trades required to generate a profit are:

- **Initiation.** Buy the futures contract at $9700. Sell or short the bond at $10 000 and invest the proceeds at 6%.
- **Settlement.** Take delivery of the bond and pay $9700 plus $200 in accrued interest. Receive $10 150 from repayments on loan. Net profit is $250.

As usual the action of arbitrageurs will eliminate the arbitrage opportunity and with all other factors unchanged the futures contract should trade at $9950.

Others

The range of possible arbitrage opportunities is limitless. In efficient markets, however, theoretical strategies are often difficult to execute. Speed and low transaction costs are essential and many of these trades have to be executed automatically using computers. There was a time when interest rate arbitrage provided a material source of trading profits at a handful of international banks with a competitive advantage in terms of global telecommunication networks and expertise in trading systems but those days are long past.

Most theoretical parity equalities assume that parties can lend and borrow at the risk-free rate and this is clearly wrong. Real differences in lending and borrowing rates mean that arbitrage-free prices should lie within a narrow range rather than be at a single price.

In a business where "margins" are very narrow transaction costs can make the difference between an arbitrage being profitable and loss making. Stock market index arbitrage that works in countries where markets are run highly efficiently, and orders placed and trades made automatically by computer, do not work in developing markets where markets and exchanges are paper-bound, transaction costs are relatively high and settlement failures are not uncommon.

OUTRIGHT FUNDAMENTAL SPECULATION

While arbitrage is risk free, in the sense given above, traders also take outright positions, and in this sense they are speculative. These positions may be justified on fundamental grounds reflecting different views on valuations, on expectations of reversion to mean or on technical or chartist grounds.

Equities

Trading in equities may be in the actual instruments concerned or be achieved using options and futures contracts. Options provide a much greater level of gearing when they are trading close to being at-the-money than buying or shorting the underlying stock:

- **Fundamentals.** Long-term investors look for opportunities to buy stocks that on the basis of fundamentals (earnings growth expectations, discount rate, risk) appear to be undervalued and sell or short stocks that are overvalued (short selling is explained in detail later in this chapter).
- **Rumors.** Stock prices do move as a result of rumors, particularly if those rumors have some reasonable rationale. If the rumors are positive then stocks are likely to move up until a firm announcement that the rumor has no substance is made. It is easier for speculators to make money if prices are relatively volatile, whatever the cause, than if they remain largely static.
- **News event driven.** There are a number of possible events where the timing of an announcement is known well in advance but the outcome is uncertain. Examples include the conclusions and recommendations of a competition inquiry, a change in tax policy, the announcement of awards for licenses or results of a bidding process. The market will price in an expectation of the outcome but if the result is opposite to that expectation the stock is likely to either rise sharply or correct.

    Earnings releases are subject to brief but intense scrutiny. People who do not understand how stock markets work are perplexed when the stock of a company falls after it reports a good set of results with strong earnings growth. The market reaction to earnings releases depends largely on any differences between what the market was expecting and what the company actually delivered. Strong earnings growth can be disappointing if the market was expecting even stronger growth. Losses may be viewed positively if they are less than the market had feared. Analysts are frequently asked in the run-up to earnings releases if they are expecting any surprises. Remarkably, this is not quite as asinine as it appears.
- **Takeovers.** Takeover bids can provide rich pickings for speculators. Friendly agreed offers may precipitate a hostile offer from a counterparty. Hostile bids will almost always be rejected and a higher bid demanded. Other stocks in the same sector will also be affected depending on whether the market believes a specific company is likely be the next target or bidder, or stands to lose or gain from the announced bid succeeding. Speculators may be able to sell their holdings in the target company to either the target company or bidder at a premium to market prices. The bid may be referred to regulatory scrutiny.
- **Indexation.** From time to time the constituents of stock indices are adjusted. Some stocks are dropped from an index while other stocks are added. In the case of some indices the criteria for inclusion are very clearly defined, such as by market capitalization, and the changes are

automatic. In other cases the index provider may have more leeway to act to try to ensure that the index is genuinely representative.

Traders will buy stocks they expect to be added to an index and sell or short those most likely to be dropped. They do so in the expectation that tracker funds will have to buy or sell these stocks after the index changes are put into effect.

- **Gray market.** The gray market is an OTC market where new issues can be traded before opening on an exchange. Successful subscribers may prefer to take a guaranteed price in the gray market rather than sell in the market after the stock starts to trade. Traders will buy in anticipation of a higher opening price than that in the gray market. The time between the stock being traded on the gray market and on the market leaves the trader exposed to the risk of an overall market correction.

Foreign Exchange

The foreign exchange market is one of the largest financial markets in the world but it has no exchange. Trades are done by phone or by using computers and it is a 24-hour market. Major foreign exchange centers include London, New York, Tokyo and Singapore. The introduction of the euro seriously reduced the opportunities for foreign exchange traders to make profits as the number of opportunities for cross-currency trades fell.

Trading currencies is arguably one of the most basic trading activities of most large commercial banks. We have already examined ways in which countries can attempt to manage their exchange rates against other currencies. In fundamental terms, however, exchange rates are determined by balance of payment deficits (or surpluses), capital inflows (or outflows) and perceptions of likely future inflation and real interest rates:

- **Currency fundamentals.** Currency strategists attempt to forecast the level and direction of foreign exchange rates over the medium term based on economic fundamentals such as economic and productivity growth, inflationary expectations, country risk, real interest rates, capital inflows/current account deficits and capital outflows/current account surpluses.
- **Managed exchange systems.** Managed exchange systems such as those with a currency peg or those that try to keep a currency within a defined band are potentially vulnerable to speculative attack. All foreign currency transactions have to go through the central bank, which manages its country's foreign currency reserves. A speculative attack on a US$ base pegged system usually involves borrowing the local currency and selling it to buy US$. This is usually achieved by using the forward markets. Once the central bank runs out of US$ the pegged system is bound to collapse. Speculators do not act alone and do not have to have the financial resources to bet against the central bank, they are more akin to surfers riding a particularly strong wave.

Interest Rate and Credit

We looked at interest rate products in some detail in Chapter 10 "Managing interest rate and FX risk". These are used in trading strategies to speculate on the following factors:

- **Interest rate direction.** If a trader expects the general level of interest rates to rise there are a number of ways to take a position on this. These include buying an interest rate swap where the trader is a fixed rate payer and floating rate receiver, buying FRAs, shorting liquid long-duration risk-free bonds and selling interest rate futures.

- **Basis spreads.** The spreads between benchmark rates such as LIBOR and Treasuries vary over time. This creates opportunities to bet on whether these spreads will widen or narrow. The most practical way to trade on US$ rates is by using Eurodollar versus US Treasuries interest rate futures. If the spread between LIBOR and US Treasuries is expected to widen buy Eurodollar interest rate futures and sell Treasury futures.
- **Term spreads.** The yield curve is not static and may experience parallel or non-parallel shifts. When an economy is overheating and inflationary expectations are rising the rates at the short end tend to rise further than rates at the long end. Central bank open market operations are more effective at the short end of the yield curve than the long end. When an economy is slowing or moving into recession central banks tend to cut rates at the short end aggressively. These shifts provide opportunities to bet on the spread between short-term and long-term rates widening or narrowing.
- **Credit spreads.** Credit spreads on corporate bonds will widen in the event of a ratings downgrade or a general flight to quality, in other words prices will fall. In these circumstances an appropriate strategy is to short lower-quality corporate bonds and buy high quality bonds of similar duration. If, however, corporate asset quality is expected to improve then a viable strategy is to write credit derivatives with spread-based payouts. If credit spreads narrow the options will expire unexercised.

Other

Most banks trade only in vanilla interest rate and foreign exchange products. Large investment banks and specialist trading operations are, however, active in trading convertible instruments and commodities:

- **Convertible bonds.** The value of a convertible bond is equal to the value of an equivalent straight bond plus the value of an equity call option. The value of a close equivalent straight bond can be relatively easily obtained from market prices and taking this away from the market price of the convertible bond gives an implied price for the call option. Using a standard options valuation model, such as Black–Scholes, the value of this option can be estimated independently. If the value of the option estimated from the valuation model is greater than that implied from the convertible's price then the bond is considered cheap or undervalued and traders will look to buy the convertible bond.
- **Commodities.** The first traded futures contracts were based on agricultural produce. Today futures contracts are available on a wide range of both commodities and financial instruments. Most commodity speculators are specialists in a small number of particular commodities. They buy and sell futures contracts not because they have any intention of taking actual delivery but as a way to trade on the price of the commodity.

  El Nino is a large-scale weather phenomenon, first observed in the Pacific, that appears at irregular intervals and has a severe impact on weather patterns in many parts of the world. Some countries experience drought, others flooding. These in turn affect output of agricultural commodities such as coffee, cocoa and palm oil. It is said that the prices of futures contracts on orange juice concentrate is the most accurate medium-term weather forecast available for Miami, for example. In this way commodity futures provide a way to bet on the weather.

OPPORTUNISTIC

Some hedge funds actively seek out one-off opportunities. The following is based on an actual case. A state-controlled bank, First Bank, wished to acquire Bank Two, a smaller bank based in a second country, trading at $70 per share and with a market cap of $3.4bn. A majority shareholder owned 75% of Bank Two's issued shares and was prepared to consider a bid in the region of $100 per share. First Bank was prepared to pay this but had problems with meeting its own capital adequacy requirements at this price and proposed to make payment in two stages. Stock exchange rules meant that it had to make an all cash offer to the minority shareholders.

Working with its investment bank it made an offer in the following form. Bank Two shareholders could opt for an all-cash payment now or a second option that gave them part of the consideration in cash now and shares in an unlisted company, set up solely for this purpose, that would pay the second installment one year later. The all-cash offer was worth $100 and the second offer a total of $105 with $70 payable now and the balance one year's hence. Annualized one-year Treasury yields at the time were approximately 4%.

The majority shareholder had already committed to the second offer but this alternative was of very little interest to the minority shareholders. Most of the institutions were prohibited from holding unlisted shares and the extra $5 did not appear overly generous for having the cash tied up in an illiquid asset. The stock traded at around $96 per share after the offer. This discount to the $100 cash offer can be explained by concerns that regulatory approval, although widely regarded as a foregone conclusion, had not yet been given.

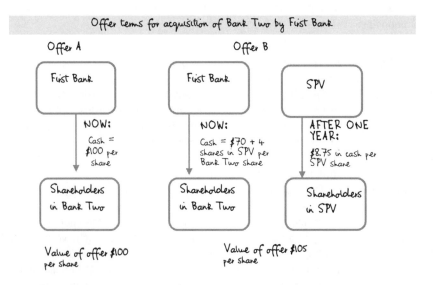

Offer terms for acquisition of Bank Two by First Bank

Offer A — Value of offer $100 per share

Offer B — Value of offer $105 per share

Offer A: First Bank → NOW: Cash = $100 per share → Shareholders in Bank Two

Offer B: First Bank → NOW: Cash = $70 + 4 shares in SPV per Bank Two share → Shareholders in Bank Two; SPV → AFTER ONE YEAR: $8.75 in cash per SPV share → Shareholders in SPV

After regulatory approval had been obtained the stock continued to trade up and on its last day of trading closed at $102 per share, a premium to the cash offer price. This can be explained by the structure of the cashflows associated with the second option. The following table shows the

IRR (internal rate of return) for a new investor buying the stock in the market at $98, $100 (the value of the first option) and $102 (the price at which the stock closed on its last day of trading).

Cashflows and internal rate of return (*IRR*)			
Market price ($)	−98	−100	−102
Cash in 1 month ($)	70	70	70
Cash in 13 months ($)	35	35	35
Internal rate of return (*IRR*)	17.5%	12.1%	7.1%

At a market price of $98 buying the stock and opting for the second alternative produced a 17.5% internal rate of return, even at $100 at 12.1% this was still well above yields on Treasuries.

The only risks were that First Bank defaulted on the second payment but this was highly unlikely as the bank's major shareholder was the government. Hedge funds bought out all of the mutual fund holdings before the offer closed. Those that got in early achieved annualized returns above 20%.

First Bank did not expect minority shareholders to take the second option. This provides an example of market inefficiencies. Approximately 50 sell-side analysts covered either First Bank and Bank Two, because they were listed in different markets, but few took the effort to fully analyze the second option open to Bank Two shareholders because they assumed that none of their clients could opt for it. It took two to three weeks before the market priced out the opportunity to lock in a guaranteed virtually risk-free profit with returns well above that available from risk-free investments.

When swaps were first developed there were no swaps markets or swaps dealers and banks relied on finding clients with complementary needs or taking the risks onto their own account. Risks were higher then but so were returns. If an investment bank sees an opportunity to buy an asset on its own account and almost immediately sell it to another party it will usually do so.

BUYING AND SELLING VOLATILITY

Common options trading strategies involve what is referred to as buying or selling volatility. This needs an explanation of a key driver of traded options' values.

The more volatile the price of the underlying instrument the more valuable the option. This arises in part from the asymmetry of returns. If the price of the underlying instrument subject to a call option is below the strike price we will not exercise the right but may if the price rises above the strike price.

If an option has an exercise price of $70 and the stock is currently trading at $70 there is a 50% probability that the option will be in-the-money and a 50% probability that it will be out-of-the-money. This does not take account of by how much the option may be in-the-money and it will be worth more if there are wild swings in prices from lows of, say, $40 to highs of $100 than from $50 to $90.

The shaded areas of the following charts represent the probability that the stock price will be above $80 assuming first a standard deviation of $5 and second a standard deviation of $10. The probability that the stock's price will be greater than (say) $80 is much higher for the second option than for the first. In other words the chances of a larger payoff are much greater for the option on the more volatile stock and this is reflected in its value.

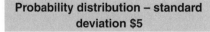

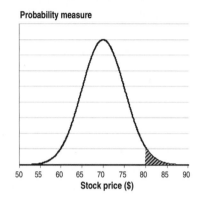
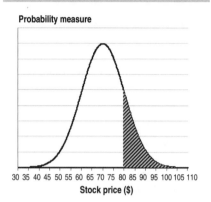

We can turn this on its head. Option valuation models, such as Black–Scholes, can be used to estimate the level of volatility of the prices of underlying instruments implied by current option prices. The higher an option's price the higher the implied volatility.

Buying and selling volatility is a method used by many traders that compares implied volatility measures with historic levels. If the level of implied volatility is higher than the historic level then this suggests that options are overvalued and if lower that they are undervalued. If overvalued the trader would look to sell (write) options and if undervalued to buy them.

Advanced Options Trading Strategies

There are many advanced options trading strategies that use various combinations of call and put options to generate profits based on volatility expectations rather than on the actual direction of stock prices. The return diagrams for these combinations are arrived at by simply adding together the return diagrams for the components.

Outright positions in either call or put options would leave the trader exposed to absolute price movement. Instead the trader would look to create (write) a straddle or strangle position.

- **Straddle.** A straddle is created by buying a call option and a put option with the same strike price ($45 in this case) and exercise date. A trader will use a straddle when he or she expects an increase in volatility. The straddle makes a profit if the stock's price either rises or falls sharply but makes a loss if prices remain relatively stable.
- **Strangle.** A strangle is used to the same end but involves buying a call option with a higher strike price, in this example $50, and a put option with a lower strike price, in this example $40. This is a cheaper combination as both options are less likely to move into the money than the options at a $45 strike price.

If the level of implied volatility is lower than the historic level the trader would look to buy a butterfly spread. A butterfly spread is created by buying two call options, one with a high strike price and the other with a low strike price, while simultaneously writing two options with strike prices between those of the two call options purchased. Returns and motives are similar in

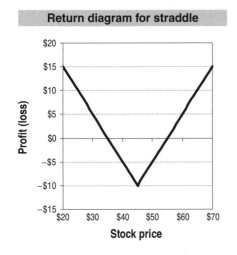

Return diagram for straddle

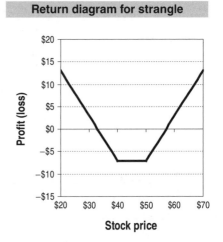

Return diagram for strangle

structure to those obtained from writing a straddle. The holder of a butterfly spread profits if prices remain tightly bound.

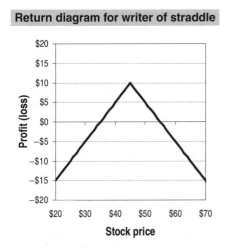

Return diagram for writer of straddle

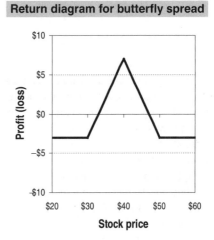

Return diagram for butterfly spread

HOLDING COMPANY DISCOUNTS

Companies whose assets are largely made up of holdings in other listed companies are normally subject to a "holding company" discount. The argument in favor of conglomerates and holding companies is that diversification reduces their risk. "Modern" portfolio theory suggests that investors can diversify their own holding better through the market.

A similar discount applies to listed closed-end funds but in the cases of listed holding companies the situation is almost always more complicated because the holding company also owns other, unlisted assets. Consider the following example. Company A owns major stakes in two other companies but also owns some unlisted operating assets directly. At a price of $140 the value of its listed assets is equivalent to 67% of its market capitalization.

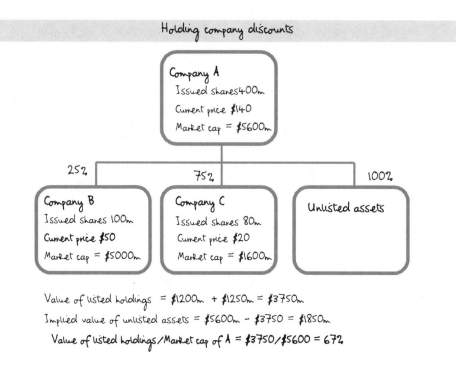

Holding company discounts

Company A
Issued shares400m
Current price $140
Market cap = $5600m

25% 75% 100%

Company B
Issued shares 100m
Current price $50
Market cap = $5000m

Company C
Issued shares 80m
Current price $20
Market cap = $1600m

Unlisted assets

Value of listed holdings = $1200m + $1250m = $3750m

Implied value of unlisted assets = $5600m - $3750 = $1850m

Value of listed holdings/Market cap of A = $3750/$5600 = 67%

A trader seeking to take advantage of a potential arbitrage opportunity will track all three stocks closely, and in particular monitor the percentage of the holding company's market cap that is accounted for by the market value of its listed holdings.

When this is high compared with historic levels the implication is that the holding company is undervalued relative to Company B and C. To take advantage of this the trader could buy Company A while shorting B and C in proportion to their value. This is not a risk-free arbitrage as the reason for the discount widening or narrowing may be due to changes in the perceived value of its unlisted assets but more in the nature of a long–short trade.

Another way to identify potential long–short trades is to monitor relative performance of closely related stocks operating in the same sector. A widely used valuation measure for banks, for example, is price-to-book. A trader looking for relative performance within the sector may compare current price-to-book ratios (PBRs) between individual banks and between individual banks and the sector against historic levels.

TECHNIQUES TO PROFIT FROM FALLING PRICES

Short Selling

Shorting a stock involves selling a stock that an investor does not hold in the expectation that it can be bought back at a later date at a lower price. This provides a way to make absolute returns when stock prices are falling.

Custodian banks act as facilitators to this process. Custodian banks approach their fund management clients to make stock lending agreements. Stock lending provides a means for fund managers to enhance returns, they lend the stock to the short seller, but retain all of their rights to the stock (dividends, rights issues etc.). In return the short seller pays a fee for this facility.

The custodian bank is exposed to counterparty risk and will also require a margin deposit from the short seller. The short seller sells the borrowed stock into the market. The proceeds from the sale cover the margin requirement and fees and leave a balance that can be invested elsewhere, usually in the money market.

Closing a short position requires a reversal of these flows. The short seller withdraws their money market deposit, buys back the borrowed stock in the market, returns the stock to the custodian bank and receives back its margin deposit. The cash and stock flows involved in initiating and closing a short position are shown in the following diagram.

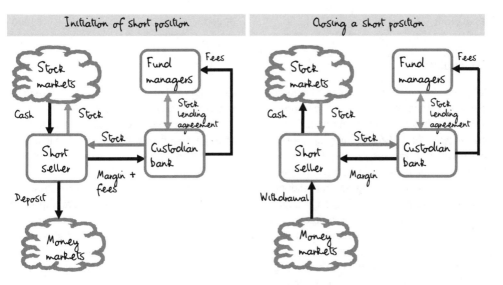

Example of Short Selling

We will use a simple example to show how a short sale may result in a profit irrespective of how the market moves. In this example we have $1m to invest. $200 000 is set aside as a buffer to meet any margin calls arising from the short position. We use $800 000 to buy Stock A and $800 000 to enter a short-sale agreement for Stock B. We receive $800 000 from the short sale of Stock B and invest this in a money market instrument.

We will assume that we earn 2% interest on the $1m we now have invested in cash equivalents.

In the first case the market rises by 7.5%, our long position rises by 10% giving a gain of $80 000 while our short position rises by 5% giving a loss of $40 000. Total profit from the transaction is $60 000. If on the other hand the market falls by 7.5% and our long position by 5% and our short position by 10% we get the following. The long position posts a loss for $40 000 but we make a profit of $80 000 on the short position. Total profit remains $60 000. Systematic risk has been eliminated (or at least reduced).

This does of course depend on us getting the relative movement of the two stocks correct of course but does not require us to forecast whether they will go up or down.

		Market up 7.5%			Market down 7.5%		
		"A" up 10%	"B" up 5%	Total	"A" down 5%	"B" down 10%	Total
Buy Stock A	800 000	80 000		80 000	(40 000)		(40 000)
Sell Stock B short	(800 000)		(40 000)	(40 000)		80 000	80 000
Total profit				**40 000**			**40 000**
Plus interest on deposit				20 000			20 000
Total profit				**60 000**			**60 000**

Long–short returns ($)

Constraints

In some countries the practice of shorting stocks is illegal. This is not rational but reflects perceptions that rising equity prices are "good" and falling equity prices are "bad". In similar vein many individuals and media organizations see a strong currency as "good" and a weak currency as "bad". Strong currencies tend to benefit importers and parties with foreign liabilities while weak currencies benefit exporters and parties with foreign assets. Weak stock prices benefit potential investors at the expense of current investors.

Even in the US, where free-market doctrine usually prevails, there is frequently an outpouring of cries of "foul" when markets fall sharply. These calls come from investors blaming short sellers for pushing prices down. Such cries of pain are understandable, as it is always bad luck or somebody else's fault when investors lose money. These cries are at their most shrill when accompanied by reports that a few investors have acted together to illegally push down an individual stock's price. Nobody ever suggests that buying stocks should be investigated when evidence of creating false markets emerges during a bull market.

What is surprising is that the Securities and Exchange Commission (SEC) continues, from time to time, to respond to these complaints by talking about looking into short-selling practices when it should simply ignore this whining. Even now short selling of equities in the US is restricted and it is illegal to short sell a stock on a "down-tick", i.e. when prices are falling. To be consistent perhaps it should look at banning buy orders on "up-ticks".

There may also be practical restrictions on shorting stocks such as a limited availability of stock to borrow. This may be due to a low "free float", this is the level of stock that is freely traded. Companies sometimes react negatively when they find out about funds short selling their stock.

TECHNICAL ANALYSIS

Technical analysis constitutes an alternative approach to trading than that provided by arbitrage and fundamental analysis. The underlying rationale for technical analysis is that markets are human systems and that prices of instruments traded in these markets are determined to a large extent by mass psychology.

Fundamental equity analysts work alongside economists and technical analysts. They respect the methods used by economists while retaining a healthy skepticism about their forecasts. Most are duty bound to mistrust the methods used by technical analysts but, if they are honest, accord their conclusions with a degree of respect. A fundamental analyst will hesitate before putting out a report advocating a strong buy on a stock where the technical analyst says that technical indicators are strongly indicative of a likely sharp stock correction. Among the features of technical analysis are the following:

- Prices move in cycles, and in cycles within cycles.
- Prices move in a series of "waves" and trends can be distinguished from cyclical effects.
- Specific price levels can be identified that act as resistance levels (for rising prices) or as support levels (for falling prices).
- Identifiable patterns can be recognized in prices tracked over time and likely turning points can be identified in advance.

Specific factors that technical analysts take into account are:

- The current market price versus moving averages of prices over defined time intervals, typically 30 days, 90 days, 180 days and one year.
- Daily opening and closing prices and intra-day highs and lows. Charts showing these are referred to as "candlestick" charts by virtue of their appearance.
- Trading volumes and whether these are rising or falling.

Technical analysis is diametrically opposed to widely accepted mainstream dogma on market efficiencies which claim that in efficient markets price changes are essentially random and that it is impossible to predict future prices from historic prices.

Technical analysis is better at explaining past price behavior than predicting future price movements (isn't that always the way). It is easier to see price patterns with the benefit of hindsight and most forecasts are qualified in some way. A support level, for example, may be tested. If the support level is breached then technical analysis can be used to identify the next support level. If on the other hand it is tested but fails to break the support level this may lead to a new resistance level. If technical analysis provided a guaranteed way to make money then there would be more technical analysts working for their own account and less employed by brokerages and speculators.

Most financial academics studiously avoid any mention of technical analysis, treating it much as scientists would treat alchemy. A variation on Shakespeare comes from David Mamet, an American dramatist: "The poker player learns that sometimes both science and common-sense are wrong; that the bumblebee can fly; that, perhaps one should never trust an expert; that there are more things in heaven and earth than are dreamt of by those with an academic bent."

12

Managing Market Risk

When playing Russian roulette, the fact that the first shot got off safely is little comfort for the next.
Richard Feynman, Nobel laureate in physics,
in relation to the causes of the space shuttle Challenger disaster

MARKET OR TRADING RISK

Every year a handful of banks make sufficiently large trading losses to make the non-business sections of the media take note. The surprising thing is not that some banks make large trading losses but how few very large losses are incurred, given the sheer volume of financial trading activities. Very few of the actual losses reported have been sufficiently large to threaten the solvency of the financial institutions concerned.

This state of affairs owes less to the skills of traders and more to the effectiveness and generally high standard of controls put in place to manage market risks. Most of the reported large losses have occurred as a result of fraud at banks where line management has not understood the nature of the risks being taken and failed to implement some of the most basic controls necessary. Single traders have been able to run up losses amounting to several hundred million dollars without anyone noticing. The traders concerned have, of course, taken the rap but the real finger of blame should be pointed in the direction of management.

Trading portfolio risks can be conveniently broken down into three parts: first order price risks, realization risks and model risks. These incorporate our more familiar definitions of interest rate risk, foreign exchange risk, counterparty risk and so on.

First Order Price Risks

Most basic valuation models assume that the change of the price of a financial instrument is directly proportional to the change in an underlying factor, in other words that a linear relationship exists. In many instances this is a first order approximation only and is equivalent to measuring the slope of the price graph against this factor. This ignores any effects due to curvature of the graph arising from higher order and secondary relationships:

- **Local currency interest rate instruments.** Interest rate instruments include bonds, asset backed securities, short-term paper, forward rate agreements (FRAs) and interest rate swaps. The value of these instruments varies with the discount rate applied to their cashflows:
    - **Risk-free rates and term spreads.** The discount rates applied to risk-free government Treasury bonds and bills are based on yields-to-maturity taken from the yield curve. These yields are affected by the overall economic environment, inflationary expectations and monetary policy. Yields may change in equal amounts across all maturities or in a non-parallel way as shown by changes in term spreads. Term spreads are defined by the difference between yields on short- and long-duration risk-free instruments.

- **Credit and basis spreads.** The discount rate applied to corporate and other non risk-free debt issues can be viewed as the yield on an equivalent risk-free instrument plus a credit spread. Credit spreads reflect the higher returns investors demand to compensate for the higher risks. In general, credit spreads tend to widen as an economy heads into recession and narrow during recovery. Individual issuer and issue credit spreads also vary depending on conditions at a single company.

  Basis spreads are the spreads between benchmark rates such as those obtained from government securities and those from an interbank rate, such as LIBOR, against which floating rate debt instruments are priced.

  The value of interest rate instruments is also affected by secondary factors such as the passage of time and the effects of embedded options such as those present in callable and putable bonds.

- **Foreign currency exposures.** Exposures to foreign exchange risk may be direct, as in a US bank having an outright cash position in euros or being committed to deliver a quantity of foreign currency at some specified future date. They may also be indirect arising from positions held in other instruments priced in a foreign currency, such as bonds and equities. First order price changes are the result of changes in exchange rates. Other effects may arise because of changes in the discount rate used to value positions in foreign currency and convexity:

  - **Spot rates.** Spot rates are determined by supply and demand and by macroeconomic fundamentals. These are used to mark-to-market values of assets and liabilities concerned. Some currencies tend to move together when their economies are closely interlinked and affected by similar external factors.

  - **Interest rate differentials.** Forward rates are determined by spot rates and by the differential between foreign risk-free interest rates and those of the base currency.

  Both spot and forward positions can be affected by central bank actions, by the use of managed exchange rate systems and from the imposition of capital controls.

- **Equity positions.** Stock prices are determined by supply and demand which in turn are affected by changes in the macroeconomic and interest environment and perceptions of the intrinsic value of stocks:

  - **Supply and demand.** Stock prices in general are affected by overall demand for equities. This is, arguably, determined by changing expectations of future earnings prospects and by perceptions of the value of the discount rate, as "determined" by risk-free rates plus an equity risk premium to compensate investors for the higher risks taken. The discount rate may change as a result of changes in risk-free rates or from a widening or narrowing of the equity risk premium.

  - **Intrinsic value.** Individual stocks are affected by investor perceptions of intrinsic value. These are affected by changes in the equity market discount rate, by expectations of future earnings growth and by the perceived riskiness of returns at one company versus the equity market as a whole. This is captured by a stock-specific measure called beta. Beta affects the discount rate applied to individual stocks according to the capital asset pricing model (CAPM). This is explored in more detail in Chapter 15 "Fund management".

  - **Corporate actions.** Individual stock prices are also affected by corporate actions such as rights issues, special dividends, share buy-back programs, takeovers, mergers, dividend payouts and the exercise of rights and other dilutive issues.

Derivatives and Hybrids

Derivatives and hybrids include options, warrants, futures, convertible debt instruments and callable and putable bonds. These are affected by two broad sets of factors:

- **Prices and volatility of underlying instruments.** Derivative instrument values are affected by changes in the prices of underlying instruments and by changes in the volatility of these prices. Stock call options, for example, will increase in value if the underlying stock price rises or the level of volatility increases.
- **Discount rate and time.** Values are also affected by changes in discount rates used and by the passage of time. The value of a call option, for example, tends towards its intrinsic value as the expiry date approaches.

The values of hybrids, such as convertible bonds, are affected by the values of the principal instruments and the value of the option-like component taken together. First order price risks are usually taken as being those due to changes in the price of the principal instrument.

REALIZATION RISKS

First order price risks show themselves in their impact on the appraised value of holdings on the basis of marking their value to market prices. This does not take into account whether such values could actually be realized and how quickly. Specific realization risks include the following:

- **Liquidity and price impact.** Liquidity and price impact risks are determined by the size of a bank's position in a particular financial instrument against its trading volume. When liquidity is relatively thin and the position relatively large unwinding the position may have a direct adverse impact on market prices for the instrument. It is possible to unwind, liquidate or hedge positions virtually instantaneously in certain positions, such as foreign exchange, where markets are very deep. Other positions may be virtually impossible to unwind quickly. OTCs, for example, usually have only one market-maker and the holders of such contracts are exposed to both price impact and liquidity risks.
- **Scheduled trading hours.** Some markets, such as the foreign exchange market, are open for trading 24 hours a day, 7 days a week around the year. This is not the case with many exchanges that have definite trading hours, are usually closed at weekends and on local public holidays. Stock markets in some emerging markets open only one morning a week!
- **Automatic dampers.** Automatic dampers exist in many markets and are intended to stabilize prices of stocks that have gone into freefall. Trading in individual stocks is suspended when they fall by a specified amount (often referred to as limit-down) in a single trading session. Trading resumes after a defined cool-down period. In some markets other restrictions exist such as the prohibition of shorting stocks when prices are falling.
- **Exchange suspension.** In extreme circumstances exchanges, financial regulators or governments may act to suspend trading on exchanges or to prohibit certain otherwise legitimate financial transactions. Exchanges may be closed as a result of panic selling or for other reasons such as civil disorder or terrorist action. Stock markets in countries with tropical climates

are often forced to close as a result of natural weather conditions such as hurricanes or typhoons.

- **Market crashes.** When prices of financial instruments fall sharply this can trigger further selling as a result of margin calls and prices hitting trigger levels of automated computer trading systems. In many market crashes trading volumes rise sharply and then collapse. At these moments of exceptionally high volumes exchange systems' capacity is tested to the limits. If an exchange's trading system crashes then all trading activities will grind to a halt.
- **Settlement failures.** Even when trades can be completed there remains the risk that they cannot be settled. Back-office settlement systems, both human and automated, are severely tested at these times. Most settlement failures require human intervention to resolve and may also have a knock-on effect with one failure leading to successive failures. It can take days to clear such backlogs.
- **Counterparty risks.** Counterparty risks are an ever-present concern for banks. Losses experienced by counterparties from a widespread collapse in asset prices may affect their ability to make the payments due on their trades and other exposures they have with the bank.

In "normal" circumstances realization risks need to be managed but are rarely the source of material losses. When markets crash, however, they become of vital importance. Realization risks are highest when their potential impact is greatest.

MODEL RISKS

Model risks are present in both appraised price estimates and the assessment of realization risks:

- **Second order price risks.** Model assumptions that prices change in a linear way with an underlying factor can lead to material differences when curvature is present. This occurs with bonds and can be taken account of by using the measure convexity. Callable bonds with embedded options exhibit negative convexity as prices approach the call price. Tranches of mortgage backed securities provide particular challenges depending on pre-payment rates.

  These risks are also present with options where this is referred to as gamma risk where the rate of change does not simply vary with the underlying factor but may even reverse sign, as we saw in Chapter 2 "Introduction to securities valuations".
- **Price distribution.** Most methods used to assess downside risks from particular trading positions are dependent on price changes being essentially random and having a "normal" distribution. This is not always the case. Some distributions are skewed, with a "long tail" in one direction, while others have a distribution close to that of the normal distribution but have "fat tails". Fat tails occur when the incidence of occurrences at the extremes is greater than would be expected from a normal distribution.

  A further implicit assumption is that price changes are not serially correlated, that is that price changes in one period are independent of price changes in prior periods. This assumption does not always hold.

Trading portfolio risks

FIRST ORDER PRICE RISKS

Local currency interest rate instruments

* Bonds, bills, FRAs & swaps
* Risk-free rates (government bonds & bills)
  - General level of interest rates
  - Term spreads
* Corporate debt issues
  - Risk-free rates
  - Basis spreads (e.g. LIBOR versus Treasuries)
  - Credit spreads

Foreign currency positions

* Direct outright spot & forward position & indirect through other exposures
* Spot exchange rates
* Forward rates
  - Base risk-free rates versus foreign risk-free rates
* Discount rates
  - Base risk-free rates

Equity positions

* Stock fundamentals
* Corporate actions
  - Dividends, dilution
* Discount rate
  - Risk-free rates
  - Equity risk premium
  - Stock betas

Derivatives/hybrids

* Options, futures, convertibles, callable bonds
* Prices of underlying instruments
* Volatility of prices of underlying instruments
* Discount (risk-free) rates
* Time left to expiry

REALIZATION RISKS

* Liquidity & price impact
  - Depth of market
  - Size of position versus volume traded
  - Trading opening hours
* Automatic dampeners
  - Trading suspension (e.g. limit-down)
  - Restrictions on short selling
* Regulatory/government actions
  - Exchange suspension
  - Capital controls
* Execution & settlement risk
  - Capacity versus actual volumes

MODEL RISKS

* First order versus second order
  - Convexity, gamma
* Statistical price distributions
  - Assumed versus actual
  - Normal versus skewed, fat tails
  - Serial correlations
* Reversion to mean
  - Price volatility
  - Correlation coefficients
  - Equity risk premium & stock betas
  - Trading volumes

- **Reversion to mean.** A further assumption often made is that of reversion to mean. This means that past relationships between factors will continue to apply in the future. Examples of these include the following:
  - **Price volatility.** Methods to determine the likelihood of losses in a given period exceeding a particular level depends on the volatility of prices of the instruments concerned. A

common assumption is that future volatility levels will revert back to historic levels or if they do change over time they change slowly.

- **Correlations.** The level of potential losses for a portfolio of financial assets depends not only on price changes of individual instruments but the way in which such changes are related to one another. The prices of two instruments may tend to move together, or if the price of one instrument rises the price of the other tends to fall. These relationships are core to overall portfolio risks. These relationships are captured in a quantitative way through the use of correlation coefficients calculated on the basis of historic prices. These correlation coefficients are assumed to remain stable over time.
- **Risk premiums.** The same considerations apply to the market equity risk premium and stock specific betas.
- **Trading volumes.** In estimating the time necessary to unwind a position the historic average daily trading volume is usually assumed.

We will concentrate in this chapter on those risks that relate to trading portfolio price risk and ignore those relating to other risks such as counterparty, settlement and operational risk.

VALUE AT RISK (VaR)

Banks have to manage a variety of trading risks and over the past 20 years a number of the tools have been developed to better quantify these risks and their potential impact on the bank. Of these the most widely used is the "value-at-risk" approach, commonly referred to as VaR and sometimes as VAR. For the sake of clarity we will use VAR to denote the actual value at risk and VaR the technique itself in this text. VaR has the following features:

- VaR uses historic data to determine past price volatility and relationships between variables. It depends to a large extent on historic correlations between instruments being maintained.
- VAR is usually quoted as an absolute dollar amount.
- VaR requires that the time frame over which the VAR estimate is made be specified. This time frame is often referred to as the holding period.
- VAR is defined at a specific confidence level expressed in terms of probabilities.
- VAR is also highly model dependent and two banks estimating VAR for an identical portfolio of financial assets will almost always end up with different estimates even though the same holding period and confidence level have been specified.

Statistical Skeletons

In order to fully understand VaR modeling it is necessary to get to grips with some fundamental statistical theory. This is not to everyone's taste, however, and in this chapter we will keep theory to a bare minimum. These bare bones are fleshed out in the statistics primer which provides a more formal treatment.

The way in which the data is distributed has an important bearing on the effectiveness of statistical methods to measure risks. Most VaR methods assume:

- **Normal distribution.** That the data in the form of price changes of instruments has a normal distribution. A normal distribution is one that has a mean equal to its mode and median and is symmetric about the mean. The price changes may be expressed in absolute or percentage terms.
- **Stable standard deviation of returns.** That the variation of returns about the mean is stable and does not vary over time. The variation of returns is measured by the distribution's standard deviation.
- **No serial correlation.** That there is no serial correlation between returns. This is particularly important when extrapolating results for a single holding period to multiple holding periods.

The first of the following two charts plot frequency of daily returns for two stocks, Blue Sky and Bore Inc. Both have the classic bell shape characteristic of normal distributions. Both have a mean of 0% reflecting the likelihood of a stock rising on a particular day being the same as the likelihood of it falling.

Blue Sky's returns are more volatile than those of Bore Inc. and this is reflected in a higher standard deviation of 1.21% versus 0.55%. The standard deviation is usually denoted by the Greek lower-case letter sigma (σ).

The normal distribution has useful statistical properties that allow one to determine probabilities that values will fall with a defined range or interval relatively easily. The second chart, for example, shows that the probability that returns on a specific day will be negative or less than 2 standard deviations above the mean is 97.725%. Turning this round this can also be expressed in other words that there is a 2.275% probability that returns will be greater than 2 standard deviations from the mean.

This is an example of a one-tail test where we are only interested in outcomes at one or other extreme. Because the distribution is symmetric there is also a 97.725% probability that losses on a specific day will not be worse (greater) than 2 standard deviations from the mean. Taking our two examples, at the 97.725% confidence level and one-day holding period, losses (prices falling) on Blue Sky and Bore Inc. holdings will not be greater than 2.42% and 1.1% respectively.

Frequency distribution of daily returns

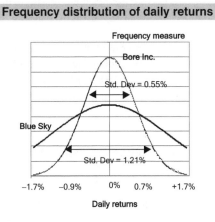

Daily returns

One-tail confidence test

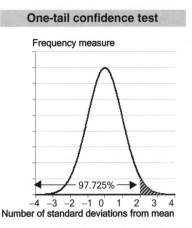

Number of standard deviations from mean

The following table shows confidence levels for various numbers of standard deviations from the mean. These are normally expressed in terms of Z-scores where:

$$Z\text{-}score = \frac{Mean\ value - Actual\ value}{Standard\ deviation} = Number\ of\ standard\ deviations\ from\ the\ mean$$

Confidence levels for one-tail test for normal distribution							
Confidence level	99.87%	99.5%	99%	98%	97.73%	97.5%	95%	90%
Z-score	3	2.58	2.33	2.05	2	1.96	1.645	1.28

Two-tailed tests differ from one-tailed tests in that they are concerned with occurrence probabilities at both extremes at the same time. For example, we would use a one-tailed test if we were interested in what proportion of the adult male population was taller than 2 meters. We would use a two-tailed test if we were interested in what percentage of this population were either overweight or underweight relative to the average (mean) weight.

The symmetrical nature of the normal distribution means that it is easy to switch between one- and two-tailed tests. In the above example of a one-tailed test the probability that returns will be greater than 2 standard deviations from the mean is 2.275%, the probability that returns or losses will be greater than 2 standard deviations from the mean is 4.55%. This is equivalent to a confidence level of 95.45%. At a 95% confidence level the Z-score for a two-tailed test is 1.96.

The general equation for calculating the value at risk for a position in a single instrument is given by:

Value at risk = VAR = (Value of position) × (Standard deviation of change in value for one holding period) × (Factor determined by required confidence level) × (Factor determined by number of holding periods)

Individual Bond Holding

With the basic theory out of the way we can now consider how to apply it. We will start with an individual bond holding and show how VAR for a single period can be calculated.

A US bank has a long position in Treasury bills with a current market value of $100m and has a duration of 0.5 years. The daily standard deviation of changes in short-term risk-free rates is 4.62 bpts.

We are interested in how much the value of this holding could fall in one day to a 99% confidence level. Our one-tailed test tells us that there is a 1% probability that short-tem risk-free rates could rise by more than 2.33 standard deviations (10.76 bpts) from the mean. The formula for calculating the change in the bills' price (value) for a change in yields is given by:

$$\frac{\Delta P}{P} = -D \times \Delta Y$$

Applying this formula the maximum daily VAR to a 99% confidence level is $53 820 as given by:

$$One\text{-}day\ VAR_{T\text{-}bill} = \$100\,000\,000 \times 0.5 \times 0.000462 \times 2.33 = \$53\,820$$

It is always important to bear in mind that these tests do not tell us anything about how great the losses could be, only the likelihood that that they will be less than the specified amount.

Our confidence test can be expressed in a different way, that in one day in every hundred we should expect losses to be greater than $53 820 but we cannot say by how much.

Extrapolation of Holding Period

If we want to know how much is at risk over a 10-day holding period (10 trading days) we can extrapolate from the result for one day. This relies on the statistical result that given the standard deviation for a single period the standard deviation for N periods is given by the following.

$$Standard\ deviation_{Nperiods} = \sqrt{N} \times Standard\ deviation\ for\ 1\ period$$

This is usually written in the following form:

$$\sigma_{Nperiods} = \sqrt{N} \times \sigma_{1\ period}$$

The 10-day VAR is then calculated by multiplying the one-day VAR by a factor equal to the square root of 10 (3.1623):

$$10\text{-}dayVAR_{T\text{-}bill} = 3.1623 \times \$53\,820 = \$170\,310$$

This extrapolation needs to be qualified, however. The basic calculation of VAR is a first order approximation only. The extrapolation only works when the rate of change of price (delta) is approximately stable as the underlying factor changes. In the case of a bond delta is denoted by duration. We can get a better approximation taking account of the curvature of the price–yield graph if we also take convexity into account but this does not eliminate the problem completely as both duration and convexity change with yield.

Options usually pose particular problems. When an option is either deep-in- or out-of-the-money the first order approximation that the price of the option varies in an approximately linear way with that of the price of the underlying instrument works well. If an option is close to being at-the-money this breaks down, however. Delta changes rapidly as the price of the underlying instrument changes and may even reverse sign. This is referred to as gamma risk.

A further practical problem arises from the asymmetric nature of returns from options. The potential losses to the holder of a call option have a floor equivalent to the premium paid for the option but unlimited potential upside. The potential losses to the writer of the call option have no theoretical limit. Finally, the assumption that there is no serial correlation is critical and if this is not the case then the result may be significantly understated.

ASSET PORTFOLIO DIVERSIFICATION

We have shown how to estimate VAR for an individual security holding but most investors hold a number of different securities or positions. They are less concerned about the changes in the value of individual holdings and more concerned about changes in the total value of all their holdings. In general, VAR for a portfolio of financial assets cannot be calculated from the simple sum of the VARs for the individual holdings.

We need to take another statistical diversion and introduce another concept, that of the correlation (or the relationship) between changes in a number of different variables.

Correlation

Correlation can be loosely defined as the mutual relation between two or more variables. This is captured in a quantitative way in statistics by a measure defined as the correlation coefficient, usually represented by the letter "r". The linear correlation coefficient is used to examine whether there is any evidence of a linear relationship between two variables and defines two qualities:

- **Nature of relationship.** A positive correlation coefficient means that the two variables tend to move in the same direction. If it is negative it implies that the relationship is inverse and that when the value of one variable rises the value of the other tends to fall.
- **Strength of relationship.** The value of correlation coefficient provides a measure of the strength of the relationship, if any exists. The correlation coefficient cannot be greater than $+1$ or less than -1:
  - **Perfect linear relationship.** A correlation coefficient of $+1$ means that there is a perfect linear relationship. If one variable rises then so does the other and the ratio of the rise or fall remains constant. If, for example, the price of one bond increases then the price of the other bond always rises. If the increase in price of the first bond for a given fall in yields is 1% and the price of the second rises by 2% then if the first bond falls in value by 3% the value of the second bond will fall by 6%.
  - **Perfect inverse linear relationship.** A correlation coefficient of -1 means there is a perfect inverse linear relationship. In the above example a 1% rise in the value of the first bond would be associated with a 2% fall in the value of the second bond. If the first bond falls by 3% the value of the second bond increases by 6%.
  - **Independent variables.** A correlation coefficient of zero suggests that no linear relationship exists and that the variables move independently of one another.

This is illustrated with the following charts. The first chart plots daily changes in implied credit spreads for a BAA-rated bond against changes in 10-year Treasury bond yields. Note that these are expressed in absolute terms. A "trend line" has been added to the scatter graph. This is defined as the line of best fit and is the line about which the variation of values is minimized. Credit spreads and long-term risk-free rates appear to have an inverse relationship. When long-term risk-free rates rise credit spreads tend to narrow and when yields fall tend to widen. The second chart shows the correlation of daily returns between the two stocks, Blue Sky and Bore Inc. The variation around the line of best fit is far greater than it is for the plot of change in credit spreads versus changes in long-term yields. There is a weak positive correlation.

In more technical terms the square of the correlation coefficient r^2 defines the "goodness of fit" of the trend line. It measures the proportion of the values that can be explained by the inferred linear relationship. Methods exist to assess whether the results are statistically significant, whether it is likely that a linear relationship does in fact exist or whether the results can be explained by chance alone.

A widely used rule of thumb is that if the value for r^2 is less than 0.4 ($r = 0.63$) the evidence for any linear relationship is very thin. A large value for r is not in itself proof that a relationship exists and a useful simple check is to calculate r over a range of time frames to determine whether its value remains stable.

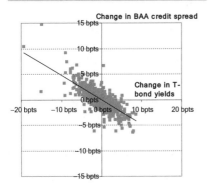

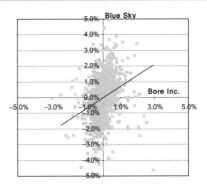

Application to Portfolio VARs

We have already stated that the VAR for a portfolio of financial assets is not in general given by the simple sum of the individual VARs. There are three specific cases we should examine in order to see how we can go about estimating a portfolio's VAR:

- **Perfect positive correlation.** If the two assets have a correlation coefficient of $+1$ then the portfolio VAR actually is the simple sum of the individual VARs. This is not surprising, as this is equivalent to simply adding more of the same asset:

$$VAR_{A+B} = VAR_A + VAR_B \quad where\, r_{A,B} = +1$$

- **Perfect negative correlation.** If the two assets have a correlation coefficient of -1 then the portfolio VAR is given by the difference between the individual VARs. In this case losses on one asset are offset by a matching proportional increase in the value of the other position:

$$VAR_{A+B} = |VAR_A - VAR_B| \quad where\, r_{A,B} = -1$$

- **Zero correlation.** If the correlation coefficient is zero then the two variables are independent of one another. In this case the value of the combined VAR has an upper bound equal to that given in the case of perfect positive correlation and a lower bound given by that in the case of perfect negative correlation:

$$VAR_A + VAR_B > VAR_{A+B} > |VAR_A - VAR_B| \quad where\, r_{A,B} = 0$$

The actual solution is derived from the underlying statistical theory and readers interested in its derivation should refer to the statistics primer for the formal treatment. The sum of the standard deviation for two variables is given from the following equation where W_i represents the weighting of each value:

$$\sigma^2 = W_A^2 \sigma_A^2 + W_B^2 \sigma_B^2 + 2 \times r_{A,B} \times W_A \times W_B \times \sigma_A \times \sigma_B$$

The VAR for each asset is based on a standard deviation (σ) multiplied by a sensitivity factor and hence the above result can be applied directly to the VAR problem (the weighting is already taken care of by the individual multiplication factors):

$$VAR^2_{A+B} = VAR^2_A + VAR^2_B + 2 \times r_{A,B} \times VAR_A \times VAR_B$$

It is easy to see how the cases of perfect positive and negative correlations are derived. For perfect positive correlation we get:

$$VAR^2_{A+B} = VAR^2_A + VAR^2_B + 2 \times 1 \times VAR_A \times VAR_B \Rightarrow VAR^2_{A+B} = (VAR_A + VAR_B)^2$$

and for perfect negative correlation we get:

$$VAR^2_{A+B} = VAR^2_A + VAR^2_B - 2 \times 1 \times VAR_A \times VAR_B \Rightarrow VAR^2_{A+B} = (VAR_A - VAR_B)^2$$

If the two variables are independent of one another (they have a correlation coefficient of zero) then the combined VAR is given by:

$$VAR_{A+B} = \sqrt{VAR^2_A + VAR^2_B}$$

An essential consequence of these results is that the VAR for a portfolio of assets is always less than the simple sum of the individual VARs provided there is anything less than perfect positive correlation. There does not have to be negative correlation for this diversification benefit to be gained.

Interest Rate Holdings Diversification

We will now look at a practical example of estimating the VAR (10-day holding period, 99% confidence level) for a portfolio with two assets; a holding in short-term T-bills and another in long-term T-bonds:

- **Long position in Treasury bills.** The value of the holding is $100m. Its duration is 0.5 years and the standard deviation of daily changes in short-term risk-free rates is 4.62 bpts. We have already made these calculations:

$$VAR_{T\text{-}bill} = \$170\,310$$

- **Long position in Treasury bond.** Value of position $20m, duration 8 and standard deviation of long-term risk-free rates 3.33 bpts:

$$VAR_{T\text{-}bonds} = \$20m \times 8 \times 0.000333 \times 2.33 \times 3.1623 = \$392\,847$$

The simple sum of the VARs of the two positions is $563\,157. The calculated historic correlation coefficient between T-bill and T-bond yields is 0.53 suggesting a modest positive linear relationship. The sum of the portfolio's VAR after taking diversification into effect is $504\,343 after taking diversification effects into account as calculated below:

$$VAR_{A+B} = (170\,130^2 + 392\,847^2 + 2 \times 0.53 \times 170\,130 \times 392\,847)^{1/2} = \$504\,343$$

This can be conveniently represented by a matrix. This is a useful way to look at the problem as the number of assets increases.

Matrix for portfolio VAR-squared sum		
	T-bills	**T-bonds**
T-bills	$+1 \times 170\,310^2$	$+0.53 \times 392\,847 \times 170\,310$
T-bonds	$+0.53 \times 170\,310 \times 392\,847$	$+1 \times 392\,847^2$

We will now add a third position, a short position with a value of \$10m in a BAA-rated corporate bond with duration of 4. The standard deviation of yields on BAA bonds of similar duration is 1.97 bpts. The VAR for this position (assuming the usual 10-day holding period and 99% confidence level) is \$58 032:

$$VAR_{BAA} = 3.1623 \times \$10m \times 4 \times 2.33 \times 0.000197 = \$58\,032$$

The simple sum of the VARs of the three positions, ignoring signs, is \$621 119. To take account of the new asset the portfolio matrix has to be adjusted to reflect the new covariance terms. The correlation coefficient table is shown in the following.

Correlation coefficient matrix			
	T-bills	**T-bonds**	**BAA bond**
T-bills	+1	+0.53	+0.35
T-bonds	+0.53	+1	+0.80
BAA bond	+0.35	+0.80	+1

The table to give the sum of the portfolio's VAR-squared is then adjusted as follows. The effect of the short position is taken into account by the negative sign of the correlation coefficient.

Matrix for portfolio VAR-squared sum			
	T-bills	**T-bonds**	**BAA bond**
T-bills	$+1 \times 170\,310^2$	$+0.53 \times 392\,847 \times 170\,310$	$-0.35 \times 170\,310 \times 58\,032$
T-bonds	$+0.53 \times 170\,310 \times 392\,847$	$+1 \times 392\,847^2$	$-0.80 \times 392\,847 \times 58\,032$
BAA	$-0.35 \times 170\,310 \times 58\,032$	$-0.80 \times 392\,847 \times 58\,032$	$+1 \times 58\,032^2$

This gives a portfolio VAR of \$462 893, which is less than the portfolio's VAR when there were two assets only. The number of covariance terms increases much faster than the number of self-variance coefficients. A portfolio with 16 members has 16 self-variance terms and 240 covariance terms while one with 30 members has 30 self-variance terms and 870 covariance terms. In large portfolios the covariance factors become the major determinant of the portfolio's VAR.

Multiple Variable Dependency

Some individual VAR positions are dependent on more than one underlying factor, many derivatives, for example, are sensitive to both the price of the underlying instrument and the discount rate used in calculating *NPV*. An important example of exposure to two underlying risk factors comes from foreign currency investments. An US owner of a foreign currency government bond is exposed to two principal sources of price risk, adverse movements in interest rates in the foreign currency and adverse movements in the exchange rate. To show how this is dealt with we will use a simple example.

The method used to calculate VARs for foreign exchange risks is basically the same as that used for interest rate positions. An important practical difference is that standard deviations for interest rate changes are expressed in absolute terms, in basis points, while in foreign exchange they are normally expressed as percentages:

- **Foreign currency bond.** The value of the holding is €25m, the bond has a duration of 10. The spot €:$ exchange rate is 1.25. The current value of the holding in US$ is $20m.

  The standard deviation of €long-term risk-free yields is 5 bpts. The standard deviation of the exchange rate is 0.06%. The correlation coefficient between €long-term risk-free rates and the US$:€exchange rate is 0.53.

  The price of the bond in US$ terms is given by:

  $$P_\$ = \frac{P_€ \ (Euro\ long\text{-}term\ rates)}{FX_{€,\,\$}}$$

  By splitting the value at risk into two components we can identify the VAR due to changes in euro long-term rates and that due to exchange rate changes:

  $$VAR\ due\ to\ LT\ rates = 3.1623 \times \$20m \times 0.0005 \times 2.33 = \$589\,453$$
  $$VAR\ due\ to\ FX = 3.1623 \times \$20m \times 0.08\% \times 2.33 = \$117\,891$$

  Using the standard method for VAR addition we get a total VAR of $659 556 versus a simple sum of $707 344.

- **Short euro forward contract.** A forward euro contract is for €100m for delivery against US$ in 90 days. Current spot rate is 1.25 and the daily standard deviation of the euro:$ exchange rate is 0.06%. Annualized 90-day euro rates are 8% with standard deviation of 4.8 bpts. The correlation coefficient between 90-day euro rates and euro:$ exchange rate is 0.2.

The spot equivalent of the forward exchange contract is given by:

$$US\$\ spot\ equivalent = \frac{Value\ in\ foreign\ currency}{FX_{FCY:US\$} \times (1 + R(t)_{FCY})} \cong \frac{Value\ in\ foreign\ currency}{FX_{FCY:US\$}}$$
$$\times (1 - R(t)_{FCY})$$

In this specific case we get:

$$US\$\ spot\ equivalent = \frac{€100m}{1.25 \times (1 + 2\%)} = \$78.4m$$

The value at risk for the two factors is given by:

$$VAR\ due\ to\ LT\ rates = \$78.4m \times 0.0006 \times 2.33 \times 3.1623 = \$346\,598$$
$$VAR\ due\ to\ FX = \$78.4m \times 0.0048\% \times 2.33 \times 3.1623 = \$27\,728$$

The actual VAR for the position is $353 190 versus the simple sum of $374 326.

Risk Factor Decomposition and Aggregation

The way in which the risk factor decomposition is carried out can affect the reliability of the VAR estimates and illustrate our point that VAR numbers are just that, estimates.

- **Risk factor decomposition.** There is a trade-off between the level at which risk factors are decomposed and then aggregated. In general the lower the level of decomposition the more reliable the estimates are likely to be but the greater the computational power and amount of historic data that needs to be stored.

  Each asset has to be assigned to a particular underlying risk factor. The value of all short-term bonds, for example, could be assumed to vary with changes in one short-term yield, such as a three-month T-bill rate. This process of assignment, the allocation of assets into classes defined on the basis of a common underlying risk factor, is an approximation unless there is a perfect correlation between all assets included in this category. It would be possible to break this down further into one week, one month, two months and so on. The benefit is a reduction in the approximation risk but if these assets are very highly correlated the extra effort may not be justified.
- **Decomposition method.** The method of decomposition also has an effect on the VAR result. In the case of the BAA bond we have taken the underlying risk factor as yields on BAA-rated bonds of similar duration. We could have modeled this by attributing changes in the BAA bond discount rate as due to changes in equivalent risk-free yields plus changes in implied credit spreads. The simple sum of the VARs is then given by the following.

Breakdown of individual VARs				
	T-bills	**T-bonds**	**BAA bond**	**Total**
Short-term rates	170 130			170 130
Long-term rates		392 847	98 212	491.059
Credit spreads			64 305	64 305
Portfolio				**725 494**

The $725 494 is much larger than the previously calculated sum of $621 009 but after taking account of covariances falls to an estimated VAR of $461 797, similar but not identical to the $462 893 originally calculated. We could take this one stage further and break down long-term yields into short-term yields plus a term spread. After carrying out a similar exercise we get an estimated VAR of $498 535 significantly greater than originally estimated.

- **Aggregation.** VAR positions at lower levels of decomposition are then aggregated using exactly the same method for VAR addition taking account of correlations between aggregated levels. Correlation coefficients become increasingly unreliable the higher up the aggregation level. If a portfolio has 10 000 positions and no aggregation takes place approximately 50m cross-terms will have to be calculated. If on the other hand we have first level aggregation with just 100 different categories that drops to around 5000 and if only 10 to approximately 50.

Equities

Estimating VARs for equity positions has one fundamental difference compared with estimating VARs for interest rate and foreign exchange positions in that there is no underlying risk factor that can be simply used for aggregation purposes.

A bank may have holdings in very many different debt instruments of similar duration whose price changes can be determined in a linear way from a single underlying risk factor, such as a yield taken from a specific point on the yield curve. Foreign exchange positions change with foreign exchange rates. In more formal terms we can say that the changes in the value of vanilla interest rate and foreign exchange products have perfect, or close to perfect, correlations with changes in their underlying risk factor.

This is not the case with equity positions, where stock price changes are not perfectly correlated with the market. If we take our two stocks, Blue Sky's returns have a relatively high correlation with market returns while that of Bore Inc.'s is low. These are illustrated in the following charts, which also show the equation of the trend line, otherwise known as the line of best fit.

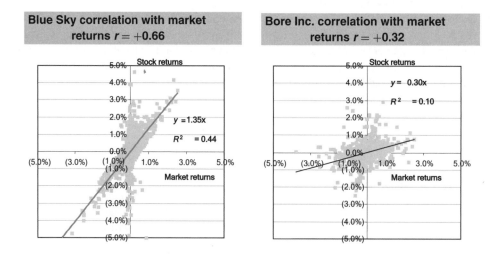

The slope of the line of best fit in this context is called beta. This may be calculated as follows:

$$\beta = r_{i,m} \times \frac{\text{Standard deviation of stock returns}}{\text{Standard deviation of market returns}} = r_{i,m}\frac{\sigma_i}{\sigma_m}$$

The betas for Bore Inc. and Blue Sky may be calculated as shown below:

$$\beta_{Bore\ Inc.} = 0.32 \times \frac{0.55\%}{0.59\%} = 0.30 \quad and \quad \beta_{Blue\ Sky} = 0.66 \times \frac{1.21\%}{0.59\%} = 1.35$$

Beta can also be calculated as $\beta_i = \sigma_{i,m}/\sigma_m^2$ where $\sigma_{i,m}$ is the covariance between the stock and the market, and this is the form most commonly shown in standard statistics textbooks.

Equity Portfolios

In order to demonstrate the key features of managing equity portfolio risk we will use a simple portfolio with one holding in Bore Inc. with a market value of $750 000 and a second holding of $250 000 in Blue Sky. The following table contains a summary of the key data concerning the individual stocks, the portfolio and the market.

Standard deviation of daily returns, correlation coefficients and betas					
	Bore Inc.	Blue Sky	Portfolio	Market	Blue Sky–Bore Inc.
Value ($)	750 000	250 000	1 000 000		
Standard	0.55%	1.21%	0.57%	0.59%	
Correlation	0.32	0.66	0.58	1.00	0.29
Beta	0.30	1.35	0.56	1	

Key features of the data are that:

- Bore Inc. has a standard deviation of 0.55%, correlation coefficient of 0.32 and beta of 0.30:

$$\beta_{Bore\ Inc.} = 0.32 \times \frac{0.55\%}{0.59\%} = 0.30$$

- Blue Sky has a standard deviation of 1.21%, a correlation coefficient of 0.66 and beta of 1.35:

$$\beta_{Blue\ Sky} = 0.66 \times \frac{1.21\%}{0.59\%} = 1.35$$

- The historic correlation of the portfolio with the market is 0.58, a standard deviation of 0.57% and beta of 0.58:

$$\beta_{Portfolio} = 0.58 \times \frac{0.57\%}{0.59\%} = 0.58$$

- The portfolio's beta can also be calculated as the weighted sum of the betas for Blue Sky and Bore Inc.:

$$\beta_{Portfolio} = 0.25 \times 1.35 + 0.75 \times 0.30 = 0.58$$

The daily VAR at the 99% confidence level for the two stocks is given by:

$$VAR_{Bore\ Inc.} = \$750\,000 \times 2.33 \times 0.0055 = \$9554$$
$$VAR_{Blue\ Sky} = \$250\,000 \times 0.0121 = \$7032$$

The simple sum of the individual VARs is $16 586 but after taking correlations into account the portfolio's VAR falls to $13 393.

It is tempting to expect that the portfolio's VAR can be calculated by multiplying the value of the portfolio times the standard deviation of the market's returns (multiplied by 2.33) and the portfolio's beta:

$$"VAR"_{Portfolio} = \$1\,000\,000 \times 0.58 \times 2.33 \times 0.0057 = \$7726$$

This is the same as the sum of the VARs for Blue Sky of $4663 and for Bore Inc. of $3064 calculated in the same way. This is the same result as if we had taken the portfolio as a whole because of beta's additive properties.

This understates the actual VAR estimate by a factor of 0.58, the correlation coefficient between the market and the portfolio. Although it is possible to use stock betas and market standard deviations of return to arrive at a notional VAR estimate this will be a lower bound only unless the correlation between the portfolio and market is taken into account.

If this approach were taken the portfolio correlation coefficient between the portfolio and the market would have to be recalculated each day. In practice banks with a material exposure to equities have no choice other than to compute correlation coefficients between each pair of stocks.

Weaknesses of VaR Approaches

It is worth concluding on the subject of VaR by reiterating that it is not a panacea and its results must be treated with caution. Ninety-nine percent confidence levels sound very impressive but for a one-day holding period mean that in one day in 100 we should expect greater losses than specified:

- Most models assume normal distributions and no serial correlation and this is not always the case.
- Correlation coefficients are calculated on the basis of historic data and there is no guarantee that such relationships will persist.
- Standard holding periods may be insufficient to liquidate or hedge all positions.
- These three concerns are all most likely to exhibit themselves at times of extremes when the level of potential losses is likely to be highest.
- The use of VaR techniques does not eliminate the risk that losses will be greater than that expressed at the stated confidence level.
- VaR models do not usually capture all material higher order price or realization risk factors.
- Most VaR models do not capture intra-day positions and the actual risk profile may be much higher than that suggested by VAR calculated on the basis of open positions at the end of each day.

VaR is a reporting and analytical tool and most banks with active trading books overlay standard VaR approaches with sensitivity analyses and stress testing. None of these remove the need for banks to put other controls in place. Only offices or branches with sufficient derivatives expertise and adequate risk control systems should be allowed to deal in derivatives, for example. Management has to put in place control systems to set and enforce limits on exposures across a range of different dimensions including counterparty, location, product, currency, country, risk type, risk factor, position limits and VAR limits.

Conversion of Reported VAR Numbers into Common Base

The following charts show the distributions of trading revenues on a daily basis for two large international banks, one a relatively conservative commercial bank and the other a relatively aggressive investment bank. The first chart shows trading revenues plotted against number of days while the second is an idealized frequency distribution chart.

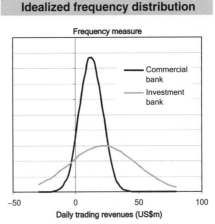

The first bank's principal activity is commercial banking although it also has investment banking and fund management businesses. It has net tangible shareholders' funds (after adjusting for goodwill) of approximately $52bn and a reputation for conservatism. The second bank's principal activity is investment banking although it also has a sizeable fund management business. Its total net tangible shareholders' funds are approximately $15bn. Total annual revenues from trading activities at the commercial banks are equivalent to approximately 6% of year-end shareholders' funds and 37% at the investment banks. Daily trading revenues at the investment bank are considerably more volatile than at the commercial bank.

Both banks disclose minimum, average and maximum VAR levels on a daily basis for the past year:

- The commercial bank's VAR numbers are reported on the basis of BIS standards and are calculated to a 99% confidence level using a 10-day holding period.
- The investment bank does not take deposits and is not subject to BIS capital adequacy requirements. It chooses to report its VAR values on the basis of a 95% confidence level and one-day holding period.

In order to be able to make any meaningful comparison between the two banks we need to convert the investment bank's VAR numbers into values reflecting a 99% confidence level and 10-day holding period. This cannot be done accurately using publicly available data but we can make a reasonable stab at this. A 95% confidence level for a one-tailed test is equivalent to 1.65 standard deviations and at a 99% confidence level to 2.33 standard deviations. A one-day holding period can be converted to a 10-day holding period by using a multiplication factor equal to the square root of 10 (3.163).

So by multiplying the investment bank's reported VAR values by a factor of 4.48 (2.33/1.65 × 3.163) we can get a reasonable basis for comparison.

Daily VAR levels ($m)								
	Commercial Bank			**Investment Bank**				
	10-day, 99% confidence			1-day, 95% confidence			10-day, 99% confidence		
	Min	Avge	Max	Min	Avge	Max	Min	Avge	Max
Interest rate	60	82	121	19	34	68	85	152	305
FX	2	21	47	5	16	35	22	72	305
Equities	20	29	40	15	22	49	67	99	220
Commodities				6	12	17	27	54	76
Total	**83**	**132**	**209**	**45**	**84**	**169**	**175**	**323**	**681**

Even at its maximum VAR level the regulatory capital requirement for the commercial bank, assuming a minimum multiplication factor of 3×, is for only $0.6bn approximately 1.2% of its total tangible shareholders' funds and 1.8% of its total 8% regulatory capital requirement. The estimated maximum VAR for a 10-day holding period and 99% confidence level at the investment bank is approximately 5% of its tangible shareholders' funds.

13

Managing Credit Risk

I would rather be approximately right than precisely wrong.

Lord Keynes, British economist

In this chapter we look at the extent to which asset portfolio theory can be applied to credit risk management, the implications for required risk capital and how banks actually provide for credit losses. Credit losses are usually treated and managed in terms of "expected losses" and "unexpected losses". Expected losses are based on the most likely level of losses arising from a particular exposure or pool of exposures while unexpected losses are those losses above that level which may occur. Unexpected losses are defined and managed using similar VaR type techniques as those used in managing market risk and covered in Chapter 12 "Managing market risk". We have already introduced the concept of the reduction of risk due to diversification effects in portfolios of assets and we will consider how this concept applies to credit risk.

The treatment of future credit losses has a critical bearing on bank capital management. In this chapter we will examine the most widely accepted approach to how this should be taken into account against the varying practices of banks. The main focus of the New Basel Accord is on the treatment of credit risk for the purpose of calculating bank regulatory capital requirements but is based on a collective compromise and lacks a fundamental basis.

Banks establish provisions, or reserves, for possible credit losses. The use of these provision accounts varies widely between banks in different countries and we identify the major differences in their definitions and usage.

CREDIT LOSSES ON INDIVIDUAL LOANS

Credit losses are not certain and can be divided into two parts, expected losses based on the probability of default and losses in the event of default and unexpected losses based on the distribution of losses and defined to a specified confidence level. The level of expected losses on an individual loan over a specified period is given by the following equation:

$$Expected\ credit\ losses = \sum_{t=0}^{T} P_t LIED_t = EL$$

where P_t is the probability of default at time t and $LIED_t$ the PV of the level of expected losses in the event of default at time t. Expected losses should be regarded as part of the transaction's costs. The time period chosen is usually over the term of a loan or lifetime of an exposure or a specified period, such as one year.

There are a number of ways to simplify this modeling. One way is to change the definition of the problem into a two-state (binomial) problem where the loan either defaults or it does not, the loss in the event of default is fixed and is independent of the probability of default. In this case:

$$EL = P \times LIED$$

where P is probability of default and *LIED* the loss in the event of default. The standard deviation σ of the losses can then be calculated using the following standard statistical formula:

$$\sigma^2 = \sum_{i=1}^{N} W_i X_i^2 - \left(\sum_{i=1}^{N} W_i X_i \right)^2$$

In our case with zero losses assumed if no default occurs we arrive at the following:

$$\sigma^2 = P \times (LIED)^2 + (1 - P) \times 0 - (P \times (LIED))^2 - ((1 - P) \times 0)^2$$
$$= P \times (LIED)^2 - P^2 (LIED)^2$$

The standard deviation for losses, from which an estimate of unexpected losses may be derived, is therefore:

$$\sigma_L = LIED \times \sqrt{(P - P^2)}$$

The two factors whose behavior we need to understand then are the probability of default and the loss in the event of default.

DEFAULT PROBABILITIES

There is a dearth of useful public information about delinquency and recovery rates of loans made by banks in most countries. The lack of such information in the public domain makes life difficult for analysts. There are a number of potential sources for data on historic credit default rates: credit rating agencies, central banks, other external information providers and banking associations. The availability and usefulness of such data vary considerably between countries:

- **Credit rating agencies.** The three main global rating agencies maintain extensive historic databases with default rates on bonds going back over many years that banks can use as proxies for likelihood of loan defaults. This data is proprietary but is available to subscribers who pay for their services. These are most useful for ratings of large companies in developed markets, and in the US and UK in particular.

  Few companies in developing markets fall within the scope of coverage of the global agencies although there has been some progress in establishing local agencies. Inevitably, however, even where such agencies now exist their default data only covers the recent past and is therefore of limited use.

- **Central banks.** Central banks are in a position to collect detailed data on loan defaults. Many central banks only make the system level of NPLs publicly available and if they report a breakdown it is usually restricted to the industrial classification of the borrowers. If the data is credible (and as banking crises develop this becomes increasingly open to doubt) it can be useful for identifying the rate of increase of NPLs at a particular time and confirmation of any turning points.

- **Other external sources.** Credit bureaus collect data on bankruptcies and other consumer and small company liquidations. The banks themselves are a useful source of data where they are required to disclose such data. Some information providers collate such data although great care needs to be taken in its use because of the widespread definitional problems in this area.

Securitization issues such as mortgage backed securities, credit card receivables and auto loans have made a great deal of data on default and loss rates publicly available on these types of assets than was previously the case. Such data only exists and is useful in a handful of countries where securitization issues are relatively common and have been so for a number of years.

- **Banking associations.** Some banking associations act to coordinate default data collection and dissemination between their members. This data is usually not available publicly. In the US, however, data from home lender associations is available on housing loans broken down by geographic location and type of property.
- **Proprietary databases.** Most banks now have internal rating systems and maintain historic databases on default rates. Unfortunately at many banks this is a relatively recent phenomenon (recent in the sense that to be useful the data should cover at least one full economic cycle). Other problems are that definitions of ratings or their interpretation over time may change and there is often a lack of granularity in the internal ratings used. There also have to be questions over its usefulness as a reference point when such data covers a period largely characterized by a developing banking crisis, the crisis itself and its subsequent resolution.

Even when there is a reasonably good base of historic data there are plenty of problems and issues that remain largely unresolved:

- **Economic cyclicality.** Should medium-term economic forecasts be taken into account given their high level of uncertainty? Should default probabilities be taken as some form of average over a full economic cycle? The case for taking these forecasts into account is that this gives a common base case. In the event of the economic environment showing signs of being weaker than expected this provides a reason for reassessing default probabilities across the board.

    It is not uncommon to overhear discussions between line managers and house economists where the former has been demanding GDP forecasts for the next five years. A typical economist response is that it's hard enough to make forecasts for the next six months with any real confidence given current uncertainties. Five years? Dream on. The line manager patiently explains that she understands this but needs the numbers for her business plan.
- **Time frame.** Should the time frame used be based on the term of individual loans? This may make sense when looking at the pricing of individual loans but makes production of consolidated numbers difficult. It may make sense also to look at default probabilities within a specified time frame independent of the term of individual loans. A problem here is that extrapolation over longer time intervals is problematic as changes in loss rates are not random and serial correlation is clearly present. A common time frame taken is one year and this may be appropriate in developed markets but in the context of emerging markets seems short and is definitely considerably shorter than the economic (as opposed to legal) term of many bank exposures.
- **Changing conditions.** Asset portfolio diversification theory depends on historic correlations being stable and reflecting some genuine underlying relationship. A high historic correlation on losses in two regions may have been because both regions depended to a large extent on a single, common industry. If that is no longer the case there is no reason to expect past correlations to be a good indicator of future correlations. This same argument can be

put for equity holdings in VaR type analysis but a major difference is that the time frames involved in managing market risk are very different from those for credit risk.

LOSSES IN EVENT OF DEFAULT

The level of expected losses arising from delinquencies should be viewed as a part of the costs of doing business. Actual losses may be higher or lower. Expected credit losses for individual loans depend on the probability that the loan will become delinquent and the likely level of losses in such an event. It is much harder to estimate the probability of default than likely loss rates on delinquent loans.

Loss rates on delinquent accounts depend on four variables. The actual exposure at the time the account was frozen, the level and quality of collateral, the time taken to resolve the case and other direct costs such as legal fees.

- **Exposure at time of default.** The actual exposure is likely to vary over the term of the loan. In the case of mortgages the principal outstanding falls over time. Continued drawdowns on loans for project financing or real estate will result in the principal increasing over time. Where the exposure is a credit facility it is likely that the customer in financial distress will draw down to the maximum allowed under the terms of the facility before defaulting on any other loans. Derivative and other transactions may also result in the bank having an outstanding exposure and these will need to be taken into account.
- **Collateral.** Collateral is usually the key factor in determining loss rates on secured NPLs. Not only does it have value but it is also important in determining the bank's position as a creditor in terms of seniority in any liquidation. Collateral is not without its problems. Falling asset prices will erode the value of pledged collateral. The creditor bank also has to establish its legal claim to the collateral, usually through a court ruling.

  The marketability of the pledged collateral is also important. It may be difficult to find a buyer for the collateral. Forced liquidation, usually through an auction, usually results in fire-sale prices. We have looked at the problems of real estate developers providing collateral in the form of the developments being funded in Chapter 5 "Corporate lending". Real estate companies are far more likely to fail when real estate prices are falling. In these circumstances the risks of failure rise at the same time as collateral cover is falling.
- **Time.** NPLs bear a carrying cost and the faster that they are resolved the less the losses are when expressed in *NPV* terms. This is simply one more example of the time value of money at work. The time until cases are resolved depends on many factors of which the form of the legal system is the most important. The nature of the established legal framework, the capacity and efficiency of the system and the integrity and honesty of politicians and judges all matter.
- **Other costs.** Other external costs include professional fees (lawyers, appraisers, and auctioneers) and court costs. In more complex corporate cases these costs mount and absorb a high proportion of the proceeds from collateral sales.

The loss in the event of default (*LIED*) is probably the easier and least contentious factor to model. It is, however, complicated by the fact that the *LIED* varies over the life of the exposure and to get a good estimate requires historic price data for pledged assets and recovery rates to be available. This is particularly important when it comes to estimating unexpected losses where the volatility of prices is an important factor.

In practice an estimate for the loss rate of 40%–60% of the total potential exposure for secured loans and 80%–100% for unsecured loans is probably good enough for many banks given the level of uncertainty inherent in estimates of default probabilities.

It is also self-evident that there is a relationship between the likelihood of default and the loss in event of default. The simplest credit models assume constant *LIED*, the sophisticated a variable *LIED* but all assume these variables are independent because otherwise the problem, which is already complex, becomes unmanageable.

It is also apparent that the distribution of credit losses on many types of loans is unlikely to be normal and this is confirmed by actual historic data. A lot of uncertainties exist but bank management has to make the effort to quantify as much as possible while keeping in mind the underlying weaknesses in the methodology and its implementation.

The banks with the best records in terms of keeping credit losses and credit loss volatility low are those that have:

- Applied rigorous cashflow analyses to all loan applications and made ability to repay the primary factor in the loan approval process.
- Recognized that even though the bank appears fully hedged against interest rate and foreign exchange risks the realization of those risks at the borrower will transform those risks into credit risks.
- Required a high level of overcollateralization of quality security.
- Insisted on covenants that protect their interests from action taken by the borrower.
- Obtained additional guarantees where possible (but not relied on them for the primary security). Treated historic, but implicit government guarantees, with a high degree of skepticism.
- Recognized that sovereign governments can default on their foreign debt.
- Maintained a well-diversified loan book skewed towards loans where loss rate distributions are close to normal.
- Avoided exposure to highly cyclical industries. Some leading international banks, for example, have longstanding policies to refuse to lend to real estate developers, airlines or shipping companies.

NON-NORMAL DISTRIBUTIONS

Most VaR modeling of market risk assumes normal distributions. Given the lack of normality in credit losses for many classes of exposures this cannot be assumed for credit risk assessment. A number of alternative techniques exist and a useful, simple alternative method is that given by Chebyshev's theorem (see the statistics primer for more details). This holds for any distribution of observations and as a consequence it provides a much lower level of confidence at a given number of standard deviations from the mean than that which can be derived for normal distributions.

The theorem results in a lower bound only and there is no concept of a one-tailed test. The following table shows confidence levels versus number of standard deviations from the mean. In terms of losses this can be explained as follows. There is at least a 75% probability that the actual losses will be within 2 standard deviations of the mean and a 25% probability that they will be more.

At the 99% confidence level a one-tailed test for a normal distribution is defined by 2.33 standard deviations, against the 10 standard deviations given using Chebyshev.

Confidence levels versus Z-scores for Chebyshev's theorem									
Z-score	2	3	4	5	6	7	8	9	10
Confidence level	75%	89%	94%	96%	97%	98.0%	98.4%	98.8%	99.0%
Number of years	4	9	16	25	36	49	63	83	100

Analysts lack the detailed information that individual banks possess and banks should be able to arrive at a lower number of standard deviations for a stated confidence level, particularly as loss rates on some classes of loans are close to being normal.

For equity analysts it is a useful tool because it is simple to use and can be used to generate ballpark results and reach reasonable conclusions quickly. Applying this approach to the US financial system in late 2001 produced estimates for total system credit losses over 2002–2003 that were nearly twice as large as those made by the US Comptroller of the Currency at the time. This simple exercise confirmed her assertion that the US banking system was not facing a banking crisis despite the economic downturn. Actual losses came in somewhere between the two estimates.

We can also make some rough estimates of average expected and unexpected losses based on historic quarterly write-offs and compare the implied risk capital requirements with those of the Basel Accord. The write-off numbers do not include other costs associated with default such as legal and other professional charges. Anyone can do this exercise by themselves by playing with the data downloaded from the Fed's website.

With a team of half a dozen analysts and a couple of months' work a much more rigorous result could be obtained but we would need a much bigger envelope. The following table shows the mean of the annualized write-offs and loss levels at various confidence levels for some of the major loan classifications.

Annualized write-off rates and Chebyshev confidence levels as % of loans						
	Residential	Commercial	Consumer	Credit cards	Leases	Commercial/ industrial	All
Mean	0.15	0.64	2.20	4.43	0.36	0.65	0.79
Std. dev.	0.06	0.82	0.41	0.73	0.22	0.50	0.36
75%	0.26	2.28	3.02	5.89	0.79	1.66	1.50
89%	0.31	3.10	3.44	6.62	1.01	2.16	1.86
94%	0.37	3.92	3.85	7.36	1.22	2.67	2.22
96%	0.42	4.73	4.26	8.09	1.44	3.17	2.57
99%	0.70	8.82	6.33	11.75	2.51	5.68	4.35

The mean value gives us annual expected losses (*EL*) as a percentage of loans and the confidence levels are defined using a one-year holding period. The level of unexpected losses (*UL*) at the 99% confidence level by category (once a century) is given below.

The contrast between residential mortgages and commercial real estate loans is stark. Expected losses for residential mortgages are equivalent to 15 bpts and for loans for commercial real estate 64 bpts, a difference of a factor of about $4\times$. The risk capital that should be allocated

	Residential mortgages	Commercial real estate	Consumer	Credit cards	Leases	Commercial/ industrial	All
Expected and unexpected losses as % of loans							
EL	0.15	0.64	2.20	4.43	0.36	0.65	0.79
UL @99%	0.55	7.18	4.13	7.32	2.15	5.03	3.56

for the mortgage is just 0.55% of the loan versus a Basel requirement of 4%, while that for a loan for commercial real estate is 7.2% close to the Basel requirement of 8%.

It is easy to see that this creates a large incentive for deposit taking banks to get residential mortgages off their books given that the regulatory requirement is more than 7× our rough estimate of the risk capital necessary. Some care needs to be taken in trying to apply these results in a quantitative way in other countries.

Given the heterogeneous nature of bank credit exposures it is worth looking at the main segments individually.

MORTGAGES, CREDIT CARDS AND AUTO LOANS

Retail loans and corporate exposures have very different credit characteristics. Losses on retail loans have distributions that are close to being normal and are less affected by economic cyclicality. Of data available publicly the US Federal Reserve is probably the most useful easily accessible source. It publishes write-offs as a percentage of loans going back over more than two decades. An efficient legal system and proactive approach to NPL management by American banks mean that there is very little lag between loans being classified as non-performing and the expected losses being written off:

- **Distribution of write-offs.** The following charts show the distribution of write-offs for mortgages and credit cards based on data for US commercial banks published by the US Federal Reserve. This data is available from the Fed's website on a quarterly basis dating back to 1Q91.

  The mean annualized write-off rate for mortgage loans is just 0.15%, with a standard deviation of 0.06%. The distribution is not normal and is slightly skewed to the right but is fairly narrowly bound. The coefficient of variation (σ/Mean) for housing loans is 0.36, indicating a low level of dispersion.

  The mean annualized write-off rate for credit cards is unsurprisingly much higher at 4.4% with a standard deviation of 0.73%. Its coefficient of variation is, however, lower than that for housing loans at 0.16 indicating an even lower level of relative dispersion (although in absolute terms it is much higher).

- **Mortgage characteristics.** Home mortgages are a relatively homogeneous product with the major difference being between fixed rate mortgages and those that are floating rate. Historical default rates across the world have generally been among the lowest of any asset class. There are a number of qualitative reasons why this is the case. Owner–occupiers have to live somewhere and their choice is usually between paying rent or making the mortgage payments; mortgages have a form of long-term option on property prices and given their typical term have significant time value. Mortgagors do not default simply because they have negative equity and this option is out-of-the-money. The personal consequences of

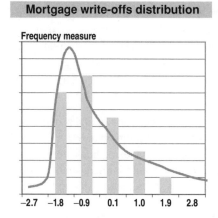

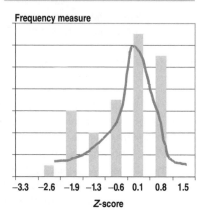

defaulting on a mortgage are extreme and mortgagors will usually default only in extreme circumstances.

For default rates to rise sharply from their very low "normal" levels usually requires some combination of falling property prices, rising unemployment, falling wages and in the case of floating rate loans higher interest rates.

There are a few examples where mortgage default rates have soared and in recent years these have occurred in countries where there has been a form of managed foreign exchange system that has subsequently collapsed. Mortgagors who took out "cheaper" foreign currency loans found that the value and servicing costs of their loan in local currency terms shot up. Other factors such as falling property prices and higher unemployment also occurred in these cases but were of secondary importance.

In countries where mortgage securitization issues are common there is a wealth of data available on both default and loss rates. In the US these are available on a regional basis and can be analyzed by type of loan and borrower. Publicly available data in most other countries is either sparse or non-existent.

LIED rates vary with the remaining term on the loan and volatility of property prices. In the event of foreclosure banks usually act to sell the properties at auction.

Industry level statistics on home loans are less useful to specialist lenders focusing on segments where most lenders are not prepared to make loans. These include loans made where standard loan-to-value criteria are lowered (and this may be as a result of upfront subsidies on mortgagors' legal and other costs), on older properties that are difficult to sell or to borrowers with an erratic earnings and employment history.

In some countries individuals may take out mortgages to purchase homes to let. These are riskier than loans to owner–occupiers and ability to meet payments is usually dependent on rental income. Such borrowers are at particular risk if they have taken out floating rate loans, interest rates rise and property prices and hence rental yields fall. Portfolio risks are particularly vulnerable to location concentration.

- **Credit card characteristics.** Credit cards are also fairly homogeneous products. Industry level data is available in countries with developed securitization markets. Many countries have specialist credit card operators and, even if individual banks do not break down their overall credit losses, typical levels for credit cards can be gauged from the specialist operators.

Their relatively small absolute dollar size and large number of accounts mean that they are particularly tractable to statistical analysis. Most banks waste little time in pursuing claims on delinquent credit card accounts. These are normally passed on to a specialist retail debt-recovery operation at which time the bank writes off the full exposure. Any subsequent recoveries due the bank are then written back. In practical terms the *LIED* can be taken as the authorized credit limit to a reasonable first approximation.

Most banks use credit bureaus to check applicants' credit history and credit-scoring systems to determine whether to approve applications. Credit card operations usually have among the highest expected loss rates of any bank assets but among the lowest level of unexpected losses relative to expected losses.

Having a lot of credit cards is a dubious luxury but in most developed countries having one working card is a necessity for many people. These people will often treat one card as their main card, usually issued through their principal bank, and will try to keep it current even as their other cards are being cut into little pieces in front of them and their friends or business acquaintances at restaurants.

Individual operators are virtually certain to experience a much higher level of expected and unexpected losses than other issuers if they relax their credit application criteria or fail to carry out diligent measures to identify and control fraud. Potential credit losses and appraised credit quality do not vary in a linear way.

New entrants or operators with no natural target customer base are most at risk. An issuer that grows its card base rapidly by approving the one-in-twenty applications that every other issuer has rejected is likely to find its credit losses spiraling out of control. Other portfolio risks arise from geographic concentration.

They are usually managed on a "pooled" basis from a credit risk perspective as one or more discrete pools. ("Gold" cards, for example, have somewhat different characteristics from mass market.) Most banks establish provisions for individual pools of exposures rather than for individual exposures.

- **Auto loans.** Auto loan credit characteristics fall somewhere between those of mortgages and credit cards. They are secured but on a depreciating asset and are relatively short-term loans. Data on default rates is reasonably accessible where auto loan securitization issues are common.

The main risk to all lenders comes from changes in tax policies that have a direct impact on the value of new and second-hand cars and a particular concentration on a particular class of vehicle or type of customer.

If a government acts to reduce taxes or import tariffs on new cars this will at a stroke lower the value of recently bought second-hand cars and the price of new cars. In cases where the reductions are extreme some people who have bought their vehicle on credit may simply return the keys for their original purchase and buy a new car.

Some lenders specialize in lending to taxi drivers or owner–drivers of coaches or trucks. The number of taxi licenses is frequently restricted and it is not uncommon for the cost of the license to be considerably more than the cost of the taxi itself. An increase in the number of licenses issued, a downturn in business or relaxation of licensing requirements will all have a negative impact on the value of the licenses and hence the lender's collateral.

Similar issues affect any financial institutions involving asset leases. These are best viewed from an economic perspective as secured long-term loans with the leased asset as collateral.

Mortgages	Credit cards
Mortgages * Homogeneous secured loans to owner-occupiers * Mitigating factors: somewhere to live, time value of "option", personal consequences of default & bankruptcy * LIED depends on time to term & volatility of property prices * Loss distribution close to "normal" * Wealth of default data in countries with developed securitization markets * Long tail does exist – but need combination of burst property market, high unemployment or falling incomes & higher interest rates * Specific problems: relaxation of lending criteria, loans for buy-to-let, foreign currency loans, indemnity insurance, geographic concentration	**Credit cards** * Homogeneous unsecured revolving credit * Industry-level co-operation – credit bureaus * Many relatively small exposures – managed on pooled basis * Wealth of default data; securitization issues, specialized issuers * LIED can be taken as credit limit * Limited attempts to recover losses, banks move fast to write off * Expected losses high * Unexpected losses high in absolute terms but low as % of EL * Relatively insensitive to economic cyclicality, rising unemployment more important * Specific problems: relaxation of approval criteria, fraud detection & prevention

Corporate, SME and Real Estate Exposures

Loans to corporates and to small and medium enterprises pose very different credit management problems to those of mortgages and credit cards. Of these two segments exposures to corporates are more complex but easier to deal with than loans to SMEs.

The first of the following two charts shows write-off distributions for loans to commercial and industrial companies. There is no readily available public data that breaks this down by company size. The second chart is for real estate write-offs. The distributions of write-offs for these loans are very different from those for mortgages and credit cards. Both of them exhibit what are referred to as "long tails". The long tails in these examples date back to the period of the recession of the early 1980s in the US.

Corporate exposure characteristic

Banks have many different types of exposure to larger corporates including the following:

- **Credit products.** Direct loans to the holding companies or subsidiaries of the group, syndicated loans and facilities. Some of these loans may be in foreign currency and booked in overseas branches. The bank may also hold some of the company's commercial paper and bonds.

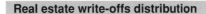

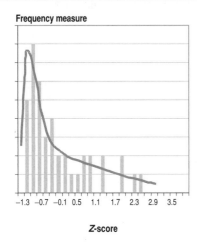

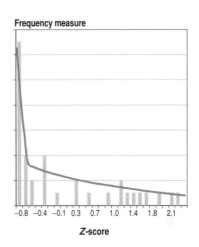

- **Guarantees.** Guarantees for letters of credit and so on. The main company of an extended group may have taken loans itself and also have acted as a guarantor for loans made to subsidiaries, associates or other companies with which it has a relationship.
- **Derivatives.** A bank may have multiple exposures in the form of derivatives such as interest rate and foreign currency swaps, futures and forward contracts. At any given moment in time some of these positions may result in a credit risk where the bank is a net receiver. Positions where a bank is a net payer and there is no current credit risk may change over time and the bank becomes a net receiver.
- **Settlement exposures.** The bank is also likely to have short-term exposures from ongoing settlement of trades and other customer-driven transactions. The level of these exposures will vary from day to day and is normally subject to bank-imposed limits.

For large complex groups collateral and guarantees also pose specific problems and for larger companies that have better credit ratings than the banks themselves many short-term exposures will in practice be unsecured at the group level.

In developed markets virtually all large corporates are subject to credit rating agency scrutiny and while this does not completely remove the responsibility for the bank to perform its own credit risk assessment these will be largely based on work already done by the rating agencies.

Some common errors that banks make are assuming that a company is too large to fail, that the government will honor historic but implicit guarantees and bail out creditors to particular companies and a failure to ensure that cross-border group-level guarantees are legally enforceable.

Large companies that default are only very rarely liquidated and restructuring agreements usually involve scores and even hundreds of financial creditors, multiple legal actions and claims. They can drag on for years and result in considerable legal and other costs.

Default probabilities can be estimated from historic bond default data, where this is available. Losses on secured loans and derivative positions can be estimated based on the volatility of the prices of pledged collateral and recovery rates.

SME characteristics

Loans to small companies terrify management at many larger banks and in many countries a small number of banks tend to specialize in lending to these segments:

- They are sufficiently large individually to require personal attention. This is not the case with retail loans where little or no attempt is made to take account of changing borrower circumstances.
- They are made to companies operating in many diverse manufacturing and service businesses. This means that they are not readily amenable to statistical analysis nor does the bank have the in-house expertise to assess prospects for all these sectors.
- They are sufficiently large collectively that a high level of losses on loans made to companies in this segment would have a material impact on a bank's financial position.
- As a group, SMEs are hit disproportionately hard by economic downturns. This can be seen by the massive increase in failures of companies in this segment as reported by bankruptcy figures through recessions.
- They are sufficiently small that they fall outside the scope of rating agencies' coverage.
- Their business risks are not well diversified and losing one major customer may be sufficient to cause an otherwise healthy company to fail.
- Collateral values often depend on the company operating as a going concern.
- In most instances a single bank is the major financial creditor. There can be safety in numbers, at least for credit officers, where the borrower has defaulted.

Banks have no real choice other than to establish their own internal rating system and collect default data going back as far as possible. With this information it is possible to estimate expected and unexpected losses. Unless the data covers at least one full economic cycle results based on it should be treated with great caution. Small and medium companies are far more sensitive to the general economic environment than any other type of borrower. We will return to the issues concerned with establishing a proprietary database later in this chapter.

These characteristics terrify management at some banks but also create considerable barriers to entry to aspiring new entrants and give lenders significant pricing power.

Real estate

Most commercial real estate loans are essentially collateral-based lending, despite protestations by bankers to the contrary. Cashflow analyses are usually based on sales (for developers) and rental yields (for investors). Both depend on the level of real estate prices. If prices drop developers will have to cut their expected asking prices and higher rental yields from lower prices are unlikely to be sustainable. Tenants will demand that their rental payments are cut.

Loans to developers of large prestige projects are generally higher risk than are those to developers specializing in small-scale landed residential developments. Many loans to real estate investment companies have bullet structures whereby there are no principal repayments until "term". In many instances there is a real difference between "economic" term and legal term as defined in a loan agreement. Many loans to companies holding real estate for investment purposes are simply rolled over at term and in practice have more in common with perpetuities than term loans.

Corporates	Small and medium enterprises (SMEs)

Large corporates
 * Many heterogeneous exposures
    - direct loans, syndicated loans, bonds, facilities, trading exposures, trade finance, derivative exposures, group level guarantees
 * Security & collateral (financial, real estate, receivables, project specific)
 * Capital market issues greater disclosure & transparency
 * Key role of credit rating agencies
 * Wealth of historic bond default & loss data by rating
 * Complex, expensive, time-consuming restructuring agreements
 * Specific problems: "too big to fail" illusion, acceptance of implicit state guarantees, intergroup relationships, appraisal difficulties
	Small and medium enterprises
	 * Many small & medium sized heterogeneous exposures primarily loans, facilities & guarantees
	 * Fall between consumer & corporate
	    - large enough to require individual attention
	    - too heterogeneous to manage on pooled basis
	    - too small for credit rating agencies
	 * Limited borrower diversification
	 * Loss rates highly dependent on economic cyclicality
	 * Low quality collateral (inventory, receivables, specialist equipment)
	 * Local & borrower-specific "know-how"
	 * Specific problems: geographic customer & industrial sector concentration

Real estate loans tend to have relatively low expected losses and relatively high unexpected losses as shown by the distribution of losses. Losses are closely correlated with the property market cycle which is influenced by overall economic and interest rate conditions but rarely exactly synchronized.

PROPRIETARY DATABASES

Most banks built transaction-processing systems in the past rather than the type of management information systems necessary to reach informed conclusions on credit-loss characteristics and default and loss rates. Few credit default databases went much beyond location, industrial classification and, in some instances, internal credit rating. If only the world were so simple.

All banks should maintain their own historic database for issuer failures, loan defaults and credit losses from other exposures that allowed for the data to be looked at in the following ways:

- **By issuer.** Industrial classification, credit ratings, net debt–equity ratios, size in terms of sales and total assets, operating cashflows to debt servicing costs, breakdown of assets and liabilities by currency, breakdown of debt by term, floating–fixed, currency.

- **By exposure.** Loan/facility/derivative etc. Size of exposure, term, floating–fixed, optionality (e.g. prepayment, repayable on demand), security (type, value), guarantees etc.

We would also want to have access to external macro-level data such as GDP growth, capacity utilization rates, interest rates, inflation, current account and fiscal positions and to industry-specific data such as property and other asset prices, auto sales, housing starts and retail sales. The shopping list of requirements could go on and on.

The intellectual tools derived from mathematical group theory to analyze such information existed 30 years ago. The technology existed at the time to store much of the data collected but the computing power to analyze and use this data did not then exist. Because it could not be used at many banks it was simply overwritten or thrown away. These basic problems with data have been compounded by the adverse effects of bank acquisitions and mergers.

This is perhaps understandable. There were costs associated with storing the data and it required a leap of vision to see that in 20 or 30 years' time that data could be used to great effect and would be extremely valuable. Newton could truthfully say "If I have seen further than others, it is by standing upon the shoulders of giants." Today people trying to work on credit risk management problems have to make do with what mere mortals have left behind.

Internal Ratings

A critical starting point for a bank seeking to develop a useful historic database on credit losses is to have an internal credit rating system and allocate a rating to each exposure. Most bank rating systems have approximately 8–12 different rating grades of which 3–4 are devoted to loans now classified in some way as problem or non-performing loans. Such a rating system is necessary to price the credit risk of an exposure. When individual ratings are reviewed on a relatively frequent basis this should provide a basis to determine changes in overall asset quality. During periods when there is a general deterioration in financial conditions this should show itself as a migration of exposures from better quality to lower quality ratings. There are some broad problems with the use of internal ratings systems.

At a minimum the definitions for individual ratings should capture the following: location (city, state, country), industry classification, type of exposure, type and value of collateral, nature of any guarantees and internal credit rating of guarantor. The original definitions are critical because if definitions are subsequently changed they may make it impossible to compare present data with that from the past. The criteria for assignment to a particular band must be clear-cut. The definitions should be largely quantitative and avoid subjective assessments. The risk arising from the latter is that interpretations are likely to change over time leading to the same problems concerning comparability.

While impossible to confirm on the basis of publicly available information, anecdotal accounts suggests that the ratings of new loans granted tend to cluster around a relatively small number of the ratings available. If this were the case it would imply that banks' differentiation between exposures from a credit risk perspective is relatively crude.

There is a natural tendency to avoid extremes and "clustering" does little to help the objective of differentiating between companies from a credit risk perspective. These classifications can become the source of much argument when they directly affect the level of expected losses, and hence pricing, and unexpected losses and hence, ultimately, allocation of capital.

DECOMPOSITION AND AGGREGATION

The process of decomposition and aggregation of credit risks involves more judgment than that required for market risk. As a general rule of thumb the better the relationship between the likelihood of a default occurring and the factor the lower down the decomposition tree it should be.

The following two schematic diagrams show possible decomposition and aggregation levels for a bank's retail loan book and its corporate exposures. The first level of aggregation is that of borrower rating.

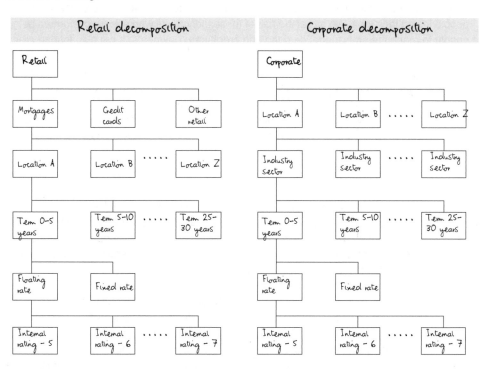

The equivalent of VAR must be estimated for each exposure at each borrower and at the lowest level. Historic correlation coefficients should be applied as we move up the tree although at the higher levels where correlations start to become weaker and less reliable it is probably better to simply make a policy decision as to whether to treat these as independent or assume perfect positive correlation.

PORTFOLIO DIVERSIFICATION

We looked at the impact of portfolio diversification of financial assets in Chapter 12 "Managing market risk" in the context of value-at-risk techniques. It makes no difference whether the assets are stocks and bonds held for investment purposes, financial instruments held and positions taken for trading purposes or loans. It is tempting to assume that the overall objective of credit management is to achieve the lowest level of expected credit losses for a given standard deviation or the lowest standard deviation for a given expected loss level. This fails to take account of the revenue side, however.

A simple example will suffice to illustrate how credit risk concentration may occur. Let us assume that we are a bank operating in one state that has made a large loan to a cement manufacturer which is the largest employer in the town in which it is located. To diversify the risk of being exposed to the cement industry we also have many loans to real estate companies and to retail customers such as mortgages, car loan and credit cards. If the cement manufacturer fails this may start a chain reaction:

- First we have the default on the loan to the cement company. But it will also lead to many people losing their jobs. We are at the risk of these individuals who are our customers being unable to make their mortgage, car loan and credit card payments. It will also lead to credit losses and loss of business at its suppliers.
- If the cement manufacturer is the town's major employer the retailers will be adversely affected. This increases the risk that they will fail. In turn this increases the risk that property investors who have borrowed to fund the retail mall will fail.
- Property prices are likely to fall as will our collateral cover. The bank can foreclose on lenders that had defaulted but could face realizing significantly lower recovery rates than originally expected from selling into a falling and illiquid property market.

This is an example of a bank that lacks geographical diversification. A bank that operates only in one city, state or geographic region is exposed to the risk that this area will be hit particularly badly by a downturn or by a decline in the competitiveness of companies operating in a single industry that is important to the local economy. A second bank that operates in many different regions is less exposed to a general, but uneven, downturn or a decline in profitability in a single industry. While some of the regions in which it operates may be hit hard, others are likely to experience a less severe impact and others may emerge completely unscathed.

The risk concentration could, however, arise from an industry exposure such as from lending to telecommunications or media companies. A bank with a mixture of fixed and floating rate assets may have managed its interest rate risk by having a similar mix of floating and fixed rate assets. That does not remove the credit risk arising from changes in the interest rate environment, however. A sharp increase in interest rates will push up the financing costs for borrowers with floating rate debt. This is likely to lead to an increase in delinquent accounts.

PROVIDING FOR CREDIT LOSSES

There is a huge gulf between theories about how banks should manage credit risk and actual practices of most banks. A few of the better managed, larger banks are able to implement many of the above approaches but even in these instances their methods are only sophisticated when compared with methods used by other banks. In absolute terms much work still needs to be done before most banks can follow such programs and be confident about the results. Market risks are more amenable to VaR type approaches but even here the core assumptions are still open to question and regulators feel compelled to add a safety factor of at least three to the actual result for the purposes of calculating regulatory capital requirements.

Provisioning has little to do with managing credit risk and everything to do with accounting and regulatory reporting requirements and efforts by bank management to report these numbers in such a way that they meet their own objectives. Most management look to report numbers that paint the most positive picture, and this often ends in them reporting numbers that understate credit losses or at least delay their recognition.

The key to understanding the economic consequences of bank provisioning for credit losses is that they affect the timing of the recognition of those losses but have no direct impact on the actual level of losses incurred. This subtle distinction has wide-ranging ramifications in terms of reported earnings and balance sheet numbers. These in turn affect investor and bank creditor perceptions of the soundness of the bank. Policies adopted also have a direct impact on regulatory capital and potentially on the need to raise capital.

The names given to the balance sheet accounts (e.g. provisions for credit losses, allowance for bad debts, reserves for credit loss) and the corresponding items in the earnings statement (e.g. bad debt charge, provision charge) are not uniformly adopted around the world. We will use the terms "provision" for the balance sheet item and "bad debt charge" for the P&L item.

In general, provisions should be established for losses that can be reasonably expected but have not yet been realized. Many banks, however, only provide for expected losses on loans that have already been identified as being impaired and some only when the loan concerned has met specific default criteria.

The bad debt charge is the sum of three principal factors:

- **New provisions.** New provisions required for the current period, these are comprised of provisions for new exposures, top-up provisions for existing exposures and additional charges for loans that have been written off during the period and where existing provisions are less than the actual losses.
- **Release of provisions.** Provisions may be released if a bank deems that they are no longer required and this may result from one of a number of factors. These include the reclassification of NPLs as performing, the removal of impaired loans that have been already been provided for from a bank's "watch" list or have reached term while remaining current. They may also be the result of a change in the assessment of the likely level of losses on NPLs, possibly due to an upward revision on collateral valuations.
- **Recoveries.** Recoveries on loans written off occur when the bank has already written off the loan and associated provisions but, in the event, actual recoveries exceed those expected.

The latter two items taken together are frequently, if inaccurately, described as write-backs.

The corresponding balance sheet provisioning item is the sum of brought forward provisions plus the above movements from the bad debt charge taken through the P&L account, less write-offs taken during the period. These write-offs are for loans that have already been provided for and these write-offs do not have any impact on the P&L account. Any differences between actual and expected losses are included within the bad debt charge.

Most banks report a much more detailed breakdown of the bad debt charge and the provision account movements but the following summary captures the key factors.

We have argued that banks should take a charge for expected credit losses for any exposure that has credit risk. In practice few banks adopt this approach. Most bad debt charges are made only once a loan has been formally recognized as impaired and many banks do not take a charge

Summary definitions of key financial statement items		
Bad debt charge	= New provisions required for current period	
	− Provisions released no longer required	"Write-backs"
	− Recoveries on loans already written off	
Carried forward provisions	= Brought forward provisions	
	+ Bad debt charge	
	− Write-offs for period	

until a loan has been classified as non-performing (past-due) under the definitions given by the local regulator.

A few banks adopt the opposite approach and consistently provide more than is necessary to meet the level of expected credit losses. To understand this rather confused state of affairs it is useful to look at motive, in terms of incentives, and means.

Incentives

More banks are underprovided than are overprovided. This matters little when credit losses are low and expected to remain low. It becomes increasingly important, however, given a period of strong loan growth, when asset quality deteriorates, NPL levels start to rise and expected credit losses increase. The main reasons why banks may underprovide for expected credit losses are as follows:

- **Ignorance and industry practice.** Many banks still operate on the implicit assumption that all loans will remain current and reach term. In effect they assume that expected losses on current loans are zero. Provisions for losses are then made only when a loan is actually identified as impaired. This may be because of a failure of management to understand the nature of expected losses or be due to a continuance of industry-level practices.
- **Unrealistic expectations.** Almost all project managers underestimate how long it will take to complete a project and how much it will cost. Even if bank management are trying to make realistic estimates of future credit losses these are likely to prove to be too low.

  A rough rule of thumb applied to failed banks is that external auditor's estimates of credit losses prior to closure will be double those of bank management. That the regulator's initial estimates immediately after bank closure will be double that of the external auditors and that the final losses after liquidation will be double that of the regulator's estimates.
- **Maintaining depositor confidence.** If the bad debt charge that should be made is so large that it pushes the bank into losses this may result in a loss of depositor confidence and result in a "run on the bank". The main bank regulator will balance the systemic risks from such a bank run against the need for the bank to report realistic levels of expected losses. It is also likely to be mindful of the inevitable resulting blame allocation if a banking crisis resulted. At such time they may well decide that as far as the public is concerned ignorance is bliss.
- **Avoiding capital raising.** Earlier recognition and higher estimates of expected credit losses may also result in the bank being unable to meet regulatory Tier I requirements because of the resultant reduction of its equity. Raising capital at such a time might be difficult to achieve at any price or result in a reduction in control of the controlling shareholders.

- **Collusion.** As asset quality deteriorates the incentives to refuse to acknowledge expected credit losses increase. This refusal is not limited to bank management but extends to external auditors and is tolerated by bank regulators.

The following factors are frequently mentioned but are of less import:

- **Management bonuses.** A lower estimate of future losses will allow the bank to make a lower bad debt charge and this will inflate reported earnings. The level of reported earnings often has a direct impact on management's bonuses and the value of their stock options.
- **No tax incentive.** This is one of the most common arguments made to explain why so many banks underprovide for credit losses, and it is also one of the weakest. Most tax authorities do not recognize bad debt charges as an allowable expense for tax purposes. Instead the tax benefits are given at the time of the actual write-off and in order to obtain this relief banks may have to demonstrate that they have exhausted all legal recovery means.

    Tax authorities argue that banks could inflate their estimates of expected losses in order to gain an unwarranted tax benefit. This may be true but is largely an issue of timing. Authorities could claw back tax relief from banks whose estimates of actual losses proved too high. The absence of a tax incentive does not, however, in itself create a disincentive for banks to reflect their expected level of future credit losses in their financial statements.

Conversely, estimates of losses at some banks may be too high. Again this may be a genuine estimation error but there may be incentives for management to deliberately overstate the expected level of losses:

- **Reputation.** Being perceived to be "overprovided" may bolster a bank's reputation for conservatism. This will hold it in good stead with credit rating agencies and lower the cost of any long-term paper it intends to issue in the future.
- **Tax incentives.** There may be a tax incentive. If tax authorities allow bad debt charges as a taxable expense there is a rational reason to keep the bad debt charge high. The longer it takes to pay a tax obligation the less it costs in terms of current value. For this reason many tax authorities do not allow the bad debt charge as a tax allowable expense but only the losses arising out of the actual write-off.

Provisions in excess of expected losses are a form of equity. In almost all cases a policy of maintaining excess provisions is misleading, distorts return measures and ratios used to determine a bank's financial condition and destroys shareholder value.

Most management at banks feel a great deal of pressure to report their earnings in the best possible light. This can lead to banks using provisioning levels as a buffer to smooth earning. When operating profits are high they dampen reported earnings growth by overprovisioning. When operating profits are under pressure bad debt charges can be kept low and the bank may move to being underprovided.

Management try to report the numbers demanded by the equity markets within the constraints of accounting and regulatory standards. Banks that report numbers that more accurately reflect economic value but whose earnings and book values are hence more volatile are punished by equity markets rather than rewarded. So where does the fault lie?

Methods

The two principal methods used to delay recognition of losses are to underestimate the level of expected losses and to delay making the associated bad debt charges for as long as possible:

- **Underestimating expected losses.** The level of actual credit losses on secured NPL depends on the realized value of any collateral, the direct legal and other costs associated with restructuring and recovery procedures and the carrying costs of the non-earning assets. For unsecured NPLs losses depend on the dividend payout from liquidation or any proceeds from completion of a restructuring agreement, plus the direct costs. Estimates of expected losses can be kept artificially low by assuming the following:
  - **Overestimating the realization value of collateral.** Most collateral is in the form of real estate. Appraised property prices are inherently subjective and only really reliable when given for smaller homogeneous properties for which there is a relatively liquid market. For large, unique developments they are at best an educated guess. Banks are often required to use external, qualified realtors for estimates of collateral values. Moral hazard rears its head again. Realtors are under pressure from banks to understate the value of collateral at the time a loan is granted and to overstate the value of collateral for NPLs. No money need change hands, although it may for the bank to be able to exert pressure for the outcome it desires.
  - **Underestimating the time to realization.** The longer that the bank keeps a non-performing asset on its books the greater the loss in *NPV* terms. Complex restructuring cases can drag on for years. Banks may retain foreclosed assets until such a time as property markets improve, and at times when serious imbalances between supply and demand exist this may be a matter of years.
  - **Underestimating direct costs.** Complex restructuring cases can result in very high legal costs and banks may simply expense these costs as they arise.
- **Delaying making charges.** Under many regulatory regimes and accounting standards banks are not required to make any provisions for losses until the loans have been formally classified as non-performing. The level of provisioning required is also often defined in terms of collateral shortfall and NPL age. We have already considered some of the differences in definitions of problem loans that exist between countries. Within these definitions there is usually still room for management to delay classification. NPL definitions usually allow considerable latitude to bank management. Impairment, for example, is usually a subjective measure. Specific examples where judgment may be used include the following:
  - A company is in arrears on one loan it has taken from the bank and this has been classified as non-performing. It also has other loans from the bank which it is servicing and are current.
  - A company has defaulted on loans from other banks but remains current on loans from this bank.
  - A guarantor of a loan has defaulted on loans from banks but remains solvent and there has been no move to liquidate the company. The borrower is servicing its loan and the loan is fully secured.
  - Collateral cover has fallen from that agreed at the time that the loan was extended and the borrower cannot "top up" the collateral but collateral cover remains well above 100%. The loan is otherwise current.

- A company is servicing its loan but has only been able to because it has drawn down against facilities granted by the bank or by other banks or has taken out new loans from other banks. None of these actions break any loan covenants.

Even when definitions appear to have hard criteria, such as day past-due, banks can often find ways such as evergreening to avoid having loans classified as nonperforming.

REGULATORY PROVISIONING REQUIREMENTS

Provisions for credit losses are inextricably tied up with regulatory capital requirements and this is acknowledged, to an extent, by the Basel Accord which allows certain provisions to be counted towards regulatory capital. In practice regulators fall into one of two camps, those that put the prime responsibility onto bank management for provisioning and where bank's behavior is determined by a combination of market forces and moral suasion and those that impose a formulaic-based framework:

- **Laissez faire.** Most regulators in developed markets leave provisioning policies up to individual banks' management to act within the constraints of local accounting standards and influenced by tax considerations. This does not imply that regulators are disinterested in bank provisioning levels but that they believe that the disadvantages of a formal framework outweigh any benefits. Where many banks have an exposure to a single counterparty (whether a company, public sector organization or sovereign) provision levels are effectively set by market forces. It would be very difficult for one bank to justify having a significantly lower level of provisioning than others in such cases. Regulators are also likely to act by having a quiet word with management at banks where they are concerned that a particular bank is underprovided.
- **Formulaic.** Formulaic provisioning requirements are common in developing markets. Most of these are based in one way or another on the following:
  - Local problem loan and NPL classifications, e.g. substandard, doubtful, loss.
  - Age, since problem loans or NPLs were classified as impaired or past-due, e.g. 90 days past-due, 180 days past-due, one-year past-due.
  - Level of collateral cover.
  - General provisions that are not allocated to any particular group of exposures.
  - General provisions for specific pooled exposures.

The following table shows a fairly standard example of the sort of provisioning requirements imposed by regulators that adopt a formulaic approach.

The rationale behind these sorts of requirements is pretty self-evident but the following are worth noting:

- **Underprovisioning.** Most of these approaches result in lower provisioning levels than would be the case if banks provided for expected losses as we have defined them. This problem is most acute when either loans or NPLs are rising sharply. A few regulators go as far as including provision requirements for *NPV* losses but these tend to be the exception rather than the rule. The same goes for providing for recovery costs.

Example of regulatory formulaic provision requirements	
Specific provisions	
Loans 0–90 days past-due	No provisioning requirement.
Loans 90–180 days past-due	
– Fully secured	10% of outstanding balance.
– Partially secured	Larger of 10% of balance and 50% of collateral shortfall.
– Unsecured	50% of balance.
Loans 180 + days past-due	
– Fully secured	20% of outstanding balance.
– Partially secured	Larger of 20% of balance and 100% of collateral shortfall.
– Unsecured	100% of balance.
General provisions	
– Of total loans	0%–1% of outstanding loans.
– Of exposures to specific countries or exposures, e.g. real estate	As specified by regulator (over and above any specific provisions established for individual exposures).

- **Provisioning lag.** Bad debt charges will remain high and provision levels continue to rise even as NPLs peak as a consequence of NPL aging provisioning requirements.
- **General provisions.** Where general provisions are made on the basis of allocation of expected losses on an undifferentiated pool of exposures such as credit cards they are completely justified. In some countries such provisions are included within specific provisions. They are also justified when used to reflect expected losses on performing assets.

    In some countries, however, banks are required to maintain a specified percentage of loans in the form of general provisions. Provisions of this form distort capital ratios and can also distort bank-lending behavior to no good effect. The requirement that they are maintained at the specified level means that they are best seen as a form of capital rather than provision for losses. This is reflected, to an extent, by their eligibility to be counted towards regulatory capital requirements in most countries.

    Where these requirements exist some banks scale back lending growth in the final months of the fiscal year on the basis that they have to take the charge for the full amount of general provisions required on new loans but only receive income for a matter of weeks or months. This scaling back of loan growth has no economic justification but is surprisingly common in countries where general provisions of this form are required. Loan growth in the early months of the fiscal year then tends to be relatively robust.

Resolution

Cases of problem loans may be resolved in a number of ways although even in this area the matter of what constitutes closure is by no means always clear-cut. The only really clear-cut cases involve either liquidation or a full payment of all due interest and payment:

- **Liquidation.** In the event of liquidation the borrower's assets are sold off either in whole or in parts. The proceeds from the liquidation are used first to pay the legal and other costs associated directly with the liquidation and then divided between the remaining creditors based on seniority of claim. This is a clean (but usually costly form of resolution). Any cash received is released for use in the bank's business. Actual losses are charged against established provisions with any adjustment for under- or overprovisioning being taken through the earnings statement.

- **Foreclosure.** If a bank owns a fully secured non-performing loan it effectively owns the right to swap that NPL for the title to the security. If the bank acts to foreclose but is unable to liquidate the pledged collateral that it has then the main impact is to reduce the level of NPLs but increase the level of foreclosed assets. Debt–equity swaps can be viewed from an economic perspective as being a particular form of foreclosure although the asset will be booked in a separate account.

    In many cases the bank has swapped an illiquid non-performing loan for an illiquid asset that does not generate income. If foreclosed assets start to increase sharply these need to be taken into account. When carried as a loan the risks to economic value result from lower provisions than actual credit losses, when carried as an asset the risks arise from a failure to take carrying costs into account and the eventual realization price versus appraised value.

- **Restructuring.** The level of disclosure of restructured loans and their reclassification as performing also creates analytical problems. There are two key issues to address. The first is whether concluded restructuring agreements have been conducted in a realistic way such that the borrowers will be able to meet the conditions and servicing requirements of the restructured loans (including principal repayments). Second, whether the bank has made a realistic assessment of the losses or haircut it has taken to reach agreement and recognized these losses.

- **Write-offs.** The speed at which the identification–resolution–liquidate–write-off process is concluded has an impact on reported NPLs and provisions. The effect of a faster cycle are as follows:
    - Reported NPLs and gross loans will both be reduced by the amount of NPLs dealt with. The percentage reduction in NPLs is, however, much greater than the percentage reduction in gross loans. The NPL level ratio will therefore fall.
    - The impact on the provision level ratio is less predictable. If the loans dealt with had a higher than average NPL cover then this ratio will fall and it will increase if lower than average.

Banks with capital adequacy problems try to delay recognition of losses when their provisions are less than the losses arising from resolution. In general terms the faster the cycle the better – provided this does not result in the bank incurring higher total losses than if it had persisted with a restructuring approach. With larger, more complex loans this is an important qualification.

IMPACT ON REPORTED EARNINGS, BALANCE SHEETS AND RATIOS

Interpreting reported NPL and NPL cover ratios is fraught with uncertainty and ambiguity. The use of common ratios to compare asset quality and NPL cover between banks in different countries is plagued with definitional issues related to problem loans, provision accounts and loans:

- **Problem loans.** The term non-performing loan has very different meanings in different countries. We look in detail at definitional differences of problem loans in Chapter 20 "Corporate failures and problem loans". This is usually the major source of comparability problems.

- **Provision accounts.** There are also differences in the definitions and use of specific and general provision accounts. There are also differences in practices within the same accounting standards that may have a material impact on derived ratios.
- **Loans.** The definition of gross or total loans as reported on the balance sheet varies between countries. The most common differences relate to whether or not interest receivables, lease financing and commercial paper are included in the definition of loans. Other differences may arise depending on how banks treat exposures to other banks and financial institutions.

This proliferation of definitions and varying degrees of conservatism in defining loans as impaired makes meaningful comparisons of NPL levels and cover between banks in different countries, and even within the same country, difficult.

A further complication is created when banks report related ratios without giving either clear definitions of numerator or denominator or their absolute values. They always try to paint themselves in the best possible light. Banks may include interbank assets in the definition of loans they are using as the denominator. Analysts then have to make the necessary estimates to adjust the numbers accordingly.

The ratios that can be calculated are constrained by what information is available but the following ratios are the ones that are most commonly used and referred to. The NPL cover ratio is sometimes referred to, albeit inaccurately, as provision cover.

Common asset quality and provisioning ratios	
NPL level	= Non-performing loans/Total non-bank loans
Provisioning level	= Total provisions/Total loans
NPL cover	= Total provisions/ Non-performing loans

When NPL levels are low these ratios provide a reasonable measure of asset quality but are paid little attention. A qualification on provisioning ratios is required, however. As we have already noted few banks provide fully for expected losses on current loans but only act when loans are recognized as impaired or non-performing. As NPL levels start to rise these ratios become the focus of analyst and investor attention but become increasingly difficult to interpret and may not provide a realistic measure of asset quality.

Using them blindly can be very misleading particularly when the use of common accounting standards and NPL definitions would appear to make such ratios between banks directly comparable. Investors and brokerage sales people do not like analysts to give answers that start with "it depends how you look at it". A low NPL level may reflect any of, or a combination of, the following:

- **Better asset quality.** The bank has been more conservative in its lending approach. Hard, but indirect, evidence for this could be loan growth well below that of the industry as a whole at a time when credit was expanding rapidly or a below average level of loans to sectors regarded as highest risk.
- **Less conservative approach to NPL classification.** We have already looked at how, even when definitions of impaired or non-performing loans appear to be completely objective, there is almost always an element of judgment. A more conservative approach to classification will lead to higher reported NPL numbers.

- **Speed of write-offs.** The faster that a bank moves to write off NPLs the lower will be the reported level of NPLs. Provision levels as a percentage of loans will also fall. The impact on NPL cover is less predictable. If the provisioning level for the loans written off is greater than its average NPL provisioning level then its NPL cover will fall. This could occur if the bank acted to write off NPLs that were either unsecured or had the lowest level of collateral cover.

  On the other hand, if the bank writes off those NPLs that were best secured reported NPL cover would be likely to increase.
- **Foreclosed assets.** If a bank acts to foreclose on pledged security for NPLs but does not sell these assets immediately then while NPLs will fall the level of foreclosed assets will rise.
- **Restructuring.** The rules on restructured loans being reclassified as performing loans vary significantly between countries. Some regulators allow these to be immediately reclassified as current while others require that borrowers adhere to the terms of the restructuring agreement for a defined number of months. The greater the level of restructured loans and the faster these are allowed to be classified as current the lower will be the reported NPL level.

Bank management comments are rarely of any help to analysts. I've never come across an example where management has admitted that low reported NPL levels and high levels of provisioning cover are due to window-dressing. It is therefore virtually impossible to determine whether or not they are lying. Even when an analyst believes that management are being "economic with the truth" the best he or she can do is to point to indirect evidence that reflects a culture of creative accounting and past sharp practices.

Other related ratios that may be disclosed usually concern collateral cover. They tend to be highlighted by banks where a high proportion of their loans are "fully" secured. The usual definitional problems apply and their usefulness is highly dependent on the appraised value of the pledged security and the ability of the bank to realize that appraised value. Other ratios using NPL aging profiles, when reported, may also be derived.

Other ratios	
Fully secured loans/Total NPLs	Total provisions/Unsecured loans
Total provisions/Collateral shortfall	NPLs/Total loans to customers and other banks
Current loans classified as NPLs/Total NPLs	

ECONOMIC VALUE

A bank that does not make provisions for expected credit losses will overstate the level of its equity from an economic value perspective. That should also include the effect of carrying costs. To calculate the *NPV* of these losses we need to use an appropriate discount rate. In principle this should be given by the yield-to-maturity of loans with the same term and structure to companies of similar credit quality. This becomes rather problematic as NPL levels rise and a simpler, approximate approach is simply to use the bank's funding costs as the discount rate.

Many banks do not provide for *NPV* losses. The accounting treatment of NPLs provides a reasonable basis for relating accounting value to economic value only when a number of conditions are met:

- **Estimates of losses are realistic.** Banks' estimates of future losses are realistic. These estimates depend largely on recovery rates and related costs.
- **Short time frame.** The time between classification of the loan as non-performing and provisioning and recovering the proceeds from the forced sale of any foreclosed assets is relatively short.
- **Low interest rates.** Interest rates are relatively low. At 4%–5% levels *NPV* losses are relatively insignificant but this is not the case when interest rates reach 15%–20%.

14

Capital Management

Capital as such is not evil; it is its wrong use that is evil. Capital in some form or other will always be needed.

Mahatma Gandhi, Indian leader

INTRODUCTION

Banks and capital markets both act as conduits for savings to be channeled to the most productive sectors of an economy. Here, productive means those sectors in which businesses can generate the highest economic returns. Bank management plays a similar role internally. Capital is a scarce commodity and management need to ensure that it is utilized effectively. External conditions are in a constant state of change and management must continually monitor the risk-adjusted returns from, and prospects for, specific businesses.

Bank management are responsible for the allocation of capital to those businesses with the highest returns and for taking capital out of businesses generating inferior returns, by restructuring such businesses to generate acceptable returns or through disposals.

The adoption of BIS standards as defined in the Basel Accord to specify minimum bank capital-adequacy levels has had a marked impact on bank approaches to capital management. Developments in finance theory have also helped managers understand the functions of capital and issues involved in its allocation better. Advances in technology have made it possible to apply at least some of these theoretical developments in a practical world. Despite this progress no-one who has studied this subject would deny that significant flaws, both theoretical and practical, remain.

Shareholder value advocacy, embodied in Anglo-Saxon capitalism, has gained considerable support in countries such as Germany, France and Italy where it has not been given the highest priority in the past. As a result capital management has gained a much higher profile in recent years. Recent is a relative term but in this context means approximately 25 years.

Capital management is complex not least because it has to find ways to accommodate the above flaws and come up with practical, effective ways to determine capital allocation. The old adage that a fool can ask more questions than a wise man can answer springs to mind. It is easy for capital managers to get bogged down in the morass of the underlying theoretical and implementation issues. The key questions for them to answer today, however, boil down to how much capital their bank needs, how it should be allocated between different businesses and what constitutes an acceptable return on this capital.

This chapter introduces key capital management issues and I would recommend Chris Matten's book "Managing Bank Capital" for a more in-depth analysis.

THE ROLES THAT CAPITAL PLAYS

All journeys start with a single step and some large problems can be tackled by breaking them down into smaller, more manageable parts. The starting point for our journey down the capital management road is to differentiate between the four roles that capital in a bank plays. These are as follows:

- **Funding capital.** Capital provides free funds in the sense that the bank does not pay interest on these funds. It is not free in the sense that shareholders require a return on their capital and it should be priced at the bank's cost-of-equity (*COE*). This role may be incorporated into financial planning and reporting though the use of hurdle rates that set minimum required returns or by explicit charges to internal business units for capital allocated to them.
- **Risk capital.** A narrow definition of risk capital is that it is the capital available within the business required to absorb a defined level of possible losses before the bank faces insolvency. Required risk capital is estimated assuming a specified holding period and confidence level. The level of risk capital required, as defined by management, may be more or less than the bank's actual level.
- **Economic capital.** Economic capital is represented by the investment that shareholders have made in the business (share capital and premium accounts and retained earnings). Under this definition economic capital is equal to actual risk capital plus any unamortized goodwill resulting from past acquisitions. As we will show risk capital makes up a large part of regulatory capital.
- **Regulatory capital.** One of the main objectives of bank regulators is to protect depositors from losses resulting from a bank failure. There are many possible ways to go about achieving this objective. In broad terms there are two levels of prime bank regulation in use today. National regulators act as the prime regulatory bodies for banks incorporated in their country. These responsibilities are overlaid on a set of global standards defined in what is known as the Basel Accord and to which all OECD banks are bound to observe and many other countries have adopted.

  For our purposes we will treat the Basel Accord as a set of arbitrary rules that specify the absolute minimum amount of capital that a bank must hold overall given its mix of assets and level of trading activities. This minimum requirement is calculated on the basis of the application of detailed but fairly arbitrary rules to individual exposures. This means that individual exposures have a notional amount of regulatory capital associated with them but this is likely to be different than the amount of capital that management actually allocates.

  Management may deem it necessary to allocate more capital to some exposures than indicated under the Basel rules. For other exposures that allocation may be less. The fundamental constraint is that the total capital held must be greater than the total regulatory capital calculated for all exposures. The Basel Accord is in a state of transition and we will deal with it by giving a summary of its key features and current status in this chapter and a more detailed account in Appendix I.

The amount of capital allocated to a business unit has a direct impact on its ability to meet return targets set by senior management. An overallocation of capital (whatever that means!) can make a viable business unit appear to be destroying shareholder value, for example.

We will look at each of these four roles in turn and address the issue of why a failure to clearly distinguish between these roles can lead to the misallocation of capital and poor management business decisions.

CAPITAL AS A FUNDING SOURCE

The equity portion of bank capital provides a source of "free funds" in the sense that it does not bear interest expense. Shareholders, however, require a return on their investment and in this sense it is not free but is actually the most expensive source of funds. This required return is called the bank's cost-of-equity (*COE*).

Failing to take the cost of capital into account can distort the assessment of the viability of a particular transaction, exposure or business. The following simple example demonstrates how the treatment of the costs of the equity portion of the funding impacts on the presentation of a transaction's profitability.

Hurdle Rates versus Charging for Capital Approaches

As an example we will look at the case of a bank considering making a one-year $10m bullet loan to a corporate customer with a triple-A rating. It is charging an annualized rate of 9.5% and the bank's treasury is providing interest-bearing funding at 8.5%. Equity equivalent to 4% of the loan's principal has been set aside for the loan (this is consistent with the 4% minimum Tier I requirement under the Basel Accord). The bank's pre-tax hurdle rate and its pre-tax cost-of-equity are 24%.

There are two ways to look at this transaction. These are equivalent from a theoretical position but present the results in different ways. We have been using both presentation methods already depending on which seemed to illustrate the features of a particular example better. To recap, these methods are as follows:

- **The hurdle approach.** In the hurdle approach we allocate capital, treat it as free funds but set a target return on this allocated capital often referred to as the hurdle rate. If the hurdle rate is set at the cost-of-equity then providing the actual returns are higher than the target rate the business is creating economic value. Some people find this the easier of the two methods to understand and it is often used in communicating return objectives at the business level and consolidated levels to employees, shareholders and analysts. It has the advantage that it can be used to avoid making reference to absolute dollar amounts.
- **Capital funding cost approach.** In this approach we allocate the same amount of capital but charge the business for the cost of this capital. This is charged at the hurdle rate. If the business makes a positive absolute profit it is creating economic value. The two main advantages of this approach are that it makes the cost of capital more explicit and that the results are expressed in absolute dollar amounts. The latter feature makes it easier to see materiality and consolidated results can be arrived at by simply adding together the absolute dollar amounts. This is so even if we have different *COE*s for different businesses.

The following table shows the results for each approach. In the first treatment the equity is treated as free funds. The transaction has a profit of approximately $82 000, and returns on allocated capital of 20.5%.

In the second treatment where the allocated capital is charged at 24% the business makes an economic loss of approximately $14 000 after taking the costs of the capital allocated to it into account.

Impact on *ROE* of treating equity as free versus charging at *COE* ($000s)		
	Equity as free funds	**Equity charged at *COE***
Loan principal	10 000	10 000
Interest-bearing funding	9600	9600
Allocated equity (4% of loan)	400	400
Operating profit		
Interest income (@9.5%)	950	950
Cost of interest-bearing funds (@8.5%)	(768)	(768)
Pre-tax cost of equity (@24%)		(96)
Operating costs	(100)	(100)
Operating profit	82	**(14)**
Return on capital allocated	**20.5%**	−3.5%

Managers used to the first approach may argue that their unit is profitable – it is making a profit in accounting terms. The reality is that it is failing to cover its cost of capital and making an economic loss. This of course begs two questions, how much capital should be allocated to specific exposures and businesses and the rate that should be charged for that capital.

RISK CAPITAL

The definition of risk capital appears to be relatively straightforward and is based on the VaR concepts we explored in the previous chapters on managing market and credit risk. In this framework we can define risk capital as follows:

Actual and required risk capital definitions	
Actual risk capital	= Reported capital **available** to absorb losses arising from a fall in the market value of assets, or increase in the market value of liabilities or losses arising from derivatives or other exposures.
Required risk capital	= The capital that management **determines necessary** to absorb losses arising from a fall in the market value of assets, or increase in the market value of liabilities or losses arising from derivatives or other exposures within a **defined time period** and to a **defined confidence level**.
Actual risk capital − Required risk capital	= Risk capital excess (shortfall).

In layman's terms this can be paraphrased as the amount of "cash" that should be put aside such that we can be reasonably sure that if we have a run of bad luck it is sufficient to cover the resulting losses without forcing the bank into insolvency.

As we know, our more formal definition begs the questions as to what time period and confidence levels are appropriate to use. This definition does not in itself help us determine the appropriate level of risk capital. Senior management can, however, make the judgment calls on the time horizon we should be looking at and the degree of uncertainty acceptable without having to get into the detail of how these are applied to arrive at a level of risk capital.

That detail is important, of course, but here the colonial edict of divide and conquer comes into play. The work necessary to come up with the best method to determine estimated VARs can be broken down and delegated to people specializing in different businesses and exposures with different risk characteristics. Others can work on looking at the impact of the relationship between these different types of risk and how these may affect results on a consolidated basis.

If we just take the component relating to credit losses then provisions, or reserves, for credit losses should be determined by the present value of expected losses over the life of the exposures. The risk capital, however, should be based on the standard deviation of credit losses (standard deviation of default probability times loss in the event of default) and a confidence level and holding period determined by management. In practice this is complicated by the somewhat fuzzy border between provisions and risk capital. This border varies with differences in local accounting and regulatory requirements and by management stance in terms of conservatism.

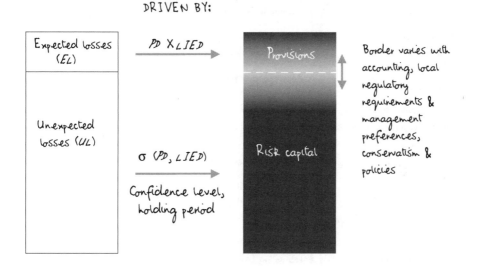

Expected and unexpected credit losses versus provisions for credit losses and risk capital

DRIVEN BY:

Expected losses (EL) — PD X LIED → Provisions

Unexpected losses (UL) — σ (PD, LIED) → Risk capital — Confidence level, holding period

Border varies with accounting, local regulatory requirements & management preferences, conservatism & policies

ECONOMIC CAPITAL

We have already defined a bank's economic value as the difference between the market value of its assets less that of its liabilities. Economic capital can be defined as the capital that shareholders have provided for the business and includes both direct inflows (initial capital raised plus capital from rights issues and placements and from the conversion of stock options and convertible bonds) and accumulated earnings not paid out as dividends (retained earnings). It is important to distinguish between economic value and economic capital given their very different definitions. Where risk capital is defined as that available to absorb losses economic capital can be defined as follows:

Economic capital = Risk capital − Unamortized goodwill

This is "sort of" equivalent to net tangible assets (NTAs), and would be equivalent to economic value if all assets and liabilities were marked to market and we assume a value of zero for intangible assets (i.e. goodwill).

Economic, risk and regulatory capital	
Economic capital	= Capital invested by shareholders
	= Actual risk capital + Unamortized goodwill
Required economic capital	= Required risk capital + Unamortized goodwill
Actual Tier I regulatory capital	= Actual risk capital + Hybrid equity

The following schematic summarizes the main roles that bank capital plays.

Roles of bank capital

Regulatory capital

* Main objective of regulators is to protect depositors & taxpayers from possible bank losses

* Secondary objective to create flat playing field for OECD banks

* Framework for calculating minimum required capital adequacy ratios (CARs) based on BIS Basel Accord – formulaic method

* Differences in implementation at national level

* Ongoing negotiations to shift towards more sophisticated framework

Economic/risk capital

* Main focus is on shareholders' interests

* Level of capital that management believes should be maintained to reflect economic risks arising from transactions & exposures (unexpected losses)

* May be less or more than regulatory capital for specific exposures

* Must maintain minimum regulatory CAR at consolidated level

* Amount of capital that should be allocated to determine profitability of specific transactions & exposures

Funding source

* No explicit funding costs for banks equity

* Some bank capital (hybrid equity & long-term debt) has an explicit cost

* Implicit cost-of-equity based on returns required by investor (COE)

* Method of allocation of capital has impact on determining transaction & exposure returns and viability

CAPITAL ALLOCATION

Although there is no off-the-shelf method for allocating risk capital an effort must be made. Successful banks are likely to be those that do this well. There are accounts about some banks trying to implement relatively "sophisticated" capital allocation systems and then quietly abandoning the attempt. It is difficult to learn from these supposed failures because few organizations want to highlight their own failings. Those banks that do differentiate between risk capital and regulatory capital (and they should) rely on a mix of highly theoretical systems and rules of thumb.

We have already considered some of the key differences between regulatory, economic and risk capital. Some banks (probably most) simply allocate the regulatory capital required, possibly with some safety buffer. This can lead to significant distortions in terms of capital allocations and also in the apparent profitability of transactions and exposures.

We have seen that the regulatory Tier I requirement for a loan to a triple-A corporate is the same as that for a BB-rated company. Under the terms of our risk model, however, we may have concluded that the risk capital required for a loan to our triple-A customer is 2% of the loan, half the regulatory Tier I requirement.

When the capital allocated for the loan is reduced to 2%, rather than the regulatory 4%, the transaction adds economic value of $18 000, rather than a loss of $14 000. The pre-tax return on (free) capital allocated rises from 20.5% to 33%, well above the 24% hurdle rate.

Impact on value added at division level of capital allocation method ($000s)		
	Regulatory capital allocated (4% of loan)	Risk capital allocated (2% of loan)
Loan principal	10 000	10 000
Interest-bearing funding	9600	9800
Allocated equity	400	200
Operating profit		
Interest income (@9.5%)	950	950
Cost of interest-bearing funds (@8.5%)	(768)	(784)
Pre-tax cost of equity (@24%)	(96)	(48)
Operating costs	(100)	(100)
Value added: pre-tax operating profit	**(14)**	**18**
Value added: expressed as % annualized	**−3.5%**	**9.0%**

At this level of risk capital allocation the exposure adds value. This is a loan that would have appeared profitable if equity had been treated as free and would have been rejected if we assumed that the regulatory minimum capital had been allocated and we had taken its cost into account and been approved if we had allocated a lower level of risk capital and taken its costs into account.

RETURN MEASURES

The problem of how to measure and assess profitability and financial performance is not unique to banks. For this reason we will only highlight the key issues and refer readers to specialized texts on performance measurement. Many concepts used in valuation techniques for non-financial companies such as weighted average cost of capital (WACC), enterprise value (EV) and cashflow are largely meaningless in the context of banks. Some efforts have been made to define a WACC for individual banks using debt allowed as regulatory capital but these are relatively uncommon. Some of the few return measures that banks have in common with non-financials include return-on-equity and cost-of-equity.

There is also general agreement that returns should in some way take account of the risks taken to generate these returns and that they must be measured against the level of capital tied up in a business. An additional measure often used for internal purposes at banks is risk-adjusted returns on capital (RAROC). This is just one of a number of measures that come within the broad scope of Risk Adjustment Performance Measures (RAPM). Definitions of RAROC vary, however, but are most commonly found in the following form:

$$RAROC = (Income - Costs)/Risk\ capital$$

Costs should include expected losses that occur in businesses such as a bank's lending activities. Performance measures are important for many reasons. They are used internally to help determine resource allocations, provide a basis for performance-based compensation and optimize returns. They are also used in valuing both stand-alone businesses and listed banks' stock:

- **Internal measures.** We have already examined the cost-of-capital and the use of hurdle rates as target minimum returns. In most companies all businesses, irrespective of different levels of risk, are given the same hurdle rate. Some advantages are that it is simple to determine and communicate. A highly successful American company had an enterprise-wide hurdle rate of 12% that remained unchanged for many years. The rationale for the 12% number was that it was equivalent to 1% each month. This made it extremely easy to communicate across the company.

  A more sophisticated approach is to draw on CAPM and estimate the beta for each business using external sources. This can be done by identifying listed companies that operate largely in the same areas and taking a measure of their betas as determined from return correlations with the stock market. This approach is generally used more for valuation purposes when a company is considering selling a particular business than as a means to set hurdle rates. At a psychological level targets must stretch managers but have a realistic chance of being achieved if they are to be useful as a motivational lever.

- **Valuations.** Quantitative equity valuation methods depend on two variables, the nominal value of future cashflows and the rate at which they should be discounted to arrive at a present value. Future cashflows in turn depend upon the level of growth expected, the amount of capital required by the business and the returns on this capital. In most stock valuation methods equity is used rather than risk capital.

  The cost-of-equity can be estimated based on risk-free rates, an estimated equity risk premium and the standard beta measure. The issue here is to determine what is an average return level through an economic cycle. This is largely driven by estimates of the average level of expected losses through a cycle, expressed as a proportion of loans.

  Most of these theoretical measures of risk-adjusted returns try to take some account of the volatility of earnings over time. This creates its own problems. The volatility of earnings at commercial banks is determined largely by the volatility of charges taken for bad debt losses. These tend to be low and quite stable during periods of steady economic growth but rise sharply during recessionary periods. The time period chosen to determine earnings volatility is therefore critical.

EXCESS REGULATORY CAPITAL

Regulators monitor compliance with capital adequacy requirements at consolidated levels and do not monitor explicitly how a bank allocates its capital internally. A capital allocation method that is based on risk capital will result in either an excess of risk capital or a shortfall as follows:

Risk capital excess (shortfall) = Required Tier I regulatory capital − Hybrid equity

$$-\Sigma \text{ (Risk capital allocations)}$$

This is derived from the following equations and the fundamental inequality that a bank must maintain more capital than the required minimum regulatory requirement:

Risk and regulatory relationships
Σ(Risk capital allocations) = Required risk capital at consolidated level
Actual risk capital = Required risk capital $\pm$ Risk capital excess (shortfall)
Actual risk capital + Hybrid equity > Required Tier I regulatory capital
Actual Tier I capital = Required Tier I capital $\pm$ Regulatory capital excess (shortfall)

A bank should find itself in a position where it has either excess risk capital or a shortfall. If a bank finds itself in a position whereby the amount of capital that management determines it needs to hold is less than the capital it needs to maintain to meet its regulatory requirements. It has two options it can try to increase its risk capital requirement or accept an excess of risk capital.

The divisions together are achieving a 31% pre-tax return, well above the 24% cost of capital. After taking account of the unallocated excess regulatory capital that falls to 24.8% at the consolidated level, slightly higher than the bank's cost of equity.

Impact of excess regulatory capital versus required regulatory capital on *ROE*	
Pre-tax operating profits from divisions	$550m
Risk capital allocated to operating divisions	$2000m
Pre-tax return on risk equity at divisional level	**31.0%**
Required regulatory equity at consolidated level	$2500m
Pre-tax return on total equity at consolidated level	**24.8%**

There is a wide variation in returns between the divisions as shown in the following table. All three divisions are achieving returns above their cost of equity. The Star division is making a return 50% higher than its target (which may beg the question as to whether the estimate of the risk capital required is realistic) while the Ready Steady division is just achieving the hurdle rate.

We will now show how ill conceived capital allocation policies can destroy profitable businesses and the bank itself. The excess capital held at the head office level is not being charged for and results in the head office "absorbing" the associated "costs". Meanwhile the division heads are happy because they are meeting their targets.

A reasonable solution would appear to be to allocate this excess capital to the revenue generating businesses. This is the most common method used to deal with head office expenses. A

Breakdown of contributions and profitability by division ($m)			
	Revenue contribution	Risk capital allocated	Return on capital
Risk capital allocated to operating divisions			2000
Ready Steady division	150	620	24.2%
OK Boys division	150	500	30.0%
Star division	320	880	36.4%
Pre-tax operating profits from	**620**		**31.0%**

simple method in this case would be to spread this excess capital to the groups on a pro-rated basis using the current level of risk capital requirement.

After spreading this excess capital around the bank the situation at the divisional level appears very different. The Ready Steady division appears to be failing to meet the bank's cost-of-equity. The returns at the total divisional level are of course the same as that at the consolidated level.

Breakdown of contributions and profitability by division ($m)				
	Income	Risk capital allocated	Excess capital allocated	Total capital allocated	Return on total capital
Ready Steady division	150	620	155	775	19.4%
OK Boys division	150	500	125	625	24.0%
Star division	320	880	220	1100	29.1%
Total divisional level	**620**		**500**	**2500**	**24.8%**

The rational act for any hard-nosed manager would appear to be to close down the Ready Steady division. Although the bank loses Ready Steady's contribution the division is achieving substandard returns and appears to be destroying value.

The capital tied up in the Ready Steady division will, under this allocation policy, have to be redistributed between the two divisions hitting their targets. The position will then look as shown in the following table. Things are going from bad to worse! Overall bank return-on-equity has

Breakdown of contributions and profitability by Division ($m)					
	Income before Ready Steady closure	Capital after Ready Steady closure	Capital allocated before Ready Steady closure	Capital re-allocated to OK Boys and Star division	Total capital allocated	Return on total capital
Ready Steady division	150		775			
OK Boys division	150	150	625	281	906	16.6%
Star division	320	320	1100	494	1594	20.1%
Total divisional level	**620**	**470**	**2500**	**775**	**2500**	**18.8%**

now fallen below its cost-of-equity. Both divisions are performing poorly, should be closed down and the remaining capital returned to shareholders. It does seem strange, however, that before the change in capital allocation policy the bank appeared to be putting in a solid performance. This example is wildly exaggerated, of course, but it is closer to the bone than many managers would like to admit. Capital allocation policies (like accounting) do not directly affect cashflows but they can have a powerful impact on how managers measure performance and assess the viability of particular businesses.

ALLOCATION OF CAPITAL AND DIVERSIFICATION

We have already argued that expected losses should be treated as part of the costs of doing business and that risk capital should be determined by the level of unexpected losses based on a specified holding period and confidence level. There are two problems that need to be "flagged" but whose detailed resolution is beyond the scope of this work.

The most profitable (as measured by return on capital) transactions or business units are those that maximize the following generalized equation:

$$Return\ on\ risk\ capital = \frac{Expected\ income - Expected\ losses}{Unexpected\ losses} \propto \frac{Expected\ income - EL}{\sigma(EL)}$$

This first issue to raise is how to take diversification benefits into account for capital allocation purposes. In principle it should be possible to estimate the impact of adding a single exposure to an existing portfolio of loans. The variance of expected losses for the original portfolio $= \sigma_{P0}^2$ and after adding the loan becomes $\sigma_{P1}^2 = \sigma_P^2 + \sigma_i^2 + 2r_{i,p}\sigma_i\sigma_p$. Subtracting the standard deviation of the original portfolio from that of the amended portfolio gives:

$$\sigma_{P1} - \sigma_{P0} = \sqrt{\sigma_P^2 + \sigma_i^2 + 2r_{i,p}\sigma_i\sigma_p} - \sigma_{P0} = \sigma_P\left(1 + \left(\frac{\sigma_i^2}{\sigma_P^2}\right) + 2r_{i,j}\frac{\sigma_i}{\sigma_p}\right)^{1/2} - \sigma_{P0}$$

Now $\sigma_i/\sigma_p \ll 1$ and therefore $(\sigma_i^2/\sigma_P^2) \cong 0$ and hence can be ignored. Using a first order binomial expansion we get the approximate result that the incremental standard deviation of an individual exposure is given by:

$$\sigma_{P1} - \sigma_{P0} = r_{i,p} \times \sigma_i$$

This can then be used, in theory, to determine how much capital should be allocated for the exposure depending on holding period and required confidence level. There are two broad theoretical alternatives to handling the effects of diversification benefits:

- **Transaction level allocation.** The diversification benefit, in terms of a lowered capital allocation, can be allocated on an incremental basis at the time that pricing is determined. Given unchanged expected losses a credit officer can offer better pricing than for a single exposure taken in isolation and still achieve the same risk-adjusted returns. There are problems with this approach. Pricing will vary depending both on how great the diversification effect is and

237

on the correlation between expected losses on the exposure and that of the portfolio. There is also no good reason why the credit officer should benefit from an effect that is outside his or her control.

- **Business unit allocation.** If diversification effects are not taken into account at the individual exposure level then the sum of the risk capital allocated to each exposure will be greater than the risk capital determined at a business unit level. A better solution may be to simply add more exposures until the excess capital due to diversification effects is used up. Under these conditions it would be possible for a business unit to have a higher return on its risk capital overall than any of the individual exposures. If it does not take on these additional exposures the business unit will end up with an excess of risk capital.

The second issue to raise concerns time. The above considers returns over a specified period and income is defined from an accounting perspective but pricing should be based on an *NPV* cash basis over the life of the exposure. Expected income, expected losses and required risk capital, as defined above, will all vary over its life.

MODIGLIANI AND MILLER REVISITED

We introduced the subject of a firm's capital structure based on Modigliani and Miller's analysis in Chapter 2 "Securities valuations". We can now revisit it in the context of our framework for risk appraisal and CAPM. We left it with proposition II:

$$R_{Equity} = ER_{Project} + D/E \times (ER_{Project} - R_{Debt})$$

The reader will recall that the beta of a portfolio of securities is given by the weighted average of the securities betas:

$$\beta_{Portfolio} = \Sigma W_i \beta_i$$

Applying this we get:

$$\beta_{Project} = D/(D+E) \times \beta_{Debt} + E/(D+E) \times \beta_{Equity}$$

Rearranging this equation gives an equity beta that is directly proportional to the project's (or firm) debt–equity gearing. In other words the effect of higher gearing on equity expected returns is completely matched by the increase in risk. The application of this framework to financial institutions is of great interest to analysts, of course. The concept of debt at a bank is ill defined. The principal economic role of bank capital is as a buffer to absorb unexpected losses.

Some bank analysts do calculate a weighted cost of capital using long-term debt instruments (bonds, subordinated debt) issued as debt. This is not an unreasonable working approach, particularly if this debt is defined as that allowable to count towards regulatory capital. There is little evidence for a linear relationship between observed bank betas and debt–equity (as defined here) ratios. The imposition of mandatory equity and long-term debt requirements, as currently defined under the Basel Accord and deposit insurance schemes complicate the formulation of a theoretical framework.

THE BASEL ACCORD – SOMETHING OLD, SOMETHING NEW

A consensus means that everyone agrees to say collectively what no one believes individually.
Abba Eban, former Israeli foreign minister and
ambassador to the United States and United Nations

Context

The Basel Accord is the name of an international agreement, whose origins date back to 1988, to define mandatory, minimum regulatory capital requirements for OECD banks and which many non-OECD countries have subsequently chosen to adopt. The Original Accord was concerned primarily with Credit Risk. It has been subject to a number of minor amendments and one major amendment in 1996 that focused on the treatment of Market Risk. A further major revision is planned for implementation in 2006, referred to as the New Accord or Basel II, which involves major changes in the way regulatory capital for Credit Risk is to be determined.

The origins of the Basel Accord can be traced back to the collapse of the fixed foreign exchange rate systems in the early 1970s. This led to an environment where exchange rates and, as a result, interest rates were both far more volatile than at any time since the end of the Second World War. This coincided with a widespread shift towards deregulation, liberalization and internationalization. There was a perception that individual banks and banking systems did not hold sufficient capital given the more volatile, and potentially unstable, global financial environment.

A key objective in writing this book has been to cut through superficial detail and get to the heart of financial transaction structures by focusing on underlying principles. It is very difficult to do this with the Basel Accord because it lacks fundamental principles and has no overall coherent framework. Its minimum requirements are largely arbitrary in nature. The detail of the Basel Accord is like quicksand and once caught in its hold it is virtually impossible to avoid getting sucked in. The total number of pages of formal releases from the Committee on the Accord in its current form and the New Accord proposals runs to 500+ pages.

A capital management specialist needs to understand all of the BIS rules, options and qualifications and take account of any local variations compared with the base Basel Accord. A legal background would probably be useful to make sense of the multiple level of clauses and sub-clauses. The generalist needs only to get a reasonable sense of the Basel Accord's key concepts and measures, how it is intended to work and what impact its adoption has, and is likely to have. We will start by exploring the nature of the original Basel Accord and then move to briefly review how the 1996 amendment for Market Risk differs in approach from the Original Accord. We will then outline the main proposals of New Accord. Finally we will ask the question as to whether there is any need for a Basel Accord in either its current or proposed form, and whether the arguments in favor of global minimum capital requirements are greater than those against.

THE ORIGINAL BASEL ACCORD

The Basic Framework

More than quarter of a century after the event, historians are better placed to determine what the actual motives and objectives of the original authors of the Basel Accord were than contemporary bank analysts (analysts are better placed to determine whether those objectives remain valid). The key features of the Original Accord were, however, as follows:

- **Risk weighted assets.** It introduced a concept of risk-weighted assets (RWAs). This was a very crude attempt to come up with a measure that reflected a bank's on-balance credit risk. It did so by defining four major classes of assets: sovereign debt, interbank assets, residential mortgages and all other on-balance sheet exposures to companies and individuals (loans, bonds, commercial paper and so on). Each asset class was assigned a risk weighting (0%, 20%, 50% and 100% respectively) and by applying these factors to all of a bank's assets a total risk-weighted asset figure for a bank could be calculated. No attempt was made to justify the chosen values of the risk-weighting factors.

  In isolation the value of RWAs had no significance but in practical terms meant that given two banks with the same total assets the one with the higher proportion of government bonds and residential mortgages versus corporate loans would have the lower total RWA. This was never anything other than a very crude attempt to differentiate between banks on the basis of credit risk and to quantify that difference in some way.
- **Risk-weighted asset equivalents.** Banks also had credit risk exposures arising from derivatives and off-balance sheet activities (guarantees and facilities). The Original Accord specified rules to follow to convert these exposures into risk-weighted asset equivalents. The conversion rules themselves were essentially formulaic and largely arbitrary. As was the case with on-balance sheet RWAs the result was very crude but a big difference was that the rules to apply to effect the "conversions" were pretty complicated.
- **Market risks.** Banks were also exposed to Market Risk arising from their trading activities (interest rate instruments, FX and equities). A very crude, but detailed, set of rules was specified that "converted" these exposures into RWA equivalents. On-balance sheet RWAs and RWA equivalents from off-balance sheet assets, derivatives and market risk were then added together to give a total risk-weighted asset equivalent for the bank as a whole.
- **Capital.** The definition of capital was extended beyond that of simple equity to include various forms of long-term debt and hybrids whose claims were subordinate to all other bank creditors save equity holders. Bank capital was broken down into two major classes, Tier I and Tier II. Tier I capital was largely made up of equity and Tier II of long-term debt. The people actually doing the work on the Basel Accord have always struggled with how, and whether, to take into account provisions for credit losses. Some allowance was made for "general provisions" to be treated as a form of Tier II capital.
- **Capital adequacy ratios.** Three capital adequacy ratios (CARs) were then defined. The Tier I CAR was calculated by taking the value of Tier I capital and dividing it by total bank RWA equivalent. A Tier II CAR value was also calculated in like manner. A total CAR could then be calculated by adding together the Tier I and Tier II values. A more detailed explanation of the process as it is currently defined and as revised in the "Standardized Approach" in Basel II is given in Appendix I.
- **Minimum CAR requirements.** The original Basel Accord then specified a mandatory minimum CAR level of 8%. At least 50% of the total ratio must came from Tier I capital. There were also some detailed qualifications on the mix of debt instruments within Tier II capital that could be counted towards meeting this total requirement. Why 8%? Why not 6%, or 10%? The Basel Committee does not publish minutes of their meetings or discussions but the level was such that most banks could either already meet the requirement or, if they couldn't, the amount of equity that would have to be raised in order to comply was relatively modest.

The Tier II allowance and total requirement also put pressure on banks operating close to the 4% Tier I level to issue eligible long-term debt instruments. It is clear that there is no fundamental rationale for the 8% level. It is highly likely its level was determined by a perceived need at the time to avoid setting a limit above what banks could meet and that might risk a loss of confidence in individual banks and banking systems and short-term instability.

- **Enforcement.** All OECD bank regulators agreed to be bound by the terms of the original Basel Accord. Individual bank regulators were given responsibility for ensuring that those banks within their purview met these minimum requirements. Many non-OECD central banks subsequently signed up to the terms of the Accord although there are widespread detailed differences in its application, reflecting variations in local accounting standards and legal frameworks.

Exclusions

The Original Accord did not address any of the following:

- **Interest rate risk.** The bulk of a bank's interest rate does not result from its trading operations (and here there is a clear distinction between a bank's trading book and its banking book). No attempt was made to include the effects of changing interest rates on a bank's economic value and potential economic losses.
- **Prime regulatory responsibility.** The prime responsibility for bank regulatory supervision continued to lie with individual national regulators. In well-regulated countries, such as the US with its hands-on approach to supervision and well-established CAMEL rating system, the Basel CAR requirements added an extra risk dimension to banks' operations but did not add an additional weapon to such regulators' armory. Less experienced regulators may have been given a false sense of security if they relied largely on the ability of their charges to meet the Basel requirements for their individual bank assessments.
- **Management responsibility for capital allocation.** The Basel CAR ratios for a bank are calculated by summing up a regulatory capital requirement for individual exposures and transactions. It did not, however, impose a capital requirement on individual exposures or transactions, this was imposed at consolidated levels. Bank management were left free to allocate however much capital they deemed appropriate to individual exposures. These individual allocations might be more or less than the value calculated for the purposes of arriving at a total regulatory CAR.

Law of Unintended Consequences

Over time the law of unintended consequences began to exert its effect:

- **Regulatory arbitrage.** Some banks acted to structure transactions such that that they left the actual level of credit risk unchanged but resulted in a lower value for the number to be used in calculating their total RWAs. A good example being where a bank had launched an asset securitization issue resulting in 90% of the assets being transferred off-balance sheet but retained a "first-loss" tranche equivalent to 10% of the exposures by value.
- **Distortions in competition.** The lack of differentiation between individual corporate and re-tail exposures put banks that focused on lending to high-quality companies at a disadvantage relative to financial institutions that did not have to meet Basel capital requirements and those focusing on higher risk segments. Loans to blue-chip and companies with junk status were

both subject to the same 8% requirement. The former could be put in a position where the total capital they had to hold for BIS purposes was greater than that which management believed was necessary given their risk profile. Banks focusing on high-risk segments could meet minimum regulatory CAR levels but still have a level of capital below that which most regulators would regard as prudential.

The lower risk weighting for residential mortgages appeared to favor housing loans specialists but this is not necessarily the case given the very different loss characteristics of mortgages compared with other segments. Everyone agrees that they should have a lower capital requirement than other exposures but just how much lower is open to question. It is easy to argue that the original Basel Accord forced such banks to hold more capital than they needed to.

- **Hedging disincentives.** Some transactions that were done for hedging purposes, and reduced overall risk, resulted in an increase in the regulatory capital requirement rather than a reduction. This clearly provides no incentive for banks to take such action and may even create a disincentive under extreme conditions.
- **Regulatory forbearance.** The Basel CAR trigger level has almost certainly led to a higher level of regulatory forbearance by regulators of distressed banks than would otherwise have been the case. There is a real case that the level of risk capital held by a bank should fluctuate through the credit cycle. It should fall to its minimum level around the time that NPLs peak while provisions for credit losses should move in the opposite direction.

The more immediate the need for a bank to raise capital the harder it is to do so and the more expensive the cost of that capital. Regulators are likely to increase the level of forbearance at distressed banks if full recognition of credit losses meant that banks were forced to raise capital for the sole reason of meeting the Basel requirements.

The Basel Accord began life as a very crude, and simple, attempt to differentiate between banks from a credit risk perspective and encourage banks to raise long-term debt. It also promoted the concept of a "level playing field" for internationally active banks, by putting a lower limit on their overall risk-capital level. Its nature started to change as it evolved into a far more complex, legalistic set of procedures that attempted to resolve detail-level inconsistencies and the types of specific problems identified above. The increasing level of detail lent a spurious sense of meaning and accuracy.

Over the years a number of detailed amendments have been made. The core approach for calculating on-balance sheet RWAs was left largely unchanged. Many of the amendments were made in the detailed rules for calculating RWA equivalents and fine-tuning the eligibility of various forms of long-term debt and hybrid instruments for inclusion as regulatory capital. The first major amendment was, however, not implemented until 1996.

THE MARKET RISK AMENDMENT

After the various tinkering with detailed parts of the Original Accord the Market Risk amendment implemented in 1996 appeared to herald a new approach. Two approaches are allowed, a "standardized approach" and one using internal models. The standardized approach was similar to the original Accord in that it was rule based and formulaic in nature. The latter, however, had a sound theoretical basis and the resultant capital requirement had a fundamental basis. The Internal Models approach was based on industry practices of using value-at-risk approaches for managing market risk. It has the following features.

- A value at risk in dollar terms for each risk factor (e.g. interest rate instruments, FX and equities) had to be calculated to a 99% confidence level and using a 10-day holding period.
- The total VAR was the simple sum of the three major risk classes. This is equivalent to assuming that they have perfect positive correlation.
- The total VAR is equivalent to "unexpected losses".
- The base minimum regulatory capital requirement was set to be equal to the higher of the previous day's VAR and the average daily value calculated over the previous 60 days.

The resultant capital requirement was then multiplied by a factor of at least three to provide a 'safety" buffer. The Basel Accord committee has justified this buffer, in part at least, to compensate for model and realization risks that were not fully captured in VAR estimates. This comfort factor is arbitrary in nature but is not hidden in the detail as is the case with so much of the arbitrariness of the rest of the Accord.

The only real problem with the Market Risk amendment is that the regulatory capital required is only a very small fraction of that required for credit risk and this is the case even at banks with very extensive trading operations. So much good work to so little effect.

BASEL II – THE NEW ACCORD

Basel II runs to more than 200 pages and can be broken into a number of relatively discrete parts. The most important parts concern the Standardized Approach (a series of changes to the treatment of credit risk based on the Original Accord approach). A proposed capital charge allocated, in name at least, to operational risk. Finally, the part of Basel II receiving the most attention and involving a major change in the way in which credit risk may be quantified, driven in part by banks' own estimates of likely credit losses and referred to as the Internal Ratings Based (IRB) approach. The other parts are concerned with the closure of certain loopholes concerning securitized assets, some well-meaning words on bank management and bank regulator responsibilities and new minimum disclosure requirements.

The Internal Ratings Based approach is receiving the most attention because it appears to represent a fundamental shift in the way that regulatory capital for credit risk is to be determined. We will deal with the other parts of the New Accord first, they are simpler and build on approaches already embodied in the Basel Accord and deal with the IRB approach as a separate topic.

There are no explicit changes in the definition of regulatory capital but there are some effective changes in the definitions arising from changes in the treatment of provisions for credit losses. There are no material changes in the treatment of Market Risk. Interest rate risk in the banking books continues to be ignored.

THE STANDARDIZED APPROACH

What Basel II refers to as the "Standardized Approach" is basically an extension of the approach taken for Credit Risk defined in the original approach with the following major changes:

- **Increased number of exposure classes.** The Original Accord only had four different classes (sovereign, banks, residential mortgages and others). The number of classes is expanded significantly. Corporate and retail loans are treated separately. Corporate loans are further broken down to commercial real estate loans and others. The residential mortgage class is retained but a new class of other retail loans is created. The definition of retail extends beyond individuals to include small companies with sales below €50m. Loans that are past-due are treated as a separate class.

  Securitized assets were also separated out into two classes. Those where the bank was the issuer and had provided some form of credit enhancement and all others. The total value of securitized assets in the first tranche is to be subtracted directly from eligible capital.
- **Use of external ratings.** Sovereign, bank and corporate (excluding commercial real estate) are further broken down into five grades, based on issuer ratings as specified by recognized external credit rating agencies. In terms of S&P ratings these correspond to AAA to AA−, A+ to A−, BBB+ to BBB−, BB+ to B−, and below B−. Exposures where the counterparty has no external rating are assigned to an "unrated" grade. A major beneficiary of the use of external ratings will of course be the credit rating agencies whose owners must be rubbing their hands together in anticipation of the bonanza in store.
- **Overall greater granularity of weightings.** The combination of more classes and the introduction of five grades based on external rating (plus the unrated grade) provides a huge increase in the level of granularity. The lack of granularity had been one of the most common criticisms of Basel I and these changes address that specific complaint. Each combination of class and grade has been assigned its own risk-weighting factor.
- **Credit risk mitigation.** Exposures where the bank has obtained certain legal rights to reduce losses arising from default may be subject to an adjustment to reflect the lower resultant risk. These are limited to financial collateral, third-party guarantees and credit derivatives. They do not include other collateral, and in particular real estate, pledged. The effects of these credit mitigants are taken into account by adjusting downward the size of the exposure used to calculate the risk-weighted asset equivalent.
- **Off-balance sheet items.** Off-balance sheet assets are translated into risk-weighted asset equivalents by applying a conversion factor determined by maturity and revocability of the commitment. Unconditional commitments with an original maturity of up to one year receive an adjustment factor of 20% and those above one year 50%. Those that can be cancelled unconditionally at the bank's discretion at any time are zero weighted.

  Securities lent by a bank or lodged as collateral receive a 100% weighting subject to any credit risk mitigation factors. Short-term, self-liquidating letters of credit associated with the shipment of goods are subject to a 20% weighting to both issuing and confirming banks.
- **Lower risk-weighting factors.** It is a feature of the evolution of the Basel Accord that each amendment results in a lower absolute capital requirement. This is achieved while keeping the definition of regulatory capital largely unchanged by reducing the calculated value for RWA equivalents. The Standardized Approach upholds this proud tradition. The proposed risk weighting for exposures to corporates in grades 3–4, those that are unrated and for commercial real estate are 100%, the same as in the Original Accord.

Weightings for exposures to corporates in the top two grades are cut to 30%–50%, while those for residential mortgages fall from 50% to 35% and for retail exposures from 100% to 75%. The only exposures that have a higher risk weighting than in the Original Accord are exposures to counterparties in the lowest grade where the weighting increases from 100% to 150% and for underprovided NPLs. The overall impact will be a reduction in total RWA and corresponding reduction in the regulatory capital requirement. The exact level of the reduction will vary depending on a bank's asset mix.

The actual values of the risk-weighting factors are of course fairly arbitrary but all of the changes save one are understandable at least. The exception being for the retail class. It is not immediately clear why loans to small companies should be given a lower risk weighting than loans to unrated larger companies.

Banks are likely to welcome these changes. There will be implementation costs and ongoing costs in particular associated with payments to rating agencies. The reduction in regulatory capital requirements will be material. That does not mean we should expect banks to start returning capital to shareholders but it would ease constraints that might be imposed by such requirements in the future.

OPERATIONAL RISK

The Original Accord did not address capital requirements related to operational risk. The Committee has proposed a specific regulatory capital requirement against losses arising from operational risk. The base method to be used to quantify this requirement is as follows, where operating income is used as a "proxy":

Operational risk capital requirement = Operating income × Weighting factor

In this context operating income is the average over the past three years and is taken as net interest income plus net non-interest income, in other words excluding bad debt charges and operating expenses. The weighting factor in the base case as determined by the Committee is 0.15. This charge is equivalent to assuming a standard deviation of losses attributed to operational factors equivalent to between 2.5% and 10% of operating costs at a typical commercial bank and an increase in the minimum capital requirement of approximately 6%–7%. Some estimates, however, suggest that for certain banks the burden may be much higher.

SUPERVISORY SCOPE AND DISCLOSURES

The Accord refers rather grandly to the three "pillars" of bank regulation: quantitative minimum capital regulatory requirements, bank supervision and market discipline in the form of minimum required disclosures. In the section on the "Pillar Two" of Basel II the Committee states its view that banks' boards and management should manage their risks in a professional manner and ensure that they are able to meet regulatory capital requirements. In addition, supervisors should check that bank management are doing their job properly and force them to take remedial action if they aren't and have them replaced if they do not do so. The only surprising thing about any of this section is that the Committee feels it necessary to spell out these responsibilities.

Along with the usual exhortations on the need for greater transparency to ensure that market disciplines can act some detailed mandatory disclosure requirements are identified. These are actually rather important and merit more attention than many other parts of the New Accord. Disclosure is the key and we will have to see how this works in practice. Analysts will want to see the inputs to the Basel II black box formulae as well as the outputs. Banks always resist such disclosures on the questionable grounds of commercial sensitivity.

THE INTERNAL RATINGS BASED (IRB) APPROACH

Fundamental Theory and Best Industry Practices

The most important part of Basel II is the proposal for a method of calculating absolute capital requirements for credit risk based in part on banks' own estimates of default probabilities and resultant credit losses. When people talk in general terms about Basel II they are usually referring to the IRB approach. Ill-informed observers have hyped these proposals claiming that they "allow banks to determine their own regulatory capital requirements". It does no such thing.

There is widespread agreement between bankers and also between academics about the "right" way to reflect credit risk in financial statements. It is worth reviewing that consensus before looking at the IRB approach itself:

- A value for expected losses (*EL*) over a specified period (commonly one year) should be estimated equal to the probability of default (*PD*) multiplied by the loss-in-event-of-default (*LIED*):

$$EL = PD \times LIED$$

- A value for the standard deviation of expected losses should be calculated. Given a specific holding period management must specify a required confidence level. A value for unexpected losses (*UL*) should be calculated by multiplying the standard deviation of *EL* by a factor determined by the nature of the distribution of *EL* (normal, Chebyshev etc.):

$$UL = Factor\ determined\ by\ EL\ distribution\ and\ confidence\ level \times \sigma(EL)$$

- Expected losses should be recognized by taking bad debt charges through the earnings statement and by the use of provisions for credit losses on the balance sheet:

$$Provisions\ on\ balance\ sheet = EL$$

- The capital to be held against credit risk should be determined by the level of unexpected losses:

$$Capital\ required\ for\ credit\ risk = UL$$

Within that consensus there are a range of views concerning virtually every factor. Some of these differences are fundamental but most are based on practical considerations of the best way to go about putting theory into practice. The most important fundamental difference concerns provisions for credit losses. Everyone agrees that they should reflect expected losses on loans that have already been identified as having default status or where exposures are managed on a pooled basis (e.g. credit card receivables). There are differences of opinion as to whether expected losses on performing loans (i.e. *PD* does not equal +1) should be reflected in provisions.

Summary of Internal Ratings (IRB) Approach

The starting point for the Internal Ratings Based approach is the establishment of an internal credit rating system with a number of clearly defined grades. Banks should maintain a database on credit default history that is broken down by both exposure class (as defined by the Accord) and internal grade.

Each new exposure is allocated to a particular class and grade. The base probability-of-default, exposure-at-default and loss-given-default may be determined by reference to the bank's own historic experience, to default data provided by third-party credit rating agencies or in certain conditions set by default values determined by the relevant bank supervisor. Banks must be able to demonstrate that they have sufficient historic data and the necessary expertise to base these estimates on their own internal ratings. Where data from external agencies are used their ratings scheme must be mapped onto the bank's own grades.

We will go through each of the core steps involved in the IRB approach to determining regulatory capital in more detail in Appendix II but in essence they are as follows:

- **Allocate exposure.** Each exposure must be allocated to a specific exposure class and within exposure class to an internal ratings grade.
- **Estimate core default parameters.** The core default parameters are default probability (*PD*), loss-given-default (*LGD*) and exposure-at-default (*EAD*). The loss-in-event-of-default (*LIED*) is thus defined as $LGD \times EAD$. There are three potential sources to help estimate these factors for each class and grade; internal historic data, external data sources and supervisory defaults. The Accord specifies the conditions under which each source may, or has to, be used.

  The Accord differentiates between an "Advanced" approach where banks have most freedom to determine these parameters and a "Foundation" approach where only certain parameters may be set by the bank itself and others have to be taken from supervisory or Accord defaults. The definitions of these parameters and other key IRB terms may be found in Appendix II.
- **Calculate base regulatory capital requirement.** These default parameters are then used as inputs to a "black-box" formula defined for each exposure class and specified in the Accord. These formulae are used to calculate a base regulatory capital requirement for each exposure. The formulae have little, if any, fundamental basis.
- **Apply adjustment factors.** The base requirement may, if necessary, be subject to an adjustment or adjustments. This is achieved by applying adjustment factors based on the effective maturity of the exposure and the size of the borrower. The conditions under which such adjustments may be made and the formulae to calculate these adjustment factors are specified within the Accord.
- **Convert capital requirement into RWA equivalents.** As usual, the calculated capital requirement is converted into an RWA equivalent (by multiplying by 12.5×) and used in the calculation of the bank's CAR as defined by the Accord.

There are three areas that are worth highlighting: the treatment of collateral, the treatment of provisions and the nature of the "black-box" formulae:

- **Collateral.** Where the bank has collateral (or other credit risk mitigants such as guarantees or credit derivatives), whether financial or in the form of other assets such as real estate these should be reflected in the estimate for the *LGD* parameter for each exposure.
- **Provisions.** Specific provisions and provisions made against assets that are managed on a "pooled" basis are in effect allowed to be treated as capital (half Tier I and half Tier II). The treatment of general provisions that are allowed to count towards Tier II capital remains unchanged. A higher level of specific provisions is allowed for credit card exposures than for other exposure classes.
- **Black-box formula.** The IRB approach does not explicitly differentiate between expected losses (*EL*) and unexpected losses (*UL*). The formulae vary by asset class and do not appear to have any fundamental basis. There is no explicit use made of the standard deviations of either *PD* or the *LGD* parameters, and these are not required inputs.

It is difficult to understand why the Committee did not build on the concepts successfully adopted in the Market Risk amendment and use a method to calculate a regulatory requirement for credit risk that mirrored that of the best practices of banks in their internal allocation of risk capital. The simplest solutions are usually the best and the application of these black-box formulae appears to add complexity for no good reason.

The same considerations apply to the continuing confused treatment of provisions for credit losses dating back to the Original Accord. Alexander the Great's sword would have come in handy. By trying to accommodate a range of different accounting policies, local regulatory requirements and national industry practices and taking account of possible distorting effects on particular lending businesses the Committee risks leaving everybody dissatisfied in one way or another.

One possible, simple solution would be to allow all provisions for credit losses, whether they are called general or specific, to count towards expected losses on all exposures (i.e. including *EL* on performing loans). Where these total provisions are less than total expected losses the shortfall should be subtracted from Tier I capital and, where greater, any excess allowed to count towards Tier I capital. There does not appear to be good reason why they should be treated as Tier II capital. In economic terms provisions above that required for expected losses are a form of equity.

If banks in individual countries felt they were in some way disadvantaged by the Basel Accord treatment of provisions for credit losses, and this issue was sufficiently important to them, they would lobby their regulator and the relevant accounting authorities to have the local policies changed. Given the weight of the Basel Accord, fundamental arguments in their favor and a global move to a common practice that should not prove an insurmountable hurdle.

Individual banks are not compelled to adopt the IRB approach and unless they determine that the capital requirement from doing so is less than that given by using the Standardized Approach they are unlikely to do so. If it is lower then management will have to weigh up whether the benefits of having a lower regulatory capital requirement are greater than the costs associated with implementing the IRB approach from generating the numbers required simply to meet the Basel requirement. If the regulatory capital requirement calculated under the Standardized Approach is already well below the level that individual banks' management feel comfortable with many banks, and possibly most, are likely to conclude that the additional costs do not justify adopting the IRB approach.

It does appear likely that in practice adoption of the IRB approach would be likely to lead to a lower capital requirement than that given by the Standardized Approach at most banks. Appendix II contains more detail on the actual mechanics of the IRB approach and definitions, key terms and measures. It also looks at the level of standard deviation of default probabilities implied by the IRB's black-box formulae in more detail.

WHO'S AFRAID OF THE BASEL ACCORD?

It is possible to criticize the Basel Accord at many different levels. To me, at least, the specific problems identified with the Original Accord are symptomatic of three fundamental flaws whose substance the New Accord does not alter:

- **Capital.** The minimum capital requirements are defined in terms of a percentage of RWA equivalents. The use of RWA equivalents is really a means to an end, the definition of RWA equivalents is inherently arbitrary. The real end is how much capital in absolute dollar terms should a bank hold given its risk profile. The various measures to convert exposures into risk-weighted asset equivalents tend to obscure that fact. The Basel Accord does not, however, attempt to justify how to determine in fundamental terms the level of protection against risks of losses that should be considered to be appropriate and hence capital held. Most of the arguments about Basel's distorting effects come back to this fundamental flaw.
- **Mandatory minimum requirements.** The other fundamental flaw is philosophical. Human activities can be regulated by stablishing detailed rules that must be followed, and where compliance failure will attract specific sanctions and punishment. Alternatively broad princi-ples can be spelt out and individuals left the freedom to interpret those principles in terms of their own actions. When sanctions are applied they usually take the form of peer pressure and involve negotiation rather than specific punitive measures. Both approaches have their place.

  The Basel Accord took the first approach. A lot of the specific problems with the Accord (and in particular those concerning granularity and regulatory arbitrage) could have been avoided if the Basel Accord defined recommended target capital levels and practices for estimating them rather than setting mandatory minimum levels determined by arbitrary rules. Banks would then have to report their actual level of capital against this target level. If the actual level held was below that of the target regulatory level a bank would be expected to publicly justify the shortfall. It would then be left to the discretion of national regulators and market forces to decide whether to require a bank to increase its capital.
- **Cyclicality.** The Accord takes no account of cyclicality. Provisions for credit losses and capital, as a buffer for unexpected losses, should vary with the level of problem loans. In approximate terms provisions should peak around the time NPLs peak while the level of capital necessary to hold should be at a minimum. The requirement for a fixed minimum level of capital at all times means in effect that this capital is not available as a buffer to absorb losses.

Some final observations on the Basel Accord overall:

- **Highlighted capital management issues.** A positive consequence of the Basel Accord has been that it has forced management at many banks to recognize the difference between risk capital and regulatory capital. A negative consequence is that less sophisticated banks have simply allocated the implied regulatory capital requirements without regard to the actual level of risks concerned for specific exposures.
- **Hasn't improved cross-border comparisons.** The reported BIS regulatory capital levels do not provide a sound base for comparing capital strengths of banks operating in the same market because of their arbitrary nature. The problems of comparing banks' CAR ratios cross-border are further exacerbated by differences in accounting policies and definitions.
- **Correlation with other risk measures.** There is very little correlation between banks' BIS CARs and their issuer ratings as given by credit rating agencies. There is some evidence that banks with very low Tier I ratios tend to have low credit ratings and higher betas but that appears to be the extent of the relationship between listed banks' stock market betas and their Tier I ratios.
- **Actual CAR levels.** Most banks operate with Basel CAR levels that are well beyond that necessary to meet the minimum requirements and have some safety buffer. This observation puts a question mark over the importance of some identified regulatory arbitrage problems intended to artificially reduce calculated RWAs. It tends to suggest that the minimum Basel capital requirements are well below the level at which most banks would choose to operate in any case.

  In financially stressed systems reported CAR levels at individual banks have been artificially inflated by a failure of banks to recognize credit losses and of regulators to force that recognition.
- **Costs.** The costs of implementing the Original Accord were relatively modest and the ongoing regulatory overhead relatively light. Those of the Internal Ratings Based approach proposed in the new Basel Accord, however, are likely to be significantly higher.

The need for an international agreement in the form of the Basel Accord tends to be taken for granted but is by no means self-evident. The perception in the 1970s and 1980s that the world's financial system had become less stable as a result of floating exchange rates has not endured. Most now see floating rate exchange rates as providing flexible means for economic systems to adjust to changing economic fundamentals. They avoid the periodic shocks associated with fixed rate systems that used to occur as a result of overnight currency devaluation. The range of instruments available to hedge and redistribute financial risk is much wider now than it was then. These markets now have much greater depth and liquidity. Risk management theory and its practical application at banks have come on in leaps and bounds.

It is the most basic questions that are often the most awkward. What is the Basel Accord now intended to achieve? Are these legitimate objectives? Who benefits from the costs expended from meeting Basel Accord requirements? Does it achieve those objectives and, if it does, are there cheaper or better ways to achieve the same end? The answer that it defines global minimum capital requirements for commercial banks is not a sufficient response. These are a means to an end. The arguments in its favor based on the need to create a "level playing field" and the need to "protect depositors" are not very convincing.

On a more positive note, the New Accord will result in a large increase in revenues at external credit rating agencies and stimulate competition in this area. More companies will seek and pay for external ratings. Consultancies specializing in this field are also likely to enjoy a sharp increase in demand for their services. Newspapers will benefit from additional advertising from these organizations trying to get a share of this new business. It will provide work for many systems analysts, designers and builders. It will increase demand for database application software and increase hardware requirements at banks. The size of specialist capital management groups at many banks is likely to increase and banks that lack such a unit are likely to establish one. Analysts across the world will spend a great deal of time getting to grips with the detail of the New Accord in an attempt to determine its likely impact on the banks within their coverage. And customers and bank share holders will pick up the tab.

Public criticisms from banking industry bodies of both Basel I and Basel II are remarkably low key and the language used extremely restrained. This is typical of the way that things are usually done in the upper echelons of banking but sometimes a more direct approach is justified. Many would agree with US First Lady Johnson's following assertion, and wonder who that "somebody" is at the BIS:

> *Any committee is only as good as the most knowledgeable, determined and vigorous person on it. There must be somebody who provides the flame.*

PART IV

Capital Markets

Fund management

* Drivers of demand for investment products
* Mutual funds
  - Benefits to investors (diversification & delegation)
  - Types of fund - style
* Investment objectives, constraints & charges
* Institutional funds
  - Life insurance
  - Pension funds
* Benchmarks
  - Qualities of good benchmark
  - Indexation issues
* Hedge funds
  - Common features
  - Types of hedge funds
* Other funds
* Tracker versus active management
* Returns measurement
* Investment portfolio theory
  - CAPM & diversification
* Performance measurement
  - Risk-return measures (Sharpe, Treynor, Jensen)
* Attribution analysis
  - Asset class allocation versus individual stock selection

Investment banking

* Principal business lines
* Primary markets - issuance
  - Prospectus, selling, book-building, underwriting
* Issuer objectives
  - Raise capital versus listed status
* Pricing issues
  - Bonds versus equities
  - Domestic & international peer comparisons
* Issues to get listed status
* Rights issues & bonus shares
* Secondary markets - brokerage
  - Research, sales, trading, back-office
* Mergers & acquisitions
* Proprietary trading
* Markets & the media

Securitization

* Issuer & investor incentives
* Mortgage backed securities
  - Pass through, IOs & POs
  - Prepayment modeling
  - Credit enhancement
  - CMOs & PACs
* Other securitization issues

15

Fund Management

The financial services industry has a recidivist tendency to sell duff products to dumb consumers, attributable partly to the failure of senior managers to supervise their sales forces adequately.

Martin Dickson, Financial Times Columnist

INTRODUCTION

CNN has brought world stock markets into people's front rooms. Individual portfolio managers became household names in the 1990s. The relationship between banks and fund managers is complex. Fund managers sell products that compete with bank deposits for savings but, although there are many independent fund managers, many large banks also have their own fund management business. The relationship between investment banks and fund managers is symbiotic with each feeding off the other. Many retail banks also generate fees from distributing third-party mutual funds.

Despite the increase in the level of investments held few people who work outside of financial services really understand how funds are managed and how their performance is measured. In this chapter we examine the most important principles of portfolio management, the key ratios used to analyze returns and the ways in which managers try to overstate or distort historic performance.

One of the ironies of investor behavior is that it is easier to sell mutual funds when markets are rising and stocks are becoming more expensive than it is to sell them when markets are falling and stocks are becoming cheaper. Individual investors suffer from the herd mentality and this tends to reinforce market direction. As markets rise individuals buy more mutual funds and this cash has to be invested in the stock market.

When markets fall investors are prone to panic and as a consequence to cash in, or redeem, their investments in open-ended funds. As portfolio managers respond to redemptions they have to sell stocks to meet their cash obligations. This adds selling pressure and if the scale of the redemptions is high enough will push markets lower. We have already noted how the dynamics of margin lending can also increase downward pressure following a market correction.

DEMAND FOR INVESTMENT PRODUCTS

Fund managers may manage funds for individuals, for institutions or for both. The fund management business across the world has enjoyed spectacular growth over the past three decades. Economic activity and stock markets are essentially cyclical in nature. The basic problem with acting on this understanding is that it is easier to identify peaks and troughs with hindsight. Cycles vary in length and identifying inflexion points in advance is difficult. The bear market that started at the end of one of the longest bull runs in history during the 1990s provided the investment business with a large challenge as investors who had enjoyed easy gains rued their sudden losses and licked their wounds.

Despite this setback to equity investors and the fund management industry there are a number of fundamental drivers that suggest that demand will recover although investors will act in a more cautious way. These drivers include the following:

- **Demographics.** Most developed countries have aging populations. These people have needed to invest their savings in order to generate an income when they retire. Some of these savings have been invested in insurance products, others into mutual funds and individual stock holdings.

  People, in general, are living longer. This means that the proportion of an individual's life spent actively working to generate an income has been falling.
- **Increased personal wealth.** Despite the periodic recession, and depending upon how this is measured, the global economy has grown by an average of 2%–4% per year in real terms over the past 50 years. In most countries there has been a move away from using tax as a policy tool to redistribute wealth and towards using the capital markets. While the overall burden of taxes may not have changed significantly that burden has shifted from the rich to the poor in many developed countries.
- **Shift away from state pension plans.** Many OECD countries face an increasing problem with their state pension plans as a result of their aging populations. As a result they have encouraged individuals to take out their own personal pension plans by providing various tax incentives.

  In a sense there is an element of sleight of hand at work here. Pension payments represent a transfer of income from younger generations to older generations. This may be done using tax policies or capital markets. In the latter case the older generation owns rights, through its ownership of companies, to a part of the income generated by the younger generation and paid out as dividends from corporate earnings.

  Whatever the political implications employees are increasingly recognizing that they cannot rely upon the state for their income during retirement. The issue of how developed countries will be able to support their future pensioners while leaving the then current working population satisfied is one that has received far less attention than it merits.
- **Shift away from defined benefit plans.** Many companies have been trying to move away from defined benefit plans, whereby the level of pensions that plan participants receive is guaranteed by the company, to defined contribution plans where no such guarantee is provided. Corporate bankruptcies due to a failure to manage pension liabilities have risen and are likely to increase further. This has given a further incentive for individuals to take out additional pension plans.
- **Better educated workforce.** Throughout the developed world the proportion of the population with tertiary education has been increasing. Better educated people are not only better paid but also understand better the investment process and are generally less conservative in terms of what savings products they are willing to invest in and take a more active approach to financial planning than older generations.
- **Privatization.** Privatization of services provided by the state and of state-owned utilities and companies started to become increasingly common from the mid-1980s. Many governments around the world moved to privatize state services in the belief that the private sector can deliver a better level of service at a lower cost. The poor performance of many state-backed companies led many to conclude that state ownership of the means of production was a less efficient way to allocate capital than relying on capital markets. In many cases in Europe these privatization issues were accomplished, in part at least, by selling or

giving shares to the general public. This led to a large increase in the proportion of the population with direct stock market holdings in those countries that pursued privatization most aggressively.

It is not surprising that enthusiasm for popular capitalism depends on whether the beneficiaries of privatization have profited from these issues. It has been higher in the UK, where most individuals made money from privatization issues, than in Germany where the issue of Deutsche Telecom resulted in large paper and actual losses for investors who subscribed to its huge Initial Public Offering (IPO). Despite this setback there are now more individual holders of stocks in Germany than there are trade union members.

- **Outsourcing.** Although some organizations manage their own employee pension plans, most companies outsource this work to professional fund managers. This has aided the growth in the number and size of specialist investment management companies. The trend for companies to outsource as much of their non-core business as possible has probably helped the growth of the fund management business.

MUTUAL FUNDS

Retail Investors

Retail investors seeking to gain some exposure to stock market investments can either invest directly by buying individual stocks on their own account or by buying a mutual fund product (in some countries referred to as unit trusts). These are investment funds that are run by professional portfolio managers. (The term "fund manager" is also used in the industry to identify individuals who manage investment portfolios but also refers to the firms themselves. For clarity we will refer to portfolio managers as the individuals and fund managers as the institutions.) Fund managers charge a fee for this service. The main benefits to investors are the result of diversification effects and from not having to take an active role in the detailed investment process:

- **Retail investment diversification.** The real value of mutual funds to retail investors comes from being able to diversify their holdings at a reasonable cost and avoid having to get involved with the investment process directly.

  Diversification allows investors to spread their risks more widely by owning a small portion of many stocks or other investments. A well-diversified stock portfolio requires at least 16–20 individual stock holdings. A degree of analysis and periodic portfolio rebalancing are necessary to ensure that it remains well diversified and does not have exposures with large risk concentrations.

  Most stocks have minimum "lot" sizes, these are standard blocks of shares that can be traded. An investor wishing to buy shares in a stock trading at $10 with a lot size of 1000 shares would have to make an initial investment of at least $10 000 to gain a holding in the stock. Partial lots do occur as a result of corporate actions such as rights issues but investors selling partial lots receive a price below that of the market for their shares.

- **Delegation of investment process.** Having selected and invested in a particular investment fund whose objectives best match those of the investor's requirements the investor does not play any active role in the actual investment process. This is particularly important for retail investors with limited investment experience. This also means that the selection of the most appropriate fund is critical.

Those benefits come at a cost of course. Claims that portfolio managers can add value by beating the market have to be viewed with skepticism, however:

- **Transaction costs.** Although transaction costs have fallen for all investors as a consequence of the abolition of regulated commission rates they are still lower for large institutional investors than for retail investors. A domestic investor wishing an exposure to stocks in a foreign market will almost always find it easier and cheaper to achieve this end by buying specialized mutual funds than making direct investments.
- **Better returns.** Fund managers claim that they are selling the expertise of their analysts and portfolio managers with a clear implication that this means that they will generate superior returns. As we will seek to demonstrate, fund managers are on very shaky grounds when they suggest that superior performance provides a justification for the fees they charge.

There is now a bewildering range of different funds for retail investors in developed markets to choose from. Most funds have a particular investment focus otherwise known as their "style". Examples of these include the following:

- **Bonds.** Funds that are wholly invested in "fixed-income" instruments, these may include short-dated investments such as commercial papers as well as long-term bonds. The term "fixed income" is slightly confusing as some bonds are issued in a floating rate form but fall within the definition of a fixed-income instrument. These funds may be wholly domestic or international. Some funds are constrained as to which bonds they can hold based on the credit quality of the issue or issuer. A fund may, for example, invest only in high-yield bonds from companies with a credit rating below that of investment grade (often referred to as junk bonds). Other funds may be prohibited from holding such bonds under the terms of their prospectus.
- **Growth.** A fund that concentrates on investing in the stock of companies with high growth potential. Such stocks tend to trade on high *PE* and *PBR* multiples and operate in new business areas. These funds' returns are usually driven by capital gains or losses rather than dividend income. Their returns are usually relatively volatile.
- **Value.** Value investors look for companies that appear cheap and where there appear to be prospects of a turnaround. Such companies may be loss making. They typically trade on low *PE* and *PBR* multiples.
- **Sector.** A fund that invests in stocks of companies operating in a particular sector, for example banking, technology or oil and energy.
- **Global/regional.** Many international funds are either global or regional. An EAFE fund, for example, would invest in Europe, Australia and the Far East, principally Japan.
- **Emerging markets.** The most important benchmarks against which fund performances are measured are those of the MSCI (Morgan Stanley Capital Indices). The MSCI separates markets into developed and emerging. Emerging markets are frequently less well regulated than developed markets and often more volatile. There is much debate about the level of correlation of returns between those of emerging and developed markets.

- **Income.** A fund that focuses on generating a steady income. Many of these funds invest heavily in blue chips, companies with a good track record and high dividend yield but where growth expectations are modest.
- **Small caps.** A fund that invests in small companies, where size is normally defined in terms of market capitalization.

Many funds are heavily marketed and large fund managers advertise heavily to promote their own brands. Fund managers rely on four principal distribution channels:

- **Banks.** Retail banks act as distributors for third-party mutual funds. This may be limited to simply putting marketing material and application forms on display but may also be the result of direct selling by bank personnel. The latter is particularly prevalent when the distributor is also the manufacturer and manager of the mutual funds.
- **Independent financial advisers.** Independent financial advisers and planners provide an investment advisory service to individuals. In most countries such advisers have to be registered with a central securities and investment agency. They charge for these services in one of two ways. Some agree a fixed advisory fee (often based on the value of the assets on which they are giving advise) others earn a commission from the issuers of mutual funds from persuading their clients to buy particular products. The latter method of charging for services provided creates considerable moral hazard.
- **Advertising.** Larger fund managers advertise specific funds in newspapers and periodicals. Investors can then apply directly to the fund manager, without having to go through a third party.
- **Cold calling.** Nobody likes cold calling and in some countries selling investment products by cold calling is illegal. Where it is permitted it gives another direct channel.

Closed and Open-ended Funds

Funds can be open-ended or closed. In open-ended funds the number of shares is not fixed. The value of open-ended funds is calculated on a daily basis and from this "bid" and "offer" prices are calculated. The price at which investors can subscribe for new shares in the fund is usually set at a small premium to appraised value. The price that existing investors may sell at is, on the other hand, set at a discount. This discount is often much wider than the corresponding premium and many investors find out the hard way that this bid–offer spread imposes a heavy burden on their investment returns. When investors sell their shares (redemptions) the fund has to liquidate assets in order to meet their contractual obligation. In practice funds maintain a proportion of the portfolio in cash or cash equivalents in order to meet routine redemptions without being forced to sell into the market.

Closed-end funds have a fixed number of shares, and are usually traded on an exchange. The basic issue for investors in closed-end funds is that the shares of closed-end funds usually trade at a discount to their NAV (net appraised value). It is difficult to see why investors should subscribe to a new closed-end fund. The only rationale can be that investors have so much confidence in the portfolio manager that they expect the performance of the fund to be so good that it will negate this discount.

INVESTMENT OBJECTIVES, CONSTRAINTS AND CHARGES

Investment Objectives, and Constraints

The main objectives of the fund are set out in a prospectus. The section on objectives normally includes the fund's "style", its approach to investing the assets and may specify the benchmark index against which its performance will be measured. Few mutual funds actually quantify either absolute expected returns or return objectives relative to the benchmark index.

The prospectus usually also identifies constraints imposed on the portfolio manager. Most funds stipulate the maximum amount that can be held in cash at any one time. Cash in this context usually means some sort of money market investment. The reason why most funds have an upper limit on the amount of cash, or cash equivalent, that can be held is that there is no reason why investors should pay a 100+ bpts annual management fee for an investment that they could make easily themselves. On the other hand portfolio managers need to keep sufficient liquid assets to meet normal redemptions without being forced to sell down positions. The level of cash that a fund holds has important consequences for fund performance. This limitation means that funds have little alternative other than to be fully invested, even if the portfolio manager believes that security prices are likely to fall.

The prospectus also usually defines limits on the amount that can be invested in different asset classes in terms of bonds, equities, countries and industries and in individual security holdings.

Charges

The prospectus also details the fund's fee structure. There is usually an initial fee based on the amount invested, and then annual fees based on the value of the assets under management. Some funds also charge a redemption fee.

When a fund has an initial fee this is referred to as "front loading", and when it has a redemption fee this is referred to as "back loading". Front loading means the fund manager gets the fee upfront but this is an obvious marketing disadvantage.

Back loading is a less obvious way of extracting management fees. It has the advantage that the greater the absolute performance of the fund the greater the fees. In falling markets fund managers have an incentive to front load fees and in rising markets to back load them. Back loading also provides a disincentive to investors to cash in their shares.

In efficient markets more than half, and as much as 75% by value, of active funds underperform the market index. This has created a demand for tracking funds, which have lower fees than those for active funds. An active fund manager blamed this demand on investors' inability to differentiate between fund managers likely to outperform and those likely to underperform. There is very little anyone can say to that.

Soft commissions are a source of much controversy. Soft commissions are a way in which brokerage houses provide services to a fund manager in return for getting an agreed level of business from the client. These include paying for the provision of items such as terminals and services from information providers such as Bloomberg and Reuters.

A portfolio manager charges her clients a management fee. Transaction costs, such as brokerage commissions and stamp duties, are treated as part of the fund's costs. If the fund manager had to pay for general services themselves this would come out of their management fees. Because the fund manager does not pay directly for these services in effect this acts as a direct subsidy to their own account.

INSTITUTIONAL FUNDS

Most other institutional investment funds are associated with either life insurance or pension funds. Both industries have similar profiles in the sense that they receive money today, in the form of insurance premiums or pension contributions that create a long-term future financial obligation, i.e. have a long duration. This is not the case with companies offering general insurance policies (theft, auto etc.) where most liabilities are relatively short term and have a relatively short duration and hence are less interest rate sensitive.

Life Insurance Companies

There is a wide range of life insurance policies available but most are structured to provide a payout in the event of the policyholder's death but provide a "surrender" option that allows the policyholder to cash in their policies. Life insurance products have a long duration and the presence of a surrender clause indicates the presence of an embedded option. While many life insurance schemes are marketed as investment products their returns are usually much lower than well-diversified mutual funds to compensate for the value of the insurance policy.

The value of the future liabilities arising from policyholder death relies heavily on actuarial modeling of mortality statistics. In the absence of the surrender option life insurance policies try to match asset duration with that of their liabilities. Their return objectives can be divided into those concerned with meeting their estimated future liabilities and those concerned with managing the surplus between the market value of its assets less its liabilities:

$$Surplus = Market\ value\ of\ assets - Market\ value\ of\ liabilities$$

In the case of most non-life insurance companies this surplus would be considered a part of shareholders' equity. The surplus is usually only a small percentage of the market value of its assets and estimated value of its liabilities and hence relatively small changes in the values of either assets or liabilities can have a big impact on the surplus level.

Insurance companies are highly regulated and in most regimes they are required to maintain a mandatory surplus reserve level. These reserves are intended to act as a buffer to protect policyholders from the impact of lower asset values. The level of surplus acts in a similar way to bank capital adequacy requirements as a constraint on the company expanding its business by writing new policies. If the surplus falls below that required by regulators the company will need to make up the shortfall from its own equity account and if necessary raise additional capital to do so.

In some countries accounting policies allow life insurance companies to transfer a part of the surplus through the income statement to equity each year. This can be illustrated with a simplified example where the transfer is "smoothed" over a five-year period. Each year the company transfers one-fifth of the increase (or decrease) in the change in the value of its surplus during the year. It transfers the same amount for a total of five years. The total taken through the P&L account in any year is then the sum of the calculated transfers for the previous five years.

Simplified example of smoothed transfer of surplus to equity account through P&L						
	Y-5	Y-4	Y-3	Y-2	Y-1	Y-0
Brought forward surplus	100 000	107 200	113 118	103 054	108 328	99 994
Change in surplus over year	9000	9648	(7918)	9275	(5416)	8999
– Year 5	(1800)	(1800)	(1800)	(1800)	(1800)	
– Year 4		(1930)	(1930)	(1930)	(1930)	(1930)
– Year 3			1584	1584	1584	1584
– Year 2				(1855)	(1855)	(1855)
– Year 1					1083	1083
– Year 0						(1800)
Transfer to equity	(1800)	(3730)	(2146)	(4001)	(2918)	(2918)
Carried forward surplus	107 200	113 118	103 054	108 328	99 994	106 076

Most life insurance funds invest heavily in bonds to match asset and liability durations and invest in equities largely to try to grow the surplus account. The level of equity holdings may also be limited to a specified percentage of assets by regulators.

In the event of severe market corrections less conservative companies may find that they cannot meet regulatory minimum surplus requirements. As is the case with bank regulators, insurance regulators normally practice regulatory forbearance.

When the surplus turns into a deficit and cannot be met from the company's equity and new capital cannot be raised the insurer is usually allowed to fail. The failure of one life insurance company does not bear the same systemic risks that individual bank failures have. Individual policyholders rarely consider the risk that an insurance company will fail in their long-term financial planning and that they will bear the brunt of the resulting losses. "Lifeboat" funds exist in some countries, funded by contributions from the insurance companies themselves. These funds may be regulated by the state but the level of state backing, if any, is usually much lower than is the case with many bank deposit insurance schemes.

CORPORATE PENSION FUNDS

Corporate pension funds fall into one of two categories, defined benefit or defined contribution. In recent years there has been a shift from defined benefit plans, where the investment risks lie with the employer, towards defined contribution where the risks lie with the employee:

Defined benefit schemes
Under the terms of defined benefit plans, the income that a plan member receives after retirement is specified in advance. This is usually defined as a certain percentage of the final year's income and may be inflation indexed. These benefits are guaranteed by the employer, and hence create a future liability for companies.

In the US these funds fall under the terms of ERISA (Employees Retirement Income Security Act). This states that such funds are to be run on behalf of the members of the fund.

Defined benefit pensions pose real risks to companies and indirectly to employees in the event that the company is unable to meet its obligations. While the employees are entitled to their defined benefits the company owns any pension fund surplus but is responsible for meeting any deficit. There are four key issues that have to be dealt with:

- **Investment growth rate.** A key assumption in managing a pension fund, given its long-term exposure and the compounding nature of investment returns, is the expected growth in the value of the pension assets. If a company's assumption of future growth of pension fund assets is too high it can claim and extract the pension fund's surplus but may fail to be able to meet its future pension obligations.

    There are many examples of companies that have mismanaged the balance between pension fund assets and liabilities and ended up with significant pension fund deficits. There are also examples where management has fraudulently and systematically looted the pension fund to cover deficits in other parts of the company.

- **Discount rate.** Defined benefit pension liabilities are highly interest rate sensitive as their expected future value depends on the level of discount rate used. There is always a careful balancing act between holding bonds, which are highly interest rate sensitive, and stocks that have historically provided better returns.

- **Liquidity.** The liquidity requirements of a company pension fund depend on its employee and pensioner profile. Companies with an aging, long-serving workforce will have to maintain a higher level of liquid assets than companies with a young workforce and few pensioners.

- **Diversification.** One of the least forgivable errors made by corporate management is to invest a high proportion of its employees' pension fund in its own stock. If the company fails their employees will not only lose their jobs but also their pensions. In principle pension funds should be invested in stocks and other investments that have a low or negative correlation with the company's performance. At times when the company is performing poorly and least able to contribute to its pension fund it will be able to avoid the need to do so because of the better performance of the fund.

Company management are often tempted to "play" with their employee pension fund to meet their own objectives. This temptation is greatest when a company is facing the most severe financial pressures. There would be less need for legislation of the form of ERISA if corporate management did not, from time to time, succumb to these temptations. The lower the discount rate and the higher the growth assumption the greater the surplus or the lower any unfunded shortfall. This will also reduce the contribution the company has to make, reducing operating costs. A shortfall may not become apparent for many years. A more direct, and fraudulent, abuse is simply to pilfer the fund's assets.

Company pension fund trustees are often put in a very difficult position in the event of a hostile bid. It may be in the best interests of current employees (and hence future beneficiaries) to oppose such a bid but in the best interests of past employees (and hence present beneficiaries) to support the bid. Management will also put pressure on trustees to support their own position.

Stock options have been used extensively to (allegedly) try to align executive incentives with those of the shareholder interests. Most ordinary employees should probably sell any stock they receive in the company they work for as soon as they receive it. It all comes back to risk tolerance and diversification.

Defined contribution

Defined contribution plans transfer the responsibility and risks to the employee. The employee makes a contribution to the fund on a regular basis. In some plans the employer matches the employee's contribution. A professional fund manager then manages the fund. The employee obtains all of the benefits of a good performance by the fund manager but is also exposed to the risk that the fund performs poorly. Defined contribution plans do not appear on the company's balance sheet.

Pension funds may be managed in-house or their management may be contracted out in part of in full to professional fund managers. Even when managed in-house portfolio managers may determine that they will only take an active role in managing a part of the funds under management, often the portion in domestic equities and bonds. They will then look to contract out the management of funds deemed necessary for diversification to specialist managers while retaining overall responsibility.

The trustees or pension fund managers then invite tenders for the mandate to run this money. A major difference between a pension fund mandate and a mutual fund prospectus is that the former sets out well-defined return objectives. These objectives normally define the benchmark against which performance will be measured, a return objective and the maximum level of risk to be borne.

In both bull and bear markets there are cases where portfolio managers fail to meet the targets specified in the mandate. Those portfolio managers who persisted in holding value stocks in the mid- to late 1990s and shunned technology stocks because they felt they were massively overvalued consistently underperformed broad-based benchmarks, for example. The usual result of failing to meet targets is that the fund manager is fired but occasionally the pension fund managers or trustees threaten, and even take, legal action.

In order to be able to assess a portfolio manager's performance in an objective manner it is necessary to have quantitative ways to measure performance and to determine whether a fund manager is acting within the terms of their mandate or prospectus. It is also useful to be able to determine whether apparent success or failure can be ascribed largely to chance or is due to the portfolio manager's skills. Provided a portfolio manager can demonstrate that they have acted in a reasonable and professional manner they are almost certain to be absolved of liability for losses incurred by their funds under management. On the other hand they may well be best advised to seek an out of court agreement in case of dispute rather than have the risk of being dragged into the glare of the public arena and suffer reputational loss.

BENCHMARKS AND PERFORMANCE MEASUREMENTS

Given that relative fund performance has to be measured against a benchmark index, the definition of that benchmark is clearly critical. The key properties of an appropriate benchmark are as follows:

- **Specified in advance.** It is essential that the benchmark be established before fund performance is evaluated. If it is not the portfolio manager is likely to choose those benchmark against which the fund has had the best relative performance.
- **Investable and measurable.** It should be possible to hold the benchmark portfolio and measure the returns from the benchmark portfolio on a regular basis.
- **Reflective of style.** The benchmark portfolio should reflect the fund's investment style. A growth fund's performance should be measured against that of a benchmark portfolio consisting of growth stocks in which the portfolio manager could invest.

RETURNS MEASUREMENT AND WAYS TO DISTORT PERFORMANCE REPORTING

Calculation of Returns

Take the case of a fund generating annual returns of 7.1%, 4.5%, a fall of 3.2% and 1.2% over the past four years. It is possible to calculate an "average" annual growth rate by adding these up, giving total returns of 9.2% and an average of 2.4% annual growth. This method is fundamentally flawed as it takes no account of time. A fund's time-weighted returns should be calculated using geometric returns as shown in the following equation, where R_t represents the fund's time-weighted returns and r_i the returns for each period:

$$R_t = [(1 + r_1) \times (1 + r_2) \times \ldots \times (1 + r_N)]^{\frac{1}{N}} - 1$$

Portfolio returns				
	Year 1	Year 2	Year 3	Year 4
r_i	7.1%	4.5%	−3.2%	1.2%
$1 + r_i$	107.1%	104.5%	96.8%	101.2%

The total returns over the four years are calculated as follows:

$$[(107.1\%) \times (104.5\%) \times (96.8\%) \times (101.2\%)] = 109.6\% - 1 = 9.6\%$$

The time-weighted annualized returns for the portfolio are then calculated as shown below and are 2.3% rather than the 2.4% we arrived at with a simple average:

$$(109.6\%)^{\frac{1}{4}} = 102.3\% - 1 = 2.3\%$$

In practice this exercise is more complex than indicated here because it is necessary to take into account new cash invested into the fund and any redemptions. There are also issues as to whether portfolio performance should be reported after taking account of management fees.

Methods Used to Overstate Performance

Fund managers have a strong incentive to put their historic performance in the best possible light. Although fund prospectuses and advertisements for mutual funds in most countries are required to include a statement to the effect that past performance is no guarantee of future performance few investors take any notice of this disclaimer. Many retail investors use past performance as a means to assess a portfolio manager's skills. By presenting past performance in the best possible light portfolio managers hope to attract new funds and hence increase the fees that they generate from managing these funds.

In more developed markets such as the US there have been significant steps made to improve the presentation of performance appraisal but in many countries the scope for abuse remains. There are many ways to misrepresent a fund's performance.

Portfolio managers have an incentive to "exaggerate" their funds' performance and, in the absence of formal regulatory performance measurement standards, they may use any of the following methods to achieve this end:

- **Selective time period.** A common way to misrepresent performance is only to report performance for those periods in which the fund has performed relatively well. This can be achieved by excluding periods of poor performance.
- **Inappropriate benchmarks.** The only time that a market index should be used as a benchmark is when this is consistent with the fund's stated objectives. It may well, for example, be appropriate for a single-market large-cap equity fund. Otherwise it fails to take style into account. It is not appropriate, for example, to measure the performance of a value fund against a market index when a significant proportion of the market comprises growth stocks.
- **Selective benchmarks.** We have already considered the qualities of a good benchmark. If no benchmark has been specified in advance a portfolio manager may choose to compare performance of its funds with those benchmarks against which the fund has performed well and neglect to report on performance against benchmarks that put them in a bad light.

  The popular method of "peer group" comparison is particularly vulnerable to this type of misrepresentation. The practice of comparing different funds' performance fails to meet our criteria for an appropriate benchmark. It is not possible to define in advance, is not easily measurable and fails to take investment style into account. This is by far the most common type of comparison given in newsstand investment magazines.
- **Failure to adjust for risk.** Performance should take account of risk. A high beta fund (a fund invested in stocks where prices have above-average volatility) is likely to outperform the market when stock prices are rising. The "better" performance may simply be due to having accepted a higher level of risk. These funds are likely to underperform in falling markets.
- **Inconsistent comparison.** There are several ways in which a comparison may be distorted by inconsistent definitions including the following:
- **Management fees.** Performance may be reported before or after management fees. Relative performance will be overstated if the fund's performance is based on performance before management fees while those of benchmarks are reported after management fees.
- **Dividend treatment.** Fund performance should include dividends received and reinvested. If the benchmark used is that of an index returns should also be adjusted to take these into account. A simple comparison of an index's percentage changes versus that of the performance of a fund is likely to overstate the fund's relative performance.
- **Inclusion of fund inflows.** It is tempting for fund managers to imply that a fund's performance is related to the increase in the value of the fund overall. ("Funds under management up by a compound rate of 25% over past five years!") For open-ended funds this fails to take into account new subscriptions.
- **Survivorship bias.** A fund manager reporting on the performance of all of its funds may overstate its overall performance because if it only includes funds that are currently active it may exclude funds whose performance has been so poor that they have been closed. This is generally referred to as survivorship bias.

Indexing Issues

A market index consists of a subset of stocks within the market that collectively are representative of the overall composition of the market. The performance of the index is expected to reflect the performance of the market and provide an appropriate benchmark against which fund performance can be measured. Portfolio managers seeking to reduce tracking error tend to overweight stocks within the index and underweight non-index stocks. This means that the performance of market and market indices tends to diverge and results in the latter no longer being an appropriate benchmark.

Specific problems arise when a large-cap stock is added to an index, particularly those arising from privatizations or IPOs. In many cases retail allocations are disproportionately high and once the stock starts trading many institutional portfolio managers are forced to reduce their resulting underweight position in the stock. This is most evident for tracking funds but many other pension fund mandates have investment objectives that specify a maximum tracking error against a market benchmark. This is intended to impose a constraint on the level of risks the manager undertakes but can have unintended negative consequences.

The only way to reduce the tracking error due to being underweight in this stock is to buy it through the market. This "artificial" demand pushes up the price of the stock and this exacerbates the underlying weighting problem further as the stock's weighting rises. The result is that such stocks often move into severely overvalued territory. Once the weighting imbalance has moderated these stocks are highly vulnerable to a sharp correction.

REASONS FOR TRADING

Given the importance that transaction costs have to play in portfolio performance it is worth taking an aside to review the reasons why institutional funds trade securities in secondary markets. Although companies use capital markets to raise equity and debt financing through the issue of financial securities only a very small proportion of an institutional fund's holdings can be traced back directly to subscription to a primary issue, most have been bought in the secondary market. The main reasons why institutional funds trade are as follows:

- **Money-in.** When new investors subscribe to an open-ended mutual fund the portfolio manager has to invest the new funds in stocks, bonds or commodities. Most mutual funds are constrained by the terms of their prospectus as to the amount of cash that the fund can hold.
- **Money-out.** When existing mutual fund investors decide to redeem their investments they are reimbursed in cash. Mutual funds keep a small cash buffer to meet an expected level of redemptions but once that is exhausted have to sell some of their investments. This is an example of trades carried out for liquidity management reasons.
- **Tracker funds.** Funds that track specific indices have to adjust their holdings when changes in index constituents are made. They will have to sell their holdings in stocks dropped from the index and buy stock in companies added to the index.
- **Asset-class allocation.** The investment process at many institutional funds is carried out in two parts. The first part is a top-down decision on asset-class allocation (the proportion of a fund to be held in equities versus bonds, for example) and the second part the selection of individual securities within each asset class. A shift in asset-class allocation will therefore result in many trades of individual securities.
- **Rebalancing.** Even with no change in asset-allocation policies occasional rebalancing of holdings is necessary to take account of changes in security prices and maintain the target asset-class weightings. This is also the case with bond portfolios that have a target duration as the portfolio's actual duration will adjust over time unless the portfolio is periodically rebalanced.

- **Security switching.** Active fund managers are constantly looking for undervalued securities to buy. In the absence of new money inflows such securities can only be bought by selling investments in other less attractive holdings.

HEDGE FUNDS

Common Features

Hedge funds provide an alternative investment vehicle to traditional mutual funds. The range of different hedge funds on offer has now grown so wide that the definition of the term has now become very blurred. Most hedge funds share four attributes in common, however:

- **Absolute returns.** The performance of most hedge funds is measured in terms of absolute returns rather than relative to a benchmark index. Achieving absolute returns becomes harder as a fund grows in size.
- **Performance-based remuneration.** A high proportion of most hedge-fund managers' remuneration is based on the absolute performance of funds under management.
- **Leveraged.** Conventional funds do not usually allow debt to be used to increase leverage. Most hedge funds use debt to increase gearing. Consider a fund that has $50m in funds under management. It can also borrow an additional $50m at a 10% annual interest rate. If it succeeds in achieving 15% returns on its invested funds then by borrowing it can increase the return on its fund from 15% to 20%.

  It generates $15m from the $100m invested, pays interest of $5m, giving it a profit of $10m, equivalent to a 20% return on the $50m of funds under management. Leverage will have a similar effect on the downside if the value of its investments fall.
- **Short selling and derivatives.** Most hedge funds have no restrictions on shorting stocks or the use of derivatives, such as options, to enhance returns.

Examples of Hedge Funds

The degree of risk that individual hedge funds are exposed to varies significantly. Examples of specialized hedge funds include the following:

- **Currency funds.** These are funds that take large speculative positions on the relative performance of currencies. They take reasoned bets based on fundamental analysis of the direction of currencies. They have often been blamed for the collapse of individual managed foreign currency systems through aggressive forward selling of the target currency. To the extent that their actions may be characterized as the "straw that broke the camel's back" there may be some truth in this assertion. They do not create the fundamental flaws, but they do seek to exploit them.

  Fixed exchange rate systems are especially vulnerable to such attacks when governments and central banks make the mistake of failing to recognize when a given fixed exchange rate is untenable.
- **Distressed debt.** Some funds specialize in trading in distressed debt. This may involve buying junk bonds or buying non-performing loans from banks at a steep discount to their book value. These funds hope to profit in one out of three ways:

- **Improvement in credit spreads.** The financial condition of the companies whose debt it has bought may improve resulting in lower credit spreads and higher bond prices.
- **Enhancement in bargaining position.** By buying a majority of a company's debt its position in creditors meetings will be strengthened and it may be possible to impose a restructuring on its own terms or play the part of the deal-maker.
- **Sale of debt back to borrower.** It may be possible to sell the debt back to the company concerned at a discount to its face value but at a premium to the price that the hedge fund actually paid.

- **Pairs funds.** A pairs fund is a fund that specializes in buying instruments with a high correlation where the portfolio manager believes that their relative performance is likely to diverge. Such a portfolio manager might buy Citicorp stock and short JP Morgan Chase if the portfolio manager believed that Citicorp was cheap relative to JP Morgan Chase. If the portfolio manager gets the relative direction correct then it is possible to make money even if both stocks fall.

  Suppose that the starting price for each stock is $100 and that Citicorp stock then falls by $10 and that of JP Morgan Chase by $15. The portfolio manager will lose $10 from buying Citibank but gain $15 from shorting JP Morgan Chase. The overall gain from the transactions is therefore $5.

- **Long–short funds.** A long–short fund differs from a pairs fund in that while it trades in pairs of stocks it selects stocks that are not closely correlated. These funds are more focused on leveraging investor perceptions of fundamental value.

OTHER FUNDS

Capital Guaranteed Return Funds

Capital guaranteed return funds become popular in environments when stock markets are volatile or appear to be in a "bear" phase and interest rates are low. The structure of these funds varies but most have the following features.

- **Capital protection.** Such funds guarantee no capital loss. After a period when equity funds have been falling this can be an attractive attribute to investors.
- **Fixed term.** Such funds are normally for a fixed term and usually have hefty early redemption charges.
- **Minimum return.** They also guarantee a minimum return over the investment term.
- **Upside potential.** They also offer potential upside, for example by offering a greater return than the guaranteed minimum in the event of a stock market index outperforming the guaranteed minimum return.

On the surface these funds may appear attractive but most have management fees that are disproportionately high given the level of management required. There is no active management after the initial set-up. The basic approach is for the fund to buy government and investment grade corporate bonds, to secure the guaranteed return, and to buy call options on the benchmark index to get the higher returns if the market performs well. The redemption costs are usually punitive and investors pay dearly if they have to liquidate their investment before term.

The following diagram shows the structure of a typical capital guaranteed fund.

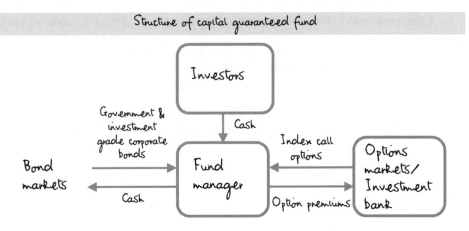

Structure of capital guaranteed fund

To understand better how such funds work we need a simple example. Suppose a three-year fund has been launched. It guarantees a minimum return of 4% per year but in the event that the S&P 500 gives a better return over that period it will pay that return:

- **Risk-free returns.** Three-year Treasury bonds have a yield-to-maturity of 6%. We will assume that we have raised $100m in funds. The first thing to do is to fix the guaranteed return. We know that at the end of the third year we will need to return a minimum of $112.5m ($100m × 1.04³). To achieve this we need to buy $94.5m ($112.5/(1.06³)) of the three-year government note.
- **Index option.** The current level of the S&P 500 is 5000. To achieve a better return than the guaranteed minimum the market would need to rise to 5624 (5000 × 1.04³). The price of three-year call options to buy the index at 5624 is $30.5 at a dollar per point. The balance of $5.5m is used to buy 1.8m of these options.

  Below an index level of 5624 the options will expire worthless. The options will be in-the-money, however, at any level above 5624. As the index returns rise above the 4% annualized guaranteed level the value of exercising the call options kicks in and makes up the additional guaranteed index return as shown in the following table.

Returns of capital guaranteed fund					
S&P index	5000	5624	5724	5824	5924
S&P returns	0	12%	14%	16%	18%
S&P annualized returns	0	4.0%	4.6%	5.2%	5.8%
Call option returns ($m)	0	0	1.8	3.6	5.4
Annualized call option returns (%)	0	0	0.6%	1.2%	1.8%
Government bond annualized return (%)	4%	4%	4%	4%	4%
Total annualized fund return (%)	**4.0%**	**4.0%**	**4.6%**	**5.2%**	**5.8%**

There are, however, problems with this structure. It is for all practical purposes impossible to get such long-dated exchange-traded options. It becomes increasingly difficult to get exchange-traded options with an expiry of greater than six months. Everything has its price, however, and the fund manager will attempt to conclude a deal with an investment bank for the latter to write an over-the-counter (OTC) option and sell it to the fund manager. The problem for an investor comes if they have to redeem their funds early. There will probably be a steep early redemption charge, this will be included in the agreement signed by the investor but frequently goes unnoticed.

The investor will receive back only the proceeds from unraveling the units. The notes will make it clear that in the event of early redemption there is no guarantee of return of capital. Most government and investment grade bonds are liquid in the secondary market although prices will have to be adjusted to take account the reduced term left and any changes in the yield curve. The only market for the OTC options will be that created by the investment bank acting as a market-maker. Prices will tend to be volatile reflecting the patchiness of demand and the investment banker will have a high bid–offer spread. The overall result is that an investor who redeems early will usually get back considerably less than their original investment.

Fund managers can get around using the OTC market with some adroit use of marketing. This can be done by guaranteeing return of capital for only a relatively short period, say six months. After the six months has passed the guarantee lapses. Instead the "guaranteed return of capital" becomes one of the fund's investment objectives. In plain language this translates as we hope that you will get your money back but we are giving no guarantee to that effect.

Another problem arises from the (unlikely) event that one of the corporate issuers fails and defaults on its bonds. The small print will normally cover such an eventuality by making the return of capital conditional on none of these corporates defaulting.

Non-life Insurance Companies

General or non-life insurance companies do not offer investment products but are instead in the business of pricing and buying general risk. They provide standard retail products (household policies concerned with fire, theft, weather and accidental breakage), auto insurance (fully comprehensive down to third-party liability cover) and medical insurance. Retail policies are highly standardized. They also provide wholesale policies for standard risks such as fire and weather and industry-specific policies (airline and maritime cover, for example) these policies vary between standardized cover against common risks and tailored products for cover for uncommon or unique risk. A telecommunications company putting a satellite into orbit is exposed to losses arising out of a launch failure. The level of potential losses will depend very much on the value of its highly specialized payload and may well run into many hundreds of millions of dollars.

They receive income in the form of premiums before they have to pay out on customer claims. Their investment objectives are therefore very different from those of life insurance companies. The most important differences between the two types of business are as follows:

- **Time horizon.** The investment time horizon for life insurance companies is much longer than that of general insurance companies. Life insurance companies invest in a higher proportion of long duration assets than general insurers. Although most general policies are of short duration there are some exceptions. The actual duration of asbestos-related liability claims, for example, had a much longer duration and time horizon than insurers realized at the time.

- **Regulatory.** Life insurance companies are subject to greater regulatory scrutiny than general insurers. A key difference is that life insurers are required to maintain a defined level of surplus (the difference between the present value of their liabilities arising from the policies they have written and the value of the associated assets) while few regulators impose any such requirement on non-life companies.
- **Reinsurance market.** Life insurance companies take individual policies onto their own account. General insurers take some policies (such as protection for retail customers against the effects of fire and theft and auto-related cover) onto their own account but only retain a part of the risks associated with the larger corporate policies. There is an active market for reinsurance whereby individual insurance companies originate policies but then immediately lay off a large part of the risk to reinsurers. In the above case of the telecommunications company these risks (and the premiums earned) would have been spread very widely. In this way insurers are able to diversify their exposures.
- **Liquidity requirements.** Payments made on claims on general insurance policies are more volatile than those of life insurance policies. Death is inevitable and when large numbers of individuals are involved is also depressingly fairly predictable. Claims from losses resulting from natural disasters, arising from the effects of a hurricane for example, are harder to predict. There may be a one in 10 chance that a hurricane of a particular severity will hit a particular city in any given year but this doesn't help in terms of knowing in which year it will occur. This lack of granularity means that the level of claims varies significantly from year to year. As a result non-life companies' liquidity requirements are greater than those of life insurers.

Non-life companies usually hold a higher proportion of their assets in the form of liquid assets of short duration than life insurers. Both companies invest a large part of their surplus in equities in order to try to grow its value.

Endowment and Trust Funds

Certain institutions such as universities, hospitals, religious orders and museums are funded to a degree by income received from endowment funds. These are long-term funds created from donor contributions. Other well-known trusts include foundations for medial research and for the award of annual prizes to individuals worthy of note in a particular field.

These types of funds have a very long time horizon. Trustees have to balance between meeting the needs of current beneficiaries while protecting the interests of future beneficiaries. They are usually managed very conservatively.

Exchange-traded Funds

So-called exchange-traded funds have been developed to meet the needs of portfolio managers to minimize "cash drag" from having to hold a proportion of funds in a liquid cash equivalent form to meet redemption requirements. Exchange-traded funds are a specialized form of tracker fund. Exchange-traded funds exist in the US but there is no impediment other than demand and liquidity for their use in other markets.

EFFICIENT FORMS OF MARKETS

Efficiency as a Measure of Transmission of Information

Analysts are employed to identify undervalued securities and fund managers are paid to manage other people's money with a core objective of "beating" the market. The efficient market hypothesis suggests that their objectives are self-defeating. Economists define markets as having one of three forms of efficiency (and we will return to the matter as to what efficient means in this context and what it doesn't mean). The generally accepted definitions of these forms are:

- **Weak form.** These are markets where current prices reflect all information contained in past security prices. In this form investors should not be able to predict future security prices from historic prices alone.
- **Semi-strong.** In the semi-strong form current prices reflect past prices and all publicly available information. Abnormal returns cannot be achieved simply by better analysis of facts already widely available.
- **Strong form.** In the strong form market prices reflect all information, both public and private. The implication being in that markets with the semi-strong form insiders can profit from inside information.

Efficiency as used here relates to the transmission and use of information. It is assumed that relevant information can be immediately and widely distributed to the investment community at low cost. This does not mean that every member of the investment community knows everything about every stock. A better way to look at this is that prices reflect everything known by members of that community collectively.

If markets are of the strong or semi-strong form this implies that stock prices should only change as a result of the emergence of new information. New information, by definition, cannot be forecast from known information and is essentially random in form. This in turn implies that stock price movements should follow a random walk.

We have already alluded to the fact that advances in technology have resulted in a wealth of digital financial data on security prices. Much academic research has been devoted to trying to determine whether security prices do have these random characteristics.

The simplest test is to determine whether evidence can be found for serial correlation between security prices over time. This can be done for many securities, in many markets in many countries using a number of different time periods with relative ease. By the very nature of the problem it is impossible to prove that serial correlation does not exist. Academics argue that the weight of empirical evidence suggests serial correlation is relatively rare. Many market practitioners doubt these results, however.

There is evidence that corporate officers acting on information have been able to profit from insider information. There would be no need for laws against insider trading if that were not the case. In an efficient market, however, there should be no way for an investor to be able to achieve returns consistently above the market based on information in the public domain.

Does Investment Analysis Add Value?

If this result holds then it poses a real question as to whether investment analysts and investment portfolio managers add any value. An answer is that they do because they don't and if they didn't they would! They do add value because they are competent and their work helps make markets efficient, if they didn't do this work then markets would be less efficient and competent analysis would allow investors to generate returns above the market.

One of the assumptions of the efficient market thesis is that all new material information is instantaneously disseminated and acted on. This is not always the case, however. Investors that can gather such information faster, analyze its consequences and take action quickly may be able to act to gain abnormal returns. This window of opportunity may close in minutes, hours or even days but does exist. There is hence huge pressure on analysts to give an immediate response to any new information because late conclusions are worth little. When investment professionals say that new information has been "priced in" they mean that the process of dissemination, analysis and action has concluded.

Some people are under the misapprehension that the existence of efficient markets implies that prices reflect a fair intrinsic value. A commonly heard expression is that "the market can't be wrong". This is not the case. Stock prices in an efficient market are determined by supply and demand, in a sense current prices represent a consensus view of value (more rigorously we really should be talking about marginal buyers and sellers but a consensus view is a useful way to look at it).

Most equity analysts arrive at a fair value target based on an estimate of intrinsic value for a stock and, formally or informally, assign a confidence level to that target. They assume that prices will both overshoot and undershoot that target but that in the long term stock prices will tend towards that level. Severe market corrections, often referred to as crashes, do not invalidate the efficient market thesis although they do appear to support the view that market prices are not a good reflection of intrinsic values.

TRACKING FUNDS

Most portfolio manager's emphasize a particular investment style that they imply will allow them to outperform the market. Fund managers who make a point of only investing in companies where they have met with the management, rather than relying on analyst reports provide a good example of this. This does give some sense of professionalism and diligence but is often more concerned with marketing than performance. The reality is that few portfolio managers outperform the market consistently.

Performance against the market is a zero sum game. For some portfolio managers to outperform the market others must underperform. On average we should expect half of funds to underperform the market, before management fees and transaction costs, in any given period. After taking account of management fees and transaction fees we should expect more than half of funds to underperform relative to the market.

This has resulted in some fund managers offering "tracking" funds that simply aim to mirror the performance of a benchmark index. As such funds do not require active management, other than periodic rebalancing, the fees that such funds can justify are lower than those charged by active managers.

Active versus tracker (passive) funds

ACTIVE	TRACKER
* Perform investment research	* No investment research undertaken
* Aim to identify & act on securities pricing anomalies	* Portfolio weightings based on benchmark or market weightings
* Actions tend to make markets more efficient - information transmitted between participants	* Occasional rebalancing
* The more efficient markets are the less opportunities for active managers	* Slightly underperform
* In efficient markets' tracker funds do better	* Reduces market efficiency & provides opportunities for active managers
	* Less efficient markets better for active funds than for passive

CAPITAL ASSET PRICING MODEL (CAPM)

Modern portfolio theory is based on two key tenets. First that returns are directly related to the level of risks taken and second that non-systematic risk can be diversified away.

The capital asset pricing model (CAPM) is a framework based on the premise that there is a direct relationship between the level of potential return from an asset and the level of risk inherent in those returns. In this context risk here is measured not in terms of losses but in terms of the volatility of returns. The core proposition of the capital asset pricing model (CAPM) is that risk and reward are inextricably linked. There are academic textbooks devoted entirely to CAPM and we will simply review the key tenets of the framework. The reader should also bear in mind that there are other theoretical models that attempt to deal with the same issues as CAPM but that CAPM is the most widely used framework among practitioners.

In formal terms the expected returns for an asset or portfolio of assets r_i are given by the following equation where r_f is the risk-free rate, β_i the asset or portfolio's beta, r_m the market's return and ε_i the stock's idiosyncratic return. (The best way to consider the idiosyncratic factor is to view it as a random fluctuation in returns. Here we are looking at the returns over a single period. Over time the mean value of the idiosyncratic return should be zero. In many texts this factor is simply ignored.)

$$r_i = r_f + \beta_i(r_m - r_f) + \varepsilon_i$$

Most of the theory concerning CAPM was developed in the period 1964–1968. No single person was responsible for its full development but credit for devising the overall framework is due to William Sharpe.

Risk-free Rate

The risk-free rate is the return that can be earned by investing in a risk-free asset. In the US this would be a long dated government bond. In the US a 20-year or 30-year Treasury note would provide such a benchmark.

In developing markets, however, bond markets are frequently underdeveloped and lack liquidity. In these cases most international analysts use currency swap rates in their place. Swap rates take account of inflationary expectations and any country risk premium. This means that the *COE* used is the required rate of return from the perspective of an institutional US dollar investor:

$$Swap\ rate = (1 + inflation) \times (1 + country\ risk\ premium + US\ real\ rate) - 1$$

Equity Risk Premium

The question as to what the equity risk premium is has dogged analysts and academics for years. Most would agree wholeheartedly that the equity risk premium is real and that it does exist but within that consensus there is little agreement on its actual value and how it may vary over time. In the latter phases of the extended 1990s US bull market some analysts argued that valuations, which appeared to be extremely extended, were in fact justified because the market's perception of the level of the equity risk premium had fallen from a historic level of 4%–5% to 2%–3%.

This is a question that cannot have an absolute answer. A key feature of CAPM is that while it is based on the premise that returns have a linear relationship with volatility of returns it does not tell us the value of the slope of the line. The stock market does not represent all risky assets and as its composition changes over time so should its risk premium. CAPM is at its most useful when treated as a conceptual framework rather than as a black-box formula to be followed slavishly.

Stock-Specific Risk – Beta

One measure of the level of risk of a security is a factor called beta. This is a measure of the variance of returns from a security versus the variance of returns from the market. We have already look at the use of beta in the context of managing trading risk in Chapter 15.

Beta can be interpreted as follows. If a stock has a beta of 1 it is likely to move in line with the overall market. If a stock has a beta of 1.5 and the stock market rises or falls by 10% the stock is likely to rise or fall by 15% and if the beta is 0.8 to rise or fall by 8%. High beta stocks are therefore more volatile (higher risk) than low beta stocks. Utilities provide examples of stocks that usually have low betas while companies in highly cyclical industries such as airlines usually have relatively high betas.

What the CAPM equation tells us is that in theory we can generate higher returns by investing in stocks with higher betas but that these additional returns are at the expense of additional risk. In a rising market a fund with a higher beta is likely to outperform the market but to underperform in a falling market.

We have already introduced the concept of a stock's beta. In formal terms beta is defined as follows:

$$\beta_i = \frac{r_{im}\sigma_i\sigma_m}{\sigma_m^2} = \frac{r_{im} \times \sigma_i}{\sigma_m}$$

This is simply the correlation coefficient between the stock and the market multiplied by the standard deviation of the stock's returns divided by the standard deviation of the market's returns.

Performance Measures

The first ratio used to adjust returns for the risk undertaken is the Treynor measure. This gives the excess returns of a portfolio per unit of systematic risk and is defined as follows:

$$Treynor\ measure = \frac{r_p - r_f}{\beta_p}$$

The next key ratio used to assess performance is the Sharpe measure. This takes the difference between portfolio returns and the returns on the risk-free rate and divides it by the portfolio's standard deviation of returns:

$$Sharpe\ measure = \frac{r_p - r_f}{\sigma_p}$$

The Sharpe measure gives the excess returns of a portfolio per unit of total risk. The Treynor and Sharpe measures are related as follows, substituting for beta. The Treynor measure can be defined as the Sharpe measure multiplied by the standard deviation of the market's returns divided by the correlation coefficient of returns between the portfolio and the market:

$$Treynor\ measure = \frac{(r_p - r_f)\sigma_m}{\sigma_p r_{pm}} = Sharpe\ measure \times \frac{\sigma_m}{r_{pm}}$$

The final measure that is used is the Jensen measure. Referred to as "alpha". By rearranging the risk-adjusted returns formula we get the following. Alpha is the excess return that cannot be accounted for by CAPM based on the portfolio's systematic risk. The search for alpha could be described as the Holy Grail of portfolio managers:

$$\alpha_i = r_i - r_f - \beta_i(r_m - r_f)$$

CAPM has its weaknesses, however. It assumes no taxes or transaction costs and that investors can both borrow and lend at the risk-free rate. Neither set of assumptions is true in reality. It is also not clear which risk-free asset should be selected to determine the risk-free rate. The returns on a one-month US Treasury bill are likely to be very different than the returns on 30-year US Treasury bonds.

It also implicitly assumes that the market consists of all risky assets, and this is clearly not the case. People applying CAPM also rely on historical data to calculate covariance coefficients and stock betas. These relationships are not stable over time and the value of beta depends on the time period selected.

Financial professionals generally accept the principles behind CAPM but are careful about their application. Financial academics have spent a great deal of time trying to empirically justify or disprove CAPM.

Diversification of Non-systematic Risk

Risk can be divided into market risk and security-specific risk. Security-specific risk can be diversified away by holding a portfolio of securities with low or negative correlation in terms of returns. It is not necessary to hold all of the securities in a market and to accomplish the objective of reducing this risk significantly it is only usually necessary to hold 16–20 stocks.

The concept of diversification of non-systematic risk is a key concept that we have looked at in detail when we looked at in the context of managing market and credit risks. We have shown that it is the cross-correlation factors that to a large extent determine the level of non-systemic risk. We have also argued that in practice this is extremely difficult to achieve with a loan portfolio. The same is not true about stock portfolios. We will use a simple example based on holdings in two companies to illustrate this point:

Suppose one of these companies is an oil producer with fixed costs that sells all of its output at market prices to a second company. The second company operates a power station. It buys oil at market prices but the price at which it sells the electricity it produces is fixed and set by regulators.

If the price of oil falls the stock of the oil producer is likely to fall but the stock of the power generator is likely to rise. Owning only one of these stocks leaves the level of returns exposed to the vagaries of the oil price. Owning equal amounts of both stocks will reduce that volatility. This is an example of a situation in which returns of the two stocks are negatively correlated.

The holder of these two stocks is still exposed to the risk that all stocks fall, perhaps due to rising interest rates, and this is what is referred to as systematic risk. We can diversify away the risks from holding individual stocks but we cannot diversify away market risk.

By way of contrast, the shares of two oil producers are likely to move together, falling when oil prices fall and rising when oil prices rise. In this case the returns on the two stocks are positively correlated.

PERFORMANCE MEASUREMENT CASE STUDY

The best way to get a handle on the practical applications of all this theory is to look at a practical example. In the following case study we will assume an equity universe that consists of just four sectors, with three stocks in each sector. To keep this relatively simple we have ignored dividends, any capital raising and transaction costs. The following table shows the key performance data over the period of measurement and historic data of standard deviation, correlation coefficients and beta for each stock within the benchmark portfolio.

The benchmark portfolio has generated 9.9% returns during the assessment period and has a historic standard deviation of returns of 5%.

Now we will take two funds and assess their relative performance. Both funds have generated slightly higher returns than the benchmark return of 9.8%. The first fund has generated returns of 12.8% versus the 10.3% from the second fund. The two areas we have to address are (1) which fund has produced the higher risk-adjusted returns? and (2) the source of the relative performance.

The first fund has overweighted banks and utilities and underweighted telecom and consumer stocks. The second fund has taken opposite sectoral positions.

		Benchmark portfolio key data							
Sector	Security	Market cap ($m)	Benchmark weight	Start price ($)	End price ($)	Performance returns	Standard deviation	r_{im}	Beta
Banks	ABC	12 400	13.8%	88.00	107.10	21.7%	4.7%	0.7	0.7
	SNB	8 500	9.5%	65.00	84.00	29.2%	5.1%	0.9	0.9
	TNB	6 000	6.7%	90.00	120.75	34.2%	5.5%	0.8	0.8
		26 900	**30.0%**			**−26.9%**			
Telecoms	Telcom	18 000	20.1%	66.25	73.50	10.9%	9.3%	0.9	1.7
	Comtel	9 000	10.0%	35.00	26.25	−25.0%	8.1%	0.9	1.5
	Telstra	8 000	8.9%	40.00	31.50	−21.3%	7.0%	0.9	1.2
		35 000	**39.1%**			**−5.7%**			
Utilities	Genpower	14 000	15.6%	60.00	66.15	10.3%	9.0%	0.4	0.8
	H_2O	5 000	5.6%	55.00	58.80	6.9%	3.7%	0.8	0.6
	Gazplus	3 500	3.9%	38.00	43.05	13.3%	4.0%	0.7	0.6
		22 500	25.1%			10.0%			
Retail	Gen store	2 500	2.8%	25.00	30.45	21.8%	4.9%	0.8	0.8
	Food.com	1 800	2.0%	15.00	19.95	33.0%	5.8%	0.8	0.9
	Head shop	900	1.0%	12.00	15.75	31.3%	5.1%	0.6	0.6
		5 200	5.8%			27.3%			
Total		**89 600**	**100.0%**			**9.9%**	**5.0%**		

The starting place for the analysis is to calculate the standard deviations and betas for the two funds. The results of these calculations are shown below. The first fund has taken lower risk than either the benchmark or the second fund which has a significantly higher standard deviation of returns and beta.

With this information we can now calculate risk-adjusted returns, assuming a risk-free rate of 5%. Based on the Sharpe and Treynor measures it is clear that the first portfolio, while generating the highest absolute returns, has outperformed its benchmark and the second portfolio on a risk-adjusted basis. This is reflected by a positive alpha, indicating higher returns for the fund given its level of risk than that implied by CAPM. The second portfolio, however, has a underperformed on all measures and with a negative alpha of 0.6% has destroyed value. The results are shown in the following table.

ATTRIBUTION ANALYSIS

Attribution analysis provides a tool to help determine the major factors in a portfolio's returns relative to its benchmark. It allows relative performance to be attributed to asset allocation or security selection decisions. The asset allocation decision may involve sectors, countries or asset class (bonds versus equities, for example). The security selection decision involves the selection of individual securities within each sector or asset class.

In many larger funds this mirrors the division of responsibilities. The Chief Investment Officer is likely to be responsible for overall asset allocation but responsibility for individual stock selection to lie with sector or country specialists. It is hence a useful tool for fund management companies to measure individual's performance.

Portfolio weightings and returns

Sector	Security	Benchmark Weight	Benchmark Returns	Benchmark Impact return	Portfolio A Weight	Portfolio A Impact return	Portfolio B Weight	Portfolio B Impact return
Banks	ABC	13.8%	21.7%	3.0%	23.0%	5.0%	0.0%	0.0%
	SNB	9.5%	29.2%	2.8%	9.0%	2.6%	6.0%	1.8%
	TNB	6.7%	34.2%	2.3%	8.0%	2.7%	14.0%	4.8%
		30.0%	**26.9%**	**8.1%**	**40.0%**	**10.4%**	**20.0%**	**6.5%**
Telecoms	Telcom	20.1%	10.9%	2.2%	12.0%	1.3%	37.0%	4.0%
	Comtel	10.0%	−25.0%	−2.5%	5.0%	−1.3%	8.0%	−2.0%
	Telstra	8.9%	−21.3%	−1.9%	8.0%	−1.7%	8.0%	−1.7%
		39.1%	**−5.7%**	**−2.2%**	**25.0%**	**−1.6%**	**53.0%**	**0.3%**
Utilities	Genpower	15.6%	10.3%	1.6%	15.0%	1.5%	8.0%	0.8%
	H_2O	5.6%	6.9%	0.4%	12.0%	0.8%	8.0%	0.6%
	Gazplus	3.9%	13.3%	0.5%	3.0%	0.4%	8.0%	1.1%
		25.1%	**10.0%**	**2.5%**	**30.0%**	**2.8%**	**24.0%**	**2.4%**
Retail	Gen store	2.8%	21.8%	0.6%	3.0%	0.7%	0.0%	0.0%
	Food.com	2.0%	33.0%	0.7%	0.0%	0.0%	3.0%	1.0%
	Head shop	1.0%	31.3%	0.3%	2.0%	0.6%	0.0%	0.0%
		5.8%	**27.3%**	**1.6%**	**5.0%**	**1.3%**	**3.0%**	**1.0%**
Total		**100.0%**	**9.9%**	**9.9%**	**100.0%**	**12.8%**	**100.0%**	**10.3%**

Benchmark and portfolios' returns, standard deviation and betas

	Benchmark	Portfolio A	Portfolio B
Returns	9.8%	12.8%	10.3%
Historic standard deviation of returns	5.0%	4.6%	6.0%
Beta	1.0	0.9	1.2

Sharpe, Treynor and Jensen measures

Benchmark	Portfolio A	Portfolio B

Sharpe measure $= (r_p - r_f)/\sigma_p$

$(9.9\% - 5\%)/5.0\% = 0.98$ $\qquad (12.8\% - 5\%)/4.6\% = 1.69$ $(10.3\% - 5\%)/6.0\% = 0.89$

Treynor measure $= (r_p - r_f)/\beta_p$

$(9.9\% - 5\%)/1.0 = 4.9\%$ $\qquad (12.8\% - 5\%)/0.9 = 8.5\%$ $(10.3\% - 5\%)/1.2 = 4.5\%$

Jensen measure alpha $= r_p - r_f - \beta_p(r_m - r_f)$

$9.9\% - 5\% - 1 \times (9.9\% - 5\%) = 0$
$\qquad 12.8\% - 5\% - 0.9 \times (9.9\% - 5\%) = 3.3\%$
$\qquad 10.3\% - 5\% - 1.2 \times (9.9\% - 5\%) = -0.6\%$

The following equation shows how to calculate the asset allocation effect and can be used to determine how much of the relative performance is due to the portfolio manager overweighting sectors, or asset classes, with superior performance and underweighting those with below average performance:

$$Asset\ allocation\ effect = \sum_{i=1}^{N}(W_{pi} - W_{bi})(r_{bi} - R_b)$$

Where W_{pi} and W_{bi} are the weightings of the sector or asset class within the portfolio and benchmark respectively, r_{bi} the returns from the ith sector or asset class and R_b the total benchmark return. The following equation can be used to determine how much of the relative performance is due to individual security selection within an asset class:

$$Security\ selection\ effect = \sum_{i=1}^{N} W_{pi}(r_{pi} - r_{bi})$$

Attribution analysis is a powerful analytical tool but it does not take risk into account. A derivation of attribution analysis is provided in an exhibit at the end of this chapter. In practice attribution analysis has to be performed on a daily basis and the results geometrically linked. Dividends, taxes and transaction costs also need to be taken into account.

Next we turn to the question of how these returns were achieved and the application of attribution analysis. We will start by considering the two funds' holdings in the bank sector. The total benchmark returns were 9.8% while those of the banking sector were just 2.7%. The first fund underweighted the sector, which proved to be the correct decision, but put all of its weighting into the worst performing stock in the sector. The second fund overweighted the sector, which arguably was a mistake, but invested its funds in the two best performing stocks in the sector.

	Benchmark			Portfolio A			Portfolio B		
Security	Weight	Returns	Impact return	Weight	Impact return	Less benchmark	Weight	Impact return	Less benchmark
ABC	13.8%	21.7%	3.0%	23.0%	5.0%	+2.0%	0.0%	0.0%	−3.0%
SNB	9.5%	29.2%	2.8%	9.0%	2.6%	−0.2%	6.0%	1.8%	−1.0%
TNB	6.7%	34.2%	2.3%	8.0%	2.7%	+0.4%	14.0%	4.8%	+2.5%
Total	**30.0%**	**26.9%**	**8.1%**	**40.0%**	**10.4%**	**+2.3%**	**20.0%**	**6.5%**	**−1.6%**

Bank sector stock impact returns

In quantitative terms the impact of the decision of the first fund to overweight the banking sector added 1.7 percentage points to the fund's relative performance while the decision of the second fund to overweight the sector cost it 1.7 percentage points. This is shown in the following table.

Asset allocation impact – banking sector stocks

	Portfolio weight (W_{pi})	Benchmark weight (W_{bi})	Sector benchmark return (r_{pi})	Total benchmark return (R_b)	Asset allocation impact $\sum_{i=1}^{N}(W_{pi} - W_{bi})(r_{bi} - R_b)$
Portfolio A	40.0%	30.0%	10.4%	8.1%	$(40\% - 30\%) \times (10.4\% - 9.9\%) = 1.7\%$
Portfolio B	20.0%	30.0%	10.4%	8.1%	$(20\% - 30\%) \times (10.4\% - 9.9\%) = -1.7\%$

Exhibit: Attribution analysis derivation

The following provides a formal derivation of the attribution formulae and may be skipped by those with no interest in its proof. The total returns of a portfolio are given by the sum of the returns r_{pi} of the portfolio's *i*th asset multiplied by its weighting W_{pi} within the portfolio:

$$\text{Portfolio return} = \sum_{i=1}^{N} W_{pi} r_{pi}$$

The portfolio returns relative to its benchmark are therefore given by the following equation:

$$\text{Relative performance} = \sum_{i=1}^{N} (W_{pi} r_{pi} - W_{bi} r_{bi})$$

The following equality should be evident as both portfolio and benchmark weighting add up to 100%:

$$\sum_{i=1}^{N} W_{pi} R_b = \sum_{i=1}^{N} W_{bi} R_b \quad \text{and hence} \quad \sum_{i=1}^{N} W_{pi} R_b - \sum_{i=1}^{N} W_{bi} R_b = 0$$

This means we can express relative performance as follows:

$$\text{Relative performance} = \sum_{i=1}^{N} [(W_{pi} r_{pi} - W_{bi} r_{bi}) + (W_{pi} R_b - W_{bi} R_b) + (W_{pi} r_{pi} - W_{pi} r_{pi})]$$

This can then be rearranged into two separate terms:

$$\text{Relative performance} = \sum_{i=1}^{N} (W_{pi} - W_{bi})(r_{bi} - R_b) + \sum_{i=1}^{N} W_{pi}(r_{pi} - r_{bi})$$

The first term tells us how much of the relative performance is due to the portfolio manager overweighting sectors, or asset classes, with superior performance and underweighting those with below average performance:

$$\text{Asset allocation effect} = \sum_{i=1}^{N} (W_{pi} - W_{bi})(r_{bi} - R_b)$$

The second term tells us how much of the relative performance is due to individual security selection within a sector or an asset class:

$$\text{Security selection effect} = \sum_{i=1}^{N} W_{pi}(r_{pi} - r_{bi})$$

In terms of security selection, however, the two funds' performance is reversed. By selecting the two best performing stocks in the sector the second fund added 1.2 percentage points to its relative performance while the first fund lost 0.4 percentage points through its heavy weighting in the worst performing stock in the sector.

Security selection impact – banking sector stocks			
	Portfolio banking sector weight (W_{pi})	Sector portfolio return (r_{pi})	Sector benchmark return (r_{bi})	Security selection impact $\sum_{i=1}^{N} W_{pi}(r_{pi} - r_{bi})$
Portfolio A	40.0%	25.9%	26.9%	$40\% \times (25.9\% - 26.9\%) = -0.4\%$
Portfolio B	20.0%	32.7%	26.9%	$20\% \times (32.7\% - 26.9\%) = 1.2\%$

The overall results of the attribution analysis for the two funds are shown below. They show that the outperformance of the first fund was entirely due to asset allocation decisions while that of the second fund was entirely due to security selection decisions.

Attribution analysis results											
		Benchmark		**Portfolio A**				**Portfolio B**			
Sector	Security	Weight	Return	Weight	Return	Sector	Security	Weight	Returns	Sector	Security
Banks	ABC	13.8%	21.70%	23.0%	4.99%						
	SNB	9.5%	29.23%	9.0%	2.63%			6.0%	29.23%		
	TNB	6.7%	34.17%	8.0%	2.73%			14.0%	34.17%		
		30.0%	26.86%	40.0%	10.36%	1.69%	−0.39%	20.0%	32.69%	−1.70%	1.16%
Telecoms	Telcom	20.1%	10.94%	12.0%	1.31%			37.0%	10.94%		
	Comtel	10.0%	−25.00%	5.0%	−1.25%			8.0%	−25.0%		
	Telstra	8.9%	−21.25%	8.0%	−1.70%			8.0%	−21.25%		
		39.1%	−5.66%	25.0%	−1.64%	2.19%	−0.22%	53.0%	0.66%	−2.17%	3.35%
Utilities	Genpower	15.6%	10.25%	15.0%	1.54%			8.0%	10.25%		
	H$_2$O	5.6%	6.91%	12.0%	0.83%			8.0%	6.91%		
	Gazplus	3.9%	13.29%	3.0%	0.40%			8.0%	13.29%		
		25.1%	9.98%	30.0%	2.77%	0.00%	−0.23%	24.0%	10.15%	0.00%	0.04%
Consumer	Gen store	2.8%	21.80%	3.0%	0.65%						
	Food.com	2.0%	33.00%					3.0%	33.00%		
	Head shop	1.0%	31.25%	2.0%	0.63%						
		5.8%	27.31%	5.0%	1.28%	−0.14%	−0.09%	3.0%	33.00%	−0.49%	0.17%
Total		100.0%	9.95%	100.0%	12.76%	3.74%	−0.93%	100.0%	10.31%	−4.36%	4.72%

16

Stock and Bond Issuance and Brokerage

The power of accurate observation is commonly called cynicism by those who have not got it.

George Bernard Shaw, Irish playwright

INTRODUCTION

The main intermediation function of commercial banks is to take deposits from investors and lend these out to borrowers. The main focus of investment banking is to facilitate the use of capital markets (stock and bond markets) to bring together investors and borrowers directly. Universal banks provide both commercial and investment banking services. There are far more stand-alone commercial banks than there are either universal banks or stand-alone investment banks. The influence of investment banks, however, is out of all proportion to their number.

Investment banks specialize in helping companies and state enterprises to raise funds through issues made in the equity or bond markets. Their client base encompasses governments, state-backed organizations, private-sector corporations and other financial institutions such as commercial banks and insurance companies. Investment banks can generate huge fees from managing and underwriting these issues.

They take an active role in the secondary markets by helping investors to buy and sell financial instruments in these markets. They also offer advisory services to companies seeking to make acquisitions and those that are subject to a takeover offer. They also specialize in "financial engineering" and advise on ways for companies to improve their balance sheet structure. This may involve the reorganization of a company's legal and capital structures.

They help to arrange the securitization of assets, both physical and financial, for their clients. Securitization issues result in a redistribution of risks and returns between companies seeking to change their financing and risk profiles and investors looking to change their own profiles.

Their in-depth knowledge of capital markets and capital market instruments help them to manufacture synthetic financial products. These are put together by people working in their structured financial product divisions.

Most investment banks are opportunistic and are active traders in all of the markets in which they specialize. While providing execution-only services for customers they also take trading positions in a wide range of instruments (equities, bonds, interest rate instruments, foreign exchange, convertibles and derivatives). Their proprietary trading activities have to be kept separate from those departments that are customer driven for both ethical and in many cases legal reasons.

Investment banks attract some very bright and some very avaricious people. Bonuses are very important to investment banking professionals. The business is, however, highly cyclical. With the exception of bonuses, costs are largely fixed while revenues are highly variable. In downturns revenues can fall sharply and the main way to bring costs into line is to fire staff. It can be a roller-coaster ride for employees, huge bonuses in one year followed by being laid off in the next.

Investment banking is primarily a wholesale business, although some have retail broker-age operations. They are funded from equity, bonds, the money markets and short-term loans from commercial banks. The following diagram illustrates the principal investment banking busi-nesses.

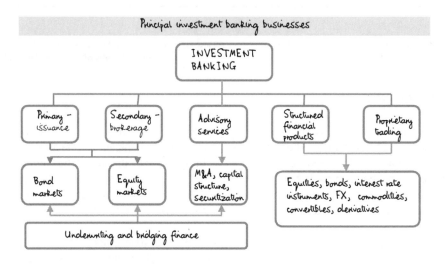

PRIMARY MARKETS, SECURITIES ISSUANCE

There are three ways in which companies can raise medium- to long-term financing. They can borrow from commercial banks, issue bonds or raise equity. Investment banks provide the principal interface between companies and institutional investors eliminating the intermediary role of commercial banks in the process:

- **Beauty parades.** A company may invite a selection of investment banks to tender for the management of a specific capital issue they are considering making. Each investment bank puts together a formal presentation to make to senior management at the company that "sells" their relevant expertise and experience. The resulting series of presentations is com-monly referred to as the "beauty parade" for obvious reasons. The company then makes a decision on which investment bank is to lead the issue. Other investment banks may also be identified to take lesser parts. After management and underwriting fees have been finalized an initial pricing structure for the structure is determined and a draft prospectus drawn up.
- **The prospectus.** The prospectus, whether for a bond or equity issue, lays out the terms of the issue and provides a fairly comprehensive description of the company's operations plus financial statements. Indicative pricing is sometimes included in the draft or may be given via word of mouth to allow the investment banks to get a sense of interest and likely demand. Final pricing is left as late as possible.

   The formal, completed prospectus is intended to help to achieve three objectives. First, to meet regulatory disclosure requirements, second to shield the company and investment banks involved from possible future litigation and finally, at a distant third, to sell the issue to potential investors.

Analysts find prospectuses very useful because they usually provide more information than is disclosed in the usual periodic company financial reports.

- **Pricing.** There are two principal ways in which pricing can be established. The first is to simply set an issue price. This is the only practical method to use for issues where there is likely to be significant retail demand. This leaves investment banks that have underwritten the issue at significant risk from a market correction occurring in the interval between the price being fixed and close of application date, however.

The second method, known as book building, is used extensively for issues aimed at institutional investors. Book building is a form of Dutch auction and best explained with an example. Suppose we have an issue comprising 100m shares with an indicative price of $100 per share. Investors are asked to submit bids in terms of price and volume for the issue. The investment bank then receives bids for 200m shares from interested investors with offers ranging between $96 and $106.

The investment bank starts with the highest offers and then works backwards. Once the 100m shares have been placed the price is set at the lowest price that allows the issue to be completed. In this example the count-back gives a price of $102 per share. All bids above this level receive their full allotment at a price of $102 per share. All bids below $102 fail and receive no allocation.

Book building example										
Price	$96	$97	$98	$99	$100	$101	$102	$103	$104	$105	$106
Applications	1m	1m	3m	5m	15m	20m	15m	15m	40m	25m	5m
Accumulated	145m	144m	143m	140m	135m	120m	100m	85m	70m	30m	5m

- **Road shows.** Investment bankers organize road shows to sell the issue to institutional investors. For smaller issues these may be confined to one market but for larger issues these are global, arduous events. Global is perhaps an exaggeration. Marketing is concentrated on the USA, the UK, continental Europe and Japan. These are the countries with the largest investment funds looking for a home.
- **The pitch.** Investment bankers are rarely passive and spend a lot of time looking for possible deals. These include possible opportunities for potential clients including acquisitions, disposals, mergers and ways to improve balance sheet structures by, for example, retiring one form of debt and replacing it with another that is cheaper and more flexible. Few of these proposals ever see the light of day.

Objectives of Issuers

The issuers (current owners) may have a number of reasons to want to make a primary equity issue, these reasons include the following:

- **Raise capital.** The need to raise capital to fund business expansion is the most common reason given for a primary issue. Most expanding businesses require capital to finance research and development, new products, new or upgraded production facilities, vendor financing, new marketing and distribution capabilities and increased working capital (primarily accounts receivable and inventory less accounts payable). In some cases the current owners may be seeking to build up a "war chest" to finance potential future acquisitions. These financing requirements may be met through debt or equity. Equity provides the longest-term, most stable form of finance. Some companies may be looking to restructure their balance sheet through the retirement of debt and its replacement with equity.

When the current owners determine that these financing requirements are best met with equity, but they are either unable or unwilling to commit new capital to the business, they may attempt to raise that capital through the equity markets. In return they will have to give up a share of the ownership of the company to the new shareholders.

The following diagram shows the changes in ownership levels and equity for a company with current equity of $1bn that raises $500m from a primary issue and ends with successful subscribers owning 20% of the company. We have ignored any related issue costs.

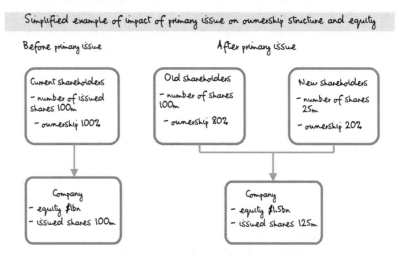

Simplified example of impact of primary issue on ownership structure and equity

Before primary issue

Current shareholders
- number of issued shares 100m
- ownership 100%

Company
- equity $1bn
- issued shares 100m

After primary issue

Old shareholders
- number of shares 100m
- ownership 80%

New shareholders
- number of shares 25m
- ownership 20%

Company
- equity $1.5bn
- issued shares 125m

After the issue the number of shares issued increases from 100m to 125m and book value per share from $10 to $12.50. The subscription price of $20 means that the new shareholders have paid a 60% premium to the new book value.

There is another way to look at the premium paid. The new shareholders have paid $500m in cash for their 20% stake. Cash should be priced at a valuation multiple of $1\times$ so the value of the new shareholders' 20% stake in the cash held is $100m. This implies that they have effectively paid $400m for their 20% stake in the underlying business, which had a book value of $1bn. This implies that new shareholders have paid an effective 100% premium to book for their stake in the underlying business.

Both methods are mathematically correct and most analysts will use the method that best supports their case. Underwriters will highlight the 60% number and counter arguments that a 100% premium is a more appropriate way to look at the pricing by pointing to the ways in which the company will use the new capital. Although such arguments are common they miss the point. Book value is not a good reflection of intrinsic value based on discounted future earning in any case.

- **Take profits and get secondary market listing.** Where an entrepreneur has invested most of his own capital (and it almost always is a "his") in a start-up business and established it as a profitable, viable operation there may be an incentive to realize some of those gains and take profits. The paper value of an unlisted company is simply its book or net tangible asset value. The stock of a successful company will usually trade at a significant premium to this value.

Incentives for the entrepreneur may include freeing up capital for the purchase of a dream house, meeting a trophy wife's demands or simply investment portfolio diversification. In such circumstances new investors normally seek to "lock in" the management for a specified period. By gaining a secondary market listing existing shareholders will be in a position to reduce their stakes through the market, gradually over time. A secondary market listing may also provide more flexibility for any future capital raising. It should also make future acquisitions using its paper as currency easier.

- **Divestments.** There are many reasons why a company may wish to divest a particular business or division. This may be achieved through a direct sale to a buyer or a management buyout but occasionally a division may be spun off as a separate listed entity. Some of the reasons why this may be done are as follows:
  - **Strategic direction.** A large company may have a division operating in a business that does not fit into management's vision for the strategic direction of the company. Where this division is viable as a stand-alone operation the optimal solution may be to spin it off.
  - **Low returns.** Another driving motive is that management believes that the sum of the parts is worth more than the whole as reflected by market valuations. A UK chemicals company with a fast growing biotechnology business felt that the higher valuations justified for its biotechnology business were not being achieved because its strong growth was being obscured by the lack of growth in its mature businesses.
  - **Regulatory requirements.** A regulator or government organization such as a monopolies or anti-trust commission may force the divestment. An example is that of AT&T, the giant US telecommunications company, spinning off the seven "Baby Bells".
- **Privatization of public sector services.** Governments have a number of potential motives for privatizing public sector services and companies and we will look at these in detail when we consider the subject itself. The main rationale put forward by proponents of privatization is that many services traditionally provided by the public sector can be better provided by the private sector. In the larger privatization issues the government often remains the largest single shareholder. This may be because the primary capital markets lack the capacity to take all of the issued shares or the government regards majority control to be in the country's strategic, national interests.
- **Demutualization and partnership dissolution.** Mutual societies exist in one form or another, and under a variety of names, in many developed capitalist countries. These are organizations where ownership rests with the members. Prime examples are savings and lending societies, thrifts, insurance societies and stock, commodity and other exchanges. The establishment of many of these mutual societies dates back to the nineteenth century when these countries industrialized.

When management of mutual societies put the case for demutualization the usual grounds are that, for a variety of reasons, they cannot compete on price, service levels or product range with the private sector. Mutual society status can result in barriers to mergers and acquisitions, limit access to capital markets and make it harder to attract suitable management talent. Many of these complaints have validity but it is also true that demutualization usually improves senior management career prospects and compensation.

Many professional firms including accounting, legal and medical practices and securities operations were established as partnerships. Many of the arguments put forward by proponents of demutualization apply to partnership dissolution. They also usually result in windfall gains for the current generation of partners. The blue-chip investment bank Goldman Sachs provides one of the most high profile examples of a partnership dissolution when it became a publicly listed company in the late 1990s.

CAPITAL RAISING PRICING ISSUES

The most common primary objectives of an issuer are to raise as much capital, and at as a high a price or lowest cost as possible, while minimizing the existing owner's control and ownership dilution. (There are occasions when these are not the overriding priority and we will consider these cases separately.)

The pricing of debt issues is less complex than that of equity issues and we will focus here on the latter. Debt issues are usually priced off a risk-free benchmark yield curve used to determine the term yield, new corporate issues are then priced to give a credit spread reflecting the credit-worthiness of the issuer. In deep markets and where most issuers have been given a formal rating by an external agency this credit spread is driven by the current prices of outstanding issues of similar quality and term or duration. In developing markets swap rates are often used in the place of a risk-free yield curve based on government bond issues. Supply and demand are, of course, the ultimate determinant of pricing with auctions and book-building exercises the most common methods used to arrive at prices.

Putting a market value on an unlisted company's equity as a going (and growing) concern is as much about psychology as it is about mathematical financial modeling. The key question for the underwriters is whether there are enough investors willing to pay a specific price so that they do not have to earn their underwriting fee. If an issue is not fully subscribed underwriters will have to take the balance onto their own books at the issue price. The existing owners will be more concerned about whether the buyers would have been prepared to pay more.

Despite the subjective nature of the valuation and pricing process there still has to be some basis for the proposed pricing that can be pointed to – and the more supporting evidence the better. The first step is to identify listed companies that can be regarded as being members of the company's peer group. These companies may be domestic or international. They may produce similar products or services, operate in the same markets or have common customer bases or similar growth expectations:

- **Domestic peer group.** Despite the continuing trend towards cross-border sector-level analysis by fund managers most valuations are still made relative to stocks and sectors within a domestic market. There are a number of reasons why this should be the case, of which the most important are differences in the cost of capital between countries, in the local competitive and regulatory environment and investor preferences.

  Sometimes it is a straightforward exercise to classify a company and identify domestic listed companies that are directly comparable. This is easiest to do when the company's operations are clearly defined and can be classified within a recognized industry sector. Most markets, for example, have a retail sector comprising local companies operating largely in their domestic market.

- **International peer groups.** It may be more appropriate to consider an international peer group for companies operating in certain industries. Two obvious candidates are industries with a high degree of global concentration and commodity plays:
  - **Global concentration.** Industries with very high capital requirements, short product cycles, a high degree of specialization and absence of close substitutes are usually highly concentrated. There are only a handful of semi-conductor manufacturers in existence worldwide, for example. Their profitability and prospects are largely determined by a common balance between industry-level supply (competition between the companies) and demand (from a common global customer base).
  - **Commodity plays.** Companies whose main business activity is the production or extraction of commodities are usually valued on the basis of costs of production, asset values and global US$ commodity prices. Gold production stocks and oil exploration stock prices depend largely on prices of gold and oil respectively.

Far more cross-border sector valuation work is now done on European stocks than it was as recently as the mid-1990s but this can largely be explained by the establishment of a single European market and the adoption of the euro as a common currency. Where the strategic market is national and, given different national currencies, most valuation comparisons will continue to be made within individual markets.

Sometimes the industry classification is straightforward but there are no comparable local, listed peer companies. A telecommunications company providing fixed line services is easy to classify but most countries only have one or two such operators. (Mobile operators have very different operating characteristics and would not normally be treated as part of a fixed line operator's peer group.) There are, however, many fixed line operators around the world and putting together a global list of 10–20 companies should not be too difficult. The challenge then comes from understanding the variations in valuations due to differences in local market and regulatory conditions, the cost of capital and so on.

Some new issues break virgin ground and may be difficult to classify based on current definitions of sectors or lack of comparable listed companies. Companies in new technologies such as nano-technology provide examples in the former group. The first stock exchanges to demutualize and obtain a listed status had a very clear business classification but a complete absence of exchanges that were already listed on exchanges:

- **Valuation methods.** A musician can play the same tune on many different instruments. There is a wide range of valuation methods available. Each one may have a different focus but most concentrate on reported earnings, cashflow, growth or asset values.

  Examples of common ratios used in valuation comparisons include price–earnings ratios (*PER*), *EV/EBITDA* (enterprise value divided by earnings before interest tax and depreciation) price-to-free-cashflow, *PBR* (price-to-book ratio, price-to-*NTA* (price to net tangible assets, usually after revaluation of assets and liabilities), *PEG* ratio (price-to-earnings ratio versus compound earning growth rate), dividend yield, earnings yield.

  Conglomerates pose particular problems. The usual approach is to try to break the company down into a number of specific businesses and value each part separately. Most analysts would then look at other conglomerate valuations to try to determine a "holding company" discount to the whole in order to arrive at a value for the firm.

Additional ratios specific to particular sectors may also be used. Price-to-subscribers (telecommunications), price-to-reserves (upstream oil companies), and price-to-deposits (banks) provide a few examples.

- **Operating and financial ratios.** There are many bulk-standard operating ratios that apply to most non-financial corporations. These include items such as inventory turnover and debt–equity ratios. There are also additional operating ratios that apply to companies operating in a particular industry. Most of these ratios only have real meaning when used to paint a picture of relative operating performances between companies.

- **Finessing.** Most standard valuation ratios have to be included in any research report or prospectus but there is usually sufficient latitude to highlight those that put the company in the best light. Care can also be taken in the selection of the peer group. There is, however, no point in excluding companies that investors will obviously consider as direct peers even if the comparison is not flattering. Such omissions can be counterproductive in any case, as investors will then start to question what else has been omitted!

The real ethical issue arises if retail investors use such reports to arrive at investment decisions. Institutional investors know that reports produced by analysts working for firms involved in an underwriting exercise are highly likely to be biased. Portfolio managers make allowances for this bias and are usually fairly forgiving of the individual analyst concerned because they are aware of the pressures they are working under. They are less forgiving of bad deals at the firm level, however. In extreme cases fund managers will "blacklist" the offending party and prohibit portfolio managers and dealers from giving them any business.

Analysts working for investment banks that are not involved in the deal are not working under the same constraints, but nobody likes a party-pooper. What goes around, comes around and analysts at competing investment banks are still likely to be wary of being too scathing about another firm's deal, at least in writing. Analysts tend to have more loyalty to their clients than they have to their employers (and this is not surprising given investment banks' hire-and-fire mentality) and another investment bank is not simply a competitor but is also a potential future employer.

PRIMARY ISSUES TO GAIN LISTED STATUS

When the current owners need to raise capital for business expansion but have no intention of selling down their stake further their primary goal will be to raise the required capital while ceding as little control as possible to new shareholders. The price at which the stock trades in the secondary market is more important to the new, minority shareholders than it is to the majority shareholders. This is not always the case.

Where the current owners are actively involved in the company's management but are seeking to reduce their exposure pricing issues become more complex. New shareholders are likely to seek assurances that the current management team will remain in place and that the interests of the majority shareholder are aligned with those of the minority shareholders. They may also have reasonable concerns that the current owners are trying to cash out because they know something negative that is not yet public knowledge.

These concerns can be met in part by the existing owners agreeing to "golden handcuffs" that keep them working at the company and to a "lock-up" period where they agree not to sell their shares into the secondary market before a specified date.

In many such issues the capital raised is relatively modest and only a small percentage of issued shares are to be placed. A secondary market listing accomplishes a number of objectives. It establishes a market-based valuation for the firm's stock, it makes it easier to use its stock as acquisition currency or collateral. Access to debt markets may also be facilitated. The paper value of existing shareholders will be determined directly by the price in the secondary market. The company's listed status also allows the existing shareholders to sell down their stake in the future, at a time of their choosing, without having to go through the formal issue process again.

Under these conditions existing shareholders will be directly affected by future secondary market prices. A successful primary issue will then be one that has the following:

- **Oversubscription.** A real, but modest, level of oversubscription where the number of shares that investors subscribe for is greater than the number of shares on offer. The excess of demand over supply normally means that the stock starts trading at a premium to the issue price.
- **Premium.** A real, but modest, premium should ensure that subscribers make a paper profit after taking into account the financing costs associated with their applications.

If these two objectives are achieved then all parties to the deal can be reasonably happy. A modest price premium implies that the market feels that the issue was fairly priced. A modest level of oversubscription means that investors get a high proportion of the shares for which they applied. It also means that the underwriters do not have to take any of the stock onto their own books in order to meet their underwriting commitments. Apart from being evidence of an unsuccessful issue this would create a share overhang as the investment banks will have to find buyers for these shares in due course either through placements or through the secondary market.

Heavily oversubscribed issues hit the headlines but are rarely good for the company or new investors. A heavily oversubscribed issue may occur because the issue has been mispriced, because the company's prospects have been overhyped or because the company is operating in a sector where an investment bubble has formed.

There may be scope for the size of the issue to be increased but in most instances of oversubscription a process of paring back application sizes is applied. The way in which this is done is normally defined in the prospectus and may vary depending on the level of oversubscription.

When the level of oversubscription is very high some subscribers may receive no allocation of shares while others receive only a small percentage of the shares they applied for. Subscribers may find that financing costs associated with their applications exceed profits made from "stagging" the issue even though the stock opens at a significant premium to the issue price in the secondary market. Issuers may be unhappy because the issue appears to be underpriced while subscribers may make a loss. The investment bank concerned may suffer a "reputational loss".

Privatization Issues

Privatizations have a political dimension that is largely absent from private sector new issues. These were pioneered and championed by UK Prime Minister Margaret Thatcher's government in the 1980s and privatization has since become mainstream political dogma in many countries, at least of publicly owned manufacturing companies. Arguments remain, however, on which services are best provided in the private rather than public sector, how to organize and regulate these privatized services such that the rights of recipients are protected given the goal of private companies to maximize shareholder returns. This is further complicated by monopolistic and competition concerns. The full impact of privatization of services may not be recognized for many years.

Politicians have short-term concerns that frequently take precedence over long-term visions. One of the most emotive arguments made against privatization is that the government is selling something to the people that the people already own. One way to counter these arguments is to bribe large parts of the electorate. It is therefore often regarded as a political necessity to achieve a high level of individual participation in high profile privatization issues and to ensure that these applicants are effectively guaranteed to make a profit from their holdings, at least in the short term.

Another reason why governments may go down the privatization road is that proceeds from the issues end up in the Treasury's coffers. These proceeds can be used to affect fiscal policies. Governments may use these proceeds to give tax breaks, to reduce the current fiscal deficit (the difference between what it receives in revenues and what it spends) or to lower the public sector borrowing requirement (PSBR). Where countries are in financial crisis IMF support may be conditional on privatization policies being pursued.

In an ideal world most politicians in power would probably like voters to pay as little as possible, to give a boost to their electoral popularity, and institutions to pay as much as can be extracted to increase the level of flexibility in the government's fiscal policy. In practice this is difficult to get away with but large privatizations are often structured such that there are separate institutional and retail allocations. In the event that the issue is oversubscribed small investors are likely to be allocated a higher proportion of the shares they applied for than institutions receive.

Despite the hyperbole of "shareholder democracy" and "popular capitalism" the level of retail holdings in these privatized companies tends to fall over time. This suits many companies that regard individually registered investors as little more than a nuisance and who bear an administrative cost out of all proportion to the value of their holdings.

The large-scale privatizations that took place in Western Europe in the 1980s and 1990s generated huge fees for investment banks, professional firms and consultancies. As the negative effects from privatizations have become more evident popular support has waned and many of the most obvious candidates have already gone. Investment bankers have had to go further afield for new business and attention has switched to the "transitional" economies of Eastern Europe, the countries that made up the former Soviet Union, China, the rest of Asia and Latin America.

Rights and Bonus Issues

Rights issues are issues made by companies that are already listed to raise capital from their shareholders. Rights issues are usually made at a steep discount to the market price. The following is a typical example of the structure of a rights issue.

A company with 1000m shares is currently trading at $20 per share giving it a market capitalization of $20bn. The company wants to raise an additional $2bn. It can do this by offering existing shareholders the "right" to subscribe to new shares at $10 per share on a one for five basis. This means that for every five shares held existing shareholders have the right to subscribe to one new share. At first glance this appears to be a real bargain being given the opportunity to buy shares currently trading at $20 for just $10. The reality is that it is a civilized form of extortion.

If all existing shareholders subscribe the number of issued shares will increase to 1200. As the only change in the firm is that it now has an extra $2bn in cash its market value should adjust to $22bn (assuming that the market does not interpret the rights issue as a form of "signaling"). The market price per share should fall to $18.33 once the rights issue has completed. The rights issue itself neither creates nor destroys shareholders' value although what is done with the proceeds may.

A shareholder with 5000 shares, and $10 000 in cash before the rights issue has total wealth of $110 000 (5000 × $20 = $100 000 + $10 000). After the rights issue they will have 6000 shares trading at $18.33 giving unchanged total wealth of $110 000.

If on the other hand the shareholder decides not to exercise their rights their wealth will fall to $101 667 (5000 × $18.33 plus the $10 000 in cash). This is solely the result of the dilution in their share of the company. This is the main reason why very few rights issues are underwritten.

Rights may be stripped away from the actual stock and traded as separate instruments. These trade as call options. All historic per share numbers, and in particular earnings per share, have to be adjusted to be comparable with the forecast and future reported numbers.

In many developing markets the media reports bonus issues as something positive for stockholders. This is not the case. The proportion of the company that each investor owns is unchanged as is the firm's value. The increase in number of shares is exactly compensated for by the fall in the value of each share. Analysts dislike bonus issues because they create work for the analyst in adjusting historic numbers but have no effect on the firm's value or operations.

Some argue that bonus issues are justified when a stock's price has risen so much that given a minimum lot size defined in terms of number of shares the minimum lot size in dollar terms has made it increasingly difficult for retail investors to invest in the stock. A simpler solution would be to reduce the minimum lot size.

There is no evidence that corporate actions, such as bonus issues or stock splits, which alter form but not substance, have any lasting effect on stock price performance.

BROKERAGE, THE SECONDARY MARKET

Although the real money comes from primary market transactions, investment banks have to provide a secondary market brokerage service. This is one of the ways in which they maintain their equity research and primary institutional distribution capabilities. The equity brokerage market has, however, broken down into three distinct segments:

- **Institutional business.** Institutions such as investment management firms, running mutual funds and pension funds, and insurance companies, are all active in the equity markets. They usually look for two services from investment banks: investment research and an efficient execution capability. Commission rates are low but the size of individual trades is large.
- **High net worth business.** In the high-end retail market there are investors who require an active investment advisory service. Private banks, retail brokers and independent financial advisors all compete with one another for their business.
- **No frills execution.** The development of the Internet has encouraged the growth of brokerage businesses that specialize in providing a low-cost execution-only service.

We will concentrate on institutional brokerages. These are organized into four broad functional areas, research, sales, trading and the back-office.

Research

The research function underpins much of investment banks' businesses. Most research analysts are highly specialized and focus on a specific sector or financial instrument. Most of them have a Masters in Business Administration (MBA) and Chartered Financial Analyst (CFA) designation. Their main job responsibilities are as follows:

- **Earnings forecasts and credit analysis.** The most basic skills that an equity analyst has to have are to be able to interpret company financial statements and provide realistic forecasts of future earnings. Fixed income analysts have a somewhat different focus. Their main concern is the ability of companies to meet their debt obligations.
- **Valuations.** The process of valuing financial assets lies somewhere between an art and a science, depending on the nature of the asset. When this is in the form of the common stock of a company it is skewed towards the art end. Despite the inherent difficulties, being able to put a credible value of the intrinsic worth of a company is a critical skill. This is a skill that can be taught, but cannot be learned, in a business school. Some financial analysts are better at this than others. Large numbers of books have been written on this subject. In this book we will restrict ourselves to valuation approaches for commercial banks (see Chapter 18 "Bank valuations").
- **Recommendations.** Analysts live and die by the sword. Equity analysts are judged by their ability to identify stocks that will outperform or underperform, credit analysts by their ability to identify issuers or issues at risk from suffering a ratings downgrade, which are likely to default on their debt or where credit spreads are likely to widen or narrow.
- **Reports and notes.** Analysts are expected to write in-depth research reports on their sectors and on individual companies or debt issues within their sector. They also have to write shorter, but timely, notes on new developments and earnings releases.
- **Marketing.** A top institutional analyst based in Asia is likely to undertake two or three global marketing trips a year. There are investment funds in Tokyo, Hong Kong and Singapore but the big money is in the US first and Europe (and in particular London) second. The trips sound glamorous but are anything but. A typical three-week trip for such an analyst involves about 50 hours in the air (this takes no account of time spent getting to and from airports) and 60–100 presentations to clients. The analyst as traveling salesman.
- **Priority client calls.** Many of the larger fund management firms also have analysts specializing on specific sectors. A sell-side analyst will typically make 100–150 calls a month to their buy-side counterparts. Of these, probably three-quarters of the calls will be end up being voicemail.

    The increased focus on marketing related activities has proved a very mixed blessing. The amount of time available for analysts to conduct fundamental research has fallen. A common portfolio manager complaint is that they receive too much research to read but it would probably be more accurate to say that they find it difficult to separate the wheat from the chaff. Many have banned brokerages from sending commodity e-mails and most voicemail is immediately deleted.
- **Corporate finance support.** Analysts get pulled in to support corporate finance deals. They may get involved in the initial pitch and then the actual issue. Most professional investment

banks have established formal procedures to take analysts "over the wall" as soon as their involvement risks them being privy to insider information. Once taken over the wall the analyst cannot write any further research on the company or even talk to investors about it.

Companies affected are placed on "blackout" status. This restricts what, if anything, can be published on a company where an investment banking relationship exists. Different regulatory regimes exist around the world and it is common to see international research with a notice "Not for distribution in the US, Canada or Japan". This used to be relatively easy to enforce but the Internet has changed that. We will return to the matter of the ethical issues that such collaboration creates.

- **Specialist roles.** In addition to fundamental credit and equity analysts there are two specialist roles worthy of note. Strategists and heads of research offer a top-down view starting with a recommended split between equities, bonds, cash and markets and ending with recommended weighting by sector within markets. Technical analysts on the other hand have a strictly bottom-up approach looking for patterns in price performance from which to infer likely future behavior.
- **Economists.** Economics may be the "dismal science" but economists have their role to play. They set out the framework for the likely economic outlook and direction of interest and foreign exchange rates. Of course they regularly get it wrong but to err is human. They also speak a language that few understand. This just adds to their prestige.

Private sector economists lack the huge models that government Treasuries run to help generate their forecasts. Few economists would admit to this but most monitor what "consensus" is saying and make their own forecasts relative to consensus. The actual numbers are secondary to this relative call.

This is probably a contributory factor in the poor track record that economists as a whole have for failing to predict major points of inflexion. It is worth noting that the "consensus" numbers at such times are largely meaningless as economists change their forecasts faster than the consensus numbers can keep up with.

Institutional Sales

Salespeople are in the business of "selling" this research to clients and getting orders from them to buy or sell financial instruments. As research analysts have become increasingly marketing oriented and many clients have increasingly demanded direct access to analysts the nature of the sales job has changed. There are basically three different styles:

- **Relationship broking.** "Relationship" broking is widely seen as old-fashioned and of questionable ethical merit. It involves wining and dining, playing golf and taking clients to expensive sporting and entertainment events. In return the client gives the broker part of their business. A $1000 dinner may be rewarded with an order earning $3000 in commission.
- **Intensity.** A more modern approach is to provide an intensive service to priority clients. This involves activities such as arranging regular analyst visits, facilitating contact with corporates and summarizing recent research and market developments. Portfolio managers are bombarded with research, most of which is of questionable merit and thrown away unread. A good sales person can act as an effective filter by understanding the portfolio manager's needs, for example by only passing on research from analysts that they know the portfolio manager respects and on sectors or stocks in which they have a particular interest.

- **Independence.** At many brokerages salespeople are required to "sell" the house research. No deviation from the party line. Everyone singing from the same songbook. Not all salespeople accept this. An experienced salesperson may feel they have a better understanding of a stock than a young, naïve analyst. They may well be right. They may receive flak for taking this approach and their only real defense is that of the P&L account.

Trading and Dealing

Trading is split between sales traders and dealers. Many fund managers have centralized dealing desks, in such cases orders are placed directly with the sales traders who then place the orders with the floor dealers. The latter are then responsible for the actual execution of the order in the market.

Orders may be placed in a number of ways. "Best efforts" or "At the market" are orders executed at the current market price. The actual average price paid will depend on the skills of the dealers. For large orders dealers will usually divide the trades up over the course of the day. Placing a single large order is likely to have an impact on the stock's market price.

Other orders may specify a maximum buying price or minimum selling price. Such orders may be valid only for the day the order is placed or may be valid until completed.

There are two distinct dealing systems in place around the world. In some markets investment banks act as market-makers giving bid and offer prices. In other markets order matching applies where buyers and sellers give their bid and offer prices and trades can only be completed when buy and sell prices meet.

The dealers report the success, or failure, of the trades to the sales traders who then pass that on to the centralized buy-side dealing desk or to the relevant salesperson who passes it on to the portfolio manager. Confirmations are also generated automatically by the exchange and brokerage's systems.

The following diagram summarizes the organization of an institutional brokerage's front-office and shows its principal interactions with fund managers.

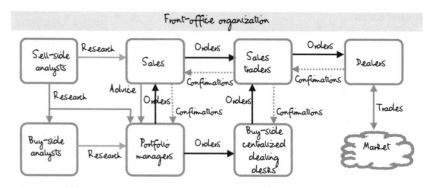

The Back-office

The back-office is a vital part of a brokerage operation although its contribution frequently goes unnoticed until things go wrong. Having agreed a trade there has to be a subsequent exchange of cash and paper between the two parties. (People in the industry still use these terms even though most cash transactions are carried out via electronic transfers and most records formerly kept in paper form are kept on computers.) There are large variations in settlement terms and the methods used between developed and developing markets.

In most developed markets trading is carried out in a scrip-less form where there are no paper certificates documenting ownership. Transfers of ownership are achieved through changes in computerized book entries. Settlement may take place on the day after the trade is confirmed (T + 1) or up to three days after the trade (T + 3). Most exchanges seek to minimize the time between the trade being executed and settlement as this reduces systemic risk. This also, however, requires relatively sophisticated infrastructure and systems at the market participants (brokerages, fund managers and custodian banks).

In many developing markets, however, the market infrastructure is relatively basic and paper bound. Settlement failures, where either the buyer fails to provide the consideration or the seller to deliver the stock, are not uncommon.

MERGERS AND ACQUISITIONS (M&A)

Industries and companies, like empires, rise and fall. Mergers and acquisitions are one of capitalism's ways to weed out the weak and they contribute towards the efficient allocation of resources. The terms merger and takeover are frequently used synonymously but have different meanings in different contexts. They have specific meanings when used in an accounting context, a transaction will be accounted for in one way if treated as a merger than if it is treated as a takeover. There is, of course, no difference in the underlying reality, however.

A takeover may be presented as a merger where management and shareholders of the target (and there usually is a target) support an agreed takeover. This is also called a "friendly" takeover. A hostile takeover attempt occurs when one company makes an unsolicited bid for another company where management of the target are opposed either to the takeover itself or to the terms offered.

Investment banks act for both would-be acquirers and target companies. They advise on the structure and pricing of the bid and on any legal and regulatory considerations. They will put the formal offer document together and facilitate most of the communications with major institutional investors:

- **Offer strategy.** The investment bank and acquirer set out an overall offer strategy. This will need to take into account several related issues:
  - **Counteroffer.** Any takeover bid has to take into account how other interested parties may respond. The most important factor to consider is whether the acquirer's initial bid will force or stimulate a bid from a third party. Other companies may feel compelled to act to protect their own competitive position. Where three companies of similar size compete in the same market a consolidation arising from a combination of any two of the companies will leave the third company at risk of being marginalized.

    By making an offer the acquirer puts the target into play. Other companies that are not currently competitors may have considered making a bid for the target themselves but have not yet reached any firm decision. They will be forced to decide whether to let those plans lapse or act on them. These parties may include financial investors whose aim is to break up the company and sell its parts.

The motives for a counteroffer vary but the outcome of takeover battles are never 100% certain. One of the bids may succeed but at a higher price than appears justified, weakening the successful acquirer's financial condition. If one of the counterbids succeeds the initial bidder's financial condition will be unchanged but it may end with a significantly weaker competitive position and tarnished management reputation.

- **Competition issues.** Many takeovers and mergers are of companies providing similar products or services in the same markets. Some takeovers raise few competition concerns but in the event that they do a bid is likely to be referred to the relevant competition or anti-trust agency. The bid will usually be frozen until the conclusions of the regulators have been released. This may, and often does, take many months to complete.

  The whole process exposes the bidder to significant risks. If the application is turned down the acquirer will have wasted considerable management time and incurred large costs from investment bank and professional fees. The delay will result in considerable uncertainty and make it difficult for the acquirer to take other actions that depend on whether the application is approved or rejected.

  Senior management on both sides may opt to take offers from outside their firms rather than accept the risks associated with the acquisition proceeding. Changing circumstances may mean that the rationale for the acquisition no longer holds water or that the terms of the initial offer now appear unattractive.

  An acquisition that depends on subsequent asset disposals to justify is exposed to the risk that prices of these assets (such as real estate) fall between the initial offer and the decision on their application being approved. Where part of the offer comes in the form of the acquirer's paper (traded equity) and equity markets fall this will lower the value of the initial offer.

  The application may receive in-principle approval but require the acquirer to take specific steps before full approval is given. These conditions may require the acquirer to sell off the very assets that justified the acquisition offer in the first place or take other measures that make the acquisition less attractive.

- **Takeover codes.** Most stock exchanges have detailed takeover codes to which aspiring acquirers and targets must adhere. These specify the documents that must be produced over the course of the takeover attempt, what those documents contain, who they are sent to and by what date. They may impose restrictions on both parties' actions, such as the acquirer buying stock in the target's firm and asset disposals by the target's management.

  They also define trigger ownership levels. These specify when an acquirer has to declare its shareholding, when an offer is deemed to have succeeded and when it becomes unconditional and the acquirer has the right to buy all of the shares issued by the target at a specified price (even though the holders of those shares voted against the bid). Transgressions of takeover codes are subject to exchange censure and possible regulatory action. One of the most basic responsibilities of the investment banks involved is to make sure that both target and acquirer comply with the relevant codes.

- **Pricing.** We have already looked at pricing and valuation issues when we looked at ways to determine IPO pricing. The same factors have to be taken into account with the major difference coming from how to finesse the multiples. The bid may be a cash-only offer, may offer shareholders in the target to exchange their shares for ones issued in the acquirer's company or by a combination of the two methods.

The value of an all-cash offer is fixed but the value of those with a paper element will vary as the prices of the acquirer's and target's stock vary. This is easiest to see with an example.

"Gobble-Them-Up" and "Eat-Me" are both fast food companies. Gobble-Them-Up has 1000m shares issued currently trading at $10 a share, giving the company a market capitalization of $10bn. Eat-Me has 200m shares trading at $15 with a market capitalization of $3bn. Gobble-Them-Up is considering three forms of offer; an all-cash offer of $20 for each of Eat-Me's shares, an equivalent all-paper offer and a combination offer where half of the consideration is in the form of cash and half in paper:

- **All cash.** The all-cash offer is at a 33.3% premium to the current market price of Eat Me putting a value of $4bn on the firm.
- **All paper.** An equivalent all-paper offer requires Gobble-Them-Up to offer 400m shares (400m × $10 = $4000m) for all the Eat-Me shares. Gobble-Them-Up would therefore offer two shares in Gobble-Them-Up for every Eat-Me share.
- **Combination.** The combination offer would have to offer $2bn in cash, equivalent to $10 for each Eat-Me share and one Gobble-Them-Up share for each Eat-Me share as the paper part of the offer.

If the market does not like the initial terms of the offer it is likely to sell down the stock of Gobble-Them-Up and buy Eat-Me stock in anticipation of a higher bid. If the price of Gobble-Them-Up falls 10% to $9 and that of Eat-Me rises to $25 the values of the original bids are as follows:

- **All cash.** No change in absolute terms but the value of the offer is now at a 20% discount to Eat-Me's current market price.
- **All paper.** The value of the all-paper offer falls to $3.6bn compared with the $5bn that the market has placed on the value of Eat-Me's shares. To simply match the current market value of Eat-Me's shares it would be necessary to offer 1.39 Gobble-Them-Up shares for each Eat-Me share. If the deal went ahead on these terms current Gobble-M-Up shareholders would own slightly less than 60% of the combined firm. (This is calculated as follows: new shares issued = 200m × 1.36 = 272m, plus existing shares of 400m shares, total shares issued = 672m, 400m/672m = 59.5%.)
- **Combination.** The cash part of the offer ($2bn) is unchanged while the paper part falls to $1.8bn. Total offer is now worth $3.8bn compared with Eat-Me's market cap of $5bn.

All-paper offers are usually only attractive to the acquirer when its stock is on a much higher valuation multiple (for example, price–earnings ratio) than the target's. The investment bank has to advise on the value of the offer, take account of the likely reaction of the market to the offer and advise on the maximum amount that the acquirer may have to pay if its bid is to succeed ultimately.

- **Buying in the market.** Where allowed under the relevant takeover code the investment bank may be instructed to buy stock in the market or attempt to make block purchases from shareholders with large individual stakes on behalf of the acquirer.
- **Bridging finance.** Investment banks may provide short-term financing in order to facilitate the completion of a deal. As this short-term finance is likely to be replaced with longer-term funds from a bond or equity issue this can be an attractive, albeit risky undertaking. The investment bank stands to generate fees from the original transaction and the subsequent refinancing.

PROPRIETARY TRADING

Many commercial and investment banks take proprietary trading positions in a number of different financial instruments. These include instruments and derivatives relating to foreign exchange, interest rates, equities and bonds. This is a highly specialized activity and such trading is normally carried out in huge trading rooms.

In many of these areas banks are also providing an execution service to their customers. This creates potential conflicts of interests and provides an example of the need for banks to erect "Chinese walls" between departments in order to prevent the sharing of information that could be used against a client's interests. There is no doubt that such Chinese walls do help to reduce the degree of such collusion but the old investment banking saying is that grapevines have a tendency to climb over Chinese walls. Proprietary trading can generate both huge gains and losses. Income tends to be volatile and management has to impose tight controls to shield the bank from potentially disastrous losses.

ETHICAL ISSUES

Investment banks face many ethical issues and are subject to significant regulatory constraints. All banks have compliance departments whose objectives are to ensure that their business activities remain within legal limits and that related internal guidelines and procedures are followed. Risks to a bank are not simply due to regulatory disciplinary action but concern the consequences of reputation loss. The following are some of the ethical issues raised:

- **Insider trading.** Insider trading is a criminal offence in many developed markets but is a common practice in many developing markets. Research analysts, salespeople, corporate financiers and portfolio managers are all in positions where they may have knowledge of information about a listed company that is not in the public domain. In itself this is not an offence but may become one in some countries depending on whether this information is acted on.

  Corporate financiers who know that a takeover bid is likely but not yet public knowledge may be tempted to buy shares in the target company in the realistic expectation that a bid will push up the target's stock price. Salespeople and analysts may act on such information, however obtained, by either trading on it themselves or giving investment advice to clients. Any of these actions breaches ethical limits generally accepted in developed markets.

  Analysts are not guilty of insider trading where their investment recommendations are based on publicly disclosed information. This is sometimes referred to as the "mosaic" principle. An analyst may conclude that a bid is likely given available information without having any knowledge that such a bid was in fact being prepared.
- **Front running.** A large order to buy a particular stock is likely to push up its price. This provides an opportunity. Salespeople and traders may be tempted into front running, also known as rat trading. This involves putting in his or her own buy order before submitting or executing the client's order.

  Ethical brokerages have rules that require client orders to be completed before those from staff or close relatives of staff. They also require any staff dealing to be conducted through their own firm. Greed, however, can result in extreme behavior and corrupt personnel may seek to circumvent such restrictions by dealing through other brokerages using friends or relatives as proxies.

This is one of the reasons why phones in most dealing rooms are taped and mobile phones banned. Unfortunately this does not stop people using their mobile phones outside the dealing room.

- **Research and corporate finance.** Primary transactions, such as IPOs, generate significant fees for investment banks. Huge pressure, whether implicit or explicit, is exerted on analysts to ensure that they have positive recommendations and put forward upbeat views on companies in which the investment bank has an interest.

  Few, if any, people within the investment bank can be allowed to stand in the way of such a deal being concluded. It is a brave, and usually short-lived, equity analyst who puts a "sell" recommendation on a company whose proposed bond or convertible issue is being underwritten by his or her employer. With mortgages to pay and families to support few have such courage or are so foolhardy.

  The failure of many dot.com companies and collapse in the share prices of many technology stocks in 2001 exposed the seedier side of Wall Street. Analysts were putting out research reports with an upbeat, positive spin on companies in which their investment bank was either pitching for or arranging an issuance. At the same time they were sending e-mails to selected clients rubbishing these companies.

- **Research comments on corporates.** The pressures that some corporate management put on research analysts to avoid publishing negative views on their firms are frequently underestimated. Where there is a corporate finance relationship the pressure tends to come from within the investment bank itself. The following are a few examples of the types of sanctions either applied or threatened. Such threats do not need to be explicit to be effective:
  - **Legal action.** An analyst may have a well-founded view that the management of a company is either fraudulent or incompetent. Publishing such allegations without firm evidence that would stand up in court leaves the analyst and brokerage at risk of being sued for damages. Such direct evidence is difficult to obtain. So analysts rarely publish research that contains such views and rely on word of mouth to communicate highly negative opinions using phones that are not recorded. They avoid making comments about specific individuals when casting doubt on management's competence.
  - **Cut off.** Legal action is, however, high profile and may result in a company being forced to reveal more of its operational and financial details than it would like. The outcome of such action is never certain. In most cases companies express their disapproval of negative analyst comments through the use of sanctions. Analysts find it impossible to get appointments to meet with management and stop being invited to briefings. E-mails and phone calls go unanswered. Management makes disparaging comments to fund managers about the offending analyst waging a vendetta against their firm and try to bring into doubt their rationality and competence.
  - **Commercial bank pressure.** Many brokerages are part of larger commercial banking groups. The business relationships between the commercial bank and a major corporate client are likely to be more important to group management than supporting an individual analyst's opinion. Pressure for analysts to modify views and downplay criticisms can be, and is, exerted through these commercial banking relationships.

The smartest corporate management do take note of individual analysts' negative comments but either ignore them or, when they have some validity, take remedial rather than coercive action.

- **Priority clients.** Most institutional brokerages have active account management and identify priority clients. These are the clients with the biggest "wallets" and everybody wants a share of their business. As a result they are given a higher standard of service than other clients.

  The large fund-managers are as much to blame for this state of affairs as the investment banks. Many have formalized voting systems by which the level of brokerage commission is determined. The brokerages respond by providing services that generate the highest level of votes. Analysts and sales people call priority clients to advise of breaking news, a change in recommendation, target price or earnings forecasts before the actual note is distributed to the whole client base. This gives priority clients a timing advantage over other clients. This is understandable from a business perspective but completely unethical.

- **Primary issue allocation.** Many primary issues are deliberately underpriced. There are several reasons why this may be the case but it reinforces the symbiotic relationship between fund managers and investment banks. The investment banks have underwritten the issue and need to get it all away to avoid having to take stock themselves, they therefore have an incentive to ensure the pricing is competitive. The fund managers want a bargain so that the opening price of the stock in the secondary market is at a premium to the issue price.

  This creates an incentive for investors to try to get the highest allocation of such issues as possible. Investment banks get paid by the company making the issue but may be able to use the allocation process to "reward" for business they have been given in the past by clients or to create a future obligation.

- **Entertainment and gifts.** Most investment banks now impose limits on the amounts that can be spent on client entertainment and gifts. This has not always been the case. Even now brokerages arrange corporate junkets and these can create real ethical issues.

  Some conferences are very well organized and provide an opportunity for many institutional investors and management of companies to meet. Other events such as taking clients to major sporting, theatre and music events have nothing to do with the investment process and everything to do with sophisticated bribes by brokers to gain business. It is difficult to say who is more culpable, the brokers for offering the bribes or the portfolio managers for accepting them. Neither of them are acting in the best interests of the end investor.

  In markets where brokers do not have seats on the exchange they have to act through local sub-brokers, with commission being split between the two firms. Sub-brokers also have an incentive to provide entertainment to the sales traders and dealers at international brokerage houses.

- **Dealing errors.** Dealing errors may arise from any of a number of sources. The fault may be due to the client or the brokerage. This is another reason why dealing room calls are taped. Disputes can be resolved by replaying the call from the client placing the order.

  The costs of dealing errors have to be taken somewhere. A brokerage may absorb the losses even if the fault lies with the client. This is a subtle form of blackmail. In return the brokerage will expect to be given a minimum level of business from the fund manager.

- **Churning.** Trades generate commissions. Churning is the practice of persuading clients to trade when there is little or no fundamental reason to do so. This is more of a problem in retail where brokers have been given discretionary powers than in institutional broking. Trading costs can, however, have a significant impact on a fund's performance. Investors should take into account fund churn rates.

- **Other ethical issues.** These make up the most important common ethical issues that an investment bank face but is not an exhaustive list. Other important issues that we have examined elsewhere include the use of soft commissions and money laundering. Egregious examples of primary issues made on the basis of inaccurate and misleading information are relatively rare these days, but this is largely due to the weight of regulatory requirements imposed and market disciplines in developed markets. This is not the case in many developing markets, even ones as large as China and Russia.

There is a strong case that no analyst should trade in, or hold, stocks they cover or where they may have a significant influence on investment recommendations. There are two overriding reasons. First, it leaves the analyst open to possible accusations of bias. Second, it leaves the analyst exposed to the risks of being accused of front running. These arguments appear, to me at least, to outweigh the argument that analysts should "put their money where their mouth is". The most valuable attribute that any analyst has is integrity. Once that is gone academic and professional qualifications and technical skills count for little.

MARKETS AND THE MEDIA

There are many different media channels: television, radio, newspapers, magazines and the Internet. Most of them provide some form of business news coverage. The *Financial Times* and *Wall Street Journal* are at the top of the class in terms of financial reporting. Most of their articles are well researched and well written. Bloomberg and Reuters do a pretty good job at disseminating information but are not in the business of offering views. Although there are isolated pockets of excellence unfortunately it's largely downhill from there.

The business pages of the quality press are of course in a different league from the popular press but the overall quality is very patchy. There is a plethora of glossy magazines purporting to be serious and studied guides to current investment opportunities. These can normally be found next to the glossy bloke, specialist car and computer magazines. Bloke magazines are amusing (in a puerile way of course) and the auto enthusiasts and technology nerds do understand their subjects. Few, if any, mass-market investment magazines are either amusing or well informed.

CNN changed the ground rules. Its coverage of the 1991 war in Iraq gave it an insatiable hunger for instant news. Financial markets provided a golden opportunity. Markets somewhere in the world were open 24 hours a day. The fact that a stock price or exchange rate remained unchanged achieved newsworthy status. There was always a pundit available for an instant analysis and authoritative (or at least confident) view.

Such reporting tends to be short term with an unhealthy concentration on daily price movements. There are many factors that affect prices but the media tends to look for a single factor to explain why a stock's price has risen or fallen. There are occasions when it is clear why a stock price has fallen or risen sharply. A profit warning or a takeover bid, for example, will have a clear impact on a stock price. These are the exception rather than the rule, however. Most daily stock price movements follow broad market trends but also track a random path.

As in any other market, stock prices are determined by supply and demand. Why do stock prices go up? More buyers than sellers! Unless a daily price change is greater than two standard deviations from its mean it's not newsworthy. On average this should occur about once a month in any event. Anything less than this and it's just noise.

Journalists in large parts of the media take pride in being a part of a cynical, profit-oriented industry (like investment bankers) whose key goals are to increase viewer levels or circulation and hence advertising revenues. There is therefore an understandable tendency to sensation-alize. Prices don't rise, they soar and sometimes they rebound. Profits don't fall, they plummet or collapse. Any unexpected event becomes a shock. Boost. Surge. Sink. Just as with snack foods, audiences have become hooked on these sound bites.

Many newspapers provide stock tips and lists of "top" mutual funds even though the reporters concerned usually lack formal investment analysis training or relevant experience. Analysts, fund managers and other investment professionals are highly regulated but in many countries there are no restrictions on press tipsters front running their own recommendations.

In many developing markets a major factor is the lack of formal training for financial journalists. Many do their best but are unable to do much more than report what they are told. At worst they become little more than management mouthpieces. Analysts are wary of being quoted in the press in general, and in particular when they are critical of management actions.

The use of the Internet to spread rumors has generated real concern about retail front running. An anonymous investor may buy a stock then post a positive rumor on the Web and as other investors buy the stock, pushing up its price, start to sell down their holding. Caveat emptor.

17

Securitization

The creation of something new is not accomplished by the intellect but by the play instinct acting from inner necessity. The creative mind plays with the objects it loves.

Carl Gustav Jung, Swiss psychologist

INTRODUCTION

Securitization involves the issue of securities that give the holders of the securities the right to receive a stream of payments based on, or guaranteed by, the cashflows generated on a pool of underlying assets. These payments may be in the form of principal or income. The underlying assets may be physical, for example an office block, or financial such as loans. The securitization can be done with or without recourse. In the former case the issuer continues to bear the default risks, in the latter those risks are removed from the issuer. Almost all securitization issues are done without recourse.

It is difficult to decide where to put the subject of securitization in a book such as this because it crosses so many boundaries between financial institutions. The main roles that commercial banks play are as originators of loans and servicing agents for asset backed securities (ABSs) but some are involved in packaging and many invest in financial ABSs for a variety of reasons. Investment banks are active in the packaging and distribution of ABSs and are also major players in the secondary market. Insurance companies sell products to enhance the credit-worthiness of ABSs and are also large investors in ABSs.

Examples of the most common asset backed securities include the following:

- **Mortgage backed securities (MBSs).** The issue of mortgage backed securities involves the packaging of many individual mortgages. This pooling of individual mortgages means that statistical methods can be employed to attempt to quantify the risks involved.
- **Other financial asset backed securities.** Auto loans, credit card receivables and other loans.
- **Collateralized debt obligations (CDOs).** CDOs represent a pool of secured commercial loans.
- **Asset backed securities (ABSs).** Real estate is the most common form of securitized physical asset but other forms include ships, airplanes, toll roads and bridges.

A subtle, but key, distinction of asset backed securities is that they do not involve any change in title. Rather they transfer the rights to the cashflows generated from the asset from the title holder to the security holder.

These securities are usually issued in a number of classes or tranches. Each tranche will have a different mix of risk and return. In some cases tranches may have augmented protection in the form of a guarantee from a third party that the payments will be made. By structuring asset backed securities into a number of tranches issuers are able to attract a wide range of investors with varying degrees of tolerance to risk. The complexity of the structure of securitization issues is limited only by the creativity and imagination of the structured finance professionals and investor demand for these products.

Asset securitization has developed into a huge industry over the past 30 years. The US has by far the most developed industry and the pace of development in other countries has been uneven. In some OECD countries such as the UK and Italy issues of asset backed securities have become increasingly common.

It has, however, been slow to take off in emerging markets. Currency issues remain a problem for international investors, there are limited numbers of potential domestic investors in most of these countries and few natural potential guarantors. Investment bankers have been trying to sell securitization services around Asia since the early 1990s with very limited success.

Issuer and Investor Incentives

For asset securitization to be successful there must be benefits and incentives for both issuers and investors. The principal benefits to issuers are as follows:

- **Redistribution of risk.** In most countries banks continue to be the largest originators of mortgage loans. However, holding such loans leaves them heavily exposed to prepayment risk, interest rate risk and default risk. Prepayment risk is the risk that the mortgagors pay off these long-term loans early. Their exposure to interest rate risk comes from the fact that most banks rely upon short-term deposits for the bulk of their funding. If rates on short-term deposits rise then their spreads on long-term fixed rate mortgages will fall. Banks that operate in a relatively small geographical area are exposed to default risk because their portfolio of mortgage loans lacks the benefits of portfolio diversification.

  In principle it would be possible for banks to sell individual mortgages but in practice this has serious practical problems. The process is cumbersome, involving the transfer of physical documents and incurs significant legal costs. Investors would also be concerned about moral hazard risks, banks would be likely to try to sell those mortgages that had most prepayment and default risk. Investors would also be concerned about the lack of secondary market liquidity.
- **Liquidity.** Asset backed securities may be traded in a secondary market. Securitization enables the issuers to take an illiquid asset such as a mortgage loan and transform it into a liquid security.
- **Balance sheet management.** Asset securitization allows issuers to get the assets off their balance sheet. Correctly structured this means that banks do not have to allocate regulatory capital against these assets. In addition banks do not have a natural source of long-term fixed rate funding. This means that issuers of fixed rate mortgages have significant interest rate risk in the event that interest rates rise. They also face significant prepayment risk in the event that rates fall.
- **Income enhancement.** The issuers (originators) usually act as the collection and payment agents. For performing this function they are able to extract servicing fees or spreads. In effect, asset securitization allows issuers to transform an asset that generates interest income, but also requires capital, into one that generates fee income but does not require capital.

The benefits to investors can be summarized as follows:

- **Comparative advantage.** Banks are subject to two "hidden" taxes, due to regulatory capital and reserve requirements. They have to set aside capital against their risk exposures, even though that capital may be well above the level of risk capital that management deems necessary. This requirement will only be waived in the event of assets being taken off balance sheet if the transfer is done without recourse and the bank retains none of the credit risk.

  Deposits used to fund the assets have formal reserve requirements that push up the banks' effective funding costs. Non-deposit taking organizations are not subject to such requirements and in effect may benefit from a form of regulatory arbitrage.
- **Complementary needs.** While banks lack a natural form of long-term fixed rate liabilities this is not necessarily the case for other institutions. Insurance companies, for example, sell annuities to their customers. These are long-term investment products that pay out a fixed rate of return.
- **Hedging.** The segmentation of risks afforded by the issue of a number of tranches with different risk characteristics allow both issuers and investors to use asset banked securities as tools to hedge specific risks.
- **Diversification.** Investors can buy mortgage backed securities from a number of issuers operating in different parts of the country, or even between countries, in order to gain portfolio diversification. The low or negative correlation between losses on assets in different regions reduces overall portfolio risk.

MORTGAGE BACKED SECURITIES

Mortgage backed securities represent by far the highest proportion of asset backed securities issued. The US has the most developed securitization market and in the case of residential mortgages this has been helped by the prevalence of fixed rate loans. These have much greater interest rate and prepayment risk than other loans in general, and floating rate mortgage loans in particular.

Mortgages have the longest term of any class of loan that commercial banks make, typically 20 to 30 years. The right of borrowers to prepay their loans is equivalent to the bank writing an embedded call option to the borrowers and as a result when yields fall the price–yield graph exhibits negative convexity. The present value terms of such a mortgage can be expressed as follows:

PV of mortgage = PV of equivalent straight loan – Value of call option

As with all loans, credit risk also has to be taken into account. The structure of securitized mortgage issues has grown increasingly complex and diverse over the years but we will concentrate only on their most important features.

Pass-through Mortgage Backed Securities

Mortgage backed pass-through securities represent claims on a defined pool of individual mortgages. Payments made to investors are directly based on payments made by individual mortgagors. The servicing agent collects the individual payments, consolidates them and, after subtracting servicing and any guarantee fees, passes these on to the holders of the mortgage backed securities. There is hence a short delay between the mortgagors making their payments and the receipt of cashflows by the holders of the securities.

We have already examined in Chapter 7 "Mortgage lending" how the level of principal payments versus interest payments for mortgages varies over time. In the early years of the mortgage the bulk of the payments made are interest payments and only a small proportion for capital repayments. As time proceeds, and ignoring prepayments, capital repayments become increasingly important.

MBSs may be issued in a "stripped" form. Stripped mortgage backed securities are created by separating principal from interest payments through the issue of two types of securities. One of these is based on the cashflows arising from principal repayments and is referred to as principal only (PO) and the other from interest payments known as interest only (IO) securities.

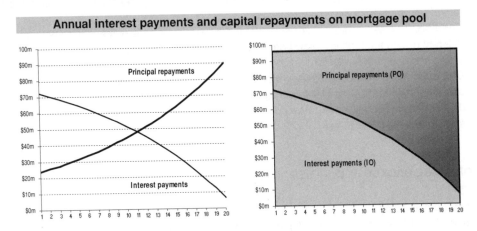

Annual interest payments and capital repayments on mortgage pool

These two securities have very different characteristics. A simple examination of the distribution of the cashflows shows that, ignoring prepayments, the PO tranche has a much longer duration than the IO tranche. Rising interest rates will result in a higher discount rate and this will have a much greater adverse effect on the present value of the PO tranche than the IO tranche.

In the real world prepayments have a significant impact. Mortgagors may choose to pay off their mortgages before they come to term. In most countries penalty charges for prepayments are relatively low and in some are prohibited by law.

Bank lenders are exposed to reinvestment risks from prepayments. As borrowers repay their loans the proceeds can only be lent out at lower rates. This is reflected in the value of a mortgage loan given by:

Value of mortgage loan = Value of equivalent straight loan − Value of call option

Holders of stripped MBSs are exposed to both reinvestment risk and also to risks due to the changing value of the securities they hold. The impact on the present value of the PO and IO classes is as follows:

- **Principal only (PO).** The value of the PO tranche enjoys a "double whammy" from lower interest rate. First, the lower discount rate increases the present value of the payments it receives. Second, and of more importance, prepayments shift the distribution of principal payments forward in time. When mortgagors repay their outstanding principal the payments made to PO holders rise. Over the life of the PO the nominal principal amount paid is unchanged but prepayments accelerate the receipt of the principal payments.

- **Interest only (IO).** The situation for IO holders is virtually the opposite. The faster that mortgages are repaid the less principal is left on which interest payments must be made. The level of IO payments made therefore falls as prepayments rise and this normally outweighs any positive effect from a lower discount rate on the present value of the IO tranche.

The following diagram is a schematic representation of the change in value for a mortgage loan, an equivalent loan with no prepayment option and PO and IO securities.

Schematic diagram illustrating PO and IO values versus yields

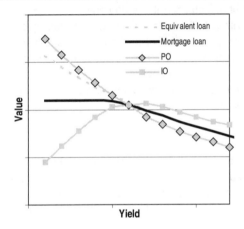

Prepayment Rate Modeling

Given how sensitive the values of PO and IO securities are to prepayment risks it is not surprising that considerable effort has been expended on prepayment rate modeling. The two principal causes of prepayments are changing mortgagor circumstances and changing financial incentives:

- **Mortgagor circumstances.** Mortgagor circumstances change as part of the normal course of life. These include the following examples. A young couple may need to move to a larger apartment to meet the needs of a growing family. A couple divorces and the communal home has to be sold. The mortgagor gets a job in another part of the country. An older couple may look for a smaller apartment now that the children have left home.

There have been attempts to create models based on mortgagor profiles to predict prepayment rates due to changed mortgagor circumstances. Given the psychometric nature of such models it would be reasonable to expect their detailed predictive capabilities to be relatively poor. To an extent the law of "big numbers" helps them. Provided historic prepayment rates due to changed mortgagor circumstances can be separated from those due to financial incentives a reasonable top-down forecast should be possible. There are, however, significant variations in prepayment rates between countries and results for one country cannot be assumed to have validity in another.

- **Financial incentives.** Financial incentives arise when interest rates on new mortgages are lower than rates on existing mortgages and the mortgagor determines that the resulting savings outweigh the costs associated with the refinancing itself. The likelihood, and hence rate, of prepayments in a portfolio of mortgages due to financial motives depends on two major factors:

  - **Spread between rates on new and existing mortgages.** The most important factor is the spread between the interest rates available on new mortgages and those on existing mortgages. There is a disincentive to refinance when rates on new mortgages are higher than on existing mortgages. Rates on new mortgages may, however, be lower than rates on existing ones. This may be due to a lower interest rate environment or the result of price competition.

    Prepayment rates in the US do not start to rise noticeably until the spread reaches about 100 bpts but rise sharply above 200 bpts.

  - **Portfolio seasoning.** Individuals with fixed rated mortgages have different levels of price sensitivity or simply different levels of understanding of potential savings from refinancing as interest rates fall. The percentage of mortgagors that refinance when interest rates fall is lower for a pool of mortgages that has already been through past periods of lower interest rates. This phenomenon of portfolio seasoning is sometimes referred to as "burnout".

Pricing and valuation of mortgage backed securities is both difficult and complex due to the presence of these embedded options. The main method used compares the attractiveness of MBSs relative to government securities. This is achieved by estimating the value of these embedded options by estimating option-adjusted spreads (OASs) as follows.

- The first step uses scenario analysis to estimate an expected present value for a security. This involves forecasting a distribution of interest rate scenarios and looking at the impact of different interest rate scenarios on portfolio cashflows by assigning probabilities to each possible path. This has to take into account interest rate volatility and expected prepayments. Summing over all the possible paths gives an estimate of the expected present value.

- The second step is to calculate the discount rate implied from the expected present value and the security's market price. This discount rate represents the security's option adjusted yield.

- The option-adjusted spread is the difference between this yield and that of a Treasury bond with a similar duration. This gives a measure of the security's relative attractiveness. It can also be used to compare the attractiveness of different MBSs.

By its very nature estimating option-adjusted spreads involves many subjective assumptions. Two experienced analysts given the same security may arrive at similar OAS values but they will never be identical. Despite its inherent weaknesses it is widely used in the industry.

Credit Risks

Although default rates and their associated losses in the event of default are the lowest of any class of loan they are still real. If we relax our assumption that the mortgage pool is not exposed to credit risk then potential buyers of the PO and IO classes will have a genuine concern about the asset quality of the underlying loans in the pool. Default rates vary with the economic environment but if we compare rates on two different pools of fixed rate mortgages we get the following:

- **Loan-to-value.** The level of default is lower when the loan-to-value ratio is lower. This means that default rates on older mortgages tend to be lower because as the level of principal payments rises the loan-to-value ratio falls, assuming stable property prices.
- **Grace periods.** Default rates also tend to be lower on mortgages that have not been subject to "grace periods". These are periods where lenders have allowed the borrower to skip payments in times of financial stress. There are probably two reasons behind the higher default rates associated with grace periods. The first is that such grace periods inflate the loan-to-value ratio. The second is that they may reflect an underlying lack of borrower financial stability.

Holders of both PO and IO classes are exposed to losses arising from defaults. The transfer of the credit risk from issuers to the buyers of the securities creates an obvious case of moral hazard. Banks have an incentive to put loans that have above average prepayment or credit risks into the securitized pool and to retain those that are below average.

There are at least two ways in which these concerns may be assuaged:

- **Senior and subordinated classes.** One possible solution is to add a senior–subordinated structure whereby the mortgage originator sells a senior claim on a large part of the cash-flows, 85%–95% levels being typical, but retains a subordinated claim on the remaining balance. This is often referred to as a "first-loss" structure. The structure of the securitization issues gives the senior claim a level of protection from losses resulting from default on mortgages in the pool.

  Given that the mortgage originator has better information on the composition of the pool this signals the originator's confidence in its asset quality and should be reflected in the pricing of the securities. The feasibility of such a structure is dependent on the banking regulator's view as to how this affects the originator's risk-weighted assets and hence regulatory capital requirements. The Basel Accord has been amended to try to close such loopholes.
- **Credit enhancement.** The losses arising from credit risk to holders of the securities can be avoided though the use of a form of credit enhancement. The mortgage originator buys a policy from an insurance company or other guarantor that the latter bears the default risk. Credit risk is shifted away from the mortgagors to the guarantor. Given the long-term nature of mortgage loans guarantors need to have high credit ratings.

The following diagram provides a summary of the typical features of the structure of a pass-through mortgage backed security. The roles of originator, packager and servicing agent may be carried out within a single bank or may be carried out separately. Origination and servicing are usually performed by commercial banks while packaging and securities dealing reside within investment banks. Guarantors may be private sector insurance companies or state sponsored agencies such as Ginnie Mae (the Government National Mortgage Association) in the US.

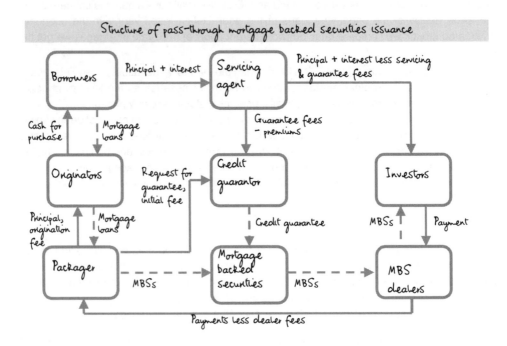

COLLATERALIZED MORTGAGE OBLIGATIONS (CMOs)

A key difference between pass-through mortgage backed securities and collateralized mortgage obligations (CMOs) is that the latter allows the sale of rights to sequential parts of the principal and interest payments. They also have a residual class that creates a degree of over-collateralization for the holders of other classes. The residual gets any payments left over after the claims of all of the other classes have been met.

By bundling and unbundling payments from the mortgage pool securities can be created with structures that mimic those of other securities. This segmentation produces securities that are potentially attractive to investors with different requirements.

We will ignore prepayments and credit risks for the moment and look at how PO and IO securities can be subdivided. The unbundling of the rights to the cashflows from a pool of mortgages into PO and IO classes can be taken further. The following is an example of a securitization with four major classes (A, B, C and Z) each of which has been subdivided into PO and IO tranches:

- The holders of A class securities are guaranteed to get back a defined amount of principal, they also receive a portion of the interest payments until they have received all of their principal due.

- The C and B classes have similar characteristics. Holders of the B class receive no a fixed interest payment but no principal payment until the holders of A class have had their principal due paid. They then receive all of the principal payments until their principal due has been paid.
- The Z class holders receive no payments until all of the claims of the A, B and C holders have been met. They then receive all principal and interest paid until there is no outstanding balance due.

Structure of annual payments for multiple security classes

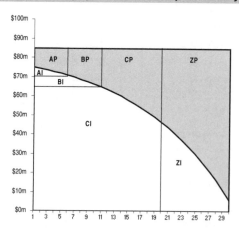

The actual cashflows will, however, vary from those scheduled and shown above as a result of prepayments. The different tranches have characteristics of other fixed income instruments:

- The A class payments have the structure of a short-dated mortgage.
- The B class payments have the approximate structure of a straight corporate bond.
- The C class structure is similar to that for the B class but with a longer term. This structure is analogous to that of a long-dated government bond.
- The Z class payment structure is close to that for a zero coupon bond (hence the standard use of the term "Z class").

Planned Amortization Classes (PACs)

Planned amortization classes (PACs) provide another way to cut the payments generated from a pool of mortgages. Two securities are issued, the PAC security itself and its "companion". The PAC is a tranche that has a planned schedule of principal and interest payments with amortization based on a sinking fund schedule. This schedule is based on an expected (likely) prepayment rate. The companion tranche acts as a buffer to ensure that the planned schedule of payments to the PAC class are met to a high degree of probability irrespective of the actual prepayment rate.

The structures of the payments given faster-than-expected and lower-than-expected pre-payments are shown in the following chart.

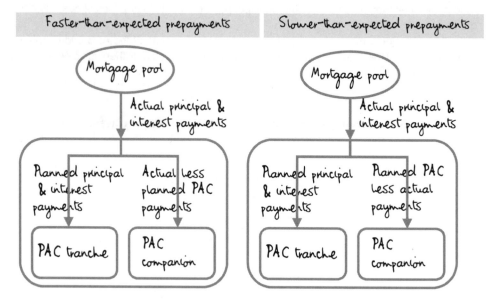

This works as follows, depending on whether the prepayment rate is faster or slower than expected:

- **Faster-than-expected prepayments.** If the prepayments come in faster than expected then the actual payments received from the mortgagors will be higher than expected. The PAC continues to receive its planned payments with the balance going to the holders of the companion tranche. The result is that the companion tranche is paid off sooner than expected.
- **Slower-than-expected prepayments.** If the prepayment rates are lower than expected then the PAC continues to receive its planned payments and the companion receives whatever is left over.

The result is that there are two tranches with very different characteristics. The PAC payments are highly predictable unless the difference between the expected prepayment and actual rates is extreme. The payments to the companion are much less predictable and can be significantly different than originally expected. These differences are reflected in pricing with the companion being priced to give higher yields to compensate for the higher risks.

OTHER FINANCIAL ASSET BACKED SECURITIES

Other common retail securitization issues are for auto loans and credit card receivables. Most of the concepts explored with regard to mortgage securitization issues also apply to these issues. Prepayment risks for auto loans issues are lower than for mortgage issues due to their much shorter term. Statistical modeling is more important for credit card receivables issues due to the nature of principal repayments.

Many issues also have some form of "clean-up" call. This is an option to terminate the issue, usually when the total value of the underlying assets falls below a certain value. The option is usually at the discretion of the issuer or servicer but may be mandatory. The clean-up conditions are specified at the time of the original issue and in most cases involve the issuer or servicer buying back the outstanding value of the assets. It is possible to structure clean-up calls in such a way that they provide a form of credit enhancement. Most regulators would regard such issues to have been done with some form of recourse.

Some issues are made with "early amortization" provisions. These are similar to clean-up calls but usually involve a pro-rata sharing of the proceeds rather than requiring the issuer to buy back the outstanding exposures.

Collateralized debt obligations (CDOs) usually represent a pool of secured commercial loans. They normally consist of loans from issuers with a range of different external credit ratings. These may then be separated into a number of different tranches. Collateralized bond obligations (CBOs) take a similar form but consist of rated bonds rather than loans.

Real Estate Invested Trusts (REITs)

Real estate invested trusts, generally referred to as REITs (pronounced "rights"), originated in the US. To create a REIT a property company, investment bank or investment company puts together a portfolio of real estate, which might include condominiums and commercial real estate. It packages them together and then sells shares in these securitized assets to investors in the form of REITs.

Such REITs may or may not be leveraged, that is partly financed with debt. A fund that invests solely in equities may gain a further diversification benefit by adding REITs to its holdings as REITs provide an alternative asset class that has a relatively low correlation with stock market performance.

PART V

Bank Valuations and Acquisitions

Bank valuations

* Book, market, economic & intrinsic value
* Market value versus intrinsic value
  - Discounts & premiums
* Return objectives
  - Public listed banks
  - Listed bank with controlling shareholders
  - State-controlled banks
* Dividend discount model (DDM)
  - Form of valuation measure, perpetuity

  $$PBR = (ROE-g)/(COE-g)$$
  - Strengths
* Key assumptions
  - Cost-of-equity, return-on-equity & growth
  - Time & gearing
* Excess capital
  - Impact of return on ROE, COE and valuations
* Multiple-stage DDMs & time
* Other valuation measures
  - Price-to-book, PER, VFO, implied factors (COE, ROE, g)
  - International banks

Bank acquisitions

* Consolidation pressures
  - Liberalization, lower barriers to entry, disintermediation
  - Scale economies & economies of scope, credit risk diversification
  - Regulatory & political pressures
* Cost savings
  - Branch closures, head office & IT rationalization
* Revenue enhancements
* Strategic benefits
* Management incentives
* Barriers to takeovers
  - Regulatory, political & defensive ownership structures
* All-cash versus all-paper offers
  - Practical constraints on cash as means of payment
* Acquisition accounting
  - Goodwill treatments
* Impact on regulatory CARs
  - Regulatory constraint on cash level of offer
* Impact on valuations
  - Value accretive versus destructive
  - Rules of thumb

18

Bank Valuations

Reality is merely an illusion, albeit a very persistent one.

Albert Einstein, physicist

VALUE MEASURES

There are four different ways to measure the "value" of a bank's equity: book value based on accounting standards, economic value based on the market value of its assets and liabilities, market value based on the price at which its stock trades and intrinsic value based on discounted future earnings:

- **Book value.** Book value is the reported value of the bank's equity based on the prevailing accounting standards. A bank reporting under three different accounting standards (US FASB, IAS and its local national standards) is likely to report three different values for its book value. In all cases book value reflects some assets and liabilities carried at their original cost and others where their value has been marked to a market or appraised price.
- **Economic value.** Economic value is defined as the difference between the market value of a company's assets and liabilities at an instant in time. In principle bank management can arrive at an estimate of this value although appraised rather than market values will have to be used for the many assets it has that lack a secondary market. (If they do make such estimates they choose not to make them public.)
- **Market value.** Market value is the most clearly defined of the four measures, can be calculated easily, has an exact value and is given by the bank's current share price multiplied by the number of shares issued.
- **Intrinsic value.** The intrinsic value of a bank is defined as the discounted value of future earning. A major difference between intrinsic value and economic value is that the former takes future growth into account. Estimating intrinsic value for equity is part art, part science. No two analysts would normally arrive at the same intrinsic value for a stock. Estimates are highly sensitive to relatively small changes in base assumptions.

Market Value versus Intrinsic Value

In Chapter 15 "Fund management" we argued that there is no direct relationship between market prices and intrinsic values. Efficient markets assume perfect transmission of information and that prices reflect a balance between supply (sellers) and demand (buyers).

Equity analysts attempt to estimate the intrinsic value of bank stocks and hence identify stocks that are overvalued (market price greater than intrinsic value) or undervalued (market price less than intrinsic value). They also use these estimates to help make relative investment recommendations between sectors and between stocks. Price targets are rarely based directly on estimates of intrinsic values but take account of other factors that are more qualitative in nature.

Equity analysts' fair value targets may have an indirect impact on stock market prices in two ways. First, they may influence investors' perceptions of potential upside or downside. Second, if enough institutional investors are using the same method to derive fair value targets and are making the same assumptions then they will tend towards the same fair value targets and stock prices will tend towards this level.

Premiums and Discounts

There are two ways to try to explain why banks that appear to have very similar financial attributes (*ROE* and growth expectations) and operate in the same country trade at very different multiples to some common valuation measure such as price-to-book:

- **Qualitative factors.** There are a number of qualitative factors that may be pointed to explain these differences. These include size, liquidity, corporate governance, asset quality, speculation and management quality. Differences are then referred to in terms of premiums and discounts. These may be relative to intrinsic value or relative to one another. In the latter case the more expensive stock may be said to be trading at a premium to the cheaper stock or the cheaper stock at a discount.
- **Cost-of-equity.** It is also possible to argue that no premium or discount exists but that pricing differences due to these qualitative factors are captured in a stock's effective cost-of-equity. This argument rapidly becomes one of semantics. The question then comes back to what are the factors that lead to a lower or higher *COE*.

Many analysts and portfolio managers talk in terms of premiums and discounts and this is a useful way to try to identify the specific factors that may justify either.

Discounts

A sell-side analyst always has problems arguing a case for buying a particular stock on value grounds alone. A common retort is that there are usually good reasons why a stock appears to be "cheap", and there often is. Some of these reasons include the following:

- **Size.** Large funds tend to avoid small cap companies because they can only account for a very small proportion of the fund and many funds' performance will largely be determined by making the right calls on a relatively small number of large cap stocks. This is a variation on US industrialist Andrew Carnegie's view that "The wise man puts all his eggs in one basket and watches the basket." The larger the number of benchmark stocks held the lower the tracking error is likely to be but the harder it will be to outperform the benchmark. Taking large positions in small caps is frequently proscribed by the terms of funds' mandates. These usually impose a limit on the proportion of issued shares in any stock that can be held (a common limit is 5%).
- **Liquidity and free float.** Many institutional investors place a significant value on the ability to get out of stocks when they need to and are unwilling to invest in stocks where this is not the case. One reason for this is the need to be able to respond to redemptions quickly. If a fund's holdings are a relatively high proportion of the free float of a stock there is likely

to be a significant adverse price impact if the fund chooses, or is forced, to sell down its position.

- **Asset quality.** Asset quality may be measured by disclosed numbers on problem loans but differences in definitions and the fact that many of these numbers are based on management judgment means that these published numbers are rarely directly comparable. A bank with poor asset quality or where there is little confidence in the disclosed numbers will tend to justify a discount.

- **Balance sheet structure.** The level of interest rate risk at a bank depends on its asset and liability mix. Few, if any banks, disclose values for estimated effective duration and hence investors have to rely on less sophisticated measures, such as the level of fixed rate to floating rate loans, to differentiate between banks. Banks with a high proportion of fixed rate assets relative to their liabilities are likely to be most affected by rising interest rates. The risks arising from liquidity management are also difficult to quantify, as is their possible impact. Banks with a lower level of liquid assets may achieve better returns but only at the expense of higher operating risk.

- **Capital raising risks.** Banks that are operating close to regulatory capital requirements may have to raise equity. This may be necessary to allow for future balance sheet growth or because the actual level of credit losses is higher than has been recognized and recognition would mean that the bank would be unable to meet these requirements.

- **Ownership, corporate governance and transparency.** We look in detail at the issues raised by ownership structures later in this chapter, and in particular at the risks to minority shareholders arising from the existence of a single controlling shareholder, whether private or public sector. Controlling shareholders have to be squeaky clean in their treatment of minorities if they are to avoid their stock being given a material discount by minority institutional investors. Portfolio managers have very long memories when it comes to actions that breach that trust. Once lost it is virtually impossible to recover. The level of disclosure and the quality and credibility of information released is also important.

- **Holding company and conglomerate discounts.** It is widely accepted that companies whose main assets are holdings of other listed companies merit a valuation discount. A similar discount is usually justified for conglomerates where the holding company is the only listed entity but the operating units have very little in common and lack a collective synergy. Most investors and financial investors reject arguments made by management of such holding companies and conglomerates that they provide diversification benefits on the grounds that investors can diversify their own holdings better through the market.

- **Management quality.** Many of the factors specific to an individual bank are often captured in a single term, management quality. This is an ill-defined term but one that has real meaning to investors. At its core are competence and credibility. It is easier to point to specific factors at individual banks that result in these attributes being compromised than it is to define them precisely.

- **Demand.** Many institutional investors treat the banking sector as a relatively homogeneous group. Having made a decision in terms of sector weighting individual bank security selection is made within the sector, rather than relative to other stocks in the market. If institutions favor certain banks' stocks over others then, even if portfolio managers are overweight banks as a whole and believe that individual bank stocks are cheap relative to the rest of the market, they may still be underweight in these less favored bank stocks.

Premiums

There are also grounds to be able to argue that individual bank stocks should trade at a premium to their intrinsic value including the following:

- **Weight of money.** Market value is arrived at through supply–demand forces. There are a number of ways in which demand may be inflated compared with "normal" levels:
  - **Mutual fund inflows.** Most mutual fund are only allowed to keep a specified proportion of their funds in the form of cash equivalents. Having to be fully invested means that when equity funds receive inflows from new subscriptions these funds have to be used to buy stocks. The level of mutual fund inflows and outflows varies over time. If these inflows are large enough they will tend to push up the prices of equities as a class irrespective of whether portfolio managers believe that individual stocks are overvalued relative to their intrinsic worth.
  - **Asset-class allocation.** Most mutual funds are run on a top-down basis with individual security selection being the last step of the process. Asset-class allocation may affect the level of equities versus bonds, country weightings, sector weightings and so on. The largest stocks in the smaller markets are most affected by these allocation changes. A relatively small increase in the weighting given to equities in developing markets made by the largest US funds is likely to have a large impact on the level of demand for stocks in these markets. This increase in demand can result in daily turnover in dollar terms in these markets rising by a factor of 2–4 times from average levels.
  - **Liquidity and free float.** Just as it is possible to argue that some stocks trade at a discount to their intrinsic value because they are relatively illiquid it is also possible to argue that some stocks will attract a premium because of their size and liquidity. Whether increased institutional demand is driven by inflows or asset allocation decisions the main beneficiaries are the largest, most liquid index stocks in the markets or sectors affected.
- **Excess capital.** Banks that are operating with capital well above that required by regulators and above that they may need to hold for planned balance sheet growth may be regarded as having excess capital. Excess capital depresses return on equity. Management may choose to return part of that excess capital through special dividends or share buy-back programs. Bank policies to maintain provisions for credit losses that are much higher than necessary to cover expected credit losses also result in a form of excess capital. The expectation of a change in provisioning policies or the actual return of capital may justify a premium.
- **Index issues.** We have looked at the effects of index-related factors on the prices of all firms in Chapter 14. Banks in developing markets are more often subject to restrictions on the level of foreign ownership than other companies. Where a local and foreign board exists the two classes of stock frequently trade at different prices even though they have the same economic interests. The price of the stock on the foreign board is almost always greater than that on the local. It is always a matter of contention as to whether the foreign board is trading at a premium or the local at a discount in particular cases.
- **Takeover speculation.** Stock values may also be inflated by speculation that a bank is likely to be subject to a takeover bid. It is usually relatively easy to draw up a short list of the banks in a single market where a bid is most likely. This may be because of fundamental weaknesses or because they have particular strengths that are attractive to a potential acquirer. The problem for investors with most such event-driven factors is forecasting the timing of the event. In the long run a bid may well be inevitable but in the long run we are

all dead. The result is that these premiums tend to come and go as other events appear to increase or reduce the likelihood of a bid in the short term.

- **Other speculation.** The main other source of speculation that affects bank valuations in particular is regulatory change. Regulators usually give an indication of the overall direction of policy and which particular areas may be subject to review and change. Many regulatory changes are preceded by lengthy consultative periods. Analysts and investors will try to identify those banks that are most likely to benefit from these changes and if the benefit appears to be material their stock may warrant a premium, those where the likely effect is negative, a discount.

THE DIVIDEND DISCOUNT MODEL (DDM)

The Basic Perpetuity Model

The dividend discount model, in one form or another, is probably the most common valuation method used by bank analysts. The perpetuity form of the DDM provides a very simple way to value a bank using publicly available information. The fair, or intrinsic, value of a stock is given by the sum of its future dividends discounted at the stock's cost of equity as follows:

$$\text{Intrinsic value} = P = \frac{D_1}{(1 + COE)} + \frac{D_2}{(1 + COE)^2} + \frac{D_3}{(1 + COE)^3} + \cdots + \frac{D_n}{(1 + COE)^n} + \cdots$$

The basic perpetuity model assumes that earnings grow indefinitely at a steady rate g, that it maintains a constant return-on-equity (ROE) and its gearing remains unchanged. Under these conditions future dividends are defined by current dividends and growth, D_1 for example is given by D_0 multiplied by $(1 + g)$. Intrinsic value can then be expressed as the following:

$$P_{Intrinsic} = \frac{D_0 \times (1 + g)}{(1 + COE)} + \frac{D_0 \times (1 + g)^2}{(1 + COE)^2} + \frac{D_0 \times (1 + g)^3}{(1 + COE)^3} + \cdots + \frac{D_0 \times (1 + g)^n}{(1 + COE)^n} + \cdots$$

Where the growth is expected to be to perpetuity, and with a mathematical sleight of hand, this equation can be simplified to the following equation (see Exhibit at end of this chapter for derivation).

$$P_{Fairvalue} = Book_1 \left(\frac{ROE - g}{COE - g} \right)$$

Bank valuations are frequently referred to as a multiple of book value and the fair value price-to-book ratio is then given by the following:

$$PBR_{Prospective} = \frac{ROE - g}{COE - g}$$

A bank with a sustainable ROE of 18%, long-run growth of 4% and a COE of 11% would thus have a fair prospective PBR given by $(18\% - 4\%)/(11\% - 4\%)$, or $2\times$ prospective book.

The following is an example of this method applied to ABC Bank (the ratios for this bank are realistic but if the absolute numbers were correct it would be one of the world's largest banks). All financial statements used in this example are as of 31 December 2006.

Balance sheet ABC Bank (2005–2007) ($m)			
	2005A	**2006A**	**2007E**
Assets			
Liquid assets	96 154	100 000	104 000
Loans	769 231	800 000	832 000
Other assets	19 231	20 000	20 800
Total assets	**884 615**	**920 000**	**956 800**
Liabilities			
Deposits	797 163	829 050	862 530
Other liabilities	28 846	30 000	31 200
Hybrid Tier I capital	7 644	7 950	7 950
Total non-equity liabilities	**884 615**	**920 000**	**956 800**
Share capital	5 000	5 000	5 000
Share premium	8 000	8 000	8,000
Retained earnings	37 962	40 000	42 120
Shareholders' funds	**50 962**	**53 000**	**55 120**
Total liabilities	**884 616**	**920 000**	**956 800**

The following shows a summary of the bank's earnings statements for 2005 through to 2007. Again, the statements for 2005–2006 are actual reported and for 2007 are forecasts based on 4% growth. There are no exceptional items in any years and the bad debt charges at 0.4% of loans is a typical charge through the economic cycle. The dividend payout ratio is assumed to be maintained at 67.8%. Its Tier I ratio is 8.83%.

Total number of shares issued is 5000m and there are no dilutive instruments present.

ABC Bank earnings statements (2005–2007) ($m)			
	2005A	**2006A**	**2007E**
Net interest income	23 990	24 950	25 950
Non-interest income	13 933	14 490	15 070
Operating income	37 923	39 440	41 019
Operating expenses	−22 292	−23 184	−24 111
Operating profit	15 631	16 256	16 908
Bad debt charge	−3 077	−3 200	−3 328
Profit before tax	12 554	13 056	13 580
Income tax	−5 021	−5 222	−5 431
Net profit	7 533	7 834	8 149
Dividend	5 573	5 796	6 029
Per share measures ($)			
Book	10.19	10.60	11.02
EPS	1.51	1.57	1.63
DPS	1.11	1.16	1.21

Based on an assumed sustainable *ROE* of 14.8%, a *COE* of 10% and perpetuity growth of 4% the perpetuity model gives a fair value of 1.8× prospective book. If the stock were trading at its intrinsic value of \$19.84 (1.8 × 11.02) it would be on just over 12× prospective earnings. The workings are shown in the following table.

ABC Bank perpetuity DDM valuation summary	
ROE	14.8%
ROE − g	10.8%
COE − g	6.0%
Fair value price-book$_{Prospective}$ ratio	1.80×
Prospective book (2007F)	×11.02
Intrinsic value per share (\$)	=19.84
Prospective EPS (2007F)	÷1.63
Fair PER prospective	12.2×

Case of *ROE* less than *COE*

If the *ROE* is less than the *COE* then the bank is destroying value. Such a bank should stop growing and pay out all of its earnings as dividends. That gives a *PBR* target of *ROE/COE*. This is the equation for a perpetual bond that pays a fixed coupon each year (i.e. $g = 0$):

$$PBR_{fv} = \frac{ROE}{COE}, \textit{no growth}$$

STRENGTHS OF DDM VALUATION APPROACHES

The DDM valuation approach is by no means the only way to try to value the equity of a bank as a going concern. In many cases these methods share the same intellectual foundation but are expressed in different ways. Most institutional equity bank analysts use it because it has a number of clear strengths:

- **Communicability and basis.** The idea that a stock should be valued ultimately on the basis of the discounted value of its future dividends is well established. In the short-term, of course, investors may buy stocks for capital returns but those capital returns depend on expectations that the discounted value of future dividends will rise due to growth higher than the market is expecting.

  Analysts are in the business of communicating views. Portfolio managers are busy people and have to cover a wide range of sectors. They do not have time to come to grips with individual analysts' proprietary valuation methods. They are well versed with CAPM and using the DDM framework removes one obstacle to communications. As a result they can focus on whether the analyst's short-term forecasts and the drivers of the long-term assumptions are reasonable and on the underlying business story.
- **Absolute valuations.** Some other valuation methods (for example, price–earnings ratio) give recommendations and values relative to the sector or market but do not give an absolute price target directly. The DDM framework can be used for relative valuation purposes but also gives absolute fair value targets.
- **Comparability.** Most analyst recommendations are relative to some benchmark. For a relatively homogeneous and important sector such as banks these relative recommendations

are frequently made within the sector. It is usually the strategist's job to decide to make the sector weighting recommendation. It is therefore important to have one quantitative, consistent method to justify those relative recommendations.

- **Sensitivity.** In common with all equity valuation methods the DDM framework produces intrinsic values that are highly sensitive to changes in the underlying assumptions. The following three charts show the intrinsic price-to-book ratio for each of the three explicit assumptions. We have varied each assumption in turn while keeping the other two assumptions constant.

  The first chart shows fair *PBR* assuming 10% *COE*, and 15% *ROE* and varying the growth assumption around the 5% level. In the second we keep growth at 5%, *ROE* at 15% and vary the *COE*, and in the final chart keep 5% growth and 10% *COE* and vary *ROE* around the 15% level.

The sensitivity of the DDM framework to its drivers is a double-edged sword. On the one hand results are very sensitive to the explicit assumptions. On the other hand it is easy to test the sensitivity of fair value targets to changes in these underlying assumptions.

The framework can be fairly easily adapted to deal with valuing banks with excess capital, those involved in acquisitions and distressed banks. At many times, it is speed of reaching a reasonable conclusion and recommendation that is vital. Equity analysts' time is a precious (to them anyway) and expensive commodity and the fact that once the framework has been set up it requires minimal effort to adjust and maintain is an important consideration to them.

KEY DDM ASSUMPTIONS

We have noted that the simple form of the perpetuity DDM has three explicit assumptions: an appropriate cost-of-equity, a sustainable *ROE* level and a growth level. It also has, however, two other assumptions that are frequently overlooked relating to gearing and time.

Cost-of-Equity (*COE*)

We have already considered some of the issues affecting the appropriate cost-of-equity to use and assumed that the risk-free rate and equity risk premium are given. The key question to address (using CAPM) is what value of beta to use for a bank's stock:

- **Market prices.** It is easy to get a value of beta from one of a number of information providers. There are problems, however, and these problems are greatest in the smaller emerging markets:
    - **Historic versus future.** Beta measures the correlation of historic returns between a stock and the market. A fundamental problem that cannot be avoided is that those historic correlations may not be a good indicator of future correlations. The nature of banks' businesses evolves over time and some may experience significant changes as a result of acquisitions. The composition of the market may change markedly over time as new companies are listed in sectors previously excluded.
    - **Time period and frequency.** The historic value of beta for stocks is not stable over time and varies depending on which time period and frequency (daily, weekly, monthly) are used. Any valuation method that results in intrinsic estimates of value that are more volatile than those of the price of the traded stock has to be regarded with a degree of skepticism.
    - **Liquidity.** Illiquid stocks tend to have low betas reflecting their lack of trading activity, so that even when there are sharp changes in market prices their prices may not change because the volume of transactions was so low.
    - **Earnings volatility.** It is possible to estimate a value of beta based on a bank's earnings volatility versus that of the market. Pandora couldn't resist the temptation to open her box and we should probably learn from her experience. A little peek should suffice. The first issue we would have to confront is the nature of reported bank earnings and, in particular, the use of accounting policies to smooth reported earnings and hide the true level of volatility in economic value. The second issue concerns apples and oranges and the extent to which a valid comparison between banks' reported earnings and those of other stocks can be made.
- **Judgment.** In the event that using betas from market prices proves unsatisfactory for any of the above reasons the analyst can always fall back on judgment. This is never going to produce results that are better than a first-cut approximation and is to an extent arbitrary but this may reflect the reality of what is available. One of the biggest and least acknowledged problems with many financial modeling techniques is the spurious sense of accuracy that the use of very detailed, complex methods to arrive at valuations gives. It is important in all aspects of life to recognize one's own limitations.

If this approach is taken then the analyst has to have a clear understanding about why he or she considers market-derived betas to be inappropriate, be able to argue the case convincingly and explain clearly the basis for the actual values used.

A simple way to arrive at individual betas is to start by comparing bank stocks with the rest of the market and decide whether banks are more risky and their earnings more volatile than those of the market as a whole. Looking at the betas for other sectors will provide some guidance. If banks appear to be riskier than the market as a whole but less risky than a well-defined sector with a beta of $1.4\times$ then bank betas should lie somewhere between $1\times$ and $1.4\times$.

Any differences in betas for individual bank stocks relative to this sector level beta must be justified on specific grounds. If the estimate for the sector beta is $1.2\times$ a less risky bank may justify a beta of $1.1\times$ and a riskier bank one of $1.3\times$. Great care has to be taken in making recommendations that rely primarily on the value of beta chosen by the analyst.

Return-on-Equity (*ROE*)

There are two parts to the calculation of a bank's return-on-equity, first what should be used as earnings and second what should be used as equity. As both numbers are driven not just by the bank's business but by the accounting standards used this is not a trivial matter:

- **Earnings.** The major source of cyclical volatility in reported earnings is bad debt charges. As soon as we start to get into considering how to treat bad debt charges in any context we move into headache territory. We will look in more detail at most of the factors that lead analysts to reach for the paracetomal in Chapter 20 "Corporate failures and problem loans". A decision has to be made as to what level of charge to assume for use in estimating the long-run *ROE*. Most would agree that some average should be used over an entire economic cycle. Taking a simple absolute average, however, is likely to understate the value because it takes no account of balance sheet growth. Most analysts apply a mean value expressed as a percentage of loans or risk-weighted assets.

  Trading profits and gains on disposals also present problems. In principle one-off disposal gains should be excluded and an average level of trading profits taken (usually expressed as a percentage of net interest income or some other proxy for scale) included. In practice it is often difficult to decide whether a reported disposal gain on securities should be treated with trading profits or whether a part of trading profits should be viewed as one-off gains. The accounting treatment of securities gains also affects the way in which these gains are reported.

  Goodwill is the difference between the price that a bank pays to acquire another firm less the net tangible assets of that firm. This is an example of a so-called intangible asset. Three different accounting practices are possible. Goodwill may be written off at the time of acquisition, it may be left unchanged over time or it may be written off (amortized) over a number of years by taking a charge through the income statement. Such charges have no impact on "cashflows" or tax paid and, where present, analysts agree that for valuation purposes they should be reversed.

- **Equity.** Equity as defined by accounting standards has a precise value but its main significance is the way in which regulators view it and in particular its eligibility for use in the calculation of Tier I capital under the terms of the Basel Accord. It may or may not be a good reflection of economic value for reasons we have already considered. The two areas we should focus on are the effects of mark-to-market policies on reported equity and the treatment of goodwill arising from acquisitions:

  - **Mark-to-market policies.** No accounting policies anywhere in the world require banks to mark-to-market the value of all of their interest-sensitive assets and liabilities. The main areas that do affect the reported value of equity that are affected by mark-to-market policies are securities holdings and real estate:

    - **Securities holdings.** The main source of gains (losses) on commercial bank securities' holdings comes from the impact of lower rates on the value of long-duration bonds and from the treatment of equity holding. We have already looked at the three different possible accounting treatments (carried-at-cost, balance sheet treatment and income statement treatment).

    - **Real estate.** Revaluation reserves may also result when a company revalues other assets, such as its branches, head office and long-term investments and marks them to market but does not take the unrealized gain or loss through the earnings statement. In some countries the common practice is to carry them at cost.

These revaluation reserves are held within the equity account. It is possible to argue the case for either their inclusion or their exclusion on a number of grounds.

- **Arguments for exclusion.** There are three principal arguments in favor of stripping out revaluation reserves from reported equity where banks have included this. First, it better reflects actual capital invested in the business. Second, a large part of revaluation reserves at many banks are for their premises and the going concern concept suggests that these should be stated at cost. Third, it allows us to compare banks that include these reserves within the equity account and those that don't on a consistent basis. Those who argue this case usually make one exception, which is that where revaluation reserves contain losses these should be subtracted from equity.

- **Arguments for inclusion.** The arguments for inclusion of revaluation reserves are largely based on the premise that the closer the reported book value is to economic value the more real meaning it has. From a valuation perspective it shouldn't matter if the bank premises and other assets were bought yesterday or 20 years ago. The use of the concept of invested capital should be restricted to measuring and assessing past performance and has no relevance to forecasting value based on future earnings.

  This argument can be illustrated with a simple example. Take the case of a bank that decides to sell its head office to a related third party, realizing any gains, and then immediately buys them back at the same price. The bank's reported net tangible assets will increase and its revaluation reserves fall by the same amount.

  If we stripped out revaluation reserves then we would arrive at one valuation before the transaction was completed and another after. This clearly makes no sense, as there has been no change in the underlying economic condition of the bank.

- **Goodwill.** There are differences of opinion over whether goodwill should be included or not from a valuation perspective. Perhaps surprisingly, proponents of the argument that revaluation reserves should be excluded tend to argue that goodwill should be included in the value for equity (and any amortized goodwill added back) while those that argue for revaluation reserves to be included tend to argue that goodwill should be excluded.

It all comes down to a fundamental difference of opinion as to whether equity should reflect historic invested capital or economic worth. We will look at the implicit assumptions concerning gearing and time and then return to this issue.

The diagram on the following page shows the way in which accounting policies and Basel requirements interact to affect intrinsic value. The most clearly defined role of reported book is to define a bank's legal status in terms of solvency. The Basel Accord sets a minimum target for the level of reported equity. This is turn constrains the level of sustainable dividend payout and may also result in banks being forced to raise equity to meet these requirements. These have a direct impact on intrinsic value.

Growth

A real constraint on the level of long-run growth assumed in the perpetuity model is that bank earnings growth cannot be higher than the assumed level of long-run nominal GDP growth. It

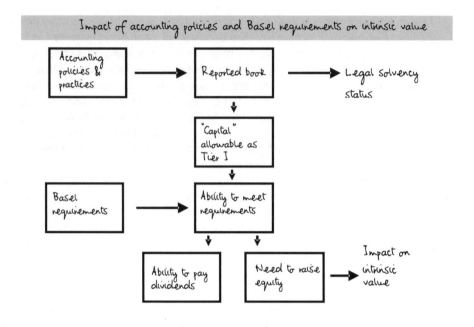

Impact of accounting policies and Basel requirements on intrinsic value

is best to err on the side of caution. Taking long-run expected nominal GDP growth over the next 20 to 30 years is both a reasonable assumption and does at least have a clear rationale. It is reasonable to assume a higher level of growth in developing markets than developed markets.

We examine how multiple-stage dividend discount models can be used to treat periods in the short to medium term when growth is expected to be well above that of the assumed level of long-run growth. In practice, analysts covering banks at the stock level always use a multiple-stage model rather than the simple perpetuity model.

Time

The assumption that the *ROE* can remain above the *COE* indefinitely does not hold up to scrutiny. If a firm is able to make a return above its *COE* then it is generating an excess economic profit. In such an event it is reasonable to assume that new entrants will seek to enter the business attracted by the higher returns on offer. Excess economic profits can only be sustained where significant barriers to entry exist. New entrants will tend to push the *ROE* down to the *COE*. If the *ROE*, however, is less than the *COE* one should expect banks to exit until the returns at least cover their cost of capital.

There are a number of ways to try to take this into account by using multiple-stage dividend discount models. We will use a simple two-stage model to show how this may be done later in this chapter.

Gearing

An underlying assumption of the perpetuity dividend discount model is that the value of equity grows at the same rate as that of earning. For this to hold the dividend payout ratio must be given by the following:

$$\text{Dividend payout ratio} = POR = 1 - \frac{g}{ROE}$$

If the actual payout ratio is less than given above then effective gearing falls, return-on-equity falls and the actual value of discounted dividends will be lower than estimated here. There is no fundamental constraint on such action but the effect is that the intrinsic value of the bank will be less than that given by the perpetuity model.

If the payout ratio is greater than this then the bank is effectively returning capital to shareholders. Effective gearing will as a result rise. As the equity base shrinks relative to earnings the return on equity will steadily increase. This cannot go on indefinitely. Regulatory capital adequacy requirements act as the ultimate constraint on the return of capital.

This provides a possible answer to the question as to what definition of equity to use. The real constraint is that equity allowable for treatment as Tier I capital under the Basel Accord. This suggests that the definition of equity that should be used for arriving at an estimate of intrinsic value should exclude goodwill and include revaluation reserves. This is not, however, standard industry practice and most analysts use cash earnings against reported equity with any amortized goodwill added back to the equity account. In the acquisition example given in the next chapter we will compare the results of using each method.

The actual payout ratio may provide some insight into the level of long-run growth expected by bank management but has to be taken in the context of its current capital level. A bank seeking to build up its capital base will have a lower payout ratio than one with capital in excess of management's target level.

EXCESS CAPITAL

Excess capital complicates the valuation process in two ways. First, it is necessary to define, identify and quantify the level of capital. Second, the possible return of excess capital introduces a valuation component that has option-like characteristics. Options are notoriously difficult to value.

In this context excess capital is usually defined as the equity which the bank maintains above that necessary to meet its regulatory Tier I requirements. This needs to be qualified, however:

- **Regulatory buffer.** Banks have to meet regulatory capital requirements at a number of different levels, within subsidiaries and at the group level. It is essential that the bank meets these minimum requirements at all levels and at all times. As a result banks maintain a regulatory buffer to ensure compliance. A typical group-level safety margin is 25%–50% of the regulatory capital requirement.
- **Capital market constraints.** A bank may have to maintain a specified capital adequacy level in order to comply with covenants arising from the issue of debt instruments, typically subordinated debt, preference shares and other forms of hybrid equity into the capital markets.
- **Credit rating agencies.** A bank may choose to target a particular level of capital adequacy in order to maintain a particular level of rating from credit rating agencies. This may make economic sense by reducing the cost of future debt issues and lowering the cost of its wholesale deposits.
- **Risk capital.** There is no direct relationship between regulatory minimum capital requirements and the level of capital that bank management is comfortable holding given the risks

in their business. This may act as a real constraint on the possible return of "excess" capital even though a bank is operating well above minimum regulatory levels.

- **Competitive positioning.** Many Swiss private banks operate with significantly higher levels of capital than required. This is a deliberate policy. Their clients require reassurance that they can safely entrust their family wealth with the bank. Maintaining a strong capital base helps to provide that reassurance.
- **Presence of hybrid equity.** Regulators set limits on the proportion of hybrid equity that can be counted towards Tier I requirements. This in turn sets a limit on the level of real equity that the bank has to maintain to meet the formal requirements.
- **Overprovisioning.** There are occasions when bank management have set aside provisions for credit losses far in excess of what is likely to be necessary to meet expected future losses on NPLs. These excess provisions are in effect a form of equity.
- **Unrecognized losses.** The bank may have unrecognized losses. In emerging markets the most common form of unrecognized losses arise from underreported NPLs and underprovisioning but can also include investments that are carried at a cost but have suffered a permanent impairment of value.
- **Unrealized gains.** There are also examples of banks that have significant unrealized gains on investments or property. Sometimes these are recognized on the balance sheet, sometimes not. If the bank recognized these gains, however, they would count towards excess capital.

In order to determine the level of excess capital or shortfall the analyst must estimate what level of Tier I capital the bank should maintain. Second, it is necessary to make any adjustments necessary to the actual level of capital. This is not a completely scientific exercise and requires the use of judgment.

The next stage involves estimating the value of the bank if it returned this excess capital to shareholders. Stock markets do not appear to reward banks for operating with capital much above that required to meet regulatory requirements. If this is the case then the return of excess capital will have minimal impact on a bank's cost-of-equity. This working assumption that the cost of equity will remain relatively stable as gearing increases becomes increasingly questionable on theoretical and practical grounds the larger the increase.

The return of excess capital will, however, result in a lower book value and, in most cases, a higher *ROE*. This will have a positive impact on valuations provided that the return being generated on its excess capital is below that of the bank's *ROE*.

Calculating *ROE* at Different Gearing Levels

For modeling purposes it is usually sufficient to assume that excess capital is returned via special dividends although in practice the bank may use share buy-backs or a combination of the two methods.

The return of excess capital will reduce the bank's net income and equity resulting in a different *ROE* than at current gearing. The question is how to model the impact on net income. There are two ways to look at this:

- **Reduction in assets.** The first option is to assume that the capital returned will be accompanied by a corresponding reduction in assets. For example, we could model the loss of interest income by assuming the bank sells government bonds and returns the cash it then receives to shareholders.

- **Increase in interest-bearing liabilities.** The alternative is to assume that the bank raises more wholesale deposits or borrowings. This will result in an increase in interest expense while leaving interest income unchanged.

There is no right way to model this. We are modeling a hypothetical event and there may well be practical constraints or specific circumstances that favor a particular approach at a particular time. A very liquid bank with an excess of retail deposits and a long net interbank position might be able to simply reduce this position.

Life is too short to spend too much time trying to figure the optimal way for a particular bank to return excess capital when it may well not do so in any case. Even if it were to do so this would be at some stage in the future.

It is also much easier to justify relative comparisons between banks by using a uniform approach rather than having to justify different assumptions between individual banks. All we are really trying to do is get a sense of the magnitude of the potential impact on fair value.

A simple approach is to take a domestic, long-dated risk-free rate and assume a reduction in interest income. The risk-free rate will normally be based on a long-dated government bond. Apply the standard corporate tax rate and we've got the impact on net income. The following equation shows the adjusted *ROE* at the chosen target gearing level to use in the perpetuity DDM:

$$ROE = \frac{NP - XSC \times r_f \times (1 - T_r)}{(E - XSC) \times (1 + g)}$$

Where *NP* represents forecast annual net profit for the following year, *XSC* the excess capital, T_r the marginal tax rate and *E* the current equity and *g* the forecast long-run growth.

Having calculated *ROE* at current gearing and at the higher gearing level it is a relatively simple exercise to calculate fair value for the two different levels. The higher fair value target gives us an upper bound, as the return of excess capital may or may not happen and even if it does it will happen at same future date reducing the value in terms of present value.

We could get sophisticated and discount the value of future potential special dividends. The effort involved in carrying out this work is simply not justified and it is questionable whether it would add any value to the investment decision process in any case.

We will use ABC Bank as an example. Its current Tier I level is 8.83%. Management has indicated that it is considering lowering this to 5.5%. The bank has $61bn in Tier I capital, including $8bn in hybrid equity, versus a regulatory 4% requirement of $27.6bn. It has no goodwill on its balance sheet. If it were allowed to count all of its hybrid equity towards its Tier I requirement it could return $23bn in equity to shareholders and still achieve its 5.5% target.

In our base case we will assume that it is only allowed to count hybrid equity up to 15% of its equity towards its Tier I requirements (the level allowed is actually 17.6% under the Basel Accord, i.e. 15% of total Tier I capital). It can therefore return only $15bn in excess capital to shareholders, equivalent to $3 per share compared with our estimated intrinsic value of $19.84 (see previous example).

ABC Bank capital and equity positions end of 2005 ($m)			
		5.5% Tier I	
	8.8% Tier I	**Hybrid equity restricted**	**All hybrid equity available**
Equity	53 000	33 012	30 014
Available hybrid Tier I	7 950	4 952	7 950
Total Tier I	**60 950**	**37 964**	**37 964**
Required Tier I (@4%)	27 610		
Required Tier I (@5.5%)	37 964		
Excess equity		**15 036**	**22 986**
Number of shares (m)		÷5 000	÷5 000
Excess equity per share		**3.01**	**4.60**

Note: numbers do not add up due to rounding.

The first stage in the valuation process is to calculate prospective equity and book value. Prospective equity is simply calculated by increasing the adjusted current equity to take account of the long-run growth forecast of 4%.

ABC Bank adjusted forecast equity ($m)		
	Hybrid equity restricted	**All hybrid equity available**
Equity (2006A)	53 000	53 000
Excess equity	−15 036	−22 986
Adjusted equity	**37 964**	**30 014**
Growth	×1.04	×1.04
Prospective equity (2007)	**39 483**	**31 215**
Number of shares	÷5 000	÷5 000
Prospective book ($)	**7.90**	**6.24**

The second step is to estimate the reduction in forecast net profit due to lost interest income from the returned equity. Dividing this adjusted forecast net profit by adjusted prospective equity gives the adjusted *ROE*. The adjusted *ROE* increases from 14.8% to 19.5%.

ABC Bank adjusted forecast net profit ($m)				
	Hybrid equity restricted		**All hybrid equity available**	
Forecast net profit (2007F)		8 149		8 149
Lost (taxed interest income)	$15\,036 \times 0.05 \times (1 - 0.6)$	−451	$12\,986 \times 0.05 \times (1 - 0.6)$	−690
Adjusted net profit		**7 698**		**7 459**
Prospective equity (2007)		÷39 483		÷31 215
Adjusted *ROE*		**19.5%**		**23.9%**

The forecast long-run 4% growth is unchanged. Putting all of these revised values into the perpetuity DDM model and taking account of the $3 returned to shareholders gives a total fair value of $23.42 versus the estimate of $19.84, 18% higher. If on the other hand there were no restrictions on the use of its hybrid equity to meet its Tier I requirement this target would increase to $25.30, more than 25% higher than the original estimate.

There are plenty of examples of banks around the world operating with Tier I ratios in the mid-teens and show no interest in increasing their gearing. If an analyst believes that this is unlikely to change then there is no basis for a higher fair value target than $19.80. If, however,

ABC Bank adjusted forecast net profit ($m)		
	Hybrid equity restricted	**All hybrid equity available**
ROE − *g*	15.5%	19.9%
COE − *g*	÷6%	÷6%
Fair value PBR prospective	**2.58×**	**3.32×**
Prospective book	7.90	6.24
Fair value at higher gearing	**20.41**	**20.70**
Excess capital returned	+3.01	+4.60
Total	**23.42**	**25.30**

management has given a credible assurance that it intends to lower its Tier I ratio to a particular target level, within a given time frame, then a higher target is likely to be justified.

One final word on excess capital is necessary. Management of companies that have excess cash, or in the case of banks, capital, often find it remarkably difficult to return it to shareholders. There are two reasons why this may be the case:

- **War chest.** Having excess capital may allow banks to consider possible future acquisitions. Anyone who has ever come into some easy money knows that the temptation to buy something extravagant can be irresistible. In similar vein it always seems much less painful to pay for expensive meals with a credit card than it is to pay with cash. Investors have good reason to be nervous about any company that has cash to burn.
- **Fear.** It is not uncommon for companies to hoard excess cash and banks excess capital rather than return it to shareholders because they fear that the market will regard such action is a sign of management weakness or demonstrate a dearth of possible future opportunities. Most portfolio managers would prefer to see such funds returned to shareholders than risk having it squandered away on misconceived or overpriced acquisitions.

MULTIPLE-STAGE MODELS

Two-stage models are a common variation of the perpetuity model. The following example has three years of explicit forecasts, a 10% cost-of-equity and assumes 4% growth and 14.8% *ROE* thereafter. In the early years the bank is forecast to enjoy faster growth than the long-run estimate and makes very low dividend payments in the first two years. From the third year onwards it is assumed to have a payout ratio of 73% (1−4%/14.8%).

		Base case for two-stage DDM example			
		Explicit forecasts			**Perpetuity**
Year	**2006A**	**2007F**	**2008F**	**2009F**	**2010F**
Equity	53 000	61 484	70 859	73 803	76 755
Earnings	7 834	8 931	9 868	10 904	11 341
Dividend		447	493	7 960	8 279
Earnings growth		14%	11%	11%	4%
ROE		14.5%	13.9%	14.8%	14.8%

The valuation process is in two parts. In the first part we calculate the present value of the forecast dividends for 2007 through 2009, giving $6794m, as shown below.

Discounted values of dividends ($m)					
Year	2006A	2007F	2008F	2009F	Total
Dividend		447	493	7960	
Discount rate		1.1	1.21	1.33	
PV of dividends		**406**	**408**	**5981**	**6794**

The starting point is to estimate the fair value of the stock going into the perpetuity model at the end of the third year. The workings are shown in the following table and should be self-explanatory. This gives a fair value target of around $22.12 versus our original $19.80 target in the simple perpetuity example.

Discounted value of perpetuity target at end of 2009 ($m)	
Equity at the end of 2009	**73 803**
Growth of 4%	×1.04
Prospective book (as of end of 2010)	**76 755**
Fair value multiple of 1.8×	×1.81
Fair value at end of 2009	**138 159**
Discount factor	÷1.33
Present value at end of 2006	**103 801**
Plus present value of dividends (2006)	+6 794
Total *PV* (2006)	**110 596**
Number of shares (m)	÷5000
Fair value per share ($) (2006)	**22.12**
Forecast equity (prospective) 2007	61 484
Number of shares (m)	÷5000
Prospective book value per share ($)	**12.30**
Price to prospective book	**1.8×**

We have already argued that the assumption that the *ROE* remains above the stock's *COE* indefinitely is unrealistic. A simple way around this is to use the perpetuity approach for a defined number of years and then cut the *ROE* down to the *COE*. Once the *ROE* equals the cost-of-equity growth is assumed to fall to zero. The nominal value at that time is the value of equity at the end of the growth period.

The following example assumes an *ROE* of 15%, *COE* of 10% and 10 years of 5% annualized growth. The present value of the terminal value (equity) at the end of the 10th year is $598.1 ($1551 ÷ 2.6). The present value of the discounted dividend stream is $744 giving a total present value of $1342 or a fair value prospective *PBR* of 1.34×.

The following table shows the variation of *PBR* with the length of the growth period. With 30 years' growth and zero growth thereafter gives a prospective fair *PBR* of 1.74× versus the perpetuity result of 2.0×.

More sophisticated models can be developed that "fade" the *ROE* down to the *COE*. Whether the additional work and potential for model errors is worth the additional "sophistication" is, however, open to doubt.

Valuations of base case – ten years' growth ($)											
Year	1	2	3	4	5	6	7	8	9	10	PV
Equity	1000	1050	1102	1157	1215	1276	1340	1407	1477	1551	**598.1**
Earnings	150.0	157.5	165.4	173.6	182.3	191.4	201.0	211.1	221.6	232.7	
Dividends	100.1	105.1	110.3	115.8	121.6	127.7	134.1	140.8	147.8	155.2	
Discount factor	1.1	1.2	1.3	1.5	1.6	1.8	1.9	2.1	2.4	2.6	
Present value	**91.0**	**86.8**	**82.9**	**79.1**	**75.5**	**72.1**	**68.8**	**65.7**	**62.7**	**59.8**	**744.4**
Total											**1343**
Prospective fair PBR											**1.34×**

Valuations of base case versus growth period ($)					
Number of years	10	15	20	25	30
Prospective fair *PBR*	1.34×	1.48×	1.59×	1.67×	1.74×

The DDM framework when used by an experienced practitioner provides a simple, extremely flexible, bank valuation tool. The arguments that it is sensitive to relatively small changes in assumptions are fair but miss the point. The real value of equities comes from their future earnings over a very long period. Small differences in assumptions will result in relatively large variations in the results given by any quantitative valuation method. Que sera, sera.

OTHER VALUATION MEASURES

Analysts and investors use a number of value measures, including the following:

- **Price-to-book (*PBR*).** In the DDM framework the price-to-book target is a derived number based on estimating a dollar fair value target and dividing this by book. This fair value target is driven by three primary factors *ROE*, *COE* and *g* (growth):
  - **Consistent definitions of "book" and "equity".** Care has to be taken to ensure that the definition of shareholders' funds on which book value is based and the equity value used in the *ROE* estimate are done on the same basis. We have already considered the issues concerning the two most common cases where this is a factor, namely the treatment of goodwill and revaluation reserves.
  - **Meaningful comparisons.** It never ceases to amaze me to hear relatively bright people in the industry talk about one bank being cheap relative to another bank on the basis of its price-to-book without putting that measure into context. A low relative price-to-book ratio is often explained simply by differences in the level of profitability (as measured by *ROE*) between two banks operating in the same market. We have already looked at other factors that may play a part earlier in this chapter.

    When comparisons are made cross-border differences in the market cost-of-equity are often important. A bank in a market with a low *COE* may justify a higher price-to-book multiple than a bank with a higher *ROE* but operating in a market with a relatively high *COE*. Similar issues affect expectations of future growth.

- **Price-to-adjusted-book.** Some ignorant salesmen and portfolio managers who should know better become obsessed with price-to-adjusted-book measures at distressed banks. If we use the analogy that the best place for a bank's financial statements in a library is with other works of fiction then the best place for adjusted-book values is in the fantasy section. This value is based on reported book (and all of the problems of that accounting definition) and provisions, reported NPLs (which the analyst almost certainly believes are understated) and analyst estimates of loss rates that may vary from 40% to 70% of NPLs.

  There comes a point at which analysts stop trying to educate these people and simply give them the numbers they are being asked for. To avoid having to deal with such questions in the future they also include these measures in their reports as a matter of course. History has shown that if a lie is repeated often enough some people will end up believing it.

- **Price-to-earnings ratio (*PER*).** There is nothing inherently different about price-to-earnings and price-to-book ratios as they are both derived from the same common factors. This is shown below:

$$PER = \frac{P}{E} \quad but \quad ROE = \frac{E}{B} \quad and\ hence \quad E = B \times ROE \quad therefore \quad PER = \frac{P}{B} \times ROE$$

Most bank specialists on both the buy and sell side tend to talk using the *PBR* measure because it is intuitively simpler to use when expressed in terms of the three fundamental drivers and this is demonstrated in the following equation. The *PBR* varies in a linear way with *ROE* while that of the *PER* with its reciprocal:

$$PER = \left(\frac{ROE - g}{COE - g}\right) \times \frac{1}{ROE}$$

Non-bank specialists sometimes use it as a way to compare bank valuations with those of other non-financial companies or the market as a whole. Given that few non-financial companies today are valued on a simple *PER* basis it is difficult to see the validity of such comparisons.

- **Value of future opportunities (*VFO*).** *VFO* is another variation based implicitly on the DDM valuation framework. We have already noted that in the absence of growth the target fair *PBR* is given by *ROE* divided by *COE*. This assumes a 100% payout ratio and that all earnings are paid out as dividends. The absolute dollar value of such a bank is simply capitalized earnings. The difference between the actual market value of the bank's stock and this value is thus the value that the market is placing on cashflows generated by growth:

VFO = Market capitalization − Value of capitalized earnings

This has the virtue that it is very easy to calculate. It provides a simple way to look at valuations of distressed banks by adjusting it as follows:

VFO = Market capitalization − Value of capitalized after tax operating profits

    − Capital necessary to be raised to cover credit losses and reach required Tier I level

This will give a very conservative value as operating profits are likely to be depressed by NPL carrying costs in any case. If the *VFO* is positive this is a clear sign that the bank, even if it is technically insolvent, has value above that ascribed by the market. We should flag that there are questions about the appropriate *COE* to apply in such cases but leave it at that for now.

- **Implied *ROE*, *COE* and growth values.** Given the values for any two of the three value drivers (*ROE*, *COE* and growth) the value of the third factor implied by market valuations can be inferred. This can be a useful way to compare intrinsic value with market value. If the implied *COE* appears to be much greater than that implied by the assumed level of the market and stock-specific equity risk premium then this suggests that there is something missing from the approach used to estimate the *COE* – or that the stock is cheap.

  We have already discussed most of the issues concerning back testing of valuation approaches in Chapter 15 "Fund management" but it is worth reiterating the key point. It is impossible to back test valuation approaches because market prices reflect market expectations and these cannot be measured with any real confidence.

- **Large international and universal banks.** There are only a handful of truly international banks but their size and importance are such that more effort in exploring alternative valuation methods is worthwhile. One of the key issues with their valuation involves determining an appropriate cost-of-equity to apply. Such a bank may have only 50% of its earnings in US$ denominated or linked currencies and the rest in other currencies. The most common approach is to apply a cost-of-equity that reflects that of the markets in which it operates, weighted by the proportion of its earnings that come from each currency bloc.

  Some analysts also attempt to put a value on large international banks by trying to value the individual parts of its operations around the world and then determine the sum. A similar approach may also be used to break down the valuation of a universal bank into its commercial banking, investment banking and other businesses.

  The main objective of these exercises is to try to understand better which factors are most important in driving valuations and the analysis may throw up apparent anomalies that are worth pursuing.

- **Other methods.** Price-to-deposits as a valuation measure is used in a similar way as price-to-assets-under-management is used in looking at stand-alone fund manager valuations. Neither method has much going for them. Occasionally individual analysts or even entire houses will come up with a "proprietary" method. If they were anything other than variations on the same theme and added real value to the process then others would adopt them.

Exhibit: Derivation of perpetuity dividend discount model (DDM)

The fair value of a stock is given by the sum of its future dividends discounted at the stock's cost of equity:

$$P = \frac{D_1}{(1 + COE)} + \frac{D_2}{(1 + COE)^2} + \frac{D_3}{(1 + COE)^3} + \cdots + \frac{D_n}{(1 + COE)^n} + \cdots$$

We can simplify this equation in a number of steps, assuming steady, sustained future earnings growth. D_1, for example, is given by D_0 multiplied by $(1 + g)$. This gives us the following equation:

$$P = \frac{D_0 \times (1 + g)}{(1 + COE)} + \frac{D_0 \times (1 + g)^2}{(1 + COE)^2} + \frac{D_0 \times (1 + g)^3}{(1 + COE)^3} + \cdots + \frac{D_0 \times (1 + g)^n}{(1 + COE)^n} + \cdots$$

This simplifies to the following:

$$P = \frac{D_0 \times (1+g)}{(1+COE)} \left(1 + \frac{(1+g)}{(1+COE)} + \frac{(1+g)^2}{(1+COE)^2} \cdots + \frac{(1+g)^n}{(1+COE)^n} \cdots + \cdots \right)$$

Now this is an equation that is easy to solve. We start with a series S_0 of the same form, and a second series S_1 obtained by multiplying S_0 by x:

$$S_0 = 1 + x + x^2 + x^3 + \cdots + x^n + \cdots \quad and \quad S_1 = x \times S_0 = x + x^2 + x^3 + \cdots$$
$$+ x^n + x^{n+1} \cdots$$

We then subtract the second equation from the first equation. All of the intermediate factors cancel each other out save for the term $1 - x^{n+1}$. Provided that x is less than 1 the factor x^{n+1} tends to zero as $n \to \infty$. The value of the infinite series S_n simplifies as follows:

$$S_0 - S_1 = S_0 - x \times S_0 = (1-x) \times S_0 = 1 - x^{n+1} \Rightarrow S_0 = \frac{1 - x^{n+1}}{1-x} = \frac{1}{1-x}$$
$$as \; x \to \infty$$

Our perpetuity DDM series can then be expressed as follows:

$$P = \frac{D_0(1+g)}{(1+COE)} \left(\frac{1}{1 - \left(\frac{1+g}{1+COE} \right)} \right) = \frac{D_0(1+g)}{(1+COE)} \left(\frac{1+COE}{COE-g} \right) = \frac{D_0 \times (1+g)}{COE-g}$$

The dividend is simply earnings multiplied by the payout ratio (*POR*). Earnings are given by return on period-end equity multiplied by period-end equity:

$$D_0 = EPS_0 \times POR = ROE \times Book_0 \times POR$$

Substituting for the dividend we get the following:

$$P = \frac{D_0 \times (1+g)}{COE-g} = \frac{Book_0 \times ROE \times POR \times (1+g)}{COE-g}$$

If a bank's earnings are to grow by g and given a constant *ROE* its book must also grow by g. This puts a constraint on the payout ratio. If the company makes a higher payout ratio than this its gearing will increase. If the payout ratio is less than this then its gearing will fall:

$$g = \frac{(1 - POR) \times Earnings_0}{Book_0} = (1 - POR) \times ROE \Rightarrow POR = \frac{ROE - g}{ROE} = 1 - \frac{g}{ROE}$$

Substituting for the payout ratio the equation for the fair value of a bank simplifies as follows:

$$P = \frac{Book_0 \times ROE \times (1 - g/ROE) \times (1+g)}{COE-g} = \frac{Book_1 \times (ROE - g)}{COE-g}$$

Rearranging we get the fair price target and price-to-book multiple for the bank:

$$P = Book_1 \left(\frac{ROE - g}{COE - g} \right) \Rightarrow Price\text{-}to\text{-}book_{Prospective} = \frac{ROE - g}{COE - g}$$

RETURN OBJECTIVES

There is a very wide range of return-on-equity (*ROE*) values reported by banks around the world. Some of these variations can be explained by differences in the competitive or regulatory environment between different countries, and by economies being at different points of the economic cycle. But this is rarely the full story. There are often wide variations in returns between banks operating in the same market and facing the same external pressures. Two factors that play important parts in explaining differences in returns are management quality and stakeholder objectives.

Stakeholder objectives are largely determined by ownership structure. The primary divide is that between banks controlled by the state and those controlled by private sector interests. A secondary divide exists between private sector banks that have a controlling shareholder and those that don't.

Private Sector Banks with no Controlling Shareholder

Almost all large banks in Anglo-Saxon countries such as the US, the UK, Canada and Australia are held within the private sector, are listed on the domestic stock exchange and have no majority shareholder. In all of these countries no single shareholder is allowed to own a stake greater than 5% of issued shares without regulatory approval. In practice the only time this restriction is lifted is when approval is granted for one bank to acquire another.

The standard management mantra is that they are "committed to maximizing shareholder value". This has different meanings to different people. Some investors interpret this to mean a focus on stock price, others on the bank's operating performance. Some management go as far as quantifying performance targets of which return-on-equity and earnings growth are most common. A few set medium-term stock market objectives such as doubling the bank's stock price within three years or defined in terms of total shareholder returns (taking account of stock appreciation and dividends paid).

In my experience the smartest bank CEOs and senior managers studiously avoid making any comment on the current level of their stock price or its likely future performance. Analysts often ask senior management whether they consider their stock to be either under- or overvalued. The best response from bank management is to point out that it is the analyst's job to make that assessment – not theirs. The only time to break this rule is when mounting a defense against a hostile takeover. I wish I had the copyright for the phrase "this bid is opportunistic and fails to recognize the underlying value".

There is very little that management can do, other than delivering on operating level promises and targets, to influence the bank's stock price in a positive way. This is almost entirely out of their control although many resort to giving earnings "guidance" that they will try to (and know they should be able to) beat, providing a quarterly "positive earnings surprise". Under bull market conditions a company that only meets its guidance is often seen as providing disappointing results.

External factors usually have a much greater influence. If interest rates start to fall unexpectedly, for example, stocks in general may perform well as investors switch from bonds to equities. Stock of companies that benefit most from lower interest rates are likely to perform better than that of companies where lower interest rates have a neutral or negative impact on earning. A bank's stock is likely to increase in absolute terms and outperform the market in these circumstances but management has little reason to claim the credit for the stock's performance.

It is easier to argue that bank management should be held responsible for bottom-line earnings. Even when unexpected external events occur that have an adverse impact on the bank, such as a change in regulatory requirements or the initiation of a price war by a competitor, management should have made contingency plans against such eventualities. The economic cycle also has a direct impact on the level of credit losses.

There is no doubt that quality of management is probably the single most important factor in determining operating performance that is within a bank's control. An individual bank can usually do little to influence the external operating environment, however. In a recession non-performing loans (NPLs) will rise at all banks and the differences between individual banks will only be ones of degree.

Management compensation schemes at some banks have evolved to reward management for stock price performance that may have little to do with management performance. They also encourage acquisitions as management at bigger banks get paid more than management at smaller banks. Finally they encourage risk taking because of the asymmetry of returns; executives get big bonuses in years of bumper profits but do not have to pay compensation to shareholders in years when the bank reports lower earnings or even losses.

In practice it is difficult to change senior management at private sector banks unless they fail in dramatic style and there are few such examples. Many countries impose limits on the level of holdings that an investor can hold, typically 5%, and this makes it difficult for shareholder activists to influence management behavior. It is sometimes said of dissatisfied bank shareholders that they do not vote at annual general meetings but with their feet. Eventually private sector banks performing badly tend to be acquired by banks with stronger management but this may be preceded by years of poor performance and strategic blunders.

Private Sector Banks – Family Controlled

Family-controlled banks tend to act differently than banks with professional management and no controlling shareholder. Plenty of academic studies have shown that individuals differ from institutions in the way that they assess risks and rewards. In general, individuals tend to weigh losses on their own account more heavily than gains.

The usual stated primary objective at banks with no controlling shareholder is to "maximize shareholder returns". In order to achieve this objective management has to be prepared to accept a level of risk. If management at family-controlled banks act in the way that behavioral theory suggests, the returns that they will generate are likely to be lower than at banks in the former group because of their lower risk tolerance.

This appears to be borne out by actual experience of analyzing family-controlled banks in Asia. They are generally relatively conservative and maintain higher than average capital adequacy ratios and below average dividend payout ratios. They tend to be hierarchical with most decisions being made at the top and have limited delegation. They are cost conscious, which is a good thing, but are also slow to adjust to a changing environment whether it is in terms of technology or new financial products.

They have little incentive to act in ways that directly disadvantage minority shareholders (unlike banks whose controlling shareholder has other interests) but are frequently not unduly concerned about their interests.

It is rare to see family control of any business last more than two generations, however. This is probably due to two factors. First, a divergence of interests within the family often develops, which means that the founder's descendants have no interest in running a bank. Second, there is usually a dilution in the size of individual family members' holding as a result of inheritance through the generations. The result is that professional management is then brought in who have no direct links with the majority shareholder. In the fullness of time the family will either start to reduce its holdings by selling into the market or it will be open to potential offers to buy the bank.

Private Sector Banks with Controlling Shareholder

In most countries regulators do not allow conglomerates to own banks. There is a very good reason for this restriction as there are significant risks arising from related lending and other transactions to the bank's minority shareholders, its depositors and other creditors. In some emerging markets many banks with a controlling shareholder exist. A controlling (or majority) shareholder may have no other interests than the bank or it may be a non-financial company. In some cases the controlling shareholder is a family or individual who also owns other non-financial interests.

Related lending is the act of a bank, controlled by a conglomerate, lending to the conglomerate. Management's interests are aligned with those of the conglomerate rather than the minority shareholders. In these countries regulators generally try to limit the risk to depositors by imposing single borrower limits. These are typically set at 10% of shareholders' funds. Such limits can be circumvented, however, as shown in the following diagram. In this example, the reported exposure of $100m complies with the regulatory single borrower limit but the actual economic exposure of the bank to the conglomerate is $200m.

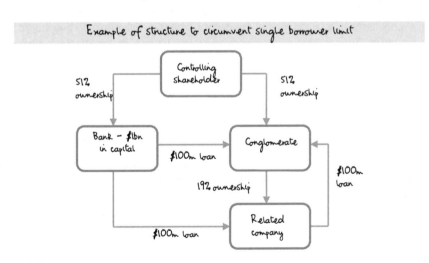

The risks to minority shareholders should be clear:

- **Moral hazard.** The bank may offer more favorable terms for loans to the conglomerate than to other borrowers. These may be in terms of the level of collateral required or the actual level of interest rate or fees charged.

- **Credit risk.** There is a potentially higher risk of default on such loans, in fact the bank is likely to be pressured to lend when the conglomerate is in the most trouble.
- **Asset sales and purchases.** The controlling shareholder may inject assets into the bank from the conglomerate at an inflated price, or sell assets from the bank to the conglomerate at a price below market value.

Public Sector Banks

Outside the Anglo-Saxon markets, state control is common although the trend in many countries has been towards privatization. This has been especially pronounced in Europe where the EU commission for competition supports arguments from private banks that the use of state guarantees effectively lowers state-controlled banks' cost of funds and creates an unfair competitive environment.

While a major objective of private sector banks is to earn an economic profit (returns above their cost-of-equity), this is rarely the case at state-controlled banks. Governments use their control to ensure that banks act in support of government policy. This support may be very specific in terms of action or general. Examples of specific action to support government policy include the following:

- **Directed lending.** Directed lending is the practice of banks lending to particular companies, strategic industries and particular groups of retail customers such as farmers. This practice was particularly prevalent in Korea in the mid-1990s and was a major factor in the financial crisis that enveloped that country in 1997–1998. Debt–equity gearing at many companies had reached a staggering $4\times$ and banks were used to support large companies that in other countries would have been liquidated, restructured or sold.
- **Market support.** In some countries market indices are taken as a barometer of the governments' popularity. In a falling market the government may ask banks to buy stocks to prop up the market. Such market support activities rarely have a lasting effect but simply result in a weaker financial system as the banks usually end up with significant unrealized losses on their equity portfolios.

Central banks and governments also use these banks in terms of providing more general support for economic and political objectives. These include the following:

- **Loan growth targets.** Banks may be given a specific minimum target for loan growth or asked to rein in loan growth. The former is usually dictated when the economy is in recession and there are fears of a credit crunch as banks become increasing risk averse in the face of deteriorating asset quality and reluctant to lend to companies that are experiencing financial difficulties. The latter is normally an attempt to slow down economic growth being fuelled by a sharp rise in bank credit.
- **Deposit rates.** In countries with ill-developed pension systems many pensioners rely on income from interest on deposits. When interest rates fall to low levels banks may be asked to maintain retail deposit rates above the wholesale market rates to offset the political outcry from pensioner groups hit by lower income.
- **Free retail banking services.** In most countries basic banking services are provided at a loss to a large proportion of retail customers. The trend in many countries has been for banks

to introduce account and transaction fees. These are frequently conditional on the level of the balance held in the customer's deposit account. These fees are highly unpopular, however, and hit the poorest members of the community hardest. In some countries legislation mandates a certain basic level of service that banks must provide for free.

- **Subsidized loans.** Banks may also be pressured to offer subsidized loans to particular groups of customers such as loans for low-cost housing and educational loans to students.
- **Deferring action on loans in default.** Banks may also be put under pressure to defer taking action on borrowers in default. These borrowers may include specific large companies where liquidation would results in massive job losses or specific groups of individuals affected by some natural catastrophe, farmers affected by drought or victims of earthquake, for example.

While these actions may be defensible, to an extent, using banks as political tools or for social engineering is regarded as inappropriate in most countries. Both state and private banks may be forced to act in accordance with the government's requirements even if the government and central bank have no legal mandate to make such demands. Central banks and regulators have considerable discretionary powers and can choose to make life very uncomfortable for banks that do not cooperate fully with their requests. State-controlled banks are also vulnerable to actions that are most definitely not defensible, these include the following:

- **Loans to politicians.** Banks may also make undisclosed loans to politicians or political parties on terms more favorable than those given to other customers in return for political favors. These terms may involve interest rates well below those charged on other loans or waiving collateral requirements.
- **Money laundering.** In the more corrupt countries many politicians receive significant cash payoffs from business interests seeking political favors or seeking to avoid criminal investigation. The politicians in turn need the banks to launder these transactions and in many cases arrange for the money to be transferred offshore. This usually involves operating secret accounts on behalf of the politicians or political parties involved.

Many politicians in opposition campaign for a reduction in the level of state control but find the opportunities afforded by this control irresistible once in office. In addition to leveraging the banks' economic impact they can also exploit the opportunity to use the banks for political patronage. Governments can reward political supporters by giving them highly remunerative, senior positions in state-controlled banks. In many instances these appointments are highly inappropriate, simply jobs for the boys. This is often a contributory factor in the generally poor performance of state-controlled banks.

It should come as no surprise, given the controlling party's interests, to find that most state banks can be characterized as follows. They are highly hierarchical with limited delegation of decision making and a distinct lack of individuals prepared to take responsibilities for decisions or initiative. They are not customer driven and have poor service levels. Listed state-controlled banks generally trade at a significant discount to private sector banks because their operating profitability is lower, they have inferior asset quality and higher levels of unrecognized credit losses. Finally there is always the risk that minority shareholders will be hurt in a future government directive. The following diagram summarizes the key characteristics of listed private and public sector banks.

Listed bank characteristics

No overall control

* Common form in Anglo-Saxon countries

* Limit of 5% on shareholding level

* Returns (ROE) and EPS growth focus

* Mantra - "shareholder value"

* Quality of management key

* May be difficult for shareholder activists to influence management behavior

* Management compensation schemes distorted by asymmetry of returns

* Ill-managed banks tend to get taken over

Family controlled

* Common in many developing markets

* Control rarely lasts more than two generations

* Conservative & risk averse, lower returns & higher CARs than other banks

* Close attention to costs but slow to embrace change

* Difficult to attract & retain quality professional staff

* Control reinforced via cross holding structures

* Little concern for minorities but rarely actively looking to pull a fast one at their expense

Majority control

* Majority shareholder may be conglomerate or have stakes in other companies

* Prohibited in most developed markets

* Moral hazards abound

* Related lending - loans to companies owned by majority shareholder

* Circumvention of single borrower limits, more favorable terms, collateral cover, credit appraisal, fees etc.

* Risk of asset sales/purchases between bank & related companies

* Minority shareholders at significant risk

PUBLIC SECTOR

* Common in developing markets becoming less common in OECD

* Act to support government policies
  - Directed lending
  - Stock market support
  - Free banking & minimum retail deposit rates
  - Subsidized lending rates
  - Support for lame ducks

* Poor asset quality, underreported but high NPLs, returns secondary objective

* Inefficient & bureaucratic

* Politician support
  - Secret accounts
  - Money laundering
  - Transfer of funds offshore

* Patronage - political appointments

In quantitative terms they usually have below average interest spreads, below average non-interest income as a proportion of operating income, poor efficiency ratios and lower capital adequacy ratios than private sector banks. They tend to understate the level of actual non-performing loans (NPLs) and this frequently leads to the need for periodic recapitalization due to credit or trading losses.

19

Bank Acquisitions

Hostile bids are a bonanza for the shareholders of the acquiree, they add to the income and status of the acquirer's management, and they are a honey pot for the investment bankers and other professionals on both sides. But, alas they usually reduce the wealth of the acquirer's shareholders, often to a substantial extent.

Warren Buffet, portfolio manager

Around the world there are pressures driving banking sector consolidation. Some of these pressures come from the inherent advantages that size can (but does not necessarily) afford but other pressures are political in nature. The latter is particularly prevalent in developing markets where domestic banks have been protected from foreign competition through regulatory barriers to entry and those barriers are being steadily eroded as a result of WTO liberalization. We examine the economic incentives in terms of cost savings, revenue enhancements and strategic benefits. We will also look at management incentives and how their misalignment with shareholders' interests can lead to value destroying actions on the part of management.

We will also look at the practical constraints imposed on cash offers and the fundamental constraints on the cash part of any bid that may be imposed by regulatory capital requirements. We look at how acquisitions are accounted for and at the treatment of goodwill. Finally we look at the impact of acquisitions on valuations.

ACQUISITIONS

Consolidation Pressures

Banking industry consolidation has been an ongoing reality in many countries for over a century. In the past two decades the pace of consolidation among larger banks has accelerated. This can be explained by looking at the worldwide pressures for consolidation:

- **Interest rate liberalization.** Banks have always been highly regulated and continue to be so, but in many countries there has been a move to liberalize measures that impeded competition between banks. Individual banks are allowed to set their own lending and deposit rates rather than following rates set by regulators or banking cartels. This liberalization has put downward pressure on spreads and profitability.
- **Lower barriers to entry.** In many countries banks face increasing competition from non-bank institutions in areas that had traditionally been the exclusive preserve of banks. The pricing of credit risk has always been a core banking competency, but insurance companies have moved into this arena by selling credit derivatives and loan guarantees. Auto manufacturers provide the bulk of auto financing in many countries. Many relatively small, developing countries are being forced to lower barriers to entry, such as restrictions on branching, to foreign banks as a result of World Trade Organization (WTO) agreements.
- **Disintermediation.** The wider range of financing options available to corporates has eroded banks' role as intermediaries. Capital markets provide a means for corporate borrowers to

go directly to investors, bypassing banks. Corporates can also use techniques such as asset securitization to reduce their asset base and hence financing needs. There are also more alternatives to bank deposits for savings. These include money market funds, direct investment in the stock market, mutual funds and investment products from insurance companies such as life insurance policies and annuities.

- **Scale economies.** All of the above factors have made price more important. This in turn has forced banks to lower unit transaction costs to maintain profitability and earnings growth. As banks have become more automated there has been a shift in terms of cost structure. The level of fixed costs versus variable costs has been, and will continue, to rise. This encourages the formation of larger banks as they seek to spread these fixed costs over a larger number of transactions.

  The absolute entry price, in terms of upfront investments in systems, has risen sharply. As smaller banks struggle to make the investments necessary to maintain their competitive position they become increasingly willing to consider offers.

- **Economies of scope.** Larger banks can offer a wider range of products to customers than smaller banks. This can be measured in terms of the number of different products sold each year on average to each customer. A bank selling four to six products to each customer on average each year is clearly leveraging its customer base more than one selling only two to three products.

  Larger banks can also afford to pay skilled specialists to develop advanced products that may only be attractive to a relatively small proportion of customers. The development of such products is only possible when a bank has a capability in a number of diverse areas.

- **Credit risk diversification.** As credit risk management techniques and internal capital allocation policies have developed the recognition that credit risk diversification reduces the level of unexpected losses and capital requirements has grown. Single market banks are exposed to higher levels of concentration risk and this puts them at a pricing disadvantage to well-diversified banks.

- **Government and regulatory pressure.** Governments and central banks in many developing countries have put pressure on their domestic banks to merge and consolidate. This is intended to ensure that some domestic banks will be able to compete with more advanced foreign banks once full liberalization takes place.

  In many Asian countries banking industries have been highly fragmented. Indonesia, for example, had more than 150 commercial banks before the Asian financial crisis hit. This made it virtually impossible for the central bank to supervise them given its limited resources even if its personnel had had the skills and integrity to do so (and they didn't).

- **Shareholder pressure.** Investors, both domestic and international, in many markets have stepped up pressure on banks' management to set and meet or exceed future performance targets. These normally translate into generating a return above the bank's cost-of-equity and a target level of earnings growth. Individual bank performance is usually monitored against the performance of the bank's peer group.

  There are active investors who seek out companies that are performing poorly, but are capable of being turned around, and take significant stakes to force management to take corrective action. This is very difficult to do at banks because most regulators impose a 5% limit on the level of any individual shareholder holding. Investors tend to simply vote with their feet and sell their holdings in such banks. This is likely to push the target's stock price down and leave the bank more vulnerable to a hostile bid.

Cost Savings

The actual level of cost savings that banks are able to achieve from in-market mergers is usually in a range between 25% and 40% of the target's operating expenses. These savings tend to be highest when the acquirer is much larger than the target and when there is a high degree of geographic overlap. Examples of specific savings that are typically identified include the following:

- **Closure of co-located branches.** In the case of in-market mergers where both banks have a significant presence, many branches from the two banks are likely to be co-located. Branches of different banks tend to cluster with a high concentration in town and business centers. These co-located branches can be closed and staff laid off.
- **Elimination of duplicate administrative head office functions.** These include departments such as the finance division, internal audit, human resources, payroll, investor relations and facilities management. The number of people required to work in these functions does not scale with the size of a bank's balance sheet.
- **Rationalization of IT and processing divisions.** Duplicate data centers, call centers, networks and settlement departments can be rationalized. Again these are largely fixed cost operations.
- **Other savings.** Other savings include external audit, director fees, advertising and marketing expenses, regulatory reporting and compliance costs.

Government restrictions, political pressures and the strength of bank unions in some countries may impose constraints on the ability of the acquirer's management to make cost savings from job losses.

These ongoing cost savings will be offset to an extent by the costs involved in the rationalization. In most cases the largest part of these costs comes from redundancy payments. As most severance terms are based on length of service and current salary these will tend to be higher at banks with a low historic turnover of staff and higher wage bill.

It is reasonably easy for analysts to judge, after the event, whether management succeeded in achieving their targeted benefits. The operating expense line is one of the easier line items for analysts to forecast. Simply comparing the future actual operating expenses against the total of those forecast for the two banks separately will show the extent to which the identified cost savings have been achieved.

Revenue Enhancements

Out-of-market takeovers are usually justified on the grounds of revenue enhancements or on strategic grounds. Targeted revenue synergies are fequently, though not always, less tangible than hard cost savings. In general opportunities may exist when the following apply:

- **Cross-selling.** This is one of the most common justifications for takeovers where the acquirer or target is operating in different markets, whether those markets are different geographically or different in terms of financial services segment. A bank acquiring an insurance company or a fund manager is likely to make much of its opportunity to sell the insurance company's or fund manager's products to its existing bank customer base.

Where the two entities are in the same business management will claim that each bank has some expertise or product line that the other bank either does not have or with which it has a relative weakness. An example would be where the acquirer claims a better understanding of selling consumer finance products than the target bank.

- **Marketing benefits.** Marketing benefits arise when both target and acquirer are operating in the same business segment and spend heavily on marketing and advertising. If the spend is maintained but focused on one brand only it is likely to be more effective.
- **Scale benefits.** Some operations, such as Treasury, require a certain critical mass to operate effectively. If properly managed, greater scale can result in an increase in revenues without a corresponding increase in costs.
- **Disposal of assets.** The acquirer may be able to extract value by selling operating assets that are no longer required such as the target's head office and redundant branches. This will allow the capital that is tied up in these assets to be used more productively.
- **Equity and associate disposals.** In addition to actual gains benefits may be derived from a restructuring of assets from both target and acquirer prior to disposals. It may be possible, for example, to inject assets from the acquirer into the target's associates to make them more attractive to potential buyers. It is also possible that there are listed subsidiaries or associates trading below NAV (net asset value) where value can be unlocked.

Strategic Benefits

Most acquirers will try to justify acquisitions to their shareholders by first identifying quantified projected cost savings and revenue synergies and second by pointing to how the acquisition fits into their overall strategy. This is usually the case even if these arguments are presented in the opposite order at investor presentations. It is difficult to think of a case where management recommended an acquisition and didn't say that there was a sound strategic fit.

There are, however, a number of occasions when management justifies an acquisition largely on strategic grounds, rather than value. These include the following:

- **Remove a competitor.** Most companies praise competition because it spurs them on to innovate more and become more efficient. They then do everything in their power to reduce or eliminate such competition. Banks are no exception. It may make sense to acquire a competitor simply to reduce the level of competition. This may allow them to enjoy what economists refer to as monopoly profits or at least to increase the effective power of an oligopoly. Governments, regulators and monopoly commissions tend to frown on such acquisitions.
- **Improve competitive position.** Two banks may agree to combine in order to take a dominant position in a particular market or business segment. Higher market shares tend to give greater pricing powers.
- **Protect competitive position.** If three banks, of similar size, are operating in the same market and one bank makes a bid for another the third bank has little choice. It must launch a counterbid, if it can, or risk being marginalized. The unspoken argument that management make is that even though a higher counterbid may destroy shareholder value the level of destruction would have been even higher if it had not acted.

- **Once-in-a-lifetime opportunity.** As we have already noted, many countries have erected regulatory barriers to entry, imposed restrictions on branching, limited the level of foreign ownership in domestic banks and prohibited foreign banks from taking over local banks. Domestic financial crises often require foreign capital to resolve. This may provide opportunities for foreign banks to acquire domestic banks. Those barriers may be reimposed once the crisis is over, slamming the door in the face of other interested foreign banks.
- **Dealing with weaknesses.** A bank that finds that it had failed to identify the area of greatest potential future growth and profitability may find that it has little choice than to look for acquisition candidates. This can also be the result of a change in the regulatory environment. A bank may find that it is able to undertake a business that had previously been disallowed. It these cases it may be better to buy the necessary expertise and customer base rather than to try to build them itself. In such cases sellers generally extract a heavy control premium.
- **Buying market share.** In business segments where scale is important, banks may attempt to buy market share in order to achieve a position of dominance. This works in segments where the industry dynamics are changing and there is a bifurcation between very large players and niche operators with middle ranking companies finding their competitive position deteriorating. In such instances the need to have scale and critical mass results in barriers to entry that allows the incumbents to generate super-economic returns.
- **Filling the gaps.** International banks may be able to generate additional synergies from having a global network. The acquisition of a bank in a country where a global bank has only a token presence may be justified on strategic grounds, on the benefits to the network as a whole, rather than on a stand-alone basis.

Management Incentives

When the management of the acquirer makes a bid for a company and management at the target recommends acceptance both parties will argue that they are acting in the best interests of their respective shareholders. It is possible that both are correct but more likely that one has either overpaid or one sold too cheaply. The former probably occurs more frequently than the latter. In most cases it is better to be a shareholder in a company that is acquired than in the one making the acquisition.

Nevertheless there are examples of bank acquisitions where the acquirer has extracted value and this has been recognized in terms of subsequent price performance. It is possible that these occur more frequently in acquisitions involving banks than in other sectors (but would be very difficult to demonstrate conclusively). There are two reasons why this might be the case.

The first concerns the effect that the standard 5% shareholder limit has in preventing "organic" changes in mediocre management. The second is that many acquisitions occur in circumstances of a forced sale. A bank with sufficient experience of making acquisitions of distressed banks is likely to have a better insight into the risks of, and potential upside, from such a deal than other potential bidders.

Although private sector banks are supposed to be run for the benefit of shareholders there are frequently powerful, personal incentives for the various stakeholders and other players. These include the following:

- **Management at the acquirer.** Management at the acquiring bank gain status from being in charge of a bigger bank. There is also a high correlation between bank size and executive and directors' total remuneration. In some cases management have been paid bonuses simply for making an acquisition rather than for achieving the targeted benefits. There may also be an incentive for them to overstate the level of synergies that can be achieved in order to justify the bid price.

- **Management at the target.** Most successful bids are made at a significant premium to the current market price of the target bank. Senior executives at the target bank are likely to have been given share options in the bank's stock as part of their remuneration. The value of these options is hence inflated by a bid. This can create an incentive for management to accept a bid. They are also in a position to negotiate a severance package (golden parachute) before recommending acceptance to shareholders.
- **Investment bankers.** Investment bankers and other professionals earn huge fees from advising both the target and the acquirer. The level of these fees is usually conditional on the deal going through.

Management still needs to "justify" their actions to shareholders. The management of the acquirer usually points to cost savings, revenue enhancements or strategic benefits as justifications for paying a steep control premium.

Management at target banks usually succeeds in generating a take-out price that is well above the value of the bank as a stand-alone business. They frequently extract a control premium that is well above the present value of the projected synergies.

In many bids the acquirer only needs board-level approval to proceed. Where shareholders' approval has to be sought bids may leave shareholders at the acquirer in a quandary. They may feel that their management is overpaying but recognize that if they vote to reject the offer then this is tantamount to a no-confidence vote. This may have a greater negative impact on the bank's stock price than supporting the bid.

An in-market takeover is one in which the acquirer already operates in the same market as the target. An out-of-market takeover is one in which the two banks are operating in different markets. Cost savings are usually the main justification for in-market bank takeovers while revenue synergies and strategic benefits are usually the main justifications for out-of-market takeovers.

BARRIERS TO TAKEOVERS

There are two principal barriers to takeovers. The first are those resulting from regulatory and political constraints and competition concerns and the second from attempts by controlling shareholders to protect themselves from the effects of hostile takeover bids.

Regulatory and Political Constraints

The main regulatory and political constraints on takeovers arise from concerns about foreign ownership, monopolistic effects and job losses:

- **Foreign ownership.** Most countries aim to maintain control of the bulk of the domestic banking system in local hands. There are at least three possible reasons why this may be the case:
  - **Central bank influence.** It is much easier for central banks to apply moral suasion to banks that are locally owned.

- **Stability.** There are often concerns that because foreign banks owe no particular loyalty at the first signs of financial system stress they will cut back exposures and that such action will increase the level of instability.
- **Xenophobia.** Few countries are exempt from political exploitation of xenophobic tendencies. The usual criticism made of governments that seek to attract foreign capital by allowing foreign banks to takeover local banks is that they are being sold too cheaply, will lead to huge job losses and make it harder for customers to borrow from banks.

- **Monopolies.** As consolidation proceeds, and the level of concentration of a banking industry increases, monopoly and competition concerns become more important. When bids are subject to formal competition or anti-trust inquiries they are usually far ranging and go well beyond simple considerations of total market share of loans or deposits. They will usually consider the potential impact in terms of local monopolies and on particular customer segments such as small and medium enterprises.
- **Job losses.** In-market takeovers are usually justified on the grounds of cost savings. Job losses are always a sensitive matter and if they take place at a time of generally high unemployment levels this sensitivity is heightened. Pressures are likely to be exerted to block bids or make them conditional on the acquirer making significant concessions in this area.

We have already looked at the use of foreign and local classes of shares to prevent foreign interests from owning a majority of the shares of local banks. Most bank regulators have to approve any individual holding of a bank in excess of 5% of issued shares. They usually also have the power to turn down proposed board and senior management appointments. They thereby have the legal power to block any takeover bid. Few bids are actually made where the potential acquirer has not talked about a possible bid with the main bank regulator and been given an informal nod of approval. The results of political factors and those of monopoly inquiries are less certain.

A real business constraint on cross-border acquisitions is that imposed by the consequences of different currencies and regulatory environments. In Euroland that is changing and we should expect to see more European cross-border acquisitions over time now that the single currency has been well established and national central banks have lost their powers to manage money supply. Even in the case of Euroland, however, different national supervisory and regulatory conditions still exist and there is no single clearing and payments system and these will tend to moderate the pace of the consolidation that appears inevitable there.

Defensive Ownership Structures

There are many examples of banks that are both listed and controlled by a single family. Many of today's largest banks have their roots in a family-controlled bank. Family-controlled banks tend to have a fairly clear lifecycle. In the early years an individual starts a bank using his own capital and that of a few other business associates, family members and close friends. As the bank grows, however, it soon becomes clear that the bank cannot generate enough capital internally to grow as fast as the family would like. Having already put all of their own capital into the bank they have a need to raise capital from external sources, and this means going public and raising additional equity.

The problem that the founder faces is one of dilution and possible future loss of control. It is at this time that he looks at way's to maintain effective control without having to maintain the same level of his economic interest. Many of these banks developed cross-holding structures with associates to achieve this end. The following example shows how a controlling party is able to increase its effective control above that of its actual economic interest. The controlling shareholder owns only 10% of the bank, but the bank has a 20% controlling interest in an associate that also owns 10% of the bank. The controlling shareholder's economic interest in the bank is 12% but the cross-holding structure means that the effective control is 20%.

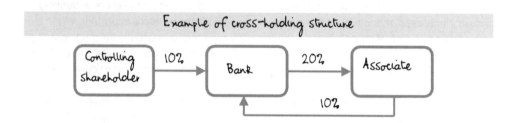

In countries such as the USA where such structures are prohibited it may seem surprising that such structures are quite common in Asia, Latin America and parts of Europe. Where new laws are passed that prohibit such structures current structures are often "grandfathered". In other words, companies that already have such structure are allowed to maintain the status quo provided they were created prior to the enactment of the prohibition.

It was tempting to use a real example, where the cross-holding structure looks very much like a circuit diagram, but all that the complexity would illustrate is the extent to which some controlling shareholders will try to cling to control. The basic techniques are the same, however, and are better shown with a simpler example. Where such structures do exist it usually requires considerable legwork to identify all of the cross-holding relationships. The controlling bank shareholder has no interest in making this easy and it is normally necessary to go to the published financial reports of associates and related companies to find out their holdings in the bank.

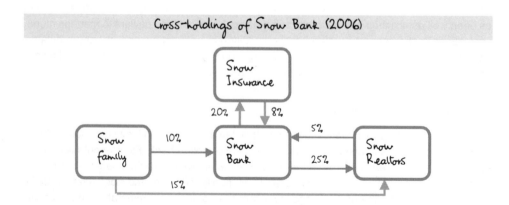

In this example the Snow family has a direct investment in the bank equivalent to 10% of the bank's equity. This is the family's direct economic interest in the bank. It also has an indirect economic interest of 3.1%. The family's effective control is, however, 23.1%, as shown in the following table.

Snow family economic interests versus effective control				
	Economic interest in Snow Bank		Effective control	
	Direct	Indirect	Total	
Snow Insurance	0%	$10\% \times 20\% \times 8\% = 1.6\%$	1.6%	8%
Snow Realtors	$15\% \times 5\% = 0.75\%$	$10\% \times 25\% \times 5\% = 0.75\%$	1.5%	5%
Snow Bank			10.0%	10.0%
Total			**13.1%**	**23.1%**

Other Measures

Other measures used in the past are the creation of two classes of shares with the same economic rights but different voting weights. These are still permitted in some developed countries but are becoming less common as institutional investors have campaigned about their existence and effect.

There are egregious cases where the most obvious factor has been the desire of management at a firm to protect their own, rather than shareholders', interests. The following is based on a real-life example:

- Company A has made an agreed cash and paper bid for Company B requiring approval from both sets of shareholders.
- Company A itself has then been subject to a hostile cash bid from Company C at a modest premium to market price.
- Management at Company A have responded to this bid by increasing the cash part of their takeover offer for Company B while reducing the paper part of the offer.

The effect of the changed terms of the initial offer by Company A for Company B in this case is as follows. The reduction in the amount of paper involved meant that management at Company A no longer required approval from its own shareholders for the bid to proceed. The higher level of cash meant that Company B shareholders were more likely to accept the revised offer.

If this first bid went through then the absolute dollar amount that company C would have to pay to acquire the two companies together would increase, stretching its ability to finance its bid without taking on more debt. In addition it would have the problem of trying to integrate two companies rather than one.

Management at Company A tried to argue that they were acting in the interests of their shareholders but their very actions took away the shareholders' rights to decide this for themselves. People become increasingly creative when their own interests are threatened. The above is simply one example of such creativity at work.

PAYMENT AND FINANCING OPTIONS

There are three broad payment options available to potential acquirers. The first is an all-cash offer, the second an all-paper offer in which the currency of the bid is the stock of the issuer and the third some combination of these two methods.

All-cash Offers

All-cash offers are relatively common when the acquirer is much larger than the target. As target and acquirer become larger, however, are of similar size, have similar capital adequacy and NPL ratios they become increasingly rare. The cash required for the purchase may be obtained from liquidation of assets or by borrowing. The decision on which financing method to use for a cash offer may be constrained in a number of ways and be influenced by the cost of borrowing.

If paid for through asset liquidation the acquirer must be able to liquidate sufficient assets to pay the agreed price without their sale having a material negative impact on the market prices of these assets. The main classes of assets that may provide sources of cash are as follows:

- **Long interbank positions.** Banks that have an excess of non-bank deposits and long net interbank position may be able to finance the acquisition by reducing this position. The extent to which this is possible depends on the size and depth of the money markets. Management will also have to take account how this would impact on the bank's overall asset-liability management. In most cases this is unlikely to provide more than a small proportion of the overall consideration.
- **Government and other securities.** Another option may be to sell government securities. The viability of this option depends on how much the bank holds and the depth and liquidity of the secondary market. In some countries there are regulatory requirements concerning the level of government securities a bank must hold. This may be an additional constraint.
- **Customer loans.** The bulk of most types of customer loans are relatively illiquid. In developed markets it may be possible to raise cash by securitization of loans such as mortgages, car loans and credit card receivables. But in many countries this is not a viable option and cannot usually be done quickly.
- **Other assets.** The sale or securitization of any commercial real estate held (probably obtained following foreclosures) or the bank's own premises to finance an acquisition are unlikely to provide a viable option.

In practice other than in case of a very large, well-capitalized bank buying a smaller bank it is virtually impossible to pay the consideration in cash without turning to debt markets:

- **Interbank market.** There are many fundamental problems with using the interbank market to finance an acquisition. These include, but are not limited to, the following:
  - **Depth.** In most countries the interbank market is unlikely to have the depth or liquidity to be able to provide such funds for anything other than the smallest of acquisitions. It is also a very short-term form of financing.
  - **Credit lines.** When in-market takeovers take place other banks will cut the combined credit lines to the new entity. (This is one of those cases where two plus two does not add up to four.) As already discussed, controlling credit risk is largely a matter of the management of risk concentration. The credit lines that other banks will provide the new entity will be less than the combined total of the two original entities.
  - **Maturity mismatch.** Using the interbank market for acquisitions also leaves the acquirer exposed to significant maturity, liquidity and interest rate risks.

The interbank market can only really be used for modest amounts of short-term funding and even here there are real risks.

- **Subordinated debt and preference shares.** These types of long-dated debt instruments are the most common form of paper used for financing acquisitions. The main issues that have to be dealt with by both issuer and investors are:
  - The seniority of the debt in the event of the bank failing or being closed by regulators. The presence of any capital protection guarantees from third parties and the credit quality of the guarantor.
  - The eligibility of the debt to count towards regulatory capital adequacy requirements.
  - The pricing and term of the issued instrument and the likely liquidity of the instrument in the secondary market.

Many people confuse excess capital with excess cash. Just because an acquirer has a relatively high Tier I ratio does not necessarily mean that an all-cash bid is viable. The important point to note in all of this is that when we talk about the financing of a cash offer by one bank for another we are referring to issues relating to how it will be able to pay out the consideration in the equivalent of cash. The matter of how the deal impacts on the acquirer's capital position is completely separate.

All-paper and Hybrid Offers

All-paper offers, where the acquirer offers a certain number of its own shares in exchange for all of the target's shares, are the only practical method that can be used to finance a takeover of one relatively large bank by another. I use the word "relatively" deliberately. A relatively large bank in most African, Asian and Latin American countries is still relatively small compared with a relatively small bank in the US or Western Europe. All-paper offers are relatively uncommon for cross-border acquisitions.

All-paper offers involve the bidder offering a certain number of its own shares, usually new shares to be issued conditional on the bid proceeding, in return for a stated number of the shares in the target company. The value of these bids varies over the course of the takeover process as the prices of the bidder's and target's stock changes. Most of the detail concerning the execution of an all-paper offer is covered later in this chapter in an acquisition case study comparing the two principal payment methods.

Hybrid offers are made in part in the form of paper and in part in cash. The cash part of the offer is usually seen as a "sweetener". It also reduces the level of uncertainty in terms of the actual price that the selling shareholders will receive.

BANK ACQUISITION ACCOUNTING

Acquisition accounting for banks is no different than for other corporates. Prior to the accounting scandals that came to light in the US after the end of the 1990s technology boom it would have appeared fair to assume that goodwill is a more important consideration in bank takeovers than in corporate takeovers. That is, however, still the case in most of the rest of the world. Goodwill is defined as follows:

$$Goodwill = Price\ paid\ by\ acquirer\ for\ target - Appraised\ net\ asset\ value\ of\ target$$

Accountancy books also define goodwill as the value of a firm's intangible assets. These include the estimated value of the target's brands, patents, licenses and management reputation. Estimating the value of intangible assets is clearly a subjective exercise but, as we have shown, this is also the case with a number of tangible assets, such as loans, where no market price can be determined readily.

There are three different accounting treatments for goodwill, which are, or have been, applied in different countries around the world at some time or another. The lack of agreement on how to go about accounting for goodwill was highlighted in late 2001 when US GAAP was revised at a time when other countries were adopting the former US standard. The three methods are as follows:

- **Capitalize goodwill.** This is the current US accounting standard. Goodwill is left on the balance sheet unless there is reason to believe that the value of an acquisition has fallen below the price paid. This was the case with many telecommunications and technology acquisitions at the turn of the century.
- **Capitalize and amortize goodwill.** The former US standard required acquirers to capitalize goodwill at the time of purchase but to write off the goodwill over the course of 20–30 years. A company paying $1.8bn for a target with a net asset value of $1.2bn could therefore take an annual charge of $20m for 30 years until the goodwill of $600m was written off. This method has the effect of inflating the book value, lowering reported earnings and deflating reported *ROE*.
- **Write off goodwill immediately.** In some countries acquirers are allowed to write off goodwill directly against their equity account. This lowers the book value but also pushes up the return on equity.

Most equity analysts had already adopted the current US standard. Goodwill reflects an investment in the business. Any goodwill charge taken through the earnings statement is a non-cash item, and when reported analysts normally simply reverse it.

It is slightly more complicated at banks than other companies because of the impact of goodwill on regulatory capital, and we will return to this issue. There are two important points to note about bank acquisitions:

- **Payment means affects everything.** The method of payment (cash, paper, cash and paper) will affect cash earnings, cash earnings per share, *ROE*, Tier I capital and Tier I ratios.
- **Accounting treatment does not affect cash EPS.** The accounting treatment for goodwill has no impact on cash earnings but does have an impact on reported book value and earnings.

All-cash offers only work when the acquirer is either much larger than the target or has a great deal of excess capital. The main regulatory constraint is that imposed by Tier I requirements. We need to use an example to show how these affect the viability of an all-cash offer.

ACQUISITION CASE STUDY

I have avoided the use of case studies as much as possible in this book but in terms of looking at the detail of acquisitions a case study provides the simplest way to illustrate the most important features. The background to this case study is as follows.

Acquisition case study background

Amalgamated Bank Corp (ABC) operates throughout the country and is considering an all-cash offer for a much smaller regional bank, Second Provincial Bank (SPB). ABC operates in the same regional market as SPB and as such this is an in-market acquisition. There is a high degree of overlap in terms of branches but minimal overlap in terms of customers.

ABC is four times as large as SPB. To keep this case study simple we will assume that the balance sheet structures of the two banks are identical.

Both banks currently have Tier I ratios of 8.8%. ABC bank is unwilling to allow its Tier I ratio to fall below 5%, giving it only a 100 bpt buffer over the minimum requirement. Both banks have issued hybrid Tier I capital up to the 15% of Tier I equity allowed by the banks' regulator.

ABC has an *ROE* of 14.8% while SPB's is somewhat lower at 12.6%. This is due to a lower level of non-interest income as a proportion of operating income.

ABC has two ways in which it may finance the acquisition. It can make an all-cash offer or offer an all-paper share swap. In the case of an all-cash offer, ABC will finance the acquisition by issuing 10-year bonds with a yield of 6%. The market cost of equity is estimated to be 10%.

Assuming that these *ROE*s are sustainable and long-run growth of 4%, this gives a fair price-to-book ratio of 1.8× for ABC and fair value base perpetuity targets of $19.84 (1.8 × 10.6 × 1.04) and 1.43× for SPB and fair value target of $15.76.

There is significant scope for cost savings from branch closures and rationalization at the SPB head office. ABC management estimates that the equivalent of 40% of SPB's operating costs can be saved. In addition the minimal customer overlap means that revenue attrition is likely to be small, at 4% of SPB's operating income. ABC knows that for a bid to succeed it will need to pay a control premium.

Both ABC's and SPB's book value is $10.60. ABC's stock is trading at $19 and that of SPB's at $16. ABC has offered $20 per share, a 25% premium to the current price of SPB.

Impact on the Reported Balance Sheet

The following table shows how the balance sheet of the combined entity would look after a successful acquisition depending on whether it proceeded by way of an all-cash or all-paper offer. The important things to note are as follows:

- **Offer terms.** The $20 per share cash offer is worth $25bn and we have assumed this is financed through the issue of the same amount in long-term debt. With ABC's current share price at $19 it will have to offer 1389m shares in ABC to make an equivalent all-paper offer or 1111 ABC shares for each 1000 shares held in SPB.

- **Goodwill.** The $25bn offer is $11.75bn greater than SPB's net tangible assets of $13.25bn and is booked as goodwill on the asset side of the balance sheet.
- **Shareholders' funds.** In the case of the all-cash offer there is no impact on ABC's reported shareholders' funds. These remain unchanged, as do its book value and net tangible assets per share at $10.60 per share.

  The impact of the all-paper bid is as follows. The par value of ABC's shares is $1. The share capital account is increased by $1389m and the share premium account by $23 611m ($18 × 1389m). Total reported shareholders' funds increase from $53bn to $78bn, book value per share rises to $12.21 but net tangible assets per share fall to $10.37.
- **Other assets and liabilities.** Assets and liabilities that are not affected by the financing of the acquisition are simply added together. As the all-paper deal has no cash component all of these can simply be consolidated.

Impact on balance sheet of all-cash and all-paper acquisition ($m)				
Assets	**ABC**	**SPB**	**All cash**	**All paper**
Liquid assets	100 000	25 000	125 000	125 000
Loans	800 000	200 000	1 000 000	1 000 000
Other assets	20 000	5 000	25 000	25 000
Goodwill	0	0	11 750	11 750
Total assets	**920 000**	**230 000**	**1 161 750**	**1 161 750**
Liabilities				
Deposits	829 050	207 263	1 036 313	1 036 313
Other liabilities	30 000	7 500	37 500	37 500
Hybrid Tier I capital	7 950	1 988	9 938	9 938
Long-term borrowing	0	0	25 000	0
Total non-equity liabilities	**867 000**	**216 750**	**1 108 750**	**1 083 750**
Share capital	5 000	1 250	5 000	6 389
Share premium	8 000	2 000	8 000	31 611
Retained earnings	40 000	10 000	40 000	40 000
Shareholders' funds	53 000	13 250	53 000	78 000
Total liabilities	**920 000**	**230 000**	**1 161 750**	**1 161 750**
Reported book per share ($)	10.60	10.60	10.60	12.21
Net tangible assets per share ($)	10.60	10.60	10.60	10.37

Impact on the Capital Adequacy Ratios

While the method of financing of the acquisition is important, the impact on Tier I capital adequacy requirements is usually the ultimate constraint on the actual cash value of the offer. This in turn constrains the way in which an offer is structured between cash and paper. The following three factors have to be taken into account:

- **Risk weighted assets.** After the acquisition risk-weighted assets will simply be the sum of ABC's and SPB's risk-weighted assets, assuming the cash offer is funded by issuing debt and that the acquirer doesn't act to either sell off or securitize its assets. We will assume that regulators give goodwill a zero risk weighting. Total risk-weighted assets are the same whether the offer is all cash, all paper or a combination. This will not be the case if part of the cash offer comes from asset sales.

- **Goodwill.** Regulators require unamortized goodwill to be subtracted from shareholders' funds when calculating Tier I equity.
- **Hybrid equity.** In this example we have assumed that regulators allow hybrid equity to count towards total Tier I capital but only up to a maximum 15% of its Tier I equity. Here it makes a big difference whether the offer is cash or paper:
- **All-cash offer.** In the all-cash offer the equity account simply represents that of ABC. After subtracting goodwill from reported equity its Tier I equity falls from $53bn to $41.25bn. Although it has hybrid Tier I equity of nearly $10bn, its lower Tier I equity means that it can only count $4425m of this towards its total Tier I capital ratio. As a result of these two factors its Tier I capital ratio falls from 8.83% to 5.30%.
- **All-paper offer.** In the all-paper offer, shareholders' fund rise from $53bn to $78bn which means after goodwill its Tier I equity increases to $66.25bn. The impact of subtracting goodwill means that, although its Tier I hybrid equity increases from $7.95bn to $8.175bn, it is left with $1.8bn in hybrid equity that it cannot count towards its regulatory Tier I ratio. The total Tier I ratio falls slightly from 8.83% to 8.63%.

Impact on risk-weighted assets and Tier I ratios ($m)				
	ABC	**SPB**	**All cash**	**All paper**
Risk-weighted assets	690 000	172 500	862 500	862 500
Shareholders' funds	53 000	13 250	53 000	78 000
Less goodwill			−11 750	−11 750
Tier I equity	**53 000**	**13 250**	**41 250**	**66 250**
Allowable hybrid Tier I capital	7 950	1 988	4 425	8 175
Total Tier I capital	**60 950**	**15 238**	**45 675**	**74 425**
Tier I ratio	**8.83%**	**8.83%**	**5.30%**	**8.63%**

At an all-cash offer of $21.50, the new entity's Tier I falls to 5%, setting an absolute limit on an all-cash offer unless it raises additional equity from its shareholders to fund the acquisition.

There is no practical constraint from Tier I requirements, in this example, on the level of an all-paper offer. At an offer level of $4\times$ book the Tier I would still be more than 8.1%. At this level the SPB shareholders would own 37% of ABC.

Impact on the Earnings Statement

We will assume that the acquisition takes place at the end of the acquirer's year-end. We will also assume that it is able to generate its targeted cost savings and suffers revenue attrition from day one. The reality, of course, is more complex. It takes time to complete the detailed planning of the integration and the job cuts are likely to take place over a period of up to a year after the acquisition. In addition there will be costs associated with the integration. Most acquirers end up taking a one-off restructuring charge to cover the costs of the redundancy package and accelerated depreciation on assets, such as computers, that are no longer required.

The size of the restructuring charge will vary from case to case and will depend, to an extent, on how the tax authorities treat the charge. If management makes no statement on how large a charge it proposes to make a reasonable first approximation is that the charge will be equivalent to one year's cost savings.

The impact on the earnings statement for the full year is shown below. We have attributed the revenue attrition to non-interest income but in reality this would come from both net interest income and non-interest income. The net profit in the case of the all-cash offer is lower than that in the case of the all-paper offer because of the increase in its long-term borrowing.

Impact on forecast cash earnings statement of acquisition ($m)				
	ABC	**SPB**	**All cash**	**All paper**
Net interest income (P/F)	24150	6038	30188	30188
Financing costs			−1500	0
Net interest income	**24150**	**6038**	**28688**	**30188**
Non-interest income (P/F)	14490	2415	16905	16905
Revenue attrition			−338	− 338
Non-interest income	**14490**	**2415**	**16567**	**16567**
Operating income	38640	8453	45254	**46754**
Operating expenses (P/F)	−23184	−5072	−28256	−28256
Cost savings			1521	1521
Operating expenses	**−23184**	**−5072**	**−26734**	**−26734**
Operating profit	**15456**	**3381**	**18520**	**20020**
Bad debt charge	−2400	−600	−3000	−3000
Profit before tax	**13056**	**2781**	**15520**	**17020**
Income tax	−5222	−1112	−6208	−6808
Net profit	**7834**	**1669**	**9312**	**10212**

Note: P/F denotes pro-forma basis, the numbers for the two banks have simply been added together.

By itself the earnings statement tells us little, but is a first step in trying to determine whether either the cash offer or the paper offer adds value.

Impact on Valuations

Using this approach and our standard DDM framework and assuming a 10% *COE* we get the following. Under the all-cash offer ABC's EPS increases and as a consequence its PE falls. Its *ROE* increases and with its book unchanged its fair value increases from approximately $20 to $25, assuming 4% long-run growth. The all-cash offer appears to add shareholder value.

Under the terms of the all-paper offer there is a modest increase in EPS but ABC's *ROE* falls and although its book value rises the overall effect on our fair value target is that it drops from $19.84 to $19.26. It appears that this method results in a destruction of shareholder value. In the case of an acquisition financed solely with paper a simple method to estimate the new cost-of-equity is to use a (pre-bid) market-cap weighted cost-of-equity for the two banks, where there is an element of cash the matter of the appropriate cost-of-equity to use is more problematic.

It is not immediately obvious why ABC's fair value target falls in the event of an all-paper offer when our analysis suggests that despite dilutive effects the deal is EPS accretive. When using any valuation method it is important to remember the implicit assumptions built into the method. In this instance the key implicit assumption is that the level of gearing remains the same.

That assumption is not necessarily valid in this case. The real gearing constraint on ABC is that imposed by its Tier I capital adequacy ratio and that depends on its reported equity less

Impact on *ROE* and valuations – cash earnings versus equity plus capitalized goodwill				
	ABC	**SPB**	**All cash**	**All paper**
EPS ($)	1.57	1.33	1.86	1.6
PE (×)	11.5	11.2	9.7	11.3
ROE	14.80%	12.60%	17.60%	13.10%
Book (Reported) ($)	10.6	10.6	10.6	12.21
Book (Prospective) ($)	11.02	11.02	11.02	12.7
Price-to-book (×)	1.80	1.43	2.27	1.52
ROE/COE (×)	1.48	1.26	1.76	1.31
Fair value assuming no growth ($)	**16.31**	**13.89**	**19.40**	**16.64**
Fair value with 4% growth ($)	· 19.84	15.76	24.99	19.26
Price-to-book fair value at 4% growth (×)	**1.87**	**1.49**	**2.36**	**1.58**

goodwill. If we look at the problem from this perspective it is clear that we should be looking not at reported equity as the constraint but Tier I equity, equivalent to its net tangible assets. This has no impact on EPS or PE multiples but it affects our "book" and "*ROE*" values. This in turn affects the valuations, as shown below.

Impact on *ROE* and valuations (cash earnings versus net tangible assets)				
	ABC	**SPB**	**All cash**	**All paper**
ROE	. 14.8%	12.6%	22.6%	15.4%
Book (net tangible assets) ($)	10.60	10.60	8.25	10.37
Prospective NTA (×1.04)	11.02	11.02	8.58	10.78
Price-to-book (×)	1.70	1.42	2.18	1.74
ROE/COE (×)	1.48	1.26	2.26	1.54
Fair value assuming no growth	**16.3**	**13.9**	**19.4**	**16.6**
Fair value with 4% growth	19.84	15.76	26.60	20.49
Price-to-book fair value at 4% growth	**1.87**	**1.49**	**3.22**	**1.98**

It is always useful to have some other ways of looking at the valuation side. A simple way to look at whether an acquirer is overpaying is to take the projected acquisition synergies, capitalize these by dividing by the bank's *COE* and subtracting the restructuring charge. Then compare this value with the offer premium over the pre-bid market capitalization of the target.

The all-paper offer is worth $25bn versus SPB's current market capitalization of $20bn, a premium of $5bn. Let us assume that the current price of SPB accurately reflects the value of its business as a stand-alone entity and that it has not been ramped up on bid speculation. For the bid to add value to ABC shareholders the value of the synergies identified must be greater than the premium it is offering.

The after-tax identified synergies are estimated to be $710m. We can simply capitalize these by dividing by our 10% *COE* and this suggests that they are worth about $7.1bn. After subtracting the expected restructuring charge we arrive at a present value of approximately $6390. This suggests in effect that the SPB shareholders are getting most of the benefits from the acquisition of the two banks under the terms of the offer.

Value of offer versus value of synergies ($m)					
Market capitalization	Value of offer	Premium	Annual synergies	Capitalized synergies	Less restructuring charge
18 750	25 000	6250	710	7100	6390

An all-paper offer will be cash EPS accretive when the following holds true:

$$S_{new}/(S_{old} + S_{new}) > (NP_{target} + Synergies_{annual})/(NP_{acquirer} + NP_{target} + Synergies_{annual})$$

Where S_{new} represents the new shares to be issued and S_{old} the number of shares issued prior to the acquisition, NP the after-tax net profit and *Synergies* are after tax.

This provides a reasonable, quick back-of-the-envelope guide as to whether an all-paper offer is likely to be value creative or destructive.

As a rule of thumb an all-cash offer will be cash earnings accretive if the following holds true:

Net profit of target + After-tax acquisition synergies > Financing costs after tax

On the other hand the cash offer appears to add value even though it is equivalent in terms of price. The key difference is that there is no dilution in ABC's shareholders' position and it is considerably more gearing. It is offering 1.89× book for a bank making an *ROE* of 12.6%. Putting synergies to one side that is equivalent to an after-tax return of 6.7%. This is being funded with bonds paying 6% gross and 3.6% net of tax. Of course such an offer will be both EPS and *ROE* accretive.

All-paper deals are simply handled. These deals are EPS accretive when the following applies:

New shares issued/(Existing number of shares + New shares issued)

< (Target's net profit + Annual synergies)/(Acquirer's profit + Target's profit + Synergies)

Although the all-cash offer appears to adds value the key questions to ask are whether or not it maximizes shareholder value and whether the offer for SPB is its optimal course of action.

Following the acquisition ABC is considerably more geared with its Tier I ratio dropping from 8.8% to 5.3%, equivalent to $4.20 per share in excess capital that could instead have been returned to shareholders.

Its book value would fall from $10.60 to $6.40 and, assuming that it financed the return of the capital by borrowing at the same 6%, its *ROE* would increase to 23.5%. Its fair price-to-book multiple would increase to 3.26×. Adding back the value of the returned capital gives a fair value target of approximately $26 for ABC stock compared with our estimate of $26.60 from acquiring SPB.

This is too close to call but given that in reality the real alternative to the acquisition would likely have been that ABC Bank would have simply sat on the excess capital most analysts would tend to give a deal done on these terms a cautious thumbs up. It has not bought at bargain basement prices but neither does it appear to have overpaid, provided the identified synergies can be realized.

If another bank came in with a higher offer then it would be extremely difficult for ABC management to increase the value of its offer without passing the point where such an acquisition was clearly value destructive.

PART VI

Problem Loans and Banking Crises

Corporate failures & problem loans

* Loan lifecycles

* Causes of corporate failure
  - Cyclical versus structural

* Bank actions to minimize credit losses going into recession

* Corporate insolvency
  - Operating losses & rising financing costs
  - Falling asset values & rising liability values

* Cashflow problems
* Failure warning signs
* Problem loans
  - NPL & other definitions
* Credit derivatives
* Foreclosure & liquidation
* Restructuring agreements

Banking crises

* Nature of banking crises - insolvency in real economy

* Macro-level factors
  - Credit growth & misallocation, deregulation, asset price bubbles, foreign borrowings overreliance

* Micro-level factors
  - Supervision, management, related & directed lending, corporate financial management

* Contagion, domestic/cross-border

* Loss allocation
  - Shareholders, other creditors, depositors, taxpayers

* Resolution of crises
  - Constraints on action
  - Emergency measures
  - Asset management companies
  - Development/rehabilitation funds
  - Corporate debt restructuring agencies

Dealing with & valuing insolvent banks

* Stock versus flow solutions
* Acquisitions of failed banks
* Taking failed banks into the public sector

* Injection into solvent bank
* Breaking up failed banks
* Closure & liquidation
* Valuing insolvent banks

20

Corporate Failures and Problem Loans

Capitalism without bankruptcy is like Christianity without hell.
Frank Borman, US astronaut and former CEO of US carrier Eastern Airlines

INTRODUCTION

We have already introduced the main tenets of credit risk management in Chapter 13 and in this chapter we revisit the subject of bad loans focusing on the following:

- **Corporate failures.** Problems in the banking system usually reflect problems in the real economy. While every corporate failure is unique in its own way most fall into one of three categories. Many companies become loss making as a result of management failure to take appropriate action with respect to a changing external environment or business cycles. Some companies fail as a result of an unexpected fall in the value of their assets or increase in the value of their liabilities. Other companies can fail as a result of a failure to manage their cashflows effectively. These may include companies that are both solvent and profitable.
- **Problem loans.** Problem loans develop as a result of financial weakness at, or the failure of, borrowers. They include loans where payments due to financial creditors have fallen behind schedule or are at risk of doing so. There are no uniform international standards for classification of problem loans but most definitions allow for loans that are past-due and other loans that are in some other way impaired. Banks take action on exposures that fall into the latter category to try to prevent them from becoming past-due.

In the following chapter we will continue on the theme of bad loans and examine some of the factors that contribute to banking crises, the allocation of losses between the various stakeholders and the ways such crises may be managed and eventually resolved.

LIFECYCLE

Most loans have a clear lifecycle. The first stage is the agreement between the bank and counterparty in the form of a legal contract to which both parties are bound. This defines the terms and conditions of the loan. There is then the actual utilization of the credit line, this may take place at an instant in time or may take place over a period of time. The loan remains current provided the borrower meets the loan's servicing requirements both in terms of interest and principal payments until all interest due and principal have been repaid:

- **Initiation.** When the bank agrees pricing and other terms with the borrower it has to take credit risk into account. This is the risk that the borrower defaults. The bank normally seeks collateral to reduce any losses incurred in the event of default:
  - **Expected losses.** Bank management must estimate the level of expected losses. This is given by the product of the likelihood of a default occurring and the losses in the event

of default. This can be viewed as the cost of doing business. These potential losses should be provided for by taking a charge for potential credit losses through the P&L account and establishing a reserve against which any future losses can be charged.

- **Unexpected losses.** They must also estimate the level of certainty in the estimate of expected losses. This depends on the statistical characteristics of the distribution of losses and is measured in terms of standard deviations. The bank should then define a confidence level and holding or time period to arrive at a measure of unexpected losses. This should then feed directly into the risk capital allocated to the loan.
- **Review.** As time passes bank management should carry out periodic reviews of estimated default probability and losses in the event of default. These may result in higher expected losses than originally anticipated or lower losses. In the former case additional bad debt charges should be made to increase the level of reserves held. In the latter case the bank should write back excess reserves for credit losses held against the loan. Any changes in the time period or standard deviation of losses will result in a change to the amount of risk capital that should be allocated to the loan.

There are then one of two possible outcomes. The loan reaches term or a default event occurs. Provided the borrower services the loan according to the loan agreement and pays all interest and principal due the final stage is to write back the reserves established for possible credit losses from the loan through the P&L account. If a default event occurs then we have to travel down a very different road:

- **Default event occurs.** The most common definition of a default event for a loan is based on required payments being past-due by a specified number of days. Management should then review its original estimates for losses in the event of default. Losses in the event of default now become expected losses. Additional charges should be taken through the P&L account to increase the reserves for credit losses.
- **Review and workout.** The bank now examines the best way to seek to minimize its losses by opting for a restructuring, foreclosure or liquidation. While this process is continuing expected losses are likely to change and may require additional provisioning.
- **Resolution.** Once the recovery phase is complete the bank should compare its reserves for credit losses established for the loan against actual losses incurred. In the event of liquidation actual losses are taken against these reserves. If the value of the actual losses is greater than the value of the reserves set aside the bank will have to take an additional charge through the P&L account for the difference. If less it can write back the excess reserves.

  Gross loans are reduced by the outstanding book principal and cash increased by the amount recovered. In cases where recovery involves gaining title to another asset or security a corresponding asset account will be credited. In many countries real estate that was pledged as collateral and where the bank has obtained title are usually reported as a separate line item with a name such as "foreclosed assets".

UNDERLYING CAUSES OF BUSINESS FAILURES

Companies in Secular Decline

Corporate bankers need to understand the underlying causes of business failures as they are the critical factor in credit risk management in general and as a source of NPLs in particular.

There are many reasons why an established, profitable company may lose competitiveness and become loss making. This shift may exhibit itself as a long drawn-out decline or may occur suddenly and come as a complete shock to the company and its banker. In the most general terms declines are usually driven by changes in the balance between supply and demand, the introduction of new substitutes and changes in the competitive environment.

If the decline is due to irreversible structural changes banks are likely to lose less if they act sooner to cut their exposures, rather than later and risk throwing good money after bad. Long-term shifts are often difficult to distinguish from cyclical factors. A frog placed in a hot pan will leap out immediately but one placed in a warm pan under a low heat will soon fall asleep and eventually succumb.

There are many factors that may result in a secular decline and these can usually be attributed to one or more of the following broad factors:

- **Falling demand.** Demographic changes are one source of a secular change in consumer demand. Other secular changes may result from changed income and wealth levels and changes in long-term consumer preferences and behavior. The end of the Cold War has had a long-term impact on the structure of defense industries.
- **New substitutes.** There are many examples of the development of a particular technology resulting in close substitutes that are cheaper and better than existing products.
- **Increased supply.** Changes in supply occur for many reasons. Developments in infrastructure may result in lower transport costs from existing sources while developments in technology, such as better extraction methods from oil wells, may change the fundamental economics of a business segment.
- **New entrants.** New entrants may occur as a result of the permanent removal of tariffs and other trade barriers. They may also occur as a result of changes in cost structures between countries. Labor-intensive industries tend to migrate to countries with the lowest labor costs. Companies operating in developed countries are constantly having to move up the value-added chain. While some of these companies simply shift their production facilities many look to outsource these low value-added activities.

It is essential for bank lenders to differentiate between borrowers operating in industries experiencing a secular decline and those suffering from the effects of economic cyclicality. It is always easier to recognize secular decline after the event.

Economic Cyclicality

Economies can be looked at as systems with stores, lags and flows. Physical systems with these characteristics exhibit highly cyclical behavior. Economies have definite cycles, moving from growth to recession as the balance shifts between supply and demand. Credit losses are highest in economic downturns, although the recognition of those losses usually lags the economic cycle.

There is an argument that banks should be reining back on lending when the economy is at its strongest and expanding when the economy is at its weakest. It would take brave, and possibly foolhardy, bank management to pursue such a policy and few banks attempt this. The problem of taking economic cyclicality into account is compounded by the fact that even well respected economists find it remarkably difficult to make accurate medium-term economic forecasts and even harder to identify future inflection points.

This is compounded by human nature, which has a tendency to optimism and to expect things to continue as they are. As economic booms persist memories of past recessions start to fade. In the late 1990s, before the 2001–2002 global slowdown, business newspapers and bookshops were full of articles and textbooks on the new paradigm arguing that structural changes in the US economy and better management of money supply had abolished the business cycle. If only.

Examples of highly cyclical industries include the following: shipping, airlines, petrochemicals, oil refining, commercial real estate investment and development, residential property development, hotels, chip fabrication and steel manufacturing. All of these industries share two characteristics in common. There is a relatively long lead time between the decision to commit to adding capacity and that capacity coming on stream and, once in place, it is difficult to reduce capacity easily.

Most of these industries are also relatively capital intensive. The result is that once an imbalance develops between supply and demand it is difficult to rectify that imbalance quickly. Companies operating in cyclical industries pose particular problems for banks in terms of pricing credit risk. The level of credit losses likely varies depending on where we are in the cycle.

Companies in cyclical industries should take action before entering a downturn to ensure that their financial position is in a healthy enough state to get through the downturn. This usually means cutting capacity, reducing the level of debt, either through asset sales or raising equity, and extending the term of existing debt. Those that can should also try to reduce the length of the credit terms they offer customers to lower the risks of credit losses arising from customers that get into financial problems. Sadly, few managers have such foresight. A surprising number of failures occur because companies got the timing of their expansion plans wrong.

If an industry is affected by a cyclical downturn and banks start tightening credit they risk exacerbating the impact of the downturn. This may cause companies that would have recovered in the upturn to fail and result in higher losses at banks than would otherwise have been the case.

Bank Actions to Reduce Risks

Individual banks cannot fully avoid the effects of a downturn. The best that they can do is to take action before a recession hits to reduce the level of risk in their balance sheet. The sorts of action that prudent bank management should take are as follows:

- **Shorten loan terms.** By shortening loan terms banks reduce default risk. The longer the term the greater the risk of incurring losses if the borrower gets into financial difficulty. Banks with shorter-term loans can choose not to roll over loans at the first signs of financial distress leaving lenders with longer-term loans to bear the brunt of the credit risks and any resulting losses.
- **Reduce unsecured lending.** Collateral provides some security against losses resulting from default. Conservative banks will reduce the level of unsecured lending going into a recession and seek to increase the level and quality of collateral cover on secured loans.
- **Reduce exposure to cyclical industries.** Where possible banks should reduce their exposure to industries that are most at risk from a downturn. This may prove difficult in practice and banks have to weigh carefully the balance between maintaining corporate relationships versus the likelihood of credit losses. Banks that walk away from customers at the first sign of trouble are unlikely to gain such customers' business in the future.

- **Interest rate risk management.** Around the time of economic turning points interest rates can swing wildly. As economies start to overheat central banks normally hike up short-term rates to cool the economy and choke off inflationary pressures. If these measure start to push an economy into recession they may act just as quickly to cut them. It is quite common for yield curves to become inverted and then return to the normal upward sloping characteristic shape. The lowest risk approach is to match fixed rate assets and liabilities and floating rate assets and liabilities as closely as possible. Banks with a higher risk tolerance may, on the other hand, seek to position the bank for such anticipated changes.

INSOLVENCY

A company is by definition insolvent when its reported equity falls to zero. This may result from it operating at a loss, taking account of both operating profit (or loss) and financing costs, if the value of its assets falls or if the value of its liabilities rises.

Operating Losses and Rising Financing Costs

Company reported profits or losses do not necessarily reflect cashflows and are essentially an accounting concept, but so is equity. A profitable company may become loss making if it has operating losses or its financing costs rise, or some combination of the two factors. These total losses are charged off against equity:

- **Operating losses.** Companies can move from making an operating profit to operating losses as a result of some combination of lower unit sales, lower unit prices and higher raw material or other operating costs. Any of these occur for a myriad of reasons.
- **Financing costs.** Financing costs will increase if a company has floating rate debt and interest rates rise. They can also rise if a company has borrowed in a foreign currency and the foreign currency has appreciated relative to the domestic currency. Not only will the value of the debt in local currency terms rise but so will the actual financing costs. We will look at this in more detail when looking at cashflow problems.
- **Combination.** Profits can also turn into losses if operating profits fall at the same time as financing costs rise. A combination of a business downturn and rising interest rates will have a negative impact on most companies' financial position. The most geared companies are, of course, at greatest risk under these conditions.

Falling Asset Values

Insolvency results when the value of a company's non-equity liabilities exceeds that of its assets. This can occur either as a result of the value of a firm's liabilities rising or the value of its assets falling:

- **Real estate.** Real estate can be a gold mine for some developers, investors and speculators but it is also a graveyard for many. It is difficult to correct supply–demand imbalances quickly given the long lead times involved. In severe property downturns prices become largely indeterminate in the absence of a clearing price as liquidity dries up.

The biggest and most high-profile failures occur at developers that have staked their future on a single large development, usually of office or retail space. Large developers with a well-diversified portfolio of relatively small-scale residential developments carry a much lower risk of failing.

The economic and real estate markets do not necessarily move in tandem but when an economic slowdown coincides with a serious level of oversupply few developers, investors or speculators escape unscathed. Developments may turn out to have a market value well below that of the costs of buying the land and construction. Developers usually carry developments at cost until forced to mark to market. This actually provides an incentive for developers to delay completion to avoid having to recognize the unrealized losses and often to avoid having to pay local property taxes due when the building is completed.

- **Inventory write-downs.** Companies may be forced to write down the value of their inventories for one of a number of reasons. The most common cause in modern times is that due to technological obsolescence. This has become increasingly important in industries where competitive innovation is the major source of advantage, technical progress is rapid and product lifecycles short. The telecommunications and technology industries are prime examples.

  The clothing and retail sectors are both exposed to changing fashions and while blockbuster movies can earn more from the licensed merchandising than from the box office a flop is likely to result in warehouses full of unwanted products.

- **Investment losses.** There are many examples of losses arising from ill-conceived corporate investments in other companies' stock and from acquisitions. The most spectacular failures are the result of deals done at, or close to, bull market peaks. When euphoria evaporates and markets correct buyers suffer large, unrealized losses on their investment holdings. In most countries these losses have to be reflected in the equity account. This may be achieved through the balance sheet (using unrealized losses on securities' holdings) or via losses reported through the earnings statement.

  There are also plenty of examples of acquisitions that have been made where it quickly becomes clear that the values placed on assets purchased were overestimated. US banks paid steep prices for British brokerages and merchant banks in the run-up to Big Bang in the mid-1980s only to find that the chief asset that they had paid for was people and that people could, and did, walk.

  Many business people see little worth in a liberal arts degree. If top executives at mobile telecommunications companies had read or seen Arthur Miller's play *The Crucible* they might have avoided the tens of billions of dollars that they subsequently wrote down on the value of 3G licenses that they won at auction.

- **Foreign currency exposures.** Multinational companies operate in many countries around the globe. Where they have made significant investments in operations in foreign countries they are exposed to significant foreign currency translation and exchange risk. If the company's base accounting currency appreciates against the currencies of the countries where it has made these investments it will have to report a diminution in the value of these investments even though in local currency terms they are left unchanged. There is a long-running argument as to whether translation risks should, or should not be hedged. It is extremely difficult and in practical terms impossible to hedge long-term foreign currency risks.

- **Credit losses and fraud.** Although banks are most exposed to credit risk few companies are completely immune. A certain level of delinquencies is to be expected and seen as part of the costs of doing business. In an economic downturn, however, the number of delinquent accounts may rise sharply and with it the level of write-offs.

Having a small number of large customers usually proves a mixed blessing for companies. Credit risk at individual customers can be monitored more closely but it may be difficult to impose better payment terms and failure of just one of its customers may result in the company's insolvency.

- **Appropriation and destruction of assets.** All private property, both domestic and foreign, was appropriated by the state in Russia and China following their communist revolutions. Many oil-producing states in the Middle East acted in the post-colonial era to nationalize assets of foreign oil companies. Compensation paid in such circumstances never matches the foreign owners' valuations. War and civil unrest are both causes of widespread destruction of both private and public property. Most insurance policies explicitly exclude claims arising from either war or civil unrest.

Rising Liability Values

Corporate insolvencies resulting from rising liabilities are not uncommon although they occur less frequently than those due to falling asset prices:

- **Foreign currency exposure.** Just as some companies are exposed to the risk of falling asset prices due to an appreciating base currency others are exposed to rising liability values if the base currency depreciates. Larger domestic companies in developing countries often look abroad for financing whether in the form of equity, bond issues or bank loans. Equity raising does not represent a problem but international bond issues are usually denominated in US$, the euro or yen. Where some form of managed foreign exchange system is in operation borrowing in foreign currencies often seems cheaper than borrowing in the local currency.

  Few companies in developing markets hedge their foreign currency liabilities. In part this may be the result of it being difficult to obtain hedging instruments for long-term exposures or may be because the companies balk at the cost of hedging. In the event of the managed foreign exchange system failing and there being a sharp devaluation of the local currency the value of these foreign currency liabilities will rise and often sharply.

- **Derivative positions.** It is surprising how many companies start off using derivatives to hedge real business exposures and end up taking speculative positions. Sometimes companies having gained experience of hedging commodity prices using derivatives decide that they can beat the market and become active traders on their own account. In other cases these positions can be attributed to hard selling by investment bankers of financial products that their customers do not understand. When derivative positions go wrong they can result in huge losses.

- **Present value of future liabilities.** Some companies have future liabilities that they can reasonably expect to have to meet at some point in the future. The most obvious example is that of corporate defined benefit pension plans. These are pension schemes funded by companies for the benefit of their employees. The company acts as a guarantor that when employees retire they will receive a defined level of pension, usually based on final salary and length of service.

  The present value of this liability is reflected in the company's balance sheet. The present value of the estimated liability is highly sensitive to the discount rate applied. The required value of the pension fund's assets is highly dependent on the assumed level of returns or growth.

Warranties provide a second example and are of particular importance to manufacturing companies. The level of expected claims should be reflected in the balance sheet. If the actual level of claims is higher than expected then this will have to be adjusted upwards.

- **Unexpected liabilities.** The US is a highly litigious society and the tobacco industry, those companies whose employees worked with asbestos, hospitals and fast food operators have all had to make huge payments to cover product and service liability claims. Companies may take actions that are legal but leave them open to unexpected future civil claims. Many American companies with outstanding asbestos-related claims have sought bankruptcy to avoid having to meet those claims. No other country matches the US when it comes to propensity to litigate and in some cases legal action has been pursued in the US for offenses that have occurred outside of the US.

Corporate solvency risk factors

Increasing liability values
* Increase in value of unhedged foreign currency liabilities
* Increase in present value of future liabilities
* Losses on derivative positions

* Operating level
  – Lower profits
  – Profits turning to losses
* Financing costs
  – Floating rate debt
  – Foreign debt

Falling asset values
* Fall in real estate prices
* Inventory write-downs
* Investment losses
* Foreign currency asset write-downs
* Credit losses & fraud
* Appropriation or destruction of assets

CASHFLOW PROBLEMS

Profitable, solvent companies can fail because they are illiquid and do not have the cash to pay their suppliers, employees or financial creditors. Key factors in cashflow problems include the following:

- **Operating cashflows.** If sales or prices fall operating cashflows will also fall even when there is no increase in the time it takes for customers to settle their invoices. Falling sales are also likely to result in a build-up of inventory affecting its working capital requirement and ability to service its debt.

Companies that have long-term contracts payable in local currency or are heavily dependent on exports are exposed to risks arising from foreign exchange rate fluctuations. We have already mentioned that it is virtually impossible to fully hedge foreign exchange risks. Foreign currency swaps provide one method of longer-term hedging but even here contracts rarely extend beyond five years and then are only available for the major traded currencies.

If their local currency appreciates then it has to choose between two uncomfortable alternatives. It can keep its prices in the foreign currencies unchanged although this will lower revenues per unit sold in the foreign market. The alternative is to adjust its prices in foreign currency terms upwards to offset the effects of the changes in the exchange rate but its products will become less competitive and it risks losing volume sales.

- **Working capital.** Working capital is tied up largely in inventory and credit to customers. This is offset by credit it receives from its suppliers. If inventory levels rise, or customers take longer to settle their invoices, working capital requirements will rise. If banks will not lend to fund that additional working capital the company is likely to experience cashflow problems. If it cannot pay its suppliers or staff then the company will fail even though it is technically solvent.

One company's accounts receivable is another company's accounts payable. As companies restrict credit to their customers this in turn causes liquidity problems at those companies. This is one of the causes of contagion in financial crises.

- **Medium- to long-term financing.** A high level of net debt to equity gearing leaves a company more exposed to the impact of rising interest rates on its financing costs. It also leaves the company more exposed to the risk of any write-downs in asset values or increase in liability values. The latter may threaten the company's solvency and leave it exposed to the risk that the value of collateral it has pledged falls and that it breaches bond or bank loan covenants.

Companies that depend on rolling over short-term debt, such as commercial paper, to meet their long-term financing requirements run considerable risks that demand for such paper will dry up due to wider market-driven factors. When borrowers have unhedged floating rate debt they are exposed to the risk that interest rates rise. This will inflate the cost of servicing their debt.

- **Investment cycle.** All businesses have some sort of investment cycle as machinery and equipment wears out and has to be replaced, existing products face obsolescence and new products developed to replace them. Developers have to constantly initiate new projects as existing ones complete. Investments have to be made before returns are generated. A telecommunications company planning to sell a service that depends on it having a dozen satellites in orbit before the service can be initiated will have to make hundreds or millions, or even billions, of dollars in investment before it receives a single dollar in revenue. Drug companies need a pipeline of new drugs under development to replace those due to lose patent protection.

New developments always have risks. Common problems are that delays set in and original completion dates missed and technical and legal issues are encountered that prove difficult and expensive to solve. In a worse case these problems encountered prove insurmountable and the project is abandoned. Even when completed the project may fail if late completion has a material impact on the project (other competitors seize first mover advantages, new technologies result in obsolescence etc.) or forecasts for operating performance prove optimistic.

It is tempting to view company failures as being due to either a management failure or to some extraneous event over which management has no control. It would be difficult to blame a company that fails as a result of an act of war or terrorism. Most external factors can, however, be anticipated, their risk assessed and steps taken to minimize the extent of the impact on the company in the event that the risk is realized. Even in the case of terrorist attacks contingency plans should be in place. Most corporate failures are due to either operational or financial mismanagement, or a combination of the two.

The major factors likely to result in the deterioration of a company's cash position are shown in the following graphic.

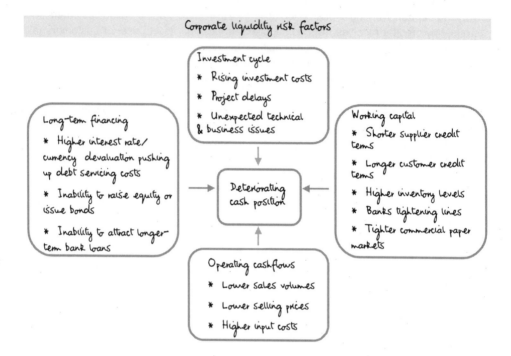

Corporate liquidity risk factors

Investment cycle
* Rising investment costs
* Project delays
* Unexpected technical & business issues

Long-term financing
* Higher interest rate/ currency devaluation pushing up debt servicing costs
* Inability to raise equity or issue bonds
* Inability to attract longer-term bank loans

Deteriorating cash position

Working capital
* Shorter supplier credit terms
* Longer customer credit terms
* Higher inventory levels
* Banks tightening lines
* Tighter commercial paper markets

Operating cashflows
* Lower sales volumes
* Lower selling prices
* Higher input costs

WARNING SIGNS OF FAILURE

Published financial statements can provide warning signs of a potential corporate failure but these provide only lagging indicators. There are other warning signs that may signal a potential default. These include the following:

- **Breaking of covenants.** A company that breaks its covenants and is unable to rectify the situation is clearly stretched financially. Even if the covenant is from another lender all creditors are at risk from deteriorating financial ratios at the borrower. Secured creditors may act to force liquidation.
- **Credit drawdown.** When companies are in financial trouble cash becomes king. A company seeking to draw down against all of its bank credit lines may be signaling an intention to be preparing to file for bankruptcy protection.
- **Credit derivative pricing.** The credit derivatives market (where it exists) is probably a more sensitive indicator of potential trouble than the rating agencies. If the rating agencies get it wrong all that they lose is reputation. The writers of credit default insurance stand to lose money in the case of a default event. The pricing of credit derivatives reflects the underwriters' and market participants' perceptions of default risk.
- **Bond pricing.** It is often difficult to get a market value for loans but most corporate bonds are traded. A sharp fall in price, the result of an increase in the credit spread on the bond,

is a strong indicator that the issuer is perceived to have become higher risk by the bond markets.

- **Significant debt repayment dates.** A company that has a significant repayment due to its bondholders or bankers and is considering bankruptcy protection is more likely to file before making the payment than after.

In like manner if a company has issued a putable bond that is approaching an exercise date but is trading at a significant discount to the put price the bond market is pricing in the risk that the company will be unable to redeem these bonds.

PROBLEM LOANS

International bank analysis is plagued by a lack of uniform definitions and accounting standards. Nowhere is this more apparent than in the realm of problem loans. The most widely used loan classifications are normal, problem loans and non-performing loans. Normal loans are those where interest income is recognized on an accrual basis. Such loans are also called "current" or "performing".

Any analyst trying to do even a half-decent job of understanding what the reported numbers actually represent has no choice other than to get hold of the relevant local accounting standards, the relevant notices from the central bank or bank regulator, and then check the actual application of those policies and standards by individual banks.

Non-performing Loans (NPLs)

The term "non-performing" is usually well defined. Unfortunately definitions vary between countries and may vary between banks in a single country! The most common definition of a non-performing loan is one where the borrower has fallen more than a defined number of days behind in the scheduled payments on the loan.

Once a loan has been classified as non-performing it is usually put onto non-accrual status and interest income is only recognized on a "cash" basis, that is when received. A loan may be reclassified as "performing" or "normal" once all payments due have been made and payments have been received as scheduled for a specified period of time:

- **Past-due.** The most widely used "past-due" period used for classification of a loan as non-performing is 90 days. In some countries regulators allow a longer period, typically 180 days. In these circumstances individual banks are usually permitted to classify and report loans as NPLs under the more conservative international 90-day norm.

  Banks reporting NPLs on a 180-day basis will report a lower level of NPLs than if they followed the international norm of 90 days. Where different past-due periods are used it is impossible to make accurate direct comparison of NPL levels between individual banks or banking systems. A rough estimate of 90-day NPL numbers for an individual bank reporting on a 180-day past-due basis can be made if industry level numbers for 90 and 180 days past-due are published:
    - A further minor difference is that while most definitions cover any payments due some only specify interest or capital payments missed.
    - Loans on which payments are erratic but in total are less than 90 days behind schedule are not usually treated as non-performing.

- In some countries banks report either "net" or "gross" NPLs. The gross number is based on the loan's outstanding principal as reported on the bank's balance sheet. This number may, or may not, include interest that has been accrued but not received. The net number is calculated after subtracting the value of any collateral held from the gross NPL number. The net number is always less than the gross number.
- A further complication occurs with revolving credit. Interest is effectively capitalized and provided the borrower keeps its borrowing below the level of its credit line need never become non-performing even though the debtor has made no payments at all.
- When using NPL numbers for comparative purposes analysts must check the local definitions carefully. It is difficult to make valid comparisons between NPL levels at banks in one country where NPLs are classified non-performing after 180 days and net of collateral with those at banks reporting on a 90-day past-due and gross basis.
- **Treatment of accrued interest.** When a loan is classified as non-performing the bank has to deal with the issue of how to treat interest income that has already been recognized but not received. In most countries this is simply reversed through the interest income line in the period when the loan is classified as non-performing. In some countries banks leave the interest in the interest receivable account, or capitalize it by increasing the outstanding principal but make a counter-entry in a provision or reserve account.

  In some countries accounting standards allow banks to continue to accrue interest income even though the borrower is well past-due provided that the bank has a realistic expectation of being able to recover the missed payments.
- **Reclassification to performing status.** NPLs can be reclassified as normal when all past-due payments have been made and the loan is current. Some regulators allow this reclassification to take place immediately the loan becomes current. Others require that the loan remain current for a specified period, which may be as long as 12 months. This also affects direct comparisons of reported NPL numbers.

Other Loans

- **Normal loans.** These are loans on accrual status where payments have been made as scheduled or when past-due do not meet the requirements to be classified as a non-performing loans. These are also referred to as current.
- **Problem loans.** Problem loans include loans classified as non-performing but also encompasses loans that are current but that in bank management's opinion are impaired in some way. Many banks maintain a watch list of current, but impaired, loans that merit particular attention and where the bank actively works with the borrowers to prevent these loans from becoming non-performing. In some countries these are reported as "special mention" loans.

  Definitions of impairment are usually subjective and may include factors such as deterioration in the financial condition of the borrower or weakening industry prospects. Hard evidence of impairment is provided when collateral cover falls below a specified level or the borrower is unable to comply with all of the covenants spelt out in the original loan agreement.
- **Substandard and doubtful.** The terms substandard and doubtful are used widely. The most common definition of a substandard loan is one classified as non-performing but where the bank has collateral pledged in excess of the book value of the loan plus any accrued interest. Doubtful loans are then defined as loans that are either unsecured or have collateral cover below 100%.

- **Restructured loans.** Restructured loans are ones where a formal debt restructuring agreement has been finalized and the loan classified as current but where the terms of the loan have been significantly changed. Examples of changed terms include an effective interest rate well below market rates, an extension to the loan's term or a moratorium of principal payments for a specified period.
- **Foreclosed assets.** These are assets, usually real estate, that banks have gained title to as a result of foreclosure action with respect to delinquent loans. Many analysts add foreclosed assets to reported NPL numbers to get a better picture of the level of non-performing assets. Neither NPLs nor foreclosed assets generate much in the way of income but both still have to be funded. In banking crises or economic downturns it is usually very difficult to sell these assets at a price close to their book value.

Problem loan terms and characteristics

Non-performing loans (NPLs)	Problem loans, special mention	Special mention, substandard, doubtful
* Classified on basis of number of days past-due	* Broad definition – NPLs form a subset	* Collateral-based classification of NPLs
* 90-day international norm	* Loans impaired in some way	* Includes all NPLs & may also encompass loans on watch list
* Non-accrual status – interest recognized on cash basis	* Hard identification broken covenants & falling collateral cover	* Substandard loans are NPLs with 100% collateral
* Some regulators allow up to 180 days past-due	* Soft identification based on weakening company financial conditions or deteriorating industry prospects	* Doubtful loans are either unsecured or have less than 100% collateral cover
* Usually reported gross but some regulators allow them to be reported net of collateral	* Placed on bank "watch list"	* Restructured loans result of work-outs
* Reclassified as normal when payments up to date – usually requires demonstrated compliance over specified period		

DEALING WITH PROBLEM LOANS

Once banks identify loans that are impaired, or are at high risk of impairment, bank management are usually faced with some hard choices. It may, for example, be possible to keep loans current and avoid any future losses by increasing credit lines, while action to rein in exposures may precipitate the company's failure and lead to large bank losses. On the other hand if the company fails increasing exposure will simply amplify the losses and give other creditors the opportunity to bail out before the final denouement.

When formal default conditions have been met, however, the pendulum swings towards minimizing losses that now appear inevitable. This may be done through foreclosure (seizure of collateral), liquidation (formal legal proceedings) or by restructuring loan and other debt agreements.

Foreclosure

The simplest way to deal with a credit default on a secured loan is to foreclose on any assets that have been pledged as collateral. We have already looked at the issues concerning the reliance on real estate as collateral with liquidity and realization of appraised values key factors.

Banks have a tendency to hold onto such real estate assets in a falling market. Two reasons. The first is the hope that the price of these assets will recover, reducing credit losses. The second is the fear that forced selling will add further downward pressure to the property market and reduce the value of collateral on other loans. This would result in greater losses on other delinquent loans and potentially result in additional provisioning requirements on both performing and non-performing loans. Many central banks impose limits on the amount of foreclosed property that banks can hold and length of time they can hold such assets to prevent banks from effectively becoming real estate investment companies.

Liquidation

The next way to deal with a loan or bond default is to take legal action against the party in question in order to force liquidation. This may, or may not, include action to have the borrower declared bankrupt. For smaller loans, whether retail or SME, obtaining legal title to the collateral and selling it is often the favored approach. This is relatively easy to do in countries such as the US and the UK with well-established and efficient legal systems. This is much harder to achieve in developing and transitional economies that lack such a legal infrastructure.

The main advantages of liquidation to the bank are that it is quick (in most developed countries) and does not tie up much bank management time. The actual process of liquidation can be contracted out to legal and accounting firms. The main disadvantage of liquidation is that loss rates on liquidated loans usually end up being higher than those resulting from the principal alternative method of restructuring. Inventory and specialist equipment is likely to be worth more as part of a going concern than if it is sold off piecemeal.

As the size of the exposure in question increases bankers will increasingly look for alternatives to liquidation and foreclosure.

Restructuring Agreements

The basic approach of a restructuring agreement is to take a company that is unable to service its debt or repay principal and to either increase its cash-generating ability or restructure its financial structure such that it is able to service this debt from operating cashflows.

In many restructuring agreements creditor banks and bondholders usually have to agree to accept a level of loss on their outstanding exposures (known as a "haircut") for the restructuring to be successful:

- **Increasing operating cashflows.** It is usually difficult to increase sales quickly and this may even exacerbate problems in the short term by increasing working capital requirements. The most common ways to increase operating cashflows are by cutting costs and closing units with negative cashflows that have no realistic chance of being turned around.
- **Additional financing.** Providing additional finance may increase the likelihood of the company eventually being able to meet its future liabilities, even though it increases risks in the short term. The extent to which banks and state agencies are willing to make more finance available depends largely on these lenders being given a senior claim relative to existing creditors.
- **Asset sales.** Any unencumbered assets that are not essential to the business should be sold. This may include sale and leaseback types of arrangements.
- **Increased security.** A lender may be prepared to take a haircut on a loan if it gains title to additional security. That may result in the lender achieving a higher recovery rate in the event of liquidation.
- **Debt–equity swaps.** Debt–equity swaps are most common in the very largest corporate defaults. There is some truth to the expression that some companies are just too big to be allowed to fail. Banks and bondholders do not welcome the prospect of taking long-term equity stakes in non-financial companies but may have little alternative.

  Debt–equity swaps occur when the company's creditors agree to take a "haircut" by writing down the level of debt to the company in return for taking an equity stake in the company. The creditors normally end up owning most or all of the company's equity in these cases. Bank regulators are less than enthusiastic about banks taking equity positions in, or control of, non-financial companies but in these sort of cases normally waive any regulatory constraints.
- **Replacing management.** In cases where the creditors can demonstrate that a company is insolvent they may seek a court ruling to write down the equity of the company to zero, inject new capital and replace the board and management.
- **Grace periods.** Creditors may agree to a period of grace whereby existing loan terms are modified waiving the requirement for the debtor to make its scheduled payments. Interest and/or principal payments can be rescheduled to match projected cashflows. The foregone interest may simply be accrued, and the borrower required to pay this interest at some point in the future. It may also simply be "forgiven" if the creditors recognize that there is no realistic means of the debtor making those future payments.
- **Extended terms.** The terms of outstanding loans may be extended. For loans with principal amortization this reduces the principal component of the regular scheduled payments.
- **Lower rates.** The creditors may agree to lower the interest rate being charged on the loans to reduce the financing burden. This may be effective where by doing so the banks increase the likelihood of eventual principal repayment. Such an approach does produce an *NPV* loss. This *NPV* loss is rarely recognized explicitly but is evidenced by lowered future interest income.

The term "debt forgiveness" is used frequently in the context of debt restructuring agreements but is completely inaccurate. The reality is that bankers never forgive borrowers that have caused them credit losses. Their memories are very long. The expression "revenge is a dish best eaten cold" could have been coined with bankers in mind.

Whatever approach is taken the key question to ask is whether there has been a genuine restructuring with banks taking a realistic view on the likely level of future recoveries. It is relatively easy to get a loan restructured such that the loan can be classified as performing. Extend the term, waive principal amortization repayments and charge a very low interest rate in early years rising over time to eliminate any *NPV* loss. Such an approach may allow a bank to avoid regulatory provisioning requirements and reduce reported NPLs. Such an approach does not provide a realistic measure of economic loss, however, if the company is unlikely to be able to make the interest payments at the higher rates or repay the principal at maturity.

In most of the developed world a restructuring agreement can be imposed on all creditors if the holders of 75% of the debt by value vote in favor of the agreement.

Restructuring Specialists

There are frequently disputes and conflicts between different classes of creditors. This has led to the emergence of a group of people specializing in resolving these disputes, liquidation and making debt-restructuring agreements.

The people who specialize in the recovery of "bad" loans can best be thought of as repo-men in suits. Their prime objective is to salvage as much as possible from the corporate or personal financial wreck.

Most banks employ their own insolvency specialists who work full time in this field but also turn to professional firms in complex cases or where the number of cases has exceeded some critical level. Most of these individuals probably make loving partners and parents and are kind to animals in their private life. In their professional life, however, there is little room for sentiment. Insolvency professionals in this field usually have to possess the following traits to be successful:

- **Directness.** Most people tend to avoid conflict. In debt recovery situations conflict is inevitable and has to be embraced rather than avoided. When banks in Thailand tried to act on bad loans following a banking crisis in the late 1990s they found that few of their own people were well suited to this task. Thailand is a highly consensual society where open conflict is avoided wherever possible. The solution for a number of domestic Thai banks was to hire 'in-your-face' Australians with extensive experience in this area.
- **Pragmatism.** In many cases liquidation, which is the one of the most straightforward methods to deal with default, is also the least effective in terms of how much the bank eventually recovers. The bank has to recognize when liquidation is the optimal choice and when a "workout" or debt restructuring is the better choice.
- **Strong negotiating skills.** In the case of the failure of a large corporate a bank is likely to find itself as just one of many creditors. These creditors usually include other banks and trade creditors. The owners of the company and its creditors have very obvious conflicts of interest but there are also major conflicts of interest between creditors of different standing (banks versus trade creditors) and within the same class (bank versus bank).
- **Decisiveness.** In most insolvency and restructuring cases the longer that action is delayed the greater the eventual losses to the creditors. When a company is hemorrhaging it is essential to take decisive action to close loss-making businesses that have no realistic prospect of being successfully turned around and to cut costs at those businesses that can be rehabilitated.

People in banks who work in this area are a breed apart from other commercial bankers. Their primary function is to clear up the mess that lending officers have left. There are two factors that protect the lending officers. The first is that in many cases they have long since moved on. The second is that, assuming they were not guilty of fraud or of failing to follow procedures, the lending decision had to be approved by higher levels of management. The more people involved in the decision-making process the lower the level of individual blame allocation. When enough people are implicated nobody need be responsible.

Banks work closely with accountancy and legal firms. These specialists are essential. In some cases they carry out the bulk of the work of recommending the course of action and formalizing the restructuring agreement or liquidation work.

Exhibit: "Chapter 11"– US corporate bankruptcy protection

The US has the most advanced legislation to provide protection for companies from their creditors while they seek to restructure their operations. "Chapter 11" refers to a section of US legislation covering bankruptcy. A Chapter 11 filing is a voluntary action taken by a company to protect its ongoing business from financial claims while it continues to operate its business without interruption. Chapter 11 protection differs from other kinds of bankruptcy proceedings (Chapters 5, 7 and 13) where the focus is on liquidation and more on retail bankruptcies than large corporates.

During a Chapter 11 proceeding, the company attempts to reorganize financially so that it can meet its financial claims. The filing freezes immediately all prior financial claims against the company. It also puts a halt to any lawsuits against the company. Under a Chapter 11 proceeding, the company maintains its normal business operations and continues to provide employees with salaries and benefits. It is also able to do business with suppliers and customers in a routine manner so that it can continue to generate funds to satisfy creditors.

After the company files for Chapter 11, a government agency, the US Trustee, appoints an Official Creditors Committee. In most cases, this committee becomes involved in a court-supervised process to ensure that creditors are dealt with in an equitable manner. A meeting of company representatives and parties that claim the company owes them money is typically held approximately a month to six weeks after the initial filing.

The company is also required to post notices, which are normally in the form of advertisements in newspapers, inviting any parties with a claim against the company to lodge such claims by a specified date. This notice period may last from three to four months. Meanwhile, the company, as the debtor, has the right to propose a reorganization or recapitalization plan in the first 120 days of the Chapter 11 process. If the company appears to be acting in good faith, and operations are stabilizing, this exclusive period may be, and usually is, extended.

Once the court has gathered all of the claims that resulted from the notice being given, hearings are held to assess the value of any disputed claims. Once the total value is estimated, the company can determine the feasibility of its financial reorganization plan. The company must then present a proposed plan with complete financial information. The court must then determine if it contains sufficient information for the creditors to consider. If approved by the court, creditors can then vote on the financial reorganization plan. If the company's reorganization plan is confirmed, the creditor claims will be satisfied as provided for in the financial reorganization plan. At this point, the company can emerge from Chapter 11 and operate its business as described in its financial reorganization plan.

21

Banking Crises

In this age of electronic money, investors are no longer seduced by a financial "dance of a thousand veils". Only hard and accurate information on reserves, current accounts, and monetary and fiscal conditions will keep capital from fleeing precipitously at the first sign of trouble.

Larry Summers, American economist

BANKING CRISES

Banking or financial crises are essentially crises of solvency, both in the banking system and within the real economy. These solvency crises are often accompanied by outbreaks of widespread panic involving depositors attempting to withdraw their funds from banks, creating runs on bank deposits. Many OECD countries have experienced periods when banks have sustained heavy credit losses but without threatening the overall solvency of the system. Such periods should not be confused with real banking crises where the solvency of the financial system is brought into question.

The world is littered with examples of financial crises in both emerging and developed markets. Examples of relatively recent crises include the following: Argentina (1980, 1986, 2001), Brazil (1984), Chile (1981), Indonesia (1997), Malaysia (1985, 1997), Mexico (1992), South Korea (1997), Spain (1987), Sweden (1992), Thailand (1983, 1997) and Uruguay (1982). In each case the date corresponds with the year in which it was generally recognized that the financial system was in crisis.

This list does not include examples from the former Soviet Union or the transitional economies of Eastern Europe. Nor does it include the 1980s crisis of US thrifts (savings and loans associations). Although the total costs to taxpayers of the S&L debacle were in the order of $350bn–400bn it had minimal impact on the core US banking system and does not meet our criteria for a banking crisis.

Crises do not occur every day but as shown above they occur sufficiently frequently, in economies at varying levels of development and have such a major impact that they merit close examination. Analysts, investors, bank management and supervisors should be aware of their likely causes, how they can be avoided and the range of options available to resolve them and recognize the warning signs of a developing crisis. No two banking crises have exactly the same root cause or dynamics but they are usually associated with a number of common factors. These can be divided into macro-level factors concerning the economic environment and management and micro-level factors concerning the management and supervision of banks.

Macro-level Factors

Typical macro factors include ill-managed deregulation, a very rapid increase in credit, the misallocation of that credit within the economy, asset price bubbles, pegged and managed currency systems and current account deficits:

- **Deregulation.** Many banking crises have followed a period of deregulation involving liberalization of controlled interest rates and the lowering of regulatory barriers to entry.

    Interest rate deregulation allows banks to compete by pushing up deposit rates and lowering lending rates. Competition is likely to be relatively restrained, however, unless liberalization is accompanied by new entrants that do not play by the old rules. Lowering barriers to entry usually results in new domestic non-bank competitors and the entry of foreign banks. New domestic competitors lack industry expertise or market experience. They have little option other than to compete in segments where they can use price to gain a foothold.

    Foreign bank entrants usually fall into one of two well-defined categories. There are those seeking to build a long-term business by using their expertise to cherry-pick the most profitable customer segments. And there are those flush with liquidity, no long-term ambitions but on the lookout for profitable short-term lending opportunities.

    Liberalization and new competition together act to destabilize the spread business. Incumbents are pressured to pursue new and higher risk businesses in order to try to maintain their margins.

- **Rapid expansion of credit.** When credit rises very rapidly it creates three related problems:
    - Bank credit appraisal standards inevitably suffer. Analysts and investors put pressure on management at banks perceived to be losing market share. Management puts pressure on lending officers to drum up business. Credit officers cannot deal effectively with the heavier volumes and are under sustained pressure to approve loan applications.
    - Such rapid growth is likely to be beyond the ability of the real economy to absorb and allocate such credit to projects that can generate an economic return.
    - Finally, excessive growth of credit frequently results in asset inflation with funds being diverted to asset classes such as real estate and the stock market. This creates its own problems down the road.

- **Misallocation of credit.** One of the roles of banks is to channel savings from depositors to projects and companies that can generate an economic profit after meeting their financing costs. When the credit goes to sectors that can not generate an economic return it is unlikely that they will be able to service their debt or make principal repayments. Some examples:
    - **Speculative ventures.** Indonesia has a low-technology economy with a history of corrupt administrations and a relatively ill-educated workforce. It attempted to develop a regional airplane business from scratch. This was always a speculative, high-risk venture intended in part to boost national prestige. Indonesia's low-cost manufacturing base gave it little competitive advantage in a high-tech business where it was competing with US specialist manufacturers. The venture was one of the early casualties of Indonesia's 1997–1998 banking crisis.
    - **National projects.** Many countries have pursued strategic initiatives to nurture the growth of companies operating in industries identified as strategic. In South Korea attempts to build national industries resulted in huge oversupply and collapse of prices in businesses such as cars, shipbuilding and semiconductors.
    - **Prestige infrastructure projects.** Many developing countries invested heavily in infrastructure but most of these investments were made in large, prestigious projects such as bridges, toll roads, airports and dams. Few of these projects were subject to any sort of rigorous cost–benefit analysis. Some countries invested billions of dollars building multi-lane highways that remained largely unused following completion while many villages had no supply of fresh water and lacked most basic public services.

- **Real estate.** Cheap, readily available credit often ends up in speculative real estate developments. In Thailand many industrial companies took out bank loans in the early 1990s that were diverted into real estate investments. Rather than being used to build mass-market affordable housing most of these developments were for high-end condominiums, shopping malls, hotels and office space.

  By the mid-1990s there was a massive imbalance between supply and demand in these segments. Many developments ended up being abandoned, leaving Bangkok littered with the skeletons of half-completed buildings. Such landscapes are common throughout the world, Spain and Greece are obvious European examples. Another reason why many projects are not completed is avoidance of property taxes.

- **Currency mismatch.** Many Argentinean mortgagors took out US$ housing loans in the late 1990s encouraged by a managed exchange system that pegged the domestic currency to the US$. The collapse of the system left most of these borrowers bankrupt as their income and the value of their assets were in Argentine pesos but their liabilities in US$.

- **Asset price bubbles.** Holders of assets experiencing asset inflation (whether in financial instruments or real estate) often see it as a good thing. Rising asset prices can create a self-fulfilling expectation. Homeowners come to expect the value of their homes to continue rising inexorably. They make borrowing decisions with that expectation in mind. Markets are cyclical, however, and when corrections occur many borrowers find themselves in a position where the market value of their assets is less than the balance of the loans that they took out to finance their purchase.

  We examined the features and dynamics of real estate bubbles in Chapter 7 "Mortgage lending". One of the consequences of a sharp correction in a real estate market is that a number of highly leveraged developers usually fail. The loans made by banks are frequently secured against the actual developments. A partially finished building has little value.

  It may not make financial sense to even complete construction if the cost of doing so is more than is likely to be obtained from selling the completed building. The development may even have negative worth if local authorities require the owners to either complete construction or clear the site.

  Rapidly rising equity prices create additional dangers when many investors buy on margin or use stock as collateral for other loans. Equity markets are reasonably good at anticipating financial crises and may fall by as much as 70%–90%. When markets fall by this order of magnitude investors and securities companies are both at risk.

- **Pegged and managed currency systems.** Globalization has been hailed by some as the source of salvation in terms of development of emerging economies and by others as a key source of instability. In many emerging-market banking crises the crisis was preceded by large inflows of foreign funds. In many instances these inflows had been encouraged by the adoption of some form of managed currency control system while restrictions on the convertibility of the currency had been lifted. The latter meant that foreign funds could flow freely into and out of the country.

  The major types of managed currency systems were introduced in Chapter 3 "Central banks and the creation of money". The central bank is responsible for managing the country's foreign reserves and money supply. Policy errors at central banks are largely responsible for creating the conditions necessary to allow financial crises to develop. It is easy to criticize after the event but such criticisms are justified when central banks ignored early warnings from external bodies such as the IMF and private sector economists of the risks that their policies were creating and the need to change them.

- **Current account deficits.** Many financial crises have been preceded by a prolonged period of current account deficits financed by capital inflows. Open capital accounts combined with managed exchange systems have been a significant factor in many emerging market financial crises.

Macro-level factors in banking crises

Credit growth & misallocation

* Rapid credit growth lowers credit appraisal standards

* Absolute limit on number of projects that can generate economic returns

* Credit growth above ability of real economy to use productively

* Misallocation of easy credit

* Speculative high-risk ventures

* National champions

* Prestige infrastructure projects

* Real estate & stock market

Asset price bubbles

* Loans diverted away from productive projects into assets (real estate & stock market)

* Result is initial asset inflation

* Real estate
  - Condominiums, shopping malls, hotels & office space
  - Growing excess of supply over demand
  - Inflated assets used as collateral for loans

* Pricking of bubble
  - Drop in liquidity, absence of clearing prices
  - Borrower insolvency
  - Bank credit losses

Deregulation

* Liberalization of controlled interest rates

* Bank deposit & lending rate restrictions removed

* Lowering of regulatory barriers to entry
  - New domestic competitors
  - Foreign banks

* Destabilizing price-based competition

* Downward pressure on spreads

* Shift towards higher risk lending activities

Foreign currency

* Managed foreign exchange systems (pegged, bands)

* Open capital accounts

* Current account deficits

* Capital inflows
  - Bank loans, foreign direct investments (FDI), portfolio investments

* Currency mismatch between corporate assets & liabilities

* Collapse of managed foreign currency system when capital inflows reverse

* Loss of foreign currency reserves

It should not be surprising that the Japanese banking crisis does not fit the pattern, or have the characteristics, of most emerging market banking crises. Japan reported substantial current account surpluses through the 1990s. Japan has to deal with problems associated with an aging and falling population, overinvestment, continuing low or negative economic growth and deflation. This is a mirror image of the problems that policy makers in most emerging markets have to deal with.

Micro-level Factors

Mismanagement at the micro-level may also play a part in exacerbating failures at the macro-level. Banks are run by people. Some of these people are corrupt, others simply incompetent. Individual bank failures do not usually lead to financial crises but such failures may be indicative of the underlying business and ethical culture and the quality of the banking supervision.

These factors include related, connected and directed lending, weak bank supervision, weak and corrupt bank management, a high level of corporate debt–equity gearing, a maturity mismatch between bank assets and liabilities and lending by foreign banks:

- **Related and connected lending.** One of the reasons why most regulators impose strict limits on bank ownership levels is to guard against the risks arising from related, or connected, lending. This involves a bank lending either directly to its parent or to companies owned by its controlling shareholder.

  There are a number of risks involved. The first is simply a matter of bank management failing to meet their fiduciary responsibilities to minority shareholders by lending on more favorable terms than to other customers. The second is more serious in that a bank may risk losing its depositors' money by making loans that threaten the bank's solvency. This risk becomes particularly acute when economic conditions deteriorate and financial problems at other members of the group start to emerge. The bank is likely to make loans to help prop up those companies in trouble but in the event of them failing the losses risk rendering the bank insolvent.
- **Directed lending.** When governments instruct state-controlled commercial banks to direct their lending to selected companies or sectors credit appraisal standards are sacrificed for political expediency. Loans are made that have no realistic chances of being either serviced or being repaid.

  Politicians may have a number of different motives for directing banks' lending. They may be seeking to prevent the failure of a large company with the attendant job losses. Such closures will result in higher unemployment and political unpopularity. They may direct loans to help develop a particular industry perceived to be in the national interests.

  The experience in the former Soviet Union and its satellites suggests that free markets are better at capital allocation than central, planned economies. If investments in a particular industry were capable of generating economic returns, at acceptable risk, after financing costs it is reasonable to assume that private sector investors would seek out such opportunities.
- **Weak bank supervision.** Even when bank regulations appear to be of a sufficiently high standard they are worth little if bank supervision itself is weak. Banks in poorly supervised countries frequently abuse constraints supposedly imposed on them by regulators. This includes actions such as circumventing single borrower limits, failing to meet minimum liquidity

requirements, understating the level of problem loans and other window-dressing exercises that conceal the true state of the bank.

This problem is compounded in most developing markets where banks do not follow internationally recognized accounting standards or standards for recognizing and reporting non-performing loans. Accounting abuses are a common occurrence.

When corruption in countries and their public institutions becomes endemic banks may simply bribe supervisory officials to accept doctored accounts and to avoid investigating problem accounts that are being reported as normal.

- **Weak and corrupt bank management.** There are many ways for banks to understate NPLs. The simplest way is referred to as ever-greening. This involves the bank making new loans to a customer at risk of default. The delinquent customer then uses the proceeds from these new loans to service its outstanding loans. Alternatively the bank can simply capitalize interest due. Where regulators require banks to identify loans as impaired when collateral levels on secured loans fall below a certain level bankers can bribe property surveyors to report inflated values.

  More sophisticated methods generally require collusion between banks. A simple, but ingenious way to avoid reporting loans as past-due is for two banks with loans to the same company to collude with one another. Each makes new, matching loans to the company. The company then uses the loans from each bank to repay existing loans from the other. There is no change in the company or banks' financial conditions but each bank now has new performing loans in place of their old NPLs. In extremes banks may even engage in NPL swaps between different companies in similar distress.

- **High level of corporate gearing.** The higher the overall level of corporate net debt to equity the more exposed they are to sudden changes in the value of their assets or liabilities. Korean companies in 1996 had average debt–equity levels of $4\times$. Many companies had levels much higher than this of course.

  In part the blame for such high gearing should be allocated to corporate management but bank management should also share the responsibility for making imprudent loans.

- **Maturity mismatch.** Banks are in the business of managing a maturity mismatch. They fund short and lend long. This exposes them to significant liquidity risk and to shifts in the structure of the yield curve. It is for this reason that they maintain a buffer of low-yielding but highly marketable assets such as government securities in order to be able to cope with an unexpected withdrawal of deposits. Even when those liquid assets are exhausted a bank can turn to the central bank's discount window and borrow additional funds, albeit at punitive rates.

  Companies have limited expertise in managing liquidity risk, however, and have no central bank to turn to in the event of their creditors cutting their credit lines and calling in short-term loans. Companies therefore take significant risk when they borrow short term to fund long-term financing needs. This risk is compounded if that funding is in a foreign currency.

- **Foreign bank lending.** Foreign bank activities pose little threat to financial system stability where they have well-established operations. Citibank, for example, has been operating in Asia for more than a century. Risks develop when foreign banks enter markets where they have no real experience. This limited experience makes it hard for them to price credit risk adequately. They frequently end up in wholesale markets, such as commercial paper or syndicated loans, usually attracted by seemingly higher returns.

Their lack of commitment to a particular market means that in the event of problems developing they are prone to attempt to effect a withdrawal as quickly as possible.

Micro-level factors in banking crises

Bank supervision
* Under funded regulators
* Ill-paid & poorly educated
* Number of examiners versus number of supervised banks
* In-fighting between departments & between regulator & Ministry of Finance
* Political interference
* Regulation of non-bank financial institutions (e.g. finance companies)
* Failure to enforce single borrower limits
* Failure to deal with reporting abuses
* Inability to comprehend and supervise complex financial transactions
* Corruption

Bank management
* Lack of credit appraisal & cashflow analysis skills
* Limited credit risk management skills
* Collateral-based lending rather than cashflow
* Failure to recognize transformation of foreign currency risk into credit risk
* Underreporting of problem loans
* Inadequate capital levels & provisioning policies
* NPL swaps
* Corruption
* Acceptance of implicit loan guarantees
* Unthinking acceptance of group guarantees

Related & directed lending
* Bank loans to related group members
* Circumvention of single borrower limits
* Exacerbated by deterioration in economic conditions
* "Bailout" loans to group members risk bank insolvency
* Directed lending
* Lame duck policies, loans to prop up loss making companies
* Loans to bolster political popularity
* Political connections

Corporate financial management
* High debt-equity levels
* Reliance on short-term funding for long-term financing requirements
* Currency mismatch between corporate assets & liabilities
* Reliance on sustainability of managed foreign exchange systems
* Failure to appreciate fully the risks of taking foreign currency loans

CONTAGION

Financial contagion can take one of two forms. The first form is that due to the direct consequences of one company failing on another and is largely a domestic phenomenon. The second form is largely due to association and crosses borders. Financial crises in emerging markets experience both forms:

- **Domestic contagion.** Domestic contagion results from the business and financial relationships between companies. All companies have customers and suppliers and in turn occupy both roles themselves. If a single company fails it is likely to result in credit losses at its suppliers. Companies can survive only a limited number of their customers failing before also failing. One company's accounts receivable is another company's accounts payable. As the number of companies failing rises there comes a point at which a chain reaction takes place and the rate of corporate failures accelerates. Banks cutting credit lines to their customers adds to the contagion. The natural response of central banks faced with such a situation would be to cut interest rates and increase liquidity. This is not usually possible in the case of distressed financial systems.
- **International contagion.** Direct contagion is possible between countries but the more common form of international contagion occurs as a result of association. The trigger for the Asian financial crisis in the late 1990s was the collapse of the Thai pegged currency system. Crises subsequently developed in Indonesia, South Korea and Malaysia but Russia and some Latin American countries were also adversely affected.

    The direct linkages between Asian economies, for example, in the late 1990s were relatively low. Their largest trading partners were OECD countries rather than each other. The common factor was their reliance on foreign funding and on international capital markets in particular. International investors who had been questioning the underlying basis for these economies' past success lost confidence in their currencies. The Thai financial crisis was not the cause of the Korean or Indonesian crises but helped to force the recognition of their underlying flaws.

    The risks involved in investing in emerging markets were brought to the fore as international investors showed their tendency to treat emerging markets as a single asset class. Russia's declaration of a debt moratorium in 1998 resulted in a flight from risk in general and from emerging markets in particular.

LOSS ALLOCATION

There are many different ways in which governments, central banks, bank regulators and private banks can attempt to solve banking crises. The key feature of banking crises is that they are primarily crises of solvency. That means that there are losses to be borne in both the financial system and the real economy. This means that someone must absorb the losses, the question is who. It is this aspect of the resolution of banking crises that makes them inherently political. The following groups are at risk of bearing these losses:

- **Bank shareholders.** Shareholders' equity is the first line of defense in protecting depositors from outright losses. Shareholders may be forced to inject more equity into a bank to absorb the losses incurred and continue to meet regulatory capital requirements. They usually plead for regulatory forbearance or for a relaxation of the formal requirements.

    Their hope is that the bank will be able to earn itself out of its insolvency problem over time without having to inject new capital (which existing shareholders probably do not have) or raise new capital from new shareholders and face a dilution of control and ownership. In the most extreme case they face having their capital being written down to some nominal value and the bank being taken into public ownership.

- **Providers of hybrid capital.** The next group at risk is the providers of other forms of Tier I and II capital. These are the holders of preference shares and subordinated debt. As we have already noted, for preference shares to count towards Tier I capital they have to be non-cumulative. This means that if the bank is unable to pay a dividend to the preference shareholders they lose the right to this payment completely. In the event of the bank being liquidated they risk losing the principal as well.

- **Depositors.** Depositors are at risk in a number of ways. The most obvious of which is that they lose their deposits. This is a risk where there is no formal deposit insurance scheme, or the deposits are not covered under the scheme or the scheme has insufficient funds to meet its stated obligations. They are also at risk in less obvious ways.

  Their deposits may be frozen, preventing depositors from withdrawing their funds. This clearly carries a utility cost but they also risk having negative real interest rates imposed on these deposits leading to a fall in the real value of their deposits when they are ultimately released. Even if the deposits are not frozen depositors may be forced to accept negative real interest rates. This is one way to transfer wealth from depositors to borrowers.

  Holders of foreign currency deposits may find that they are forced to convert their deposits into local currency deposits. This may be at a rate that is below that of the market or simply leave them exposed to a devaluation of the local currency. In many cases domestic holders of foreign currency deposits either have foreign currency liabilities to meet or hold them because they have no confidence in the local currency.

- **Borrowers.** Borrowers face similar risks to bank shareholders in terms of having to inject new capital or risk losing control. Solvent borrowers are also at risk of having high real interest rates imposed on them. This is a method that can be used to transfer wealth from the real economy to the banking system. This may be the result of a deliberate policy decision or simply a by-product of market forces. It may be necessary to keep high real interest rates in order to protect or stabilize the local currency, for example.

- **Taxpayers.** Public bailouts of private banks are not popular politically. Taxpayers risk facing higher future taxes in order to meet the financing costs of recapitalizing the banking system or from a need to reduce the government's fiscal deficit. If IMF support has been sought the latter is a common condition for being granted financial aid.

- **Employees.** Employees are at risk of having the value of their wages cut in real terms, either by actual cuts, by the imposition of longer working hours or by having their buying power eroded by inflation. This is one way to transfer wealth from individuals to corporates. The extent to which this can be achieved depends on the strength of unions, legal constraints and the level of unemployment. In severe crises even public sector employees are at risk of the government being unable to pay them.

- **Foreign banks.** Foreign banks face a number of risks. They bear similar risks of suffering credit losses as local banks although this may be exacerbated by a higher level of foreign currency lending. They risk being discriminated against in restructuring or liquidation cases. They are also exposed to the risks of the possible imposition of capital controls. This would leave them exposed to currency risks and also having to meet letter of credit guarantees without being able to collect the funds due from the buyer.

Major groups bearing losses

Shareholders & other providers of capital	Depositors
* Attempts to understate NPL & credit loss levels * Loss recognition leads to risk of failure to meet regulatory requirements * Appeals for regulatory forbearance * Mandatory conversion of hybrid equity * Injection of new capital * Loss of capital & control	* At risk of losing deposits * Retail deposits may be insured * Implicit, assumed state guarantees to be tested * Frozen accounts, withdrawals postponed * Imposition of negative real rates – transfer of wealth to banks & borrowers * Mandatory conversion of foreign currency deposits into local currency
Borrowers	**Tax payers**
* Loss sharing with banks * Injection of new capital * Loss of control * High lending rates for solvent borrowers * Losses from delinquent customers * Losses from deposits with banks	* Cost of depositor insurance claims * Costs of soft loans to banks * Bailouts & losses from nationalization of private sector banks * Recapitalization of state-controlled & nationalized banks * Higher taxes, removal of subsidies, lower level of public services

CONSTRAINTS ON ACTION

There are many ways to go about resolving a banking crisis but the methods that can be used are subject to a number of constraints:

- **Scale of the crisis.** Depending on the scale of the crisis either a stock or flow solution may be appropriate or some combination of the two. In less severe crises it may be possible to resolve the crisis with a pure flow solution. In these cases bank regulators allow banks to operate that are technically insolvent or have capital adequacy ratios below BIS standards. The main objective of flow solutions is to allow the capital base to be rebuilt from operating earnings. Conditions are normally imposed on troubled banks preventing them paying dividends until they have met the regulatory capital requirements.

  The need to use stock solutions, where banks are recapitalized by the injection of new capital, becomes increasingly necessary as the scale of the crisis increases. This is because flow solutions become ineffective above a certain level of NPLs.

- **Legal powers.** The methods used may also be constrained by the legal powers granted to the central bank and bank supervisors. This may, for example, prohibit the use of taxpayers' money to bail out private banks and other private sector corporates.

In many instances the legal powers and institutions necessary to manage the process of rehabilitating the financial system are not in place. New laws have to be passed to establish these institutions and grant them the necessary powers to be effective.

In many developing countries the legal system is biased against creditors and judges tend to act in favor of borrowers. These systems are also frequently highly inefficient, sometimes corrupt and cases often take years to be resolved.

Few developing countries have a legal framework, such as that of Chapter 11 in the US, that provides temporary protection for companies in trouble to continue receiving bank financing while they attempt to restructure to return to good health.

- **Political considerations.** The ability of the government to take action is also constrained by political considerations. As discussed in the previous section there are many different groups at risk of bearing losses. The political strength of a particular group is a major factor to the extent to which they can avoid losses. The strength or weakness of the government is also an important factor.

  It may make sense to have negative real interest rates in order to transfer wealth from depositors to borrowers. This may not be possible in practice if the country has an ill-developed pension system and pensioners depend on the income from their savings held with banks. The result could be a system where retail depositors receive a higher interest rate than wholesale depositors, the opposite of what occurs normally.

  It may also not be possible to close and liquidate companies that are not viable either because of the political connections of shareholders or because of popular opposition to large-scale job losses.

- **Markets.** Foreign currency markets may impose effective constraints on interest rate and fiscal policies. It may be advisable to keep domestic rates low to lessen the financing burden of borrowers. This may not be possible if it is necessary to keep domestic rates high either because of the existence of a currency board or simply to ward off a currency devaluation.

- **Supranational institutions.** When a banking crises involves significant levels of foreign currency debt the country's foreign reserves are likely to be depleted. This will affect its ability to pay for imports and service its foreign currency debt whether held in the private or public sector.

  In such cases the government is likely to have to appeal to the International Monetary Fund (IMF) for financial support. Such support is normally only granted provided governments agree to certain conditions for fiscal and market reforms.

  Most of these conditions are intended to help to achieve two objectives. First, to stabilize the currency in the short term and, second, to effect longer-term structural changes that lead to a more open and competitive economy and make a repeat of the crisis less likely. There is considerable controversy over the nature of the conditions that the IMF imposes and it is clear that for all their power they do not have all the answers. The IMF may force a country to keep real interest rates high in order to support the currency but higher rates will inflate corporate financing costs and are likely to push the economy into recession. These are likely to lead to more delinquencies and exacerbate the problem of domestic insolvency in both the real economy and at local banks.

- **Deposit insurance schemes.** The ability to stem short-term problems arising from bank runs is affected by the existence of a deposit insurance scheme, the level of coverage and the level of funding of such a scheme. Bank runs are more likely in the absence of such a scheme, when coverage is low and when there is a lack of confidence in its ability to cover depositors.

- **People.** The resolution of a banking crisis is a complex matter and requires individuals with different skill-sets than in the normal course of events. These include debt restructuring professionals and facilitators, liquidators and managers of distressed debt. In developing markets there is frequently a shortage of such professionals. This may constrain the development of the institutions required to turn a crisis around.

EMERGENCY MEASURES

In the early stages of a financial crisis emergency action must be taken to stabilize the situation. The actual action that needs to be taken depends to a large extent on whether the banking crisis is wholly domestic or has a large foreign borrowing component. It is much easier to deal with the former than the latter.

Domestic Banking Crises

The first things to do in a domestic banking crisis are to protect the payments systems and to prevent solvent institutions from failing as a result of deposit runs or from the failure of other, insolvent, financial institutions.

In any financial crisis there is always a "flight to quality". Depositors transfer funds from finance companies to small private banks, from small private banks to large private banks and from large private banks to state-owned banks, and from state-owned banks to foreign banks.

The role of the central bank as the lender of last resort now comes to the fore. It should pump liquidity into the system so that financial institutions suffering bank runs can continue to meet deposit withdrawals. In some cases the central bank may make a statement guaranteeing deposits at selected institutions.

This appears to pose risks for the central bank as it effectively takes on the credit risks of the weaker financial institutions but is almost certainly the most effective option. As we will see closure is usually the least effective method for dealing with failed banks and should only be used in cases of relatively small, isolated financial institution failures.

Financial crises are systemic in nature and this creates a risk of the domino effect taking place. If a large financial institution fails it creates a risk of bringing down others with it. Even if it allows a small bank to fail it risks undermining confidence, which may be shaky in any case, in the whole banking system.

Domestic and Foreign Currency Crisis

Banking crises that involve a significant level of foreign currency borrowing in excess of foreign currency assets are difficult to resolve without the intervention of the IMF. Just as national central banks act as the lender of last resort to their country's banks, the IMF acts as the lender of last resort to most of the world's central banks.

One of the biggest mistakes that central banks make when facing an imminent financial crisis is leaving a request for IMF support too late in the day. There are a number of reasons why this is often the case, however:

- **Denial.** Individuals at the center of financial crises often respond at a subconscious level as someone suffering from shock. There are three clearly identifiable phases: denial, acceptance and action. Highly educated and intelligent people are capable of remaining in denial for an extended period. No helpful actions are likely to be made until the psychological adjustment is complete.

- **Lack of understanding.** The Thai crisis provides an example of a central bank that failed to comprehend the risks that the country faced. The governor of the Bank of Thailand had been in the job for only one year. He had little relevant experience and was ill placed to assess the situation. At the heart of the growing crisis were a fixed currency peg and an overreliance on short-term foreign funds. The correct response to the escalating flight of foreign capital would have been to let the currency peg go and try to conserve its foreign reserves. Instead it made a desperate last-ditch attempt to maintain the currency peg and, with speculators adding to the pressure, lost its US$30bn in reserves over the course of a month.

  The economy had enjoyed stable and strong economic growth for most of the period since the peg was introduced. Policy makers did not recognize that the conditions under which the currency peg had been useful had changed, however. Private sector economists and officials from the IMF had warned them of the growing risks and advocating a shift to a floating rate system by introducing a currency "band" and widening that band over time. This advice was ignored.

- **Political factors.** Many left-wing politicians and leaders in developing markets have demonized the IMF. These criticisms are understandable as the policies the IMF normally advocates are to reduce the government's fiscal deficit by cutting public expenditure and raising taxes, to force the removal of subsidies, to remove restrictions on foreign ownership and to remove trade tariffs. Few of these measures are popular with the electorate. A government that has to call in the IMF is making an explicit admission of policy failure and may well fall.

The first priority in dealing with a crisis involving a significant element of foreign liabilities is to stabilize the currency. Capital flight is most acute when foreign investors fear that capital controls will be introduced, preventing them from taking their funds out, or that the central bank will exhaust its foreign reserves and be unable to meet is obligations. By granting a sufficient emergency loan the IMF reduces the immediate fears and by making the loan conditional on economic and financial system reforms attempts to restore confidence.

RESOLUTION OF FINANCIAL CRISES

Once emergency action to stabilize currencies and restore confidence in the banking system has been taken and the initial panic has subsided the hard work of dealing with the real insolvency crisis can begin. No long-term solution to the problems in the banking system can be found without dealing with the related problems in the real economy.

We have looked at the factors involved that may result in corporate failures and the ways in which banks can deal with problem loans in the previous chapter. Most of that analysis remains valid in the context of a system-wide financial crisis and does not need to be repeated here though some modifications may need to be made to take scale into account. At the system level the three areas that may require centralized initiatives are the establishment of a government sponsored corporate debt restructuring agency, a strengthening of bankruptcy law and training of additional judges and relaxation of bank secrecy laws to allow banks to share information on delinquent accounts more easily.

National Asset Management Companies (AMCs)

More than a thousand US thrifts failed during the 1980s. A common factor was a widespread failure to manage the interest rate risk arising from making long-term fixed rate housing loans funded by floating rate funds. Some failed due to high NPL levels following the collapse of real estate prices in states, such as Texas, badly hit by the recession of the early 1980s. Others failed as a result of making speculative, high-risk investments with most of the risk in effect being covered by the Federal Savings and Loans Insurance Corporation. Weak supervision also allowed a high degree of mismanagement and fraud.

The government set up a state-financed organization, the Resolution Trust Corporation (RTC), whose main objectives were to take over the NPLs of failed thrifts, and actively manage these assets in order to minimize losses following their eventual disposal. At its peak the RTC was managing assets with a book value of approximately US$1 trillion. The RTC was wound up after seven years of operation following the successful disposal of all of its assets. The RTC is a prime example of an agency commonly referred to as an Asset Management Company (AMC). Their three principal activities are the acquisition of distressed assets, their management and their ultimate disposal. Most AMCs are usually set up in response to a crisis and once they have fulfilled their objectives are wound up.

An AMC can take the form of a central state-owned agency which buys distressed assets from all financial institutions. It may be set up by an individual bank or group of banks or be a private sector agency whose main objective is to maximize profits to its shareholders rather than minimize losses as is usually the case with state-owned agencies.

It is widely agreed that establishing a central state-owned agency with similar objectives to the US RTC results in a faster, more efficient rehabilitation of a banking system in crisis than would otherwise have been the case. Mexico, Sweden, South Korea, Malaysia and Indonesia all provide examples of countries that have taken such action in subsequent financial crises. The main features of their three primary functions are as follows:

- **Acquisition of assets.** The AMC buys non-performing loans (together with the rights to any pledged collateral) and foreclosed assets (predominantly real estate) from the liquidators of failed banks, from private sector and state-controlled banks and from nationalized banks. The price paid effectively determines any loss sharing between the AMC and the banks. The AMC normally has conflicting objectives of effecting a speedy resolution of the banking crisis while minimizing costs to taxpayers. A price is determined by negotiation accompanied by incentives, disincentives and coercion.

  The carrot dangled in front of the sellers is the exchange of an asset that bears a carrying cost but generates no income for a performing asset. A possible disincentive is that bank management may believe that the price offered by the AMC is less than the value that the bank will be able to recover. In a free economy it is clearly inequitable to give a state body carte blanche to seize private sector property and dictate the level of compensation made.

  One way to deal with this is to give banks the right to decline any offer from the AMC but require it to make the provisions equivalent to the write-offs that would have been necessary if it had accepted the offer. In the event that the losses following eventual disposal of the underlying assets prove to be less than the provisions made the difference can be written back though the income statement as profits.

Where the actual or implied losses are greater than the provision for losses that the bank has established it will have to take an additional charge through the profit and loss account. This will reduce the bank's equity and hence its regulatory risk capital. This reduction may result in the bank being unable to meet its regulatory CAR requirements without raising more capital. In effect the AMC results in a higher level of transparency at individual banks and forces a more realistic recognition of bank credit losses.

The consideration is usually made in the form of government guaranteed zero coupon bonds. If payment were made in the form of cash banks would need to buy government bonds to transform the cash into income generating assets, as it would be unable to lend out such proceeds in a timely manner. The zeros are issued at a steep discount to par and usually mature in five years. Banks then amortize this discount over time and take it as interest income. The five-year term is usually chosen because it pushes back the need to finance the redemption of these bonds into the relatively distant future but is still in sight.

The underlying hope is that recoveries will be sufficient to cover the redemption of the bonds by the AMC or at least result in a manageable shortfall. This is more likely to be the case if a modest recovery in real estate prices occurs.

There is one more advantage of this approach. If the AMC overpays for non-performing assets this represents a transfer of wealth from taxpayers to private sector bank shareholders. Bailouts are unpopular with voters but this method is sufficiently subtle that it is likely to go by largely unnoticed.

- **Management of assets.** Non-performing assets must be actively managed or they will lose even more value. Physical assets must be maintained and where they generate an income (such as rental income from tenants) this must be pursued and collected. The AMC must also ensure that its position with regard to assets that it has purchased is protected. It may have to take action to defend its interests from proposed action at creditor companies with possible adverse implications such as may arise from asset disposals.

  The AMC has two broad alternatives for dealing with individual problem loans where it is the only or major financial creditor. It can move to sell part or all of the loans to a third party such as a vulture fund or attempt to impose a debt restructuring agreement.

  Where it is but one of many financial creditors it must take an active part in debt restructuring processes but in theory has no more influence than any other creditor with a similar level of exposure. In practice this is rarely the case. By buying distressed assets from a number of banks the AMC usually becomes the largest single creditor and is in a position to dictate restructuring terms not just for individual companies but also for entire industries. This may result in it forcing industry-level consolidation and the removal or destruction of excess capacity.

  In very severe financial crises the national AMC may end up owning and controlling the largest companies and most valuable assets in the country. Such powers are not without their own risks.

- **Disposal of assets.** Assets may be disposed of in one of a number of methods available. The AMC may look to sell assets through auctions. It may use the services of investment banks to securitize loans and physical assets and then sell these securities to investors. Management of the AMC has to balance between the potentially conflicting objectives of making such disposals as quickly as possible and maximizing recovery rates.

Such agencies are usually staffed with people seconded from the central bank, ministry of finance and from legal and accounting practices. There is usually also a pool of equity and credit analysts available following the failure of local securities operations.

Financial Institutions Rehabilitation Funds

It may be necessary to create a specialist state-financed agency whose main responsibility lies in the recapitalization of the banking industry, in the rehabilitation of failed private sector banks taken into the public sector and honoring depositor claims at these banks. We will use the term FIRF for such agencies but both the names of such agencies and the range of responsibilities they have vary. It may be possible to achieve some or all of these goals without actually establishing a separate agency and this depends on the nature of the crisis and on the existence of agencies that already perform some of these functions, such as a deposit insurance corporation:

- **Recapitalization.** Keeping some banks in the private sector is usually regarded as a government goal. Insolvent private sector banks have to look to the private sector for the bulk of their recapitalization needs but may be helped by the FIRF. Indirect support can be given by making "soft" loans to distressed banks. These are long-term loans made at rates well below market rates for such financing. They provide another way to give private sector banks a public subsidy. The FIRF may take minority stakes in banks to help them in their recapitalization with a view to selling down these stakes once the banks has been rehabilitated.
- **Rehabilitation of nationalized banks.** When failed banks are nationalized key objectives are to ensure that their business operations continue without creating a major dislocation to the economy, to minimize taxpayer costs and to return rehabilitated banks to the private sector as soon as possible.

    There are two possible ways to deal with nationalized banks. The first is to inject the bank into a larger, solvent bank, the second to rehabilitate the bank and then sell it as a going concern.
- **Depositor claims at failed banks.** Where an agency such as the US Federal Deposit Insurance Corporation (FDIC) exists this is used to absorb losses from depositor claims at insured, failed banks. In severe crises it may not have sufficient funds to meet all claims and hence will require additional funding.

    Where no such agency exists but the government has decided that it is in the wider public interest to meet such claims an agency such as the FDIC must be established. This is usually set up in such a way that solvent and rehabilitated banks are expected to meet at least some of these losses from future earnings.

    The level of future costs imposed on banks must not be so high that it results in the failure to achieve the ultimate goal of establishing a solvent viable banking system. Meeting uninsured depositor losses from public funds results in a transfer of wealth from taxpayers to depositors. It also represents an indirect subsidy to bank shareholders, by honoring its implicit guarantee the government allows banks to avoid having to pay depositor protection insurance premiums.

Corporate Debt Restructuring Agency

In many banking crises a relatively small number of borrowers account for a large part of system-level NPLs. These accounts are usually highly complex and in addition to trade creditors involve a large number of financial creditors when these companies had tapped the syndicated loan and bond markets for medium-term financing. These cases can only be resolved through restructuring agreements but with many conflicting interests reaching such an agreement is likely to be difficult and protracted.

The main stick that the restructuring agency has to persuade interested parties to reach agreements is to threaten liquidation of the borrower if they fail to do so. As this is usually the option least favored by most creditors such a threat can help concentrate minds but only works if the threat is credible. It is usually necessary to legislate to give such a body specific and egregious powers to be able to force liquidation even though it has no claim itself. It may also be necessary to tighten bankruptcy law to make it easier to dispose of assets and pre-empt legal procrastination.

It is highly unlikely that there will be sufficient judges and lawyers trained and experienced in bankruptcy cases to be able to cope with the much higher volume of cases they are likely to have to deal with as a consequence of the financial crisis. This is a real practical constraint as it is a problem that is difficult to rectify quickly.

Legislation in many countries makes it difficult for banks to share information on customers even when those customers have defaulted on their loans. It makes sense to relax such laws during times of crisis in order to resolve the crisis as quickly as possible.

22

Dealing with and Valuing Insolvent Banks

Failure is not a single, cataclysmic event. You don't fail overnight. Instead, failure is a few errors in judgment, repeated every day.

Jim Rohn, US businessman and author

STOCK VERSUS FLOW SOLUTIONS

The main issue in the financial sector following a banking crisis is how to deal with financial institutions of varying degrees of financial insolvency. The main decision to be made is whether a bank should be liquidated or rehabilitated. Liquidation is usually the least attractive option. It may be possible to rehabilitate insolvent private sector banks without actually having to nationalize them.

The rehabilitation of private sector banks may be achievable with a "flow" solution, whereby a bank earns itself back to health, through "stock" solutions that involve the injection of new capital or some combination of the two methods.

The following example is of a fictional bank with NPLs as a percentage of loans varying between 10% and 40%. NPL cover is 35%. The reported Tier I ratios (based on equity alone) vary from 4% to 4.3%. The main bank regulator has given all banks two years to meet a 4% minimum Tier I level and minimum NPL cover equivalent to 50% of NPLs. The question is whether a bank can meet these requirements from operating profits or whether it will be forced to raise capital.

Balance sheet ($m)							
NPLs as % of total loans	10%	15%	20%	25%	30%	35%	40%
Assets							
Other earning assets	20 000	20 000	20 000	20 000	20 000	20 000	20 000
Performing loans	45 455	43 478	41 667	40 000	38 462	37 037	35 714
Non-performing loans	4 545	6 522	8 333	10 000	11 538	12 963	14 286
Provisions @35% of loans	(1 591)	(2 283)	(2 917)	(3 500)	(4 038)	(4 537)	(5 000)
NPLs net of provisions	2 955	4 239	5 417	6 500	7 500	8 426	9 286
Other assets	2 052	2 032	2 013	1 995	1 979	1 964	1 950
Total assets	**70 461**	**69 749**	**69 096**	**68 495**	**67 940**	**67 427**	**66 950**
Risk-weighted assets	54 461	53 749	53 096	52 495	51 940	51 427	50 950
Liabilities							
Free funds	10 569	10 462	10 364	10 274	10 191	10 114	10 043
Interest-bearing liabilities	57 714	57 108	56 553	56 042	55 571	55 134	54 729
Equity	2 178	2 178	2 178	2 178	2 178	2 178	2 178
Reported Tier I	**4.00%**	**4.05%**	**4.10%**	**4.15%**	**4.19%**	**4.24%**	**4.28%**

If the higher NPL cover required was met today through a balance sheet transfer from the equity account to the reserves for credit losses accounts the Tier I level would fall sharply, as shown below. Even at a 10% NPL level the bank would be unable to meet both the higher provisioning requirement and the 4% minimum Tier I level.

Adjusted Tier I and capital shortfall ($m)							
NPLs as % of total loans	**10%**	**15%**	**20%**	**25%**	**30%**	**35%**	**40%**
Additional provisions required	682	978	1250	1500	1731	1944	2143
Adjusted equity	1497	1200	928	678	448	234	36
Required equity	2178	2150	2124	2100	2078	2057	2038
Adjusted Tier I	**2.8%**	**2.3%**	**1.8%**	**1.3%**	**0.9%**	**0.5%**	**0.1%**
Capital shortfall	**682**	**950**	**1 195**	**1421**	**1630**	**1823**	**2002**

Turning to the earnings statement, operating profits before charges for credit losses fall as the NPL level increases. If we compare the current level of operating profits with any inferred capital shortfall we can estimate how many years it would take to rebuild its capital base and meet the provisioning requirement.

At a 10% NPL level the bank only requires half a year's worth of operating profits to comply but at a 40% NPL level it would take nearly four years of operating profits to comply.

Balance sheet ($m)							
NPLs/total loans	**10%**	**15%**	**20%**	**25%**	**30%**	**35%**	**40%**
Interest income	6473	6265	6075	5900	5738	5589	5450
Interest expense	(3751)	(3712)	(3676)	(3643)	(3612)	(3584)	(3557)
Net interest income	**2721**	**2553**	**2399**	**2257**	**2126**	**2005**	**1893**
Non-interest income	352	352	352	352	352	352	352
Operating income	**3074**	**2905**	**2751**	**2610**	**2479**	**2357**	**2245**
Operating expenses	(1762)	(1744)	(1727)	(1712)	(1699)	(1686)	(1674)
Operating profit	**1312**	**1162**	**1024**	**897**	**780**	**672**	**571**
Capital shortfall	682	950	1 195	1421	1630	1823	2002
Number of years	**0.5**	**0.8**	**1.2**	**1.6**	**2.1**	**2.7**	**3.5**

A reasonable conclusion in this specific example would be that at a 10%–20% NPL level a flow solution is likely to be effective provided NPLs remain at this level. At a level of approximately 20%–30% a flow solution may still be possible if the regulator relaxes either the required capital or provisioning level or allows more time for those minimum levels to be achieved. Above 30% a stock solution is likely to be unavoidable.

Existing shareholders of private sector banks will seek to avoid raising capital if possible. If there is a majority shareholder and they lack the means to make a significant capital injection they are likely to go to considerable lengths to achieve this end in order to retain control.

If a private sector bank needs to raise capital in order to meet regulatory requirements but is unable to do so there are a number of alternatives. It can be liquidated, but this is rarely an optimal solution, the government can inject capital by taking a minority stake or it can be taken into the public sector.

TAKING FAILED BANKS INTO THE PUBLIC SECTOR

The process of taking a failed banks into the public sector is normally achieved by forcing the bank to write down the value of its shares to a nominal amount and then injecting new capital. The state then effectively has 100% control and ownership of the bank.

When failed banks are nationalized there are three principal ways to deal with them, rehabilitation, the injection of the entire bank into another bank and breaking up the bank.

Rehabilitation

The first act of a new set of shareholders taking control of a failed bank is to replace the board and senior management of the bank with their own appointees. This must be followed by action to seize possession to prevent theft and to prevent any records being destroyed. Later investigation will determine whether the failure was due to criminal fraud or simply mismanagement. In the early days this should not be the priority although a sensible precaution is to remove their passports, freeze all of their bank accounts and, if possible, get a court order restricting their ability to travel.

At this stage the level of capital injection made is not too important as the level of losses that will ultimately be borne can not be determined accurately at this time. The central bank, or its agency, has to ensure sufficient liquidity to allow the bank to continue to operate. By taking the bank into the public sector the state is effectively guaranteeing the bank's deposits and other liabilities. It is unlikely to suffer a continued deposit run and other banks are likely to be willing to extend credit lines.

After establishing effective management control there are a number of key objectives that must be achieved. These are normally achieved by bringing in accountants from the large professional firms and examiners from the bank supervisory body. These key objectives are as follows:

- **Take physical control.** Taking physical control fast is important, particularly where there are any suggestions of fraud or corruption. This is the case because not only is it necessary to protect the bank's physical assets (such as PCs and other equipment) but to keep management away from the shredder. In developing markets with ill-developed legal systems and an uncooperative management resisting being replaced getting physical control is not necessarily a foregone conclusion.
- **Review key personnel.** It is important to identify employees in key positions who are either incompetent or corrupt. The key personnel to review are those who were involved in either the appraisal or authorization process of the larger non-performing loans. If there is a suspicion of either incompetence or corruption being the case the personnel concerned should be suspended until a full, formal investigation can be undertaken.

   This is particularly important when loans to related companies, to companies associated with management or to management have been made.
- **Freeze credit lines.** The central bank normally has the power to issue "cease and desist" orders that will allow management to break the terms of any loan agreements with its customers. This is normally done both for customers with non-performing loans and for credit lines above a certain limit.

   Corporate customers know that their accounts will be subject to a detailed review. If their financial condition is weak or if they believe their lines of credit will be reduced it is rational for them to draw down against the full limit of their lines. In times of financial crisis cash is king. Other off-balance sheet exposures should be closed off, where possible, and the use of derivatives other than for hedging heavily restricted. The main goal is to avoid increasing current customer exposures until the major accounts have been reviewed.

- **Review all major corporate accounts.** Freezing credit lines risks causing companies to fail that might otherwise have survived. The first accounts to be reviewed are those with the largest outstanding loans where the bank is one of the largest creditors. At a minimum the review should establish whether loans outstanding are current or not!

  For current loans it is also necessary to determine whether any of the loan covenants have been broken and to assess the overall financial condition of the firm. The latter is to make an initial assessment of the likelihood that the loan will remain current and principal repaid on time. Loans where important covenants have been broken or where it is likely that future interest or principal payments will be missed are classified as impaired.

  It is not necessary to review exposures arising from a syndicated loan where the bank has a relatively small part of the total loan in detail at this time. No matter the size of the actual exposure. It will soon be clear whether such a loan is current or not. Doing a more detailed review is likely to be a wasteful diversion of resources that are urgently needed elsewhere within the bank. Such cases are complex and the bank's ability to influence the outcome extremely limited.

- **Release credit lines.** As the review process progresses credit lines for accounts whose loans are all current should be released. This should be done as quickly as possible to prevent creating problem loans that could have been avoided.

- **Set up bad bank.** The organization of the bank has to be split in two through the establishment of a "good" and a "bad" bank. Loans that are current are kept within the good bank. Impaired loans are transferred to the bad bank. This separation reflects not simply the difference in nature between current and impaired loans but also the different priorities and skills required of the management of the two banks. It also speeds up the process of recapitalizing the good bank and selling it back to the private sector.

  Management of the bad bank's main objective is to minimize losses arising from the bank's impaired loan portfolio. This may involve restructuring, liquidation, and collateral disposal and asset sales. They are usually best advised to hire insolvency and restructuring specialists from an international accounting practice. The transfer of impaired loans to the bad bank frees up management at the good bank for the job of generating income and keeping performing loans current.

- **Review controls and procedures.** Management has to satisfy itself that existing controls are robust and, if not, rectify any weaknesses or deficiencies immediately. As most of the losses from banks that fail in banking crises come from credit losses it is highly likely that credit appraisal and authorization policies of failed banks are weak or open to abuse. They must be reviewed and either tightened or replaced.

- **Cut costs.** Costs should be cut wherever this can be done without damaging the long-term business of the good bank or the ability of the bad bank to operate effectively and maximize recovery rates. These cost-cutting measures have two objectives, they will lower costs but probably of more importance they communicate a very clear message of the severity of the problems that the bank faces to its staff.

All of these measures need to be taken as quickly as possible. They are designed to reduce potential losses from making more loans to customers that will become non-performing, eliminating the risks from fraud and control weaknesses while establishing a structure for the rehabilitation of the bank and the management of its non-performing loans.

Other Options

Other options that may be considered include the following:

- **Injection into a solvent bank.** An injection of a failed bank into a larger, solvent bank is often considered. Such injections are viewed with great suspicion, as there is always a fear that poor asset quality at the failed bank will drag down that of the bank forced to absorb it. (A common, simply stated belief is that if you add one good bank and one bad bank together you end up with one larger bad bank.)

    Domestic private banks usually resist pressures to absorb a failed bank's operation and balance sheet. State-controlled banks are usually given no option. Using the largest state-controlled bank as the "national good bank" has the advantages that it is relatively straight-forward, and to an extent can be ring-walled. The disadvantage is that management at these banks are usually incompetent.
- **Breaking up the bank.** Another option is to break up the failed bank. This can be achieved by transferring non-performing assets to the national AMC and injecting performing financial assets and related bank liabilities into a larger bank or selling off the assets. Operating assets such as branches are usually disposed off separately.
- **Sale.** An option is to sell the bank as a going concern. Private sector banks are extremely wary about buying failed banks, and with good reason. When NPLs are rising it is extremely difficult to forecast with any certainty at what level they will peak. Even when identified NPLs have already been transferred to a national AMC it is extremely difficult to be confident about the results of a due-diligence exercise.

    Successful sales usually require the state to transfer impaired assets to an AMC, and then selling performing assets and other assets of the bank as a whole. Buyers usually insist on a form of loss sharing on loans that are currently classified as performing but subsequently turn sour. This may give the buyer a put option to sell such assets at book value to the AMC.

ACQUISITIONS OF DISTRESSED BANKS

When a bank cannot deal with its problems using a flow solution and cannot raise the capital for a stock solution the authority responsible for dealing with failed banks will often look at the option of selling it. There are few, if any, hostile bids for distressed banks. The risks are too high. Prospective acquirers should follow these guidelines, as best as possible:

- **Do a full credit review.** Potential acquirers should demand the right to do due diligence. In simple terms this means going through the target bank's loan portfolio to try to determine the current level of NPLs and future credit losses. If the acquirer's management fails to do a full due-diligence exercise and then proceeds with the acquisition they should be sacked and sued for negligence.
- **Buy a clean bank.** Get the seller (who is usually a state AMC) to take identified NPLs onto their own books before agreeing to the purchase. This will remove the problem of managing

these problem loans and also eliminate the matter of estimating expected loss rates on these loans.

- **Get a put option on future NPLs.** The buyer should also seek to get a put option on future NPLs. This is particularly important when system NPL levels are continuing to rise. Under these circumstances the due-diligence process never ends. It is extremely unwise to buy a bank where NPLs have not stabilized without getting a put option on possible additional future NPLs.
- **Loss sharing.** Where the acquirer has bought a bank with NPLs it is prudent to try to get a loss-sharing agreement with the seller on these NPLs. This will reduce the risks arising from collateral that is of lower quality than originally assessed and proves harder to dispose of and collect on than expected at the time of purchase.

Buying into distressed banks is clearly a relatively high-risk undertaking but may also result in high returns. As we have noted, the seller is usually a state-sponsored AMC. They are in the position of a forced seller. Their objective is usually not to get the maximum price possible but the best price possible as quickly as possible. There are also usually only a small number of serious interested bidders.

CLOSURE AND LIQUIDATION OF FAILED BANKS

The Case Against Bank Liquidation and Closure

When a bank is technically insolvent the first, and simplest, option is to close it. This is rarely the optimal solution. For this reason this option is seldom taken and when it is usually leads to greater losses than would otherwise have been the case. The reasons for this are as follows:

- **Dislocation to financial system.** Individual banks are a part of that complex creation called the financial system. Each bank has many outstanding transactions and positions with other banks at any moment in time. The closure by authorities of an individual bank will cause a dislocation to the financial system. Off-balance sheet agreements such as swaps, FRAs and foreign exchange contracts will fail. Deposits that other banks have made with the failed bank will be frozen.

  The closure of accounts and freezing of customer deposits is also likely to further undermine confidence in the banking system.
- **Dislocation to real economy.** Customers with deposits with the bank will have their deposits frozen. They may or may not get those deposits back eventually but, at least in the short term, access to their accounts is frozen. Payments by customers of the bank will also be blocked to customers of other banks. As a result members of the latter group may not be able to meet their own short-term liabilities and as a consequence fail even though they are solvent.
- **Higher level of defaults.** If the bank is closed borrowers of the bank who are current have little incentive to remain so. Without regular monitoring of these accounts and taking early

action to address payment problems the level of NPLs will rise higher than if the bank continued to operate. This will increase the eventual losses of the bank.

- **Loss of customer knowledge.** Closure of the bank will result in staff being laid off. With them will go a great deal of knowledge about the bank's customers and loans. That knowledge includes factors such as the seasonality of cashflows at particular businesses, sources of collateral other than that stated in the loan agreement, the reliability of customers in terms of payment regularity and timeliness, family ties and any special conditions attached to particular loans.

   This loss of knowledge will make it harder to determine whether the optimal way to deal with a default is through a restructuring or liquidation. Combined with the loss of knowledge on collateral this will inevitably push up loss rates on non-performing loans.

- **Loss of resources and personnel.** Closure of a bank will also result in the temporary loss of the physical resources of the bank such as branches. Without maintenance the value of such resources is likely to decline. Other resources such as computer systems may be lost permanently following the loss of their support personnel.

For all of the above reasons when the central bank, government or agency set up by central bank to handle liquidations decides to close and liquidate a bank it is vital for them to act fast. Loan documentation must be secured. Measures must be taken to prevent staff from shredding records. Bad loans must be transferred to the agency responsible for managing bad debts.

Current loans must be transferred to the agency responsible for managing current assets or sold to a solvent bank. The sale of current assets may be financed in a number of ways but a typical method would be for the central bank or agency to provide a medium-term loan. We will look at these issues in detail when we look at the option of injecting a failed bank into a solvent bank.

HUMAN COSTS

None of the above really captures the sense of panic and desperation that result from real banking crises. Indonesia's financial crisis of 1998 coincided with a meteorological phenomenon called "El Nino". This led to a devastating drought in parts of the country and the failure of the rice crop just as the government was taking action to remove subsidies on staple commodities and other basic goods such as cooking and heating oil. These actions were taken in order to comply with IMF conditions for financial support. Many hospitals ran out of essential drugs and other medical supplies because the country lacked the foreign currency reserves to pay for them. Few noticed the sporadic reports of people starving to death in the countryside.

Most blame for these crises can be laid at the feet of rich and powerful people driven by greed and compounded by ignorance. International lenders knew that parts of the loans they were making were being siphoned off into politicians' and officials' offshore accounts. Many of the loans made in the run-up to crises in developing countries were used to buy equipment from OECD companies that won their contracts by paying off the right people. The people who suffer most in these crises are ordinary decent people, raising families, trying to get educated and get on with their lives. It is easy for investment and banking professionals and finance academics to forget that banking crises are also human tragedies.

VALUING DISTRESSED AND INSOLVENT BANKS

On the surface it is not obvious that technically insolvent banks may have an intrinsic value, and indeed in many cases they do not! Where value does exist it comes from what is commonly referred to as "franchise" value. Franchise value arises from a bank's branch network, from having the licenses necessary to conduct business, from its systems and people and from its customer base and brand. In combination these provide a base for future earnings.

Technical solvency at a bank is largely a concept associated with accounting and economic value. Value from an equity investment standpoint comes from the value of discounted future cashflows.

The art of valuing distressed banks usually requires what may accurately be described as heroic assumptions. The key factors are as follows:

- **Credit losses.** The first estimate to make is the level and timing of the recognition of credit losses. This breaks into three parts:
  - **Peak NPL level.** When NPLs are rising it is extremely difficult to forecast the level at which they will peak. In cyclical downturns they are likely to continue to rise after the economy turns round. The best an analyst can do is to monitor the rate of increase of reported NPLs to attempt to identify when NPLs are close to peaking.

    Valuing banks when NPLs are rising, based on public information, is extremely difficult. Acquirers looking to buy distressed banks before NPL levels have stabilized would find it difficult to conduct the requisite due-diligence process. They would be taking a significant risk if they proceeded at this stage without an iron-clad loss-sharing agreement with the government or a state-backed organization.
  - **Loss rate.** Estimating loss rates accurately is also difficult. The actual level depends on several factors. The degree of conservatism of NPL classification, the level of secured loans, the actual value of the pledged collateral and the ability of the bank to realize that value (which depends on the nature and efficiency of the legal system and liquidity of the pledged collateral).

    It is best for the analyst to keep it simple. An assumed loss rate in the region of 40%–60% of peak NPLs is a reasonable starting point. Whether the loss rate is 40% or 60% does, however, make a huge difference in the estimates of the value of banks with NPL levels above 10%–15% of loans.
  - **Timing.** The timing of the recognition of losses matters because it has an impact on the bank's ability to meet regulatory capital requirements and hence on its need to raise equity.
- **Operating profitability.** Distressed banks suffer from a drag on operating profits that comes from the carrying costs of their NPLs and the lower yields on their restructured loans. Funding costs are determined largely by the market. Other operating expenses are largely fixed. Most of these relate to people costs. A downsizing will reduce the cost base but may be impractical given government or union constraints on layoffs. In addition any voluntary severance scheme will involve one-off charges as a result of redundancy payoffs. This will put

further short-term pressure on operating profits or losses, and hence on regulatory capital adequacy requirements.

Operating profits are crucial. With positive operating profits distressed banks can start to absorb their credit losses. As they provide for, or write off, their bad loans operating profits should start to recover. This improvement will be accelerated if the bank is able to start making new loans that remain current. In financial crises this is usually difficult, however, for three reasons:

- **Lack of opportunity.** When the system level of NPLs rises above 15%–20% of loans it becomes extremely difficult to assess the credit-worthiness of companies. At these levels contagion is at risk of setting in.
- **Loss of confidence.** Lending officers become increasingly risk-averse. The lax credit appraisal standards that prevailed in the run-up to the crisis are replaced with ones that put every loan application under extreme scrutiny.
- **Capital adequacy constraints.** The final constraint is that imposed by capital adequacy requirements.

Combined with tight liquidity the overall result is usually a credit crunch.

- **Capital adequacy requirements.** Most regulators relax capital adequacy requirements during financial crises. They frequently also reduce the requirements for banks to recognize loan losses. The most common means are to push back the past due criteria from say 90 days to 180 days and ease the conditions under which restructured loans are defined as performing.

They also tend to widen the range of hybrid equity instruments that can be treated as regulatory capital. Unfamiliar instruments such as CAPS (capital augmented preference shares) and SLIPS (subordinated limited irredeemable preference shares) and ICULS (irredeemable convertible unsecured loans) started to appear in Asian bank balance sheets in the aftermath of the late 1990s financial crisis.

The basic structure of these instruments was that the bank paid interest at a specified rate for the first five years but if it failed to redeem them at that time the interest rate payable would automatically rise to a punitive level. Clearly the banks will seek to avoid this occurring but it leaves them with the future problem of refinancing these instruments at that time.

These convertible instruments just add additional complexity to the valuation process. In broad terms, however, the value of a distressed bank is given by the following:

Value of distressed bank = Discounted value of (future dividends − capital to be raised)

Valuing distressed banks is so complex potentially that the analyst must make simplifying assumptions and use judgment and creativity. A key question to answer is whether the bank can earn itself out of the crisis. There is no single, right way to deal with this problem and the following provides just one possible approach.

We will start with a distressed bank with $20bn in NPLs out of a total loan book of $70bn. Provisions are just 25% of NPLs versus our estimate that they should in fact be 50%. Our estimate is that the bank is earning 350 bpts over its cost of funds on its performing loans and 100 bpts on its other earning assets. The bank is reporting a Tier I ratio of 6% based on an equity base of just over $4bn. That falls to −1% after taking account of our estimate that there is a $5bn provisioning shortfall. Pre-provision operating profits are less than $900m suggesting that it would take five to six years to make good the provisioning shortfall from operating profits.

Now take the same bank and assume it has been rehabilitated. The cost base has been assumed to remain unchanged but the NPLs have been replaced with performing loans and the Tier I level has been pushed up to a more conservative 8%. Under these assumptions the bank is making an *ROE* of nearly 20%, and assuming a 15% *COE* and 5% long-run growth assumption is worth nearly $9bn. The problems to solve are how to get there and whether it is worth it.

Balance sheet ($m)			Earnings statement ($m)		
	Distressed	Rehabilitated		Distressed	Rehabilitated
Other earning assets	20 000	20 000	Interest income	5700	7500
Performing loans	50 000	70 000	Interest expense	(3506)	(3627)
Non-performing loans	20 000	0	**Net interest income**	**2194**	**3873**
Provisions	(5000)	0	Non-interest income	438	438
NPLs net of provisions	15 000	0	**Operating income**	**2632**	**4311**
Other assets	2550	2550	Operating expenses	(1751)	(1751)
Total assets	**87 550**	**92 550**	**Operating profit**	**881**	**2560**
			Bad debt charge		(560)
Risk-weighted assets	**71 550**	**76 550**	**Pre-tax profit**		**2000**
			Income tax		(800)
Free funds	13 133	13 883	**Net profit**		**1200**
Interest-bearing liabilities	70 125	72 544			
Equity	4293	6124	*ROE*		19.6%
Total liabilities	**87 550**	**92 550**	*COE*		15%
			Growth		5%
Reported Tier I	6.00%	8.00%	**Fair value**		**9382**
Additional provisions	5000	0			
Adjusted equity	(707)	6124			
Adjusted Tier I	−1.06%	8.00%			

We will take two extremes. First, assume that the bank is rehabilitated today and second that it drags out the process over five years.

On our working assumptions the bank is $1.8bn short of the capital to meet an 8% Tier I requirement and $5bn short of the provisions necessary to achieve 50% NPL cover. We will assume it raises that $6.8bn today. We have already estimated that the rehabilitated bank is worth $9.4bn. Subtracting the capital raised puts a value on the bank of $2551m or a fair price-to-book target of 0.6× (based on reported or "unadjusted" book).

Value of bank with immediate capital raising ($m)	
Capital shortfall	1831
Provision shortfall	5000
Capital raising requirement	**6831**
Fair value	9382
Value of reported equity	2551
Price-to-book target	0.6×

Next we will assume that any capital raising takes place in five years' time. This example is being deliberately kept simple to keep it manageable. Tax implications, including any tax shield, have been ignored. The level of operating profits should increase as the level of equity and provisions edges up. We can safely assume no dividends and minimal balance sheet growth. The shortfall drops to $1.6bn. Subtracting this from our assumed fair value of $9.4bn gives a value in five years' time of $7.8bn. We now need to discount this back to today giving a current value of $3.9bn or a price-to-book target of 0.9×.

	Value of bank with capital raising in five years ($m)							
	Operating profit	Equity plus provisions	Required equity plus provisions	Shortfall	Fair value	Fair value less shortfall	Discounted value	Price-to-book target
Year 1	881	10 174						
Year 2	960	11 133						
Year 3	1046	12 179						
Year 4	1140	13 320						
Year 5	1243	14 563	16 124	1561	9382	7821	3888	0.9×

We now have a working price-target range of between 0.6× and 0.9× reported book. Below 0.6× book potential rewards probably outweigh risks. Above 0.9× the stock's valuation appears stretched.

This may come across as a rough and ready approach because that is what it is. The assumptions are pretty clear, however, as is the valuation approach. There are at least two traps that analysts can fall into:

- **The detail trap.** Modeling solvent banks involves a lot of numbers but is actually reasonably straightforward. A well-constructed model will self-adjust as banks report earnings and re- quire little maintenance. This is not the case with models for distressed banks operating in stressed financial systems. Getting the appropriate level of detail is difficult particularly as regulators have a habit of changing the rules on a frequent basis. It is easy to get swamped with this detail.

  Discounted models can become incredibly complicated as analysts try to take account of new NPLs, restructured loans, NPL aging, provisioning requirements, new capital instru- ments, changing capital adequacy requirements and so on. All of this detail can lead to a spurious sense of accuracy. It can also lead to that well-known condition, paralysis by analysis.
- **The sensitivity trap.** A modest amount of sensitivity analysis can be useful to highlight which assumptions are most important. In the above example a table showing valuations against assumed loss rate would probably be of use. There is a tendency for analysts to write reports on distressed banks that comprise largely of sensitivity tables. These work fine when there is one variable and one dependent function. In analyzing distressed banks there are just too many variables. At the end of the day analysts are paid for opinions and to make judgment calls.

The prices of listed distressed banks tend to fall into one of two categories. They are either highly volatile or not traded actively. In the former case this usually indicates that analysts and investors are uncertain whether the franchise value of the bank is greater than the costs of rehabilitating the bank. The volatility arises from there being many variables that affect perceived value and many differing views on the value of those variables. In the latter case analysts and investors have concluded that the costs of rehabilitation outweigh franchise value. When the investment community decides that this is the case the bank will find it virtually impossible to raise new equity at any price.

PART VII

Supervision and Financial Statements

Regulation, supervision & policing

* Regulatory objectives & approaches
* Commercial bank regulation
  - Requirements
  - Cost overhead
  - Transaction complexity
  - US CAMEL assessment

* Securities market regulation
  - Issuance
  - Secondary market trading
  - Investment research
  - Mergers & acquisitions
* Regulatory weaknesses
* Accounting authorities
* Audit bodies

The balance sheet

* Accounting standards, disclosure & truthfulness
* key assets
* key liabilities
* Derived items

  - Interest earning assets, interest bearing liabilities, interest rate-sensitive assets, interest rate-sensitive assets,

* key ratios

  - Asset quality, CAR, liquidity, loan-to-deposit, free-funds, asset-equity gearing
* Meetings with management
* Forecasting the balance sheet
  - Loans, equity, others

The income statement

* Interest income & asset yields versus interest expense & funding costs
* Net interest spread & margin
* Market forces & Treasury positioning
* Forecasting net interest income
  - Forecasting errors
  - Cost plus spread approach
* Forecasting non-interest income
* Forecasting operating expense
  - Efficiency measures
* Forecasting bad debt charges
* Profitability measures (ROAE, ROAA)
* Relationship between net interest spread & margin

23

Regulation, Supervision and Policing

Everything not forbidden is compulsory.

Thomas White, "The Once and Future King"
notice at the entrance to each tunnel in the ants' nest

REGULATORY OBJECTIVES

Financial institutions are among the most highly regulated of all commercial businesses. In most countries banks and other financial institutions are subject to oversight by a number of different regulatory bodies, each one responsible for regulation and supervision of a particular segment of financial services.

Other parties such as accounting standards bodies and auditors also have important roles to play with the former group agreeing the most appropriate way to present financial transactions and the second group acting to ensure the accuracy of data released by companies.

The terms regulator and supervisor are used as synonyms with flagrant disregard to their actual definitions and we will follow that convention. The division of responsibilities between financial regulators varies from country to country and usually reflects the historic evolution of the institutions, practical considerations and political factors.

The overall goal of financial institution regulation is to achieve three primary objectives:

- **Safe and sound.** To maintain a safe and sound financial system.
- **Consumer protection.** To protect customers from abuse by financial institutions and to ensure that they are treated in a fair way.
- **Business conduct.** To establish and communicate clear guidelines, and when necessary procedures to follow and measures to meet, for financial institutions to follow in order to discharge their responsibilities in terms of meeting the first two objectives.

Regulators operate under political constraints and business pressures that are rarely explicitly stated. Neither maintaining an efficient financial system nor the protection of financial institutions' shareholders are explicit regulatory objectives. These constraints include the following:

- **Costs versus benefits.** That the regulatory costs imposed are commensurate with the public benefit gained from achieving these objectives both in general and for specific instances.
- **Innovation.** That the regulatory approach is sufficiently flexible to allow for continuing innovation.
- **Market and price distortion.** That procedures and measures defined do not hinder free competition or result in a distortion of market prices.

Although the way in which regulators are organized varies from country to country most regulations are divided between commercial banking, the securities business (investment banks, brokers and fund managers) and insurance companies (both life and non-life).

Regulatory Approaches

There are three principal issues concerning the regulatory approaches taken to achieve the above objectives:

- **Regulation versus market forces.** A fundamental regulatory issue to deal with is the extent to which regulation is necessary to correct for "market failures". There is an ongoing debate between those arguing for the use of formal measures to regulate financial institutions and those who favor allowing market forces to run their course.
- **Principles versus rule-based systems.** There is a fundamental divide between authorities who favor establishing broad principles to guide institutions' behavior, backed up by on-site examination to assess how these principles are applied, and those that favor the use of very detailed rules that institutions must follow backed up by audits to check compliance.
- **Recommended targets versus mandatory limits.** Specific regulatory requirements may be met by defining best practices and recommending target levels or by setting mandatory limits (whether minimum or maximum) for those measures.

Regulation versus Market Forces

We will use the example of bank regulatory capital requirements to contrast the views of those favoring market forces versus those arguing for greater regulation.

Those in favor of allowing the market to operate argue that formal capital adequacy requirements are both unnecessary and distort competition. Banks taking greater risks will have to operate with higher capital ratios or the market will act to make it more expensive for it to fund from wholesale sources. They will also find it difficult to transact business with other banks because the latter will impose very tight counterparty limits and may refuse to deal with them. A bank recognized by the market to be more conservative will be able to operate with lower capital ratios and less restrictive limits on exposures imposed by counterparties.

Those in favor of a higher level of regulation argue that for market forces to be able to act the market must have access to far more information on banks' financial condition than banks are willing to disclose. Such information is rarely less than six to eight weeks old and hence of limited value. Under these circumstances formal minimum regulatory requirements policed by regular bank examination are the only viable method of protecting depositor and wider public interests.

A combined approach is possible. A formal regulatory requirement could be set that required banks to maintain a specified, minimum credit rating issued by a recognized credit rating agency or risk losing their banking license. The actual assessment of the bank's capital strength would be determined by these agencies.

Principles versus Rule-based Systems

The Basel Accord is a rule-based system. Those in favor of rule-based systems point to the risks arising from the liberal and creative interpretation of principles and the more scope for abuse than occurs with principle-based systems. They also argue that it is relatively easy to check compliance with rule-based systems but difficult to assess whether individual institutions' interpretations of principles and resulting actions are appropriate.

Those is favor of principle-based systems argue that it is impossible to define all of the rules necessary to cover all eventualities and in doing so they become so complex that they risk becoming unmanageable and risk losing sight of the larger objectives. They also create incentives for institutions to seek means that comply with the letter of the regulation but not their spirit. Their use creates the incentives for regulatory arbitrage. Where such rules are essentially arbitrary they also risk distorting market prices.

This divide is fundamental. An obvious example is given by comparing the use of US accounting policies, which are largely rule-based, with those of countries such as the UK and Canada where their application is largely principles-based.

Recommended Target versus Mandatory Limits

Many countries have formal minimum liquidity risk management requirement for banks that are defined in terms of them having a defined minimum level of liquid assets against its liabilities. The eligibility of assets to count as liquid assets and liabilities to be included in the denominator are defined explicitly.

A problem with these measures is that they take no account of the likelihood of a deposit run or a bank's liquidity management capabilities. Better managed banks are penalized relative to other banks by having to hold a higher level of liquid assets than management believes are necessary to have the same level of protection against deposit runs as their less well-managed competitors.

In general, regulators in developing countries rely more on mandatory requirements than those in developed markets where regulators allow banks' discretion to determine their own level but assess banks' overall condition and level of bank competency. They may set minimum limits for those banks perceived to be either weak or lacking capable management.

COMMERCIAL BANK REGULATION

In many countries the prime responsibility for commercial bank supervision rests with the central bank. It is by no means self-evident that these two functions should reside in the same institution. Such an institution may seek to encourage banks to lend during an economic slowdown to support its central bank monetary policy objectives. This may conflict with its responsibilities as a bank supervisor, however, where to protect the solvency of the banking system banks would be better advised to be showing restraint in terms of credit growth.

Most banks are subject to oversight by a relatively large number of regulatory bodies. This is due to the fact that most banks provide a wide range of financial services and in many countries regulation is divided between commercial banking, investment banking, asset management and insurance.

Banks in most countries are also subject to regulation to prevent them from assisting criminal organizations, whether deliberately or not. The main focus of these regulations is on money laundering.

Around the world these regulatory and supervisory functions reside in the public sector, there is, however, a wide variation in the level of political independence, particularly in the supervision of commercial banks. In addition to meeting regulatory reporting requirements most banks are required to publish periodic externally audited financial statements. Many banks are listed on one or more exchanges and also have to comply with the relevant stock exchange reporting requirements.

All of this regulation is designed to protect bank stakeholders and customers. It does, however, impose a regulatory burden on banks in terms of the effort necessary to ensure that a bank complies with its legal requirements and meets its reporting requirements in a timely manner. Most banks and other financial institutions have a separate compliance department responsible for ensuring that they do not fall foul of their legal obligations.

Commercial Bank Regulatory Requirements

The following are examples of typical commercial bank regulatory requirements:

- **Capital adequacy requirements.** Regulators require banks to maintain a minimum level of capital based on the size of a bank's assets and the level of risk. In developed markets these requirements are based on rules drawn up by the Bank of International Settlements (BIS), currently based on an amended version of the 1988 Basel Accord. The implementation of these standards varies from country to country, such as the definition of what banks can treat as capital to meet regulatory requirements.
- **Liquidity requirements.** Banks face the risk that they may be subject to a "deposit run". This involves an unexpected withdrawal of deposits by customers. Loans are effectively illiquid, this means that a bank cannot simply call its loans at short notice. In order to mitigate these risks banks have to keep a portion of their assets in the form of liquid assets. These generally include short-term deposits with other banks and holding government bonds that can be readily sold in the market.

    In some countries regulators actually define specific liquidity requirements that must be met. These are usually based on a standard ratio such as liquid assets (marketable government securities and short-term deposits with other banks, for example) to customer deposits. In more developed markets the trend has been away from regulation and towards supervision. In these countries banks are allowed to determine their own level of liquid assets.
- **Restrictions on investment holdings.** In many countries banks are restricted in terms of the level of listed equities, commodities and real estate investments that they can hold. These restrictions have two major and unrelated objectives. First, to protect depositors from the risk that the values of these investment holdings and trading positions will fall risking bank insolvency. The second objective is to reduce the risks arising from equity cross-holdings between banks and related companies.
- **NPL classification.** Definitions of NPLs can vary significantly from country to country. In some countries this is simply based on a 90-day past-due basis. As the level of NPLs has a crucial bearing on economic solvency the exact definition of what constitutes a NPL is important. Many supervisors use terms such as substandard, doubtful and loss to subdivide problem loans but in many instances even when these terms are used the definitions vary between countries.
- **Provisioning requirements.** When banks make loans one of the biggest risks that they face is that the borrower will default. In many countries banks are required to put loans into one of a number of classifications based on the likelihood and level of future losses. While banks in more developed markets are generally allowed to determine the level of provisions that should be set aside for potential future losses in emerging markets the central bank

frequently defines minimum provisioning requirements that must be made based on a loan's classification.

- **Single borrower limits.** Most regulators impose limits, defined as a percentage of shareholder funds, on the total exposure to a single company or group. These are referred to as single borrower limits. Banks that are controlled by non-financial institutions are at particular risk of breaching such limits. Even when regulators do not proscribe such limits most banks set limits as part of their overall risk management policy.
- **Money laundering.** Money laundering may be carried out through banks, brokerages and fund managers. The most important regulatory imposition is that of the "know your customer" principle. This puts the responsibility for ensuring that financial transactions are legitimate onto the financial institutions involved.
- **Consumer marketing.** In many countries legislation has been enacted to prevent banks from publishing misleading marketing materials aimed at retail customers. In particular banks and other financial institutions are usually required to clearly indicate effective annualized interest rate charged on consumer credit products.

Cost Overhead

All banks have to produce a wide array of regular financial reports for different external bodies. Most of these are produced on a quarterly basis although some are required on a monthly basis or even more frequently. In more developed countries these are produced in a digital form but in many countries banks still have to lodge printed reports. Under the terms of the Internal Ratings Based (IRB) approach of the Basel Accord banks will have to maintain duplicate credit risk management databases and systems to be able to comply with regulatory conditions and produce the numbers in the form dictated by the Accord. Meeting regulatory reporting requirements is just one example of the cost overhead imposed, there are others.

All individual cash deposits in the US, for example, above a certain minimum level ($10 000 at the time of writing) have to be reported. This is intended to help combat money laundering by drug dealers and organized criminal organizations. One has to wonder whether this particular measure does anything more than create a mild inconvenience to money launderers. Any self-respecting drug dealer will make more deposits of a lesser value rather than hit this well-known trigger level. Banks still have to report all other transactions above this limit of which almost all are legitimate.

These regulatory reporting requirements impose a significant cost overhead on financial institutions. There is an ongoing tussle between regulatory authorities and financial institutions on this issue. In general terms regulators require as much information as possible, delivered in a form and at a time of their choosing. The role of a bank chief information officer has become increasingly challenging as they try to provide systems that meet the needs of both their internal and external clients.

Regulators are less concerned about the costs that their requirements impose on the organizations being supervised. Eventually these costs are passed on to customers reducing the efficiency of the financial system overall.

Transaction and Instrument Complexity

Most banks seek to operate within the law but are constantly looking for legal ways to increase competitive advantage and profitability and to minimize taxes paid. When authorities close one loophole banks will change their behavior and look for another. A financial institution or its customers may be prohibited from holding a particular instrument but a bank may be able to find a way around this prohibition by using derivatives and other instruments that are allowed to create an equivalent synthetic position.

Regulators and accounting bodies are generally one step behind current market practices and operating in catch-up mode. Individuals in the private sector are usually paid significantly more than those in the public sector and attract very bright, highly motivated individuals at the higher levels. There are frequently genuine intellectual disagreements on how to treat a particular financial transaction and how this should be presented in a bank's financial statements. Regulators, accounting bodies and market participants generally try to reach a consensual agreement on an appropriate treatment although this may take years to achieve. At the end, however, authorities with legal powers are in a position to impose a solution.

Fraud

Fraud occurs in all walks of human life and financial services are no exception. Fraud may be perpetrated by or with the knowledge of senior management, or by individuals acting alone. Frauds carried out by external parties are much easier to prevent and detect than those carried out by "insiders".

Fraud is of particular concern at financial institutions because its scale usually dwarfs that possible in non-financial institutions and because of the knock-on effect of bank failures on the system as a whole.

US Bank Examination and the CAMEL Assessment Method

The US has a highly sophisticated regulatory infrastructure, but it is unrivalled in terms of the sheer scale of the financial services industry (there are literally thousands of banks) and the diversity of its financial institutions ranging from simple community banks through to financial giants active in all areas of the business and on an international basis. The bank regulatory approach is very much hands-on but the actual framework used to assess and communicate an individual bank's overall position is deceptively simple.

Federal and state regulators conduct regular on-site examinations of banks. Banks have internal audit and compliance functions and are also subject to external audits. One of the many objectives of the examiners is to confirm that the information being reported is accurate and that adequate controls are in place. The overall objective is to assess the financial condition of each bank. This is not a trivial exercise given the increasingly complex nature of financial operations and the large number of risks that banks are exposed to.

The level of detail available can be overwhelming to both analysts and regulators. In an attempt to simplify the presentation of the results of the assessment each bank is awarded a numeric overall rating to help identify sound and impaired banks. This is known by the acronym CAMEL where C stands for capital adequacy, A for asset quality, M for management quality, E for earnings and L for liquidity.

The best rating in each category is "1" and the worst "5". These assessments are then used to determine an overall rating. An overall rating of "1" or "2" indicates a sound bank with a clean bill of health. A bank with a rating of "3" has an underlying weakness that requires corrective action. Banks with a rating of "4" or "5" are perceived to be at risk of failing.

Problem banks are subject to a higher level of regulatory scrutiny, may be required to raise capital or risk losing their banking license. They are also likely to be subject to restrictions on deposit taking and credit extension.

This framework is most useful when applied to banks that are primarily concerned with the spread business – making most of their earnings from the difference between what they pay for their funding and what they are paid on loans. It is less useful when applied to financial institutions with extensive investment banking or trading activities or that use derivatives extensively.

As banks in developing markets tend to fit into the former category it is not surprising that many regulators in these countries have assessment frameworks based on the CAMEL approach, although few make such information publicly available. A major weakness in many of these countries is a lack of suitably qualified examiners. While the American model has been adopted on an informal basis by many countries the global minimum standards are determined by a committee working under the auspices of the Bank for International Settlements (BIS) and known as the Basel Accord.

SECURITIES MARKET REGULATION

Overall regulatory oversight for securities markets usually lies with one public body, usually called the Securities Exchange Commission (SEC) after the US body. More detailed responsibilities are usually delegated to individual exchanges and representative self-regulatory bodies. These have to act within overall guidelines set by the SEC. The main areas of supervisory focus are as follows:

- **Primary issuance.** All new issues that will be publicly traded are required by securities' regulators to be registered and sufficient information about the issuer's financial and operating situation disclosed to allow investors to make an informed decision on whether or not to subscribe to the issue. In the US laws of this kind intended to prevent securities fraud are known as "Blue Sky" laws. This information is contained in a formal prospectus. The issuer and leading investment banks are responsible for compliance and for the accuracy of information provided. They are liable for any inaccurate or misleading information.

  Regulations may also cover the methods used for new issue allocations to ensure that all investors receive a fair treatment. Investment banks have an incentive to give favored clients a higher level of allocation in "hot" issues in return for future business.
- **Secondary trading.** Most trading regulations are set by the relevant exchanges. These regulations are intended to result in an orderly market where all investors are treated fairly and prices reflect all publicly available information. Abuses occur in many areas including:
  - **Front running.** Front running occurs when market participants execute their own orders before acting on those placed by their customers. A large customer buy order is likely to push up the price of the stock concerned.
  - **Priority of treatment.** Giving favored clients priority in the execution of orders before acting on those from less important clients is inherently unfair. This is difficult to police effectively but most respectable firms have procedures established to give an appearance, at least, of fair treatment in terms of execution to all clients.

- **Suspense-account transfers.** Brokers may book customer-driven trades to suspense accounts and if profitable over the course of the day close the position and take a proprietary profit and if loss making transfer it to the client's account.
- **Acting on insider information.** Insider information is material, price-sensitive information that is not in the public domain, such as knowledge that one company plans to make a takeover offer for another. Acting on such information is illegal in some countries (although prosecutions are rare). Company board members and senior management are exposed to such accusations but anyone who acts on such information is potentially liable under some regulatory and legal regimes.
- **Creation of false markets.** The creation of false markets may be achieved by a group of investors acting together to push up the price of a specific stock's price or to push it down through short selling. Small-cap, relatively illiquid stocks are particularly vulnerable to such action. Investment banks have an incentive to underreport the level of stock they have been left with following an unsuccessful issue that they have underwritten. Market knowledge of this overhang would depress the stock's price at a time when the bank is trying to minimize any losses by disposing of this stock in the marker at as high a price as it can obtain.
- **Window dressing.** Many derivative products are based on prices of financial instruments at the close of dealing and often on specified dates. An arbitrageur who has bought an index future, for example, and taken short positions in some of the constituent stocks may put in large buy orders in one index stock just before the market closes. Few of these orders will actually be executed but the effect of the orders will be to push up the price sharply at the close. Such price movements on dates when common derivative products expire are particularly suspicious.
- **Short selling.** Restrictions on short selling exist in many markets. In the US, for example, short selling is prohibited on "down ticks" when stock prices are falling. In many markets short selling is not permitted under any circumstances.

Markets can be dirty places and when abuses take place they usually benefit market insiders at the expense of investors. Greedy dealers are constantly looking for loopholes to exploit that are either legal or where they believe it will be difficult to prove guilt. Procedures have to be established to resolve trade disputes and most exchanges require all dealing room calls by members to be recorded.

Certain actions are prohibited in some regimes but tolerated in others. Insider trading is a criminal act in most developed countries but is accepted as common practice in many developing markets. This does create ethical, and in some instances legal, problems for some international investment houses. These hold investments in stocks in other countries where there are less regulatory and legal restrictions than in their home country. They are in a position where they can act in a local market in a perfectly legitimate manner but where if they took such action at home they would be at risk of being prosecuted.

Such conflicts are not restricted to financial services and exporters often face the problem of having to make bribes, in one form or another, in order to win contracts. These are often made in the form of commissions to middlemen.

- **Investment research.** Most investment research is produced with institutional investors the main target audience. Retail-oriented research has to be simpler and is often produced by pulling together extracts from institutional research. A key difference lies in investment recommendations. Institutional-oriented research tends to make recommendations relative to specified benchmarks or indices while research intended for retail investors is concerned more with absolute returns.

Most analysts, from time to time, find themselves in positions when personal acquaintances ask them for investment advice and stock tips. Smart institutional analysts never give either. A "buy" recommendation suitable for an institutional investor does not readily translate into a buy recommendation for a retail investor. Investment advice has to be made in the context of what is appropriate for an individual's requirements. It is also true that retail investors have highly selective memories. The easiest way for analysts to get out of such positions is to make some vague statement alluding to regulatory licensing constraints on investment advise rather than get into an entire debate on what constitutes ethical behavior on their part.

The fundamental issues affect both retail and institutional investors, however. The most important are as follows:

- **Independence.** Brokers may under certain conditions produce research on companies in which their investment bank has a corporate finance relationship, its proprietary desk may have trading positions or it makes a market in securities issued by the company. All of these create potential conflicts of interest. At a minimum brokers have to publicly disclose that they have such interests. It is relatively easy to construct Chinese walls between research and the trading and market making functions. Such walls can be built between research and corporate finance but tend to be rather porous.

  Corporate finance deals can generate substantial fees and even when research analysts have not been involved in a particular issue there are ways in which pressure can be exerted to obtain a more positive spin from analysts. An investment bank looking to get a bond issue away for a company is unlikely to be pleased if one of its equity analysts downgrades his or her forecasts, writes a negative report or downgrades the stock recommendation from a "buy" to a "sell" just before the issue is launched. Even when direct management pressure is not applied, analysts may practice a form of "self-censorship". Management tends to regard analysts who are not "team players" with suspicion. Suspicion in this context translates into a lowered bonus.

- **Facts and opinions.** A basic requirement of research reports is that they clearly differentiate between fact and opinion. If they do not they may leave the firm at risk from being sued by investors who claim to have acted on the basis of the research but have since lost money. Few of these cases reach the court-room but it is difficult to determine the number of cases that are settled out of court.

- **Thoroughness and basis.** On a related matter, analyst research has to be conducted in a thorough manner and where opinions or judgments are being made the basis for such conclusions must be clear.

- **Black out.** When an investment house is undertaking corporate finance work production of research may be curtailed. Most securities regulators allow factual, historic information to be published but ban any research that contains views and makes "forward-looking" statements. Earnings forecasts can no longer be made and investment recommendations suspended. Analysts may be prohibited from making any statements about the company whether verbal or written.

- **Distribution.** Countries have different regulations and laws regarding distribution of research. The US, in particular, poses particular problems with restrictions on such detailed matters as from where printed research is posted. An international broker may have to courier its research in bulk to a US-based location before it can be sent out to individual investors.

These restrictions can run counter to requirements that all investors are treated fairly and receive research and broker changes in forecasts and earnings at the same time. These requirements are intended to ensure fair treatment for all clients.

- **Mergers and acquisitions.** Most stock market regulators specify various trigger levels for stock holdings. These include the level of holding when the shareholders must declare their interest (typically 5%–10% and when the potential acquirer is compelled to make a general offer (often referred to as a "Gee-O") to all shareholders and the level of acceptance required before the offer becomes unconditional. At this stage the acquirer has the right to compulsorily buy all of the issued shares, even those held by investors in the target company who had rejected the offer.

  Most stock exchanges have detailed takeover codes to which potential acquirers and target must adhere. These codes specify the manner in which a bid should be launched, the detailed documents that must be produced (in particular the offer and defense documents). They also specify under what conditions a counterbid may be made and how other offers affect the initial takeover timetable.

  There are normally restrictions placed on the would-be acquirer as to when it can make a subsequent bid if its first attempt fails. Many of the articles of takeover codes are intended to ensure that the rights of minority shareholders are protected.

- **Investment funds and advisory services.** Investment fund regulation focuses largely on the measures necessary to protect retail customers. As a result a lot of emphasis is placed on the nature of marketing materials and the methods used to sell these products. Many of these restrictions also apply to retail brokerage businesses:

  - **Marketing materials.** Marketing materials should point out downside risks, and point out that past returns on funds are not necessarily indicative of likely future returns. There should be a clear statement of the investment characteristics and objectives of the fund. Front-loading and redemption fees must be clearly stated. Where units have a bid–offer spread this must be stated. Annual management fees should be clearly identified.
  - **Historic returns.** There is a wide range of techniques available to present investment fund past performances. Fund managers have an incentive to choose those that show the performance of their funds in the best light.
  - **Sales techniques.** In some countries cold calling potential customers to try to sell an investment product is illegal but in many is not. Some regulators impose a "cooling-off" period between a customer signing up for a policy and being bound by its terms. The cooling-off period is intended to give customers an opportunity to change their minds.
  - **Independent financial advisors (IFAs).** IFAs provide advice to retail clients on how to manage their funds. There are usually restrictions on how these individuals can advertise their services. In developed countries most of the independent financial advisors have to be registered with a central securities regulatory body and to have gained a specified qualification (a common qualification in the US is that of a chartered financial planner, or CFP). Some IFAs are paid on a fee basis while others are paid on the basis of commissions they can generate. As some investment products have higher commission rates than others this creates a conflict of interests between advisor and clients. IFAs are only supposed to recommend, or sell, investment products that are appropriate to the client's individual circumstances and investment objectives.

REGULATORY WEAKNESSES

Some central banks and regulators are very good but in emerging markets there are a lot that are not. It is useful to start off by asking what factors contribute to making a bad regulator. It is difficult to get empirical evidence to support the following assertions but these are my observations:

- **Underfunded.** Weak bank regulators tend to be paperbound, bureaucratic and have a level of IT that is usually years behind that of the private sector banks that they are supervising.
- **Low pay.** Pay peanuts, get monkeys! The tendency of regulators to pay salaries well below those that can be obtained in the private sector has two implications. The first is that better qualified, more able potential candidates are likely to be attracted by better paid positions in the private sector. Second, it leaves central bank employees more open to bribery.
- **Low level of education.** Education levels in emerging markets are much lower than in developed markets. This means that there is usually stiff competition for the minority of people who have been educated to degree level. It may be politically incorrect to say so but it is nevertheless true that a degree from a top university in a developed country has little in common with one taken in a developing market.

    In emerging markets two of the most important criteria generally applied by many international brokerages for hiring local analysts are whether the applicant has been educated abroad and whether they have had experience of working for a foreign firm.
- **In-fighting.** At many weak central banks it is difficult to get a coherent, single view because of departmental in-fighting. This is frequently due to a lack of a clear definition of departmental responsibilities but can also be compounded by individual senior bureaucrats' desire to "empire build".
- **Political interference.** Two of the most important forms of political interference are directed lending and bailouts of failed banks.
- **Lack of political mileage.** Regulation is unpopular with institutions and of limited concern to voters. It only hits the headlines when a regulatory failure takes place. Politicians know that memories of such events are short and the issue can usually be disposed of by setting up a committee to investigate the matter. Occasionally (but only occasionally) this leads to action and actual change.

The structure of the banking and other financial industries can also have a significant impact on the effectiveness of regulatory authorities. The three most important factors are as follows:

- **Number of regulated banks.** Regulators depend upon required returns, normally monthly, from banks for their core data. Bank examiners usually have unlimited powers of investigation. They can turn up unannounced at a bank branch or head office and require management to bring forward all of the records of its loan book to be examined. Their fectiveness, however, depends on the number of skilled, well-educated individuals that they have available for their task.

    Regulators in developing markets only have a limited number of bank examiners and these people are frequently of poor quality. A problem that bank supervisors in many emerging markets face is the sheer number of banks that they are required to examine given the scale of their resources. When the regulator has to supervise many banks its resources simply become too stretched.

- **Regulation of non-bank financial institutions.** Other problems may arise when the banking regulator does not have responsibility for supervision of other non-bank financial institutions offering products with deposit and credit features. These may include finance companies providing consumer finance and other non-deposit-taking financial institutions.
- **Complexity of transactions.** The more complex a bank's transactions, such as taking derivative positions, the harder the regulator's job is to assess the risks that individual banks are exposed to. Some transactions may be taken to hedge existing positions while others may have been taken for proprietary trading positions.

A few failures have occurred as a result of confusion between different supervisors as to which one was responsible for a particular institution's activities. Barings, a bank incorporated in the UK, failed as a result of losses incurred by its Singapore-based subsidiary arising from trading futures contracts on the Japanese Nikkei index.

ACCOUNTING AUTHORITIES

The use of double entry bookkeeping in both Europe and China dates back nearly a thousand years. The oldest published book on accounting principles is believed to have been written at the end of the fifteenth century by a Venetian monk. Those fundamental principles enunciated then have remained largely unchanged over time but their detailed application has expanded massively.

There are two key areas where there is considerable controversy and debate over the definition and application of accounting policies and practices:

- **Economic versus accounting value.** This is an area we have looked at in detail but is of sufficient importance that the key issues are worth repeating and a new one is worth introducing. Bank's reported book value does not reflect economic value because only small parts of its interest rate-sensitive assets are marked-to-market. The level of book value also depends on the level of provisions held versus the present value of expected future credit losses.

  Companies are required to include the present value of future liabilities, such as arise from defined benefit pensions, but do not attempt to include the present value of expected future earnings. Even if a bank's book value reflected its economic value it would still not reflect its intrinsic value. This is not a matter to pursue here but rather an issue to raise for the reader to consider at their leisure.
- **Reported earnings.** Just as there are arguments on the extent to which reported book should reflect economic value there are also arguments as to how changes in economic value should be treated and in particular the extent to which they should be included in bank reported earnings.

The use of different accounting practices does not affect the underlying economic reality but rather the way in which it is presented. Mapmakers had to struggle with a similar problem when they tried to represent the world in two dimensions. The Mercator projection is the most familiar of these representations. It was extremely useful for navigators because the shortest route between two points on the surface of the world could be determined by drawing a straight line between the two points. Unfortunately it does this at the expense of distorting distances and area, particularly close to the poles.

There are many different users of a firm's published financial statements (shareholders, suppliers and other industry creditors, lenders, customers, credit and equity analysts, employees and trade unions, regulators). Financial statements required by tax authorities normally differ from those published. Management also require different reports that provide information on how to manage the firm going forward. Published financial statements reflect history, which cannot be changed, and a balance sheet that represents a snapshot in time.

The two most important accounting authorities are the US Financial Accounting and Standards Board (FASB – pronounced fas-bee) and the International Accounting Standards Board. FASB is responsible for drawing up and maintaining US General Accepted Accounting Policies (GAAP).

The International Accounting Standards Board is an independent, privately funded accounting standard setter based in London, UK. Board members come from nine countries and have a variety of functional backgrounds. The Board is committed to developing, in the public interest, a single set of "high quality, understandable and enforceable global accounting standards" that require transparent and comparable information in general purpose financial statements. In addition, the Board cooperates with national accounting standard setters to achieve convergence in accounting standards around the world. Noble aims.

The problems of agreeing accounting standards at financial institutions are usually greater than at traditional manufacturing companies because so much of a financial institution's business is conceptual. Accounting standards do have an impact on reported earnings and book value and when used improperly they may distort investors' perceptions of the company's financial condition and management's understanding of business unit profitability and hence future allocation of capital.

Some philosophies are based on a belief that life is but a dream. It is ironic that accountants, who are normally seen as such down to earth individuals, should have done so much to make that belief a reality when it comes to bank financial statements.

AUDIT BODIES

Banks have internal audit and compliance departments. Their main functions are to ensure that:

- Internal procedures and controls are established to ensure that the information captured is accurate and kept in a secure manner.
- Authorization limits are established and observed and that access to data and particular functions is controlled in a secure way.
- Measures to combat fraud are in place and that there are clear divisions of responsibilities, that checks and balances are built into systems (both manual and automated).
- Appropriate contingency plans are in place and records backed up to protect the business from unexpected events such as a power failure, fire, terrorist attack, flooding and so on. Many financial institutions have separate groups responsible for contingency planning and disaster recovery.
- The organization is acting within the law and requirements set by regulatory authorities.

The function of line management and supervisors is to ensure that personnel follow established procedures and take corrective action when necessary. The finance division is responsible for establishing accounting policies and ensuring these are followed. It also produces most of the reports required by regulatory and other external bodies. The financial division is not usually responsible for ensuring the accuracy of the information provided from other departments other than at the most basic level of ensuring that financial statements balance and can be reconciled.

The role of external auditors is frequently misunderstood. There is a widespread mistaken belief that an external audit involves every transaction being investigated and verified. These audits have a much narrower scope in reality. Their four most important objectives are:

- To confirm that internal audit has been doing its job properly and that appropriate procedures and controls have been established.
- To confirm that such procedures are being followed and controls have been implemented.
- To review accounting practices against established accepted accounting policies.
- To identify any weaknesses in the above and recommend remedial action.

Exhibit – US regulatory environment

It is not surprising that the US has one of the most complex and comprehensive regulatory environments. This is due to a number of factors including the size of its economy, the number of banks operating in the country, the division of legal rights and responsibilities between state and federal authorities and the impact of lobbying efforts by special interest groups and politics. Regulators and financial institutions have to operate within the confines of a raft of legislation that has been passed and, in many cases, amended over the past century.

Despite this high degree of supervision banks continue to fail and in the 1980s many Savings and Loans institutions incurred heavy losses and required a huge government bailout.

Commercial bank supervision is split largely between the Office of the Comptroller of the Currency (OCC), a semi-autonomous office of the US Treasury department, and state-level organizations. The OCC supervises and examines "national banks", these have a federal charter issued by the OCC and have to be members of the Federal Reserve System. Other commercial banks operate in one state only and are state chartered. Memberships of the Federal Reserve System and FDIC coverage are optional for these banks. Banks under OCC supervision account for around 60% of total domestic loans. The FDIC can also be regarded as a form of regulatory authority by virtue of its powers to impose constraints on activities of banks under its coverage.

The Fed also has its part to play, in particular from setting reserve requirements. In an example of the blurred boundaries between US regulators the Fed imposes minimum initial margin requirements for securities purchases, while minimum maintenance requirements are set by the self-regulatory organization the National Association of Securities Dealers (NASD), by individual exchanges and by individual brokers. The latter three organizations are all subject to SEC oversight.

The US banking industry structure has been shaped by three major pieces of historic legislation affecting cross-state banking, linkages between commercial and investment banking and community banking:

- **Cross-state banking.** One of the earliest pieces of banking legislation imposed restrictions on cross-state branching. This impeded the development of national banks. Large commercial banks operated on a regional and international basis rather than across the whole country. Bank of America, for example, continues to operate largely in California while Citibank's branches are based mainly in New York.
- **Glass-Steagal.** Following the 1929 market crash US lawmakers introduced (Glass-Steagal) legislation in 1933 to prevent commercial banks from offering most securities' services. The intention was to protect depositors at commercial banks from any adverse effects arising from speculative investment banking activities. There was also a widespread belief that there was a dangerous concentration of power at a small number of banks.

  The historic separation of investment banking activities from commercial banking activities has resulted in the survival of some of the few pure investment banks left in the world. These included Goldman Sachs, Merrill Lynch, Morgan Stanley and Lehman Brothers at the time of writing.
- **Community banking.** Under US community banking law banks are required to lend out the bulk of the deposits raised in the particular area from where they were gathered. This makes for good politics, and may even be good for the economy overall, but is potentially poor business for private banks. Banks concerned with high expected credit losses in a particular area will simply avoid taking deposits there.

  Many US community banks are often single branch operations servicing the needs of a particular community. The US is unique in having literally thousands of such banks. These banks lack the scale economies and product range of regional or national banks. The number of these banks continues to fall.

Large US banks lobbied hard in the 1980s and 1990s for the repeal of Glass-Steagal and for cross-state banking restrictions to be relaxed. They argued that Glass-Steagal put US banks at a competitive disadvantage relative to their European rivals where universal banking was the norm. They also argued that technology changes and effectiveness of anti-trust measures meant that cross-state restrictions had little purpose now.

The political climate was already shifting towards deregulation and liberalization at that time and Glass-Steagal was effectively repealed in the mid-1990s. Many formerly independent US investment banks have been bought by commercial banks since its demise. Citicorp bought Salomon and integrated it with Smith Barney, Deutsche Bank bought Bankers Trust, Union Bank of Switzerland bought Dean Witter and Chase Manhattan bought J.P. Morgan, a commercial bank that had tried to reinvent itself as an investment bank.

Restrictions on cross-state banking have been relaxed but not removed entirely. Federal restrictions have been removed but individual states can block the entry of banks from other states. The rise in the use of credit cards, ATMs and electronic banking had already eroded many of these restrictions in a practical sense.

One of the consequences of this relaxation was a spate of mergers and acquisitions between large US regional banks during the 1990s as banks sought to take advantage of the greater opportunities from cross-state branching to gain economies of scale.

The Securities and Exchange Commission (SEC)

The US Securities and Exchange Commission (SEC) was established in 1933 following the October 1929 market crash. Its prime responsibility is to maintain a regulatory environment for capital markets that protects the rights of both individual and institutional investors. It provides a model framework that many other countries have adopted.

Its powers are set out in broad terms and it has considerable freedom to act within its legal boundaries. Market practices are constantly changing and the SEC needs to be responsive to those changes. Its three primary areas of responsibility are as follows:

- **Market operations.** Stock, commodities and futures exchanges are largely self-regulated but the SEC retains ultimate oversight.
- **Primary issuance.** The SEC requires companies selling securities in the US to register such securities. Companies have to provide a description of their businesses and properties, audited financial statements and details of management. Small and private issues are exempted from these requirements.
- **Investor protection.** The SEC regulates the licensing of individuals and institutions providing investment advice.

The SEC has allowed the establishment of a number of self-regulatory bodies, such as the National Association of Securities Dealers. This delegation of responsibilities is more in the nature of a loan than a gift. Ultimate responsibility continues to reside with the SEC.

24

The Balance Sheet

A lie told often enough becomes the truth.

Vladimir Ilyich Lenin, Soviet revolutionary leader

INTRODUCTION

Banks and other financial institutions are very different commercial animals than manufacturing and other non-financial companies. It is therefore not surprising that many of the analytical tools and ratios used to assess the health and performance of the latter group of companies have little relevance to the analysis of banks.

Few business schools include bank analysis as part of their core MBA programs. Even organizations such as the US-based Association for Investment Management and Research concentrate almost wholly on manufacturing companies, asset managers and insurance companies in their global Chartered Financial Analyst program and barely touch on banks.

Our main objectives in this chapter are to introduce the most important balance sheet line items and the key ratios that bank analysts, management and investors in bank stocks use to assess a bank's condition. As a secondary objective we will outline the type of approaches analysts take to forecast banks' balance sheets. A few words of caution are called for at this point, however:

- **Accounting standards.** Published financial statements are based on the accounting standards applicable in a particular country. In the USA these are based on US GAAP (Generally Accepted Accounting Principles), in some countries on IAS (International Accounting Standards) and in many other countries on policies specific to that country, frequently based on some variant of either US GAAP or IAS. These accounting policies and standards and regulatory definitions can significantly affect the reporting of the underlying condition of a bank.
- **Disclosure.** There are significant variations in the level of disclosure required from banks between different countries. Even within a single country some banks will disclose only the minimum information legally required while others may provide more information. The frequency of reporting also varies from country to country. In the USA listed banks are required to report on a quarterly basis while in the UK and much of Europe most banks report on a semi-annual basis. The longer the gap between reporting the older the information and the less useful this information is to analysts.
- **Truthfulness.** One final note of caution relates to the accuracy and veracity of reported numbers. This problem is particularly acute in emerging markets where regulatory supervision is frequently lax. Management at banks with the greatest problems has the greatest incentive to understate the degree of the problems. Cases such as the collapse of Barings and BCCI demonstrate that this problem is not unique to emerging markets and show that the external auditor's sign-off is no guarantee of the integrity of the audited financial statements.

THE BALANCE SHEET

The starting point in any analysis of a bank's financial statements is the balance sheet:

- **Assets.** Any item that the bank owns, or is owed, is an asset. These include cash held, deposits held with other banks, financial assets such as stocks and bonds and physical assets such as its branches. A loan made to a customer is a bank's asset. This is the reverse of what you would find looking at a corporate balance sheet (where loans are debt and hence a liability) or even your own bank statement (where a deposit is an asset). Loans are the largest asset class by value for the vast majority of commercial banks.
- **Liabilities.** Any item that the bank owes is treated as a liability. Deposits from customers are the largest liability class. Other liabilities include deposits from other banks and long-term financing such as bonds issued and subordinated debt. Equity represents the difference between the value of its assets and non-equity liabilities based on the relevant accounting standards and is owed to shareholders.

Off-balance sheet items are more important at banks than they are at the vast majority of non-financial institutions. Off-balance sheet assets and liabilities represent payments to or from the bank due at some future date. These payments due may be committed or contingent on specific conditions being met.

Most banks in most countries report enough detail to be able to identify the values for the following summary balance sheet items. The names of the items may and do vary from country to country.

Summary of key commercial bank balance sheet items	
Assets	**Liabilities**
Cash and cash equivalents	Deposits from non-bank customers
Deposits with other banks	Deposits from banks
Securities	Long-term debt
Repurchase agreements	Interest payable
Loans	Other liabilities
Reserves for credit losses	Equity
Associates	Minorities
Fixed assets	**Total liabilities**
Interest receivable	
Other assets	
Total assets	

Each of these items represents a consolidation of a number of more detailed balance sheet items. There is a wide variation in the level of detail disclosed for each of these items. Some of the more detailed breakdown is available from notes to the accounts. The level and type of disclosure constrains what ratios can be calculated and the extent to which bank financials can be compared. We will look at what each of these summary items represents and how they may be reported.

THE ASSET SIDE OF THE BALANCE SHEET

Cash and cash equivalent

Cash and cash equivalents
Deposits held with central bank
Cash

Deposits held with central bank to meet bank reserve requirements. May be mandatory or may not be required disclosures. May or may not earn interest. Level held depends on central bank requirements and hence there is a wide variation between 0% and 10% of assets. Also known as Reserve Deposits.

Cash held in branch vaults and ATMs. Does not earn interest and kept to a bare minimum. Typical level 1%–2% of total assets.

Deposits held with other banks

Deposits with other banks

Deposits held with correspondent banks
Deposits held with other banks
By maturity
  Overnight, 1–30 days, 31–90 days, 91–180 days,
  6 months–1 year, 1–3 years, 5–7 years, 7+ years
By currency
  Local currency, $, euro, yen, other

These are deposits held with other banks to facilitate provision of services such as payments by banks with which the bank has a correspondent banking relationship. Usually do not pay interest. The larger the bank and the more extensive its operations geographically the smaller the proportion of assets held in this form.

Other deposits held with other banks in the interbank market. Most are very short term and the percentage with a term above 90 days is very small. They earn interest. Used by banks for interest rate and liquidity risk management.

Some banks do not break down deposits held with other banks in any way.

A breakdown by maturity and currency may be provided.

Securities

Securities
  Equities
  Trading equities
  Listed equities held for long-term investment
  Unlisted equities held for long-term investment

Only large banks with extensive trading operations normally have any equities held for trading purposes. Trading equities are usually reported at market prices with any changes from historic cost taken as gains or losses through the P&L account.

Equities held for long-term investment may include stakes held in strategic partners or may be associated with venture capital investments made by the bank.

Listed equities held for long-term investment may be reported at historic cost or current market value. Where reported at current market price the historic cost, revaluation reserves and any provisions for diminution in value may also be disclosed.

Where reported on the balance sheet at historic cost revaluation reserves may still be reported as notes to the account. Most accounting standard require any "permanent impairment" in value to be reflected in the balance sheet numbers.

(*continued*)

Bonds

By issuer

OECD governments, non-OECD governments

Government

State and municipal authorities

Corporations

By maturity

0–30 days, 31–90 days, 91–180 days,

1–3 years, 5–7 years, 7+ years

By currency

Local currency, euro, yen, other

By pricing

Fixed, floating, zero coupon

Asset backed securities

Mortgage backed securities

Auto finance securities

Collateralized debt obligations (CDOs)

There are a large number of ways in which bond holdings can be broken down. The way in which, if any, these are reported varies from country to country.

Where a breakdown is provided the most common are by issuer, maturity, currency and pricing method.

Convertible bonds may or may not be reported separately.

It would be possible to break these securities down further, bonds issued by corporations could be broken down by credit rating and could be divided between callable, putable and straight bonds. Some bonds may be in the form of flip-flop notes whether by currency or interest rate basis.

In practice few, if any, banks report the latter breakdowns in their publicly released financial statements.

In some countries asset backed securities may not be reported as a separate line item and may be included within total loans or within securities under the usual catchall item "other securities".

Repurchase agreements

Federal funds purchased

Securities bought under agreements to resell

Federal funds purchased arise from central bank reserve requirements. When two banks calculate how much they should hold as reserve deposits with the central bank and compare this with what they actually have one may find it has a shortfall and the other an excess. The bank with the shortfall may buy the other's excess paying the "Fed Funds" rate.

Securities bought under an agreement to resell are in effect securities that the bank has borrowed for a specific period of time and agrees to return. These are common agreements when the securities concerned fall within the central bank's definition of reserve requirements. The borrowing bank earns interest on these securities for the period of the agreement but also pays a fee to the lender.

Loans

Loans

By industrial classification Manufacturing, service, trading, retail, hotels and restaurants, agriculture and mining, real estate, housing loans, consumer loans, other financial institutions

Almost all banks report loans broken down by some form of industrial classification. Most of these conform to a somewhat archaic international form. There are three major analytical problems with this classification scheme.

By usage
  Working capital, project finance, construction, real estate development, real estate investment, financial investment, housing, home improvements, asset financing
By currency
  Local currency, euro, yen, other
By country
  Local, US, UK, France, Italy, Argentina, Brazil, South Korea, Japan etc.
By term
  6 months or less, 6–12 months, 2–5 years, 5+ years, revolving
By pricing
  Fixed
  Floating
    Government bond yield, interbank rate, cost of funding, industry rate (prime)
Commercial paper
Interest receivable

The first is that it classifies loans on the basis of the industrial classification of the borrower. This means that if a manufacturing company takes out a bank loan in order to finance a speculative real estate development the level of credit being channeled to real estate development will be understated.

The second is that the actual classifications as originally defined defies rational explanation. Loans for real estate and to non-bank financial institutions were lumped together, a detailed breakdown is given for loans for agriculture, mining and fishing even though these together account for a minute proportion of total system loans in a modern economy. The last problem is that countries do not all follow exactly the same classification scheme making cross-border comparisons very difficult.

Very few banks report a breakdown of loans by usage – which is what most bank analysts are interested in. There are examples of banks reporting some or all of the following breakdowns; by currency, country, term and pricing method.

The numbers for loans classified by country have to be treated with care. A loan may be booked in one country and used in another (this is a common distortion in countries with a significant offshore banking presence). In the case of loans actually made directly to companies operating in a foreign country a key issue is the breakdown between loans made to local companies and those made to subsidiaries of MNCs, where the parent has guaranteed the loans. None of this detail is usually reported.

Commercial paper is the equivalent of short-dated zero coupon bonds issued by corporations at a discount to par. They may be reported separately or included within loans.

Interest receivable is normally reported as a separate item but may be included within an individual bank's definition of total loans.

Reserves, provisions and allowances

Provisions
  Specific provisions
  General provision
  Provisions for credit losses
  Provisions for securities losses
  Other provisions

Provisions are accounts used to report unrealized losses or other unfunded liabilities.

These accounts go under a range of different names. In some countries they are defined as "allowances", in others as "reserves".

(*continued*)

They are usually contra-asset items, i.e. they are negative numbers on the asset side of the balance sheet. In a few countries they are reported as positive liability items, however, South Korea is a prime example.

They are usually netted against loans and securities to give net loan and securities figures. Not all banks disclose the breakdown between provisions for credit losses and those for other assets.

Definitions of specific and general provisions vary from country to country and we have already looked at this issue in some detail in Chapter 11.

Other provisions may have to be made for items such as a shortfall on a bank's defined benefit pension plan. In the few instances where such provisions exist they are usually material and have to be analyzed.

Associates

Associates

The treatment of associates at banks is exactly the same as at any other company. The definition of associates and the point at which equity rather than dividend accounting can be applied does vary from country to country. Most bank associates are companies with related businesses where the bank is prohibited from operating itself (insurance companies, realtors, real estate companies).

Goodwill

Goodwill

Goodwill is the difference between the price the bank paid for any acquisitions less the net tangible assets of the acquisitions at the time of acquisition and less any amortized goodwill.

Fixed assets

Fixed assets
Bank premises
Real estate investments
Foreclosed property
Other fixed assets

Fixed assets account for a much smaller proportion of total assets than they do at a manufacturing company.

Bank premises may include the bank's head office and its branches although many of these will actually be leased.

Real estate investments include land intended for development and other assets generating a rental income. Few banks in developed countries have material real estate investments but they do crop up at some banks in emerging markets.

Foreclosed property represents real estate that was pledged as collateral for a loan on which the borrower has defaulted and the bank has gained legal title to. The value placed on foreclosed property is normally an appraised value at the time of foreclosure. In most countries banks are discouraged from holding real estate and may be required to dispose of such assets within a certain number of years from the date of foreclosure.

Other fixed assets include computers, furniture, ATMs, printers and so on.

THE LIABILITY SIDE OF THE BALANCE SHEET

Deposits from non-bank customers

Deposits from non-bank customers
By product
 Demand, savings, time, NOW, checking, FRCD
By type
 Interest bearing, non-interest bearing
By currency
 Local currency, euro, yen, other
By maturity
 Overnight, 1–30 days, 31–90 days, 91–180 days, 6 months–1 year, 1+ years

Interpretation of reported non-bank deposit numbers has been complicated by the effects of deposit rate liberalization. Most banks continue to report deposits by product type when the definitions of those products no longer have any real meaning.

The key breakdowns are whether the deposit is interest bearing or not, the currency mix and the maturity profile. Some banks report all of these, others some and many none of them.

It would be useful if banks reported the split between deposits priced against wholesale rates (such as interbank rates) and those priced by the bank.

Floating rate certificates of deposit (FRCD) may be treated as a time deposit or may be reported separately. The major difference between an FRCD and a time deposit is that the former is usually a liquid, negotiable instrument.

Deposits with banks

See note on Deposits from banks under Assets heading.

Long-term debt

Long-term debt
 Bonds
 Debentures
 Straight bonds
 Convertible bonds
 To maturity
 6 months or less, 6–12 months, 2–5 years, 5+ years

By currency
 Local currency, euro, yen, other

Although long-term debt is usually reported in a summarized form on the balance sheet details of all medium- to long-term debt issues are usually disclosed in full in notes to the accounts.

Long-term financing is usually issued as part of the bank's capital management rather than as a form of long-term financing for the business. Long-term debt is normally only a small fraction of customer deposits.

(*continued*)

Subordinated debt
  By remaining term
  6 months or less, 6–12 months, 2–5
  years, 5+ years
By currency
  Local currency, euro, yen, other

Interest payable and other liabilities	
Interest payable	Just as banks account for interest earned using the accrual concept they treat interest paid in the same way.
Other liabilities	Other liabilities include the usual items such as accounts payable (for utility bills etc.), tax payable and dividends payable.

Shareholders' funds	
Shares issued	Value of the number of shares issued at par. Par is usually set at $1 or the equivalent in the local currency so that the value of the shares issued account is the same as the number of shares issued. If 10 000 shares are issued with a par value of $1 and issue price of $10 the shares issued account will show $10 000.
Share premium account	Difference between the price actually paid for new shares less the par value. In the above example the share premium account would show $9000.
Retained earnings	The difference between total earnings of the bank over time less the value of any dividends paid to shareholders.
Revaluation reserves	The difference between the market value of a bank's fixed assets and its long-term investments and their historic cost where the unrealized gain has not been taken through the P&L account.
	The use of revaluation reserves depends on local accounting standards. In some countries fixed assets (less any depreciation) and long-term investments are left on the balance sheet at cost. The appraised or market value may or may not be included as a note to the account in this case.
	Conservatism suggests that if the historic cost is greater than the current market price the value in the balance sheet should be adjusted downwards by taking a charge through the P&L account and reflected in lower retained earnings.
Minority interest	Bank's share of the equity accounts of their subsidiaries.
Preference shares	Also referred to as preferred stock. Class of security that pays a fixed dividend and has seniority over equity holders in the payment of dividends and any liquidation of the bank. Holders do not have voting rights. Dividends may be cumulative or non-cumulative. If cumulative any missed dividend payments have to be made up before the company can pay a dividend to equity holders. If non-cumulative any dividends skipped are lost.

OTHER DERIVED BALANCE SHEET ITEMS AND RATIOS

Interest-earning Assets and Interest-bearing Liabilities

Two of the most important derived balance sheet items are average interest-earning assets and interest-bearing liabilities. These items are difficult for an analyst to estimate accurately, based on public information, unless the bank includes them as a public disclosure. In some countries breakdowns of interest-earning assets and liabilities by asset and liability class (the US is an example) are also disclosed. There is no international standard for the definition of average interest-earning assets, however. Definitions and the level of disclosure usually apply at a national level only.

One of the reasons why these items are important to analysts is that they are used to calculate the yields earned on assets and bank funding costs. These in turn give the bank's net interest spread, a key measure of a bank's intermediation power and, hence, driver of a bank's profitability. When making cross-border comparisons it is necessary to check the local definitions for interest-earning assets and liabilities as relatively small differences in definitions can have a large impact on the calculated values for spreads and margins:

- **Average interest-earning assets.** These are given by the sum of those assets that paid interest averaged over the relevant period corresponding to the income statement. The key items here are loans to customers, government and corporate bonds and deposits with other banks.

    In countries where reserve deposits do not bear interest and have not for many years it is not surprising that the usual convention is to exclude these from the definition of interest-earning assets. Zero coupon bonds do not pay interest and hence it might appear reasonable to exclude them from the definition but, given that their discount to par is amortized through the interest income line, in practical terms they justify inclusion.
- **Average interest-bearing liabilities.** These are the complement to interest-earning assets on the liability side of the balance sheet, for funding on which the bank pays interest. The key items here are deposits from customers, deposits from other banks and other forms of short-term and long-term debt. The definition of interest-bearing deposits has become increasingly blurred. It is possible to argue that demand deposits should be treated as non-interest-bearing liabilities or as interest-bearing liabilities with a zero percent interest rate. On balance the latter definition appears to have more merit.

The averaging is usually done on a daily basis for the entire relevant accounting period. Most regulators and accounting standards bodies require this to avoid the distortion that results from using period-end numbers.

Interest-earning assets and interest-bearing liabilities
Average interest-earning assets   = Average assets on which interest is earned
Average interest-bearing liabilities = Average liabilities on which interest is paid

Interest-earning Assets and interest-bearing Liabilities

Many texts define a measure of a bank's interest rate sensitivity by taking the ratio of interest rate-sensitive assets to interest rate-sensitive liabilities. This could also be defined as floating rate assets and floating rate liabilities.

Derived interest rate-sensitive items and ratios

Interest rate-sensitive assets	= Sum of floating rate assets
Interest rate-sensitive liabilities	= Sum of floating rate liabilities
Interest rate sensitivity	= Interest rate-sensitive assets/Interest rate-sensitive liabilities

Many texts refer to the interest rate sensitivity measure and state boldly that when it is greater than +1 bank earnings will be adversely affected in a falling interest rate environment but benefit from rising rates. The reality is more complex. In practice this measure is of limited utility for the following reasons:

- **Definitional.** A more granular breakdown of floating rate assets and liabilities would be those that are:
  - Clearly floating rate and priced relative to a well-defined external benchmark, such as LIBOR or Treasuries, and repriced according to terms specified in advance.
  - Clearly floating rate but defined against a bank's benchmark rate, such as its published "prime" rate, where the bank has discretion over adjusting this rate.
  - Usually fixed rate but where rates can be adjusted at the bank's discretion, in many countries rates paid on "savings" deposits are only adjusted infrequently.
  Rates on these three different types of assets and liabilities are unlikely to all move together by the same amount.
- **Non-parallel and basis shifts.** External benchmark rates, such as three-month LIBOR and five-year Treasuries, may not all change by the same amount and rates may even move in opposite directions. These differences may be due to term shifts (three-month versus five-year, for example) or basis shifts (LIBOR versus Treasuries).
- **Stickiness.** This measure does not capture stickiness of rates or the speed at which individual floating rate assets and liabilities are repriced. When pricing is based on external benchmarks the repricing terms are usually defined in advance. Loans priced against Federal Fund rates may be repriced virtually instantaneously while those priced against a more volatile rate, such as interbank, may be priced every 30 or 90 days. Some benchmark rates, such as those based on actual, historic bank funding costs, adjust relatively slowly over time.
  Where repricing is at the bank's discretion it will seek to reprice its assets faster than its liabilities when interest rates rise and the reverse when rates fall. Where the interest rate sensitivity measure is less than +1 banks will try to cut rates on their deposits faster, and by more, than they cut rates on loans when rates fall.
- **Derivatives.** The expansion in the range of interest rate derivatives (FRAs, swaps and futures) and greater depth of derivative markets has given bank treasuries tools to manage on-balance sheet interest rate risk. A simple measure such as the interest rate sensitivity ratio has become increasingly irrelevant as a consequence.

Asset Quality and NPL Cover

Non-performing loans and provisioning for losses are covered in detail in Chapter 13 "Managing credit risk" and Chapter 20 "Corporate failures and problem loans". The key ratios are as follows.

Common asset quality and provisioning ratios	
NPL level	= Non performing loans/Total non-bank loans
Provisioning level	= Total provisions/Total loans
NPL cover	= Total provisions/Non-performing loans

Capital Adequacy and Gearing Ratios

Definitions of regulatory capital and regulatory capital adequacy ratios were introduced in Chapter 14 "Capital management" and are covered in more detail in Appendix I on the Basel Accord. The key items and ratios are as follows.

Key capital adequacy and equity gearing ratios and definitions	
Tier I capital	= Capital allowable as Tier I capital
Tier II capital	= Capital allowable as Tier II capital
Tier I ratio	= Tier I capital/Total period-end risk-weighted assets
Tier II ratio	= Tier II capital/Total period-end risk-weighted assets
Total CAR	= Tier I ratio + Tier II ratio

Other Balance Sheet Ratios

The basic gearing ratio assets-to-equity has largely fallen out of use for two principal reasons. The first is that bank's have increasingly moved business off-balance sheet. The second was the adoption of BIS standards; with all its weaknesses it still brought a measure of adjustment for risk which the assets-to-equity ratio fails to do. The ratio of "free" funds to total liabilities is little used but in markets where there is limited use of derivatives for hedging interest rates indicates those banks whose earnings stand to rise as interest rates increase from the so-called endowment effect.

The two most common other ratios used in connection with liquidity measures are the loan-to-deposit ratio (LDR) and liquidity ratio. The loan-to-deposit ratio is easy to define but has to be looked at in the context of the level of equity versus other non-deposit sources of funding. The liquidity ratio is difficult to define precisely.

Basic balance sheet ratios	
Asset equity gearing	= Period end assets/Period end equity
Free funds ratio	= (Demand deposits plus equity)/Total liabilities
Loan-to-deposit ratio	= Gross non-bank loans/Non-bank deposits
Liquidity ratio	= Liquid assets/Non-bank deposits

MEETINGS WITH BANK MANAGEMENT

Before looking at how to go about forecasting it is worth spending a little time on what can be gained from meetings with bank management to help achieve this objective. In the late 1990s most bank analysts, including myself, listened in disbelief as analysts in some other sectors appeared to base their forecasts almost entirely on detailed guidance provided by corporate management. The competitive advantage for analysts in these sectors appeared to be how close they were to management rather than how well they could analyze industry fundamentals and apply them to particular companies. Bank analysts might fall victim to such temptations if banks' management were in the habit of giving such detailed guidance but in the vast majority of cases they are not.

Most meetings between bank analysts and bank representatives are of limited use, although they may provide an insight into the likely caliber of staff employed. There are a number of reasons why this may be the case:

- **Investor relations.** In many banks senior management is too busy to meet all save the largest funds and most influential analysts. At the same time most want to give an impression of accessibility. One approach is to have a separate investor relations department with a prime contact who handles most meetings with investors and analysts. To be fair to them most of them do a competent job at answering, or getting answers, to factual questions on past performance. They are also usually well briefed in terms of being able to repeat the bank's long-term strategic objectives (where they exist).
- **Line management.** At smaller banks it is not uncommon for such meetings to be held with line managers. They are usually expert in their particular field but few treasurers, for example, have an overall understanding of the bank as a whole. A good bank analyst usually knows more overall about a bank they are covering than individual line managers who simply work for it.
- **Detailed numbers.** Trying to get detailed numbers for items such as internal loan growth targets is fraught with problems. It may be management's policy not to make public such numbers. The bank may not set targets. The bank does set targets but the particular person doesn't know what they are or can't remember exactly what they are. They may be lying. The internal targets given may be as stated but be unachievable.

  A fundamental problem is that even when detailed numbers are given definitional problems are such that it is often difficult for an analyst to be certain that they are talking about the same items. This is particularly true when talking about items relating to asset quality and provisioning and derived items such as margins.

It is usually much more useful to analyze by "wandering" and using one's eyes. A couple of visits to some branches is usually enough to check on claims by management about their "highly effective use of cross-selling techniques to increase the number of products sold to each customer" and their "commitment to a world-class level of customer service". Piles of cardboard boxes with files in the corridors of the head office usually say more about their operations than management claims about "their success in implementing straight-through processing and increasing productivity".

The result is that most bank analysts rely largely on their own judgment for forecasts, other than for specific items such as the provisions a bank intends to set aside for a particular high-profile exposure or gains to be booked from an asset disposal, rather than management guidance. There is usually a relatively wide dispersion of forecasts around the consensus mean.

FORECASTING THE BALANCE SHEET

Although analysts are usually primarily concerned with getting their earnings forecasts right this is difficult to achieve without getting the forecasts for the balance sheet approximately right. The starting point is therefore the balance sheet. Forecasting net interest income, for example, is a two-stage process. The first stage involves estimating balance sheet components, the second stage forecasting market prices for (broadly speaking) loans and deposits.

The most important driver of growth of interest earning assets is loans. Any unexpected expansion or contraction of interbank assets is likely to result in an error in the forecast for total assets but the very thin spreads on these assets means that the error in the net interest income forecast will be much lower.

The first step in the process for a single-market bank is to arrive at an estimate of total market loan growth. This is at best an educated guess because there are so many factors involved and (horror of horrors) usually means having to talk with an economist. For an analyst the only thing worse than this is having to find an accountant to get an explanation of a particular accounting treatment. That is usually an act of desperation, and definitely a last resort. It is, however, nice when the banking analyst and economist at a single house can agree to a common view on credit growth and the interest rate outlook:

- **Economic cycle.** Demand for credit is highly dependent on the level of economic growth. Loan growth usually lags the economic cycle. At times when economies are expanding rapidly loan growth usually outstrips nominal GDP growth. In turn when economies experience a downturn loans may remain flat or even contract. In the recovery phase it may take 12–18 months for loan growth to resume.
- **Monetary policy.** Central bank monetary policy also has an important bearing. An increase in reserve requirements or increase in the discount rate will result in a slowing of loan growth.
- **Sectoral demand.** Loan growth is not uniform across sectors. In an economic boom demand for housing loans, car loans and consumer finance is likely to be strong but fall sharply in a downturn. Demand for car loans is also affected by the replacement cycle and for housing loans by the balance between supply and demand. A decent bottom-up forecast has to be at the sector level.
- **Disintermediation.** We have already examined how disintermediation and asset securitization affect banks' businesses. They also complicate estimating system-level loan growth.

The next step is to estimate loan growth at individual banks. It's pretty simple really, there are only three options. Loans can either grow in line with the forecast at the industry level, or the bank lose market share or gain it. The estimate itself is usually based on balancing management comments, changes in the competitive environment and what the numbers appear to suggest.

For a bank that has a loan book breakdown in line with that of the industry the lowest risk assumption for an analyst to make is that loan growth will be in line with the industry average. Anything different has to be justified on specific grounds but there may be cause. Management at a conservative bank may deliberately choose to cut back its loan growth targets when demand is strongest, anticipating a downturn. Another bank with strengths in the fastest growing segments is likely to be able to expand its loan book faster than the industry average.

It is also useful to compare the sectoral breakdown of the bank's loan book against that of the industry average. By applying the estimates at the industry and sector level to this loan book a bank level forecast can be made.

It is difficult to apply the bottom-up approach to large international banks. There are a number of reasons why this should be the case. The first is a matter of disclosure. Most of these banks report exposure by country and sector but do not disclose the breakdown by sector within individual countries.

Where they operate through subsidiaries these may be required local disclosures, but it is hard and time-consuming work to try to collate this information. There is always a "hole" – the difference between what is reported at the consolidated level and that arrived at by adding together the numbers reported by subsidiaries. This problem is exacerbated by differing definitions of loan segments between countries. In practice analysts focus on the key markets in which the bank operates and make an overall estimate for growth in the remaining markets.

Another factor that needs to be taken into account are expected changes in exchange rates. Reported overall balance sheet growth may be solely due to such changes. It is also necessary to check whether individual banks use end of accounting period rates or average rates over the relevant period.

EQUITY AND INTEREST-BEARING LIABILITIES

Equity provides a source of "free" financing. Changes in this base therefore will have a direct impact on the level of interest-bearing liabilities necessary to fund a bank's assets. This in turn will affect net interest income. There are several ways in which the equity account may be adjusted:

- **Retained earnings and dividends.** Retained earnings are simply the difference between reported earnings and dividends paid. This can be forecast by estimating the dividend payout ratio based on past performance and management indications of intentions. Most companies try to at least maintain their dividend payout. This may not be possible for distressed banks.
- **Special dividends and capital reductions.** Banks with excess capital may decide to return a part of this to shareholders. Two of the ways in which this can achieved are through special dividends and capital reductions. There are legal differences between these two methods but in economic value terms they are equivalent.
- **Share buy-backs.** Share buy-backs became an important method of returning excess capital for US banks in the late 1980s. Whether buy-backs add, reduce or have no economic effect on banks' value remains open to debate. In some countries share buy-backs are not allowed.
- **Capital raising.** The principal ways in which banks can raise capital are through rights issues, private placements and the exercise of convertible instruments. Employee stock

Forecasting the balance sheet	
ASSETS	
Cash & reserve deposits	Same percentage of deposits as previous period, unless changes in central bank reserve requirements
Deposits with other banks	Balancing item. Calculated as Total Liabilities less sum of all other asset line items
Gross loans	Brought forward loans + forecast increase in loans less loans written off
Reserves for credit loss (negative item)	Brought forward reserves + new provisions from earnings statement less net write-offs
Net loans	Gross loans + reserves for credit losses
All other assets	Growth in lines with total assets
LIABILITIES	
Customer deposits	Forecast growth or based on loan-to-deposit ratio
Long-term debt	Same as previous period
All other liabilities	Growth in line with deposits
Equity	Brought forward equity + retained earnings for period
DERIVED	
Interest-earning assets + Interest-bearing liabilities	Calculated
Tier I CAR	Calculated

option plans may create issues of corporate governance and result in overstated earnings, but at banks are rarely material in terms of the capital base.

- **Asset revaluation.** In some countries unrealized gains or losses on assets can be reflected through a revaluation line item contained within the equity account. This may include effects from currency translations. Changes in this account have no impact on a bank's free funds as the assets concerned will be increased or reduced accordingly.

Banks' balance sheet growth may be constrained by a lack of loan demand, problems in raising funding or meeting capital adequacy requirements. The balance sheet must balance, however, and that means that any model has to have a "balancing item". In building an earnings model an analyst has to decide whether to put this on the asset or liability side of the balance sheet.

There is no "right" way to do this. A good rule of thumb, however, is to put the balancing item on the liability side of the balance sheet when a bank is constrained by deposit taking. The balancing item in this case would by "Borrowings from other banks". For a bank with an excess of deposits compared with its loans it makes sense to put the balancing item on the asset side of the balance sheet and in this case the item would be "Deposits with other banks".

25

The Income Statement

It contains a misleading impression, not a lie. It was being economical with the truth.
Robert Armstrong, senior British civil servant

THE INCOME STATEMENT

In common with the balance sheet the presentation of the income or earnings statement and the names of line items vary from country to country. All of which further increases the problems that analysts have in making meaningful cross-border comparisons between banks. This usually involves restating the published reports to a common format. Even in the USA and other OECD countries banks are frequently given some discretion in the way that they present their financial statements.

The earnings statement provides a breakdown of a bank's income and expenses based on a set of accounting standards to arrive at a profit attributable to shareholders. The definition of operating profit is the most contentious item.

Operating income comes from the income generated by the bank's core spread management business (net interest income), its success at generating fees from providing services to its customers and success in its trading operation. Operating expenses are restricted largely to the direct expenses of running the business. Operating profit, as defined here, is therefore a reasonable measure of the bank's operating performance. There are, however, two areas of contention concerning the treatment of bad debt charges and disposal gains/trading income:

- **Bad debt charges.** There is an argument that bad debt charges should be included within operating expenses as part of the costs of doing business. There are three arguments against this. The first is that in practice bad debt charges reflect past mistakes rather than current performance, most banks still only make provisions for bad debt losses once specific problems emerge. The second is that the level of the charge varies significantly over the course of an economic cycle. The third is that a key measure is the ability of a bank to provide for additional credit losses from its operating profits.

  US banks include bad debt charges as an operating expense but they are much faster at recognizing problem loans and moving through the identification, resolution and write-off process than banks in other countries. For cross-border comparisons it seems to make more sense to calculate an operating profit number that excludes this charge.

- **Disposal gains and trading income.** It is sometimes difficult to distinguish between "trading income" and "disposal gains". Some analysts argue that both should be included as operating profits, others that both should be excluded. Trading income is inherently volatile but is still a part of operating income. That its inclusion means that operating profits are also volatile is irrelevant. Where gains result from a one-off sale of an asset such as a long-term equity holding or a fixed asset such as a head office then it is probably better to exclude them from operating profits.

The following is a standard form of the breakdown of the earnings statement that should be suitable for all commercial banks.

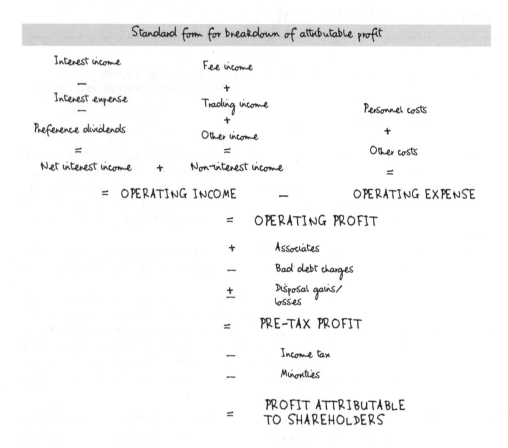

Standard form for breakdown of attributable profit

Interest income

—

Interest expense

—

Preference dividends

=

Net interest income   +   Non-interest income

Fee income

+

Trading income

+

Other income

=

Personnel costs

+

Other costs

=

= OPERATING INCOME   —   OPERATING EXPENSE

= OPERATING PROFIT

+   Associates

—   Bad debt charges

±   Disposal gains/losses

= PRE-TAX PROFIT

—   Income tax

—   Minorities

= PROFIT ATTRIBUTABLE TO SHAREHOLDERS

As should be expected there are plenty of detail differences in accounting standards between countries and there are also some major variations in the form of the summary earnings statement. These need to be taken into account when making cross-border comparisons:

- **Accounting standards.** Some differences in accounting standards have only a small impact on reported numbers and can be safely ignored. Different accounting standards result in differences in individual line items and also in derived items down to and including net profit.

  Some material differences can be identified and the reported numbers adjusted to a common basis. Some material accounting differences can be identified but it is not possible to quantify these differences and fully adjust for them. In this case the best an analyst can do is to be aware of why certain derived ratios are not strictly comparable and whether the distortion overstates or understates the relevant ratios.

- **Presentation.** Differences in the form or presentation of the earnings statement do not affect detail line items, nor do they affect net profit but they do result effectively in different definitions of intermediate, derived items such as operating income, operating expenses and operating profits. Provided the detail line items are reported the process of reformatting the earnings statement is a relatively straightforward exercise.

If the detail line items are not released this is not possible. This can be the case when banks release unaudited earnings results in a summary form and release the detail at a later date. Unadjusted, these numbers can give a completely misleading picture of the bank's operating performance and may not provide analysts with sufficient information to undertake a meaningful analysis.

There are accounting standards where there is room for informed debate as to which are the most appropriate methods to use, and even in the case of the nature of the presentation we have already identified two specific areas where there are arguments for and against a particular form used. But in some countries reporting treatments are completely inexplicable.

If the form used meant that banks' performances were consistently shown in a better light at least this would be comprehensible, instead their effect can be fairly random although the main result is to render the published numbers largely meaningless. In Asia this is the case not only in an emerging market such as the Philippines but also in an OECD country, South Korea. Banks in these countries calculate operating income as gross interest income plus non-interest income and operating expenses as gross interest expense plus staff and other costs.

There are only a few ratios derived directly from the earnings statement. Most ratios relate items from the earnings statement with items from the balance sheet. There are four specific ratios used by analysts that do come directly from the earnings statement:

- The proportion of operating income that comes from net interest income versus non-interest income.
- The costs that have to be expensed to generate each dollar of revenue.
- The proportion of operating profits that are absorbed by charges for future credit losses.
- The effective tax rate.

NET INTEREST INCOME

Interest Income

The level of detail provided for interest income line items varies from country to country. Some countries require banks to provide a more detailed breakdown by asset class, in others you simply get one line. The following may be included in the summary interest income line:

- Interest income from loans and coupon bonds is recognized on an accrual basis. This is normally done on a daily basis.
- Interest income from NPLs is usually recognized on a cash basis, that is when received.
- Discounts on commercial paper and zero coupon bonds are normally amortized and taken as interest income.

- Dividends from equity investments are frequently itemized and included in non-interest income but some banks do not itemize dividends received and include it within interest income.
- Credit-related fees such as arrangement and drawdown fees are normally recognized as non-interest income although for the purpose of assessing the profitability of the lending function they should be taken with interest income.

Exhibit: Swaps treatment

There are three possible ways to account for interest income and expense arising from a bank's position in interest rate swaps. They all have the same impact on net interest income but result in different values for interest income and interest expense:

- The first way would be to recognize gross interest income and gross interest expense in the interest income and expense lines. This has no merit as an accounting policy whatsoever.
- Interest from individual interest rate swaps where the bank is a net receiver is recognized as interest income while that where it is a net payer as interest expense. This is the US GAAP and most common international standard.
- The total of netted payments and netted receipts are taken as a netted interest income or interest expense item depending on whether overall the bank is a net payer or receiver.

- **Accounting.** The accounting for loans and interest income has four discrete elements. First, the drawdown of the loan, second, the recognition of the interest income, third, the actual payment of the interest and fourth, the repayment of the principal. The principal repayment is simply the reverse of the accounting entries associated with the drawdown.
- **Asset yields.** Asset yields are calculated as interest income divided by average interest-earning assets. In some countries the value of the derived item interest-earning assets is disclosed and may be broken down by asset class while in others the analyst has to estimate this value:

$$Interest\ income = Asset\ yields \times Average\ interest\ earning\ assets$$

The way in which banks annualize interest rates varies. US banks have a 360-day accounting (and calculation) convention while banks in most other countries use a 365-day convention. This can be very confusing initially but the simplest way to consider it is that annual rates reported by US banks are equivalent to 360/365 times the rates reported by foreign banks. In point of fact it is much easier using the 360-day convention for fairly obvious reasons.

In some countries banks simply annualize the quarterly number by multiplying by four. This results in a small error because it takes no account of compounding or the differing number of days in each quarter:

$$Annual\ asset\ yields = (1 + Quarterly\ asset\ yields)^{\wedge}(Number\ of\ days\ in\ quarter/360) - 1$$

The level of asset yields will depend on a number of factors:

- **Asset class mix.** The higher the proportion of government securities or deposits with other banks the lower the asset yield is likely to be. In such a case this begs the question as to whether this is due to holding short-dated government paper, with short duration, for liquidity requirements or long-dated paper with long duration to position the bank for expected falling interest rates.

A bank in the former case may simply be highly conservative or have to maintain a highly liquid balance sheet because it is relying primarily on wholesale funding and is vulnerable to a possible run on its deposits.

- **Loan mix.** A consumer bank is likely to have significantly higher asset yields than one with a predominantly corporate customer base. This does not mean that the consumer bank is making riskier loans, however, on the basis that risk is measured by the volatility of losses. It does, however, mean that we should expect a higher level of average loan losses at the consumer bank.
- **Currency mix.** In isolation a bank's asset yields tell us little. They are, however, useful for comparing banks operating in the same market. This is less helpful for comparing international banks whose assets and liabilities are in a mixture of different currencies. The level of asset yields will depend on the mix of its assets by currency.
- **Swap positions.** The size of a bank's swap positions can result in this measure being of limited use as they are not included in the definition of earning assets or liabilities but interest received from them or paid are included in interest income or expense.

A final note of caution concerns recognition of interest income from NPLs. Interest from such loans is usually recognized on a cash basis. Changes in definitions of NPLs may have an impact on interest income, the same is true about the treatment of restructured loans (whether classified as non-performing or not). The successful resolution of a large restructuring case may result in interest income being inflated in the period in which this occurs.

Interest Expense

The level of detail provided for interest expense is usually in line with that provided for interest income. Included within interest expense are the following:

- Interest expense on deposits and other forms of debt financing such as subordinated debt and convertible bonds.
- Preference share dividends are normally reported after pre-tax profit and are not normally included within the definition of interest-bearing liabilities but for analytical purposes should be treated as debt. Where they are present the interest expense line and interest-bearing liabilities should be adjusted accordingly.

In countries where there is either an explicit deposit insurance scheme to which banks pay insurance premiums those premiums have to be taken somewhere. In some countries these are referred to as taxes on deposits or "contributions" to rehabilitation agencies set up to deal with prior banking crises. These premiums are sometimes included as a part of deposit expenses and appear within interest expense, sometimes they are included as an item as part of operating expenses and sometimes as part of "taxes paid". The only way to find out is to check the actual accounting standard in the country concerned, even then it may be necessary to check the actual practice of individual banks.

These differences are generally very difficult to adjust for unless the charges are itemized. When they do occur they can make a significant difference to spreads, efficiency ratios and effective tax rates when trying to make meaningful cross-border comparisons:

- **Accounting.** The accounting for deposit taking and payment of interest expense is quite straightforward. Take a cash deposit for a one-month time deposit, this is credited to the cash account (asset) and deposit account (liability) increased by the same amount. Interest is normally accrued on a daily basis (although there are occasions when it may be done more frequently). Interest expense is taken through the income statement. The interest payable account is increased by a matching amount and the equity account reduced accordingly.

  At the end of the month the interest payable account is reduced to zero and the deposit account increased by the same amount. Finally when the deposit is withdrawn the cash account is reduced by the initial deposit plus the interest earned and the deposit account reduced by the same amount.
- **Funding costs.** Funding costs are defined as interest expense divided by interest-bearing liabilities. The same level of detail provided for reported asset yields will usually be provided for interest-bearing liability classes:

$$Funding\ costs = Interest\ expense/Average\ interest\text{-}bearing\ liabilities$$

The factors that determine the level of funding costs include the following:

- **Liability class mix.** The level of funding costs depends on the mix in terms of liability term. Longer-dated liabilities, such as subordinated debt, generally have higher funding costs than short-dated liabilities such as non-bank deposits.
- **Deposit mix.** Retail banks with a high proportion of deposits from individuals generally have lower funding costs than banks relying on corporate and wholesale funding. In part this may be due to the existence of a deposit insurance scheme which should lower the rate that depositors demand because they do not need to be compensated for accepting credit risk. In part this is simply due to the lower pricing power that retail depositors have compared with wholesale depositors.

  The benefits of a lower level of funding costs from attracting a higher proportion of cheaper retail deposits is usually offset by a higher level of operating expenses and in making an assessment of a bank's performance efficiency ratios must also be taken into account.

The same observations made for asset yields with respect to currency mix and swaps also apply to funding costs.

Spreads and Margins

As net interest income continues to account for more then 50% of operating income at the vast majority of commercial banks it is usually the single most important line item to both forecast and analyze. Net interest income is calculated by subtracting total interest expenses from total interest income:

$$Net\ interest\ income = Interest\ income - Interest\ expense$$

Net interest spreads are defined as asset yields less funding costs. They tell us how much a bank is paying for its funding versus how much it is extracting from its assets:

$$Net\ interest\ spread = NS = Asset\ yields - Funding\ costs$$

The second related ratio is the net interest margin (NIM). This is defined as net interest income divided by average interest-earning assets:

$$Net\ interest\ margin = NIM = Net\ interest\ income/Average\ interest\text{-}earning\ assets$$

Banks and analysts tend to use both terms in a loose sense interchangeably, I tend to concentrate on the spread because it is less affected by changes in balance sheet structure and in particular capital raising exercises than the net interest margin. A detailed explanation of the relationship between margins and spreads is included in an exhibit at the end of this chapter.

Spreads are affected by two principal factors:

- **Market forces.** Just as in any other competitive business there are usually secular downward pressures on bank margins as well as cyclical effects. These are also affected by specific factors such as price wars for housing loans and credit cards. Changes in the level of interest rates and the shape of the yield curve will also have an impact.
- **Treasury positioning.** The use of instruments such as FRAs and interest rate swaps by bank treasuries also complicates matters. Banks may position themselves for anticipated shifts in the yield curve. Analysts cannot forecast the impact of either of these two factors.

At times it is clear whether spreads are likely to narrow or widen, but it is always difficult to quantify exactly by how much. The safest approach is to assume that spreads stay flat! This is rarely the case but reduces forecasting error risk. An analyst who forecasts a contraction in spreads but the bank concerned manages to obtain wider spread will be rewarded with a large forecasting error.

A bank may be able to increase spreads by reducing the level of low-yielding liquid securities held and increasing the level of loans or by reducing its reliance on high-cost wholesale funds by attracting more low-cost retail funds. These are examples of changes in the balance sheet structure.

The net interest margin is also affected by changes in the equity base. From an accounting perspective equity provides a form of free funds. A successful rights issue will increase the level of "free funds" at a bank. In this instance even if spreads are flat we should expect to see an increase in the reported net interest margin.

If interest rates fall returns on "free" funds will fall and usually result in lower net interest income. If demand for credit remains robust, however, a bank may be able to maintain its yields on assets but be able to cut deposit rates, lowering funding costs (or cut deposit rates at a faster pace than lending rates). This will result in an expansion of spreads and may be sufficient to offset the lower returns of free funds.

Key spread and margin ratios
Asset yields   = Interest income/Average interest-earning assets
Funding costs   = Interest expense/Average interest-bearing liabilities
Net interest spread = Asset yields − Funding costs
Net interest margin = Net interest income/Average interest-earning assets

Forecasting Net Interest Income

Although net interest income is calculated by subtracting total interest expenses from total interest income only an inexperienced analyst would go about forecasting it in this way. And they would only do this once. Nobody really expects analysts to get it precisely right but they do expect them to get it roughly right. That means minimizing forecasting error is more important than getting the number exactly on the spot. The standard deviation from forecasting "interest income minus interest expense" is lower than the sum of the standard deviation of forecast interest income and the standard deviation of forecast interest expense.

The following example will show why few experienced analysts adopt this approach. The errors in forecasting asset yields and funding costs are only 5%–6%, but the error in the crucial net interest line is nearly 34%.

In this example the errors were in opposite directions but even if the analyst got the funding cost exactly correct a 5% error in the forecast for asset yields would result in an 18% forecasting error.

Errors in forecasting net interest income					
	Forecast			**Actual**		
	IEA/ IBL	**Yields/ costs**	**Interest income**	**Yields/ costs**	**Interest income**	**Forecasting error**
Asset yield	10 000	10.0%	1000	9.5%	950	−5.0%
Funding costs	9 000	8.0%	−720	8.5%	−765	6.3%
Interest spread		2.0%		1.0%		−50.0%
NII ($m)			280		185	−33.9%

Note: IEA: Interest-earning assets, IBL: Interest-bearing liabilities, NII: Net interest income.

The method most analysts use is to forecast net interest income is as follows:

- Estimate interest-earning assets and interest-bearing liabilities based on loan and deposit growth, any new sources of long-term funding and changes in equity.
- Estimate average funding costs based on interest rate outlook and any changes in the bank's interest-bearing liability structure.
- Estimate net interest spread based on direction of interest rates, magnitude of expected change, changes in composition of asset-earning assets and interest-bearing liabilities and the effects of competition and regulatory changes.
- Calculate average asset yield by adding forecast interest spread to average funding costs.
- Calculate interest income by multiplying average interest-earning assets by asset yield. Calculate interest expense by multiplying average interest-bearing liabilities by funding costs. Subtract interest expense from interest income to give net interest income.

NON-INTEREST INCOME

The level of detail that banks disclose of non-interest income varies significantly between countries. The level of disclosure also frequently varies by reporting period, more detail is usually given in annual reports than in quarterly earnings releases.

Non-interest income can be broken down into two broad categories:

- **Stable recurrent income.** Fee income (at commercial banks), rental and dividend income tends to be fairly stable. Fees are generated from credit-related activities, trade finance, trust, custody, account charges and investment banking. Investment banking fees and trading income are fairly volatile but the remaining items are fairly well behaved. The simplest way to forecast these items is to take an average over a number of accounting periods and then apply forecast growth equivalent to that of the expansion of the balance sheet.

  This approach has three advantages. It makes the modeling process simpler as any changes in assumptions for balance sheet growth are automatically reflected in non-interest income. Second, forecasts automatically adjust for actual results. This is important because when banks are reporting earnings time is short, everyone wants revised forecasts and the analyst just wants to go home. The final reason is that the basis of the forecast is easy to explain.

- **Trading and investment banking income.** Trading, investment banking income and gains and losses on investment securities tend to be highly volatile. Trading income tends to benefit from higher market volumes and greater volatility. Investment banking income depends largely on stock market turnover and the level of IPOs and M&A activity.

  It is dangerous to forecast such line items using a formulaic approach. An analyst has to read the financial journals and newspapers, talk with investment bankers and traders and then make an educated guess. Management at some banks may provide guidance.

Some transactions carried out on behalf of customers incur costs such as stamp duty and other charges that the bank pays for but passes on directly to the customer. Fee income can be treated gross, in which case these charges are included as a part of operating expenses or net. The better treatment is to report them net. Banks that report gross have artificially inflated non-interest income and operating expenses. Efficiency ratios such as operating expenses to operating income and operating expenses as a percentage of assets are also inflated.

OPERATING EXPENSES

It is generally much easier to forecast operating expenses than operating income. A large proportion of operating expenses at commercial banks relates to the costs of employing people, with the balance going on computer and telecommunications costs, rent and depreciation of equipment. These costs are difficult to change quickly.

The simplest approach is to assume that operating expenses grow in line with the balance sheet. This assumption may prove too simplistic if any of the following conditions apply:

- **Downsizing.** A bank may be seeking to cut costs actively through redundancies, branch closures and rationalization of facilities, particularly after an in-market acquisition. This may lead to one-off restructuring charges that inflate operating expenses but then result in lower ongoing costs.
- **Expansion into new businesses.** Banks seeking to enter new businesses will need to invest before they start to see the revenue streams. This is fine so long as management watch costs carefully and have realistic business plans. Unfortunately egos can get in the way of prudent management decision making.
- **Goodwill charges.** We have already looked at the goodwill charges resulting from acquisitions and it should suffice to reiterate that these need to be taken into account.

We have already discussed the issues of the reporting of deposit insurance premiums and reporting of costs, such as stamp duties, passed directly on to clients. The only way to deal with such factors is to check national accounting standards and read the notes to the accounts, but such accounting and reporting differences mean that analysts have to be wary of simple cross-border comparisons of ratios such as cost–income and cost–assets.

Key earnings statement ratios	
Cost–income ratio	= Operating expenses/Operating income
Cost–assets ratio	= Operating expenses/Average assets
Non-interest income level	= Non-interest income/Operating income
Fee income level	= Fee income/Operating income

Bad Debt Charges

We have already examined the subject of bad debt charges in depth in Chapter 13 "Managing credit risk". We have already mentioned that there is an ongoing debate between analysts as to whether operating profit, as an item, should be calculated before bad debt charges or after. This is not a debate about what is right or wrong but about what is most useful and we have already discussed the pros and cons of the two approaches.

ATTRIBUTABLE PROFITS AND PROFITABILITY MEASURES

With all of these detailed forecasts complete we can arrive at an estimate of a bank's net profit. Relevant income taxes and payments to minorities also need to be taken into account to arrive at profit attributable to shareholders. (Interest expense on preference shares is usually reported at this level but as already explained for analytical purposes should be treated as interest expense.) The key profitability measure is return-on-average-equity.

Profitability ratios	
Return-on-average-equity (ROAE)	= Net profit/Average shareholders' funds
Return-on-average-assets (ROAA)	= Net income/Average total assets

Care needs to be taken when calculating average shareholders' funds. Items such as preference issues should be excluded if they have been included. Some banks report average equity over an accounting period but many do not. The simplest approach is to take the sum of the brought-forward and carried-forward values and divide them by two. This is an approximation but usually suffices. There are, however, inevitably exceptions that need to be catered for:

- **Capital raising.** If a bank has a rights, or other capital raising, issue then this has to be taken into account, by taking a weighted average of the equity before and after the issue. The effects of the exercise of employee option schemes can usually be ignored although it is necessary to reflect changes in number of issued shares.
- **Capital returned.** Any special dividends or capital reduction programs also need to be taken into account. These are treated in much the same way as capital raising issues.
- **Exercise of convertibles.** Where the exercise of convertible instrument takes place on a modest scale over a prolonged period this rarely requires any special treatment in terms of calculating average equity. If mass conversion takes place on or around a specific date then they should be treated in the same way as capital raising exercises.
- **Acquisitions.** The effects of acquisitions also need to be taken into account. All balance sheet and earnings statement numbers for the period in which a material acquisition takes place are usually heavily distorted. It is more important to focus on getting the numbers right for periods after the acquisition has completed.

Analysts also have to take account of these factors in calculating and estimating number of shares issued and the fully diluted number of shares in order to arrive at estimates of earnings-per-share (EPS) and fully diluted earnings-per-share. The latter takes account of future dilutive exercise of convertible instruments. I am not going to deal with how to adjust numbers of shares for rights issues and convertibles in this work. Their treatment is exactly the same as at any non-financial company.

The general formula for estimating average shareholders' funds to adjust for capital raising and reduction exercises is given by the following equation. At first sight this might appear intimidating but is basically a mechanical and rather tiresome exercise. It is usually sufficient to make the adjustments on a "full-month" basis but the more anal retentive analysts may do this on a daily basis:

Estimated average equity = [*Brought forward equity at start of accounting period*

+ Estimated equity on day before capital is raised (returned)]

÷ 2 × (*Time between start of accounting period*

÷ *Total duration of accounting period*)

+ [*Estimated equity on day before capital is raised (returned)*

± *Capital raised (returned)*

+ *Carried forward equity at end of accounting period*]

÷ 2 × ((*Total duration of accounting period − Time between*

start of accounting period and capital raising (return))

÷ *Total duration of accounting period*)

BOTTOM-LINE FORECASTING

Forecasting bank earnings may appear to be something of a lottery with so many uncertain line items. In practice the market takes little notice of individual analyst forecasts but focuses on the consensus. It might appear surprising how often it is possible for a good analyst to get every line item wrong but get the forecast net profit to be within a couple of percentage points of the

---

Exhibit: Relationship between net interest margins and spreads

The net interest spread and net interest margin can be defined as follows.

$$\text{Net interest margin} = NIM = \frac{\text{Interest income} - \text{Interest expense}}{\text{Interest-earning assets}} \quad and$$

$$\text{Net interest spread} = NIS = \frac{\text{Interest income}}{\text{Interest-earning assets}} - \frac{\text{Interest expense}}{\text{Interest-bearing liabilities}}$$

The difference between the net interest margin and net interest spread is given by:

$$NIM - NIS = \frac{\text{Interest expense}}{\text{Interest-earning assets}} - \frac{\text{Interest expense}}{\text{Interest-bearing liabilities}}$$

and this simplifies to the following:

$$NIM - NIS = \frac{\text{Interest expense}}{\text{Interest-earning assets}} \times \left(\frac{\text{Interest-earning assets}}{\text{Interest-bearing liabilities}} - 1 \right) \quad or$$

$$NIM - NIS = \text{Funding costs} \times \left(\frac{\text{Interest-earning assets}}{\text{Interest-bearing liabilities}} - 1 \right) = FC \times \left(\frac{IEA}{IBL} - 1 \right)$$

A bank's net interest income margin is almost always higher than its net interest spread because interest-earning assets are almost always greater than interest-bearing liabilities. As most analysts and investors focus on changes in margins and spreads it is worth seeing how these two measures change together:

$$\Delta(NIM - NIS) \cong \Delta(FC) \times \left(\frac{IEA}{IBL} - 1 \right) + FC \times \Delta \left(\frac{IEA}{IBL} \right)$$

- In a flat interest rate environment (i.e. change in funding costs is zero) margins will increase relative to spreads if the ratio of interest-earning assets to interest-bearing liabilities increases. This would be the case if the bank raised capital through a rights issue. They would fall following a special dividend. It is actually a little more complicated than suggested here because this simple approach fails to take full account of the impact of the changes in balance sheet structure. If a bank raises capital it will tend to use it to replace its more expensive funding where possible, lowering the average funding costs on its interest-bearing liabilities.
- If funding costs increase (and asset yields increase by the same amount) the net interest margin should increase and net interest spread remain unchanged because interest-earning assets are almost always greater than interest-bearing liabilities.

---

reported number. This happens when errors compensate for one another. By now the reader should recognize the hand of diversification effects at work.

Analysts balance their bottom-up forecasts against their top-down expectations, what goes around, comes around. Most banks have considerable flexibility in reporting profits for a specific period. A larger than expected bad debt charge may well be offset by higher than expected gains on investment security disposals. Large one-off bad debt charges for specific events such as a large corporate failure or the 2001 Argentinean financial crisis can usually be identified and forecast.

The real driver of valuations is not, however, reported net profit for a single accounting period (although this may affect sentiment) but the market's perception of sustainable profitability, earnings growth and the likelihood of capital raising. While analyzing past performance forms a major part of analysts' jobs, forecasting future earnings is both harder to do well and more important to stock market investors. We can't change the past but we can try to anticipate the future.

Primers

26

Statistics for Finance

Statistics are like a bikini. What they reveal is suggestive, but what they conceal is vital.
Aaron Levenstein, US author

This primer sets out to remind those people who have already studied statistics of formal definitions and to introduce those definitions to those who do not have those skills. Most non-statisticians who have taken a statistics course at some point in their life, but do not use their techniques on a regular basis, usually refer to a standard textbook for anything other than the most basic problem. The key here is to recognize what sort of solution exists for a particular type of problem and to know where to look it up. Spreadsheet applications contain most statistical functions and these can be used without having to memorize the underlying formulae. The important thing is to know what these formulae or functions represent and the restrictions on their application rather than the detail of how to calculate them.

For practical advice a friendly economist is a useful source. They use statistical methods fairly regularly in their work and this means their suggestions are usually of a practical nature, tending to lack the complexity of advice from professional statisticians. Most of us have enough complications in our personal lives than to look for it elsewhere. This also shows, despite evidence to the contrary, that economists can have a productive role in life.

NOTATION

Statistics use many different symbols to represent various functions and values. There are also many terms whose meaning is not always intuitively obvious. The symbol "Σ" is used extensively and means "the sum of" or "add up the following". It is accompanied by the use of subscripts that indicate which values to add together. If we have a variable X with four values 2, 3, 4 and 5 then the sum of the values of X is given by the following:

$$\sum_{i=1}^{i=4} X_i = 2 + 3 + 4 + 5 = 10$$

Given a second variable Y with three values of 7, 8 and 9 the sum of their products is 336 as shown by the table on the next page.

This can be represented in a more concise form as follows. The sum of the products of values of X and Y is given by:

$$\sum_{i,j=1}^{i=4, j=3} X_i Y_j = 2 \times 7 + 3 \times 7 + 4 \times 7 + 5 \times 7 + 2 \times 8 + 3 \times 8 + 4 \times 8 + 5 \times 8$$

$$+ 2 \times 9 + 3 \times 9 + 4 \times 9 + 5 \times 9 = 336$$

Sum of the products of values of *X* and *Y*				
		Y value		
		7	8	9	Sum of products

		7	8	9	Sum of products
X values	2	14	16	18	48
	3	21	24	27	72
	4	28	32	36	96
	5	35	40	45	120
Sum of products		98	112	126	**336**

A final example shows that the sum of the values squared does not equal the square of the sum of the values:

$$\sum_{i=1}^{i=4} X_i^2 = 2^2 + 3^2 + 4^2 + 5^2 = 4 + 9 + 16 + 25 = 54 \quad while \quad \left(\sum_{i=1}^{i=4} X_i \right)^2$$

$$= (2 + 3 + 4 + 5)^2 = 16^2 = 256$$

The symbol "Σ" is the upper-case Greek letter sigma which is potentially confusing as the lower case Greek symbol "σ" is usually used to represent an important statistical measure "standard deviation" which indicates the degree of variation of the values of a variable about the mean of its values.

In formal terms, datasets can be divided into two types, populations and samples of populations. A population contains all of the data available while a sample is a sub-set of the data available. There are some differences in certain formulae depending on whether the data is a "population" or a "sample". There are also some differences in certain formulae when the number of values is small (typically less than 30–40).

Throughout this primer we will restrict the scope to populations of data with large numbers of values but readers should be aware that such differences do exist and when the data is a sample or has a small number of values refer to a standard statistics textbook to see whether, and how, any formulae need to be adjusted.

Although the terms probability, frequency and weighting all have different specific meanings, in the context of statistics they are all used for the same purpose. Frequency and weighting are commonly taken as proportions of the whole. There is, however, a key conceptual difference, probability is forward looking while frequency is often based on actual results. A key assumption, often implicit, is that historic results using frequency may be extrapolated into the future.

AVERAGES AND VARIABILITY

Averages

There are three types of average, the mean, median and mode. Each has advantages and disadvantages in their use for describing a set of data depending on the shape of the distribution of the data:

- **Mean.** The weighted arithmetic average ($\bar{X}$) of a set of numbers $X_1, X_2, \ldots, X_n$ with weightings or frequencies of $W_1, W_2, \ldots, W_n$ or $f_1, f_2, \ldots, f_n$ respectively is given by:

$$\bar{X} = \sum_{i=1}^{N} W_i X_i \Big/ \sum_{i=1}^{N} W_i \quad \text{or} \quad \bar{X} = \sum_{i=1}^{N} f_i X_i \Big/ \sum_{i=1}^{N} f_i$$

If the numbers of the set have equal weightings or occur with the same frequency this simplifies to:

$$\bar{X} = \sum_{i=1}^{N} X_i \Big/ N$$

- **Median.** The median is the value at which half of the numbers of the set have greater values and half of them have lower values.
- **Mode.** The mode of a set of numbers is the value that occurs most frequently. For a given set of numbers there may be no such value or there may be more than one value. A set with two modes is called bi-modal.

Variability

An important characteristic of a set of data is the extent to which its members' values are spread about some average value. This is sometimes referred to as variation and sometimes as dispersion. A set of data with a high level of dispersion has many values far from that of the average. In a set of data with a low level of dispersion the values are closely clustered around the average.

In formal terms, dispersion is defined by a set's variance and its standard deviation. The variance is calculated from the values of the data set and the standard deviation derived directly from the variance:

- **Variance.** The variance is calculated as the sum of the square of the difference between the value of each member of the set and the set's mean. Squaring this difference gives equal weight to values that are greater than the average and those where it is less:

$$\text{Variance } \sigma^2 = \sum_{i=1}^{N} W_i (X_i - \bar{X})^2$$

The variance for a population can also be calculated using the following formula:

$$\text{Variance } \sigma^2 = \sum_{i=1}^{N} W_i X_i^2 - \left(\sum_{i=1}^{N} W_i X_i \right)^2$$

- **Standard deviation.** The standard deviation is defined as the square root of variance and has statistical properties that make it a very useful measure. The standard deviation gives a result that is analogous to the "average" distance of the variable's values from the mean. Standard deviation is normally represented by "σ" (the Greek lower-case letter sigma):

$$\text{Standard deviation} = \text{Square root of variance} = \sqrt{\sum_{i=1}^{N} W_i (X_i - \bar{X})^2} = \sigma$$

The standard deviation is measured in absolute terms but it is also useful to represent it in terms relative to the mean, particularly when comparing results between a number of sets of data. A useful and widely used measure is the Z-score. This gives the distance of the value of a variable from the set's mean expressed in units of standard deviations. A Z-score of 3 would indicate that the value was 3 standard deviations away from the mean:

$$Z\text{-score given by: } Z = \frac{X_i - \bar{X}}{\sigma}$$

DISTRIBUTIONS

The values of the numbers in a set of data may be distributed in one of many ways. Some of these distributions occur naturally in both nature and human systems. These distributions have been studied extensively and the characteristics of the most common defined. Of these some of the most important are the normal, skewed, random, exponential and Poisson distributions:

- **Probability distribution charts.** These distributions are shown using frequency distribution or probability density function (pdf) graphs where the y value gives a measure of frequency or probability for specific values of x. The values of the probability measure are not important in isolation. The best way to consider their interpretation is that the area under the whole graph represents a cumulative probability of 100%. This is best illustrated with an example. The following chart shows the distribution of trading prices over time for a stock with a mean of $45. The shaded area represents the probability that the price will lie between $37 and $42. This probability is equal to the shaded area divided by the total area.

  When plotting two different distributions on the same chart it is necessary to normalize the x values so that they are both expressed in terms of standard deviations.
- **Effect of different standard deviations on shape.** The second chart shows the probability functions for two stocks with the same mean price but different absolute standard deviations. The lower the standard distribution the more the prices are clustered around the mean.

Probability distribution graph	Absolute frequency distribution graph

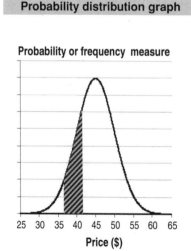

Probability or frequency measure

Price ($)

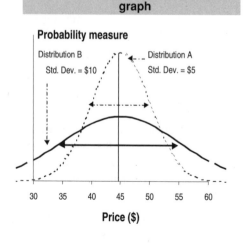

Probability measure

Distribution B
Std. Dev. = $10

Distribution A
Std. Dev. = $5

Price ($)

Both of the above charts show "normal" distributions. The key features of normal and skewed distributions are as follows and are illustrated in the next two charts:

- **Normal distributions.** The normal distribution has a bell-shaped curve, it is symmetric about its average value. The values of the mean, mode and median are identical. It is useful to plot the probability density function against the Z-scores (the difference measured in standard deviations from the mean). The total area under this curve is $+1$ or 100%.

  The normal distribution has the unique properties that approximately 68% of the values lie within one standard deviation of the mean, 95% within two standard deviations of the mean and 99.7% within three standard deviations. The traded prices of many financial instruments often have the characteristics of normal distributions. Many theories and some trading strategies rely on this assumption holding true but this is not always the case.

- **Skewed distributions.** In skewed distributions values are shifted away from the mean. A business example of distributions skewed to the right is the level of credit losses. These are normally very low but infrequently can be very high. An example from life is the frequency of sexual intercourse by age. Both distributions are said to have a long tail.

  Distributions can be skewed to the left or right. The mean, mode and median have different values and the methods used to determine probabilities that work with normal distributions do not always work.

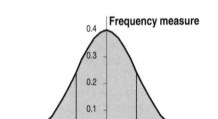

| Normal distribution – Z-scores | Skewed distribution – right hand tail |

- **Other.** Other distributions include exponential and random. An example of an exponential distribution is given by radioactive decay. A random distribution has a flat line where probabilities of occurrence are equal for all values of X.

  The distribution of the height of human adults will have two peaks, one centered on the average value for adult males and the other for adult females. Such a distribution is termed "bi-modal" and the mean and median values are largely meaningless.

Problems

A real problem for statisticians analyzing financial data is that of distinguishing between datasets with normal distributions and those with slightly skewed distributions. It seems trite to say that this problem arises because infrequent events don't happen very often! "Often" is a subjective term and in this context needs to be put in terms of human time frames.

The probability of a particular subatomic event happening may be very small but when billions of events take place every second may be observed on average once a day. Individual business events that have a much higher probability of occurring than the event in our subatomic example may not, however, take place within the space of a single human generation.

This means that for many distributions the likelihood of improbable events has to be inferred from the behavior of the frequent events. In many cases a normal distribution is assumed in order to quantify estimates of the probability of remote events occurring. Small errors can result in large differences between estimated probabilities and the actual levels at the extremes.

Other problems arise because external conditions may change and affect the distribution resulting in the standard deviation varying over time. It is easy to come to likely conclusions concerning future events based on past results without recognizing the implicit assumptions that lie in historic analyses.

CONFIDENCE LEVELS AND HOLDING PERIODS

Confidence Levels

This leads us to the subject of confidence levels or confidence intervals (the terms confidence level and confidence interval have slightly different technical definitions but are often used synonymously). When a building contractor is asked whether he will be able to get the work on our kitchen finished on time we demand a "yes" or "no" answer and get frustrated with his inevitable "well it depends" response.

The contractor may lack the benefits of a college education but he knows that there are things that could go wrong. A better answer would have been "I am 95% confident that it will be completed by then based on past projects. For the other 5% I can't tell you when it will then get finished or whether it will ever get finished." The irony of the real exchange is that the builder would probably confirm that the work would be done on time, we will then refuse to believe him and he will miss the deadline in any event.

Some of the very few quantitative measures that people remember from statistics courses is that "the value of a number in a dataset with a normal distribution will lie within 2 standard deviations of the mean to a 95% confidence level". The 99% confidence level is also frequently referred to and this has a Z-score of 2.58.

Given a normal distribution the probability that a value will fall within 2 standard deviations of the mean is 95.45% as shown in the following table. At the 99% confidence level 2.58:

Confidence levels versus number of standard deviations from mean (Z-score) for normal distribution										
Confidence level	99.73%	99%	98%	96%	95.45%	95%	90%	80%	68.27%	50%
Z-score	3.00	2.58	2.33	2.05	2.00	1.96	1.645	1.28	1.00	0.674

One-tail Tests

The above tests have all been "two-tail" tests, where we are interested in the probability of events occurring within given standard deviations from the mean, either lower or higher. A common requirement, however, is to determine the probability of a value being either greater or less than a given number of standard deviations from the mean. A good example of that is a trading operation where we are interested in assessing the probability that a given level of losses will be exceeded.

The following two charts show the difference between a two-tail and one-tail test. The charts both show identical distributions of trading losses. The first chart shows the probability that trading gains or losses will lie within 2 standard deviations of the mean to be 95.45%.

The second chart shows the probability that losses will exceed 2 standard deviations from the mean. The probability that they will be less than this is 97.725% (95.45% + 4.55%/2) and subtracting this from 1 gives a probability that they will exceed 2 standard deviations from the mean of 2.275%.

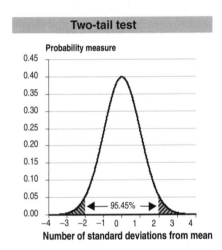

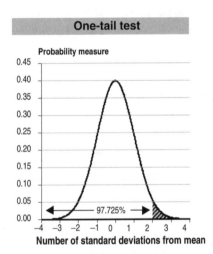

Chebyshev's Theorem

A little knowledge can be dangerous and some analysts blithely assume normal distributions for the data they are looking at and then assert the confidence levels given above. Where we cannot say what the nature of the distribution is we can still arrive at confidence levels using Chebyshev's theorem. (If we know the nature of the distribution it may be possible to use more advanced statistical methods to obtain a more precise solution.)

Chebyshev's theorem holds for any distribution of observations and as a consequence it provides a much lower level of confidence than that which can be derived for normal distributions. In addition the value the theorem gives is a lower bound only. In terms of losses this can be explained as follows. The probability, P, that a random variable X will lie within n standard deviations of the mean is equal to or greater than $1 - 1/n^2$. More formally, this is expressed as follows:

$$P[(\bar{X} - n\sigma) < X < (\bar{X} + n\sigma)] \geq 1 - 1/n^2$$

The following table shows confidence levels versus number of standard deviations from the mean. There is at least a 75% probability that the actual losses will be within 2 standard deviations of the mean.

Confidence levels versus Z-scores for Chebyshev's theorem									
Z-score	2	3	4	5	6	7	8	9	10
Confidence level	75%	89%	94%	96%	97%	98.0%	98.4%	98.8%	99.0%
Number of years	4	9	16	25	36	49	63	83	100

PORTFOLIO ANALYSIS

Covariance and the Correlation Coefficient

The starting point for portfolio analysis are the relationships between the members of the portfolio. These portfolios might be loans, bonds, equities and other traded assets.

Covariance measures the extent to which the values of two variables "covary" and is defined as follows:

$$Covariance = \sigma_{i,j}^2 = \sum W_i W_j (\bar{X}_i - X_i)(\bar{X}_j - X_j)$$

The correlation coefficient $r_{i,j}$ between two variables is then calculated using variance and covariance as follows:

$$r_{i,j}^2 = \frac{\sigma_{i,j}^2}{\sigma_i \sigma_j} \Rightarrow r_{i,j} = \pm \sqrt{\frac{\sigma_{i,j}^2}{\sigma_i \sigma_j}}$$

The correlation coefficient has three fundamental properties:

- The value of r must lie between $+1$ and -1, this can be demonstrated mathematically quite easily.
- The correlation coefficient defines the degree to which a relationship exists between two variables, it does not, however, provide any proof that such a relationship exists. When the value of r is close to ± 1 this suggests a strong relationship, when positive values tend to move together in the same direction. When r is negative it suggests an inverse relationship, when one value increases the other tends to fall.
- A correlation coefficient close to zero suggests that the two variables are independent of one another. The value given by r^2 defines the extent to which changes in the two values can be explained by the assumed relationship. A rough rule of thumb is that when r^2 is less than 0.4 there is no meaningful relationship of this form between the two variables.

The total variance between two members of a portfolio is given by the following, where $r_{1,2}$ is the correlation coefficient between the two variables:

$$\sigma_{1,2}^2 = W_1 W_2 r_{1,2} \sigma_1 \sigma_2 + W_1^2 \sigma_1^2 + W_2^2 \sigma_2^2 + W_2 W_1 r_{2,1} \sigma_2 \sigma_1$$

The variance of a portfolio can then be generalized as the following sum.

Double summation to give portfolio variance				
$W_1 W_1 r_{1,1}\sigma_1\sigma_1$	$+$ $W_1 W_2 r_{1,2}\sigma_1\sigma_2$	$+$ $W_1 W_3 r_{1,3}\sigma_1\sigma_3$ $\ldots$	$+$	$W_1 W_N r_{1,N}\sigma_1\sigma_N$
$W_2 W_1 r_{2,1}\sigma_2\sigma_1$	$+$ $W_2 W_2 r_{2,2}\sigma_2\sigma_1$	$+$ $W_2 W_3 r_{2,3}\sigma_2\sigma_3$ $\ldots$	$+$	$\ldots$
$\sigma_p^2 = W_3 W_1 r_{3,1}\sigma_3\sigma_1$	$+$ $W_3 W_2 r_{3,2}\sigma_1\sigma_3$	$+$ $W_3 W_3 r_{3,3}\sigma_3\sigma_3$ $\ldots$	$+$	$\ldots$
$\ldots$	$\ldots$ $\ldots$	$\ldots$ $\ldots$ $\ldots$	$\ldots$ $\ldots$	$\ldots$
$W_N W_1 r_{N,1}\sigma_N\sigma_1$	$+$ $\ldots$	$+$ $\ldots$	$\ldots$ $+$	$W_N W_N r_{N,N}\sigma_N\sigma_N$

W_i and W_j represent the proportion of the portfolio held in the ith and jth members, N is the number of assets, r_{ij} is the correlation coefficient between the ith and jth members and σ_i and σ_j the standard deviations. In the shorthand of mathematics this can be written as:

$$\sigma_p^2 = \sum_{i=1}^{N}\sum_{j=1}^{N} W_i W_j r_{ij}\sigma_i\sigma_j = \sum_{i,j=1}^{i,j=N} W_i W_j r_{ij}\sigma_i\sigma_j$$

As we add members to a portfolio the covariance factors between different members become increasingly important. A portfolio with only two members has two own-variance terms ($r_{i,j}$ where $i = j$) and two covariance terms ($r_{i,j}$ where $i \neq j$). A portfolio with four members has four own-variance terms and eight covariance terms. A portfolio with 16 members has 16 own-variance terms and 240 covariance terms and one with 30 members has 30 own-variance terms and 870 covariance terms.

In order to explore this equation's properties further it is easiest to consider a portfolio with two members giving:

$$\sigma_p^2 = \sum_{i,j=1}^{2} (W_i W_j r_{ij}\sigma_i\sigma_j) = W_1 W_1 r_{1,1}\sigma_1\sigma_1 + W_2 W_2 r_{2,2}\sigma_2\sigma_2 + W_1 W_2 r_{1,2}\sigma_1\sigma_2$$
$$+ W_2 W_1 r_{2,1}\sigma_2\sigma_1$$

This simplifies further, after taking into account that $r_{1,1}$ and $r_{2,2}$ are both equal to $+1$ and $r_{1,2} = r_{2,1}$:

$$\sigma_p^2 = W_1^2\sigma_1^2 + W_2^2\sigma_2^2 + 2W_1 W_2 r_{1,2}\sigma_1\sigma_2 = \sum_{i=1}^{2} W_i^2\sigma_i^2 + \sum_{i,j=1}^{i,j=2} W_i W_j r_{ij}\sigma_i\sigma_j$$

The first term is the simple weighted sum of the variances, assuming no correlations between members of the portfolio (i.e. they are independent and $r_{i,j} = 0$). The second term is that due to the existence of cross-correlations. The first extreme cases we should look at is where there is perfect positive cross-correlation ($r_{i,j} = +1$). This will define an upper limit to the level of standard deviation for a portfolio as a whole. If there is a perfect positive correlation then all cross-correlation coefficients will be $+1$. For our sample portfolio with two members this gives:

$$\sigma_p^2 = W_1 W_1 r_{1,1}\sigma_1\sigma_1 + W_2 W_2 r_{2,2}\sigma_2\sigma_2 + W_1 W_2 r_{1,2}\sigma_1\sigma_2 + W_2 W_1 r_{2,1}\sigma_2\sigma_1$$
$$\sigma_p^2 = W_1^2\sigma_1^2 + W_2^2\sigma_2^2 + 2W_1 W_2 r_{1,2}\sigma_1\sigma_2 = (W_1\sigma_1 + W_2\sigma_2)^2 \Rightarrow \sigma_p = W_1\sigma_1 + W_2\sigma_2$$

The standard deviation of a portfolio whose members have perfect positive correlations is given by the simple sum of the weighted standard deviations of the members of the portfolio. This means that in any case where there is less than perfect positive correlation the portfolio standard deviation will be less than the weighted average of the standard deviations of the members of the portfolio. The cross-correlation coefficients do not have to be negative for diversification to have a benefit in terms of reducing risk as measured by standard deviation.

This is the keystone of modern portfolio theory. It is used widely in portfolio investment management, credit risk management, some value-at-risk techniques and hence capital management.

The variance, and hence standard deviation, of a portfolio with a large number of members is determined primarily by the covariances between those members. The correlation coefficients may be calculated as follows:

$$r_{ij} = (W_i W_j (X_i - \bar{X}_p)(X_j - \bar{X}_p)) \left/ \left(\sum_{i,j=1}^{i,j=N} W_i^2 W_j^2 (X_i - \bar{X}_p)^2 (X_j - \bar{X}_p)^2 \right)^{1/2} \right.$$

A final point, the above is sometimes illustrated using the term covariance, this is defined as follows:

$$Covariance_{i,j} = \sigma_i \times \sigma_i \times r_{i,j}$$

Beta is used extensively in the capital asset pricing model (CAPM) and its formal definition is as follows:

$$\beta_i = \frac{\sigma_{i,m}^2}{\sigma_m^2} = r_{i,m} \frac{\sigma_i}{\sigma_m}$$

Beta for a portfolio is given by the sum of the simple weighted betas of the individual betas of the members of the portfolio.

$$\beta_p = \sum_{i=1}^{N} W_i \beta_i$$

REGRESSION

It is tempting to expect regression to be something that happens to students of statistics but it turns out to be a particular statistical technique used to investigate the relationship between an independent variable "Y" and one or more dependent variables "X_i" based on a sample of data.

The first step is to postulate (i.e. assume or guess) a form of the relationship between the two variables and by far the most common form of regression is linear regression where the assumed relationship is of the following form, where "a_0" and "a_1" are constants:

$$Y = a_0 + a_1 X$$

The aim is to find the values of a_0 and a_1 that give the best fit between the actual values of Y for a given value of X and the value of Y obtained at the same value of X from using the above equation. The values of a_0 and a_1 can be easily obtained using a spreadsheet function.

This uses a technique called the "least squares" method. This method can be used to derive the constants for equations with higher powers or with more than one variable, such as the following:

$$Y = a_0 + a_1 X + a_2 X^2 \quad and \quad Y = a_0 + a_1 X + a_2 Z^2$$

With computers allowing regression to be performed very easily these are potentially dangerous tools in the wrong hands as they may be used to suggest that relationships exist when that is not the case. Fortunately there are ways to determine just how well the selected equation explains the relationship between the variables.

Correlation defines the extent to which variables are related or the degree to which a particular equation describes the relationship between variables. If the values of Y tend to increase as X increases a positive correlation exists. If all of the values of the variables satisfy the equation exactly the variables are perfectly correlated.

The correlation can be broken into two parts, the extent to which the actual values are explained by the equation and the part that is not. The correlation coefficient (r) is defined as the square root of the ratio of the level of variation that is explained by the equation to the total variation of the actual values:

$$Correlation\ coefficient = r = \pm \sqrt{\frac{\sum_{i=1}^{N} \left(X_i^{Est} - \bar{X}\right)^2}{\sum_{i=1}^{N} (X_i - \bar{X})^2}} \quad and \quad r^2 = \frac{Variation\ explained\ by\ equation}{Total\ variation}$$

A quick examination of this equation shows that r can only take values between $+1$ and -1. A simple rule of thumb is that if r^2 is less than 0.4 there is no real evidence of a relationship indicated. Even when r is close to $+$ or -1 this does not prove anything, spurious correlations do occur where the high value of r is simply due to chance.

OTHER TERMS

Other terms that may be helpful to be familiar with include the following:

- **Multiple periods.** The monthly variance of a member is given by the simple product of its daily variance and 30 days (this is Dreamworld and all months have 30 days):

$$Variance = \sigma^2_{(Monthly)} = \sigma^2_{(Daily)} \times 30$$

The monthly standard variation is therefore given by the square root of the monthly variance:

$$Standard\ deviation\ \sigma_{(Monthly)} = \sigma_{(Daily)} \times \sqrt{30}$$

This is a simple but important result of application in VAR problems where it is used to extrapolate results for one holding period to multiple holding periods:

$$Standard\ deviation_{N\ holding\ periods} = \sqrt{N} \times Standard\ deviation\ for\ one\ holding\ period$$

- **Serial correlation.** Serial correlation occurs when the values of a variable in some way depend on prior values. An example of serial correlation would be if it was more likely to rain on a given day if it had rained on the previous day and more likely to be dry if it had not rained the day before. Where serial correlation exists various statistical methods are no longer applicable. This is the case in the example above where we inferred a standard deviation for multiple periods from the results for a single period.

- **Expected value.** The expected value (*EV*) of a number of independent events, each with probability P_i and value V_i, is given by the following equation:

$$EV = \sum_{i=i}^{N} P_i V_i$$

The same formula applies for a portfolio with a number of assets each comprising W_i of the total portfolio's value and substituting W_i for P_i:

$$EV = \sum_{i=i}^{N} W_i V_i$$

- **Idiosyncratic terms.** Idiosyncratic terms are sometimes shown in the full form of the CAPM equation. The best way to consider idiosyncratic terms is to view them as a random fluctuation in time. They may have a non-zero value for a specific period but over time the mean value of an idiosyncratic term should be zero.

27

Derivation of Duration and Convexity

I have a truly marvelous demonstration of this theorem which this margin is too narrow to contain.
Pierre de Fermat, French mathematician

DURATION AND CONVEXITY

In this appendix we provide a formal derivation of the factors duration and convexity that we introduced in Chapter 10 on managing interest rate risk. Duration and convexity are factors used to determine the change in price of a bond, given by ΔP or dP, for a given small change in yield, ΔY or dY.

Zero coupon bond portfolio value versus yield

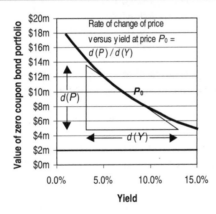

The derivation of duration and convexity relies on the application of a mathematical series, called the Taylor series. This can be used to derive the price (P_1) of a bond given a small change in yield (ΔY) from a given level of yield and assuming we know its price (P_0) at that yield. This is shown in the following equation:

$$P_1 = \sum_{n=1}^{\infty} P_0 + \frac{dP}{dY}\Delta y + \frac{1}{2}\frac{d^2 P}{dY^2}(\Delta y)^2 + \frac{1}{3 \times 2}\frac{d^3 P}{dY^3}(\Delta y)^3 + \cdots + \frac{1}{n!}\frac{d^n P}{dY^n}(\Delta y)^n$$

To a first approximation, this simplifies to the following equation. The first differential is simply the slope of the price–yield curve at the starting yield:

$$P_1 = P_{Y0} + \frac{dP}{dY}\Delta Y \Rightarrow P_1 - P_{Y0} = \frac{dP}{dY}\Delta Y \Rightarrow \Delta P = \frac{dP}{dY}\Delta Y$$

Dividing both sides by P we get the following equation. This gives us the percentage increase in price for a given change in yield:

$$\frac{\Delta P}{P} = \left(\frac{1}{P}\frac{dP}{dY}\right)\Delta Y$$

This rate of change of price versus yield is called the bond's duration, D, as shown below. (Note that many financial textbooks refer to this term as modified duration, I will explain later the source of the confusion over this term.) Note that bond duration is always positive in the absence of embedded options because the slope of the price–yield curve for a straight bond is always negative. This assumes you are the holder of the bond, of course:

$$\frac{\Delta P}{P} = -D\Delta Y \quad \text{where } D = -\left(\frac{1}{P}\frac{dP}{dY}\right)$$

To understand the concept of duration better it is instructive to look at its units. Both price and the change in price are measured in units of currency and cancel each other out. The change in yield is a number divided by time. Numbers have no units and therefore duration is measured in units of time. Because we are using the annual yield-to-maturity duration is measured in years:

$$\$\left/\left(\frac{1\times\$}{t}\right)\right. = t$$

We already know that the theoretical market price P of a single future cashflow or a zero coupon bond at a given yield Y is given by the following:

$$P = \frac{Par}{(1+Y)^n}$$

We are interested in the rate of change of the price with change in yield. This can be derived using simple calculus and gives us the following result for a zero coupon bond:

$$\frac{dP}{dY} = -\frac{n\times Par}{(1+Y)^{n+1}} \quad \text{and after substituting for price} \quad \frac{dP}{dY} = -\frac{n\times P}{(1+Y)}$$

Rearranging this equation we get the rate of price change for a given change in yield. The term $n/(1+Y)$ gives the percentage change in a zero coupon bond's price for a given change in yields. This gives us a way to calculate duration for a single future payment:

$$\frac{dP}{P} = -\frac{n}{(1+Y)}dY \quad \text{and hence:} \quad Duration = \frac{n}{(1+Y)} = D$$

A zero coupon bond with a face value of $10 000 matures in 10 years. It has a current market price of $5084 and yield-to-maturity of 7%. Its duration is 9.3458 as shown below:

$$D = 10/1.07 = 9.3458$$

A 100 bpt increase in yields will reduce the value of the bond by approximately $475 and if they fall by 100 bpts an increase in value, also of $475:

Change in price for a 100 bpt change in yields $= \$9.3458 \times 5084 \times 0.01 = \pm\$475.14$

This gives an implied price of $5559 at a 6% yield and $4609 at 7%. The actual price should be $5584 at a 6% yield ($10 000/(1.06)^{10} = 5584) and $4634 at 8% ($10 000/(1.08)^{10} = 4634). This difference between the theoretical price and that calculated using duration is the result of an approximation error from failing to take the curvature of the price–yield graph into account. To do so we need to introduce the concept of convexity.

Convexity

To reduce the approximation error we need to take account of the curvature, or convexity, of the price–yield graph. This requires us to take account of the second differential (the rate of change of duration). Differentiating the first differential and substituting for P we get the following:

$$\frac{dP}{dY} = -\frac{n \times Par}{(1+Y)^{n+1}} \Rightarrow \frac{d^2 P}{dY^2} = +\frac{n(n+1) \times Par}{(1+Y)^{n+2}} = +\frac{n(n+1) \times P}{(1+Y)^2}$$

To take account of both duration and convexity of a zero coupon bond we need to add the following term:

$$\frac{\Delta P}{P} = -\frac{n}{(1+Y)}\Delta Y + \frac{1}{2} \times \frac{n(n+1)}{(1+Y)^2}(\Delta Y)^2$$

This is usually expressed as follows where D represents duration and C convexity:

$$\frac{\Delta P}{P} = -D \times \Delta Y + \frac{1}{2} \times C \times (\Delta Y)^2$$

Taking our zero coupon bond example, convexity is given by the following:

$$C = \frac{10 \times (10+1)}{(1+.07)^2} = 96.1$$

Plugging this into our equation the impact of convexity on the change in bond price is $24.4:

$$\frac{1}{2} \times 96.1 \times \$5084 \times (0.01)^2 = \$24.4$$

Taking both duration and convexity into account gives a very close approximation.

Zero coupon bond prices given by duration and convexity versus actual prices ($)					
Yield	Duration	Convexity	Duration alone	Duration plus convexity	Actual
At 6%			5559.1	5583.5	5583.9
At 7%	9.3458	96.1			5083.5
At 8%			4608.9	4633.3	4631.9

It should be clear from the above that given a choice of two bonds with the same duration it is preferable to own the bond with the higher convexity as its price will rise more when yields fall and drop less when yields increase.

So far we have concentrated on a single zero coupon bond but we can view any single future payment as the equivalent of a zero coupon bond. A bond portfolio will contain many different types of bonds with differing maturities and coupon rates. It turns out that duration and convexity have additive properties that make them much more powerful tools to manage interest rate risk than yield-to-maturity.

To calculate the yield-to-maturity for a portfolio of bonds it would be necessary to take the coupon and principal payments from each bond, add them together in each time period and then calculate the portfolio's yield-to-maturity. There is no way to do this by simply adding together the yields-to-maturities of the individual bonds.

The *NPV* of a portfolio of assets is given by its future cashflows discounted at the portfolio's yield-to-maturity, as shown below:

$$NPV = \frac{Cf_1}{(1+Y)^1} + \cdots + \frac{Cf_n}{(1+Y)^n} + \cdots + \frac{Cf_N}{(1+Y)^N} = \sum_{n=1}^{N} \frac{Cf_n}{(1+Y)^n}$$

The change of the value of this portfolio for a change in yields is given by the following:

$$\Delta(NPV) = \left(\frac{-D_1 Cf_1}{(1+Y)^1} + \cdots + \frac{-D_n Cf_n}{(1+Y)^n} + \cdots + \frac{-D_N Cf_N}{(1+Y)^N} \right) \Delta Y = -\sum_{n=1}^{N} \frac{D_n C_n}{(1+Y)^n} \Delta Y$$

Dividing both sides of this equation by *NPV* we get the following. This is simply the *NPV*-weighted duration of the individual assets divided by the *NPV* of the total portfolio:

$$\frac{\Delta(NPV)}{NPV} = -\sum_{n=1}^{N} \frac{D_n Cf_n}{(1+Y)^n} \Delta Y \Big/ \sum_{n=1}^{N} \frac{Cf_n}{(1+Y)^n}$$

This can be expressed more formally as shown below. This is simply the time and *NPV*-weighted duration of the individual assets, divided by the *NPV* of the total portfolio and divided by $(1+Y)$:

$$\frac{dP}{P} = -\left[\frac{1}{(1+Y)} \left(\frac{\sum_{n=1}^{N} \frac{n \times Cf_n}{(1+Y)^n}}{\sum_{n=1}^{N} \frac{Cf_n}{(1+Y)^n}} \right) \right] \times dY = -D_p \times dY$$

We can demonstrate this using our example of a coupon bond with a 7% yield and current price of $10 000. We can calculate the *NPV* change in the bond for a 1% point drop in yield by adding together the changes in the *NPV* of the individual payments. This gives us a price of $10 702.

If we add together the time- and *NPV*-weighted durations of the individual payments we get 7.02. This gives us the duration of the entire portfolio. This holds true for any distribution of future cashflows.

		Portfolio *NPV* change implied by duration ($)						
		NPV at yields of:			Duration	Implied *NPV*	Implied	*NPV*-weighted
Year	Payment	6.0%	7.0%	8.0%	at 7%	change	*NPV*	duration
1	700	660	654	648	0.93	6.1	660	0.06
2	700	623	611	600	1.87	11.4	623	0.11
3	700	588	571	556	2.80	16.0	587	0.16
4	700	554	534	515	3.74	20.0	554	0.20
5	700	523	499	476	4.67	23.3	522	0.23
6	700	493	466	441	5.61	26.2	493	0.26
7	700	466	436	408	6.54	28.5	464	0.29
8	700	439	407	378	7.48	30.5	438	0.30
9	700	414	381	350	8.41	32.0	413	0.32
10	10 700	5975	5439	4956	9.35	508.3	5948	5.08
Total		10 736	10 000	9329		702.4	10 702	7.02

DURATION, MODIFIED DURATION AND EFFECTIVE DURATION

MacAuley was among the first people to look at how changing interest rates affected the value of bonds in the first half of the last century. His method to calculate duration (also known as MacAuley) is close to the one used today but overstated duration by a factor of $(1 + Y)$. Unfortunately, this definition of duration persisted and when the error was recognized and corrected the resulting factor was called "modified duration". Throughout this book, in common with market practitioners but not all academics, when we use the term "duration" this is in reference to the correct or "modified" method.

"Effective" duration simply takes into account the impact of embedded options where negative convexity results in price truncation close to any call or put price.

The fundamental concept of duration is critical to understanding how banks can manage their balance sheet. Convexity is generally of more importance to bond portfolio managers than bank treasurers but is an important factor to be taken into account in bond trading operations.

28

Financial Institutions

I have called this principle, by which each slight variation, if useful, is preserved, by the term of Natural Selection.

Charles Darwin, The Origin of Species

UNIVERSAL BANKS

Universal banks operate in countries where there are no regulatory restrictions on banks combining both commercial and investment banking functions. They have been particularly prevalent in Europe. The demise of Glass-Steagal (US legislation that prohibited banks that took deposits from operating in the securities business) led to some traditional commercial banks in the US buying formerly independent investment banks. Examples of such deals included Citicorp buying first Smith Barney and then Salomon Brothers. Many large European banks (Deutsche Bank and Union Bank of Switzerland being examples) made acquisitions of US investment banks (Banker's Trust and Paine Webber respectively) to try to establish their presence in the world's largest capital market.

Universal banks usually consist of a commercial bank, a private bank, an investment bank and brokerage operations, and may have a division manufacturing and managing investment products such as mutual funds.

Commercial Banks

Commercial banks are at the heart of all universal banks. They are licensed to take deposits from the public and lend these funds to individuals and corporates. In this sense they are widely viewed as "spread managers" with most of their income coming from the difference in the rate they pay for their funding and the rate at which this is lent out. They also provide support to companies to finance trade. In the US under the 1923 Glass-Steagal legislation commercial banks were prohibited from undertaking investment banking business. The main activities of commercial banks are as follows:

- **Deposit taking.** Banks provide a safe haven for individual and corporate savings. They offer a reassurance to depositors that they can safely entrust their funds with the bank and be able to withdraw them on demand or as specified in the account terms. In some countries deposit-taking banks are required to pay insurance premiums to a government-owned insurance agency that guarantees retail deposits against losses arising from a bank failure. In other countries an implicit government guarantee is frequently assumed.

  Many of these deposits are interest bearing and provide depositors with a return on their savings. Commercial banks are in competition with other forms of savings, such as stocks, mutual funds and bonds, and with other financial institutions such as brokerages and insurance companies. The latter offer investment products, such as annuities (perpetual investments that pay a fixed return) and guaranteed capital protection products that provide investors with alternatives to bank deposits.

Banks also provide depositors with means to withdraw funds and settle bills by issuing checkbooks, providing withdrawal facilities at branches and cash dispensing machines via Automated Teller Machines (ATMs).

- **Lending.** Banks are intermediaries and they lend out the deposits that they take to individuals and companies seeking finance. Banks charge interest on these loans. The difference between the rate that they can extract from making loans and the rate at which they pay for deposits is the spread that they earn for providing this intermediation service.

  This spread has to be sufficiently wide to cover the operating expenses (head office, branches, computer systems, telecommunications, people and regulatory costs) associated with providing the intermediation service. It must also be wide enough to take account of losses experienced as a result of borrower defaults while providing a return to shareholders on the capital invested in the bank.

- **The creation of money.** Banks play an important role in the process of creating money although this is controlled largely by the country's central bank. In the case of the US this function is the responsibility of the Federal Reserve Board and in the Eurozone by the European Central Bank. The management of the money supply is critical to the stability and well-being of a currency and economy.

- **Clearing and settlement services.** Banks provide the basic clearing and settlement services that enable individuals and organizations to make payments to one another in a safe, secure and controlled manner. They do not give this service for free but impose a pricing structure to cover their costs and provide a return on capital employed.

  Some of these clearing and settlement systems are owned and run by independent organizations, including ones owned by the state but most are owned and run by bank consortiums.

- **Remittances and money transfer.** A basic service that banks provide is that of transferring money from one account to another. This may be within the same country or cross-border. This is an important service to foreign workers who need to remit their earnings back to their family in their home country.

- **Foreign exchange.** International trade and cross-border investment have created a growing need to be able to exchange one currency for another quickly and efficiently. Banks provide this service and also provide the liquidity to ensure an efficient market by actively trading currencies for their own account.

- **Trade finance.** Banks facilitate trade, both within countries and cross-border, by providing guarantees of payment. This ensures that producers can be certain of payment for goods shipped to customers. Banks charge fees for these services.

- **Guarantees.** Banks can also generate fees by providing other guarantees. These include posting surety bonds on behalf of individuals or companies. The bank guarantees to pay the value of the bond if the customer fails to meet the bond conditions. The bank gets the client to indemnify the bank in the event of the terms of the bond being broken. The bank charges a fee for the issue of the bond.

- **Hedging.** Non-financial institutions face a range of financial risks. These include interest rate risk, exchange rate risk and commodity price risk. A company that borrows at a floating rate faces the risk that if interest rates increase so will the company's cost of servicing this debt. Banks are able to provide a range of products, at a fee, that allow these institutions to hedge risks such as these.

- **Cash management.** Large international companies have to manage deposit accounts at their subsidiaries around the world. This is a highly complex operation because it usually involves many different currencies and most of the future cashflows cannot be forecast with certainty. At any one moment in time a company may have an excess of Argentine pesos but be short of Philippine pesos. Banks provide cash management services to maximize the returns on any excess funds and minimize interest expense on any borrowing.

- **Lease financing.** Many companies such as airlines and shipping companies do not own their airplanes or fleet but instead lease them from specialist finance companies. In some countries banks are prohibited from providing lease financing, in others this is allowed through the use of a bank holding company and separate leasing subsidiary.
- **Factoring.** Many smaller companies experience cashflow problems as a result of late payments from customers. Some banks offer factoring services whereby they buy the rights to the company's accounts receivables at a discount to their book value.
- **Custody.** Banks provide safe custody in terms of a highly secure vault and data centers. The most basic custody service that banks provide is that of a safety box where individuals and companies can entrust relatively small valuables and critical documents.

Investment Banks

Investment banks are wholesale businesses and normally do not take deposits from retail customers. Their main business activities are related to "capital markets", that is the bond and equity markets. They generate fee income from the "primary" business of underwriting new issues, and commissions from executing customers' orders to buy or sell securities on their behalf in the "secondary" market. They also generate income (and sometimes losses) from trading on their own account. Investment banks are referred to as "merchant" banks in some countries. Prominent examples of US investment banks are Goldman Sachs, Merrill Lynch, Morgan Stanley and Lehman Brothers:

- **Securities issuance.** When a company is looking to raise funds either from equity or bond markets it appoints an investment bank to manage the issue. The investment bank will put together all of the information required by securities regulators in the form a prospectus that sets out the terms of the proposed issue. It will also advise on the pricing of the proposed issue.

  In most cases the bank leading the issue will put together a syndicate of other investment banks. Between them they will give a guarantee to the issuer to buy any paper left outstanding in the event of the issue being undersubscribed. Investment banks are able to charge significant fees both for the management of the issue and also for the underwriting service.
- **Brokerage.** Brokerage is another intermediary business. In its most basic form this may simply be an execution-only service whereby the brokerage takes orders from clients to buy or sell securities (these may include equities, bonds, futures and options) traded on an exchange. The rise of the Internet led to a large expansion in the number of no-frills brokerages offering a low-cost execution service.

  In its most advanced form brokerages offer an investment research service targeted at large institutional clients such as managers of mutual funds, pension funds and insurance companies. These institutions pay very low commission rates but on very large order size. The issuance of securities is referred to as the primary side of the securities business while brokerage itself is referred to as the secondary side.

- **Mergers and acquisitions.** Investment banks also act on behalf of companies that are seeking to acquire another company, merge with another company or are subject to a bid from another company. They advise on the structure and pricing of the bid and on any legal and regulatory considerations. They will put the formal offer document together and manage most of the communications with major institutional investors.
- **Advisory services.** Many investment banks also provide advisory services to companies. Most of these services relate to the financial and legal structures of companies. They will advise on the optimal way to manage the company's balance sheet and recommend particular courses of action.
- **Securitization.** Securitization is the term given to the process of taking an asset, or pool of assets, that generates a stream of future cashflows and selling the rights to those cashflows to institutional investors. Investment banks structure the securitization and, using their sales force, sell the issue to investors.

  Mortgages make up the largest class of securitized assets. In countries, such as the US, with developed securitization markets many commercial banks find that it is more profitable to originate mortgage loans and then sell those loans than it is to hold them. Securitization does not affect the overall risks and returns on the assets concerned but it does allow these risks and returns to be redistributed and this is positive overall.
- **Proprietary trading.** Many larger commercial and investment banks take proprietary trading positions in a number of different financial instruments and commodities. These include instruments and derivatives relating to foreign exchange, interest rates, equities and bonds. Exchange-traded commodities include traditional products such as oil and agricultural staples, for example grain and orange juice concentrate, but have expanded into new areas such as energy and bandwidth.

  In many of these areas banks also provide an execution service to their customers. This creates potential conflicts of interest and provides an example of the need for banks to erect "Chinese walls" between departments in order to prevent the sharing of information that could be used against a client's interests. There is no doubt that such Chinese walls do help to reduce the degree of such collusion but the old investment banking saying is that grapevines have a tendency to climb over Chinese walls.

  Proprietary trading can generate both huge gains and losses. Income tends to be volatile and management has to impose tight controls to shield a bank from potentially disastrous losses.
- **Research.** Most of investment banks' income-generating businesses are built on the strength of their investment research capability. Most analysts are highly specialized with the major division being that between fixed-income (bonds) and equity research. They also tend to specialize in a specific sector (in the case of equities) or product (for example derivative instruments such as convertible bond). The most highly regarded private sector economists work for investment banks.

Private Banks

Private bankers provide a dedicated and discrete wealth management service to very rich individuals, referred to in the industry as high net worth clients. Most private bank clients would be expected to have at least $1m in investable assets. At the more exclusive banks an individual would probably need at least $5m in liquid assets to be taken on as a private client. Traditionally, private banking has been very much the domain of Swiss banks but in recent years global banks have become increasingly important and the world's largest private bankers in terms of assets under management are now Union Bank of Switzerland, Citibank and HSBC.

The service provided ranges from an execution-only service, through advisory up to full discretionary investment management. The rise of the "mass-affluent" as a segment has blurred the boundary between the rich and the mass market in recent years. These are wealthy individuals who fall below the level to be given the full private banking service but who nevertheless can provide profitable business.

Private banking has been one of the fastest growing segments over the past decade and is expected to continue to enjoy strong growth driven largely by changing demographics in developed countries and continued global economic growth. This strong expected growth arises from the properties of the bell-shaped curve representing a population's wealth distribution. A relatively modest increase in the median level results in a much larger percentage increase in the number of very wealthy individuals.

Fund Managers

Fund managers manage investments for other institutions and for individuals. These funds include equity funds (invested primarily in stocks), fixed-income funds (invested primarily in bonds) and money markets funds (invested in short-term wholesale deposits and commercial paper). These also extend to less traditional funds, such as hedge funds, that offer alternative investment styles and invest in a wider range of financial instruments and other assets such as real estate.

Although the management of portfolios of stocks and bonds is not a traditional commercial banking activity many larger banks own subsidiaries that provide this service to both institutional clients, such as pension funds, and retail clients. Most retail banks also try to sell their own and third-party mutual funds to their customers. They charge an upfront fee for this service that is normally split between the bank, acting as a distributor, and the actual fund manager.

NOT-FOR-PROFIT INSTITUTIONS

Supranational Institutions

There are a relatively small number of supranational financial institutions such as the World Bank, the Asia Development Bank and the European Development Banks. These three are all examples of development banks and are funded largely by international agencies and governments. Their brief is to provide the longer-term financing required for projects in developing markets. Commercial banks are generally reluctant to take on such risk in terms of the maturity mismatch arising from the short-term nature of their deposit bases. In more developed markets such funding would normally be raised from bond markets but in developing markets bond markets generally lack the depth to allow for such issues.

The IMF (International Monetary Fund) is a particular form of an international bank. It is funded by the world's central banks. Its main role is to act as the lender of last resort to national central banks. This is usually associated with exchange rate and foreign reserve problems. The IMF makes such loans conditional on structural reforms intended to return the country to financial health. Its focus is very much on macroeconomics and the most common requirement is for governments to reduce fiscal deficits. This may require a reduction in military spending, reducing consumer subsidies on commodities such as oil and rice, raising taxes, privatization and implementing other austerity measures.

Competition Institutions

The combination of politics, microeconomics, money and power often creates an explosive mix. The urge to create monopolies comes as naturally to capitalists as the urge to push in childbirth. Some private monopolies are very obvious and many were created in the rush to privatize public utilities. Others are subtler, such as Microsoft's efforts to use software bundled into its Windows operating systems to restrict competition. Financial services' cartels are relatively common and may be explicit and condoned by regulatory authorities, or implicit and tolerated by regulatory authorities.

US legislators acted at the end of the nineteenth century and the early part of the twentieth century to pass federal anti-trust laws intended to combat national and local monopolies, price fixing and restraint of trade. The Federal Trade Commission (FTC) was established with powers to investigate possible infractions and to mandate companies to take any corrective action necessary to comply with these laws.

At the time of writing the division of responsibilities in Europe between EU and national monopoly commissions is somewhat unclear. This, in part, reflects changing perceptions of what constitutes a strategic market and monopolistic behavior. Much of these commissions' work is concerned with considering applications for mergers and takeovers. The power of the EC monopoly commission is such that it is able to block the proposed merger of two US companies because of the impact such a merger would have on competition within Europe. Approval may be granted without conditions, be subject to the parties involved taking specific actions to reduce any negative impact on competition or be rejected outright.

Banking system consolidation brings with it particular risks of the creation of localized monopolies (whether these are geographic or by customer segment). The practice of "tying", where commercial bank units of a universal bank offer cheap loans to specific customers in order to gain investment banking business, is illegal in the US but difficult to prove. In the rest of the world such practices are generally legal even though they may raise pricing and competition concerns.

The World Trade Organization (WTO) was established to aid in the liberalization of trade and removal of tariffs. It does this through the enforcement of GATT (General Agreement on Trade and Tariffs) agreements. Newspapers report that progress on liberalization of all services has been slow, but journalists work to daily deadlines and getting multinational agreement on these areas, where there are significant vested and perceived national interests, was always likely to be a marathon rather than a sprint. Not all WTO members have signed the current GATT Financial Services annex and a number of those that have signed have negotiated exemptions from some of the terms, mainly on grounds of "prudential concerns".

Central Banks

The main objective of most central banks is to manage money supply in order to control the level of price inflation. The central bank has a number of tools to help it achieve these objectives. It can impose reserve requirements on commercial banks that effectively limit the amount of loans they can make. It is able to influence domestic interest levels directly by adjusting the rate at which it will lend to banks that have a funding shortfall. It also conducts open market operations where it buys or sells government (Treasury) bonds in the market in order to inject or take out cash from the monetary system. The central bank also has the role of "lender of last resort" to domestic banks.

The central bank is also responsible for maintaining the country's foreign currency and gold reserves. Some central banks (such as the US Fed and the European Central Bank) have effective political independence when it comes to interest rate and monetary policies. Other central banks may be directly responsible to the government's Treasury department or Ministry of Finance.

The World Bank is not in fact the world's central bank but is a development bank. The closest to that is the International Monetary Fund (IMF) with its ability to act as the lender of last resort to individual national central banks.

Depositor Insurance Institutions

In some countries institutions have been established that guarantee customer deposits in the event of a bank failing. The most prominent example is the US Federal Deposit Insurance Corporation (FDIC). The FDIC is funded by premiums paid by banks that choose to seek such insurance. Not all US banks are FDIC covered and retail depositors at such banks risk losing their deposits in the event of bank failure.

Regulators and Supervisors

The function of financial services regulation is so important that almost every country seems to have developed its own, unique way of performing it. A universal bank may find itself under the watchful eyes of several regulatory bodies. Most financial institutions dread the arrival of the regulators whose job it is to examine how a business is being run and to look for ways in which regulatory requirements are being breached.

Some have the power to determine regulations within broad legislative guidelines, others have very specific mandates with very limited discretion. Some have the power to issue enforcement orders while others can only recommend action to a higher authority such as the Ministry of Finance.

Where possible financial businesses cooperate to establish self-regulatory bodies. Their actions are still under the authority of the appointed regulatory body. The Securities and Exchange Commission (SEC) in the US, for example, has extensive powers in regulating market activities but allows organizations such as the National Association of Securities Dealers to establish market rules and practices up to a certain, ill-defined limit. At the end of the day the SEC still calls the shots.

Government

The overall framework in which financial institutions operate is established through legislation. In most countries this legislation is changed only very occasionally and then involves a major revision. The reason why this is the case is because such legislation is normally based on a wide consensus and involves the delegation of most detailed responsibilities and powers to specific organizations set up for this purpose.

Under the terms of the relevant banking and finance laws the legislation will cover the establishment of various bodies (a central bank and a prime bank supervisor, for example) and delineate their responsibilities and powers. The legislation may, for example, require banks to maintain a minimum capital level but also state that this level is as determined by the bank supervisor at the time. Additional more specific detailed legislation may be enacted such as those concerning data protection, the rights of consumers to check credit records and money laundering.

Governments also have a direct impact on the economy through the application of fiscal policy. Fiscal policy concerns the level and nature of taxes that the government intends to impose to generate its revenues and its plans for public expenditure. If its expenditure is greater than its revenues it will have to make up the difference by borrowing or by selling public assets. The Treasury department is responsible for managing the government's finances. In many countries the equivalent of the US and UK Treasuries is often called the Ministry of Finance (MoF).

Accounting Standards Authorities

Accounting policies have a direct impact on the way that companies report their earnings and financial condition. The complexity of many financial transactions is such that a huge effort is expended to agree common accounting standards. The two most important accounting authorities are the US Financial Accounting and Standards Board (FASB) and the International Accounting Standards Board. FASB is responsible for drawing up and maintaining US General Accepted Accounting Policies (GAAP).

Most countries also have national accounting standards bodies. There have been attempts to move towards consistent global accounting standards. Everybody involved agrees that this is a good idea but good intentions cost little. A UK company with dual listings in the UK and US will be required to publish two sets of financial statements, one conforming to US GAAP and the other to UK national standards. It may also choose to provide accounts to IAS. The end result is three headline earnings numbers, all of which are "correct"!

Bank financial statements can be used to tell a story about a bank's performance but for all save the simplest bank these stories have more in common with novels than they do with works of non-fiction.

Thrifts and Mutual Societies

Mutual savings societies are quite common in many countries. These not-for-profit organizations go under a wide range of names including credit unions and credit associations and in the us, thrifts. They usually have very little interaction with the mainstream financial system. They are often small and lightly regulated and in a number of countries this has led to significant management abuses and fraud. In a few countries some of these cooperative organizations have become as large as mainstream commercial banks. The trend in such countries has been towards demutualization, however.

OTHERS

Insurance Companies

Insurance companies write an increasingly wide range of insurance policies. These include retail policies such as life cover, general household and fire insurance, auto insurance and medical insurance. They also offer investment products that compete directly with mutual funds and bank deposits. They provide cover to corporates against a wide range of business risks. In recent years they have become increasingly involved with writing protection to banks and bondholders against losses arising from credit defaults.

Bancassurance is the term given to the business of banks leveraging their retail customer base by selling insurance products. In many countries banks are restricted from owning insurance brokers in which case, as with mutual funds, commercial banks typically act as distributors only.

Finance Companies

Finance companies raise their funding from equity and wholesale money markets. They do not usually have licenses to take deposits. They specialize in loans for autos, other consumer goods, second mortgages and loans to small companies. The rates they charge are often higher than banks offer.

Retail Brokerage

Institutional brokerage is dominated by a relatively small number of investment banks, most of which operate on a global basis. Retail brokers fall into one of two broad categories. Many brokerages offer both investment advisory and execution services to clients and these "value added services" are charged accordingly. The abolition of regualated minimum commissions rates in many markets has created opportunities for discount brokers that offer a low-cost execution-only service.

Few retail brokers operate in more than one country. Institutional brokerages tend to regard them with affectionate disdain. The affectionate part comes from a belief that when markets are due for a sharp correction, and the institutions are trying to get out, the retail brokers have a large client base waiting to buy. Retail brokerages provide a service to the "little people", institutional brokerages to "big money". It's not much of a contest. The disdain comes from recognition that what retail brokers pass off as research has even less merit than that produced by the institutional brokers.

In many developing markets foreign institutional brokers are not members of the local stock exchange and rely upon a domestic retail broker to act as their sub-broker responsible for execution of the institutional broker's trades.

Financial Holding Companies

Financial holding companies usually take one of two forms. In the first form they are largely bank holding companies set up to circumvent regulatory restrictions such as restrictions on cross-border branching. The second form is less common where a company is set up that is comprised of unrelated financial businesses. GE Capital, for example, can be viewed as a holding company with a finance arm, an asset management arm and a venture capital division.

Asset Management Companies (AMCs)

Asset management companies (AMCs) specialize in buying and managing problem loans. These are loans where the borrower has run into financial problems and is unable to meet its contractual interest payments on the loan. There is usually considerable doubt as to the ability of the borrower to repay the loan's principal. Some of these loans are backed with collateral pledged by the borrower and some are unsecured.

The sellers of these loans may be banks, finance companies or a state-run institution responsible for managing the assets of banks that have failed and been nationalized. AMCs buy at a discount to the face value of these problem loans.

Their main objective is to sell these loans or the underlying security for more than they paid for the loans. This may be achieved by restructuring corporate operations such that they are able to service their debt or through liquidation and sale of the collateral.

AMCs may be established as a separate division within a bank suffering from a high level of problem loans. When this occurs this division is usually colloquially known as the "bad bank" and the rest of the bank the "good bank". This separation reflects the different focus of the individuals working in the two areas. The bad bank concentrates on maximizing recovery rates on bad debts while the good bank concentrates on keeping performing loans current and making new loans.

Some AMCs are run as private companies financed by venture capitalist organizations, others as public sector institutions. An example of the latter is the Resolution Trust Corporation (RTC) established in the US in 1989 to deal with the problem loans resulting from failures of domestic savings and loans associations in the 1980s.

Venture Capitalists

Venture capitalists may be individuals, a division within an investment bank or a privately owned company. They specialize in making high-risk investments with the potential to generate high returns. Venture capitalists are best known for taking equity stakes in start-up businesses and funding their initial growth before selling out. In this role they are sometimes, for obvious reasons, referred to as "incubators". In some countries they are referred to as "private equity" investors. Any difference that exists between private equity and venture capital is largely a matter of semantics.

They are opportunistic and will consider any investment that meets their selection criteria. Opportunities often exist in the midst of financial crises and venture capitalists are active in corporate restructuring and bank rehabilitation. They do not look to run the businesses they invest in, simply to make a financial profit. They usually take minority stakes only.

Venture capitalists get a bad press. When they make successful investments the rewards can be phenomenal but for every such success story there are a dozen stories of modest success or failure that go unremarked. When they look to invest in assets in countries in the midst of a financial crisis they are often painted as voracious asset-stripping vultures. This portrayal is intended to be derogatory but even vultures play an important part in nature. Few critics pause to consider that they are often responding to desperate pleas from these countries for foreign investment and venture capitalists will consider taking such risks when conventional investment funds are nowhere to be seen.

SERVICE PROVIDERS

Exchanges

Many exchanges operate that facilitate trade between buyers and sellers in many different financial products, commodities and even services. Exchanges range from huge, regulated, highly automated operations through to informal, unregulated street markets. Many of the larger exchanges in developed countries date back more than 100 years. Some of them rely on methods such as "open outcry" and have a physical trading floor but many have moved to automated or screen-based trading.

Examples of stock exchanges are the New York Stock Exchange (NYSE), the London Stock Exchange (LSE) and NASDAQ. Major futures and derivative exchanges include the Chicago Board of Options Exchange (CBOE), the Chicago Mercantile Exchange (CME) and the London International Financial Futures and Options Exchange (LIFFE). The London-based Baltic Exchange is one of the oldest exchanges and provides rates to shipbrokers for freight and shipping prices and related derivatives.

Most exchanges were established as mutual societies. In recent years there has been a move away from national exchanges towards more integrated regional exchanges and demutualization. The LSE, Paris Bourse, Frankfurt, Hong Kong Exchange, Australian Exchange and SIMEX are all now public, listed companies. The Chicago Mercantile Exchange was the first US exchange to opt for demutualization and the stock of its parent company is now listed on the NYSE.

Clearing Houses and Depositories

All developed financial markets have clearing houses that allow participants to settle financial transactions between themselves, normally on a netted basis. These clearing systems may be real time or run at the close of the business day. Specialist clearing houses exist for clearing corporate and governmental Eurobonds.

Depositories operate to maintain records of securities ownership. Ownership rights may be established via certificates or by using computer records. Most depositories in developed countries have switched from paper records to centralized databases. This process is called "dematerialization" which sounds like something that would happen on *Star Trek*. Many developing markets still have physical depositories and besides from being inefficient they bear much higher risks of settlement failures.

Information Providers

Knowledge is supposed to be power and the sale of accurate, fast information is big business in financial services. Reuters is probably the best known news provider but it is also strong in foreign exchange and the bond markets. Bloomberg's strengths lie more in the equities field. Thomson Financial has amassed a huge database of historic financial and economic information. Some exchanges provide a real-time price service to subscribers and members with prices for non-subscribers deliberately delayed.

Global Network Providers

Three organizations provide specialized global network services to financial institutions. SWIFT (Society for Worldwide International Financial Telecommunications) provides a global message switching system to enable financial transactions and payment instructions to be successfully transmitted and completed. VISA and MasterCard, in addition to branding and marketing support, also run networks that enable credit cards to be used around the world. These organizations are owned by, and run on behalf of, their members.

Rating Agencies

Rating agencies provide reports and conclusions on the credit-worthiness of national governments, companies and other institutional borrowers and specific issues of debt (bonds) from those borrowers. These ratings are important because they affect the price that new debt can be issued at (and whether it is possible to issue new debt) and the market price of debt already issued. The three best known global ratings agencies are Standard and Poor's (S&P), Moody's and Fitch. Each one uses a slightly different rating system based on an alphabetic "score". The top grade issued by Standard and Poor's is AAA (or simply triple-A) indicating a very high level of credit-worthiness and minimal risk of default. The top three grades down to BBB are classified as "investment grade". Debt issues with ratings below this are commonly referred to as "junk bonds".

Large companies usually ask these agencies to rate them. A rating may be necessary if it intends to issue new debt or be a condition imposed from past debt issues. Bond issuers may be required to maintain a specified minimum rating level to comply with bond issue prospectuses or covenants. The ratings agencies are given inside access to company accounts in order to provide these ratings.

The agencies may also provide ratings that have not been asked for based on publicly available information. These are known as PI ratings and are provided as a service to subscribers. It is also true that this may well put pressure on such companies to pay the fees demanded by the agencies for a full rating, particularly as the PI rating is likely to be lower than a full rating. Many expect the widespread adoption of Basel II to result in a sharp increase in the number of rated firms and institutions.

Debt issues cannot have a higher (better) credit rating than their issuer and issuers cannot have a higher rating than the relevant sovereign debt. This created a few problems when the former British colony Hong Kong became a Special Administrative Region within the People's Republic of China. Hong Kong had a better rating than China as did some of its most financially secure companies.

Some countries have their own national rating agencies. They focus more on smaller companies that are not included in the global agencies' coverage. Many of these agencies in developing markets receive training and other support from the global agencies. Credit bureaus provide a similar service to credit rating agencies but collect credit history for individuals and small businesses. They may be run as commercial firms, mutual societies or be government administered. Dun and Bradstreet is one of the largest commercial firms active in this business.

Index Providers

A number of competing institutions maintain indices on a range of financial instruments and commodities. These provide a way to assess overall performance of the constituents of the indices. Market stock indices comprise a sub-set of stocks that are representative of the market as a whole. Performance of the index is taken as indicative of performance of the entire market.

Many fund managers' portfolio performance is measured against these indices. The origins of some of them are reflected in their names. The FTSE 100 (pronounced "footsie") for the largest stocks traded on the London Stock Exchange is maintained by the *Financial Times* newspaper. The origins of the Dow Jones All Ordinary index (which gives a broad coverage of the NYSE) lie with the *Wall Street Journal*. Many exchanges now also provide these services. Arguably the most important global equity indices are provided by an organization established by investment bank Morgan Stanley and the fund management powerhouse Capital International. There are scores of MSCI indices at global and regional levels and by industry sector classification.

Changes in the composition of indices can have a significant impact on stock performance. A stock being included in a widely followed index may enjoy a period of strong performance, as tracker funds will have to buy the stock to maintain their benchmark weightings. In practice this outperformance may come before the actual announcement as investors buy in anticipation of the stock's inclusion. Changes in composition occur periodically and are announced on scheduled dates.

Most stock market indices are (and should be) market capitalization weighted. Some providers apply a downward adjustment factor to stocks with a low level of free float. These are tightly held stocks where only a small proportion of issued shares is traded. This adds a further source of speculation about possible changes in these adjustment factors. A notable exception is the Dow Jones Industrial Average (DJIA) which is based on a simple price-weighted average of 30 US blue chips. There is no intellectual basis for using a price-weighted average and it is surprising that it remains such a widely quoted index. No index provider would seriously consider launching a new price-weighted index.

Legal and Accounting Practices

Clifford Chance and Linklaters are hardly household names but they are leading members of a small elite of global legal practices. These global firms are organized as partnerships and compensation for senior partners matches that of the best paid traders and corporate financiers working on Wall Street. Their bread and butter work comes from drawing up iron-clad contracts for their clients. These contracts include documents such as loan agreements and account opening forms. Where there is a legal dispute they become involved in subsequent litigation or in reaching an out-of-court agreement.

Their most remunerative work comes from initial public offerings (IPOs), mergers and acquisitions (M&A) and corporate and debt restructuring. They also advise on tax-related issues. A poorly drafted IPO prospectus may leave issuers and underwriters open to regulatory censure or possible litigation from investors based on claims of false, inaccurate or misleading information. Mergers and acquisitions also involve a high level of legal work. Acquirer and target companies both appoint their own investment banks as advisors. Legal firms may work for either side. Investment banks have their own legal departments but lack the specialization and expertise that the big firms can offer. They will not only work on the compliance side, by ensuring that the offer and defense comply with relevant takeover codes, but identify particular legal aspects that may afford an advantage or are potentially an obstacle. They recommend ways that such obstacles can be overcome.

Large corporate failures and banking crises provide a potentially lucrative source of income for these firms particularly as their clients have little choice other than to rely on them. The legal and accounting professionals brought in have their fees paid before other creditors. It is always difficult to get a debt restructuring agreement concluded in the larger cases as there are many different creditors each with a different agenda and set of objectives. Negotiations can drag on for years and through all of that time the professionals' meters are running.

The accounting firms provide the usual external audit service and also advise on how to interpret accounting policies as defined by organizations such as FASB and apply them to a financial institution's transactions. Given the complexity of some of these transactions this is by

Organizations involved in the financial services industry

INSURANCE	FINANCE COMPANIES	RETAIL BROKERAGE	AMCs	VENTURE CAPITALISTS
* Life & general * Investment products * Credit enhancement & loss insurance protection	* Auto loans * Consumer & SME loans	* Investment advice * Execution service * Margin loans	* Buying, selling & managing problem loans * Private or public sector, e.g. RTC	* Start-ups & turnarounds * Distressed debt

NOT FOR PROFIT

SUPRA-NATIONAL	COMPETITION COMMISSIONS
* IMF * World Bank * BIS	* Anti-trust * Anti-monopoly * World Trade Organization (WTO)

DEPOSITOR PROTECTION	CENTRAL BANKS
* Retail deposit insurance * Deposit Insurance Schemes, e.g. US FDIC	* Monetary policy, foreign reserves * The Fed, European Central Bank

REGULATORS	GOVERNMENT
* Implementation of legislation * Regulations * Examinations, enforcement, censure	* Fiscal policy * Government finance * Legislation * Treasury, MoF

ACCOUNTING STANDARDS	THRIFTS
* International Accounting Standards (IAS) * National bodies (e.g. US FASB)	* Credit unions / thrifts * Mutual societies * Savings & loans * Co-operatives

UNIVERSAL BANKS

COMMERCIAL BANKS

* Deposit taking (demand, savings, time, checking accounts)
* Loans (& credit lines) to corporates & SMEs
* Housing loans (origination, servicing, funding)
* Home equity loans, second mortgages
* Consumer loans
* Credit cards
* Payment & clearing services
* Mutual fund distribution
* Distribution of insurance policies (Bancassurance)
* Foreign exchange & trading
* Trade financing & third-party guarantees
* Products to hedge client exposures
* Cash management, trust custody & factoring

INVESTMENT BANKS

* Primary securities issuance
* Equities & bonds
* Underwriting issues
* Secondary market trading (retail & institutional brokerage)
* Mergers & acquisitions (M&A)
* Corporate advisory services
* Asset securitization
* Structured financial products
* Proprietary trading

FUND MANAGERS

* Retail & institutional mutual funds
* Pension fund management
* Hedge funds
* Vulture funds

PRIVATE BANKS

* Wealth management services
* Portfolio investment & tax planning advice
* Trust services
* High net worth clients

EXCHANGES	PAYMENTS, CLEARING & DEPOSITORIES	INFORMATION	LEGAL
* Financial & commodities * Buy-sell order matching * Derivatives (options and futures contracts)	* Cash payments * Securities delivery & ownership transfer	* Foreign exchange & interest rates, securities & derivative prices * News, economic & financial data	* Contracts & prospectuses * Opinions * Litigation services * Debt recovery & restructuring
NETWORK PROVIDERS * International payment messages (SWIFT) * Credit cards (VISA & MasterCard)	RATING AGENCIES * Sovereign, corporate & individual credit-worthiness * Collation & distribution of credit information, e.g. Standard & Poor's, Moodys, Dun & Bradstreet	INDICES * Establishment & maintenance of financial & commodity price indices * Composition * Distribution of index levels & history to clients	ACCOUNTING * External audit * Tax planning * Application of accounting principles * Debt restructuring & receivership

no means a trivial exercise. They both compete and cooperate with legal firms on restructuring deals and both try to get the work involved in advising on tax issues.

Consultancies provide a range of services ranging from strategic planning, branding, customer relationship management, data security, project implementation to basic outsourcing of services. Many consultancies are run as independent practices but some consultancy services are delivered by a division within a larger group such as an IT services organization or an accountancy firm.

Linkages between firms offering external audit and consulting services have raised concern about moral hazard, particularly in the US. The main concern being that the integrity of external audits risks being compromised from allowing sharp corporate accounting practices to go unchallenged in order to retain more profitable consultancy business. The most surprising aspect of these attacks is that anyone believed that external audits could be compromised further. In the US firms were required to separate the two businesses after a number of high-profile corporate accounting scandals.

Appendix I

The Basel Accord

Dealing with complexity is an inefficient and unnecessary waste of time, attention and mental energy. There is never any justification for things being complex when they could be simple.

Edward de Bono, British psychologist

INTRODUCTION

The way in which bank capital adequacy ratios (CARs) are determined is outlined in Chapter 14 "Capital management". To recap, there are two major parts to the calculation of risk-weighted assets. First, the risk weighting of assets held on balance sheet and second, the calculation of risk-weighted asset equivalents from off-balance sheet exposures.

The proposals for the New Accord were not finalized at the time of writing. There is always a risk of errors arising due to misinterpretation of the specific parts of any document of this size and complexity. There is also a possibility that, although the proposals are in their final stages of development, changes may be made before their formal adoption, and readers should bear that in mind. The views expressed in this chapter are my own.

DEFINITION OF CAPITAL UNDER BASEL ACCORD

The definition of regulatory capital under the terms of the Basel Accord extends beyond that of simple equity to include various forms of long-term debt instruments. It is divided into Tier I and Tier II capital and Tier II capital is further divided into upper and lower Tier II.

Tier I Capital

Tier I capital is comprised of the following major elements:

- **Equity.** The principal part of Tier I capital is equity. Equity is the sum of the value of shares issued at the time of their issue (whether through a primary issue, rights issue or exercise of stock options or convertible instruments) plus retained earnings. The first term is often shown in the accounts under the headings of "Issued and fully paid shares" and "Share premium account". In some jurisdictions regulators require banks to maintain "statutory" or "general reserves". In these cases banks are required to maintain such identified reserves as a condition of keeping their banking license. They are usually not distributable as dividends. From an economic perspective these statutory reserves are best viewed as a form of retained earning. They are usually allowed to be treated towards Tier I capital.
- **Preference shares.** Non-cumulative preference shares are fixed rate debt instruments that have a higher seniority than shareholders but lower than all other creditors. A bank has no obligation to pay the fixed dividend on these shares in any particular period but if it fails to make the payment it cannot pay its shareholder a dividend either. In most countries

the dividend payment on preference shares is not allowable as a tax expense. This makes it a relatively expensive form of financing, but is still cheaper than the cost of equity.

Preference shares are normally required to be both perpetual and non-cumulative to be treated as Tier I capital. Perpetual means that while the issuer may have the right to buy them back the holder has no put option and cannot redeem them. The non-cumulative characteristic means that if the bank misses a dividend payment on the preference shares it is has no obligation to make up that payment. Equity analysts treat these dividend payments as a part of interest expense, irrespective of how it is reported.

- **Hybrid equity.** Hybrid equity is a catchall term for instruments that meet Tier I requirements but fall somewhere between debt and equity and are usually perpetual. They are some-times referred to as "innovative capital instruments". Non-cumulative preference shares are often treated as hybrid equity. Other allowed innovative instruments are allowed structured such that provided the bank is operating normally they can be viewed as debt but in the event of the bank getting into financial trouble they convert into equity. The use of hybrid equity (including non-cumulative preference shares) is restricted to 15% of total Tier I capital.
- **Minority interests.** Minority interests in the subsidiaries of a consolidated bank's accounts are allowed.

Finally, any unamortized goodwill has to be subtracted. This has an important bearing on the price that banks can pay for acquisitions and the form of payment, whether cash, paper or some combination.

Tier II Capital

Eligibility of liabilities for inclusion as Tier II capital varies widely between non-OECD countries. What one regulator may allow another may disallow. To complicate things further the Basel Accord subdivides Tier II capital into upper and lower. Under the core Basel Accord Tier II capital falls into one of the following categories:

- **Hybrid debt.** The main difference between hybrid debt and hybrid equity is that there is no mandatory conversion into equity in the event that the bank defaults. Hybrid debt includes convertible bonds and cumulative preference shares. These instruments have to meet sev-eral requirements to meet the Basel Accord standards.
- **Revaluation reserves.** These may include both property and investment revaluation re-serves. Many regulators only allow 45% of these reserves to be treated towards Tier II capital. Where these are allowed it creates an incentive for banks to revalue assets in a rising property market even though significant costs may be associated with the revaluation process. When banks depend on these reserves to meet capital adequacy requirements, as with the Japanese banks, and financial markets turn south banks may face considerable challenges meeting their target ratios.
- **General provisions.** Under the original Basel Accord these are eligible to be treated as Tier II capital but are restricted to 1.25% of risk-weighted assets.
- **Subordinated debt.** While all of the aforementioned are treated as upper Tier II capital, subordinated debt is treated as lower Tier II. For good reason, but to add to complexity, this is subject to a rolling 20% discount after its maturity falls below five years. Only 80% of

subordinated debt would be eligible to be counted towards Tier II capital if its maturity had fallen to four years, 60% at three years and so on.

- Basel II states that there are no explicit changes in the formal definition of capital but this is largely a matter of semantics. The value of securitized assets where the bank is the issuer and has the equivalent of a "first-loss" position are to be deducted from capital. Under the terms of the IRB approach specific provisions for credit losses may be treated towards capital under certain conditions and up to a defined level.
- The Basel Accord also defines a third Tier of capital but for all practical purposes it can be ignored and that is exactly what we are going to do.

The following shows the inverted pyramid structure of regulatory capital and other liabilities of a typical commercial bank operating in an OECD country with a Tier I capital adequacy ratio of 8%–9% (equity 6%–7% and hybrid equity of 2%) and Tier II of 4%. The diagram is approximately to scale based on area.

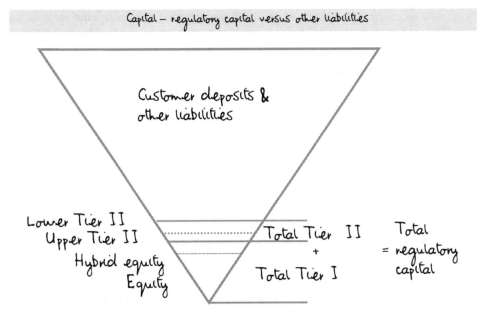

The basic approach for calculating risk-weighted asset (RWA) equivalents for credit risk is the same for the Original Accord and the Standardized Approach of Basel II. These can be broken down into two parts. A calculation of RWAs for on-balance sheet exposures and a calculation of RWA equivalents for off-balance sheet exposures.

Original Accord – Calculation of RWAs

The basic approach has already been explained in Chapter 14 "Capital management":

- **On-balance sheet.** Under the terms of the Original Accord there are four separate risk buckets for assets held on the balance sheet. Each bucket has been assigned separate weighting. The buckets are cash, reserve deposits and government securities (risk weighting 0%), deposits with OECD banks (20%), housing loans (50%), loans and all other assets (100%).

The total value of the assets in each bucket is then multiplied by the relevant risk-weighting factor to arrive at a risk-weighted asset number. The risk-weighted values for each bucket are then added together to give a figure for on-balance sheet risk-weighted assets.

No allowance is made for the presence of any collateral, financial or otherwise.

- **Off-balance sheet exposures.** Many banks have significant off-balance sheet exposures in the form of contingent claims, and these are converted into equivalent risk-weighted assets. These conversion factors vary between 0% for standby facilities of less than one year that can be canceled at any time before being drawn down against and 100% for forward purchases.

The Standardized Approach

The general approach to on-balance sheet credit risk embodied in Basel II is the same as that of the Original Accord in its use of asset classes, risk-weighting factors and the calculation of risk-weighted assets. The major differences are as follows:

- Increase in number of risk buckets by increasing number of asset classes and introducing five credit rating grades. These are to be mapped on ratings provided by recognized external credit rating agencies.
- Make some allowance for the effects of financial collateral, guarantees and credit derivatives.
- Risk weightings to be assigned at level of asset class/credit grade.
- Reduction in weightings for all residential mortgages and other retail loans.

Risk Buckets

The response to demands for a greater level of granularity in the number of risk buckets has been expanded by increasing the number of asset classes and introducing the use of five grades based on credit risk:

- **Asset classes.** The number of asset classes has been greatly expanded, and in particular in the area of loans made to individuals and corporates. These are now divided into the following: corporate, commercial real estate, residential mortgages and other retail credit. Past-due loans are afforded a different treatment from performing loans.
- **Credit grades.** Exposures for each asset class are to be allocated to one of five credit rating grades. These grades are to be defined with reference to ratings ascribed by independent credit rating agencies, such as Standard and Poor's. In terms of S&P ratings these correspond to AAA to AA−, A+ to A−, BBB+ to BBB−, BB+ to B−, and below B−.

Credit Risk Mitigation

Exposures where the bank has obtained legal rights to reduce losses arising from default may be subject to an adjustment to reflect the lower resultant risk. In specific terms these are limited to financial collateral, third-party guarantees and credit derivatives.

Collateral, guarantees and credit derivatives all come under the broad heading of "Credit Risk Mitigants", or CRMs, under the terms of the accord. Eligible financial collateral is restricted to deposits held with the lender, debt securities, repos and equities. All three categories are subject to additional qualifications on eligibility and some very detailed formulae for taking the impact of such instruments into account. Banks may calculate an adjusted exposure for the purpose of calculating risk-weighted assets using a form of the following general equation:

Adjusted exposure at default = Exposure × Haircut adjustment factor − Value of collateral × Haircut and foreign exchange haircut adjustment factors

The Accord specifies standard haircuts to be applied to debt securities and equities based on issue quality and maturity (the lower the quality and the longer the maturity the greater the factor). These factors vary from 0.5% through to 25%. The standard haircut for currency risk where the exposure and collateral are denominated in different currencies is 8%.

Supervisors may allow individual banks to calculate their own haircut factors to take account of market price and foreign exchange volatility, based on a standard VaR approach. The precise conditions that banks must meet to be able to apply for their own assessments are also defined within the accord and cover the usual sort of detailed conditions and also address the way in which exceptions identified from back-testing may occur.

The eligibility of certain types of financial collateral is also affected by the existence and enforceability of netting agreements with counterparties, and this is covered in depth in the Accord.

Only credit derivatives whose main economic objective is that of principal protection (credit default and total return swaps) are allowed. Only a few of the detailed conditions relating to eligibility are worthy of specific mention and to a large extent simply make explicit conditionality that is largely based on common sense.

Asset Classes

The number of asset classes has been increased sharply, compared with the Original Accord:

- **Sovereign and banks.** The crude division between OECD and non-OECD sovereign and bank risk is replaced by one based on reference to external ratings. This removes the anomaly that debt from stressed OECD countries (which has included South Korea and Japan) has received a lower rating than certain non-OECD countries with strong financial condition as measured by balance of payments, fiscal position and foreign reserves.

  Banks may opt to assign the same ratings to banks in a given country or to assign different ratings for individual banks. If they opt for the latter approach a distinction is also made between short-term and longer-term exposures.
- **Corporate and commercial real estate.** A higher level of granularity has been provided based on external credit rating buckets and dividing corporate loans into those for commercial real estate and those for other purposes. This additional granularity will have most impact on banks operating in countries where most corporates have solicited and been given external ratings. In most developing countries this is not the case and for these banks there is no significant difference between Basel I and Basel II.
- **Residential mortgages.** The risk-weighting factor for residential mortgages has been reduced from 50% to 35%. This is an implicit acknowledgement that the level of both expected and unexpected losses on such loans is much lower than was recognized under Basel I.

- **Other retail loans.** A new class of other retail loans has been defined. The major types of exposures included are forms of revolving credit (credit cards and overdrafts) granted to individuals and term loans such as auto and consumer loans but also extends to relatively small (€1m) exposures to individuals and relatively small sales (less than €50m). No specific justification is given for the lower 75% risk-weighting factor applied to these loans against that of the standard 100% weighting for loans to unrated larger companies.
- **Past-due loans.** Specific requirements are defined for past-due loans based on the level of NPL cover defined as follows:

$$NPL\ cover = \frac{Specific\ provisions}{Exposure - Eligible\ CRMs}$$

The risk-weighting factor is determined largely by whether NPL cover exceeds, is less than or greater than 20%. The capital requirement will be based on the unsecured portion of the exposure less specific provisions. If we assume no eligible collateral is held:

- An NPL with no specific provisions will attract a weighting of 150% and capital requirement of 12% (8% × 1.5).
- One with 20% cover will attract a lower weighting of 100% and capital requirement of 6.4% (100% × 8% × 0.8). Total provisions plus capital required as a percentage of the exposure are then 26.4%.
- At a 50% NPL cover level provisions plus capital required reach 54%.

On the surface, at least, this treatment does not provide any real incentive for banks to increase the level of their NPL cover.

- **Securitization issues.** Basel II, somewhat belatedly, closes a number of regulatory loopholes concerning banks' securitization issues and in particular where banks retain a "first-loss" position. The most blatant form of this type of regulatory arbitrage is provided by this simple example:

- A bank creates two tranches of securities backed by a pool of assets with value $100m. The first tranche with value of $90m is sold to third-party investors while the bank retains the second tranche with value of $10m. This second tranche absorbs any losses arising from the pool of assets up to a maximum of $10m, any losses after that level is reached are to be absorbed by holders of securities in the second tranche.
- In addition to various benefits (relating to origination fees and any servicing spread) the level of regulatory capital required to be set aside falls from $8m to $800 000 even though there has been no substantive reduction in the level of its economic credit risk exposure.

There are many different ways to achieve this end. The bank, for example, could issue the whole $100m in securitized assets but provide a guarantee against losses up to the first $10m. Some of these methods go beyond the scope of the rather cursory explanations of clean-up calls, early amortization and other forms of credit enhancement contained in this book.

Basel II defines explicit conditions that must be met for securitization issues to be considered to have been done without any form of recourse. It also states clearly that even when these stated conditions have been met supervisors have the right and responsibility to consider the economic reality behind securitization issues rather than their stated form when determining whether this has been achieved. These types of behavior, where affected parties look for ways to circumvent the spirit of the Accord but follow the letter, are present in most rule-based systems.

At one level this is one of the more droll parts of the Accord because it gives a sense of the way in which creative structured finance professionals have given bank supervisors the run-around and the latter's increasingly desperate measures to prevent this in the future. The Vatican is rumored to have an entire work devoted to proscribed sexual behavior. Needless to say this work is not publicly available because of realistic concerns that it would give people ideas!

Under the terms of the Standardized Approach two different tranches are defined, one with issuer credit enhancement and the other for all other securitized issues held:

- **Tranches with issuer credit enhancement.** Where an issue has been done with an element of credit enhancement by the issuer the outstanding value of this portion is to be deducted from regulatory capital (half from Tier I and half from Tier II).
- **Other tranches.** Where the bank holds securitization issues (whether it is the originator or simply an investor) and where it is not providing any form of credit enhancement itself these are to be treated in a similar manner to other corporate exposures with risk weightings based on external ratings.
- **Other assets.** All other on-balance sheet assets are to be given a 100% risk weighting.

The following table provides a summary of the risk-weighting factors for on-balance sheet assets.

Risk weightings by grade for on-balance sheet assets under Standardized Approach						
	1	2	3	4	5	Unrated
Sovereign banks	0%	20%	50%	100%	150%	100%
Option 1 (National)	20%	50%	—100%—		150%	100%
Option 2 (Individual)						
Short-term claims	—20%—			50%	150%	20%
Other claims	—20%—	50%		100%	150%	20%
Corporates	20%	50%	—100%—		150%	100%
Commercial real estate	—100%—					
Residential mortages	35%					
Other retail	75%					
Past-due loans (based on unsecured portion)						
NPL cover < 20%	150%					
NPL cover 20%–50%	100%					
NPL cover > 50%	50–100%					
Other assets	100%					
Risk weightings for securitized assets by rating						
	1	2	3	4	5 or Unrated	
Long term	20%	50%	100%	350%	Deduction from capital	
Short term	20%	50%	—100%—		Deduction from capital	

- **Off-balance sheet items.** Off-balance sheet assets are translated into risk-weighted asset equivalents by applying a conversion factor determined by maturity and revocability of the commitment. Unconditional commitments with an original maturity of up to one year receive an adjustment factor of 20% and those above one year 50%. Those that can be canceled unconditionally at the bank's discretion at any time are zero weighted.

- Securities lent by a bank or lodged as collateral receive a 100% weighting subject to any credit risk mitigation factors. Short-term, self-liquidating letters of credit associated with the shipment of goods are subject to a 20% weighting to both issuing and confirming banks.

REGULATORY CAPITAL REQUIREMENTS FOR MARKET RISK

Market risk is concerned with the bank's trading operations and the trading book (as distinct from the bank's non-trading book). No changes in the treatment of regulatory capital are planned under the terms of Basel II.

Banks may opt to apply a standardized, rule-based approach to calculate the regulatory requirement for Market Risk or one based on their own internal VaR models. Both approaches have their weaknesses but those of the standardized model are more serious. Regulators have encouraged banks to use the internal model where they are qualified and capable of doing so. The internal model approach usually results in a lower regulatory capital requirement than the Standardized Approach and this provides a further incentive to banks to adopt this approach.

Both approaches break down trading exposures into four major risk classes: interest rate, foreign exchange rate, equities and commodities. Very few commercial banks are active commodity traders and for practical purposes this class can be ignored.

The Standardized Approach

The Standardized Approach defines a series of rules and procedures that banks must adopt for each major risk class in order to calculate regulatory capital requirements:

- **Interest rate risk.** The rules used to determine capital requirements for interest rate risks are the most complex of the classes. Gross positions within each currency are put into one of a number of time bands, defined within the Accord, based on an approximate measure of duration. The net position in each time band is then calculated. These net positions are then subject to some complex and detailed adjustments intended to take into account in a rough manner a part of the duration mismatch.

  The capital requirement is then calculated by applying a conversion factor for the adjusted net position in each time band. These conversion factors vary between zero for time bands with very short duration to 12.5% for those with the longest duration. The converted values then translate directly into a capital requirement.

  It is worth stressing that this only captures interest rate risk arising directly from a bank's trading operations. By far the largest part of interest rate risk lies within the bank's non-trading operations and there is no specific capital requirement for this.
- **Foreign exchange.** Foreign currency positions are calculated by taking the net spot long and short position in each currency after converting forward contracts and derivatives into spot equivalents. These net positions are then converted into the bank's base currency. All of the bank's net positions, irrespective of currency, are then added together. The process is repeated for the net short positions.

  The capital requirement is then calculated as 8%, the standard BIS minimum capital requirement of the larger of the total long and short positions. Currencies may depreciate or appreciate against the base currency and this approach is intended to take the position with the largest exposure. If, for example, a bank has a total net long position of $1bn and total net short position of $600m the regulatory requirement would be for $80m.

- **Equities.** The first step is to calculate the net positions in each stock taking into account current spot positions and converting any derivative positions into spot equivalents. The standardized model defines the rules to be followed for the conversion of derivative positions into spot positions in each market. The capital requirement is then calculated as a defined percentage of the net positions, whether long or short, by default 8%.

The major weaknesses of the standardized model are that:

- The approach fails to take account of any correlations that exist between risk factors and positions. This is a fundamental defect.
- Many of the rules and conversion factors are essentially arbitrary, although this same criticism may also be leveled at aspects of the internal model approach.
- The failure to differentiate between individual currencies in assessing foreign exchange risk means that differences in exchange rate volatility between currencies is not taken into account.
- The rules result in the imposition of additional regulatory capital requirements for some positions taken for hedging purposes that actually reduce economic risk. A bank may have a long position in a stock but a matching position in a put option. Both positions would have a regulatory capital requirement imposed.

Internal Models Approach

We have examined some of the ways in which VaR techniques may be applied to assess market risks. The internal models approach allows these techniques to be used to calculate a total VAR for the trading book and the capital requirement is equal to this value. Banks must demonstrate that they are competent to use internal models effectively to be allowed to calculate their regulatory capital requirements on this basis.

Regulators take into account qualitative factors such as the way in which risk is managed from an organizational point of view. There are also hard standards that define the type of models (VaR, simulations, Monte Carlo etc.) that are permitted. They also specify the way in which risk classes are to be subdivided into lower risk factors and the minimum acceptable level at which aggregation can start. Other key standards include the following:

- The VAR for each risk factor must be calculated to a 99% confidence level and use a 10-day holding period.
- Individual VARs at lower levels of risk factor decomposition are to be consolidated within asset classes taking into account correlations between risk factors.
- The total VAR is the simple sum of the three major risk classes. This is equivalent to assuming that they have perfect positive correlation.
- The resultant VAR is then multiplied by a factor of at least three to provide a "safety" buffer.

The required minimum regulatory capital requirement is equal to the higher of the previous day's VAR and the average daily value calculated over the previous 60 days.

The last-minute application of the comfort multiplication factor of at least three is unfortunately typical of the uneven level of detail contained within the BIS standards. Across all major risk areas there are examples of very detailed treatments to take specific factors or possible situations into account that are then completely submerged by sweeping, arbitrary "adjustments" which render much of the detail work irrelevant.

That is not to say that in the case of market risk a safety factor is unnecessary but does demonstrate the level of confidence that regulators have with the detailed VAR estimates. The multiplication factor of three is a minimum and regulators are at liberty to increase this factor for individual banks. A similar result would have been obtained if a 100-day holding period had been specified. The value for the adjustment factor to be used is justified by regulators on two principal grounds:

- **Model deficiencies.** The first grounds for concern relate to modeling weaknesses. We have already considered a number of the major criticisms leveled at VaR techniques. Even in "normal" times the actual frequency of losses may be greater than that defined at the specified confidence level. At the 99% confidence level losses greater than that estimated from VaR should occur only once in every 100 days. Historic success can be determined by back-testing and this is the main tool used by regulators to help them determine whether a higher multiplication factor appears warranted.
- **Extreme circumstances.** The potential for trading losses is greatest under extreme conditions when everything seems to go wrong at the same time. In an increasingly interconnected world a market crash in one country may have a direct knock-on effect on other markets. It does appear that market crashes are becoming increasingly highly correlated but they are sufficiently rare that there is only limited historic data to back up this impression. In the event of a market crash historic correlations that underpin VAR estimates may break down and liquidity dry up. Under such circumstances the 10-day holding period specified may not be sufficient to liquidate or hedge all positions.

Although market risk is important to manage at larger banks with extensive trading operations the resulting regulatory capital requirement is usually only a small fraction of that required for credit risk.

CAPITAL ADEQUACY RATIOS

- The Tier I and Tier II capital adequacy ratios are then calculated by taking Tier I and II capital and dividing by total risk-weighted assets. The total capital adequacy ratio is the simple sum of the Tier I and Tier II ratios. This is, however, qualified.
- The minimum capital adequacy requirement (CAR) under the Basel Accord is that banks must maintain a total CAR of at least 8%, of which at least 50% must be in the form of Tier I capital. Tier II capital cannot be greater than Tier I capital and lower Tier II cannot be more than 50% of Tier I.

The following diagram summarizes the entire process under both the Original Accord and the Standardized Approach proposed in Basel II.

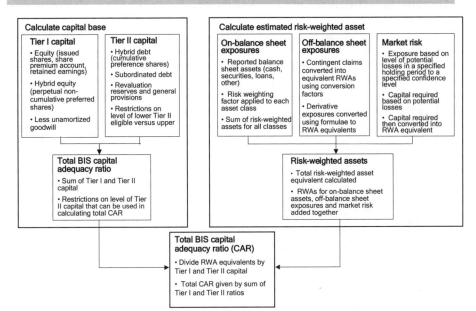

This means that a bank with $1bn in both Tier I and Tier II BIS capital can support the equivalent of $25bn ($2bn multiplied by 1/8%, 12.5×) in risk-weighted assets and meet the BIS minimum standards. That is equivalent to roughly $30bn in reported balance sheet assets for a typical commercial bank.

Most large banks have a separate capital management group to carry out this work and try to ensure that the bank complies with regulatory requirements at all levels. Most banks operate internationally by establishing foreign branches rather than subsidiaries. The main reason being that local regulators will usually waive BIS requirements for branches of foreign banks provided they are satisfied that the head office will honor its branch's commitments. The bank still has to satisfy capital requirements at consolidated levels, of course, but this gives greater flexibility overall. From time to time local regulators raise the specter of "subsidiarization" for foreign banks operating in their market whereby the foreign bank would have to provide capital to support a separate banking business rather than the minimal requirements for a branch.

THE INTERNAL RATINGS BASED (IRB) APPROACH

Asset Classes and Internal Grades

The IRB approach defines a number of assets classes as shown in the following diagram. This breakdown is important for two reasons. The first is that it defines the structure for the way in which exposures must be classified and hence one of the ways in which historic default data must be organized and against which key default historic parameters must be kept. The second is that different rules in terms of the way in which the regulatory capital requirement are calculated apply to exposures classified within certain classes. Banks must also allocate each exposure within each class to one of six internal grades.

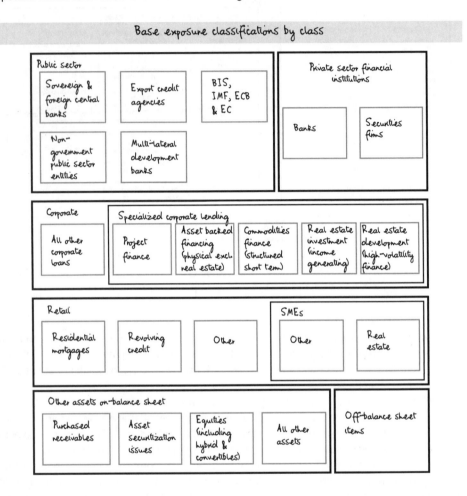

calculated apply to exposures classified within certain classes.

DEFAULT PARAMETERS

Expected losses in general are defined as the expected probability of default multiplied by the loss in the event of default:

$$EL = PD \times LIED$$

There are many ways in which to approach an estimate of *LIED*. The Accord is based on an approach that assumes that the loss in the event of default is directly proportional to the exposure at the time of default, with some allowance being made for any credit risk mitigants.

The four key related definitions are the conditions for an exposure to be deemed to have default status, the probability of default (*PD*), the exposure-at-default (*EAD*) and the loss-given-default (*LGD*) expressed as a percentage of an adjusted *EAD*.

Definition of Default

A loan (exposures) is deemed to have a default status when either of the following apply:

- **Past-due.** The standard 90-day past-due rule is to be applied for term exposures. Overdrafts and other forms of revolving credit are to be treated as past-due once the customer breaches its limit or the bank cuts the limit below that of the current value of the drawdown.
- **Likelihood of repayment.** If the bank considers that full repayment is unlikely under the terms of the loan agreement the exposure is to be counted as being in default. Factors that would normally be taken as indicative of this having occurred include:
    - Loans put on non-accrual status.
    - Specific provision made against the exposure (or write-off).
    - Bank enters into discussions for debt restructuring where the bank is likely to realize economic losses from such a restructuring.
    - Bankruptcy petition against borrower filed or company has filed for Chapter 11-type protection.
    - Covenant violations.

The Accord implies that recognition of a default event occurring on one exposure to a borrower should lead to all other exposures being classified as default other than in the case of retail borrowers. The second definition concerning likelihood of repayment is highly dependent on management conservatism.

Probability of Default (*PD*)

The *PD* is based on an estimate over a one-year period based on a long-run average of all exposures to the specified class of borrower and exposure type in the relevant internal rating grade. By long run the Accord states that the data should cover one full economic cycle but that a minimum of five years of historic data must be used, but where a longer observation period exists the longer period data should be used.

The *PD* definition is highly ambiguous when it comes to cyclicality. While requiring a long-run average to be used it requires banks to be able to demonstrate that historic data used is relevant to both current and foreseeable conditions. Given the close relationship between economic cyclicality and default rates this complicates the interpretation. Banks are also encouraged to add a conservative buffer to their long-run estimates to take account of the volatility in the estimates.

Exposure-at-Default (*EAD*)

The exposure-at-default (*EAD*) for an on-balance sheet item should be equal to at least the current drawdown, adjusted for any netting agreements or eligible financial collateral. Banks using the advanced approach must estimate *EAD*s for off-balance sheet items (excluding derivatives) taking account of possible future drawdowns both up to and beyond that authorized.

EAD estimates must be based on seven years of historic data or five years in the case of retail exposures. Just why five years of historic data are deemed sufficient for the purposes of estimating *PD* for corporate exposures but an extra two years are needed for estimating *EAD* is not clear.

Loss-Given-Default (*LGD*)

There are a number of ways to approach the estimate of the expected loss-in-event-of-default (*LIED*) for an exposure. It will clearly depend upon a number of factors: the exposure at the time of default (*EAD*), carrying costs, the realizable value and liquidity of collateral and the direct (legal and other recovery) and indirect (management time) costs of resolution. The overall approach taken in IRB for estimating expected *LIED* is as follows:

Expected LIED = Expected EAD adjusted for eligible financial collateral

× *Loss-given-default (LGD) adjusted for guarantees and collateral, where allowed*

LGD as used above is defined as a fixed percentage of the expected *EAD* adjusted for eligible collateral, or in the terminology of the accord "credit mitigating factor" where this takes into account the effects of any credit derivatives and guarantees. Implicit in this approach is that *PD* and *LGD* are independent.

Where banks are not qualified to estimate *LGD* under the more liberal form of the Foundation Approach they must apply the following default *LGD* values. Senior unsecured exposures to corporates and banks are assigned a 45% *LGD*, subordinated claims a 75%.

In addition to financial collateral an allowance may be made for some other types of collateral, primarily receivables and commercial and residential real estate. The *LGD* is adjusted as follows:

Adjusted LGD = Original LGD × (Exposure − Allowance for collateral)/Exposure

The detailed explanations of just how to arrive at the *LGD* under either the Foundation or Advanced options are extremely obtuse and littered with qualifications.

Non-financial Collateral

Non-financial collateral may be eligible for consideration provided three key conditions are met:

- The ability of the borrower to repay its debt does not depend in a material way on the performance of the pledged collateral. (This excludes its use in project financing-type transactions.)
- The value of the collateral must not depend in a material way on the performance of the borrower overall. (This puts effective limits on collateral such as forms of work-in-progress and specialist equipment.)
- The bank can demonstrate that its claim on the collateral in the event of default is legally enforceable.

The value of the collateral must be based on a market price based on the willing-buyer principle and should be revalued on a regular (at least once a year) basis. Sampling methods and use of property indices are permitted for collateral valuation purposes other than in cases of default, or where there has been a material deterioration in the value of the asset. In these cases a professional (and by implication independent) valuation should be obtained.

The Accord also specifies how to treat exposures where a bank has both collateral and some other form of credit protection.

Guarantees may be reflected in loss-given-default (*LGD*) estimates. The condition of both borrower and guarantor must be monitored separately and both assigned to internal ratings. In no case can the resultant risk-weighted asset be less than that of an equivalent direct exposure to the guarantor.

Sources of Default Parameters

There are four sources for default-related parameters:

- **Internal historic data.** The Accord contains detailed conditions for banks to meet to be able to use their own historic databases. None of these conditions contain any surprises and cover issues that we have already considered when looking at the use of historic internal data. Where banks use statistical modeling to generate forecast default probabilities based on analysis of historic data and current and expected conditions internal statistical modeling methods may be used.
- **Mapping to external sources.** Banks may map their own internal grades onto those of an external credit rating agency and use their default rates as the base. Such data should be issuer rather than issue specific.
- **Supervisory defaults.** Some banks that do not qualify for the full IRB approach must apply supervisory *PD*s to certain classes.
- **Exposure itself.** The *EAD* may be adjusted for eligible financial collateral and *LGD* for other collateral pledged by the borrower.

From here on the calculation is formulaic, but overly complicated. A number of potential adjustments may be made to take some account of collateral, maturity of exposure and firm size:

- **Recognition of collateral on *LGD*.** The *LGD* may be adjusted in two ways. In the first method a direct reduction of the factor may be made to reflect the presence of certain financial collateral. In the second method, which takes account of certain credit risk mitigants (other collateral, guarantees and credit derivatives), the adjustment is indirect but the effect is basically the same.
- **Maturity adjustment.** A further adjustment may be made based on the effective maturity of the exposure. The accord does not say so but one way to consider this is that it is effectively an attempt to adjust the single one-year holding period defined for the probability of default (*PD*) for multiple periods. The practical effect is that exposures with a longer maturity have a higher capital requirement imposed.
- **Firm size.** A further adjustment factor may be applied for exposures to small firms that fall outside the definition for retail exposures. These adjustment factors lower the capital requirement compared with larger firms.
- **Application of black-box formula to *PD*.** The Accord defines a function to be applied for most classes of exposures that when applied to the probability of default produces a new value to be used in its place. This function has no fundamental rationale but is the major determinant of the capital requirement.

Taken together the general form of the capital requirement is given as follows:

Capital requirement = Result of Accord function for (PD) × Base EAD adjusted for eligible financial collateral × Base LGD adjusted for non-financial collateral × Adjustment factor based on maturity of exposure × Adjustment factor based on firm's size

In the language we have been using the resultant capital requirement is based on the sum of the expected losses (*EL*) plus some ill-defined (but quantifiable) value for unexpected losses (*UL*). Some allowance is made for general provisions to be included within the definition of capital and for specific provisions for loans already defined as being in a state of default to be allowed. Unexpected losses are, however, not defined explicitly in terms of historic volatility of losses but are based on a function whose only input is *PD* (probability of default).

The Accord then goes further and throughout applies a multiplication factor of 12.5× (equivalent to dividing by 8%) to translate this capital requirement into a risk-weighted asset equivalent which is then multiplied by 8% to arrive at the capital requirement! I'm going to stick with the actual capital requirement.

Maturity Adjustment Factors

Some recognition is made for differences in risk due to term. Banks are required to calculate an estimate of effective maturity (*M*) for each exposure as the time-weighted average of the expected cashflows over the life of the exposure as follows:

$$\textit{Effective maturity} = M = \sum_{t=0}^{T} t \times CF_t \bigg/ \sum_{t=0}^{T} CF_t, \text{ where } CF \text{ represents cashflow at time } t$$

It is convenient to regard the base case as being for an exposure with an effective maturity of one year where the maturity adjustment factor is +1. The maturity adjustment factor is calculated using the following formula:

$$\textit{Maturity adjustment factor} = \frac{1 + (M - 2.5) \times (0.08451 - 0.05898 \times \ln{(PD)})^2}{(1 - 1.5 \times (0.08451 - 0.05898 \times \ln{(PD)})^2)}$$

The maturity adjustment factors for a range of effective maturities between 90 days and five years and default probabilities between 0.25% and 5% are shown below. The capital requirement for an exposure with an effective maturity of five years and default probabilities between 0.25% and 1% are between 1.6× and twice that of the base one-year case.

Maturity adjustment factors										
	Effective maturity (*M*) years									
PD	**0.25**	**0.50**	**1.00**	**1.50**	**2.00**	**2.50**	**3.00**	**3.50**	**4.00**	**4.50**	**5.00**
0.25%	0.80	0.86	1.00	1.14	1.27	1.41	1.54	1.68	1.81	1.95	2.08
0.50%	0.84	0.90	1.00	1.10	1.21	1.31	1.42	1.52	1.62	1.73	1.83
1.00%	0.88	0.92	1.00	1.08	1.16	1.24	1.32	1.39	1.47	1.55	1.63
1.50%	0.90	0.93	1.00	1.07	1.13	1.20	1.27	1.33	1.40	1.47	1.53
2.00%	0.91	0.94	1.00	1.06	1.12	1.18	1.24	1.29	1.35	1.41	1.47
3.00%	0.93	0.95	1.00	1.05	1.10	1.15	1.20	1.24	1.29	1.34	1.39
4.00%	0.94	0.96	1.00	1.04	1.09	1.13	1.17	1.21	1.26	1.30	1.34
5.00%	0.94	0.96	1.00	1.04	1.08	1.11	1.15	1.19	1.23	1.27	1.31

SIZE ADJUSTMENT FACTOR

Exposures to relatively small firms (defined in Basel II as firms with sales (turnover) between € 5m and €50m), may have their capital requirement adjusted requirement reduced by multiplying by the base requirement by the following factor:

$$Size\ adjustment\ factor = 1 - \frac{S-5}{45}\ where\ S = sales\ in\ €m$$

The size adjustment factor is approximately 0.8 for a company with turnover of €5m rising to approximately 0.9 at a turnover around €25m and 1.0 for a company with sales of €50m.

ALLOWANCE FOR PROVISIONS TO TREAT TOWARDS CAPITAL

Although Basel II states that there are no changes in the definition of capital the reality is that there have been due to changes in the proposed treatment of specific and general provisions. The explanation for their treatment is very convoluted but the gist appears to be as follows:

- **Exposure-specific provisions.** The base black-box formulae for exposures in default (i.e. $PD = +1$) gives a capital requirement equal to expected losses (EL). This capital requirement can be fully met from specific provisions established against those exposures.
    If the specific provisions set up for some exposures with a default status are greater than the expected losses on those exposures the excess may be used to meet capital requirements for other exposures in the same asset class with default status where there is a shortfall.
- **Portfolio "specific-general" provisions.** Where a general provision has been established for a specific risk factor (e.g. exposures in a particular country or to companies operating in a particular sector) it may be treated as capital.
- **General provisions.** If general provisions exceed the level given by the standard 1.25% of RWA allowed for Tier II capital these can be counted as capital provided that the surplus exceeds the total expected losses for all exposures (save retail revolving and special lending) less specific provisions.

The actual mechanism used to effect the above is to multiply the capital allowance by 12.5× and subtract this from the total RWAs. The effect is the same whichever way you look at it. The treatment of retail revolving credits is different from that given above and there are some minor differences in the way that special lending exposures are treated.

BLACK-BOX FORMULAE FOR SPECIFIC ASSET CLASSES

Corporate Loans

The regulatory capital requirement (CR) for exposures to banks and corporate loans (ignoring adjustments relating to maturity and firm size) is given, in general, by the following equation.

(The form of this equation differs from that given in the Accord because I have simplified it in the mathematical sense of the term. They are equivalent.) In Basel terminology this is called a "supervisory credit risk function" but the term "black-box formula" appears more appropriate:

$$CR = Normsdist \left[(0.88 - 0.12e^{-50 \times PD})^{-0.5} \times Normsinv(PD) \right.$$

$$\left. + 3.09 \left(\frac{0.12 + 0.12 \times e^{(-50 \times PD)}}{0.88 - 0.12 \times e^{-50 \times PD}} \right)^{+0.5} \right] \times LGD \times EAD$$

The function "Normsdist" gives the confidence level for a one tailed test on a normal distribution for a given number of standard deviations from the mean. Normsdist(0.999) is equal to 3.09, for example. Normsinv is the inverse, giving the number of standard deviations from the mean for a given confidence level. Normsinv(3.09) is equal to 99.9%, for example.

Unfortunately, there is no obvious intuitive explanation of either the form of the equation or any *a priori* reason for the value of the constants contained within it. The black-box formulae for two other classes of exposures (real estate development and other retail) is based on the above form with the only difference being the values of some of the constants. The black-box formulae for residential mortgages and retail revolving exposures are different in both form and substance.

The only way that I can see how to understand how this function behaves is to express the capital requirement in the form of expected and unexpected losses and see how the latter varies with *PD*:

$$Capital\ requirement = EL + UL = PD \times LIED + n \times \sigma(PD) \times LIED$$

(*LIED* is simply *LGD* × *EAD*). From this we can work out an implied standard deviation of the default probability versus probability as shown below for all asset classes. Trying to reach any conclusions from this chart without having a wealth of actual data is virtually impossible.

Real Estate Development (High Volatility Commercial Real Estate (HVCRZ))

All corporate exposures are subject to the same basis for the calculation of the capital adequacy requirement, save for exposures related to property development (in Basel II terms High Volatility Commercial Real Estate). These are subject to the following formula and contain a small quantitative modification to the base black-box formula:

$$CR = \times Normsdist \left[(0.88 - 0.18e^{-50 \times PD})^{-0.5} \times Normsinv(PD) \right.$$

$$\left. + 3.09 \left(\frac{0.12 + 0.18 \times e^{(-50 \times PD)}}{0.88 - 0.18 \times e^{-50 \times PD}} \right)^{+0.5} \right] \times LGD \times EAD$$

This is equivalent to multiplying the base requirement calculated for other comparable corporate exposures by the relevant factor as shown in the following table. The effect for most such loans will be to increase the requirement compared with comparable straight corporate exposures by approximately 20%–30%.

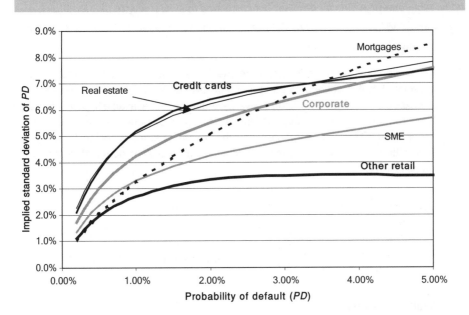

Implied standard deviations of *PD* versus *PD* by asset class

Adjustment factors for capital requirement for real estate development exposures												
PD	0.1%	0.2%	0.3%	0.4%	0.5%	0.6%	0.7%	0.8%	0.9%	1.0%	2.0%	3.0%
HVCRE factor	1.33	1.31	1.29	1.27	1.25	1.24	1.23	1.21	1.20	1.19	1.11	1.07

Residential Mortgages

Exposures that are secured by residential mortgages (whether to owner–occupiers or for buy-to-let) are subject to a much lower capital charge than other classes of exposure. The adjusted formula is as follows:

$$CR = Normsdist[1.085 \times Normsinv(PD) + 3.09 \times 0.42] \times LGD \times EAD$$

Retail Revolving Credit

By far the largest part of revolving retail credit is that from credit cards. We have already observed that these represent a well-defined class that differs from most other bank exposures in a number of ways.

The confusion within the Accord concerning the treatment of expected losses versus un-expected losses is evident in the convoluted way in which these exposures are treated for the calculation of regulatory capital.

The capital requirement is reduced by a factor constrained by the level of expected income of the pool of credit cards being managed. (In Basel terminology expected income is called "margin future income" or *MFI*.) The proposed "solution" also reflects the success of bankers' associations lobbying. The regulatory capital is to be treated in this general way:

Capital requirement = Capital requirement calculated in similar way to that for other exposures − Value determined by PD but constrained by the level of expected income from performing assets in this class

In Basel II terminology expected income is referred to as "future margin income" or *FMI* and represents annual profits defined as the amount of revenue less "normal business expenses" that a bank expects to generate from the relevant exposures and available to be applied against credit losses from the portfolios. It excludes income that may be generated from new accounts. For full recognition *FMI* must be greater than the annual level of expected losses plus two standard deviations from the mean level of annualized losses. In quantitative terms this is expressed as follows:

$$CR = Normsdist\left[(0.98 - 0.09e^{-50 \times PD})^{-0.5} \times Normsinv(PD) \right.$$

$$\left. + 3.09\left(\frac{0.02 + 0.09 \times e^{-50 \times PD}}{0.98 - 0.09 \times e^{-50 \times PD}} \right)^{+0.5} \right] \times LGD \times EAD - 0.75 \times PD \times LGD \times EAD$$

Other Retail Exposures

Other retail exposures include other term loans (often referred to in the context of consumer finance and auto financing as installment loans) made to SMEs and individual personal customers. The equation is in form on the black-box formula for corporate exposures with some differences in the values of some of the constants, as shown below:

$$CR = Normsdist\left[(0.98 - 0.15e^{-35 \times PD})^{-0.5} \times 3.09\left(\frac{0.02 + 0.15 \times e^{-35 \ PD}}{0.98 - 0.15 \times e^{-35 \times PD}} \right)^{+0.5} \right]$$
$$\times LGD \times EAD$$

If we simply compare the resulting capital requirement for "other" retail exposures based on those for corporate exposures then we see that they vary from between 66% and 76% across a range of default probabilities between 1% and 4%.

Other retail exposure capital requirements as percentage of requirements for corporate exposures versus probability of default (*PD*)							
PD	1.00%	1.50%	2.00%	2.50%	3.00%	3.50%	4.00%
Retail/corporate	76%	75%	73%	71%	69%	67%	66%

OPERATIONAL RISK

The Original Accord did not address capital requirements related to operational risk. The Committee has proposed a specific regulatory capital requirement against losses arising from operational risk. The base method to be used to quantify this requirement is as follows, where operating income is used as a "proxy":

$$\textit{Operational risk capital requirement} = \textit{Operating income} \times \textit{Weighting factor}$$

In this context operating income is the average over the past three years and is taken as net interest income plus net non-interest income, in other words excluding bad debt charges and operating expenses. The weighting factor in the base case as determined by the Committee is 0.15. Individual banks may be allowed to apply a more "sophisticated" formula where a bank's operating income is allocated among eight specified business lines with weighting factors varying from 0.12 through to 0.18 against a "norm" of 0.15 for the commercial banking business line. The Committee is responsible for determining these factors based on their assessments of relative "riskiness":

Appendix II

Glossary of Terms

What's in a name? That which we call a rose. By any other name would smell as sweet.
William Shakespeare, Romeo and Juliet

Allowance for bad debts. See "Reserves for credit losses".

Alpha. Alpha provides a measure of any investment returns that cannot be explained by the level of risk (as measured by beta) taken.

Arbitrage. Arbitrage is the act of buying a security or commodity and simultaneously selling another related instrument to lock in a guaranteed profit.

Asset allocation. The proportion of an investment fund to be held in each of a number of different asset classes. In many investment organizations the responsibility for asset allocation is separated from that of security selection.

Asset backed security. A security issued that entitles the holder to a stream of payments that are based on, or guaranteed by, the cashflows generated on an underlying asset or pool of assets.

Asset classes. Asset classes are usually defined by their risk and return characteristics and by factors such as term and liquidity. Common asset classes are equities, bonds, real estate and cash (money market).

Asset-liability-management (ALM). The management of the risks associated with a bank's, fund's or other organization's assets and liabilities.

Asset quality. A generic term to describe the credit quality of a bank's assets. A bank with a high standard of asset quality will have a low level of problem loans and well-diversified portfolio.

Asset yields. Asset yields are defined as gross interest income divided by average interest-earning assets.

Association of Investment Management and Research (AIMR). A US-based organization that administers and awards the Chartered Financial Analyst (CFA) designation to qualified investment professionals.

At-the-money. A traded option whose strike or exercise price is equal to the current price of the underlying instrument.

Bad debt charge. A charge taken through the earnings statement to reflect changes in expectations of future credit losses. Also known as the provision charge or charge for credit losses.

Banker's acceptance. A time draft drawn on a bank, normally used to finance export or import transactions.

Banker's draft. A check written by a bank on behalf of a third party that is guaranteed by the issuing bank. Such drafts may be post-dated.

Bank of International Settlements (BIS). An international organization owned by the world's central banks based in Basel that coordinates and facilitates cooperation on issues such as capital adequacy requirements and settlement systems between central banks.

Bank runs. Bank runs occur when many customers at a bank attempt unexpectedly to withdraw their deposits at the same time.

Barbell bond portfolio. A portfolio of bonds made up of a combination of bonds with short and long durations.

Basel Accord. An agreement made between OECD central banks to standardize minimum bank capital adequacy requirements. Most other countries have adopted standards based on these standards. The Original Accord dates back to 1988 but has been subject to a number of amendments. A major revision (Basel II) is currently being worked on with earliest implementation planned for late 2006.

Basis point. Basis points provide a useful way to describe small fractions of percentage points. 100 basis points is equivalent to 1 percentage point. For example, if the yield on an asset increased from 4.5% to 5% it would be said to have widened by 50 basis points. Frequently abbreviated as bpts or bps.

Bearer securities. Securities where physical possession represents the claim to the security rather than some form of registration.

Benchmarking. A method used to measure a portfolio's performance against a representative benchmark of similar investment style.

Beta. Beta provides a measure of the volatility of returns for a stock against the market. Beta plays an important role in the capital asset pricing model (CAPM).

Bid price. The price that a buyer is willing to pay for a security.

Bid–offer spread. The difference between bid and offer prices for a security. Also known as bid–ask spread.

Black-Scholes model. A theoretical framework used for valuing options.

Book entry securities. Securities where registration of ownership claims is held in the form of entries in computer records rather than by paper certificates.

Bonus issue. Bonus shares are additional shares issued to current shareholders without the latter having to invest more capital. These issues have no impact on a firm's economic value but increase in the number of shares issued and reduce book value and earnings per share. Stock prices adjust to take the additional shares issued into account. Effectively a synonym for stock-split.

Bullet loan. Loan made with the same structure as a zero coupon bond.

Callable bond. A bond in which the issuer has the right to call (redeem) the bond before it reaches term. Such redemptions are usually done at par and redemptions are only permitted on pre-specified call dates.

Call option. A call option gives the holder the right, but not the obligation, to buy a financial or physical asset at a specified price within a specified time period. The holder pays the issuer (writer) a fee (the option's premium) in advance for this right.

Call–put parity. Call–put parity ensures that the value of a stock call option is determined by the price of an equivalent put option (common expiry date and exercise price), a risk-free rate and the stock's current price.

Cap. A cap provides the holder with protection against adverse price movements. A borrower taking a floating rate loan may purchase a 10% cap. In the event that the base floating rate rises above 10% the costs to the borrower will be capped. At this point higher interest rates will have no impact on the borrower's funding costs.

Capital. A measure of a bank's ability to absorb losses before depositors face loss. Under the Basel Accord capital is divided into Tier I and Tier II capital. Most Tier I capital is provided by shareholders' funds (equity) and Tier II capital by forms of long-term debt.

Capital adequacy ratios. Regulatory capital adequacy ratios provide a measure of a bank's capital relative to its risk-weighted asset equivalents. There are usually based on standards defined in the Basel Accord.

Capital asset pricing model (CAPM). CAPM is the underlying framework for most modern financial asset valuation methods. Its key tenet is that risks and returns have a linear relationship.

Capital guaranteed return fund. Funds that guarantee no loss of capital and may give some minimum return over a specified period but have upside potential if stock markets perform well.

Capital markets. The capital markets comprise the bond and equity markets and provide alternative, and longer-term, form of financing to bank loans.

Capital reduction program. A capital reduction program is one of a number of ways in which banks with excess capital can return part of that capital to shareholders. The principal differences between a capital reduction program and special dividend concern legal and tax issues.

Cash-drag. Cash-drag on portfolio returns occurs because of the need to keep a proportion of the portfolio in the form of cash or cash equivalents. Given lower returns on the cash component than the rest of the portfolio this results in a "cash-drag".

Cashflow matching. Cashflow matching involves a manager with a stream of future expected payments on liabilities holding a portfolio of fixed-income assets where the cash received from those assets (both interest and principal) matches those for the liabilities in both time and value.

Certificate of deposit. Certificates of deposit (CDs) are issued by banks and are close to the equivalent of time deposits. They may have fixed or floating interest rates. The major difference between CDs and time deposits is that the former have a secondary market.

Chapter 11. "Chapter 11" is the name of a part of the US Bankruptcy code that provides a legal means for distressed companies to seek interim protection from creditors while undertaking a financial and operational restructuring to restore the firm to financial viability.

Chartered Financial Analyst (CFA). The CFA designation is awarded by the AIMR and has become widely recognized as the global professional qualification for securities analysts and portfolio managers.

Chartered Financial Planner (CFP). The CFP designation is awarded by the US-based CFP board. Many CFP holders work as independent financial advisors.

Churning. The act of brokers or other financial agents encouraging, or acting on behalf of, clients to trade simply to generate commissions. Portfolio managers are also assessed by the churn rate on their funds, that is how fast they turn over the investments in their portfolios.

Closed end funds. Closed end funds are funds where the number of shares in the fund is fixed. Redemptions are not possible nor can new shares normally be issued. Such funds are usually listed and traded on a stock exchange.

Collar. An options combination created by buying an in-the-money put option and selling an out-of-the-money call option on the same underlying instrument. This effectively puts limits on both potential upside and downside.

Collateral. Collateral comprises assets that a borrower owns and pledges to a lender as security for a loan. In the event of a failure by the borrower to make the payments as specified in the terms of the loan agreement the bank has the right to seize and dispose of these assets.

Commercial paper. Commercial paper are short-dated (less than one-year term) debt securities issued by companies to raise funds. Commercial paper is issued in the form of a zero coupon bond.

Contingent liabilities. These arise when banks provide guarantees or are committed to making conditional future payments. These may result from writing letters of credit, providing facilities or loan guarantees. They are recorded off-balance sheet.

Convertible security. A convertible bond is a form of long-dated fixed-income instrument that may be exchanged for an equity stake in the issuer. Depending on the issue terms, this conversion may be optional or mandatory and such rights reside with either the issuer or the holder.

Correlation coefficient. A quantitative measure of the extent to which a relationship between the values of two variables exists (usually denoted by "r").

Coupon rate. The interest rate on a coupon bond that the issuer pledges to pay based on the face (or par) value of the security.

Coupon bond. A fixed-income security that makes regular defined payments, normally annual or semi-annual, and the principal at term. A coupon bond is the most common form of bond issued.

Covenant. A restrictive condition that a borrower agrees to in a loan agreement that, if broken, will entitle the bank to call in (demand immediate repayment) its loan or impose revised terms.

Collateralized bond obligation (CBO). Most CBOs take the form of a bond backed by a diversified pool of bonds from individual issuers. These individual bonds normally cover a range of credit quality from junk through to investment status. A CBO is structured in such a way that it normally has investment status and is issued in the form of a number of tranches based on asset quality. Collateralized debt obligations (CDOs) have similar structure but are backed by loans rather than bonds.

Convexity. While duration is used to calculate the change in the value of a bond for small changes in yields, convexity measures the rate of change of duration against yields.

Cost-of-equity (COE). A company's cost-of-equity is defined by a risk-free rate plus a stock-specific equity risk premium.

Credit derivative. A credit derivative is a form of insurance policy against a default or deterioration in asset quality of a loan or bond. Credit derivatives usually take one of two principal forms. In the first form the payout is based on any principal loss due to borrower default. The second form involves restoring the yield on a corporate bond when credit spreads widen by a specified amount against a benchmark yield.

Credit enhancement. The credit-worthiness of a securitization issue can be enhanced by a company with a high credit rating guaranteeing holders of the securities against a defined level of possible credit losses.

Credit leverage. Universal banks may seek to use their commercial banking relationship with a company in order to win more profitable investment banking business. In the US this practice is sometimes referred to as "tying".

Credit lines. A generic term for the total of any loans made or facilities provided by a bank to a client.

Credit spread. The credit spread on a loan made to, or bond issued by, a company is the difference between the yield on the loan or bond and that of an equivalent risk-free security.

Cross-hedge. A cross-hedge is a partial hedge achieved by using a security or commodity that has a high correlation with the security or commodity being hedged. A fund manager with a long position in a corporate bond for which no futures contract exists should be able to achieve a partial hedge against rising interest rates by selling futures contracts on a Treasury bond of similar duration.

Currency swaps. A currency swap is an agreement made between two parties to make netted payments between themselves based on two notional principals (one for each currency) and the exchange rates between two specified currencies.

Custodian. A bank providing a securities' safe-keeping service. Custodians provide a range of services related to the ownership of these securities. Custodians may act in one market only or on a global basis.

Daily-earnings-at-risk (DEAR). The daily-earnings-at-risk gives a measure of the maximum amount that a bank in its trading operations may lose in a single day to a specified confidence level. DEAR is a specific sub-set of value at risk with a holding period of one day.

Defined benefit pension plan. A pension scheme provided by an employer for its employees. Pension benefits are defined in advance (usually based on salary in final year of employment) and are guaranteed by the employer.

Defined contribution pension plan. A pension scheme based on employee and employer contributions. Pension benefits depend on investment performance. Defined contribution plans shift investment risk from the employer to the employee.

Delta. Delta is a measure of the relationship between changes in option prices and those in the underlying security. A delta of 0.5 implies that the value of the option should increase by 50 cents for each dollar increase in the price of the underlying security. The value of an option's delta varies depending on the extent to which the option is in- or out-of-the-money.

Demand deposit. A term used for a deposit that normally does not pay interest and where funds can be withdrawn without prior notice.

Deposit insurance schemes. Deposit insurance schemes provide a (usually state-backed) guarantee that customers will get their deposits back in the event of a bank failure. Most schemes only cover retail deposits. Banks are usually required to pay a premium in order to obtain such cover.

Dilution. Dilution is the term given to the effect on financial measures per share, such as earnings and book value, arising from exercise of warrants and stock options or conversion of convertible securities into ordinary shares.

Disintermediation. Disintermediation is the process whereby borrowers and savers are brought together directly rather than through a bank taking deposits and making loans. Capital markets and mutual funds provide the most important sources of disintermediation.

Diversification. Portfolio diversification is the process of spreading risk by holding assets or asset classes with a low or negative correlation.

Dividend discount model (DDM). A standard method used to value stocks by discounting forecast future dividends at a defined discount rate to determine an estimate of their present value.

Duration. Duration (also known as modified or MacAuley duration) measures the percentage change in price for a given change in yields measured in basis points. It only provides a first approximation, only works for small shifts in yields and assumes parallel shifts in the structure of the yield curve.

Economic value. A measure of a bank's value based on the current market value of its assets less the current market value of its non-equity liabilities.

Effective duration. The calculation of duration adjusted for the presence of embedded options in assets such as callable and putable bonds. The value of callable bonds is truncated when interest rates fall but provides a floor for putable bonds when interest rates rise.

Embedded options. Many financial instruments and products contain embedded options. Some of these, such as with callable and putable bonds, are explicit while at others such as fixed rate mortgages and time deposits the embedded options are less obvious.

Employee Retirement Income Security Act (ERISA). The key piece of US legislation covering the management and operation of employee pension plans.

Equity risk premium. The higher returns investors demand for holding equities rather than risk-free instruments. A key part of CAPM.

Eurobond. A bond issued and traded outside the country of its denominating currency, e.g. a US$ bond issued in London.

European Central Bank (ECB). The bank established to manage monetary policy in the Eurozone. Its prime responsibility is to ensure price stability.

Exercise price. The price at which the holder of a call option can buy an underlying instrument or the holder of a put option can sell. Also known as strike price.

Expected losses. The level of losses expected on a loan based on the product of the probability of default and the expected losses in the event of default.

Facility. A facility gives a customer the right, but not the obligation to borrow up to a specified limit from a bank, up to a specified date. Also referred to as a line of credit. May be conditional (committed) or unconditional (uncommitted).

Fat tail. Distributions that are approximately normal but where the probability or frequency of events at either end of the distribution are greater than would be expected from a perfect normal distribution are said to have fat tails.

Financial Accounting Standards Board (FASB). US accountancy body responsible for determining US accountancy standards.

Finance company. Non-deposit taking financial institutions funded through wholesale markets that concentrate on niche businesses such as auto financing, consumer loans, and loans to small and medium enterprises (SMEs).

Financial Standards Authority (FSA). UK regulator responsible for all bank, insurance, investment management and other financial services.

Fiscal policy. Stance taken by government with regard to taxation, public expenditure and borrowings.

Floating rate note (FRN). A debt instrument whose interest rate is based on a prespecified benchmark such as LIBOR. The rate is adjusted on regular predefined dates. Also known as adjustable rate notes.

Foreclosure. Foreclosure is the act of a bank taking legal action in the event of default to gain title of collateral pledged by a borrower.

Foreign currency swap. An agreement between two parties to make (or receive) regular, netted payments based on the exchange rates between two currencies where each side has a notional principal denominated in one or other currency.

Forward contract. A forward contract differs from an exchange-traded futures contract only in being a private agreement between two parties.

Forward rate agreement (FRAs). An FRA is an agreement between two parties to exchange a single netted interest rate payment on a specified date based on a notional principal. FRAs may take one of two forms. Fixed–floating, where one participant pays a fixed interest rate and the other a floating rate based on an agreed benchmark, such as three-month LIBOR. The second form, a basis swap, is a floating-floating swap based on two benchmarks such as three–month LIBOR against yields on 10-year Treasury bonds.

Free float. The proportion of shares in a listed company that are effectively available for trading within a market.

Front loading. The practice of fund managers' charging an initial fee when customers invest in a mutual funds. Back loading requires the investor to pay a fee when they redeem (cash in) their investment.

Front running. The act of salespeople or traders at brokerages placing orders for themselves before completing execution of client orders. In most countries such actions are illegal. Also known as rat trading.

Funding costs. Funding costs represent the average price that a bank pays for its non-equity funds. Calculated as interest expense divided by average interest-bearing liabilities.

Funding spread. The difference between a bank's funding costs at a given maturity and the cost of raising funds of equivalent maturity through the wholesale money markets.

Futures. Contractual agreements between two parties, mediated through an exchange, to buy or sell commodities or other financial instruments on a fixed future date and at a fixed price. Settlement may be on a cash-only basis or may involve the physical delivery of commodities.

Generally Accepted Accounting Principles (GAAP). Recommended principles for accounting treatments to be followed by US companies as defined by the US Financial Accounting and Standards Board (FASB).

Gray market. An OTC market where securities are traded before their official start of exchange trading.

Guarantee. A commitment from a guarantor that in the event of one party failing to meet its contractual obligations to a second party it will honor the terms of the agreement or pay a defined amount in compensation.

Hedge funds. Hedge funds come in many forms but most focus on absolute returns, are leveraged, and make widespread use of derivatives and short selling.

Hedging. Action taking to neutralize financial risks arising from changes in the prices of financial instruments or commodities held in an outright position.

Hybrid equity. Hybrid equity comprises forms of long-term debt that can be used to absorb potential future losses at a bank before depositors are affected. Examples of hybrid equity include preference shares, convertible bonds and subordinated debt. Most regulators allow banks to use hybrid equity to enable them to meet their regulatory capital adequacy requirements.

Immunization. Techniques used to protect economic value of a bond portfolio from parallel shifts in the yield curve.

Index arbitrage. Trading technique whereby a trader sells stock index futures and buys the individual constituents of that index.

International Accounting Standards (IAS). Independent body responsible for gaining agreement on internationally accepted accounting principles.

International Monetary Fund (IMF). The IMF is best viewed as the world's lender of last resort. It is funded by its member countries and its main responsibility is to provide short-term finance to countries experiencing balance of payment or foreign reserve difficulties.

Insider trading. The act of taking advantage of information that is not in the public domain to buy or sell a stock. In most developed markets this practice is illegal but it is endemic in many emerging markets.

Interest rate parity. Interest rate parity ensures that forward foreign exchange rates adjust to take account of interest rate differentials between currencies in such a way as to eliminate arbitrage opportunities.

Internal rate of return. The interest rate that when applied as a discount rate to an investment's cashflows takes the value of that investment back to its current market value.

Interest rate swaps. Interest rate swaps are simply multiple-period forward rate agreements.

In-the-money. A call (put) option with an exercise price below (above) that of the current market price of its underlying security is said to be "in-the-money".

Intrinsic value. The intrinsic value of a stock is the estimated value of discounted future earnings.

Intrinsic value of option. The value of an option if exercised that is in-the-money and zero if it is at- or out-of-the-money.

Investment grade bonds. Bonds issued by blue chip companies where default risk is minimal. Issues require at least a BB rating from Standard and Poor's.

Junk bonds. Bonds issued by companies where there is a degree of risk of default. All issues below BB as rated by Standard and Poor's are called junk. Also called "high yield bonds".

Letter of credit. A guarantee of payment in the event of delivery of goods, made on behalf of an importer (buyer) to an exporter (seller).

Leveraged buyout. A takeover, or management buyout, that relies primarily on debt for financing.

Lien. A legal claim on an asset pledged as collateral. Where the asset is property the claim is lodged with the central land registry – where one exists.

Limit order. Order given to buy (or sell) a security up to (or down to) a specified price.

Liquidation. A legal ruling to wind up a company, sell its assets and pay off its creditors. Liquidation may be voluntary or result from action by creditors.

Liquidity requirements. Requirements by some regulators for banks to hold a certain level of liquid assets (e.g. government bonds), based on the size of their deposit base.

Long–short strategy. Investment strategy of buying stocks perceived to be undervalued while simultaneously short selling others perceived to be overvalued.

Long tail. Distributions that are approximately normal but are skewed are said to have a long tail in one direction.

Margin call. A demand by a bank or brokerage on a customer to increase the level of collateral held against a margin loan. Usually results from a fall in the value of positions financed by the loan.

Margin loan. A loan made to an institution or an individual to finance the acquisition of a stock or other financial instrument. Borrowers have to hold collateral (cash and securities) specified as a proportion of the stock's value with the lender.

Market order. An order to buy or sell a security at the prevailing market price. Also referred to as "best efforts".

Mark-to-market. Practice of marking the value of traded assets to their market price. Unrealized gains or losses may be taken through the earnings statement or reflected in a reserve account in the balance sheet.

Monetary policy. Stance adopted by a central bank to control money supply. Monetary policy may be tight, neutral or expansionary. Tools available to effect policy are open market operations, the discount rate and reserve requirements.

Money laundering. The act of taking money earned through illegal activities, such as drug trafficking, and converting it into money apparently gained through legitimate means.

Money market. The wholesale market between banks, corporates and brokers to lend or borrow short-term funds.

Morgan Stanley Capital Indices (MSCI). Series of global bond and equity indices widely used as performance benchmarks for investment funds.

Mortgage. A loan made to a borrower to purchase a property, secured by the property. Such loans usually have a 20–30 year term and may be fixed or floating (adjustable) rate.

Mortgage backed securities (MBS). An asset backed security giving its owners claims to cashflows generated from a pool of mortgage loans.

Mutual funds. Mutual funds are widely marketed retail investment products. There is a huge range of different styles on offer. Funds may invest in stocks, bonds or money market instruments.

Negative convexity. Impact of embedded option on rate of change of price (duration) of a callable bond as it approaches the bond's call price.

Net interest margin. Widely used measure of a bank's ability to extract value between what it has to pay for its funds and receives from its assets. Calculated as net interest income divided by average interest-earning assets.

Net interest spread. The net interest spread is a simple measure of the difference between what a bank pays for its funds and what it receives on its assets. Calculated as asset yields minus funding costs.

Non-performing loan (NPL). A problem loan that has met a bank's or regulator's conditions to be classified as non-performing. Definitions of NPLs vary widely but most are based on payments falling past-due for a specified period, usually 90 days.

Net present value. The difference between the initial price of an investment and the sum of the discounted cashflows generated from that investment.

Normal distribution. A symmetric statistical distribution where the mean, mode and median have the same value.

Off-balance sheet. Claims on and commitments made by an institution that are conditional on certain conditions being met at a future date.

One-tailed test. Statistical test used to determine likelihood of occurrences at one end of a normal distribution.

Open-ended fund. A mutual fund where the number of shares in the fund are not fixed. New investors are issued new shares based on a bid–offer price.

Open market operations. Methods used by central banks to influence money supply. May involve buying (selling) government securities to increase (reduce) money supply. Also used to describe central bank intervention in foreign exchange markets.

Option. An option gives the holder the right, but not the obligation, to buy or sell a commodity or financial instrument at a predetermined price by, or at, some future date. Options take many forms.

Option premium. Premium paid by the buyer of an option to the seller or writer of the option.

Origination fee. A fee earned by a bank or other financial institution for originating a loan, typically a mortgage.

Over-the-counter (OTC). A contract or transaction between two parties that is not carried out through an exchange.

Performance attribution analysis. A method for analyzing an investment portfolio's performance relative to a benchmark. Used to determine the extent to which performance differences are due to asset class or market allocation and how much is down to individual security selection.

Portfolio presentation standards (PPS). Standards promulgated by the Association of Investment Management and Research for the presentation of investment portfolios' performance.

Prepayment risk. This is the risk arising from borrowers repaying their loan before it comes to term. Prepayment risk exposes banks and other financial lenders to significant reinvestment risk. It may also be a significant risk to holders of asset backed securities.

Present value. The current value of an asset when its future forecast cashflows are discounted at an appropriate discount rate.

Price impact. The effect of a large buy or sell order on the market price of a security when executed.

Primary market. Term for the market for the issue of new securities.

Private placement. A placement of securities made off-market.

Property indices. Indices that reflect price movements of specified classes of real estate such as residential properties in defined locations.

Proprietary trading. Trading carried out on financial institution's own account rather than that done to provide an execution service to clients.

Prospectus. A legal document containing detailed information on the terms and conditions of a new issue of securities together with information on the issuer and its financial condition.

Prudent man versus prudent investor. US legal terms concerning fiduciary duties of trustees and fund managers. The prudent-man principle prohibits investments in high-risk securities while that of the prudent-investor allows them as part of portfolio diversification.

Putable bonds. Putable bonds are bonds that give the holders the right to sell the bonds back to the issuer before the bond is due to mature. Most put prices are set at par and the dates of exercise of such options defined at the time of issue.

Put option. Option that gives the holder the right but not the obligation to sell a financial security at a specified price.

Real estate investment trusts (REITs). A fund set up with real estate, both retail and commercial, as the underlying asset. REITs are normally funded with a mix of equity and debt.

Rebalancing. Periodic exercise performed by bond portfolio managers to adjust duration to bring it back to some target level.

Red herring. Draft prospectus intended to help gauge investor interest and likely demand for a new planned issue.

Regulatory arbitrage. Actions taken by international banks to conduct business in centers where regulatory requirements (e.g. capital adequacy and reserve requirements) and taxes are lowest.

Regulatory capital. Regulatory capital under the terms of the Basel Accord is divided into two principal forms: Tier I capital, comprised principally of shareholders' funds and Tier II capital made up largely of long-term hybrid equity such as preference shares, certain convertible bonds and subordinated debt.

REPO agreement. More formally referred to as government "securities sold under an agreement to repurchase".

Reserves for credit losses. Reserves set aside for expected future credit losses. Usually booked as a contra account on the asset side of the balance sheet. They may be split between general and specific reserves. In some countries referred to as "allowances" or "provisions".

Reserve requirements. Regulatory requirement set by most central banks that commercial banks maintain a specified percentage of their deposits and certain other liabilities in the form of cash, deposits with the central bank and holdings in government securities.

Revaluation reserves. Revaluation reserves are balance sheet accounts, held within shareholders' funds, used to reflect differences between the market value of assets and their historic cost.

Revolving credit. A type of credit that has no formal term. Credit cards make up the most important source of retail revolving credit.

Rights issue. An offer made by a company to its current shareholders to subscribe for more shares at a specified price usually made at a steep discount to the current market price.

Risk-weighted assets. A quantitative measure of a bank's absolute risk profile. The basic framework for calculating risk-weighted assets is based on BIS guidelines but actual methods used vary between countries.

Secured revolving credit. In effect an overdraft to finance working capital and often secured against assets such as accounts receivable or inventory.

Secured loan. A loan made in which the bank has obtained a right to a security or asset, in the form of collateral, that the bank can claim in the event of the borrower defaulting.

Serial correlation. Serial correlation occurs in a set of data when the values of the data depend in some way upon prior data values.

Settlement date. Date on which securities and consideration are to be exchanged between buyers and sellers.

Share buy-backs. Action taken by a company to buy its own shares in the market, usually in order to retire and cancel them.

Shorting. The act of borrowing stock to sell it into the market with the borrower's expectation that when the time comes to return this borrowed stock they will be able to buy it in the market at a lower price. Also known as short selling.

Short covering. The act of buying stock in the market to close out a short position.

Single borrower limit. A regulatory or internal limit on the maximum exposure that a bank is allowed to have to a single company or group of related companies. This is normally defined as a percentage of the bank's equity, typically between 10% and 20%.

Sinking fund. Fund from which a part of the principal of a bond is repaid on a number of specified dates. Similar in structure to a term loan.

Skewed distribution. Asymmetric statistical distribution with an approximately normal distribution in one direction but a long tail in the other.

Soft commissions. Services provided, or paid for, by brokerages for fund managers that provide an indirect subsidy in return for future business.

Special dividend. Dividend paid to shareholders that is unlikely to be repeated and is usually the result of some exceptional gain, such as that arising from an asset disposal, where the company has no need for the cash.

Special purpose vehicles (SPVs). Legal business entity with no operating assets established for a specific purpose. Frequently set up to aid securitization issues.

Spot. Current market price for commodities, financial instruments or interest or foreign exchange rates.

Standard deviation. A measure of the level of dispersion of the values of a variable set around their mean value. Defined as the square root of variance.

Style. The investment approach of a particular mutual fund focusing on investments with defined characteristics such as growth or value stocks.

Stop-loss order. An advance order given to sell a stock holding in the event of the stock's price falling to a particular level.

Straight through processing. Method of automated transaction processing that eliminates duplicate manual data entry.

Surety bond. A form of guarantee issued by a bank on behalf of a third party guaranteeing payment in the event of a defined set of conditions being met.

Swaption. An option that entitles the holder to enter into a future swap agreement.

SWIFT. The Society for Worldwide Interbank Financial Telecommunications (SWIFT) provides the principal means for international banks to send payment and other financial transaction instructions and confirmations, in the form of standardized messages, cross-border.

Syndicated loan. A large loan made to a single borrower by a group (syndicate) of banks. The terms of the loan are usually the same for all banks but the actual level of participation will vary between banks.

Synthetic instrument. A synthetic instrument can be created by combining positions in a number of financial instruments.

Telegraphic transfer (TT). Electronic transfer of funds from one bank account to another often, but not exclusively, cross-border.

Term loan. A loan made for a specified period in which the borrower both pays interest and makes regular principal repayments over the life of the loan.

Time deposits. A deposit made for a specified period. Early withdrawal is usually subject to some form of a penalty fee or may be prohibited.

Tombstone. An advertisement taken out by the lead manager and other members of a group of investment banks to announce the success of an new issue or other corporate transaction.

Treasury stock. Stock bought by a company and held by its treasury to meet needs created by schemes such as employee stock option plans.

Value at risk (VAR). A statistical technique used to assess a bank's potential market risks, within a defined period to a specified confidence level.

Value of future opportunities (VFO). The difference between the value of a company's current earnings capitalized at its cost-of-equity and its market capitalization. This is the value the stock market is implicitly assigning to future earnings growth.

Variance. The sum of the squares of the difference between the individual values of variables in a dataset and their mean.

World Bank. A supranational financial institution whose main role is to provide long-term project finance to developing and transitional countries.

Write-backs. Write-backs arise when banks conclude that they have overprovided for expected credit or other asset losses. These write-backs are netted against bad debt charges.

Write-offs. Write-offs are made when banks recognize losses on loans or other assets, and are normally taken against provisions established for expected losses.

Yield-to-call. The equivalent to the yield-of-maturity but for a callable bond where term is given by the next call date.

Yield-to-maturity. Yield-to-maturity is defined as the internal rate of return of a bond or loan.

Zero coupon bond. A bond issued that pays no interest but is issued, and trades, at a discount to its par or redemption value. Also known as a bullet bond.

Sources and Further Reading

ORGANIZATIONS WITH WEBSITES USED AS SOURCES

US Federal Reserve Board (US bond yields, exchange rates and bank write-offs)

Office of the Comptroller of the Currency (US banking regulatory environment, CAMEL scoring method)

Securities Exchange Commission (US regulatory environment)

Federal Deposit Insurance Corporation (operation of US FDIC)

US Department of Justice (bankruptcy code)

Bank for International Settlements (BIS Basel Accord)

INVESTMENTS AND SECURITIES

The Great Crash, J. K. Galbraith: Houghton Mifflin.

Principles of Corporate Finance, Brealey & Myers: McGraw Hill.

Investments, Z. Bodie, A. Kane and A. Marcus: Irwin.

A Random Walk Down Wall Street, B. Malkiel: W. W. Norton and Company.

Handbook of Fixed Income Securities, Editor F. Fabozzi: Irwin.

The Global Asset Backed Securities Markets, C. Stone, A. Zissu and J. Lederman: Phobus Publishing Company.

COMMERCIAL BANKING

Money, Whence It Came. Where It Went, J. Galbraith: Replica Books.

Managing Bank Capital: Capital Allocation and Performance Measurement, Chris Matten: John Wiley and Sons.

Understanding Market, Credit, and Operational Risk: The Value at Risk Approach, A. Saunders, J. Boudhoukh and L. Alllen: Blackwell Publishers.

The Bank Valuation Handbook, A Market Based Approach to Valuing Banks and Bank Branches, H. Johnson: Irwin.

Bank Financial Management: Strategies for a Changing Industry, George H. Hempel and Donald G. Simonson: John Wiley and Sons.

Bank Management, Timothy W. Koch: The Dryden Press.

Commercial Banking: The Management of Risk, D. Fraser, B. Gup and J. Kolari: West Publishing Company.

DEREGULATION AND CONSOLIDATION

The Bank Merger Wave: The Economic Causes and Social Consequences of Financial Consolidation, G. Dymski:

Financial Sector Deregulation: Banking Development and Monetary Policy, The Indonesian Experience, Binhadi: Institut Bankir Indonesia.

Banking in an Unregulated Environment: California 1878–1905, L. P. Doti: Garland Publishing.

Banking Redefined, How Superhouses are Reshaping Financial Services, J. Speigel, A. Gart and S. Gart: Irwin.

CREDIT LOSSES, BANK FAILURES AND CRISES

Bank Restructuring: Lessons from the 1980s, Edited by Andrew Sheng: The World Bank.

Banking Crises: Cases and Issues, Edited by V. Sundararajan and Tomás J. T. Balino: International Monetary Fund.

The Banking Crises of the Great Depression, Elmus Wicker: Cambridge University Press.

Bank Failures in the Major Trading Countries of the World: Causes and Remedies, Benton E. Gup: Quorum Books.

Banking Scandals: The S&LS and BCCI, Edited by Robert Emmet Young: The Reference Shelf.

Asia in Crisis: The Implosion of the Banking and Finance Systems, Philippe F. Delhaise: John Wiley and Sons.

Banking Crises: in Latin America, Edited by R. Hausmann and L. Rojas-Suárez: Inter-American Development Bank.

Workouts & Turnarounds II: Global Restructuring Strategies for the Next Century, Edited by Dominic DiNapoli: PriceWaterhouseCoopers.

Bankruptcy & Distressed Restructurings: Analytical Issues and Investment Opportunities, Editor E. Altman: Beard Books.

Credit Derivatives and Credit Linked Notes, Editor and principal contributor Satyajit Das: John Wiley and Sons.

Index

Index compiled by Annette Musker